The Extermination of the European Jews

This major reinterpretation of the Holocaust surveys the destruction of the European Jews within the broader context of Nazi violence against other victim groups. Christian Gerlach offers a unique social history of mass violence that reveals why particular groups were persecuted and what it was that connected the fate of these groups and the policies against them. He explores the diverse ideological, political and economic motivations that lay behind the murder of the Jews and charts the changing dynamics of persecution during the course of the war. The book brings together both German actions and those of non-German states and societies, shedding new light on the different groups and vested interests involved and their role in the persecution of non-Jews as well. Ranging across continental Europe, it reveals that popular notions of race were often more important in shaping persecution than scientific racism or Nazi dogma.

Christian Gerlach is Professor of Contemporary History at the University of Bern. He has published several award-winning books that deal with the persecution and murder of Jews and non-Jews in Nazi-occupied Europe. He is also the author of *Extremely Violent Societies: Mass Violence in the Twentieth Century World* (Cambridge University Press, 2010).

New Approaches to European History

Series editors
T. C. W. Blanning, *Sidney Sussex College, Cambridge*
Brendan Simms, *Peterhouse, Cambridge*

New Approaches to European History is an important textbook series, which provides concise but authoritative surveys of major themes and problems in European history since the Renaissance. Written at a level and length accessible to advanced school students and undergraduates, each book in the series addresses topics or themes that students of European history encounter daily: the series embraces both some of the more "traditional" subjects of study and those cultural and social issues to which increasing numbers of school and college courses are devoted. A particular effort is made to consider the wider international implications of the subject under scrutiny.

To aid the student reader, scholarly apparatus and annotation is light, but each work has full supplementary bibliographies and notes for further reading: where appropriate, chronologies, maps, diagrams, and other illustrative material are also provided.

For a complete list of titles published in the series, please see:
www.cambridge.org/newapproaches

The Extermination of the European Jews

Christian Gerlach
University of Bern

Shaftesbury Road, Cambridge CB2 8EA, United Kingdom

One Liberty Plaza, 20th Floor, New York, NY 10006, USA

477 Williamstown Road, Port Melbourne, VIC 3207, Australia

314–321, 3rd Floor, Plot 3, Splendor Forum, Jasola District Centre, New Delhi – 110025, India

103 Penang Road, #05–06/07, Visioncrest Commercial, Singapore 238467

Cambridge University Press is part of Cambridge University Press & Assessment, a department of the University of Cambridge.

We share the University's mission to contribute to society through the pursuit of education, learning and research at the highest international levels of excellence.

www.cambridge.org
Information on this title: www.cambridge.org/9780521706896

First published 2016

A catalogue record for this publication is available from the British Library

Library of Congress Cataloging-in-Publication data
Names: Gerlach, Christian, 1963– author.
Title: The extermination of the European Jews / Christian Gerlach.
Description: New York : Cambridge University Press, [2015] | 2015 |
Series: New approaches to European history |
Includes bibliographical references and index.
Identifiers: LCCN 2015041669 | ISBN 9780521880787 (hardback) |
ISBN 9780521706896 (paperback)
Subjects: LCSH: Holocaust, Jewish (1939–1945) | Germany–Politics and government–1933–1945. | World War, 1939–1945–Atrocities.
Classification: LCC D804.3. G4675 2015 | DDC 940.53/18–dc23
LC record available at http://lccn.loc.gov/2015041669

ISBN 978-0-521-88078-7 Hardback
ISBN 978-0-521-70689-6 Paperback

Contents

Tables

Acknowledgments

Historians depend for their works on many others. As so often, these include archivists and librarians. I am grateful to the collaborators of all archives used for this study and their helpful suggestions. The same goes for the staff in the many libraries that I used for the research that forms the basis of this book, especially the librarians at Hillman Library at the University of Pittsburgh, at the BTO and the Schweizerische Osteuropabibliothek at the University of Bern, particularly Therese Meier-Salzmann, and at the Josef-Wulf-Bibliothek at the memorial site Haus der Wannsee-Konferenz in Berlin.

Many colleagues were kind enough to discuss their work and mine with me, comment on the latter and give me suggestions for further readings. I am indebted to Götz Aly, Frank Bajohr, Ralf Banken, Hans Blom, Florent Brayard, William Brustein, Marc Buggeln, Marina Cattaruzza, Raya Cohen, Tim Cole, Markus Eikel, Bert Jan Flim, Stig Förster, Odd-Björn Fure, Alfred Gottwaldt‡, Heiko Haumann, Sanela Hodzic, Alexander Korb, Patrick Kury, Irina Livezeanu, Wendy Lower, Christian Axboe Nielsen, Kathrin Paehler, Nicolas Patin, Berna Pekesen, Dieter Pohl, Julia Richers, Peter Romijn, Dirk Rupnow, Hans Safrian, Vladimir Solonari, Wichert Ten Have, Gregor Thum, Feliks Tych, Krisztián Ungváry, Anton Weiss-Wendt and Franziska Zaugg. Marcus Gryglewski, Anna Hájková, Helene Sinnreich and Nicholas Terry gave me access to their important unpublished works. Special thanks for pointing me to relevant documents go to my friends Andrej Angrick and Christoph Dieckmann, who also shared their insights with me.

I am grateful to Daniela Heiniger and Florentina Wirz who helped me in various ways during my research. Michael Wildt provided helpful general feedback to my manuscript, and Alexa Stiller (who also suggested further directions of reading to me) provided helpful detailed suggestions; many thanks to them! I also owe many insights to the unknown readers who reviewed my proposal and manuscript for Cambridge University Press. Gregory Sax and Peter Kenyon tried to prevent me from committing crimes against the English language. They and Michael Watson from CUP invested much work when trying to make this a better book through their thoughtful and valuable suggestions. Any remaining deficits of the book in terms of the use of language and its content are, of course, entirely my responsibility.

Several academic institutions gave me the opportunity to present partial results of this study, including the history departments at the University of Pittsburgh and at the University of Leiden, as well as at the Institute for Human Sciences in Vienna and the Mémorial de la Shoah at Paris. Such partial results were also presented at the following conferences: "Territorial Revisionism and Revisionism Inside: The Politics of the Allies of Germany, 1938–1945," organized by the Universities of Tübingen and Bern at Blaubeuren, Germany; "Towards an Integrated Perspective on Nazi Policies of Mass Murder," at the Center for Studies of Holocaust and Religious Minorities at Oslo; "The Holocaust and Other Genocides," organized by the ITF Academic Working Group at Den Haag; "Vernichtungskrieg, Reaktionen, Erinnerung: Die deutsche Besatzungsherrschaft in der Sowjetunion 1941–1944," at the Deutsch-Russisches Museum Berlin-Karlshorst; "Rationierung: Logiken, Formen und Praktiken des Mangels," at Goethe University, Frankfurt a.M.; "Umkämpfte Vergangenheit und Deutungskonkurrenzen: Geschichtspolitik und Forschungsperspektiven in Ungarn," University of Bern; and at the 8th Central Seminar of "Erinnern.at" at the University of Graz. I thank all the organizers of these conferences and guest lectures.

Finally, with their love, my family helped me immensely to finish this work. I owe Magdi, Nina and Emilia more than I can express.

Abbreviations

ADAP	Akten zur deutschen auswärtigen Politik
AIPN	Archiwum Instytucie Pamięci Narodowej – Komisji Ścigania Zbrodni przeciwko Narodowi Polskiemu, Warsaw
AMV	Archiv ministerstva vnitra (Archive of the Interior Ministry, Prague)
BA	Bundesarchiv (German Federal Archive), Berlin
BA D-H	Bundesarchiv Dahlwitz-Hoppegarten
BAK	Bundesarchiv, Koblenz
BA-MA	Bundesarchiv-Militärarchiv, Freiburg
BAS	Bundesarchiv (Swiss Federal Archive), Bern
BBGFW	Bulletin der Berliner Gesellschaft für Faschismus- und Weltkriegsforschung
BDC	Berlin Document Center (in the German Federal Archive, Berlin)
BdS	Befehlshaber der Sicherheitspolizei und des SD
BGN	Beiträge zur Geschichte des Nationalsozialismus
BNGS	Beiträge zur nationalsozialistischen Gesundheits- und Sozialpolitik
CdS	Chief of the Security Police and Security Service
CChlDK	Center for the Storage of Historical-Documentary Collections, Moscow
CEH	Central European History (journal)
DRZW	Militärisches Forschungsamt der Bundeswehr, ed., Das Deutsche Reich und der Zweite Weltkrieg
GuG	Geschichte und Gesellschaft
HGS	Holocaust and Genocide Studies
IMG	Der Prozess vor dem Internationalen Militärgerichtshof, vols 1–42 (Nuremberg, 1947–49)
JfW	Jahrbuch für Wirtschaftsgeschichte
JASF	Jahrbuch für Antisemitismusforschung

JGR	Journal of Genocide Research
JSS	Jewish Social Studies
KG	Kammergericht (higher court)
LBIY	Leo Baeck Institute Yearbook
MadR	Boberach, Heinz, ed., *Meldungen aus dem Reich: Die geheimen Lageberichte des Sicherheitsdienstes der SS 1938–1945*, 17 volumes (Herrsching: Pawlak, 1984)
MGM	Militärgeschichtliche Mitteilungen
OKW	Supreme Command of the German Armed Forces
PA AA	Politisches Archiv des Auswärtigen Amtes (of Germany)
RBD	Reichsbahndirektion (Reich Railway Directorate [regional])
RHS	Revue de l'histoire de la Shoah/le monde juif
RMO	Reich Ministry for the Occupied Eastern Territories (of the Soviet Union)
RSHA	Reichssicherheitshauptamt (Head Office of Reich Security)
SA	Sturmabteilungen (storm troopers)
SD	Sicherheitsdienst (Security Service, of the SS)
SDIY	Simon Dubnow Institute Yearbook
SS	Schutzstaffeln (Protective Squads)
SSPF	SS and Police Leader
StA	Staatsanwaltschaft (State Prosecutor's Office)
SWCA	Simon Wiesenthal Center Annual
TSD	Theresienstädter Studien und Dokumente
VfZ	Vierteljahrshefte für Zeitgeschichte
WVHA	Economic and Administrative Head Office of the SS
YVS	Yad Vashem Studies
ZfG	Zeitschrift für Geschichtswissenschaft
ZStL	Central Authority of German States for the Investigation of National Socialist Violent Crimes, Ludwigsburg

1 Introduction

This book offers a particular perspective on the destruction of the European Jews. It places the persecution of Jews in the context of interdependent policies regarding warfare, occupation and policing, social issues, economics, racist thought and popular racism. The study also describes the murder of Jews amidst massive violence against other groups and attempts to make connections among these different sorts of violence. This differs from narratives that examine the persecution and murder of Jews alone with little regard to the fate of other groups, on the basis of a history of ideas with relatively few other forms of contextualization. In addition, this book gives more prominence than many other works to the persecution of Jews by non-Germans and tries to provide a general analysis of this persecution across national boundaries.

This book's perspective is derived from a new approach to understanding mass violence that I have recently suggested.[1] In brief, I find the prevailing explanations too state centered, too focused on the intents and plans of rulers and too concentrated on race and ethnicity as causes, and they are usually concerned with the persecution of one group that is treated in isolation from other victim groups. Historically, by contrast, various population groups in many countries were victims of massive physical violence in which diverse social groups, acting together with state organs, participated for a multitude of reasons. These three aspects – the participatory character of violence, multiple victim groups and multi-causality – were interconnected. Simply put, the occurrence and thrust of mass violence depends on broad and diverse support, but this support is based on a variety of motives and interests that cause violence to spread in different directions and in varying intensities and forms. In emphasizing that mass violence is based on complex participatory processes, I speak of extremely violent societies. These phenomena can be traced through many important historical cases of mass

[1] For this paragraph see Gerlach 2010, esp. Chapter 1. This introduction also takes up some ideas mentioned in ibid., pp. 236–8.

violence such as the Soviet Union from the 1930s through the 1950s, the late Ottoman Empire (including the destruction of the Armenians), Cambodia, Rwanda and North America in the nineteenth century.

The same traits – broad participation, multiple motives and several victim groups – can also be found in the violence of Germans and people from other nations during World War II. I shall elaborate on this shortly, but it is important to note that it is of little value simply to mark these as extremely violent societies. Rather than being the goal, this classification should be the point of departure in thinking about how that persecution and violence came about.

A multitude of victims

Around Christmas of 1944, Buchenwald concentration camp made a monthly list of its and its sub-camps' inmates. In a printed table, the 63,837 prisoners from 28 European countries, plus "others" and "stateless," were listed in 13 categories: persons in protective custody (who were mostly political prisoners, many of them French), Jehovah's Witnesses, homosexuals, members of the German military, clergy, "Red Spaniards," "foreign civil workers," Jews, "anti-socials," professional criminals, habitual offenders, "gypsies" and (Soviet) prisoners of war (POWs). The three largest categories, in order, were political prisoners (a specialty of Buchenwald), foreign workers and Jews. Together they accounted for close to 90% of the prisoners; Jews alone numbered about 20%.[2] Many of these prisoners, whether Jews or not, did not live to see liberation. They perished from privation and disease, especially in the overcrowded main camp; and from exhaustion and killings, above all during the death marches.

It wasn't just Jews who were killed under the Nazi regime. Contrary to popular belief, except for the period November–December 1938 most concentration camp prisoners were not Jewish. After mid 1944 more than a third were Jews again. From 1938 to 1941 – in Buchenwald and its sub-camps – 14–19% of the inmates were Jews; by June 1, 1942, it was 11%, and 2.4% by late December. In 1944 their numbers rose again – from less than 1% in May to more than 24%; by the end of February 1945 the figure was 32%.[3] Generally, there were multiple groups under persecution – victims of a variety of policies, subject to different fierce resentment, and struggling to evade repression and maintain their livelihoods

[2] "Schutzhaftlager-Rapport," KL Buchenwald, December 15, 1944, facsimile in Rose 2003, pp. 192–3. See also Gerlach 2010, p. 236.

[3] Stein 1998, pp. 169–71, 182, 184, 187. For Jewish victims of the concentration camp at Neuengamme see Bauche 1991, p. 130.

by interacting with German occupiers, national and local authorities, and diverse other social groups.

In this the German case is not unique. Not only did other regimes in Europe in the early 1940s stage (and other societies allow) anti-Jewish persecutions, usually a variety of groups were simultaneously stripped of their jobs, robbed and expelled, exposed to forced labor or murdered.

In many European countries the number of non-Jewish victims of German and Axis violence – even putting military losses aside – far surpassed that of Jews who were murdered. In the Soviet Union (as constituted by its borders of May 1941), about 30% of all German-induced loss of human life outside of battle were Jews; in France, 40%; in Greece, 20–22% and in Italy and Yugoslavia 6% each. Among Germans, about a third of the victims of Nazism were Jews.[4] In Poland, Belgium (38%) and the Czech lands (32%), non-Jews were a sizable minority of the victims. In Hungary the civilian dead were mostly Jewish.[5]

During World War II, Germans (and people from other powers) killed not only 6 million Jews but also 6–8 million other non-combatants. The largest among these non-Jewish victim groups were Soviet POWs – of whom 3 million died. Anti-guerrilla warfare in the countryside (especially in the occupied Soviet territories, Yugoslavia and Greece) claimed about a million lives. Another million, mostly urban dwellers, perished in famines caused directly by German policies. The death toll from urban terror was high, but I am not aware of reliable Europe-wide figures. Out of about 12 million people deported to Germany in the forced labor program, 300,000 may have perished – a figure that surpasses the number of disabled people and Roma and Sinti who were murdered.[6]

When non-Jewish victims appeared on the radar of historians in the past, many works focused on certain of these groups: the disabled, Sinti and Roma ('gypsies'), homosexuals, Jehovah's Witnesses or political

[4] About 500,000 Germans were killed by their own regime, or by their compatriots, between 1933 and 1945 – including about 180,000 disabled people and 165,000 Jews. See Pohl 2003, esp. pp. 35, 109. The number of Germans who fell victim to their own regime equaled the number of German civilian victims of Allied aerial bombing. For Greece, see Gerlach 2010, p. 238; for Yugoslavia, see Cvetković 2008 and Biondich 2002, p. 41 note 2; for Italy, see Klinkhammer 1993, pp. 552–3, 573–4; for Soviet Ukraine, see Kumanev 1991, p. 66; for France, see Lagrou 2002, esp. pp. 318–20, Lieb 2007, pp. 306, 412–13 and Lafont 1987, pp. 60–8. Approximately 75,000 French Jewish residents were murdered; among France's non-Jewish victims, about 10,000 were executed in France, 35,000 resisters died in German concentration camps, up to 20,000 civilians were victims of anti-partisan warfare, at least 30,000 mentally disabled people starved to death and 21,000 POWs died. (In addition, aerial bombing claimed up to 60,000 victims.)

[5] For Belgium, see Brachfeld 2005, p. 44 note 16; for the Czech lands, see Brandes 2006, p. 459.

[6] See Pohl 2003, p. 153; Spoerer 2001; and my own estimates.

opponents. This had much to do with a research perspective concentrating on violence against Germans and, in some cases, with pressure groups promoting the memory of their fate, a memory which served the construction of group identity. Among Germans, the focus on German victim groups served a nationalist view that excluded victims who were not compatriots and ignored German imperialism as much as possible. The disabled and Roma seemed to be worth investigating because methods similar to those used against Jews were employed to kill them, or because it was, in part, the same personnel who conducted the mission. By contrast, this book, dealing with the persecution of Jews, will otherwise largely be devoted to the quantitatively deadliest phenomena: the destruction of Soviet POWs, anti-guerrilla warfare, famines and the forced labor program.

Of course, given that much research remains to be done, one could investigate the fate of these groups one by one. In the long run, however, neatly treating each group separately will not be sufficient.[7] This study is, rather, concerned with such questions as why a variety of groups suffered from mass violence, what connected the fate of these groups, the policies against them and motives underlying the deeds. To what degree did violence against different groups occur in the same context? What did it mean for each group that they had to operate within a wider web of persecution? What was going on in societies where not just one group, but many, were excluded, stripped of their rights, dehumanized or declared hostile elements? What relationships were there between victim groups, German officials and non-German authorities? And how well integrated within their societies were those under persecution? By understanding these connections we may reach a better understanding of not only the general picture but also the persecution of each group, including the fate of the Jews.

Ways to do research on multiple victim groups

This book puts the persecution and murder of the Jews at the center and searches for links to other persecutions, and for common contexts between violence against Jews and other groups. It also offers comparative views, but it goes beyond the not uncommon, but unproductive, 'who suffered most?' approach.

Other avenues would be possible. Henry Friedlander pursued continuities of policies, ideas and perpetrators among the murders of the disabled, Jews and Roma; Dieter Pohl has offered a general account of

[7] See Friedlander 1995, p. 295 (with reference to Jews, the disabled and Roma).

different Nazi crimes one by one; Doris Bergen presented a short narrative providing a limited glance at policies against other victim groups; and Donald Bloxham placed the destruction of Jews primarily in the context of what he called "ethnopolitics."[8]

One can imagine still other approaches – such as putting no victim group, or a group other than the Jews, at the center.[9] But the reality looks different. There are thousands of books in English devoted to the destruction of 6 million European Jews. One cannot really say how many – although one can say with certainty how many books there are in the English language dealing exclusively with the second largest group of victims of Nazism, the 3 million Soviet POWs who perished: none. In English, there is neither a single monograph nor a single collected volume on this subject. So there are good reasons to talk a bit more about non-Jewish victims and not to put Jewish victimhood at the center every time one writes about German violence. This book, however, is not so avant garde as to establish this as an overall structural principle. It does not really consider non-Jewish victim groups in their own right, as they deserve. Yet the fact that the fate of Europe's Jews lies at the heart of this book by no means suggests that Jews were necessarily at the center of the thoughts of historical actors. In fact mostly they were not.

Other potential ways to approach the multitude of victims include examining those who faced persecution in one country, region or city. For example, an expert forensic commission reported about German atrocities in Černigov, Ukraine, in September 1944:

> In November 1941 there was a three-day so-called campaign to shoot the Jewish population of the city. In January 1942 the mentally disabled were shot, in the spring of 1942 the gypsies, and in the following months of the year of 1942 Soviet activists. In February and March 1943 were shot the prisoners of war and those civilians just held in the [local] camp.[10]

In reality, the 2,000 Roma were shot in June or August rather than in the spring of 1942, and the shooting of psychiatric patients started in October 1941. Beginning with these facts, one could explore the political, ideological, organizational and other connections between these massacres as well as their social effects, possibly also in conjunction with the large-scale deportations of forced laborers from the town in 1942–43 and with anti-guerrilla warfare in the vicinity.

[8] Friedlander 1995; Pohl 2003; Bergen 2003; Bloxham 2009.

[9] For all of the major victim groups in a single country see Gerlach 1999 (for Belarus) and Dieckmann 2011 (for Lithuania).

[10] Quoted in Holler 2009, p. 74; for corrections to this statement see pp. 74–6.

One can research about how one German organization, institution or unit (or individual) acted against different sorts of people. For example, there have been discussions about the motivations of 'apolitical' men in German Order Police battalions when shooting Jews in great numbers in 1941 and 1942.[11] In the debate about how these men could kill, hardly any of the authors took into account that the same units also used extreme violence against other groups. Before shooting Jews in Poland, the hotly debated Reserve Police Battalion 101, for instance, had participated in deporting almost 37,000 non-Jewish and Jewish Poles from western to central Poland in 1940, guarded the starving ghetto of Warsaw in 1941 and accompanied transports of fatally exhausted Soviet POWs in the same year.[12] Police Battalion 322, which also incited such arguments, deported or killed civilians during anti-partisan warfare in the same months when it shot Jews in the western Soviet Union in 1941, and it took part in bloody operations against guerrillas in Yugoslavia and Albania in 1943–44.[13] The approach of considering the violence of one unit against different groups has proven illuminating in respect to the 253rd Infantry Division, a German frontline division deployed to the Soviet Union. This unit killed stragglers of the Red Army, took civilians hostages, carried out reprisals against, or looted, villages near sites where there was partisan activity, employed first Soviet POWs and then civilians as forced laborers, shot some POWs and sent others back after having used them to the point of total exhaustion, forced civilians to clear mines, recruited civilians as forced labor for the Reich, helped concentrate 33,000 women and children in an improvised camp that was mined and intentionally infested with typhoid (killing 9,000) in 1944, and destroyed housing on 5,000 km^2 while in retreat. A study showed that virtually all sub-units took part in violence against non-combatants and that some of the relevant policies and strategies were developed within the division without detailed instructions from above.[14] The German 1st Mountain Division was involved in the pogrom against Jews in Lvov, Ukraine, in 1941, killed thousands of civilians during anti-guerrilla warfare in Yugoslavia, Greece and Albania in 1943–44, shot hostages, massacred Italian officers and soldiers in Kephalonia, Greece, after Italy had withdrawn from

[11] See the controversy about Reserve Police Battalion 101 between Browning 1993 and Goldhagen 1997.

[12] Keller 2011, pp. 132–3; Mallmann 2004, p. 81; for certain aspects see also Browning 1993, pp. 41–3. Curilla 2006 (pp. 125–702) mentions other victims for many Order Police units, especially during anti-partisan warfare.

[13] See the extensive files of that unit in BA D-H film, p. 812–27.

[14] Rass 2003, pp. 331–402; Rass 2005, pp. 80–6.

the war, and helped deport Jews from northwestern Greece who would later be killed at Auschwitz.[15]

Another set of questions could be linked to documents such as the aforementioned Buchenwald roll call report. Here, the Germans had herded people from different backgrounds into a single place. But were they really in a position to treat them differently according to their thirteen neat categories? Did they receive different food rations, clothing or medical treatment? Could the guards keep them spatially separate? Could the prisoners be forced to do distinct sorts of work? In the cramped camp, did the guards have time to mete out different kinds of beating, or torture, to prisoners from each category? Or did the conditions tend to level the maltreatment in such a way that it converged to become the same for everybody?[16] How far, then, were things under control and going according to plan in Buchenwald? Were imaginations of racial-social stratification actually being carried into effect (as it was indeed often possible for German organizers in forced labor camps and POW camps)? And what were the crucial dynamics among the prisoners, who comprised – according to prisoner categories and nationalities – one hundred groups and included native speakers of at least twenty-four languages?

There were other multi-purpose camps for civilian inmates, some of which were run by the German military.[17] Here too it would appear that managing violence turned out to be more difficult than expected and that people who had started out as being subject to distinct types of persecution were thrown together. Analogous observations can be made about other camps such as the German camp in Semlin (Zajmiste), Serbia, or the Croatian camp of Jasenovac. Even what may appear as a single group often consisted of different sub-sets – like the non-Jewish Polish prisoners in Mauthausen who included members of the intelligentsia, forced workers, political resisters and forced evacuees from Warsaw.[18]

Not all of these approaches can be taken in this book, and not all these questions can be answered. As a synthesis, it cannot offer a comprehensive study of individual localities, units or institutions. Rather, this study traces the fate of one group and tries to establish systematically how this fate was related to the treatment of other people. This has not been done

15 Meyer 2008, pp. 58–65, 113–27, 159–224, 384–95, 463–555, 567–609.

16 Blatman 2011 (pp. 416–18) makes the latter argument for death marches from concentration camps in 1945.

17 For example, see Commander of Rear Army Area 580 (2nd Army), directive of January 14, 1943, in Müller 1982, pp. 144–5.

18 See Mataušić 2006, p. 48; Mihovilović and Smreka 2006, pp. 218–9; Pavlowitch 2008, p. 70 note 19; Cvetković 2008, p. 367; for Mauthausen see Filipkowski 2005, pp. 129–36.

before. Jews found themselves in what could be called a labyrinth of persecution that was almost inescapable; but simultaneously, other groups wandered around trapped in their different mazes. Thus, I will also compare survival and coping strategies of the different groups.

A variety of contexts and motivations for violence

As with the persecution of the Jews, whoever considers the non-Jewish victims of German and Axis violence in their entirety must also take account of imperialism. Some 300,000–350,000 of the 6–8 million non-Jews killed were German; that is, about 95% were foreigners from the German point of view. Of the 6 million Jews slain, about 165,000 were German, meaning 97% were foreign.[19] Quantitatively, non-German non-Jews were at an almost tenfold greater risk of being killed under the Nazi regime (3–4% out of a population of 220 million) than German non-Jews (0.4–0.5%). To a degree, this tendency can also be observed among Jews, who ran a much higher risk than non-Jews: a third of German Jews died, but more than 80% of non-German Jews were killed.[20] Overwhelmingly, both the Jews and the non-Jews who were killed were foreign; most perished in German-occupied countries, and, of course, most died after September 1939. This is why it is difficult to discuss the fate of these people outside the context of war and occupation. Needless to add, Germany did not wage a war of expansion just to bring more Jews under its control.

Had the Nazi regime ended in the summer of 1939, before World War II started, it would have been remembered for causing several thousand deaths, for persecuting German, Austrian and Czech Jews and driving half of them into exile, for arresting more than 100,000 political opponents and tens of thousands of social deviants, and for sterilizing 300,000 people by force. At that time, many much bloodier regimes ruled in Europe and elsewhere. Had Nazi Germany collapsed by May 1941, it would be remembered for a war of aggression, forced labor deportations, the deportation of 300,000 non-Jews and Jews from western to central Poland, and the murder of 200,000 civilians: half the latter victims were mentally disabled people in Germany and Poland, a quarter belonged to the Polish leadership, tens of thousands were innocent victims of German aerial attacks, and many thousands were Jews who were starved to death

[19] By contrast, Melson 1992 examines the murder of Jews in Wold War II as "total domestic genocide" (pp. 5, 39, 278).

[20] These figures are based on an estimate of about 1.3 million survivors from Axis-controlled territories (including Tunisia and Libya, but excluding Soviet Jewish citizens who fled eastward and never came under German rule).

Table 1.1[21] *Temporal distribution of peaks of destruction*

Victim group	1940	1941	1942	1943	1944
Soviet POWs		----	----		
Famine victims			-------		
Jews			----	---	
Forced-labor recruitment			--------	--------	
Anti-guerrilla warfare				--------	--------
Civil wars					-------------

in large ghettos or killed in the fall of 1939.[22] By that time, Soviet and Japanese policies had caused millions of deaths, and, arguably, fascist Italy (primarily in Africa) and Francoist Spain killed more civilians than Germany did. Soldiers went into battle having watched newsreels about war and atrocities in China, Ethiopia and Spain.[23] Only later would Nazi Germany surpass the death toll of all these regimes and societies. But on May 13, 1940, when Winston Churchill took office as Prime Minister of Great Britain, it was an exaggeration to call Nazi Germany a regime "never surpassed in the dark and lamentable catalogue of human crime."[24]

Therefore, the evolutionary dimension is also important in the search for connections among different forms and directions of violence. So identifying temporal clusters may be illustrative. What is presented in Table 1.1 is a very tentative, macro-level version of them. Obviously, the bulk of German killings of civilians and other non-combatants took place during World War II; more precisely, 95% of all these deaths occurred after the German invasion of the Soviet Union in 1941. Table 1.1 shows the most intense period of violence relating to Nazi rule for each of the largest victim groups.

Persecutions clearly became more brutal as the war intensified. Geographically, violence spread from the German-occupied Soviet territories and Yugoslavia to other parts of Europe that were increasingly also treated and exploited nearly as brutally as the rear areas of the Eastern Front. With the outcome of the world conflict seemingly on knife edge in

21 For the data on Soviet POWs and famine victims, see Chapter 9; for Jews, see Chapter 4; for forced labor recruitment, see Chapter 8; for anti-guerrilla warfare and civil wars, see Chapter 11.

22 See Browning 1993, p. xv; Browning 1998a, pp. 127–8.

23 For example letter by Frank Pickesgill, September 1, 1939, in Bähr 1961, pp. 18–19.

24 See www.winstonchurchill.org/learn/speeches/speeches-of-winston-churchill/92-blood-toil-tears-and-sweat (accessed March 8, 2013).

1941–42, the German attempt to appropriate Europe's resources – first food and then labor – intensified. Food denial caused the death of millions of Soviet POWs. They were the largest victim group in 1941. In 1942 it was the Jews, and in 1943 the Jews were on a par with rural populations suspected of supporting guerrillas. Food policy was also linked to the murder of Jews in Poland and elsewhere.[25] The peak of the destruction of Jewry coincided with a giant mobilization of labor, primarily of Soviet and Polish civilians who created a reservoir large enough for Germany to be able to do without badly weakened Soviet POWs and Jews. In the second half of the war, the focus of the German leadership shifted to conscripting labor in the countryside and combating resistance to the occupation. The German regime became even harsher in rural areas than before as taxation and the collection of agricultural produce intensified,[26] and hiding became more difficult, including for Jews. Violent conflicts within societies under occupation also came to the surface. These were the result of political disagreements about the future, as well as earlier internal stress caused by the oppression and impoverishment of many, and gains for a few. Of course, these are only tendencies, and this is in no way exhaustive. Locally, events often may have evolved quite differently.

Many facts suggest that factors other than anti-Jewish attitudes influenced the fate of Jews and their chances of survival. The Nazi government largely allowed Jews to function within the economy as entrepreneurs, and as professionals, until 1938; it deported Jews to Germany as forced labor in 1944 having previously declared Germany to be more or less free of Jews before then; the great majority of British, American, French and Yugoslav Jews in German POW camps survived the war unharmed. Also, the fiercely anti-Jewish Romanian government first organized the mass slaughter and starvation of at least 250,000 Romanian and Ukrainian Jews in occupied Transnistria, but then refused to hand over another 250,000 Romanian Jews to Germany, allowing them to survive. This book examines such factors.

Participatory violence

As more victim groups enter the picture, the fact that a wide array of people took part in the violence becomes even clearer. Persecution was not only a matter of centralized government policies and a handful of state authorities, particularly the SS and police. Most Soviet POWs died

[25] See Gerlach 1998a and Chapter 10.

[26] For northwestern Russia see Hill 2005, p. 113; for eastern Belarus and western central Russia see Terry 2005.

in army custody. The conditions of forced labor were set in part by the management of private companies and sometimes by commanders of military units. Civil and military administrations organized forced labor recruitment, and they were also in charge of food policies in general and the feeding, housing and labor of Jews – at least until 1942–43, and locally even longer. They also carried out many selections of Jews either for forced labor or for death. Although the SS and police carried out most of the mass killings of Jews, this does not mean that they alone determined the underlying policies. The different attitudes, interests, life stories and education of others who co-determined these policies also matter.

Occupation policies were important given that the overwhelming majority of victims, also Jewish victims, were from occupied countries. However, there was no *single* German institution that organized the persecution of European Jews, nor was there a single Nazi office that assigned a place in the hierarchy for the peoples of Europe. "Neither was there a map showing how Europe was supposed to look after 'final victory' nor a master plan for the destruction of the European Jews."[27] This has profound consequences for analysis. The often-cited 'new order' that Germany introduced was nowhere defined. There was no planned or coherent system of occupation throughout German-controlled Europe – virtually every conquered country got a different status, and the occupation was organized differently in different places. So it would appear that we need to understand patterns in the *practice* of occupation. Multiple actors shaped this practice: the German leadership in Berlin, government ministries and other central agencies, different types of civilian and military administrations, which were given considerable autonomy, and, to a degree, also the SS and police. This in turn means that these agents acted on the basis of a variety of interests and attitudes. Many of the individuals involved were not even Nazis (i.e., members of the Nazi Party) but different sorts of conservatives, chauvinists and racists (see Chapter 6). Even among real Nazis, political and racial thinking was inconsistent; for example, there seems to have been no clear and unequivocal "racial" evaluation of Slavs (see Chapter 7).

Genocide experts and Holocaust specialists have both focused overwhelmingly on the state and on government-orchestrated crimes. The resulting narrative in Holocaust studies is a trap in which the state acts and the victims merely react or are altogether passive and powerless. Persecution, according to a widespread view, was conducted by agents of the state machinery merely to carry government policy into effect. Among the reasons why perpetrator and victim history often don't quite

[27] Hilberg 1992a, p. 22.

seem to match, one is also a methodological – perpetrator history has been written as political history, victim experience more as social history.

Overcoming this mismatch requires the writing of the history of mass violence more as one of social actors.[28] This approach also addresses the unfortunate tendency in studies of Nazism to make the state, 'the Germans,' 'the Poles,' and so on, appear as monolithic. This papers over differences between social groups and contradictions in personal, local and regional behavior. Take, for example, anti-partisan warfare. To be sure, the writing of its history should include German strategies, German attitudes toward conquered populations, and a study of the German army, SS and police units and administrations. However, in no country could German functionaries totally disregard the local population or the national government, if there was one, as a political factor. And warfare against guerrillas usually involved local authorities, police forces or paramilitaries. Germans tried to utilize these forces, yet these also tried to instrumentalize the Germans just as much. Partisan conflicts were not only rooted in the German (or Italian, Bulgarian, etc.) occupation, but also in pre-existing tensions within the societies concerned. And occupation further deepened conflicts among Greeks, Soviets, Italians, and so on. All of the guerrilla wars included an element of internal struggle, and some of them evolved into outright civil war under German occupation in the early 1940s. Often, multiple parties fought over contrasting visions of their country's future. It is possible, though too limiting, to write this purely as a history of Nazi treatment of other peoples. If one includes locals in the analysis, one could still write this strictly as a political history, but this approach would also disregard much of the broader context. Hence, I suggest including elements of a social history of mass violence, which, in this case, also facilitates a broader understanding of the survival chances of Jews caught in the middle of this pattern of conflict (see Chapter 11). I will make similar arguments about the participatory character of famines, which are complex social processes that no government – not even a Nazi one – can completely control. Market mechanisms sometimes helped Jews survive, at least for some time, but violent policies often tried to counter such survival strategies (see Chapter 9).

In connection with these two issues of 'security' and food, persecution against Jews and others took place in an environment of restrictions on movement and communication, of numerous prohibitions and threats, registrations, checks, raids, and the need for official papers, and of rationing, inflation and black markets – all of which

[28] A similar demand is made in Bajohr and Pohl 2006, pp. 10, 17.

made the struggle for survival so hard. And it happened in the context of the waning of solidarity that accompanied social fragmentation in countries ridden by conflict. Those wanting to investigate one or more of the persecutions can hardly leave aside the crises in European societies.

Even if one focuses on the German persecutors, a concentration on government policies alone will not suffice. The possibilities offered for local participation to shape policies within the apparatus, the initiatives 'from below' to do so, the opportunities given to the forerunners of violent ideas and the denunciations – all this modified or diluted the state's monopoly on violence. Many German initiators or perpetrators of violence were not Nazis, such that ideas other than those pertaining to strictly Nazi conviction (e.g., Christian, conservative, nationalist, anti-communist) motivated them (see Chapter 6). This, too, points to the need to include more social history in what is now perpetrator history. When one reconstructs a victim's perspective, it becomes quite clear that the persecuted interacted not just with structures, authorities, or offices, but with people, and tried to find a modus of survival with them.

However, looking at Germans is not enough. The violence against Jews during World War II had not only a European geographical scope, but also a European political dimension beyond German actions. German forces occupied northern France for four whole years, and all of France for one-and-a-half years; and yet three-quarters of the Jews in France survived. This demonstrates that there were limits to German power, which implies, in turn, that the influence of non-German governments and societies on mass violence in the 1930s and 1940s needs to be studied. The roles of non-Germans, as we will see, were crucial beyond merely the low numbers of direct killings (non-Germans not under German command may have killed no more than 5–6% of the 6 million Jewish victims). Foreign influences were complex, as is again shown by the case of France, which had a national government and administration that was largely hostile to Jews, and a society comprised of many citizens who were not friendly to Jews either, but where deportation and murder were often obstructed. By no means should what I call the 'European dimension' imply that Europeans acted unanimously, all of them willing to victimize Jews. Much research has already been conducted on this European dimension, but so far there is little in the way of a synthetic analysis. My attempt to produce one (in Chapters 12–14) is informed by the approach of global history, which tries to go beyond national histories and make connections and comparisons across borders to include non-state actors. In the 1990s much research focused on German agents;

in the 2000s it was more about non-Germans. My account tries to fuse these tendencies.[29]

This leads us to some of this volume's important limitations. It is a synthesis, not a comprehensive study that covers all aspects of its topic. It does not deal with the attitudes and actions of states fighting Germany and with the aftermath of persecution, and it does not discuss the many interpretations and debates in the historiography. On a certain level of abstraction, it deals with the interrelationships of different persecutions with that of the Jews, with a variety of contexts and policy issues, and with the policies of various countries. But in terms of persecutors, this book can only sketch tendencies in the behavior of groups. As a synthesis, it says little about the complexity and contradictions of individuals' motivations and personalities. As part of this approach, this study will argue often on the basis of numbers and percentages – as this introduction already has done. Works on the persecution of European Jews that emphasize quantitative arguments have often been sharply criticized,[30] yet I find them useful. It is true that statistics cannot provide a full understanding of a human life, be it a victim or a persecutor. But behind the statistics in this volume stand critical implications for human fates, and the options that persecuted people had and those that were barred for them. If read carefully, the numbers can speak volumes.

Terminology and structure of this volume

At this point, some remarks on terminology seem appropriate. There are a number of words I will try to avoid because of the serious misconceptions they might lead to. The terms 'Holocaust' and 'Shoah' are not useful since neither has any analytical value. 'Holocaust' (derived from the Greek *holókauton*, or burned sacrifice) has a religious connotation unbefitting of the event it is supposed to refer to, and users of this term may mean by it either the persecution and murder of Jews alone, or Nazi German violence against any group more generally.[31] The word 'Shoah' carries undertones of natural disaster.[32] Importantly, 'Holocaust' and 'Shoah' have also been criticized as "teleological and anachronistic" terms that convey a retrospective view that makes complex processes

[29] Aside from Europeans, north African actors also have to be taken into account. About 2,000 Tunisian and Libyan Jews may have perished: see Sebag 1991, p. 254; Roumani 2008, pp. 29–35.

[30] For example, Fein 1979. Criticisms of her study are summarized in Croes 2011, pp. 68–74 and Zeller and Griffioen 1996, pp. 35–6.

[31] See Traverso 1999, pp. 7–9.

[32] Bauer 2013, p. 345 note 2.

appear "as a single event."[33] 'Auschwitz' as a metaphor for the entire extermination of Europe's Jews is misleading precisely because it implies a more centralized, factory-like process of the persecution and annihilation than what was actually the case.[34] Only one in six who fell victim to the extermination of European Jews died in Auschwitz (and every second murdered Jew died by gas), and little more than 1% of all non-Jews who died as a result of German policies did so in Auschwitz. 'Final solution' is a popular term, but out of the question – not only because it is an expression of perpetrator language, but also because it has changed its meaning over time. In 1937 and 1940, those who used it usually meant something other than total extermination.

I shall not use the words 'anti-Semite' or 'anti-Semitic' because of the possible misunderstanding that I also mean attitudes hostile toward Arabs and other groups to be included. And despite the fact that Hitler and others called themselves anti-Semites, their thinking and policies did not necessarily apply scientific racism as much as the use of that term suggests (see Chapter 7).[35] Instead of 'anti-Semitic,' I will use expressions such as 'anti-Jewish.' Some scholars have even objected to the term 'Jew' with regard to the persecution of the 1930s and 1940s because it had no clear definition. At the time, 'Jew' could include persons converted to Christianity decades before, who did not define themselves as Jews and people not recognized as Jews by Jewish communities. Rather, it applied to people who a state's representatives or citizens *categorized* as Jews. But one doesn't want to continually repeat this qualification, and writing the word 'Jew' in quotation marks instead does not solve this problem of terminology either.[36] I will also avoid the terms 'collaboration' or 'collaborator,' since in this context they connote, for many Europeans, treason against one's country – whereas in fact most so-called 'collaborators' regarded themselves as fierce nationalists. The concept 'collaboration' has hampered research in the past. Additionally, so-called 'puppet states' did not necessarily act like puppets.[37] Finally, I will not speak of 'perpetrators' since this term – derived as it is from a legal framework that proved not very successful in analyzing or punishing the acts in question – unduly limits guilt to those few people carrying out, or responsible in a narrow sense, for violent acts, and separates them

[33] Steinberg 1998, p. 350.
[34] Here I differ from Traverso 1999, pp. 7–9.
[35] For example, see the skepticism of Strauss and Kampe 1988, p. 10, and Wistrich 1991, p. xvi. Wistrich starts his book with the phrase: "Antisemitism is a problematic term" (ibid., p. xv). Nazis used the semantic field around "anti-Semitism" less frequently than many assume: Rürup 1975, p. 112.
[36] Cole 1999; less radical is Lewkowicz 2006.
[37] See Tönsmeyer 2003, pp. 341–7; Hirschfeld 1991, pp. 8–10.

too easily from larger groups involved in such acts. Rather, I will speak of 'persecutors.' It has to be added that, in my view, 'persecution' includes official and semi-state official measures, but also the actions of non-state agents.[38]

This book's structure deviates from most studies of the persecution and murder of European Jews. Many syntheses and comprehensive studies follow a more or less chronological order.[39] Some are arranged country by country.[40] A few combine a chronological with a thematic approach.[41] My book keeps the initial chronological account (which follows after this introduction) relatively short, and then offers two larger analytical sections in addition to chapters on persecutors' and victims' responses. One section consists of chapters that each deal with one ideological, political or economic context of the persecution of Jews and also make connections with policies against other major affected victim groups. The second group of chapters deals with the persecution of Jews by non-German states and societies. In this way, the book offers more analysis than narrative; it tells few exemplary stories.

38 For Pohl, the term includes only state and semi-state policies: Pohl 2003, p. 1.

39 Longerich 1998a; Friedländer 1998 and 2006; Browning and Matthäus 2003; Bergen 2003; Bloxham 2009.

40 Hilberg 1994a; Benz 1991.

41 Dawidowicz 1987.

Part I

Persecution by Germans

2 Before 1933

In the nineteenth century, the region that would become Germany underwent profound economic, social, political and cultural transformation. Especially from the middle of the century, industrialization set in forcefully. By 1900, Germany was one of the two greatest industrial nations – together with the USA – leading in steel, chemical, and, later, electrical industries. Around 1900, about half of all Germans lived in urban areas to which many impoverished rural dwellers had moved and where a broad middle class was emerging which, by 1900, included, increasingly, many white-collar workers. From the 1840s to the late nineteenth century, streams of Germany's rural poor emigrated, particularly to the Americas. Inside Germany, a network of large cities developed linked by a railroad system that was largely complete by 1880. Imbalances remained – the northeast, still dominated by large rural estates, contained few industrial, urban centers. Germany became a leading nation also in science, technology, and, by the early twentieth century, the arts.

By 1806, the remnants of the outdated first German empire had collapsed under the Napoleonic onslaught. Under the leadership of Prussia, the largest German state, a new German nation state was founded in 1871 – a constitutional monarchy that united smaller kingdoms and duchies, but which excluded Austria. New ministries and strong bureaucratic institutions were swiftly established. In the late nineteenth century, government interference in the economy and social life increased with the first rudimentary elements of social insurance. This insufficiently addressed the so-called 'social question' of the millions of urban workers living in miserable conditions who increasingly formed their own political and social organizations which threatened bourgeois-aristocratic rule. Tendencies toward a welfare state became stronger – although without ending widespread poverty – after Germany became a republic with the introduction of universal suffrage in late 1918. The monarchy was toppled by infuriated workers and soldiers who were weary of a war effort primarily placed on their shoulders that seemed to them to make less and less sense, especially given that Germany was heading toward defeat. Red flags flew over Berlin, but then the strong working-class movement split, and the radical left was defeated. The period of the Weimar Republic was characterized by economic and political instability and fierce internal conflicts between the political left and right in which the initially strong centrist parties melted away.

In terms of foreign policy, after the Napoleonic Wars there had been decades of peace in the area that became Germany – interrupted, from 1864 to 1871, by the three wars of German unification against Denmark, the Habsburg Empire and France. Germany emerged from these as the new great power in central Europe. Often regarded with suspicion by European leaders and intellectuals for its militarism, Germany was opposed by France and, after some time, also Great Britain and Russia – while Germany allied with Austria-Hungary (previously with Russia), and for a while with Italy. Bloody warfare was not unknown during the allegedly peaceful Second Reich, but between 1904 and 1908 such conflict took place in the overseas colonies that had been acquired since 1884, with Germany hardly bothering rival European nations. Germanization policies in the east, which began in the 1870s, failed due to the resistance of Polish nationalists. When German imperialism – fueled by the desire of the ruling classes to acquire a dominant position in Europe, in world politics, and in the global economy – turned against Russia, France and Great Britain in 1914, Germany, together with her weaker allies, was defeated in World War I and subjected to substantial territorial losses, extensive disarmament and reparation payments.

Many of these developments were not limited to Germany. In the same period, other European countries also experienced industrialization, urbanization, the rise of the middle class, the social question, economic boom and then instability, the founding or strengthening of nation states, the beginnings of the welfare state and mass participation in politics, nationalism and imperialism – to varying degrees. The same was true for gradual secularization and from the 1920s the rise of the political right led to right-wing authoritarian governments coming to power in large parts of eastern, southern and central Europe.

The emancipation of the Jews was connected with the political emancipation of the middle classes. In Germany, both processes were long and conflict-ridden. Legal discrimination against Jews was largely lifted in four waves: between 1800 and 1810, in the 1840s, in the 1860s, and the rest in 1919. Before 1871 this process, driven by Enlightenment thought and skeptical bureaucracies, developed separately in each of the German states.[1] Other European states also granted Jews equal rights from

[1] Niewyk 1980, pp. 3–5; Hecht 2003, pp. 15, 34; Mohrmann 1972, p. 98; Rürup 1975, pp. 17–20, 29–30, 34, 78–9; for Baden see ibid., pp. 37–73.

the 1830s through to the 1870s.[2] Emancipation, however, was fueled by non-Jewish expectation that Jews would assimilate. The nineteenth century witnessed the acquisition of wealth by large parts of German Jewry (in contrast to the situation of most Jews in the early 1800s[3]). During the industrialization process their traditional commercial skills and educational attainments helped such Jews, together with non-Jews, to co-pioneer business expansion. Central and western European Jews became important members of their countries' bourgeoisie, middle class and intelligentsia. The Jewish underclasses shrank, relatively speaking, although much less so in eastern Europe.[4] More and more Jews moved to the cities, which made them socially and politically visible.[5] By the 1920s, between two-thirds and 92% of the Jews in Great Britain, France, Austria and Denmark lived in the national capitals; in Germany this figure was 30%.[6]

Concerning religion, Jewish communities diversified into traditional, orthodox and mostly secularized groups.[7] There were relatively few conversions to Christianity but much intermarriage in Germany and large parts of Europe (with Poland being one notable exception), the children from which became for the most part Christians.[8] This seems to indicate trust and amity.[9] In political terms, most German and Austrian Jews supported liberal parties by the late nineteenth century, and the social democrats by the 1920s.[10] Concurrently with their social differentiation, a variety of Jewish political organizations ranging from liberal to leftist to conservative, or leftist Zionist, emerged. This variety reflected discord, debate and some anxiety about where the future of Jews should lie. Zionists gained strength in Germany after 1918 and even a slight majority in Austria in the 1930s.[11] Nonetheless, just 2,000 German Jews emigrated to Palestine before 1933.[12] By the early twentieth century, the majority of German, French and Hungarian Jews were proud and more or less successful citizens of their countries

[2] Claussen 1994, p. 142; Rürup 1975, p. 80.
[3] See Rürup 1975, pp. 14–15, 26–7, 45, 55.
[4] See, for example, Melson 1992, p. 90.
[5] In Berlin, Frankfurt am Main, Breslau and Beuthen, Jews made up 4–6% of the population: Günther 1930, p. 331 and unpaginated insert.
[6] Melson 1992, p. 86.
[7] Battenberg 1990, pp. 161–2; for Prussia see Niewyk 1980, p. 123 and for lenient observance p. 102.
[8] Niewyk 1980, pp. 98–9; Barkai 1997, p. 39; Strauss and Kampe 1988, p. 9 note 1.
[9] By contrast, Jochmann (1988a, p. 183) argued that the increase in intermarriage served Jews "by forestalling danger and social isolation."
[10] Paucker 1988, pp. 143, 154–5; Niewyk 1980, p. 29; Maderegger 1973, pp. 73–4.
[11] See Almog 1990, pp. 24, 32; Niewyk 1980, pp. 149–50, 156. For Austria see Maderegger 1973, pp. 6–50, 55, 67.
[12] Niewyk 1980, p. 141.

and members of their own countries' middle classes and no longer an oppressed, persecuted and suffering people. Soviet rule in Russia formally liberated the Jews there, as did laws in some other eastern European states – but the situation of Jews in this part of the continent, where they lived in much greater numbers and often represented a larger proportion of the population,[13] was more tenuous. In many regions, their lives were characterized by small-town residency, a low degree of acculturation, low intermarriage rates, the widespread use of the Yiddish language, religious orthodoxy, a lower-middle-class or proletarian background and high birth rates.[14]

The social position of Jews

Traditions among Jews, as well as Christian laws prohibiting Jewish ownership of land and participation in many professions, had for centuries confined Jews mainly to trade and finance. After emancipation, many turned successfully to other jobs. By 1933–34, about half of the economically active Jews in Germany and Austria worked in trade as compared to more than 90% in 1817.[15] Like other citizens, Jews were affected by social changes, and while some of them managed to adapt, others, fitting less well the stereotype of Jewish adaptability, remained stuck in their families' traditional occupations.[16] Their numbers varied. In Poland in 1931, 36.6% of Jews worked in commerce and insurance. In inter-war Yugoslavia, a third of the economically active Jewish population worked in trade and commerce, 44% in the civil service, and 8% in the liberal professions.[17] Similarly, 34% of the Jews in Italy in 1931 were merchants and nearly 11% worked in the professions, while 25% were white-collar workers.[18]

Jews formed a large part of the bourgeoisie and intelligentsia in many European countries. In Poland, 58.7% of those working in commerce and industry (including the skilled trades) were Jews, but they were underrepresented in the civil service. The number of Jews among merchants

13 By 1933, Jews represented less than 1.4% of the population in western Europe, Germany and most of southern and southeastern Europe; between 2% and 3% in Austria, Czechoslovakia and Russia proper; and 4–10% in Poland, Ukraine, Belarus, Lithuania, Hungary, Romania and Latvia. See Wannsee Conference 2009, pp. 18–19. Some 19–35% of the population of large Polish cities was Jewish; in towns in eastern Poland 42–63%: Mendelsohn 1983, pp. 23–4.

14 Mendelsohn 1983 (pp. 6–7) finds this in Poland, Lithuania, eastern Czechoslovakia and large parts of Romania.

15 Genschel 1966, pp. 29, 288; for 1817 see Volkov 1990, p. 39.

16 Barkai 1997, pp. 41–2.

17 Rothschild 1974, p. 39; Gitman 2011, p. 10.

18 Schlemmer and Woller 2005, p. 170.

declined from a staggering 62.7% in 1921 due to government discrimination.[19] In many countries, Jews held a proportion of the prestigious positions far exceeding their percentage of the population. In Vienna, by 1936, 62% of the lawyers, 47% of the physicians, 28% of the university professors (as compared to only 3% in France), close to 63% of the dentists, 73% of the textile merchants and 18% of the bank officers were Jews. Jews controlled 77% of the banks, 64% of the cinemas, 63% of the daily newspapers and 40% of the jewelry stores. In Hungary the situation was similar.[20] In Romania, Jews "controlled the bulk of private capital in the export, insurance, textile, leather, electrotechnical, chemical, housing, printing, and publishing industries." Some 70% of the journalists and 99% of the stockbrokers were Jews.[21] In 1931, 56% of all private medical practices and 33.5% of the lawyers in Poland were Jewish, not unlike the situation in Czechoslovakia.[22] Compared to other countries, the position of Jews in Germany, especially in the professions, was less dominant. In 1933, 11% of the physicians and 16% of the lawyers were counted as Jews (the proportions were a little higher in Prussia), and Jews controlled a few specific business areas: 40% of the textile trade, 80% of department store sales, and nearly 20% of the private banks. Among workers and craftsmen, German Jews were underrepresented. They did not make up a large proportion of the industrialists either.[23] Whereas 21% of the employees in trade in Prussia had been Jews in 1861, the figure dropped to 5% by 1925 as non-Jews streamed into this economic sector. By 1933, 7% of the retail stores in Berlin were in Jewish hands. By contrast, a third of the board members of companies on the stock exchange registered in Berlin were Jews.[24] In western Europe, the socioeconomic role of Jews was less pronounced, but the position of the Bulgarian Jews was quite exceptional in Europe in that they were not much overrepresented among the bourgeoisie.[25]

Generally, these data tend to hide the Jewish underclass; although few Jews in central and western Europe could be called poor,[26] there were

[19] Rothschild 1974, p. 40; Melzer 1997, p. 3.

[20] Maderegger 1973, p. 220; Genschel 1966, p. 289. For France see Zuccotti 1993, p. 57; for Hungary see Rothschild 1974, p. 196.

[21] Rothschild 1974, p. 289 (quote); Brustein and King 2004a, p. 696. For the strong position of Jews as factory owners in some industries in Greece see Plaut 1996, p. 54.

[22] Mendelsohn 1983, p. 27; for Slovakia see Witt 2012, p. 103; for Bohemia and Moravia see Barkai 1997, p. 43.

[23] Winkler 1981, p. 276; Genschel 1966, p. 287; Niewyk 1980, pp. 13–15; for Prussia in 1932 see Battenberg 1990, p. 243.

[24] Barkai 1991, p. 130; Genschel 1966, pp. 21–2; Schreiber 2007, pp. 19, 24, 30. For similar proportions in Yugoslavia see Freidenreich 1979, p. 19.

[25] See the data in Brustein and King 2004a, p. 695.

[26] For Yugoslavia (excluding Sarajevo) see Gordijew 1999, pp. 58–9.

many, for example, in Poland and Romania. Still, many of the aforementioned data illustrate why Jews became the envy of European societies and how it could happen that they were collectively identified with wealth. Such envy could indicate, on the one hand, the desire to eliminate business competitors, or, on the other hand, a sheer malevolent desire to see certain sections of society lose their elevated status.[27] Although most of the figures cited above are taken from the works of scholars of Jewish background, the contemporary political right, nationalists, and indeed Nazis used them in particular ways[28] to suggest that the elite position of Jews was illegitimate and should be eliminated via government measures since Jews were standing in the way of the well-being of non-Jews. This trend began after non-Jews started to enter into business and the intelligentsia in larger numbers than they had before, placing them in direct competition with already-established Jews at a time when they were trying to forge careers.

Social mobility and European Jews

Studies often place the history of the persecution of Jews by Nazi Germany in a social historical context of Jewish ascent. The argument is supported by data from the late nineteenth century, but usually does not consider the time period after World War I.[29] In contrast, I think that the destruction of Jews in Germany and other countries occurred during a period of social stagnation and even as the position of many Jews was *declining* as a result of a complex social transformations in which new groups of non-Jews were rising in social status.[30]

In Germany, Austria, Bohemia and Moravia, Hungary and Italy, the Jewish population stagnated or decreased slightly in the 1920s and early 1930s – i.e., before the Nazis came to power. Having adopted a bourgeois urban lifestyle, Jews had fewer children, but emigration also had an impact.[31] In Germany, this seems to have been true in particular for regions where few Jews lived to begin with.[32] The German countrywide trend, which had already started in the late nineteenth century, spread to

27 Aly 2011, pp. 11, 83–93, 301; Barkai 1997 (pp. 44, 47) stresses the role of direct competitors in this context.

28 See, for example, Seraphim 1938.

29 Melson 1992 is symptomatic of this kind of analysis. For the period after 1918, he deals with political, rather than social processes regarding Jews.

30 A similar thesis can be found in Arendt 1998 [1951], pp. 32–3; Barkai 1997, see that work's title and p. 49.

31 Freidenreich 1979, p. 59; Hilberg 1992a, pp. 157–8; for Germany see Barkai 1997, pp. 37–40; Genschel 1966, p. 274, and Winkler 1981, p. 275; for Vienna and the rest of Austria see also Maderegger 1973, especially pp. 1–3.

32 Liesenberg 1995, pp. 444, 449.

Munich (the city where Hitler lived) after 1910.[33] In other European countries the strong increase in the Jewish population continued for longer.[34]

Events throughout the 1920s, and in particular the global economic crisis that began in 1929, intensified an already existing trend. Beginning in the late nineteenth century, non-Jews opened businesses and entered commerce in large numbers, and the market share of Jews decreased, particularly in trade. Jewish writers in Germany in the period 1930–33 noted a decrease of Jewish economic power, although with respect to those in positions of economic leadership the Depression affected Jews less than it did non-Jews prior to 1933.[35] But during World War I and the period of the Weimar Republic, many small Jewish merchants were as badly affected as non-Jews, and this contributed to the decline in the average real income of German Jews in general – although the number of Jewish paupers was small.[36] This loss of wealth contradicted the widespread hostile image of the Jewish war profiteer.[37] In many countries inter-war economic insecurity hit Jews especially hard, especially in Poland, a country more greatly affected than its neighbors. There, the "impoverishment of the Jewish masses and a reduction in government allocations enfeebled the [Jewish] community at a constantly growing rate."[38] The same occurred as a result of nationalizations of firms in the wake of the Soviet annexations of the Baltic states, eastern Poland, Bessarabia and Bukovina.[39] The many post-war refugees in Europe who tried to establish themselves socially – largely in urban centers – competed with Jewish businesses, often successfully, with help of Christian governments, as was the case in Salonica, Greece, from where 20,000–25,000 Jews emigrated in the 1930s.[40] But given the widespread restrictions, emigration provided less and less of an outlet for Polish Jews.[41] The "suicide epidemic" among German Jews in the 1920s, as discussed in the contemporary press, was possibly connected with a crisis of small Jewish businesses.[42] Furthermore, non-Jews increasingly pursued

33 Piper 2005, p. 39; for Munich see Cahnman 1979, p. 407.

34 Battenberg 1990, pp. 238–9.

35 Genschel 1966, pp. 16, 21–3, 29–30, 276; Barkai 1997, p. 48.

36 Barkai 1997, p. 44; Niewyk 1980, pp. 17–20, 24.

37 Hecht 2003, p. 63.

38 Alberti 2006, p. 28; for Poland in general see Mahler 1944, p. 310. Quote in Weiss 1977, p. 359.

39 In Lithuania, 80% of the commercial enterprises that were nationalized had been Jewish-owned: Levinson 2006, p. 380.

40 Rozen 2005, p. 134; Mazower 2004, p. 406.

41 Jewish emigration from Poland fell to less than 20,000 annually after 1925, down from 70,000 per year in 1900–14. See Marcus 1983, p. 388.

42 Niewyk 1980, p. 20; Kwiet 1984, pp. 142–4 (but Kwiet puts this in the context of the Jewish social "rise," ibid., p. 144).

higher education, and Jewish advantages here also diminished. By the 1920s both the absolute number and the percentage of Jewish students had decreased from what they had been in 1910. Among Polish university students, the percentage of Jews peaked in 1923–24 (at 24.4%), and the absolute number in 1932–33 (at which time Jews represented 18.7% of the total). The later *numerus clausus* laws (most of which restricted the number of Jewish students to Jews' percentage of the general population) belong in this context and served to consolidate and accelerate the gains of non-Jews.[43] A similar trend emerged in less prestigious jobs: the percentage of Jewish merchants in Poland peaked in 1921, and the number of Jewish factory workers also started to decline as new state monopolies in certain industries preferred to employ Christians. As a result, even more Jews were forced to become craftsmen.[44]

In many ways, Jews (not totally unlike the German minorities in eastern Europe after World War I) came under many forms of economic pressure. This was the flip side of a comprehensive European (as well as German) process of social mobilization among non-Jews in the early twentieth century.[45] Among those attempting to rise were some of the most intense Jew-haters. Many of the regional leaders of the Nazi Party were among these climbers. They often came from artisan or working-class families and joined the ranks of the political and social elite.[46]

Anti-Jewish attitudes

Traditional society in central Europe had been dominated by agriculture and structured by Christian beliefs which assigned a marginal social position to Jews and led to discrimination against them but which started to dissolve by the early nineteenth century. It was in this context, around 1840, that the term "the Jewish question" entered the German language.[47] Change through progress, industrialization and population growth "led to the loosening of century-old social ties, to the erosion of religious traditions and the invalidation of ethical systems."[48] In addition to religious anti-Judaism, which focused on the Jewish rejection of Jesus as the Messiah, the Jews' alleged guilt for his death, and myths about Jewish rituals involving the slaughter of Christians, prejudices against

[43] Mahler 1944, especially pp. 341, 343. For Germany see Niewyk 1980, p. 19; for a similar development in Yugoslavia, see Freidenreich 1979, pp. 66, 222.

[44] Melzer 1997, p. 3.

[45] Aly 2011, p. 192.

[46] Aly 2011, pp. 218–21, 318–21.

[47] See Holz 2001, p. 253.

[48] Jochmann 1988b, p. 99.

Jews as usurers, cheaters and exploiters had spread through Europe since the twelfth century.[49] Enlightenment thinkers' statements in favor of Jewish emancipation, as well as anti-Jewish propaganda at the end of the eighteenth and the beginning of the nineteenth centuries, provide abundant examples of how dominant the image of the Jew as cheater had become.[50]

Some scholars see a profound change in anti-Jewish attitudes in Germany in the 1870s, with a switch from a political to a racial basis as indicated by the coining of the term 'anti-Semitism' in 1879.[51] But a linguist's closer look at German anti-Jewish writings between 1789 and 1872 shows that there were earlier "attempts to justify hatred of Jews biologically-anthropologically." Jews were already then regarded as aliens who had a malignant influence on the state, culture, society and the economy, and were described in language that alluded most frequently to Jewish usury, betrayal, alienness and intrusiveness. Animal metaphors portrayed Jews variously as parasites and vermin – a threat to healthy blood.[52] The mixture of religious, socioeconomic and racist anti-Judaism observed in late nineteenth-century Germany[53] included few entirely new trends.[54] Religious elements continued to exist. By the 1920s, Christian anti-Jewish propaganda, in turn, combined religious, social, economic, political and cultural arguments.[55] However, right-wing criticism after 1918 that Germany was being subjugated by 'Jewish' politicians – which referred especially to leftist revolutionary leaders in Berlin and Munich, and to the primary author of the republic's constitution – *was* new. In reality, Jewish ministers serving in national cabinets between 1919 and 1932 were not significantly overrepresented compared to the Jewish proportion of the population more generally.[56]

In social terms, anti-Jewish sentiments have been attributed to German artisans who underwent a profound upheaval in the nineteenth century due to industrialization and the lifting of traditional

[49] Wistrich 1991, pp. 26–7, 30–32.

[50] Battenberg 1990, pp. 87–99, 124; Rürup 1975, pp. 15, 62, 76.

[51] This is the flip side of comparatively little emphasis on hostility against Jews among liberals. In this view, emancipation was completed by the 1860s and then questioned as part of a conservative backlash. Rürup 1988, p. 94; Rürup 1975, pp. 29, 73. For the term 'Anti-Semitism,' see Reinhard Rürup and Thomas Nipperdey, "Antisemitismus – Entstehung, Funktion und Geschichte eines Begriffs" in Rürup 1975, pp. 95–114.

[52] For biological arguments see Hortzitz 1988, pp. 1 (quote), 262–73; for economic, animal and blood metaphors, see ibid., pp. 120, 140–3, 148–53, 177–86, 211–14, 223. See also quotes in Rürup 1975, pp. 44, 56.

[53] Almog 1990, p. 35.

[54] See also Volkov 1990, pp. 59–60.

[55] Niewyk 1980, pp. 55–61.

[56] Hecht 2003, pp. 77–82; for the ministers see Mohrmann 1972, p. 97.

handicraft regulations. Most of them had supported liberalism in Germany for decades, before turning conservative in around 1870.[57] Several German middle-class revolutionaries of 1848, as Polish and Russian democrats, expressed fierce anti-Judaism, and in Bavaria 80,000 signatures were collected for a petition protesting against emancipation of the Jews.[58] Among conservatives, some aristocrats, military officers, state bureaucrats, clergymen and intellectuals rejected Jews because they saw their own dominance under threat. (It was a similar situation in Austria.)[59] Only in the 1890s, when some anti-Jewish activists went on to attack Christianity and the lack of legal protections for workers, did they fall out of favor of the leading German conservatives.[60] Resentment against Jews before 1914 was apparently particularly strong among rural dwellers and the lower middle class, in addition to traditional elites, and in Protestant areas of central and eastern Germany; this was also true of the early members of the Nazi Party a decade later.[61] Anti-Jewish propaganda in Tsarist Russia succeeded in swaying opinion among similar groups.[62] Among the German working-class movement (and even more so in France), there were influential figures who identified Jews collectively with the oppressive and exploitative bourgeoisie, but these were then replaced by advocates of more differentiated views, as was the case in France after 1900, and criticisms were instead directed more against the capitalist system in general.[63] Significantly, new impulses for hostility against Jews in the late nineteenth century came from elements of the German intelligentsia. The absence of the topic in journals that historians consider important would suggest that for many *Bildungsbürger* the 'Jewish question' was not important or did not exist.[64] By the 1920s, however, many in the professions, students, civil servants, small business owners and white-collar employees thought otherwise – arguing that Jews had undermined the previous war effort, supported the Versailles treaty, toppled the monarchy, created internal unrest, eroded the traditional culture, destroyed the middle class, infiltrated society with usury, and

[57] Volkov 1990, pp. 25–6, 42, 47–8.
[58] Aly 2011, pp. 20–36, 65; Rürup 1975, p. 28.
[59] Jochmann 1988a, pp. 25, 31, 40, 55; Jochmann 1988b, pp. 99, 103–10. For Austria see Pulzer 1966, pp. 223–8.
[60] Jochmann 1988b, pp. 115–16.
[61] Jochmann 1988b, p. 134; for the NSDAP see Mühlberger 2003, esp. pp. 40, 53–6, 68.
[62] But in late Russia, not only the working class but also the bourgeoisie was largely exempted around 1900: Löwe 1981, pp. 201–2.
[63] Aly 2011, pp. 126–36; Mohrmann 1972, p. 66; for France see Dreyfus 1981, pp. 231–5; Birnbaum 1992, pp. 91, 94.
[64] Zmarzlik 1981, pp. 254, 266.

fueled conflicts between rural and urban dwellers and between workers and the state.[65]

The tendencies mentioned in the previous paragraph were not all unique to Germany.[66] In other European countries, too, Jews were integrated in the modern nation-building process, but this was increasingly controversial among nationalists and especially questioned by conservatives. Controversy was especially intense from the late nineteenth century whenever the question of the true German, French or Russian nation arose. Thus, before the emergence of fascism many conservatives and reactionaries identified Jews with the undesirable uprootedness of modernity. Anti-Jewish sentiments coincided with hostility against neighboring countries or ethnicities to which Jews were linked by nationalists; and anti-Jewish propaganda was widespread.[67] The dissolution of multinational empires in the nineteenth and early twentieth centuries also put Jews in a difficult position. In those empires the principle of ethnic homogeneity had played a less important role in the foundation of the state, and Jews had been one of many minorities.

From the 1870s on, anti-Jewish policies played an important role in the foundation of certain German organizations and political parties. However, these parties remained small and collectively they enjoyed little voter support. As with Jew-baiters among the intellectuals, they remained at odds with each other because of the widely varying analyses and policies they offered, all of which was usually presented with uncompromising claims to knowledge of the truth. During World War I, and throughout the 1920s, this situation did not change much.[68] The absence of government policies against Jews and of strong anti-Jewish parties (the city of Vienna, Austria, ruled by an anti-Jewish party from 1891 to 1911, was an exception[69]) has led to an interpretation that hatred of Jews was a marginal issue in German politics – at least before 1918. Even if this were true, the fact remains that anti-Jewish attitudes were established and cultivated in civil society and among the administrative elites. Various associations such as student fraternities, sports clubs, the League of German Farmers and the German National Association of Shop Assistants excluded Jews as members, and the nationalist All German

65 Winkler 1981, pp. 272, 281–5.

66 Pulzer 1966 (pp. 109–53, 162–77) draws parallels between Germany and Austria.

67 Almog 1990, esp. p. 38; Zuccotti 1993, pp. 13–14; Löwe 1981, p. 208; see also Volkov 1990. Kallis 2009 (pp. 1–2, 99–106) locates the effort to reclaim an idealized fatherland through some kind of cleansing in facism.

68 For strong anti-Jewish tendencies in the German National Peoples Party (DNVP), one of the largest parties, see Mohrmann 1972, p. 150; Niewyk 1980, p. 49; Adam 1972, pp. 25, 42–3.

69 See Pulzer 1966, pp. 144–53, 162–77.

League produced anti-Jewish propaganda. Anti-Judaism spread from the universities via alumni to local judges, lawyers, civil servants, pastors and high school teachers, as well as military officers.[70] Tacit understandings and unofficial arrangements structured social initiatives for excluding or discriminating against Jews. It was the intensity of these social practices among academic elites (rather than party politics or official policies) that distinguished the developments in Germany from other countries in the imperial era. Anti-Jewish hostility among guests at holiday resorts and in hiking clubs in Germany, and especially in Austria, was another example of such unofficial initiatives – but such phenomena were also known in other countries, including the USA.[71] The same was true for anti-Jewish boycotts, but these had a particular quality in Germany in that they were sometimes organized by large concerns, including parts of the German media in the early 1930s.[72]

Jewish immigrants became special targets of hostility in Germany, as elsewhere in Europe. This was usually about a westward migration of relatively poor Jews who sought to establish themselves in a new home country. Often religiously orthodox, their dress styles made them stand out. Enmity focused on the so-called eastern Jews who since the late nineteenth century had sought passage through Germany on their way to western Europe or the Americas. Often they tried to earn money as laborers to finance the rest of their trip; thus, this hostility targeted Jews as poor outsiders. By 1914 there were 80,000 of them in Germany; their number peaked around 150,000 in 1919; and in 1932 there were close to 100,000 eastern European Jews in the country. Many more had passed through Germany since the 1910s.[73] Expulsions during the early 1920s seem to have been limited to a few hundred.[74] Those in 1884–86, when about 10,000 Jews and then 20,000 non-Jews from Russian Poland were evicted from Germany, had been much larger.[75] In France, members of the political right distinguished even more sharply assimilated French Jews from Jewish immigrants, but without attacking the former.[76] The period from the 1860s to the 1910s has been called the classical era of general European xenophobia, a period during which riots against working-class, non-Jewish Italian, Irish and Polish immigrants recurred in France, Great

[70] Rürup 1988, pp. 95–6; Jochmann 1988a, pp. 60, 65, 68, 146–8; Jochmann 1988b, p. 118; Battenberg 1990, pp. 196–8; Volkov 1990, pp. 15–16.
[71] See Bajohr 2003, esp. pp. 68, 139, 145, 147, 163, 167; Hecht 2003, pp. 299–331.
[72] See Rosenkötter 2003, p. 63; Hecht 2003, pp. 332–6; Wildt 2007, pp. 145–51; Barkai 1988, p. 15.
[73] Winkler 1981, pp. 274–5; Mohrmann 1972, pp. 170, 173.
[74] Walter 1999, pp. 55–6, 71–2, 76–7.
[75] Aschheim 1982, p. 43.
[76] See Birnbaum 1992, pp. 101, 243–5, 125 note 19.

Britain and Germany.[77] Beginning in the late nineteenth century, negative stereotypes about eastern Christian and especially Jewish immigrants to the USA and Germany as carriers of contagious diseases also led to the establishment of a mandatory system of health inspections – including delousing – especially on Germany's eastern borders.[78]

In nineteenth-century Germany, several, usually non-lethal, pogroms occurred – some in the years after 1819, some around 1848, and locally a few in the 1880s and 1890s, each time following new official steps toward equal rights for Jews.[79] The wave of political murders of Jewish political leaders such as Rosa Luxemburg, Kurt Eisner, Gustav Landauer, Hugo Haase and Walther Rathenau (and executions following the trials of others) from 1919 to 1922 was exceptional in modern German history before 1933.[80] Hundreds of thousands participated in demonstrations across Germany protesting against the murder of the Foreign Minister, Rathenau.[81] Non-Jewish leftists and centrists such as Karl Liebknecht and Matthias Erzberger were also killed (and Eisner's murderer had some Jewish ancestors). In total, there were about 400 assassinations. In most cases, the victims were apparently not Jews.[82] Recent studies have demonstrated that, in general, violence against Jews during the period of the Weimar Republic after 1922 was widespread; but they also show that it was usually non-lethal and that most attackers showed some minimal restraint. They give no indication of the overall number of Jews killed, but fortunately it seems to have been very few.[83] There were extensive debates on the extreme right about pogroms, but except for the food riots in mid 1919, the pogroms in the fall of 1923, and the Nazi-organized Kurfürstendamm riot in Berlin in 1931, attacks on Jews were, in reality, small scale or the work of individuals.[84] After 1848, such events, excluding those in 1923, had a local, marginal character.

Some scholars argue that aggression was channeled toward Jews as unprotected adversaries through certain conflict mechanisms in times of crisis; others, though, find the correlation less clear.[85] Others argue

[77] Kury 2003, pp. 19, 26–7; Zuccotti 1993, p. 14.

[78] Weindling 2000, pp. 16–17, 58–60, 64–5, 68–70, 79–80, 97, 117–18.

[79] Battenberg 1990, pp. 124–5; Niewyk 1980, p. 9; Volkov 1990, p. 70. (For France see Volkov 1990, p. 67).

[80] Niewyk 1980, p. 27.

[81] See Schumann 2001, pp. 163–5.

[82] Hecht 2003, p. 138; Gumbel 1922, pp. 43–9; for Eisner's murderer, Count Anton Arco-Valley, see Niewyk 1980, p. 27.

[83] See Walter 1999, esp. pp. 109, 130–6; Wildt 2007, pp. 74–7, 87–100. For exceptions see Walter 1999, pp. 203–4; Hecht 2003.

[84] Walter 1999, pp. 23–51; Hecht 2003, pp. 101–19, 163–86, 240.

[85] Jochmann 1988a, pp. 13, 20, 30, 64–5, 106, 167; Geiss 1988, p. 102; Strauss and Kampe 1988, p. 24; for Italy see Michaelis 1978, p. 6; for the latter view see Holz 2001, pp. 55–6. Geiss (1988) saw three anti-Jewish waves in Germany that were not

that middlemen minorities in general are particularly vulnerable during crises.[86] In the context of the economic crisis and famine of 1816–17 and the depressed land prices of the 1820s, Jews in Germany were accused of being responsible for the situation of indebted peasants and others; journeymen, shop assistants and the jobless participated enthusiastically in the anti-Jewish riots of 1819. Another wave of pogrom-like events occurred in 1848 in connection with inflation, famine, the failed revolution and attacks on other economic elites and on priests. This resembled the riots in Berlin in 1923 during hyperinflation.[87] The emergence of self-proclaimed anti-Semitism in the 1870s coincided, more or less, with the great depression which began in 1873, when criticism of liberalism and financial manipulations became widespread and mortality by natural causes in modern Germany reached an all-time high. Military defeat, the revolution, economic crisis and inflation between 1918 and 1923, and after 1929, were accompanied by increases in anti-Jewish hostility, and, according to one historian, economic stabilization during the period 1924–28 led to a decrease. Historians have also linked decrees restricting Jewish immigration in European states to the "political or economic crises" of 1849, 1857, 1882, 1920 and 1929.[88] Pierre Birnbaum found that Jews in France were similarly identified with decadence, decline and degeneration, especially during periods of political disorder: the 1890s, the 1930s and the 1950s.[89] Upheaval could also cross borders: German anti-Jewish propaganda may have contributed to the wave of pogroms that swept through parts of Russia in 1881, and was subsequently taken up in the form of hostility against Jews in Hungary in 1882.[90]

Imagined 'solutions'

It is often said that everybody should have known before 1933 that Hitler and the Nazis wanted to destroy the Jews. However, relevant documents

necessarily parallel to economic crises: from 1878 to 1881, 1893 to 1904 and 1912 to 1914; similarly Zmarzlik 1981, p. 254.

[86] See Fein 1979, p. 201; for Jews as a middlemen minority see Fein 1979, p. 6 and p. 360 note 5.

[87] Rürup 1988, p. 94; Rürup 1975, pp. 27, 51; Battenberg 1990, pp. 111, 124–5; Wistrich 1991, p. 55; Katz 1980, pp. 92–104. In the Scheunenviertel riot in Berlin in November 1923, non-Jews owned 70% of the stores that were looted: Walter 1999, p. 153. On a larger scale, non-Jewish estate owners, rich urbanites and members of the intelligentsia were also targeted during the pogroms in Russia in 1881 and 1905: Löwe 1981, p. 204.

[88] Strauss 1987, p. 188; Rürup 1975, p. 12; Levy 2010, p. 123; for the decrease see Winkler 1981, pp. 272, 283, 285. Hecht (2003, pp. 14, 187, 205) tries to relativize this. For the peak of mortality see Weindling 1989, p. 13.

[89] Birnbaum (1992, pp. 4–5, 286) locates a crisis of decolonization in the 1950s.

[90] Katz 1980, p. 275.

do not make this so obvious. According to the 1920 program of the Nazi Party, which was later declared "unchangeable," Jews should be stripped of their German citizenship, all Jews should be legally regarded as foreigners, and, as such, Germans should have priority over them with regard to employment, with the suggestion of a possible option to expel Jewish competitors. Jews were to be removed from the civil service, from journalism and from ownership of journals and newspapers; all immigration was to be outlawed and all immigrants (not just Jews) arriving after August 2, 1914, were to be expelled. "Usurers" and "grafters" were to be executed "regardless of their religious denomination and race."[91] There were similar Nazi demands in parliament before 1933.[92] Except for the last point, and, arguably, citizenship, these resembled many of the actual measures taken between 1933 and 1935. In May 1932, Hermann Göring told an Italian fascist newspaper that all Jewish immigrants who had arrived since 1914 would be expelled and that all Jews would be removed from leading positions in culture and education. In 1931, the Nazi daily newspaper, *Völkischer Beobachter*, carried an article that threatened to outlaw sexual contact between non-Jewish Germans and Jews. Alfred Rosenberg wrote in 1920 that Jews, who should be regarded as a separate nation within Germany, should no longer be allowed to serve in the military, or serve as politicians or as managers of cultural institutions; Germans should support Zionist tendencies.[93] Klaus Holz has argued that Hitler himself remained ambivalent in his speeches of the 1920s about the expulsion or the murder of Jews.[94]

In his book, *Mein Kampf*, Hitler did not explicitly say that he wanted to kill the Jews. His likening of Jews to vermin on several occasions was suggestive of this fact, but not unheard of in German anti-Jewish discourse. As is well known, he wrote of his regret that 12,000–15,000 "Hebrew corrupters of the people" had not "been held under poison gas" during World War I – as many frontline fighters had been – which would, as he argued, have helped prevent defeatism in Germany and reduce consequent losses at the front.[95] Of perhaps greater importance, Hitler also

[91] Nazi Party program, February 24, 1920, points 4–8, 18 and 23, www.dhm.de/lemo/html/dokumente/nsdap25/ (accessed September 30, 2013); an English translation can be found in Arad 1999, pp. 15–18; see Hilberg 1994a, p. 37; Schulle 2001, p. 50; Walter 1999, pp. 113 and 287 note 52.

[92] Meyer zu Uptrup 2003, pp. 179–80, 212–22; Adam 1972, p. 25; Graml 1988, p. 121; Walter 1999, p. 229.

[93] Piper 2005, p. 65; Niewyk 1980, p. 53; for Göring see Walter 1999, p. 235; Adam 1972, p. 27.

[94] Holz 2001, pp. 417–20; see also Walter 1999, p. 37.

[95] Hitler 1999 [1925–27], p. 679; for the remarks on vermin see Jäckel 1997 [1969], pp. 58–9; for Nazi leaders in general at this time see Niewyk 1980, p. 53.

formulated that "some day a German national court must judge and execute some ten thousand of the organizers and hence responsible criminals" of the leftist revolution and the Armistice of November 1918.[96] According to Hitler, many of these people were Jews. In reality, however, no such mass trials took place after 1933. Maybe still more significantly (and even less known), Hitler had stated that established "conceptions and ideas" could be destroyed only by brute force, after which the new holders of power must replace the uprooted ideas with new ones. "Force alone" offered no remedy, "except in the form of a complete extermination of even the very last exponent of the idea and the destruction of the last tradition." Such attempts to "exterminate a doctrine" were "doomed to failure, and not seldom end with the exact opposite of the desired result."[97] If one applies this thought to 'Jewish ideas' (which Hitler did not do explicitly), his remark can be understood in the sense that he *considered* mass annihilation but did not necessarily advocate it. As he saw things, it was unrealistic to expect that the extermination of the Jews alone could produce the complete mental-intellectual purge desired; and, if such a purge were to be carried out, it would also require the murder of all non-Jewish Marxists, liberals, and so on, something which the Nazis never undertook. Re-education was at least as important as violence.

Many of the Nazis' anti-Jewish demands were not new. In part, they echoed practices from the previous 1,500 years[98] and ideas voiced earlier by other rightist thinkers. In Tsarist Russia, for example, quotas restricting the number of Jewish university students were introduced in the 1880s and 1890s.[99] By 1880–81, university students and others were initiating public protests in Germany with the objective of having Jews excluded from the teaching professions and the civil service.[100] In his popular book of 1912, *If I Were the Emperor*, Heinrich Class – chairman of the All German League – had suggested declaring Jews to be legally foreign; prohibiting them from holding public office, serving in the military, practicing law, teaching, working in the theatre, holding important positions in banking or owning land; refusing them entry into the country; and expelling all Jewish aliens. They should also have their taxes doubled. All of these suggestions had the explicit aim of driving them from Germany as soon as possible.[101] Retired general, Konstantin Freiherr von Gebsattel, added in 1913 that sexual contact between Jews

[96] Hitler 1999 [1925–27], p. 545; see Jäckel 1997 [1969], p. 58.
[97] Hitler 1999 [1925–27], pp. 170–1.
[98] Hilberg 1994a, pp. 17–20.
[99] Prusin 2010, p. 29; Löwe 1981, p. 194.
[100] Jochmann 1988b, p. 113.
[101] Saller 1961, p. 28; Friedländer 1998, p. 76.

and non-Jewish Germans should be forbidden and that Jews should be prohibited from emigrating with their assets.[102] In the late nineteenth century, Eugen Dühring opposed intermarriage between Jews and non-Jews, although he did not call for a prohibition. In 1924, Arthur Dinter of the German-Folkish Freedom Party advocated outlawing such marriages, as well as sexual contact.[103] Achim Gercke and other Nazis declared in 1932 that it was important to segregate Jews from Germans. Jews should be put in concentration camps until they emigrated – although their complete removal abroad was possible, according to Gercke, only if a "confined national home" for them could be found.[104]

German activists were not alone in wanting to evict Jews from their country or from all of Europe. A number of public figures in Europe advocated this. In fact, some intellectuals had imagined removing all Jews from Europe since the late eighteenth century. Paul de Lagarde seems to have been the first – in the late 1800s – to suggest Madagascar explicitly as a possible destination, a thought that became widespread later and was taken up by the Nazis in 1940–41.[105] By the 1930s, however, many other Jewish settlement areas were being discussed.

Some intellectuals, such as Paul de Lagarde and Karl Paasch, called explicitly for the extermination of Jews in the 1880s and 1890s.[106] It is not always clear, though, if such radical demands were anything more than hyperbolic threats.[107] In the 1930s, some British proponents of the Madagascar plan were publicly considering the murder of Europe's Jews – including thoughts about so-called 'gentle' or 'humane' killing methods such as gas chambers.[108] Yet neither in Germany nor in Great Britain were there mass killings of Jews between the 1850s and 1933. The most lethal events for Jews in Europe during this time were probably the pogroms in Russia in 1903–05; the forced evacuation of Jews from the west of Russia in 1914–15 during World War I; the pogroms of 1917–21 in Ukraine and Poland, which took place in the context of the Russian civil war and which claimed up to 75,000 lives; and the killing of several thousand Jews in Hungary during the anti-communist repression of 1919.[109]

[102] Jochmann 1988b, pp. 137–8.
[103] Essner 1995, pp. 201–2.
[104] Schulle 2001, pp. 51–2, 56, 58.
[105] Jansen 1997, esp. pp. 35, 43, 48.
[106] Graml 1988, pp. 68, 79; see Stern 1965, p. 93.
[107] At times, de Lagarde argued instead for the expulsions of Jews (Stern 1965, p. 99).
[108] Jansen 1997, pp. 90, 95.
[109] Prusin 2010, pp. 41, 55, 57 and 104 note 2; Fischer 1988, pp. 138–41.

Pre-Nazi Germany: An extremely violent society?

Before 1933, Jews fled to Germany rather than from it. So, was Germany not relatively civilized until 1933 and the succeeding violence just a matter of one specific regime: the Nazis? In addition to the traumas of the soldiers who had fought in World War I, the consequences of which are not entirely clear, other things should be noted here. Mass destruction of civilians by Germans did claim more than a quarter of a million lives between 1900 and 1933, but few of the victims were Jews.

One complex of violence was the civil war between radical leftists and their opponents from 1918 to 1921.[110] Most of the 4,000–5,000 victims (which does not include those killed in the struggles at the Polish border) were workers and suspected leftists killed by rightist *Freikorps* irregulars in Berlin, Munich and the Ruhr area. The leftist and Nazi uprisings in 1923, and the street fighting between Nazis and communists at the end of the Weimar Republic – in which both groups struggled for control of public spaces – claimed hundreds of lives.[111] After 1929, there was also no significant rise in common criminality (in contrast to the years after the 1918 revolution). Murder rates during the period of the Weimar Republic were somewhat higher than before.[112] The level of domestic political violence was also low in inter-war Austria (1918–34), and of the at least 217 people killed, more than two-thirds were leftists. As in Germany, much non-lethal violence took place. During the failed coup of 1934, at least an additional 137 socialists died.[113] The bulk of political violence involving Germans took place outside Germany: as many as 30,000 right-wing *Freikorps* fighters may have died in the civil wars in the Baltic countries in 1918–20, and the *Freikorps* caused up to 100,000 deaths among Bolshevik troops and locals, including military deaths.[114] Some of the victims of anti-communist reprisals were Jews. German regulars had already killed about 6,500 civilians in Belgium in 1914 during mass executions for alleged irregular attacks.[115] In addition, tens of thousands of Belgians and Poles (including Jews) were used as forced laborers during World War I.[116]

110 Ziemann (2003, p. 88) speaks of a "selective civil war," but emphasizes that most militias formed after 1918 were peaceful and moderate (pp. 83–5). Similarly ambivalent is Schumann 2001, pp. 45 (chapter headline), 202.

111 See Schumann 2001, pp. 163–5, 202, 235, 245.

112 Wagner 1996, p. 31; Reichardt 2002, p. 95.

113 See Botz 1976, esp. pp. 236–7; Gedye 1942, pp. 123–4.

114 Gerwarth 2008, pp. 175–6 note 2.

115 See Horne and Kramer 2001, p. 430.

116 According to Mohrmann (1972, p. 172) 50,000 Polish Jews were brought to Germany for forced labor.

During the war, an additional 70,000 patients of German psychiatric hospitals, over what was normally to be expected, died from starvation and cold. Hospital staff accepted the lack of supplies and the consequent deaths, agreeing that food should be reserved for the more worthy members of society who lived under dire conditions during the war.[117] Approximately one in five German victims of starvation during World War I was mentally disabled.

German colonial warfare against anti-colonial insurgencies in Africa and China between 1900 and 1908 resulted in even more victims.[118] From 1904 to 1907, deeply racist German colonial authorities and troops murdered or caused the deaths of 70,000–100,000 people in German Southwest Africa (now Namibia). At about the same time, German warfare in German East Africa (now Tanzania) claimed about 100,000 lives; in some regions the mortality rates came close to those in German Southwest Africa, despite the fact that German East Africa was not a settler colony. In the former case, military operations were carried out against warriors and civilians, including women and children; people were chased into the Namib Desert; and men were starved in prison camps that served to subjugate the Herero and Nama peoples and transformed them from free pastoralists or farmers into a confined and tightly controlled workforce at the disposal of miners and German commercial farmers. Although the German military commander pursued a policy of total destruction for some months, the colonial administration and the government in Berlin prevented full-scale extermination because of the need for labor. In German East Africa, the Germans crushed resistance that rose up against the taxation and forced labor programs that had been imposed to make the colony profitable. Most of the dead were victims of a German scorched-earth policy against villages and agriculture.[119] Prior to 1914, Germany also adopted racial laws prohibiting marriages between Germans with Africans (in German Southwest Africa only) and Samoans, though not between non-Jewish Germans and Jews.[120] German colonial atrocities were among the worst of their time. Again, however, they were not unique. In around 1900, 40,000–50,000 Boers and Africans died in the so-called concentration camps of British South Africa. About 100,000 people perished in the Spanish *reconcentración* during the

[117] Faulstich 1998, pp. 25–68.

[118] Kuss (2011) offers a comparative study of certain aspects of all three cases.

[119] For German Southwest Africa see Zimmerer 2001, pp. 14, 18, 35, 40 (note 120), 42, 44–8, 57–84, 94–109; for limits of control see Zimmerer 2001, pp. 136, 148; see also Drechsler 1984; for a different interpretation see Hull 2005, pp. 5–90. For German East Africa see the contributions in Becker and Beez 2007; Kuss 2011, pp. 102–26.

[120] See the contributions in Becker 2004.

Cuban war of independence from 1895 to 1898. Hundreds of thousands of Filipinos died as a result of the US military's anti-insurgency measures. Millions fell victim to ruthless Belgian exploitation of the Congo. In the 1920s and 1930s, Italian suppression of resistance in Libya and Ethiopia claimed many tens of thousands of lives. Finally, millions succumbed to Japanese policies in China.[121] In each case, internment, expulsions, resettlement and hunger, combined with direct violence, took a major toll.

Before 1933, German mass violence carried out simultaneously against several victim groups was rare. But the mass destruction of defenseless people was not totally unknown to the Germans by then (though Austrians had less experience of it). The summary of events in this chapter shows that Nazism was not the only troubling point in German history. Although a comprehensive social analysis of these events is beyond the scope of this study, participation was quite broad and diverse. It included conscripted soldiers and volunteer warriors, colonial administrators and settlers (in Africa), medical personnel and political activists. There were remarkable parallels concerning those affected before and after 1933, although the scope of murder perpetrated during World War II was greater than that before Nazi rule. As was the case after 1939, the bulk of the earlier violence was imperialistic in character and occurred as part of the subjugation of conquered peoples or when political enemies were attacked abroad. Also, as happened later, much of the violence inside Germany targeted mental patients – who were considered to be inferior – in order to facilitate the continuation of an offensive war. And, as happened after 1933, violence and oppression against the domestic leftist opposition was harsh but much less lethal than the imperialistic violence and the destruction of the German disabled. The big difference, the great discontinuity, was the mass murder of Jews.

[121] See Gerlach 2010, pp. 182–3; Hochschild 1998; for Italy, see del Boca 2004, pp. 194–8; di Sante 2008, pp. 465–96.

3 From enforced emigration to territorial schemes: 1933–41

From the onset of Nazi rule, Jews were the targets of hostile propaganda in the German media, on posters and banners, and in mass gatherings. The central government under Hitler desired this atmosphere. However, there was no single authority in charge of the persecution of Jews. Rather, different state and Nazi Party agencies – central, regional and local – pursued their own anti-Jewish policies. These policies were related to other political areas, for no authority and virtually no single official in the government or Party was responsible for Jews alone. There was no consistent, undisputed, overall strategy.[1] Accordingly, this chapter tries to sketch anti-Jewish policies in Germany, the relevant agents from 1933 through mid 1941 on different levels, legislation and centralized action, popular violence, communal policies and Jewish behavior. The chapter also covers the first years of German anti-Jewish policies in annexed and occupied countries until mid 1941, before the systematic massacres started.

The Nazi Party was handed power on January 30, 1933, at the low point of the Great Depression. Within months, it erected a dictatorship, introduced press censorship, took control of radio broadcasting, outlawed all other political parties and suppressed leftist opposition through mass arrests and detention, partially in improvised camps. In the general elections of March 5, 1933, the Nazis, despite their intimidation, did not win an absolute majority. In the months afterwards, however, they gained the often-enthusiastic sympathy of the vast majority of Germans who often flocked to Nazism of their own accord.[2] This mass support was consolidated by an economic recovery stronger than in many other countries, a recovery that was built in no small degree on *dirigiste* measures – and especially on a massive rearmament effort – and accompanied by the rhetoric of class compromise that in reality gave entrepreneurs a free hand. By 1938, Germany enjoyed full employment. The social crisis

[1] Wildt 1995, pp. 12, 14.
[2] Kershaw 1998, pp. 594, 601–11.

seemed to be overcome. Nazi organizations and their propaganda permeated the everyday, but at the same time the regime integrated most of the traditional elites and the middle classes into its politics. The Party's relationship with parts of the Protestant and Catholic Church remained conflicted, incomes were modest, and there was repeated grumbling over scarce consumer goods and too much empty Nazi propaganda.[3] Currency problems restricted foreign trade. Still, birth rates rebounded – indicating increasing confidence. Foreign policy successes, such as the return of the Saar region to Germany in 1935, the reoccupation of the previously demilitarized Rhineland in 1936, and the annexation of Austria in March 1938, the Sudeten area in October 1938 and the occupation of Bohemia and Moravia in March 1939, further bolstered the popularity of the Nazi government.

Anti-Jewish laws

Nationwide German anti-Jewish legislation before 1941 came in three phases. Largely in April 1933, soon after their rise to power, the Nazis barred Jews from certain professions: the civil service, the arts, journalism and positions at universities. Their activities in other areas – for instance as tax advisers, lawyers and medical doctors – were restricted. Limits were put on the number of Jewish students at schools and universities. By September 1933 they were forbidden to be farmers as well as Protestant pastors.[4] The thrust of these laws was socioeconomic, freeing jobs for non-Jews. But behind them loomed a racist background, the thought that Jews were a political-ideological threat to German society and had to be removed from the media and the public sphere. The prohibition of kosher slaughter in April was religious in character; while regulations against eastern European Jews were xenophobic in their nature.[5] In 1935, when German rearmament policies again made military service mandatory, Jews were dismissed from the military. In September, the so-called Nuremberg racial laws essentially prohibited Jews from marrying Germans, outlawed Jewish/non-Jewish sexual relations, and forbade Jews to display the German national flag or the swastika banner. These laws were of a direct racist nature. They were not the

[3] For socioeconomic developments and living standards see Mason 1978, pp. 140–53; for the critical popular mood in 1934–35 and 1937 see Bankier 1996, pp. 15–20, 39–41, 48–59.

[4] Walk 1981, pp. 7, 12–13, 17–18, 53; Church law in parts of Prussia, September 6, 1933, in Hermle and Thierfelder 2009, p. 158; Neliba 1992, p. 222. For exceptions see Friedländer 1998, p. 29.

[5] Walk 1981, pp. 3–4, 15.

result of a sudden impulse of Hitler; the administration and the Nazi Party had demanded such laws, and discussed their precise forms as well as further prohibitions against inter-ethnic marriage and proposals for forced sterilizations[6] which were not adopted for years. As we will see, they were responses to the local violent actions of many Nazis. The new laws did not break up existing Jewish/non-Jewish marriages. The first ordinance of the Reich Citizenship Law of November 14, 1935, defined Jews as persons with three or, under certain conditions, two Jewish grandparents (by religion). It also created the category of persons of 'mixed blood.'[7] In 1938–39, primarily after the Reich-wide pogrom (although starting before it), a third wave of legislation led to the expropriation of Jewish-owned factories, businesses and stores and a 1 billion Reichsmark levy which amounted to about a sixth of the assets of Jewish Germans. No longer were Jews allowed to work as medical doctors, pharmacists, dentists or lawyers, except for Jewish clients.[8] Five years after the Nazi takeover, these measures largely removed Jews from the German private economy, especially once the economic boom made the takeover of Jewish-owned businesses a more attractive prospect.[9]

Other countries also had anti-Jewish legislation.[10] But Nazi Germany adopted more nationwide anti-Jewish laws and regulations (about 1,500[11]) than any other state. And most other countries adopted most of their policies later than Germany. In some of these other countries, the xenophobic aspects of anti-Jewish legislation were stronger than in Germany, but the early thrust against Jews in the professions and in the civil service, and as intellectuals, was similar. As was the case in other nations, the German government removed Jews from the economy only after some years, when full employment had been reached but at a time when financial difficulties occurred. Other countries also adopted anti-Jewish measures of a narrowly racist character, but to different degrees. About ten countries established definitions of a "Jew" more or less in terms of descent; half a dozen enacted bans on sexual relations; and three mandated that Jews wear identifying marks (as did Germany in September 1941). Some countries did not rigorously implement all

6 See Neliba 1992, pp. 199–214 for the Ministry of Interior; see Wildt 1995, pp. 21–4 for the SS and police; see Graml 1988, pp. 137–47 (for various authorities); Essner 2002, pp. 97–143; Bock 1986, pp. 101, 103.

7 Reichsgesetzblatt 1935, Part I, pp. 1333–4.

8 Seidler and Rett 1982, pp. 123–5.

9 Genschel 1966, pp. 136, 146, 211; Barkai 1988, pp. 67–8.

10 For this paragraph see Chapter 12.

11 Listed in Walk 1981.

of these laws; but in Germany they were all implemented. However, discrimination also prompted Jews from countries like Poland and Romania to leave.[12]

Persecution by local administrations

Who could make life more miserable for Jews than locals? The active role of city, county and town administrations demonstrates that the central German government, or Nazi leadership, did not prescribe everything in detail and that a considerable drive existed beyond the Nazi Party's organization. Local administrations took the initiative to exclude Jews from a growing number of aspects of public life. They dismissed local civil servants; it was they who erected the infamous signs declaring that Jews were not allowed to enter certain towns or localities. Such exclusions started in 1933, were extended in the mid 1930s to include public baths, sports grounds and park benches, and later extended to educational and recreational facilities like theatres, cinemas and libraries, as well as market stalls. In the period 1937–40, Jews were no longer admitted to public hospitals, or even segregated therein, unless their condition was life-threatening. From 1939 on, Jews were denied public welfare; and many cities, moving closer to segregation, forced them into so-called Jew houses or out of town altogether, with restrictions imposed upon where and when they could shop. Curfews were also imposed. Between 1933 and 1939, Jewish students were gradually squeezed out of the public schools.[13]

Many spa towns barred Jews within the space of a few years. Before Nazi rule, such measures resulted from the initiative of non-Jewish guests putting pressure on hotel owners and mayors; after 1933, they originated from local authorities competing with each other; and in northern Germany, more than in the south, for the reason of 'purity from Jews.'[14] Some communal authorities were more reluctant to regulate public swimming pools and parks and adopted measures covering these public spaces some years after others did. By the fall of 1939, Nazi Party functionaries in Vienna's districts took up another issue: the city's grim housing conditions. They demanded, among other measures, that Jews be concentrated in certain neighborhoods, be forced to live in basements or on upper floors that were at greater risk of damage from air raids, moved to barracks outside town, or deported to occupied Poland.[15] Building

[12] For this point see Marrus 1985, pp. 142–5.

[13] Gruner 2000b, pp. 75, 79, 85–6, 88, 94–7, 103–4, 115–19; Botz 1975, p. 67; Walk 1981, p. 256; for Jews forced out of Oldenburg in 1940 see Hoffmann 2000, pp. 38–9.

[14] Bajohr 2003, pp. 116–17, 121, 139.

[15] Botz 1975, pp. 84–5, 148, 156–7, 160–2.

owners who wished to evict Jewish tenants were aided by regional courts, especially after late 1938, which led to a nationwide law on April 30, 1939.[16] By late 1939, mayors and county chiefs had made "countless applications" to Berlin for Jewish-owned plots in order to build roads, establish schools, hospitals, nurseries and apartments for civil servants.[17] As with Jews, many of the steps taken against Sinti and Roma originated in the period 1933–38 from local and regional administrations and not the Berlin ministries.[18] The anti-Jewish measures were sometimes the result of interaction with central authorities (sometimes urged by local officials), but were also influenced by direct exchange of experiences between local administrations or via the *Deutschen Gemeindetag* (German conference of local administrations).[19] Ideologically speaking, the measures sketched here were in part motivated by the alleged 'impurity' of Jews, and they struck largely at their social status by denying them ever-more broadly defined 'luxuries.' They also aimed at segregation more than did the laws emanating from Berlin.

Violence: Nazi organizations, popular input and popular response

The persecution of German Jews did not consist only of legal and administrative measures. Recent research, based on many local studies, has highlighted the amount of direct, although mostly non-lethal, violence against Jews already occurring in the years from 1933 to 1939. The level of violence had its ups and downs, which led Peter Longerich to speak of three anti-Semitic waves in 1933, 1935 and 1938.[20] Focusing on small towns, Michael Wildt saw more continuity than other researchers did, and he relativized their perceptions of lulls in 1934 and 1936–37.[21] Still, the 1936 Olympic Games were preceded by actions against leftists, criminals, vagrants, prostitutes and "gypsies" rather than Jews.[22] It is also remarkable that an insignificant number of incidents against Jews was reported in the first six weeks following the takeover[23] (very much unlike in Austria in the spring of 1938), at a time when the Nazis were concentrating on repressing the political left.

16 Führer 1992, pp. 54–9.
17 Gruner 2000a, p. 137.
18 Zimmermann 1996, pp. 81–85, 99.
19 Gruner 2000b, esp. p. 77.
20 Longerich 1998a, pp. 23–207; see also Genschel 1966, pp. 105, 179.
21 Wildt 2007, pp. 152–66, 291–8.
22 Bergen 2003, p. 92; Pohl 2003, p. 16.
23 Wildt 2007, pp. 101–4.

When it came, the violence was first concentrated on stores run by Jews, which in many places were subjected to repeated boycotts (partially fueled by local non-Jewish competitors), smeared with slogans, and had their shop windows vandalized and were sometimes looted. This was combined with many different types of intimidation of shop owners and customers. Jews were literally chased out of courts and universities. In 1934–35, attacks on Jewish individuals, especially men, became more frequent. Increasingly, Jews were forced out of town, prevented from moving there, and assaulted for alleged sexual relations with Germans and publicly paraded through their home towns with degrading signs around their necks. In some cases, attackers also broke into and vandalized the houses or apartments of Jews. Smaller scale attacks on Jewish cemeteries and synagogues had happened before, but in the pogrom of November 1938 (which was triggered by the killing of a German diplomat in Paris by Herschel Grynszpan, a German-Polish Jew whose parents were being expelled to Poland) many synagogues were destroyed. Thousands of stores and individuals, including women, were attacked, and up to 30,000 Jewish men interned until they could provide evidence that they would emigrate. The pogrom was a clear signal that after their exclusion from public service, the public sphere and close social contacts with non-Jews, Jewish religious and economic activities were now going to become impossible.[24]

It was primarily members of Nazi Party organizations who organized this violence. Until about 1935, it was storm troopers (SA) in the cities and party members under their local leaders in towns and villages. Later, there were more attacks by boys from the Hitler Youth. For the most part, collective violence was organized locally, not ordered by Berlin. More than once events got out of hand and the violence spread more widely than was deemed good for national politics or foreign policy, and state authorities (starting with the local police) or central Nazi Party offices sometimes issued restraining orders. One reason was that the actions of Nazi groups often attracted the participation of large crowds of non-Nazis, though we know little about them.[25] For example, many looters in the pogrom of November 1938 were not Nazis. Sporadic pogrom-like events started before they were officially sanctioned and

[24] For this paragraph see Wildt 2007; for boycotts see Genschel 1966, pp. 45 (note 6), 67–73, 81–2, 89–91, 108–10; for intimidation see Cahnman 1979, p. 433; for local competitors see Bajohr 1998, pp. 33–44; for protests against the return of Jews to temporarily evacuated western border areas of Germany in 1940 see Toury 1986, pp. 436–7.

[25] Wildt (2007) describes this in detail but provides little analysis on who joined the crowd and for what motive. For participants in the November 1938 pogrom, see Graml 1988, pp. 26, 30; Benz 1994, pp. 33–9.

lasted a few days longer.[26] By contrast, the role of the SS was limited.[27] The events of November 1938 also demonstrated how great was the readiness for violence against Jews, especially within the Nazi Party and among party members, and even more especially among those with solid educations and jobs who had joined the storm troopers relatively late.[28] However, the number of riots after November 1938 seemed much smaller compared to the years before.

Some historians have emphasized the control and manipulation of these anti-Jewish riots by central agencies, but new research suggests that rioters autonomously created pressure on policy makers to adopt new laws and regulations, thus playing into the hands of the more radical factions of Nazi politicians. These new measures then *also* served to restore public order. Specifically, the Nuremberg racial laws and the harsher policy of expulsion after late 1938 were, in part, responses to pressure from below.[29] This claim gains additional plausibility when one considers that in many rural towns all of the Jews were forced out by the constant threat of violence.[30] A continuous trickle of hostile actions, not only in the countryside, wore Jewish business owners down so much that a third may have already closed their businesses before central government outlawed their activities in 1938–39. The smaller the town was, the larger was the percentage of closed Jewish businesses.[31] It was the publicly visible, and therefore often-attacked, retail stores that were first sold or closed down, while most other Jewish businesses continued in operation until 1938; meanwhile German entrepreneurs misused the official persecution to eliminate their Jewish competitors and enrich themselves.[32] Indirect pressure on Jewish firms came from locals who denounced non-Jews still doing business with them – for example in the cattle trade after 1935 – which served to enforce conformity.[33] Hitler and other important Nazi leaders in the SS, for example, had publicly rejected what they called pogrom or riot anti-Semitism and called for an "anti-Semitism of reason,"[34] but not everybody in the Nazi movement agreed. The leaders

26 Bajohr 2001, p. 105; Obst 1991, pp. 67–71; see also Benz 1994, pp. 18, 32.

27 Graml 1988, p. 33; Obst 1991, pp. 87–8.

28 Benz 1994, p. 19; Graml 1988, pp. 24–9; Obst 1991, pp. 121, 131, 137, 162.

29 Longerich (1998a, pp. 23–223) holds a middle position in this debate. Gruner (2000a, esp. pp. 90, 103) underscores central control, while Wildt (2007) provides evidence for local autonomy, as do the many "Einzelaktionen" mentioned in more than a hundred reports in Kulka and Jäckel 2004 (see their index). See Wildt (1995, p. 22) for an example of the idea of restoring order.

30 Wildt 2007, pp. 239, 242, 245, 285–90, 300; but see Bankier 1996, p. 84.

31 Rosenkötter 2003, p. 150; Bajohr and Pohl 2006, p. 29; Barkai 1988, p. 123.

32 Based on figures in Barkai 1991, pp. 132–3, 138, 140.

33 Abke 2001, pp. 101, 104–5, 326, 364–5.

34 Wildt 1995, p. 15. See also Chapters 2 and 7.

tolerated pogroms; some even incited them and instrumentalized them to drive their policies forward.[35]

In those areas incorporated into Germany where Germans formed a strong majority of the population – like Austria in 1938 – continuous, popular low-level violence (which was much harder to sustain where Germans formed a minority[36]), created so much pressure that most Jews emigrated within months of annexation. The "dejudaization" of Austria proceeded "in some respects even faster than initially planned," as one contemporary author wrote. Even Eichmann anticipated a much slower pace of emigration in May 1938. In July 1938, an officer in charge of 'aryanization' in Austria and the local Nazi newspaper estimated that all Jewish firms would be in non-Jewish hands within a period of three to four years; in fact, it did not take that long.[37] Among the up to 70,000 arrested were many non-Jews, although most were released after some months; thousands more non-Jews fled Austria.[38] So intense was the violence, plundering and public humiliation that even Heydrich repeatedly tried to curb them, and a considerable number of Austrian Jews fled to Nazi Germany.[39] Jews faced the same extremely hostile atmosphere in the fall of 1938 in the Sudetenland, where it took just weeks before virtually all Jews were forced out or had fled. In addition, many leftists and nationalists (who were also exposed to pogrom-like popular terror) were either arrested or fled. About ten times as many non-Jews as Jews left the area.[40] In Danzig, an independent city under Nazi rule, terror and the adoption of the Nuremberg laws on November 23, 1938, had prompted the great majority of the city's Jews (their number was 11,228 in 1930 and 7,439 in October 1937) to flee before the German Reich took the city over in September 1939 (when 1,660 remained); by late 1940 these were reduced to just 650, and 575 of these were later deported.[41] If there

35 A memorandum, probably by Eichmann, from January 1937, exemplifies this. Rejecting riots, he declared them useful to create and maintain pressure for emigration. Wildt 1995, pp. 99, 104.

36 Popular violence and the resulting pressure to flee were much less pronouned in areas such as Alsace-Lorraine, Luxembourg, Slovenia, and Bohemia and Moravia.

37 Rentner 1939, p. 69 (quote); see Gedye 1939, p. 326; Botz 1986–87, p. 360. For Eichmann's expectations, see Wildt 1995, p. 53.

38 Moser 1966, p. 7; Neugebauer 2002, pp. 724–5.

39 Directive by Gestapo Karlsruhe to send these refugees back, dated August 29, 1938, in Walk 1981, p. 239. For Heydrich, see Gerwarth 2011, pp. 154–5.

40 Some 37,000–55,000 people had fled the Sudeten area by October 1938; increasing to 150,000–200,000 by late 1939; less than a tenth (perhaps 27,000 Jews) remained within the period of a month. Gebel 2000, pp. 70–6, 279 (note 627); Ther 2011, p. 110. The pogrom atmosphere was in contrast to the Protectorate of Bohemia and Moravia where the German authorities also prevented 'wild aryanizations': Kárný 1994, p. 157; Oprach 2006, pp. 33–4.

41 Schenk 2000, pp. 99–100, 140, 217–18.

was any dissent in the annexed territories, it was silenced. The invading German military had no objections; abroad, the level of violence perpetrated against Jews that was acceptable to the troops that were stationed there seemed higher than at home.

Yet there are also indicators that far from all Germans agreed with the persecution of Jews in Germany. Lacking representative opinion surveys from the time, our evidence for this is scattered and indirect, like the reactions of non-Jews to major nationwide policy moves and actions against Jews. Most of these actions had a mixed echo. The boycott of April 1933 prompted not only support, but so much domestic resistance – some Germans arguing about it in public – that Nazi leaders did not consider it to be a success (although it may have been a signal for further boycotts and violence).[42] The pogrom of November 1938 drew much criticism, even from within the Nazi Party itself, for the public violence that accompanied it and for the destruction of property. Although the typical memory is that many watched the violence in silence, seemingly indifferent, the evidence suggests that the pogrom polarized society instantly and over the days that followed.[43] A wave of localized anti-Jewish upheavals in 1935 had similar effects, but it produced fewer objections.[44] The mandatory marking of Jews with a yellow star, which began in September 1941, led to individual demonstrations of non-Jewish solidarity to an extent that worried the regime; while the deportations that followed triggered discernible dissent only from small groups whose members came mostly from the middle class and the Church.[45] Yet one can argue that in general, no major differences existed in the reactions of different social groups, who were divided among themselves when it came to open violence but who largely acquiesced to – or supported – legal discrimination.[46]

However, non-Jews voiced dissent and protested individually, not in organized groups. For instance, in none of these cases was there an outright, unqualified and public protest by the Protestant Church; or even from the somewhat oppositional Confessing Church.[47] In general, criticism was voiced privately, not in public – where the atmosphere of intimidation meant that courage was required to speak out – and it was aimed at individual actions instead of a rejection based on principles. And the regime's legal steps – like the 1933 civil service law and the

[42] Bankier 1996, pp. 68–9; Wildt 2007, pp. 115–32, 144; Barkai 1988, pp. 26–33.

[43] Obst 1991, pp. 235–40, 319–30, 333–41; Bankier 1996, pp. 84–8. Kershaw (2008, pp. 175–83) and Benz (1994, pp. 47–50) see a more mixed reaction.

[44] Bankier 1996, pp. 72–5.

[45] Bankier 1996, pp. 124–8, 133–7; and see Chapter 4.

[46] Bankier 1996, pp. 89–100.

[47] Hermle and Thierfelder 2008, pp. 76, 264–5, 276.

Nuremberg racial laws of 1935 – which many citizens welcomed either because they thought the laws were necessary or because they expected them to stop the wave of local anti-Jewish violence, and the expropriations of 1938–39, seem to have been much less controversial.[48] On the whole it appears that public violence – despite considerable popular participation – produced much more discomfort and even opposition than did increasing legal discrimination. This raises an important question that this book will not be able to answer sufficiently: if violence at a relatively low level met with noticeable criticism, why was much less verbal opposition noticed among Germans operating in occupied countries after 1941 during the outright mass murder?

The policy of forced emigration

Many central agencies, local and regional administrations, and Nazi Party organizations, at all levels, pursued their own anti-Jewish policies and, thus, made their own contributions to shaping the general picture. This multiplicity was not just the result of a rational, conscious and effective division of labor of a monolithic machinery, as the Nazi apparatus has often been portrayed.[49] Rather, instructions and measures were sometimes contradictory. If there was one overarching goal of the central authorities after 1933, it was emigration. All Jews were supposed to leave Germany, and actions in the country were supposed to serve that goal. Forced emigration was the common denominator of many of the steps taken; various politicians declared it as a goal,[50] and it was the most important outcome until 1940–41 in Germany and Austria.

However, there were several obstacles. People do not lightly leave their country, and, so, the number of Jewish emigres from Germany decreased to a lower level in the period 1935–37, after an initial peak in 1933–34. A German newspaper cited Nazis complaining in 1938 that, "if figures remain constant, it will take about 30 more years until the last person of Jewish religion will have left Germany."[51] The intensified persecution of 1938–39 drove Jewish emigration to record levels. At the same time, migration opportunities were inadequate since many countries restricted the entry of foreigners, especially Jews. The international conference in

[48] Bankier 1996, pp. 69, 76–80; Wildt 2007, pp. 265–6; Friedländer 1998, pp. 162–4.

[49] See Hilberg 1994a.

[50] The following references refer to those declaring emigration as a major policy goal: Longerich 2001, p. 58 (Hitler, early 1938); Schleunes 1992, p. 29 (Ribbentrop, January 25, 1939); Schumburg, German Foreign Office, "Die Judenfrage als Faktor der Aussenpolitik 1938," January 25, 1939, PA AA R 100857, Bl. 239 (Rosenberg, January 15); Wildt 1995, pp. 66–7, 96, 99, 104, 186 (SD, various dates).

[51] Frankfurter Zeitung, June 11, 1938, excerpt in Pätzold 1984, pp. 152–3.

Evian in June 1938 did little to change that. Most governments refused to make additional commitments; even the ambitious international plans of 1938–39, and negotiations with the German government, aimed only at placing, first, the insufficiently low number of 65,000, and, then, 100,000 mostly Jewish German refugees abroad per year.[52] Against this background the German government started to evict Polish Jews residing in Germany (whom Poland wanted to strip of their citizenship) to Poland in the fall of 1938,[53] an action that prompted Herschel Grynszpan's assassination of a German the diplomat in Paris, which, in turn, increased pressure for another round of emigration. The second obstacle was that many elderly (and poorer) Jewish Germans and Austrians stayed. Some contemporary estimates put their number, with some exaggeration, at 200,000. They were less inclined to move, and they also had no realistic chance to do so because their age barred them from obtaining visas for entry into most countries. According to some plans, they were supposed to stay in Greater Germany until their natural death.[54]

The 1938 pogrom (Kristallnacht) has been cited as a sea change in Germany's anti-Jewish policies;[55] but in fact it brought about only gradual change. Still, the events were shocking. Yet in principle, the policy of enforced emigration remained in force. It was given more thrust by the mass arrest of Jewish men during the pogrom who were released if they could prove that they had a foreign visa, and by a more comprehensive expropriation and ban on Jews in the professions. Actually, these economic measures had already started in April 1938.[56] Over the course of 1938, the fiscal crisis of a regime that could no longer afford its huge rearmament effort gave making these steps an increasing urgency. Still, in the end it could only be financed by territorial expansion and the plundering of foreign countries. From this perspective, perhaps the most important anti-Jewish move was a 1 billion Reichsmark tributary payment that Göring imposed on the German Jews on November 12. (In reality, the financial authorities raised over 1.1 billion Reichsmark.)[57] Next in importance for German war preparations were the proceeds of

52 Weingarten 1981, esp. pp. 51–2, 99–100, 122–42; Adler-Rudel 1968, pp. 235–71.

53 Milton 1984, pp. 165–99; Maurer 1994, pp. 52–73.

54 Weingarten 1981, pp. 132 (Schacht, Reich Minister for the Economy), 139 (Rublee-Wohlthat agreement); SD situation report for 1938 in Wildt 1995, p. 201. At the end of 1938, 75,000 Jews remaining in Germany – probably including Austria, as the figures in Strauss (1980, p. 318) suggest – were over sixty-five years old.

55 See, for example, Gruner 2001, p. 49.

56 Neliba 1992, pp. 227–8; Gruner 2000a, pp. 126–7; Bajohr 1998, esp. pp. 134, 386; Genschel 1966, pp. 150–78; Barkai 1988, pp. 128–46.

57 Hilberg 1994a, pp. 143–5; Aly 2006a, pp. 19, 39–49; see also Mason 1978, pp. 215–22. Tooze (2007, pp. 325–8) sees only a limited impact.

the Reich Flight Tax. (Introduced in 1931 in another context, this tax, which mostly affected Jews, yielded a total of 900 million Reichsmark, 742 million of them in the period 1938–40.) Emigrating German Jews, or those who wished to leave the country, were officially robbed at an increasing rate.[58] But in a way, this, like the billion Reichsmark penalty, stood in the way of emigration because the chances for emigres to be accepted by other countries depended heavily on their financial means upon entry. Viewed from a different angle, the Reich could not afford, financially, to have large numbers of emigres transfer their money abroad since this would have overstretched Germany's hard currency reserves.[59]

Göring saw the November 1938 pogrom as a waste of national wealth (given the cost to non-Jewish insurance companies and to the German state for importing replacement shop window glass). Moreover, it made a chaotic lack of coordination obvious. During an important meeting on November 12, 1938, Göring, commissioned by Hitler, announced that "now the Jewish question shall be homogenized and resolved in this or that way" and that Hitler wanted "the decisive steps [to be] centrally coordinated" (*zentral zusammenzufassen*).[60] On January 24, 1939, Göring commissioned Reinhard Heydrich, Chief of the Security Police and Security Service, to found a "Central Reich Office for Jewish Emigration" – on the model of an organization in Vienna (directed by a mid-level SS officer, Adolf Eichmann) that had enforced a wave of emigration unprecedented in Germany. This office was to find receptive countries, facilitate emigration by procuring German documents and passports, and resolve huge financial issues such as finding the funding for the travel and visas of poor Jews that Jewish communities were supposed to provide (see Chapter 10). That the Central Reich Office for Jewish Emigration also had no unchallenged authority is indicated by the fact that it formed a coordination committee with representatives from other agencies "for the smooth cooperation in all questions of Jewish emigration with the government agencies in charge." Forced emigration was still the main policy objective, and to support this office a Reich Association of German Jews subordinate to the Central Office for Jewish Emigration was established in February.[61] Until then, the Security

[58] Hilberg 1994a, pp. 141–2; Aly 2006a, pp. 47–8; Heim 1999, pp. 107–38.

[59] See, for example, Schleunes 1992, p. 30; Tooze 2007, p. 102.

[60] Protocol of meeting of November 12, 1938, IMG, vol. 28, p. 499.

[61] A good description of this is in the indictment, StA KG Berlin 1 Js 1/65, April 23, 1971, pp. 23–30 (quote from the first committee meeting, February 11, 1939, ibid., p. 25); see Safrian 1997, pp. 47–8 (and pp. 23–67, on the Vienna model); Jasch 2012, pp. 282–3; Jansen 1997, p. 327.

Police and SD had been marginal players in anti-Jewish policies, observing political developments and making proposals without concentrating on this field. Now they gained considerable influence.[62] At the level of legislation, there were so many laws not because '*the* Nazis' thought of everything in a coordinated fashion, but rather because so many Nazi functionaries took the initiative. All sorts of central agencies had issued anti-Jewish decrees and regulations; Göring wanted this to stop, too. "For securing the necessary uniformity in the treatment of the Jewish question," he requested all authorities to inform him of any planned decree or measures, and to obtain his assent. (By contrast, a 1933 proposal by high-ranking civil servants for a coordinating institution, the *Volkswart*, had led to nothing.)[63] In any case, the events of 1939 did not come close to fully centralizing anti-Jewish policy. This left the Reich Ministries of Finance, and Economy, local authorities, and the Security Police and Security Service, among others, as major players.[64] It is worth noting that in the same period, 1938–39, policies against the Sinti and the Roma also became relatively more centralized, although in the hands of the criminal police rather than the Gestapo.[65]

Because of a lack of receptive countries in late 1938 and early 1939, leading German politicians threatened that the German Jews would be killed if no country took them in or if, as Göring and Hitler predicted, another world war broke out.[66] Yet the systematic mass murder of German and Austrian Jews did not start at the outbreak of war. This despite the fact that the number of murdered Jewish concentration camp inmates rose steeply, into the thousands.[67] However, emigration policy continued. As late as April 1940 the RSHA decreed "Jewish emigration from the territory of the Reich must continue to be supported even more strongly, also during the war," and it emphasized that Jews should emigrate to non European territories if possible.[68] The fact that the German

[62] Wildt 1995, pp. 9–64, esp. p. 18; Browning 1978, pp. 4–5; Herbert 1996, p. 203.

[63] Göring circular, December 14, 1938, BA R 18/5519, p. 281. For the *Volkswart* see Adam 1976, pp. 45–8; for the many originators of anti-Jewish legislation (of which a small and decreasing part were outright laws) see Walk 1981.

[64] Gruner 2000b, p. 110; Browning 1978, pp. 8, 213. Gruner (2000b, p. 103) finds that coordination increased already from the fall of 1937 to the summer of 1938.

[65] Zimmermann 1996, pp. 83–110.

[66] Unabhängige Expertenkommission Schweiz 1999, p. 86 (von Weizsäcker, State Secretary in the Foreign Office, November 15, 1938); Mommsen 1997, pp. 147, 154–5 (Hitler, January 30, 1939; Göring, November 12, 1938).

[67] This can be extrapolated from partial figures in Moser 1966, pp. 7–12; Freund and Safrian 2002, p. 789; Pingel 1978, p. 265 note 126; Herbert 1996, p. 222.

[68] Circular degree, IVD4–2 (Rz) 1275/40, April 24, 1940, quoted in indictment, StA KG Berlin 1 Js 1/65, April 23, 1971, p. 30; see Schellenberg's circular, May 20, 1941, BA R 58/276, pp. 273–4; Walk 1981, p. 320.

leadership pursued a policy of forced emigration cannot be reconciled with any claim that German politicians, including Hitler, were already resolved in 1933, 1939, or even 1940, to kill all of the Jews – if this were the case it would have been counterproductive to allow them to flee to areas beyond the Nazi reach, such as Palestine and North and South America.[69] Of the German and Austrian Jews who emigrated during 1933–41, 64,500 went to Palestine (about a third of the Jewish immigrants there), about 110,000 to the United States, at least 40,000 to South America, 17,000 central European Jews to Shanghai, and 6,000 to South Africa.[70] Yet while the emigration of German Jews took priority for German authorities, to expedite this they temporarily impeded the departure of Polish, Czech and French Jews.[71]

Emigration as the prevalent Jewish response

The propaganda, legal discrimination, direct violence and especially an atmosphere of threat that for some (though not all) Jews permeated everyday life, produced, as German politicians had intended, a surge in the emigration of German (and later Austrian and Czech) Jews. This violent atmosphere in the late 1930s persuaded many to leave the country who had initially decided to ride out the storm and even petition against discrimination or challenge it in court. The fact that, although many young people left,[72] the number of births among so-called 'full Jews' and 'quarter-Jews' rose again slightly from a low level in 1934 and remained stable until 1938 indicates the same pattern of attempted accommodation. Negotiation with the German state became another strategy, as is most notable in the Haavara agreement of 1933 for financing Jewish emigration through a complex mechanism that allowed the transfer of some of the assets, and even the pensions, of German Jews emigrating to Palestine.[73]

[69] See Gutman 1982, p. 15; memo (probably by Eichmann), January 1937, and note by Wisliceny in Wildt 1995, pp. 102, 109; for shifting and conflicting instructions regarding Jewish emigration to Palestine in 1937–38, which was still favored by Hitler, see Wildt 1995 pp. 40–5; Longerich 2006, pp. 102, 115; Walk 1981, pp. 196, 200; ADAP 1953, pp. 641–2, 652, 671.

[70] Strauss 1987, pp. 197, 207–8, 216–21, 226–8.

[71] Oprach 2006, p. 64; Gutman 1982, p. 18.

[72] The data are from Strauss (1980, pp. 319–20), who offered a different interpretation.

[73] Strauss 1987, pp. 199–201; Strauss 1980, pp. 319–20; Barkai 1988, pp. 62–4. For petitions, see Friedländer 1998, pp. 60–5. By comparison, people threatened with sterilization challenged the measure in court or made petitions against it, but usually they formed no organization on their own. Other individuals tried to help them, but only the Churches helped in an organized way. Bock 1986, pp. 209–30, 280–1, 285–6, 289–98, 346.

Table 2.1 *Jewish emigration from Nazi Germany (Old Reich), 1933–41*[74]

Year	1933	1934	1935	1936	1937	1938	1939	1940	1941
Refugees	37,000	23,000	21,000	25,000	23,000	46,000	78,000	15,000	8,000

Accordingly, after its initial peak the flow of emigrants slowed in 1934–37 and then quickened to its peak in 1938–39. Even during the initial years of the war, emigration continued. By 1939, this left 214,000 Jews in the Old Reich, a number that fell to 160,000 by October 1941. This compares to a Jewish population of 500,000 in early 1933. Some 104,000 Austrian Jews emigrated between March 1938 and late July 1939, and 24,500 more left in 1939–41. Approximately 26,000 Jews had left Bohemia and Moravia for foreign shores by 1941, although most of them left in 1939.[75] Emigration was a strategy primarily adopted by Jewish Germans; between 1933 and 1939, only 40,000 or fewer German non-Jews left the country, many of who were political opponents of the Nazi regime who left in 1933.[76] More than 85% of the refugees were Jews. For many of them, emigration may have been more a matter of maintaining their dignity than of flight.[77] To depict all of them as 'victims' may result in wrong conclusions being reached in this case.

In addition, the domestic migration of Jews from small and not-so-small towns to large cities rose sharply. This was often the first step to flight abroad. Given that two-thirds of the German and Austrian Jews had emigrated by 1941, any charge that they had waited passively like sheep awaiting slaughter is out of place. Most of those who could flee did so, though many did so late, in 1938–39. Of those who remained, many were either too poor, too old, disadvantaged as females, or (often because of these reasons), unable to obtain foreign visas. A few stayed out of stubborn German patriotism. Several thousand Jews who had already left returned to Nazi Germany, even from Palestine.[78] Some did not flee far enough. (The

[74] Strauss 1980, p. 326; Steur 1997, pp. 24–5; Jonca 1996, p. 275; the 1938 figure is from a Security Service annual report for 1938 in Wildt 1995, p. 202.

[75] Scheffler 1988, p. 193; Jonca (1996, p. 275) has slightly different figures; for Austria see Botz 1975, pp. 66–7; for Bohemia and Moravia see Oprach 2006, p. 75. For the SD see Wildt 1995, pp. 50–1. The difference between the figures for emigration and remaining Jewish Germans is explained by the 60,000 deaths among the elderly population in 1933–41: Strauss 1980, p. 320. Most of these deaths were not caused by murder or suicide. For suicides, see Kwiet 1984, esp. pp. 146, 155.

[76] Weingarten 1981, p. 17; Mehringer 1998, p. 124; Head Office for Reich Security, annual report for 1938, MadR vol. 1, p. 67.

[77] With this, I read Barkai 1988, pp. 30, 47 and 78 somewhat against the grain.

[78] Wetzel 1988, pp. 497–8; for women see Barkai 1988, p. 66.

Germans caught and murdered some 15,000–16,000 Austrian Jews who traveled abroad, out of a total of 130,000 emigres.) But most did get away. Already, in 1934, 40% or less of the Jews fleeing in that year remained in Europe, and this proportion continued to decrease.[79]

Violence against non-Jews before 1939

Jews were not the only group persecuted in Nazi Germany from 1933 to 1939, and they were not necessarily the worst affected. Typical before World War II were *non-lethal* persecutions, of which there were different kinds for different population groups. Jews, much more than any other group, saw themselves forced to leave the country; whereas, unlike Jews, political leftists and social outsiders (so-called 'asocials') suffered long-term internment in great numbers. In addition, 300,000 people categorized as disabled or 'asocial' became subject to forced sterilization by 1939. Beyond its anti-Jewish policies, which a large part of German society accepted, the Nazi regime waged a massive campaign against the poor, representatives of the working class, and marginalized groups of low status. This poverty is among the reasons why, unlike many Jews, few of them emigrated to evade persecution.

Initially the bulk of the violence was directed at communists, social democrats and labor unionists. In 1933 up to 100,000 leftists were arrested and sent to prisons or improvised proto-concentration camps; 500–1,000 may have been murdered. In later years the number of such arrests was still high, although decreasing: 13,000 in 1936, 9,000 in 1937 and 3,500 in 1938.[80] But the regime released most political prisoners (including most of the Jews among them) after some months or years, so their numbers dropped to less than 20,000 in 1938.[81] By 1938, 'asocials' had replaced leftists as the largest group of concentration camp inmates, with the exception of November and December 1938 when Jews were briefly the majority.[82] The blanket term 'asocial' included so-called habitual criminals, beggars, vagabonds, alcoholics, the 'work-shy,' so-called hecklers, pimps, prostitutes and other sexually deviant women, men who did not pay their alimony, parents, especially those with large families, allegedly unable to properly raise their children, and Sinti and Roma. Up to half of the 100,000 'asocials' imprisoned in camps or sentenced to death may have perished, although

[79] Moser 1966, p. 52; Freund and Safrian 2002, p. 789; Strauss 1987, p. 190.

[80] Pohl 2003, pp. 12, 16; Gellately 2002, p. 87; see also Mehringer 1998, pp. 84, 129.

[81] Wachsmann 2004, pp. 113, 118, 432 (note 21). In terms of lethality, 1945 seems to have been the worst year for German communists, with 1,800 executed: Mehringer 1998, p. 180.

[82] Gellately 2002, p. 144.

most of these deaths occurred during the war.[83] The treatment of 'asocials' resembled the permanent detention of so-called habitual criminals in other countries such as England, Norway, Italy and Finland – but there it was far less often applied and less lethal when compared to Germany after 1939.[84] Although supposed experts considered 1–1.6 million Germans as genetically deviant, or hereditary criminals, interning only a small minority of them in camps was apparently considered sufficient to intimidate the rest in a situation of labor scarcity in 1938–45. According to this somewhat contradictory view, most idlers could be re-educated for work in an industrial society. Germany's labor shortage also explains the huge difference in the proportion of people arrested as 'asocial' and 'anti-social' between Nazi Germany and the Soviet Union in the 1930s – in the latter this was much more common.[85]

The bulk of convictions for homosexuality (usually men), like the arrests of leftists and the forced sterilizations, occurred before the war (in 1936–38). Despite about 50,000 court verdicts against homosexuals, most managed to survive, and some actually thrived under the Nazi regime.[86] The result of even greater racist-biological concern, the mass sterilizations of the mentally disabled and certain groups among the physically disabled were based on a law of July 1933 and more radical regulations for women in 1934.[87] Sterilizations peaked in 1935–38; resistance grew after this period, and there was not enough money or medical personnel to carry out the necessary surgery during the war. Of the close to 1 million people recommended for sterilization, 400,000 were actually sterilized – mostly on the grounds of "feeblemindedness," schizophrenia and epilepsy.[88] The surgery was risky; according to estimates, 5,000 people (mostly women) died as a consequence of the procedure.[89] In Germany, an equal number of men and women were sterilized, whereas in Sweden, for example, 93% of the 62,868 people sterilized from 1935 to 1975 were women. There were also sterilization laws, although less radical practices, in other countries.[90]

83 Gerlach and Werth 2009, pp. 146–8.
84 Wachsmann 2004, pp. 367–8.
85 Wagner 1996, p. 375; Lotfi 2000, p. 216; Mason 1978, pp. 313–19; Gerlach and Werth 2009, pp. 144–50.
86 Pohl (2003, pp. 14–15) claims more than 5,000 homosexuals died in concentration camps); Gellately 2002, p. 164; Wachsmann 2004, pp. 144–6; Jellonnek 1990, p. 33.
87 Law for the prevention of offspring with hereditary diseases, July 14, 1933, in Hermle and Thierfelder 2008, pp. 620–3; see also Neliba 1992, pp. 162, 174–6, 189–90, 197–8; Bock 1986, pp. 87–8.
88 Bock 1986, pp. 232–7, 241, 372; Lifton 1986, p. 25.
89 Bock 1986, pp. 12, 375–81; Neliba 1992, pp. 197–8.
90 Frykman 2000, pp. 213, 229; for laws in other countries see Bock 1986, pp. 48–9, 242; Kühl 1994, p. 90.

The German sterilization program (which the International Federation of Eugenic Organizations recommended as a model for other countries in 1934) fulfilled the dreams of a number of influential medical doctors. Doctors, psychiatrists and other health personnel were often eager to implement the law. Their varying zeal seems to explain, in part, the considerable regional variation in the number of victims.[91] As with the persecution of Jews, support for the violence against leftists, 'asocials,' Sinti, Roma and homosexuals, while not being disconnected from biological ideas, drew upon a variety of older prejudices. Among them were repressive work ethics and strict controls tied to social services, the alleged criminality of 'gypsies' and popular racism against them, Christian regulations of sexuality and family life, as well as old stereotypes concerning Marxists and revolutionaries. The regime exerted a massive propaganda effort, right down to lessons on the subject in schools, in support of all of these persecutions.[92]

The start of World War II and violence against non-Jews

On September 1, 1939, Germany invaded Poland, thus starting World War II in Europe. Poland was defeated within five weeks, but France and the United Kingdom declared war on Germany. Their failure to take the offensive gave Germany the opportunity to take on its enemies individually, one after the other, in short, intense campaigns. This allowed Germany to avoid an all out armament effort and great domestic sacrifices in terms of cuts in consumption at home. Military casualties remained modest, Allied air raids limited. One could argue that before mid 1941, German society avoided a deep new crisis. The mood among Germans turned from concerned to enthusiastic in mid 1940 after the occupation of Denmark, Norway, the Netherlands, Belgium and Luxembourg, and the defeat of France. Germany consolidated her position through a network of European allies consisting of the Soviet Union, Finland, the newly founded state of Slovakia, Romania, Hungary, Bulgaria and Italy. Between April and June 1941, German troops and the armies of her allies conquered Yugoslavia and Greece. In Norway, France and Greece, British troops were defeated; only in Libya, where German troops came to the aid of Italian forces, did the British stand their ground. Germany's failure in the Battle of Britain in the summer of 1940 left the United Kingdom (supported by its dominions and colonies of 400 million

[91] For the International Federation see Kühl 2004, p. 498; for German medical doctors see Bock 1986, pp. 52, 80, 182–208; for regional differences, see Bock 1986, pp. 247–8.

[92] On this point regarding eugenics see Bock 1986, pp. 91–2, 121, 195.

people) as the only remaining enemy power in Europe, a situation that resulted in mutual strategic bombing campaigns between the two.

By mid 1941 Germany had occupied twelve countries, fully or in part. Each had a differently structured occupation administration, often with different administrative zones and regimes within a single country. Austria was completely annexed. Luxembourg, Alsace and Lorraine (in France) and parts of Slovenia (in Yugoslavia) were incorporated into neighboring German administrative areas, as were some areas of northern and southwestern Poland; whereas the rest of western Poland and the Sudeten area became separate German-incorporated administrative areas. Central Poland, Norway and the Netherlands got different sorts of German civil administration; Denmark remained autonomous, although controlled by the German Foreign Office; while Belgium, northern France, Serbia and parts of Greece fell under slightly varying German military administrations. This created different major policy players and led to varying occupation policies, which were at their harshest in Poland and, later on, Yugoslavia, but much less confrontational in western Europe.

Aside from the many thousands of civilian victims of German aerial bombing, particularly in Warsaw, London and Belgrade, some 3,000 captured African soldiers in the French army who were massacred, and the beginning of reprisals in Serbia and Crete, the main field of German violence outside of battle between 1939 and June 1941 was Poland – whose population was considered inferior. During the invasion of Poland, German army, SS and police units were very easily ready to ascribe shooting to irregulars or illicit warfare, which was linked to anti-Polish stereotypes and incited by drastic orders. By way of reprisal, these German units shot recently captured military prisoners (about 3,000 in total), civilian hostages and civilians living nearby in groups of a few to several hundred people. Civilians in particular were also abused, humiliated, robbed and tortured. The number of victims may have reached 16,000 during the five weeks of armed conflict.[93] From October 1939 to early 1940, the regional German civil administrations in western Poland directed the SS, the police and local militias under SS supervision to arrest or murder about 50,000 members of the Polish leadership and intelligentsia (broadly defined), in order to facilitate incorporation and eliminate potential leaders of a Polish resistance. The victims included Catholic priests, intellectuals, teachers, members of the professions, political party activists and post-1918 settlers. These operations centered in the region of Danzig-West Prussia (which saw 30,000–40,000 victims), where the regional administration later pursued a policy of forced assimilation of

[93] Böhler 2006, pp. 54–157, 181–5, 241; Wildt 2003, pp. 433–50.

Poles. In the Wartheland fewer were killed in 1939, but far more were displaced or deported eastward later on. In the General Government (i.e., German-occupied central Poland), still fewer killings of members of the intelligentsia were organized; the number peaked in 1940.[94] For the sake of the Germanization policy in western Poland, the SS and the police deported close to 400,000 Poles (including an unknown number of Jews), primarily from the Wartheland, to the General Government from late 1939 to early 1941. Protests by the German civil administration and the military in the General Government repeatedly moved Göring and Himmler to stop the expulsions.[95] Several hundred thousand ethnic Germans from eastern and southeastern Europe were brought to western Poland to replace Poles.

Before mid 1941 there was no need for the anti-partisan warfare that became so deadly afterwards, but by that time close to 3 million Europeans had been brought to Germany as forced laborers. The largest group, Polish civilians, were often mistreated, obliged to wear a "P" on their clothing and herded into closed camps.[96]

Non-Jewish German target groups suffered varying fates from 1939 to 1941. The persecution of leftists (who were muted by the German-Soviet alliance) picked up only slightly and temporarily. 'Asocials' continued to be interned, but foreigners, potential or actual resisters, and recalcitrant workers, soon replaced them as the largest inmate group in the prisons and the growing number of concentration camps in Germany.[97] The hunt for homosexuals abated somewhat. While the forced sterilization of disabled people and social outsiders decreased for financial reasons, inter alia,[98] the disabled became, and remained to the end, the largest civilian victim group of Nazi policies inside Germany. From the fall of 1939 to August 1941, some 70,000 patients of mental institutions (and some physically disabled) who appeared permanently unable to work, were murdered – primarily by gassing. This secret campaign was centrally organized by a branch of the Chancellery of the Führer (Hitler's chancellery in his capacity as leader of the Nazi Party) under Viktor Brack, together with many medical doctors and staff coordinated by the Reich Ministry of the Interior. Regional killing units

[94] Schenk 2000, esp. pp. 129, 150–78, 212, 291; Borodziej 1999, p. 29; for the order by Gauleiter Forster see also Böhler 2006, p. 232. For the militias see Jansen and Weckbecker 1992, pp. 35, 42–54, 60, 70, 154, 156. According to Mallmann *et al.* (2008, pp. 65 and 84), Himmler gave the orders, but they do not explain why they went so much further in Danzig-West Prussia than they did in other regions of annexed Poland.

[95] Witte *et al.* 1999, pp. 80–3; Aly 1999.

[96] Herbert 1985, pp. 67–131.

[97] Wachsmann 2004, pp. 200, 222–5; Orth 1999, pp. 67–105.

[98] Bock 1986, p. 346.

murdered 20,000 other mental patients in German-annexed Poland in 1939–40. On the one hand, this destruction of humanity was in tune with eugenic thinking and racist Nazi ideas of strengthening the German 'blood' by eliminating people with poor hereditary dispositions. On the other hand, these murders, as opposed to the earlier sterilizations, served to save money and free hospital space and medical staff for the military and ethnic Germans resettled from eastern Europe to German-controlled areas by taking the lives of unproductive people considered "unworthy of living" and unworthy of such resources. Only after unofficial (but fierce) criticism was increasing and became public in mid 1941, largely by Church representatives, was the centralized killing program stopped, but decentralized murder through food and medical deprivation and poisoning with medication would resume later on.[99]

The persecution of Jews: 1939–41

German anti-Jewish policy in the period from 1939 to 1941 has often been characterized as one of territorial schemes; that is, dominated by plans to deport all Jews within German reach into a single territory. However, these never-realized plans had, arguably, little bearing on the lives of Jews under German rule before June 1941; forced emigration (in central Europe), ghettoization and deprivation (in Poland) had far more effect. Even less than in the years before was there *one* policy of persecution and *one* Jewish experience of it. The new elements also meant that anti-Jewish measures were not a mere continuation of policies from before 1939.

The outbreak of the war exacerbated anti-Jewish policies in many ways, but, despite all of the previous utterances of Nazi leaders about what would happen in the event of war, it did not lead in the short run to a comprehensive extermination policy. One indication of a more severe policy to follow were the politicians' declarations that, given the number of Jews under German rule after the conquest of western and central Poland (more than 2 million), the 'Jewish question' could no longer be solved by emigration, although the legal emigration of German, Austrian and Czech Jews did continue. Instead, the Jews should be resettled, concentrated in a certain territory. From the fall of 1939 to mid 1940, this was imagined to be the area around Lublin in central-eastern Poland; from mid 1940 to early 1941, it was the French colony of Madagascar; and from early 1941 it was the soon-to-be-occupied Soviet territories.

[99] See Friedlander 1995; Aly 1987; on productivity as a criterion, see, for example, Grabher 2006, pp. 45, 48; on the increasing reluctance to commit funds to mental institutions after the 1930s see Faulstich 1998, pp. 101–240. For annexed Poland and hospital beds see Aly 1999, pp. 70–6, and Riess 1995, esp. p. 359.

Such thinking was not exclusively German. US, British, French, Polish and Japanese politicians suggested resettlement schemes. The Polish Prime Minister in exile, Władysław Sikorski, suggested the resettlement of 3.5 million Polish Jews to the British Foreign Minister, Anthony Eden, as late as in January 1942. Other deportation destinations suggested were Alaska, Dutch Guyana and various other South American countries, Manchuria, Angola, Ethiopia, Northern Rhodesia and the Philippines.[100] Jewish emigration to Palestine added to the territorial resettlement options. During the Evian conference, Polish and Romanian diplomats urged President Roosevelt of the US (unsuccessfully) to include the emigration of their Jewish nationals in the work of the Intergovernmental Committee on Political Refugees.[101]

The first concrete German scheme for concentrating Jews concerned the area of Nisko in southeastern Poland. Gestapo chief, Heinrich Müller, ordered that 70,000–80,000 Jews from the areas of Kattowitz (in East Upper Silesia) and Ostrava (in Moravia), and some from Vienna, be taken there. In reality, 4,600 Jews from these places of origin were deported to Nisko in late October 1939. The effort was stopped because it interfered with larger German resettlement schemes from western to central Poland.[102] The German civil administration in the General Government, and in part also the military, blocked deportation attempts with a stream of complaints and objections. Eichmann had organized the Nisko deportations, pointing to Hitler's desire that all of the 300,000 Jews in Germany and Austria be removed within nine months.[103] Near Nisko, several thousand Jews were forced to cross the demarcation line into Soviet-controlled territory, and another 150,000–200,000 fled to eastern Poland, which the USSR had annexed. Their reception there was sympathetic at first, then neutral, but many were later sent back upon arrival. Such Jewish refugees formed a large part of the 77,000 persons arrested and deported further eastward by Soviet authorities in late June 1940.[104] In February 1940, the Soviet government rejected two proposals by the Security Police's resettlement offices in Berlin and Vienna to take custody of the German (and probably also the Austrian)

[100] Pramowska 2010, p. 169; Hirschfeld 1984, pp. 163, 174 (Guyana was proposed by the Dutch fascist leader Mussert, 1938); "Dichiarazione sulla razza del Gran Consiglio del Fascismo," October 6–7, 1938, in Collotti 2006, p. 190 (Italian Ethiopia was a possibility). Picard 1997, pp. 297 and 322, mentions sixteen plans from various nations between 1926 and 1941; see also Weingarten 1981, pp. 164–72.

[101] Weingarten 1981, p. 165; for Poland see Melzer 1997, pp. 131–43.

[102] Steur 1997, pp. 30–2; Steinbacher 2000, p. 114.

[103] Longerich 2001, p. 81; Gruner 2000b, p. 112; see Mallmann *et al.* 2008, pp. 63–5.

[104] Polian 2008, pp. 15–17.

Jews and settle them in Ukraine and the autonomous Jewish territory of Birobidjan, Siberia.[105]

The idea that all European Jews should be deported to Madagascar had circulated not only among bigots but also among governments of countries like Poland and Romania, since the 1920s.[106] Nazi politicians too found Madagascar a suitable destination for all of Europe's Jews.[107] Hitler and others considered the idea, and, after the defeat of France in June 1940, the German Foreign Office seriously proposed Madagascar as a resettlement territory and the RSHA adopted the proposal after modifying it. The final proposal called for two ships, each carrying 1,500 Jews, to sail daily over four years – a total of 4 million deportees. This would have required the constant use of 120 ships.[108] The Jews were to be settled primarily in the highlands where, it was argued, conditions were more suitable for Europeans; as their numbers grew, though, they would eventually have to drain off the swamps. A statistician and a geologist were consulted. There would be a Jewish self-administration under the authority of the German Security Police.[109] By December 1940, Eichmann was speaking of moving 6 million Jews first to Poland and then to Madagascar.[110] In August 1940 Hitler still considered inserting a clause into the peace treaties with defeated countries requiring them to transport their Jewish populations outside of Europe.[111] Later, he distanced himself from the Madagascar plan. The French Prime Minister, François Darlan, still expressed interest in the scheme in August 1941.[112]

By that time, German planners had already thought of another territory. Drawing upon the earlier attempt to transfer Jews to the USSR, they intended, perhaps from as early as early 1941, to deport all the Jews within reach to the Soviet territories that were to be occupied.[113] There, planners imagined, they, the sexes separated, would have to drain swamps and build roads; some envisioned marching them to the Arctic Sea.[114] Each of these 'territorial schemes' incorporated, to

[105] Polian 2008, p. 1.

[106] Brechtken 1997, pp. 32–52, 81–164; 482–4; Jansen 1997, pp. 60–107, 114–34, 142–73.

[107] See Moser 1966, p. 15 (about Rosenberg in a press conference as early as February 7, 1939); see Longerich (2001, p. 58) about this objective of Hitler by late 1937, without reference to Madagascar.

[108] Brechtken 1997, pp. 221–83; Steur 1997, pp. 36–8.

[109] "Plan zur Lösung der Judenfrage," July 2, 1940; Rademacher to Luther, "Bisherige Entwicklung des Madagaskar-Plans des Referats D III," August 30, 1940; RSHA, "Madagaskar-Projekt," undated, all in PA AA R 100857, pp. 195–6, 199–214, 226–7.

[110] Lösener note about a conversation with Eichmann, December 3, 1940, BA R 18/3746a.

[111] See Klarsfeld (1992, p. 271) about notes from a meeting between Hitler and Abetz.

[112] Brechtken 2000, p. 489.

[113] Aly 1999, pp. 171–7.

[114] Gerlach 1998a, pp. 27–9.

increasing degrees, the adversity of living with little infrastructure in a harsh climate and its potential to kill off some of the deported Jews; few plans mentioned any precautions against this. Seyss-Inquart had already mused that deportations to the Nisko area could lead to a "stark decimation" of the Jews, and already in the summer of 1939 Rosenberg mused about sending the Jews to some place with a "deadly climate."[115]

Each of the 'territorial schemes' was utopian, and all were designed to be carried out after the war.[116] But the war did not end. The resulting failure to put any of these plans into effect contributed to the emerging pressures that would radicalize thinking about what to do with the Jews, and it also contributed indirectly to their regional concentration and subsequent worsening treatment.[117] The schemes had little direct effect on the lives of Jews, except for some smaller expulsions from certain regions on the initiative of regional Nazi Party leaders and administrations. In these cases, however, expellees' destinations were remarkably in tune with the 'territorial scheme' then in fashion. In 1938, Jews were expelled mainly to Poland, but also to Czechoslovakia and Hungary. In February and March 1940, more than 1,300 Jews from Stettin and Schneidemühl were deported to the Lublin area. By May, the chief of the Order Police in that district erroneously expected the arrival of 100,000 German Jews in the near future.[118] In July 1940, Jews from annexed Alsace (3,255, plus 17,893 refugees who had fled the approaching German troops and were not permitted to return after the armistice), Lorraine, and Luxembourg began to be expelled to France; those from the German regions of Baden and the Palatinate (6,500) in October of that year. The German military administration also forced Jews from France's occupied areas into the unoccupied zone and disallowed returns in the fall. By way of continuous protest against the deportations that had already taken place, the Vichy government at least successfully objected to German plans to bring all of the 270,000 German, Austrian and Czech Jews – starting with those from Hesse – to France.[119] There were also attempts to expel Jews from

[115] Seyss-Inquart quoted in Moser 1966, p. 15; for Rosenberg see Cecil 1972, p. 226.

[116] See, for example, Dannecker memo, January 21, 1941, in Steur 1997, p. 185.

[117] This is the central argument in Aly 1999.

[118] Westermann 2005, p. 155; see also a circular by Gottong, April 6, 1940, in Berenstein 1961, p. 56. For signs of impending large deportations in February, see Gruner 2004, pp. 38–9.

[119] Groundbreaking research on these expulsions and deportations is to be found in Toury 1986, esp. pp. 431–3, 440, 447–9, 455, 458. For protests see Browning 1978, p. 45. For forced emigration from the occupied zone see Steur 1997, pp. 46, 49–50, 52; see also Alary 2006, p. 224. For returns see Eggers 2002, p. 356. For overall deportation plans to France see Kettenacker 1973, pp. 250, 363 (note 76); Klarsfeld 1992, pp. 272–3; Hirschfeld 1991, p. 20.

certain regions within the Old Reich.[120] As soon as the general orientation pointed eastward again, 5,000 Viennese Jews were transported to the Lublin region in February and March 1941,[121] and the deportation of 70,000 Jews to Riga, Kaunas, Minsk and Łódź began in October and November of that year, all despite an unfinished war. It has to be added that German authorities deported people from other undesired groups in 1940–41 as well (which triggered as much resistance by the German administration in the reception areas as the deportation of Jews had done) – for example, Roma, who were sent mainly to Poland. In August 1940, Hitler dreamed of deporting all "truly criminal elements" to an island.[122] So, for example, Roma and Sinti, Spanish Republican veterans, criminals, 'asocials,' French citizens who had immigrated after 1918, and Alsatian nationalists were removed from Alsace. The vast majority of the more than 106,000 deportees from Alsace and Lorraine, as well as of the approximately 170,000 refugees who were refused readmittance, were not Jews.[123]

At the same time, other policies were in place. In Germany and Austria these included, as mentioned above, continuing forced emigration, concentration in 'Jew houses' and collective forced labor.[124] German policies and actions in Poland were harsher by far. In September 1939, reprisals, sadistic torture and plunder affected Poles of all denominations, with Jews suffering slightly more than proportionally – 7,000 died, primarily at the hands of the SS and police units.[125] This was mass murder, but, at first, it did not last long. German military instructions said that the "Jewish question in Poland is not yet to be solved in the short-term" because of economic considerations.[126] Beatings, humiliation, forced labor, plunder and arbitrary killings, however, persisted.[127] The deprivation of rights went further for Jews than for other Poles and included regulations making forced labor obligatory, dispossession, and

[120] Directive by Gestapo Koblenz to halt these expulsions, November 16, 1939, in Walk 1981, p. 310.

[121] Moser 1966, pp. 19–22.

[122] Zimmermann 1996, pp. 173–4, 178–9, 186, 214–17, 225. Hitler is quoted after Goebbels in Wachsmann 2004, p. 193.

[123] Peschanski 2010, pp. 40, 42; figures, according to Toury 1986, pp. 447–9. According to Heinemann 2003 (pp. 307 and 319), 165,000–168,000 people were expelled from Alsace and Lorraine. Stiller (2009, pp. 65–6, 81) gives lower figures.

[124] For forced labor in 1939–41 see Gruner 1997, pp. 19–216.

[125] Mallmann *et al.* 2008, p. 88; Böhler 2006, pp. 188–200; Rossino 2003, pp. 72–3, 88–120, 169–74.

[126] OKW leaflet, August 28, 1939, quoted in Böhler 2006, p. 39. For a similar argument see Chief of Security Police and Security Service, daily report, September 16–17, 1939, in Mallmann *et al.* 2008, p. 142.

[127] See Pohl 1993.

mandatory marking with an armband carrying a yellow star.[128] It is not clear how many Jews were among those deported from western to central Poland, but some plans suggest they were overrepresented proportionally speaking. Deportation reduced Jews and others to impoverished refugees without sustaining social networks in the reception areas.[129]

Yet no measure prior to 1941 was as grave as ghettoization. It was local German authorities, not regional administrations or authorities in Berlin, who for various reasons first forced Jews into designated neighborhoods which they could not leave without permission. In relatively few places were residents actually walled or fenced in.[130] Five to ten Jews were assigned to a single room because space was required for the German military, the administration, settlers and also the Polish non-Jews who had been forced out of their homes by the Germans and because, according to German administrators, Jews deserved no better. Ghettoization was also rationalized as preventing epidemics and curbing Jewish influence on public opinion. And once limited access was imposed on a separate quarter, deliveries of food, heating materials, medication and other essential goods could be restricted and control over the allocation of Jewish labor imposed. Small food rations, the lack of heating and hygiene, and overcrowding proved a deadly mix. By June 1941, more than 13,000 people had died in the ghetto of Warsaw and perhaps 5,000 in that of Łódź. (This was fortunately untypical for most other, especially smaller, ghettos, where control was less tight.)[131] In early 1941 financial experts predicted that the ghettos in Warsaw and Łódź would require German public subsidies in the longer run, and 'solutions,' such as using the ghetto population in productive labor or starving it to death, were discussed. Historians have interpreted these developments in different ways: as an attempt to force the Jews in the ghettos to hand over their allegedly huge assets; as a struggle between different German factions, the so-called productivists and attritionists; as a first step on the path to considering the murder of the unproductive and as a policy of extermination that had already begun.[132] But it is a matter of fact that this ruthless policy killed people who were utterly despised

[128] Weiss 1977, pp. 345–6.

[129] Mallmann *et al.* 2008, pp. 60, 63; HSSPF Posen, November 12, 1939, in Mallmann *et al.* 2008, p. 191. Some 30,800 of those deported from annexed western Poland to the district of Lublin were Jews: Kiełboń 2004, p. 124.

[130] Browning 1986, esp. p. 345; Młynarczyk 2007, pp. 112–24; Roth 2009, pp. 180–1, 189–90.

[131] Berenstein *et al.* 1961, p. 138; Snyder 2010a, p. 478 note 63 (11,837 deaths in 1941).

[132] The four arguments were made by Alberti 2006, pp. 150, 159; Browning and Matthäus 2003, pp. 189–99; Aly and Heim 1991, pp. 300–21; and Sinnreich 2004, p. 14 (in that order). See also Hilberg 1994a, pp. 246–9.

by many Germans. Ghettoization and the management of housing and food – all of this was the business of the civil administration which was, therefore, primarily responsible for the resulting deaths.

Germany went further toward implementing ideas for a 'territorial solution' than other countries did. These segregation schemes also drew on the nineteenth-century colonial practice of "reserves" for "natives" in settler colonies.[133] Likewise, establishing ghettos had an old, medieval tradition. Neither strategy was unheard of, but they did *not* belong to the standard set of Nazi or German right-wing thinkers' ideas. They went beyond earlier stated objectives. Additionally, no ghettos – with the exception of Amsterdam and Theresienstadt – would be erected outside eastern Europe. Except in Poland (and Serbia after April 1941), Jews in occupied countries faced legal discrimination but until mid 1941 not much more than that. For all these reasons, explaining German anti-Jewish policies in occupied countries as a mere continuation after 1939 of what the Nazis did inside Germany is inadequate. On the contrary, other factors arising from occupation, war, economics and other forms of racism co-determined the outcome.

By mid-June 1941, some 200,000 people had fallen victim to German mass murder, including 70,000 German and 20,000 Polish patients of mental institutions, up to 70,000 members of the Polish intelligentsia, hostages, reprisal victims, concentration camp inmates, victims of aerial bombings and about 30,000 Jews, 20,000 of whom starved to death in large Polish ghettos. The majority of these victims were non-Jews, but, in some ways, Jews were harder hit than others. In relation to their share of the overall population, Jews were overrepresented among reprisal victims in Poland; and Jews among the disabled and among the exhausted concentration camp victims who were systematically killed in early 1941 ran a higher risk of death than others in the same groups; 1,500 Jews, a disproportionately high number, were among the so-called 'asocials', political prisoners and criminals put in concentration camps in 1938; and once the war began Jews were less likely than others to be released from these camps and more likely to be murdered.[134] However, there is no evidence that Jews became victims of sterilization proportionally more often than non-Jews. The idea of 'solving' the Jewish 'problem' by sterilization was superficially considered in 1941, but no serious steps were taken toward it and the sterilization of Jews had stopped in Germany by March 1942.[135]

[133] Politicians like Heydrich (on September 14, 1939) spoke of creating a Jewish "reserve": Longerich 2001, p. 78.

[134] For the 'asocials' see Wildt 1995, p. 56; for political prisoners and criminals see Pingel 1978, pp. 72, 74; for mental hospitals see Grabher 2006, p. 50, and Neliba 1992, p. 242; for concentration camp inmates killed see Orth 1999, pp. 114–22; Pingel 1978, pp. 84, 96.

[135] Bock 1986, pp. 354–9; see also Chapter 4.

4 From mass murder to comprehensive annihilation: 1941–42

This chapter deals with a period of time that included several dramatic turns in German anti-Jewish policies and practices. Extermination was not decided upon all at once. Within one-and-a-half years, from the spring of 1941 to the late summer of 1942, the imaginations about schemes for the territorial concentration of the Jews came to include more and more violence combined with ideas for the selective mass murder of Jews in the Soviet Union that was to be occupied. This led to intentions to kill virtually all Soviet Jews; to which were then added plans to murder those Polish Jews who were regarded as unproductive, until, finally, the plan to kill *all* European Jews by 1943 was developed. Such policies came about through a complex process involving different central and regional authorities and agencies – at different levels of their hierarchies – and were the result of a number of intertwined motives. Practice evolved accordingly, though in regionally uneven ways – from selective mass shootings to almost complete annihilation in the occupied Soviet territories in 1941, though in some regions large numbers of Jews were spared for a year or longer; and from selective deportations from many countries to newly built extermination centers; and then the almost complete wiping out of Jewish communities in 1942. Other policies of mass violence also emerged and evolved during 1941–42, including the starving of Soviet POWs and others, forced labor, and anti-guerrilla warfare, all of which were, in some ways, connected to the fate of Jews. All of these developments were closely connected to the war's having become a relentless life-and-death struggle as a result of Germany's invasion of the USSR in June 1941 – and the subsequent hard-fought battles; of Germany's feverish efforts to support the Eastern Front with a wartime economy hampered by scarcity; and by the start of guerrilla uprisings in several countries. Non-German policies and actions against Jews and others must also be borne in mind.

It is important to examine the many initiatives and twists and turns in German decision-making because such patterns indirectly provide insights into more profound questions about the motives behind, the forces driving, and the political structures responsible for the extermination of Jews. For example, the later a researcher sees the general decision for extermination having been taken, the more his or her interpretation tends to emphasize the autonomy and initiative of lower-ranking German functionaries in the field.[1]

The mass murder of Soviet Jews

In June 1941, policies against Jews differed across the German-controlled areas of Europe. They were worst in Poland. Polish Jews had to wear a distinctive mark, and many were crammed into ghettos. They had lost their possessions, jobs, incomes and their homes, and they struggled to keep their dignity. They were socially isolated and lacked food, housing, heating, clothing and medicines. In mid 1941, more than 6,000 Jews starved to death each month in the large ghettos of Warsaw and Łódź. In most other areas under German control Jews did not wear an identifying sign or live in ghettos – although some were forced to live in so-called 'Jew houses' – but they were not allowed to use many public amenities, and had restricted shopping hours imposed upon them. Direct mass killings of the sort that had occurred in Poland in the fall of 1939 had stopped, but the sporadic arbitrary killing of Jews continued in some Polish areas, and the Jewish disabled and Jewish concentration camp inmates who were deemed unfit for work were selectively murdered. This situation did not change much, whether in Poland or elsewhere, when Germany attacked the Soviet Union on June 22, 1941, and German units began to massacre the Soviet Jews.

With the war against the USSR, the German leadership wanted to gain land for empire-building in the east, destroy what they saw as the home of world communism, improve their strategic position against Great Britain, and, potentially, the USA, and appropriate resources that Germany lacked like, for example, certain metals and mineral oil, grain and vegetable oils. In order to commandeer these resources, German military and economic planners had designed, before the invasion, a policy of selective mass death of Soviet citizens. Tens of millions were to be starved to death or killed in other ways. Since it was anticipated that Soviet agricultural production would plunge because of wartime disruptions, and because it seemed impossible to control such a large population tightly enough to be able simply to reduce everybody's food

[1] For more details on these patterns, reviews of existing theories, and evolving practices of mass murder, see Longerich 1998a; Browning and Matthäus 2003; Gerlach 1998a.

consumption, certain groups were to be forcibly excluded from consumption, i.e., urbanites and the inhabitants of the 'deficit areas' in north and central Russia and Belarus. Although important documents outlining this plan did not mention Jews specifically, many would suffer its effects as urban dwellers of the western Soviet Union.[2]

But that wasn't the only reason why Jews would feel its effects. The plan did not simply aim to relieve Germany's overall deficit of food and raw materials; in fact, most of the food that was supposed to be made available was to be used to supply the huge German armies on the Eastern Front. The plan, which fused military, economic, political and ideological thinking,[3] was conceived as a solution to the problem that German strategists envisaged in attacking the Soviet Union; namely, that the enormity of Soviet manpower, military equipment and territory meant that they had to be defeated quickly, before they could bring those resources to bear. Consequently, German strategists wanted to concentrate as much manpower and materiel at the front as possible, and so, Germany needed to free the few critical railway lines in the rear from transporting food eastward. Instead, they wanted to 'take the food from the country.' Thus, the success or failure of the war seemed to depend on the hunger policy, which is why that policy tended to find support among military officers. Moreover, concentrating troops at the front would leave few forces to occupy the rear. So, these would have to compensate for their low numbers with intimidation tactics and preemptive killings, and for this reason they welcomed the deployment of SS and police units here. In brief, the design of the campaign meant that victory at the front categorically required brutal policies in the rear. German generals expected that the policies of starvation and oppression would face Soviet resistance, mostly among urbanites. Communists and Jews, in particular, seemed to pose a danger to the German operation, thus reinforcing the war's anti-communist aims. Jews were believed to have inspired the prevailing Soviet system ('Jewish Bolshevism') and were expected to take the lead in defending it. Before the invasion began, therefore, the German leadership gave orders to kill Soviet political functionaries, and the SS and police gave orders to kill Jewish male members of the intelligentsia wherever they were found.

SS and police began shooting Jews in rear areas on the very first day of the invasion. Among these units were four *Einsatzgruppen* (operation units) of the Security Police and the Security Service, totaling 3,000 men – led by young academics; a growing number of Order Police

[2] See Gerlach 1999, pp. 46–76; Dieckmann 2011, pp. 192–209.
[3] Dieckmann 2011, pp. 184–92, 209–33; Gerlach 1999, pp. 72–6, 81–94, 214–15.

battalions; SS brigades, which were also supposed to serve as combat units; and soon also local auxiliary units of mostly Lithuanian, Ukrainian and Latvian origin. At first, the mass murder campaign was more or less restricted to Jewish men aged between fifteen and sixty years of age serving in the state bureaucracies, and in the liberal professions. These were seen as the Jewish intelligentsia in a broad sense. This restriction, and the rapid advance of German troops, initially limited the number of victims. In July 1941 up to 39,000 Jews in Ukraine and about 26,000 in Belarus were murdered.[4] Non-Jews were also murdered, but from the start they usually constituted only a small minority of the civilian victims (unlike among Soviet POWs). In Lithuania, locals may have massacred more Jews in June and July than the 8,000 killed by German death squads.[5] In the first weeks of the invasion, tens of thousands of Jews fell victim to pogroms conducted by locals (often strongly encouraged by German forces) from Latvia through Lithuania, the region of Białystok, eastern Galicia, and Romanian-reconquered Bukovina and Bessarabia to Moldavia. In connection with these, Romanian troops and *gendarmes* killed tens of thousands of people, most of whom were Jews. The Romanian murder of Jews registered other peaks in October 1941, in and around Odessa; and from December 1941 to April 1942, which claimed some 250,000 lives through massacre and starvation (see Chapter 14).

Beginning in August, German units in various Soviet areas targeted a wider range of Jews. For example, they began to murder women and children and, several weeks later, in some regions started to annihilate the entire Jewish community of smaller towns. Some male Jews were still exempted, but the criteria had changed: now it was those who were useful as forced laborers.[6] Accordingly, the killings increased dramatically. In Ukraine the number had exploded by the end of August, reaching its peak in September, remaining extremely high in October, and peaking again in December.[7] In Lithuania the killings culminated in August and September 1941, with more than 40,000 murdered each month.

[4] See Kruglov 2010, pp. 274–5; Gerlach 1999, p. 550.

[5] See the figures in Dieckmann 2011, p. 391; and in Einsatzkommando 3, report of December 1, 1941, printed in Klee *et al.* 1988, pp. 52–3.

[6] Good surveys are to be found in Longerich 1998a, pp. 352–403; Jürgen Matthäus's contribution in Browning and Matthäus 2003, pp. 405–28. See also Gerlach 1999, pp. 555–628.

[7] According to Kruglov (2010, pp. 274–7), and including the Romanian murders, 38,000–39,000 Jews were killed in July of 1941, 62,000 in August, 136,000–137,000 in September, 118,000–119,000 in October, 65,000 in November, and 87,000 in December.

October and November were the peak months in Belarus.[8] Killing techniques were adjusted to enable relatively small death squads to destroy many people in a short space of time. Jews were assembled under duress. Often, some were dismissed as still useful; the rest were marched or driven to a secluded place, usually a few kilometers out of town, where, with numbing brutality, they were forced to undress and hand over their valuables. They were then shot, group by group, and buried in previously prepared pits. While waiting, victims were in a state of agony. Many nevertheless remained calm and bid farewell to relatives and friends. Some prayed. Others cried or begged for their lives. In 1941, few tried to escape. Army troops or local auxiliary policemen cordoned off the sites. In the early weeks the murderers killed their victims face-to-face with rifle volleys on command – firing squad style. Later they shot their victims with pistols or rifles individually in the back of the head so that their bodies would fall into the pit; or they forced them to lie down in the pit on top of other bodies and shot them lying in that position. Increasingly, they lined Jews up in rows and shot them with machine guns or machine pistols.[9] However, such advanced shooting techniques had already been employed by ethnic German militias and SS and police in western Poland in 1939.[10] Such massacres were brutish and chaotic rather than neat and orderly. In order to save time, the killing units used automatic weapons and did not care if, as a result, many victims lying in the pits were only wounded and consequently buried alive. Often a few such victims, those who were not killed by the small team that usually guarded sites for several hours following the massacre, managed to escape.

Almost 900,000 Soviet Jews were murdered during such operations under German control in 1941. In Ukraine, in 1941, almost twice the number of Jews fell victim to *Waffen*-SS brigades and the supposedly apolitical Order Police than to the *Einsatzgruppen*.[11] This came close to the ratio experienced in the Baltic region and in Belarus.[12] Army units also massacred tens of thousands of Jews.

[8] See Einsatzkommando 3, report of December 1, 1941, printed in Klee *et al.* 1988, pp. 52–9. For Belarus, see Gerlach 1999, pp. 585–628.

[9] Angrick 2003, pp. 362–3; Gerlach 1999, pp. 562–3.

[10] Jansen and Weckbecker 1992, pp. 103, 117–18, 125, 129–31.

[11] In 1941 about 150,000 Jews were killed in Lithuania, 70,000–80,000 in Latvia, 190,000 in Belarus, more than 500,000 in Ukraine (of which 70,000 were killed in eastern Galicia (see below), close to 90,000 were killed under Romanian control, and tens of thousands in Russia. See Kruglov 2010 (pp. 274–80) for Ukraine; see Gerlach 1999 (p. 628) for Belarus; see Dieckmann 2011 (p. 1009) for Lithuania; see Felder 2009 (p. 206) for Latvia.

[12] For 1941, the Einsatzgruppen reported about 350,000 killings, mostly of Jews. See Scheffler 1997, p. 38; Gerlach 1997, p. 62; Headland 1992, pp. 98–101; Angrick 2003, p. 519.

Himmler later claimed to have decided personally to have Jewish women and children killed.[13] However, the fact that the murders of women and children started at different times in different occupied areas of the Soviet Union suggests there were some local influences. Negotiations between the military and the SS and police were one important factor.[14] The fact that the destruction was very unevenly spread in 1941 also suggests the importance of local factors. Germans, and those assisting them, killed 80% or more of the local Jewish population in eastern and much of central Ukraine, eastern Belarus, Russia, Latvia and Lithuania; but only 10–25% in western Belarus and northwestern Ukraine. Close to 900,000 Jews remained alive in these western areas, which were under civil administration.

A number of reasons have been cited for these disparities: the military administrations in the east were pushing harder than the civil administrations, at that time, for the quick elimination of Jews as security threats, and also to save food; Jews in pre-1939 Soviet territories were thought to be more committed to communism and thus more dangerous than those from the recently annexed areas; also, not many Security Police forces were deployed to some of the western areas. Moreover, in former eastern Poland, unlike in the old Soviet territories, manufacturing was dominated by small workshops, and the vast majority of craftsmen were Jews whom the civil administration and the *Einsatzgruppen* found indispensable. Further to the east, much of the economy (and civilian housing) had been destroyed by war, and, as a result, there was little demand for urban labor.[15] The enthusiastic participation of local non-Jews in German-organized killing was another factor in some areas. Lithuanian units carried out many massacres in the Lithuanian countryside, with no Germans present.[16] This closer inspection of local events – which reveals these patterns – suggests that SS and police units carried out most of the killings, but only sometimes did they act autonomously. Usually German civil and military authorities ordered, or at least co-determined, these operations.

The mass murder of Soviet Jews took place in the context of the largest war in history. Millions of Soviet soldiers fell in battle in 1941. More than 3 million Soviet troops fell into German captivity, and about 2 million

[13] Himmler's speech, October 6, 1943, BA, NS 19/4010, p. 175. For other speeches in 1944, see Longerich 2001, pp. 189–90.
[14] Pohl 2000, p. 143.
[15] See Gerlach 1999, especially p. 606; Reitlinger 1963, p. 185; Pohl 2000, pp. 144, 147–8, 154–6; for losses in Ukraine see Alexander Kruglov's data in Zabarko 2005, p. 391; and Spector 1990a, p. 186 note 63; for economic structures see Dean 2000, pp. 7–8.
[16] See Bankier 2011, pp. 96–161.

Soviet POWs had perished by late January 1942. At that time, Soviet POWs – not Jews – were the single largest victim group of German policies, and they died overwhelmingly in German army – not SS – custody. Most were starved to death between October 1941 and January 1942 after the German military had redirected the hunger policy (the blanket version of which had failed) against specific groups in the context of the military supply crisis in the fall and winter of 1941 (see Chapter 9). This change in the hunger policy, which also contributed to decisions to massacre Jews, came after it had become the basis of German planning in September 1941 that the war against the Soviet Union could not be brought to a close before the end of 1941.[17] Should the war in the east last into 1942, then Soviet partisans behind the German lines would pose a much greater political threat than previously thought. Accordingly, the Germans stepped up their anti-partisan measures in September and October 1941 (as they did in Serbia). Tens of thousands of non-Jews were killed as a result. In the occupied Soviet territories, many military officers argued on the basis of their preconceptions that Jews – collectively suspected to be spies, insurgents and agitators – should be killed for reasons of security in areas where there were many partisans, and also in some areas where this was not yet the case[18] (see Chapter 11). Whilst initially most German functionaries and politicians had not considered Jews to be a valuable labor resource, this situation changed somewhat once bases for manufacturing supplies for the Eastern Front had been set up in the rear but only a few able-bodied Soviet POWs were available to work in them. Several tens of thousands of Jewish workers, mostly men – the group initially targeted for murder – were kept, temporarily, for this purpose (see Chapter 8). In these ways, anti-Jewish violence was embedded in broader policy issues that involved violence against non-Jews as well.

Many Soviet Jews sensed that the German forces posed a great threat to them and tried to evacuate or flee on their own. This, too, took place within a broader population movement, i.e. the eastward evacuation of 10–15 million Soviet citizens. Jews' success at fleeing eastward depended on various factors: their awareness of German policies; the local success of the organization of the evacuation campaign, which, in turn, depended on the geographical location and the development of military operations; and Soviet policies for determining who was to be evacuated. Jews were overrepresented among evacuees since many of them were civil servants,

[17] Gerlach 1999, pp. 274–5; see also Jersak 1999, p. 364. Against this backdrop, any temporary excitement over the initial successes in the Battle of Moscow in early October (see Browning and Matthäus 2003, pp. 455–75) was secondary.

[18] See Gerlach 1999 (pp. 602–5, 615–20, 875–84) for Belarus; see Boll and Safrian 2000 (pp. 256–63) for eastern Ukraine; see Hasenclever 2010 (pp. 474–516) in general.

functionaries, or worked in industries essential to the war effort, and many lived in cities with railroad access. But those who lived in former eastern Poland were sometimes barred from entering pre-1941 Soviet territory. The longer the war lasted and the further east it spread, the smaller the number of Jews who fell into German hands tended to be. According to estimates, about 1.6 million Soviet Jews escaped eastward, at least 900,000 of them from Ukraine.[19]

Fall 1941: The geographical spread of mass murder begins

In some areas of German-occupied Europe, the systematic mass killing of Jews started months after the German attack on the USSR. In Serbia, mass arrests began in April 1941, but killing of Jewish (and other) hostages, held against the threat of partisan attacks, and of some Jews because of their alleged participation in the communist resistance, remained limited until late August. In either September or, more likely, October of 1941, German military units began the killing of 6,000 Jewish men who were part of the 20,000–25,000 murders that were committed in order to quell the national uprising. In early 1942 the Security Police and SD murdered the remaining Serbian Jews, mostly women and children, who could not flee.[20] In France, German measures were less harsh at this time, but 3,710 Jews of various nationalities were arrested on May 13, and at least 4,232 Polish, Czech and Austrian Jews were arrested between August 20 and 25, 1941 (together with sizable numbers of non-Jews in both cases). Some were later released; others became hostages.[21] Becoming increasingly uneasy, for political reasons, about shooting French hostages in response to the first attacks of the Resistance on German soldiers, the German military administration suggested deporting a certain number of Jews to the east instead.[22]

In the Wartheland, a part of annexed western Poland, there was special pressure to remove many of the resident Jews. Plans to evict them from the region and move them to the General Government – partly to make room for resettling ethnic Germans – had failed for the most part in 1940–41.[23] About 150,000 Jews were crowded in adverse conditions in the Łódź ghetto, where the number of deaths from starvation

[19] See Arad 2009, pp. 75–88; Pohl 2011, p. 122; Kruglov 2010, p. 273.

[20] See Romano and Kadelburg 1977, pp. 678–81; Browning 1985, pp. 39–56, 68–85; Manoschek 1993, pp. 12, 69–108; see also the telegram by Veesenmayer and Benzler, September 8, 1941 (copy), BA, NS 30/193.

[21] Peschanski 2002, p. 202; Kaspi 1997, p. 212; Steur 1997, p. 58.

[22] Herbert 1996, pp. 301–4. [23] Aly 1999, pp. 33–87, 134–84.

and disease rose to more than 1,000 per month.[24] Recent research has shown that the region's civil administration, under Arthur Greiser, was the driving force behind the mass murder of Jews in that area, a policy that was adopted in the summer of 1941 and resulted – with Himmler's permission – in the construction of the first German extermination camp at Chełmno (Kulmhof).[25] One reason for wanting "some fast working means to finish off" the Jews was to prevent further mass deaths by starvation (and consequent epidemics).[26] The SS and police reactivated men who had carried out the gassing of mental patients in the area. Jews were shot or killed by other methods in various localities between the end of September and November 1941.[27] Mass murder at Chełmno began on December 8, 1941. From January 1942, Jews from Łódź were also killed there. The civil administration planned to murder all of the Jews in the region, except those fit for work, by the end of March.[28] In reality, however, the murder of the approximately 100,000 Jews deemed unproductive took until September 1942. They were brought to a remote castle where they were first politely asked to undress, then brutally crammed into closed vans whose exhaust fumes were piped into their airtight interiors, and driven to a forest. A team of Jews was forced to unload the vans and throw the bodies into mass graves.[29]

Meanwhile, anti-Jewish policies in the General Government became more aggressive, too. In Warsaw and in some smaller places also, ghettoization led to overcrowding, starvation and epidemics. In Warsaw the number of deaths rocketed in the first half of 1941 and remained close to 5,000 per month throughout the second half.[30] Instead of substantially increasing the food ration for Jews (which was about 200 calories per day in Warsaw), the German administration decreed on October 16 that all Jews found outside a ghetto without permission should be shot. On October 13 the option of deporting Jews from the General Government to the occupied Soviet territories in the near future was ruled out. On the same day, the SS and Police Leader in the district of Lublin – Odilo Globocnik – received Himmler's order (which he probably suggested) to build the first death camp in the area. Construction at Bełżec started around November 1. The camp began operations on March 17, 1942,

[24] Unger 1998, p. 125.
[25] Klein 2009, pp. 320–2, 344, 390, 478, 504–5; Alberti 2006, esp. pp. 349–53; Epstein 2010, pp. 185–6.
[26] Hoeppner to Eichmann, July 16, 1941, printed in Pätzold 1984, p. 295.
[27] Krakowski 2007, pp. 22–6.
[28] See the memo of a meeting in the Reich Labor Ministry, November 28, 1941, printed in Pätzold 1984, p. 322; Klein 2009, pp. 442–4.
[29] For details see Krakowski 2007.
[30] Gutman 1982, p. 64.

but because of its small gas chambers it was adequate 'only' for the decimation of Jews in the region, and not yet for killing them all.[31] In the district of Galicia – former Polish territory that the USSR had annexed in 1939 and the Germans had conquered in the summer of 1941 – systematic German mass shootings of Jews, which began on October 6, had claimed 70,000 lives by the end of the year.[32] The practice here, which did not yet extend to other districts of the General Government, resembled that in most of the German-occupied Soviet territories.

Within the Old Reich and Austria, the murder of Jews in 1941 was restricted to several thousand disabled and concentration camp inmates deemed unfit for work.[33] Otherwise, the RSHA in the summer of 1941 continued to focus on political preparations for yet worse treatment of Jews. On July 31, Heydrich was commissioned by Göring to prepare and submit a draft of an "overall solution to the Jewish question in the German sphere of influence in Europe" or, as Göring also called it, a "final solution to the Jewish question."[34] A week later the RSHA started to gather data on the number of Jews in different countries across Europe (which were later used in the protocol of the Wannsee conference). Their next step was an attempt to enlarge the definition of 'Jew' with the intention that it should include so-called 'half-Jews'. This became the topic of an interagency working group in August, but its deliberations produced no agreement.[35] In August 1941, Hitler's prohibition against deporting German Jews elsewhere was still in effect, although he intended to have them removed later.[36] Based on the suggestions of many regional Nazi Party leaders, the Ministry of the Interior, and the aforementioned interagency working group, a decree, dated September 1, was issued compelling Jews in the Greater German Reich to wear a yellow star. Goebbels reasoned that this would make it impossible for Jews to voice criticism and defeatism without being recognized.[37] Before, only the Jews in the

[31] Pohl 1993, pp. 92–5, 99–106; Witte *et al.* 1999, pp. 233–4; Gerlach 1998a, p. 178.

[32] Pohl 1996, pp. 139–54.

[33] See p. 65 in this volume; Friedlander 1995, pp. 271–5.

[34] Printed in Pätzold 1984, p. 298.

[35] Essner 2002, pp. 329–46; Kreuzmüller 2008, pp. 40–1; Wildt 2003, pp. 609–11; Adam 1972, pp. 319–20. For the data, see two lists, one from August 7, 1941, in AIPN, CA 362/218, pp. 1–10. Objections against the enlarged definition came especially from the Reich Ministries for Justice and the Interior.

[36] Zeitschel to Behr, August 22, 1941, in Steur 1997, p. 190; for Hitler's intention to have Jews removed later, see the remark of the General Commissioner in the Netherlands, Schmidt, on August 20, 1941, in Michman 1986, p. 172.

[37] See the police decree, September 1, 1941, in Pätzold 1984, pp. 306–7; Goebbels 1996, II, 1, p. 265 (August 15, 1941); for the suggestions from the Party see Bormann circular Nr. 109/41, September 9, 1941, BA NS 6/335, p. 84; for the Interior Ministry see Neliba 1992, p. 344; for the working group see Essner 2002, pp. 337–8; for proposals by the HSSPF in Prague see Oprach 2006, pp. 117–18, 122.

occupied Soviet and Polish territories (and Polish non-Jewish workers inside Germany) had suffered such marking. For people defined as Jews, this was a traumatic, degrading turn of events that moved them further into social isolation.

The next, much more fateful step, followed. Between September 14 and 18, Hitler decided to begin the deportation of Jews from the Reich to the east. Originally he had envisioned taking this step after the defeat of the Soviet Union. Eichmann's office in the RSHA started to coordinate the deportations. Although this was a step toward greater centralization of anti-Jewish policies, Hitler's permission was also the result of the initiatives of several different authorities and agencies, including the RSHA and the regional party leaders in Berlin, Vienna and Hamburg (Goebbels, von Schirach and Kaufmann, respectively; the latter two wished to offer apartments to non-Jews, and Kaufmann to those who had lost their housing as a result of British air raids). The appointed Minister for the Occupied Eastern Territories, Rosenberg, suggested threatening the Soviet government with such deportations in order to deter it from repressing the Volga Germans. In fact, 400,000 of them were deported between September 13 and 15, and Hitler became interested in modifying Rosenberg's idea.[38] Allegedly, Hitler envisioned the deportation of all German Jews by the end of 1941.[39] For 1941, however, historians have discovered only permits for the deportation of 70,000 Jews and 5,000 Austrian *Lalleri* ("gypsies") to Łódź, Riga and Minsk (destinations that Hitler personally chose), of which number – between October 15 and the end of the year – 42,000 Jews and 5,000 "gypsies" were actually transported to Łódź, Kaunas, Riga and Minsk. Most of these remained alive for the time being. Protests from German authorities in the reception areas limited the number of deportations: Military Commanders complained about the problems that deportations caused to the rear supplies on the Eastern Front, civilian administrators objected because of the lack of shelter for Jews from the Reich, and no administration wanted its territory to become a dumping ground for Jews.[40] Still, these were the largest deportations of Greater German Jews thus far.

[38] See Witte 1995; Gerlach 1998a, pp. 76–8; for Kaufmann, see his letter to Görnnert, September 4, 1942, BA 34.01 FC, film no. 375, p. 6786; see Lammers and Bormann to von Schirach, December 3, 1940, and November 2, 1941, respectively, in Botz 1975, pp. 197–9.

[39] See the protocol of a Security Police meeting in Prague, October 10, 1941, in Longerich 1989, p. 176.

[40] Gottwaldt and Schulle 2005, pp. 52–130; Gerlach 1999, pp. 749–54. For Hitler choosing the destinations see Adam 1972, p. 314, note 51; Gruner 2000a, p. 75.

For eight years, Nazi Germany had practiced a policy of forced emigration. Leaving the country remained legal during the war, despite various plans to resettle the Jews in Poland, Madagascar, and even the Soviet territories. Since December 1939, German diplomats abroad had been suggesting, unsuccessfully, that emigration be discontinued because of the criticism that Jewish emigres were spreading abroad about the Nazi regime.[41] It was only with the start of deportations in October 1941 that Jewish emigration from Germany, Austria and Bohemia and Moravia was outlawed.[42] After that time, Jews from Greater Germany emigrated only in a few exceptional cases, mostly with Himmler's permission (but emigration from Vichy France was still possible, and at least 2,000 emigrated legally in 1942).[43] The remainder were trapped.

Certain categories (like decorated veterans of World War I) were excluded from deportation. The reason was the large number of petitions that German non-Jews made on behalf of Jews. Other categories were sent to Theresienstadt, which was allegedly set up as a camp for those deserving preferential treatment; Heydrich said that through this "practical solution the many interventions will be neutralized in one blow." Eichmann mailed the first restrictions on which Jews were to be deported on November 20, 1941, and a supplement came out on April 17, 1942.[44] Even Nazi Party agencies, including Bouhler's Chancellery of the Führer, supported so many requests for exemption – for example from persons of 'mixed blood' – that Hitler became infuriated.[45] In particular, the forced marking of Jews with the yellow star drew so many signals of solidarity among individuals from the middle class, intellectuals, workers in Berlin and in the Czech lands – that the propaganda machinery was mobilized against them and the Gestapo ordered on October 24 that people showing "Jew-friendly behavior" be arrested.[46] On the other hand, most German onlookers remained silent when Jews were deported

[41] Conze *et al.* 2010, pp. 176–9.

[42] Browning and Matthäus 2003, pp. 288–92, 529–30; Gerwarth 2011, p. 253; see also Browning 1978, p. 44. Passports for Czech Jews were no longer issued after October 2, 1941; see Klein 2009, p. 371 note 46.

[43] See Zariz 1987, pp. 275, 290; for France see Thalmann 1999, p. 267; Marrus and Paxton 1981, pp. 164, 247.

[44] See Gerlach 1998b, pp. 770–1; Heydrich's opinion is quoted after the minutes of the Wannsee conference on January 20, 1942; see the facsimile in Tuchel 1992, p. 130. For the planning for Theresienstadt see Oprach 2006, pp. 122–3.

[45] Bormann to Bouhler, June 2, 1942 (copy), BA 62 Ka 1, Nr. 63, p. 136.

[46] Bajohr and Pohl 2006, p. 56; Gellately 2002, p. 187; Milotova 1996, p. 171; von Hassell 1946, pp. 231, 236 (October 4 and November 30, 1941); Gruner 1997, p. 275; Goebbels 1941, pp. 1–2; MadR, vol. 8, p. 3007 (no. 239, November 20, 1941); Steinberg 1992, p. 305. Kershaw 2008 notes much displeasure but even more indifference (pp. 182, 200); see also Longerich 2006, pp. 36, 42.

from their town; occasionally, crowds (which included children) showed hostility; and a few, pity. Some clergy, elderly people and members of the bourgeoisie privately voiced criticism of the deportations.[47] But private criticism, individual demonstrations of solidarity, and particular cases of petitioning for exemption were not enough by far to challenge Nazi hegemony and reverse the increasing severity of the persecution, except for relatively small exempted groups. One scholar has credited the Christian churches with the fact that the Nazis did not annul existing marriages between Jews and non-Jews.[48] Other citizens felt no such mercy. German railway personnel, for example, were sometimes unwilling even to provide drinking water to deportees.[49]

Some historians interpret the beginning of mass killings in Serbia, plans for death camps in the Wartheland and the General Government – together with the decision to deport the Jews of the Reich, and radical anti-Jewish statements coming from Hitler and other Nazi politicians (all of which occurred in the fall of 1941) – as indicative of a general decision to murder the Jews of Europe.[50] Others reject this view, arguing that the decision was made later.[51] The question is important. If the destruction of Jews, or major preparations for it, started in a number of different areas without a general decision having been made (and no document from the fall of 1941 proves that any was), then the mass murder had a more participatory character and was fueled by a variety of initiatives and interests that came together in a general assault on Jews. As briefly sketched above, there is ample evidence of such initiatives. For each of Serbia, Wartheland, and the General Government, there is also evidence of contacts with various central authorities (Hitler, Himmler, the RSHA, the Foreign Office, Rosenberg, and the Chancellery of the Führer, respectively), but in none of these regions did the center take the lead at this time.[52]

47 Bajohr and Pohl 2006, pp. 47–51; Kershaw 2008, pp. 146–7; see also Hitler's comments on November 19, 1941 and January 25, 1942 in Hitler 1982, pp. 143, 228.

48 Essner 1995, p. 207.

49 See the report of police captain Salitter, December 26, 1941, in Hilberg 1981, p. 138.

50 See Browning and Matthäus 2003, pp. 449–535.

51 Friedländer 2007, pp. 743–4, 751–4; Longerich 1998a, pp. 441–60; Gerlach 1998a, pp. 267–79.

52 Experiments with prussic acid gas at Auschwitz – either in September or November 1941 – had no direct connection with the start of the extermination of Jews. Most of the victims of the experiments were non-Jewish Soviet POWs. The gassing of prisoners, among them Jews, started on a small scale in February 1942, but the first murder of Jews who had just arrived was in July 1942. See Orth 1999, pp. 137–40, 199–201, and pp. 97 of this volume. A speech by Rosenberg at a press conference on November 18, 1941, about the "biological elimination of all Jewry in Europe" to be carried out in the occupied Soviet territories was ambiguous in its context (Gerlach 1998a, pp. 109, 159) and understood ambivalently. See the journalist Fritz Sänger's note on Rosenberg's speech: "They [6 million Soviet Jews] have to be eliminated biologically, one can send

Hitler's decision in principle to kill all of the European Jews

By early December 1941, mass shootings of Jews were under way in the German-occupied Soviet territories and, on a much smaller scale, in Serbia. Mass killings had started in the German-annexed Wartheland region of Poland, where gassings at the first death camp, at Chełmno, began on December 8. The first large-scale massacre of Jews from the Reich took place in Serbia on October 12 and 13, 1941, when the army's 342nd Infantry Division, not the SS, shot 400 male Jewish refugees, extracting gold teeth from the corpses.[53] Large deportations of German, Austrian, Czech and Luxembourgian Jews started in October, but most of them were sent to ghettos rather than being massacred upon arrival. In Minsk and Riga many thousands of local Jews were murdered to make room in the ghettos for Jews from the Reich. But, in late November, Einsatzkommando 3 shot close to 5,000 of the Jews who had arrived at Kaunas from the Reich, and SS and police units shot another 1,000 near Riga on November 30. Himmler then ordered an end to such murders in response to protests from the civil administration that Jews who should have been exempt from deportation were being killed (such as decorated World War I veterans), and objections from within the Security Police and SD.[54] The next day, Hitler – who had met Himmler on November 30 – stated privately that some German Jews were decent.[55] The wholesale murder of German Jews appeared to require a precise specification of who was to be included, and there were doubts about whether the killing of German Jews (as opposed to eastern European Jews) was permissible in general.

The broader context included the beginning of the first major Soviet counteroffensives – near Moscow and at the southern end of the Eastern Front – in the first days of December. Hitler understood the importance of these events. He even traveled to Mariupol, Ukraine, on December 2 or 3 to visit the SS division that was named after him, and reinforce its morale in this critical situation. It took his aides some effort to prevent him from entering areas open to enemy fire.[56] In addition, Hitler

them behind the Urals or eliminate them in another way." Quoted in Dörner 2007, p. 164.

53 Manoschek 1993, pp. 91–6.

54 Gerlach 1998b, pp. 761–73; Angrick and Klein 2006, p. 162. For decorated Jews among the central European victims at Kaunas see M. Jelin, "Die Todesforts bei Kaunas" in Grossman and Ehrenburg 1994, p. 582.

55 See entry for December 1 and 2, 1941, in Hitler 1982, p. 148.

56 See an SS war correspondent's report to d'Alquen and Weibgen, Taganrog, December 5, 1941, BA NS 19/2440, pp. 2–4.

declared war on the United States on December 11, shortly after the Japanese attack on Pearl Harbor. In his speech in the Reichstag on that day, he asserted that Jewish warmongers were pulling Roosevelt's strings. The German leadership now regarded the present war as another world war. For them, Germany's situation had become still more serious than before.[57]

As a batch of documents shows, Hitler announced his decision in principle to murder all of Europe's Jews on or around December 12, 1941. He gave a speech during a meeting of about 50 regional and sectional leaders of the Nazi Party on that day, about which Goebbels noted:

> Regarding the Jewish question the Führer is determined to clear the table. He warned the Jews that if they were to cause another world war, it would lead to their own destruction. Those were not empty words. Now the world war has come. The destruction of the Jews must be its necessary consequence. We cannot be sentimental about it.

According to Goebbels, Hitler added – in reference to German military losses – that those responsible for the war "will have to pay for it with their own lives."[58] On December 16, Hans Frank, who had been present at Hitler's speech, told his administration in Kraków that it was necessary to "liquidate" the Polish Jews in Poland since, according to his conversations with those in charge of the Reichskommissariate, it would not be possible to deport them eastward to Soviet territory. (In October, Frank had been told that such deportations might be possible later.) Frank said that instead – referring back to Hitler's remarks four days earlier – an organization was to be established in the General Government in cooperation with authorities in the Reich which would, in ways yet to be determined, produce a "destructive result" (*Vernichtungserfolg*) against the Jews. The Jews had to disappear during the war because Nazi thinking demanded it and because they were "useless eaters."[59] On December 14, Rosenberg, the minister for the occupied Soviet territories, told Hitler that "now, after the decision" he did not want to talk publicly about the extermination of the Jews. According to Rosenberg, Hitler agreed with him, adding that the Jews had to bear the consequences of having brought destruction upon the German people. On December 18, Rosenberg's ministry wrote to the Reich Commissioner for the Ostland (who was also present at Hitler's speech on December 12) to say that concerning "the Jewish

[57] Gerlach 1998b, pp. 784–7.

[58] Goebbels' diary, December 13, 1941, quoted in Gerlach 1998b, p. 785.

[59] Quoted in Gerlach 1998a, p. 132. For a vague commitment from the Eastern Minister, Rosenberg, see General Governor's log, October 14, 1941, in Präg and Jacobmeyer 1975, p. 413.

question, clarity has meanwhile presumably been provided through oral conversations. Economic considerations shall not be taken into account in solving this problem."[60] (In reality, however, hundreds of thousands of Soviet Jewish workers remained alive for at least six months, and several tens of thousands in the Ostland for years afterwards.) On December 18 Himmler met with Hitler and later noted: "Jewish question/to be exterminated as partisans" (the latter part was presumably the result that Himmler noted after the conversation took place). In my view this was in reference to Jews in general, i.e., to the so-called 'Jewish threat'.[61]

Thus, Hitler's guidelines had changed. Instead of the mass murder of Soviet Jews, and the removal of the rest to a single area for slow decimation there *after* the war, he now called for the direct destruction of the European Jews *during* the war, pointing to their alleged role as enemies and as partisans by way of justification. Jews were also no longer useful as hostages against US entry into the war.[62] As has already been mentioned, other politicians pointed to long-term ideological goals and food problems. These new developments led to announcements of changes in policies concerning Jews by the administrations under whose authority most of them lived. There was a major change in policy in the General Government and a gradual one in the occupied Soviet territories. It is also likely that Himmler said – on December 14, during a meeting with Viktor Brack, the organizer of the mass gassing of the disabled – that the murder of the Jews had to be carried out as quickly as possible. On December 13 there were further conversations between Bouhler (Brack's superior), Himmler, Hitler, von Ribbentrop and Rosenberg; and on December 14 between Bouhler, Hitler, Himmler and Ribbentrop. Experts from Berlin may have been dispatched to the proposed sites of the annihilation camps as a result of these talks.[63] The events of December 1941 reflected a fundamental change in policy, which was communicated further but which did not immediately result in the intensified mass murder

[60] Quoted in Gerlach 1998a, pp. 121 (from Rosenberg's note of December 16), 130. Reichskommissriat Ostland included the Baltic countries and parts of Belarus.

[61] Quoted in Gerlach 1998b, p. 780. In his Reichstag speech on December 11, Hitler had announced ruthless measures against disturbances on the home front and against the black market, as the SD emphasized. See MadR, vol. 8, p. 3091 (246, December 15, 1941). Peter Longerich (1998b, p. 28) has suggested that Hitler's reference to partisans meant that the murder of Soviet Jews was to be intensified again. I don't think this to be the case since there were hardly any Jewish partisans at the time. Also, in most of the occupied Soviet territories, the large-scale killing of Jews did not resume for months. According to Friedländer 2006, p. 354, the "first [entirely] Jewish resistance organization in occupied Europe" (in Kaunas) came about in January 1942, two weeks after Hitler's meeting with Himmler.

[62] This point is emphasized by Hartog 1997, pp. 75–6.

[63] See Gerlach 1998b, pp. 781–3, 792; see also Berger 2013, pp. 34–6.

of Jews anywhere. No death camps sprung up and no major deportations were triggered (despite the intentions for deportations; see below). Some mass murders *had* already occurred – but despite his impulse in favor of extermination, perhaps his strongest over the years, Hitler did not, and did not have to, decide upon everything. The apparatus was not ready to implement the new policy instantly.

Richard Evans has asserted that the present author "subsequently distanced himself" from the thesis that Hitler announced a decision to kill all European Jews in December 1941.[64] I didn't; Evans's claim is pure invention. My interpretation is supported by newly discovered documents, especially a report from mid 1944 written by an unidentified German former SD officer, a man with comprehensive knowledge of the policies of mass murder who had defected to Switzerland. According to the document's author, beginning in the second half of 1941 there were

> actions for the annihilation (*Ausrottung*) of *all* Eastern Jews (for example, [in] Galicia) and the complete emptying of certain areas of the Russian population. After America entered the war, the annihilation (*Ausrottung*) of all European Jews was initiated on the Führer's order.[65]

He mentioned, among other things, the four Einsatzgruppen (although he confused their commanding officers) and that the announced reason for the general deportation of Jews – namely, that they were to be employed as laborers – was a pretext in general (which became popularly known). But some Jews were actually selected for forced labor. He provided largely accurate descriptions and drawings of seven different techniques of mass murder, including various methods of shooting, "Nebe's gas vans" (*Nebe'sche Gaswagen*), and descriptions of gas chambers into which gas containers were introduced through a hole in the ceiling, and listed the disadvantages of each method (although he also falsely described ships with opening bottoms and murder by acid). He described the systematic unearthing of mass graves and the use of crematoria, especially after the discovery of the mass graves at Katyn. He knew about mental breakdowns and alcoholism among the Einsatzgruppen men, about the death of Walther Stahlecker (the chief of Einsatzgruppe A) during anti-partisan warfare, and about the starving to death of millions of Soviet POWs. With reference to a conversation with Max Thomas, the former chief of Einsatzgruppe C, the author stated that "6,000,000

[64] Evans 2010, p. 22.

[65] "Militärisch-politische Berichte. Ueber den deutschen Nachrichtendienst" (no date, receipt stamp of August 5, 1944), BAS, EMD, E27, 1000/721/Bd. 2183, Dossier 306, pp. 58–9. The word "all" is underlined in the original. First quoted in Haas 1994, pp. 163–5, though not in this context.

people (Russians and Jews) had been 'bumped off'" by the summer of 1943.[66] Given such competence, apparently acquired via extensive conversations with RSHA personnel, his remark on the timing of Hitler's "order" gains credibility.

A German military administrator in France already interpreted Hitler's speech of December 11, in which he declared war on the USA, in such a way that "the Jewish problem gains a new, strong political importance also for France, whereas so far the elimination of the Jewish influence in the economy has been in the foreground."[67] On December 12, 743 Jews were arrested in Paris. The imposition of a levy of 1 billion francs on the French Jews, the execution of dozens of Jewish hostages, and permission to deport 1,000 Jews from France as a measure to instil terror, were approved by Hitler on or before December 12, although all of these had been previously proposed by the military commander in France.[68] Julius Streicher, the regional party leader of Franconia who had probably been present during Hitler's speech on December 12, publicly demanded the "annihilation" (*Ausrottung*) of the Jews in the journal *Der Stürmer* on December 25.[69] Some observers abroad noted that something important was going on in Berlin. The Romanian leader, Ion Antonescu, said in a speech to government ministers on December 16:

> The matter is being discussed in Berlin. The Germans want to take all the Yids from Europe to Russia and settle them in a particular area, but it will take some time for this plan to be carried out. What are we to do in the meantime with them? Are we to wait for a decision to be taken in Berlin? [...] We have to take care of them [...] Pack them into the catacombs, throw them into the Black Sea, but get them out of Odessa [...] A hundred can die; thousand can die, all of them can die [...]

so that Jews might no longer endanger the Romanian armed forces.[70]

Thus, Antonescu employed an argument similar to Hitler's. Rumors about a change in Romanian policy seem to have spread almost instantly among Jews in Bucharest. A decree for a census of Jews followed on December 16, and large-scale massacres in Transnistria started on December 21. These had claimed 70,000 lives by March 1942; and

[66] "Militärisch-politische Berichte. Ueber den deutschen Nachrichtendienst" (n.d., receipt stamp of August 5, 1944), BAS, EMD, E27, 1000/721/Bd. 2183, Dossier 306, pp. 58–61. This passage was part of a typed one hundred-page report on the German SD. Arthur Nebe, head of the Reich Criminal Police, was indeed involved in the development of gas vans.

[67] Wi/Verb for Kriegsverwaltungschef Dr Michel, December 12, 1941, facsimile in Billig 1955, p. 363.

[68] Steur 1997, pp. 67–8; Hilberg 1994a, pp. 666–8.

[69] Essner 2002, pp. 27, 396.

[70] Quoted in Deletant 2006, p. 176. Thanks to Jürgen Förster who first pointed me to this document.

regional Romanian authorities had been involved in the decision. Ethnic German militias murdered approximately 28,000 of these Jews.[71]

Toward a plan for swift, direct extermination

Hitler's decision in principle did not immediately lead to mass murder or the erection of new extermination centers. The infamous Wannsee conference of January 20, 1942 – a high-level interagency meeting about the persecution of Jews – sheds light on why not. It provides insights into the structures of the political process. But because the conference does not fit well with many historians' periodizations, some have been embarrassed by it and have concluded as a result that it was not very important. Most scholars assume that the meeting had several purposes. The conventional view is that it served to ensure that authority for the "solution to the Jewish question" rested with the Security Police and Security Service under Heydrich, who chaired the conference. He wanted to inform the ministerial bureaucracy about the plans for persecution and to gain its support.[72] Another (and probably the original) objective was to determine the future treatment of Jews specifically from the German Reich, for which it was crucial to define who was to be included. Several agencies, seeking a revision of the Nuremberg racial laws, wanted the meeting to pave the way for inclusion of so-called German 'half-Jews' in the persecution and mass murder.[73] Many of the discussions at Wannsee dealt with this topic.

The Wannsee conference was about responsibilities and cooperation, but this needs to be put into proper perspective. The persecution and mass murder of Jews was not centralized – neither before nor after Wannsee – and Heydrich did not direct all of the ongoing killing.[74] According to the summary minutes of the meeting, Heydrich called for a "parallelization of policies" (*Parallelisierung der Linienführung*),[75] which suggests an effort at coordination and, perhaps, centralization. The conference was a step toward this end, which explains Heydrich's satisfaction that it had brought "complete agreement" on "the general

[71] See Emil Dorian's diary entry for December 16, 1941, about the alleged intention to deport all Romanian Jews to Transnistria that "everybody is talking about," quoted in Volovici 1997, p. 208. The law is mentioned in a note by SS-Hauptsturmführer Richter, September 15, 1942, in Ancel 1984, pp. 407–8. For the deportations and shootings see Ancel 2011, pp. 342–5; Ancel 2007, pp. 264–5, 283–7.

[72] Roseman 2002 synthesizes much of the literature. A facsimile of the minutes can be found in Tuchel 1992, pp. 122–36.

[73] Gerlach 1998b, pp. 777–80, 795, 801–3.

[74] Angrick 2012 (pp. 249–54) emphasizes the latter point.

[75] Minutes of the meeting on January 20, 1942, are found in Tuchel 1992, p. 123.

line concerning the practical enforcement of the final solution to the Jewish question."[76] Above all, nobody expressed objection to the plan for killing the Jews. However, full centralization was not achieved. No agreement was reached, at Wannsee or afterwards, about the inclusion of German 'half-Jews,' and the Nuremberg laws were never changed. Like Hitler and the Propaganda Ministry, some central authorities rejected treating persons of mixed heritage like the Jews – primarily to avoid a storm of protest from relatives.[77] At the conference Heydrich presented only vague plans for "combing out Europe from West to East," bringing the captured Jews to eastern Europe, letting most of them die during transport and forced labor, and then killing the rest.[78] These fundamentals and methods did not go unchallenged either. This time representatives of occupied regions from the East objected. Josef Bühler, the State Secretary of the General Government, and Alfred Meyer, the Deputy Minister for the occupied Soviet territories, called for the extermination to be carried out first in their territories because – as one of Bühler's remarks was summed up, "motives of labor policy would not impede the course of this action."[79] In fact, Bühler and Meyer had their way, not Heydrich: most of the eastern European Jews were killed before those from western and central Europe, in 1942, although it had been Hitler who had suggested the clearing of central Europe of Jews to the east.[80] Instead of full centralization, the Wannsee conference thus demonstrates the participatory character of the persecution of the Jews. The conference partly defined fundamental policies, but concrete organizational steps were not clarified and agreed upon.

The Wannsee conference had another objective, one that has not received sufficient attention – which becomes obvious when one considers its aftermath. For SS and police strategists, it was supposed to be the signal immediately to begin large-scale deportations of Jews from Greater Germany. On January 19, the day before the conference, Eichmann made a dramatic appearance at Theresienstadt – the ghetto camp where Czech and elderly German Jews and potentially

[76] Heydrich's cover letter, dated February 26, 1942, to the minutes of the meeting on January 20, 1942, can be found in Tuchel 1992, p. 121.

[77] See Gerlach 1998b, pp. 795, 801–2; note on talks with Goebbels, October 26, 1942, BA R 22/4062, pp. 44–5.

[78] Minutes of the January 20, 1942 meeting in Tuchel 1992, pp. 128–9; see Longerich 1998a, pp. 469–70.

[79] Minutes of the January 20, 1942, meeting in Tuchel 1992, pp. 135–6. Killings were not explicitly mentioned, but the logic of the remarks shows that they were intended.

[80] See Essner 2002, p. 393; Gerlach 1998b, p. 799 with note 186; see also Himmler to Greiser, September 18, 1941, BA NS 19/2655, p. 3 (which says that Hitler wished Germany, including Bohemia and Moravia, to be "emptied and liberated [of Jews, C.G.] from West to East").

controversial cases were to be interned – and ordered the camp's Jewish elders to accelerate the construction of bunks by scheduling two working shifts per day.[81] Apparently he expected many new arrivals on short notice. On January 26, Himmler announced to Richard Glücks, the head of the Inspectorate of Concentration Camps, that instead of Soviet POWs, who were not available, 100,000 Jewish men and 50,000 Jewish women would be sent to these camps within four weeks to perform unspecified "great economic tasks and commissions."[82] Three days earlier, Glücks had inquired about the number of Soviet POWs fit to be employed in the concentration camps, adding that he presumed the number would be small.[83] Five days after Himmler's announcement, on January 31, Eichmann indicated that deportation plans had become less urgent since, as he wrote, "currently new possibilities for reception areas are being worked on."[84]

The background to these deportation plans consisted of plans for various economic activities. On January 24, two days before his telegram to Glücks, Himmler talked to Field Marshall Erhard Milch about using several thousand of the SS's prisoners as forced labor for the air force.[85] On January 31 Himmler ordered the establishment of SS construction brigades (composed of concentration camp prisoners, POWs, Jews and "foreign auxiliaries").[86] Given that there were only 8,900 construction workers in the concentration camps in mid-December 1941, the new SS Economic and Administration Head Office (WVHA) estimated in early February that 175,000 additional men were needed: 60,000 in the occupied Soviet territories, 67,500 in the Reich, and 47,500 in the General Government.[87] It would have made little sense to deport Jews to concentration camps located in Germany and Poland to carry out work in the

[81] Council of Jewish elders in Theresienstadt, order of the day, January 19, 1942, in Pätzold and Schwarz 1992, p. 101. Cesarani 2007, p. 112 mentions the trip.

[82] Telegram from Himmler to Glücks, January 26, 1942, BA NS 19/1920, p. 1; see Himmler's note of January 25, 1942, about a phone conversation with Heydrich in Witte *et al.* 1999, p. 327.

[83] See Otto 1998, p. 197.

[84] RSHA IVB4, "Evacuation of Jews," January 31, 1942, in Wannsee Conference 2009, p. 229.

[85] See Budrass 2004, p. 50.

[86] WVHA, February 10, 1942, BA NS 19/2065, pp. 20, 26–7 (quoted from p. 27).

[87] Ibid., pp. 28–9. Schulte's claim (2001, pp. 360–2) – that the Jews mentioned in Himmler's telegram of January 26 were to work for the settlement schemes of the SS in the occupied Soviet territories – conflicts with these numbers. Schulte argues correctly that there were no substantial SS armament activities in January 1942. Few if any concentration camp prisoners worked in the production of armaments. At the same time, however, there were no substantial SS settlement activities in the German-occupied Soviet territories either. (See Gerlach 1999, pp. 339–41 and the correspondence in BA NS 3/1367.)

occupied Soviet territories.[88] Therefore the latter option was only part of the objective.

Due to a lack of rail transportation and building materials, plans for quickly bringing central European Jews to the concentration camps (including Auschwitz, which was not yet an extermination center) were not carried out. In early 1942, Himmler also had to abandon the huge expansion planned for the concentration camp in Majdanek.[89] Also, no new concentration camps were established as planned in mid-January except for Stutthof (near Danzig).[90] SS plans for civilian construction had to be shelved as well since the success of the Soviet winter counterattack gave the manufacture of armaments priority. In mid-March 1942, the SS and the Armament Ministry again expected a "large inflow of prisoners" by the end of the month, this time as forced laborers for the armament industry. They were to include Soviet POWs, Jews and other prisoners.[91] Once more, however, things came to nothing. The first German Jews did not reach Theresienstadt before June 1942, the first month in which the number of arrivals was greater than that in December 1941.[92] All these short-term deportation plans highlight how naive Himmler's and the other chief SS and police planners' ideas for anti-Jewish policies were. In December 1941 and January 1942 neither Himmler nor Heydrich and Eichmann had a workable plan for exterminating Europe's Jews, and if they didn't have one then nobody did. Himmler's short-term efforts still reflected "attritional features"; that is, slow destruction through bad conditions.[93] It was *after* the Wannsee conference that Eichmann and his collaborator, Friedrich Bosshammer, spent weeks compiling an overall report about anti-Jewish policies across Europe, future deportations and deportation destinations.[94]

88 Schulte 2001 does not consider this point. Brayard 2004, p. 110, argues that Himmler's order of January 26 referred to the deportation of 150,000 Jews to Auschwitz and Majdanek. The context laid out here suggests that other destinations were also intended.

89 Himmler to the Reich Transportation Ministry, April 14, 1942, BA NS 19/3625, p. 7 ("in the beginning of the year"). For Speer's letter to Rosenberg on January 26, 1942, about the postponement of the deportation of Jews, see Adler 1974, p. 193.

90 Plans for "new concentration camps to be erected" are mentioned in a telegram from Kaindl (Inspectorate of the Concentration Camps), "very urgent!", January 14, 1942, BA NS 3/101, p. 1. For Stutthof's transformation into a concentration camp in January 1942 see Orth 1999, pp. 154–5.

91 Protocol by Saur, March 17, 1942, BA NS 19/755, pp. 32–3; Budrass 2004, p. 51; Allen 2002, p. 150.

92 Hájková 2013, p. 6; "Die Bevölkerungsbewegung der jüdischen Siedlung Theresienstadt in der Zeit vom 24.11.1941–31.5.1945" with enclosures, AMV, 305-633-1, pp. 272–82.

93 Bloxham 2009, p. 226.

94 See the interrogations of Bosshammer's former secretary, M.G., who started work at the RSHA on January 15, 1942, from October 4, 1967 and March 19, 1970, StA KG Berlin 1 Js 1/65, vols. 5 and 40; for Bosshammer's tasks, see also a quote from Eichmann of June 24, 1943, in the indictment against Bosshammer, StA KG Berlin 1 Js 1/65, April 23, 1971, p. 107.

The absence of a clear plan was also illustrated by high-level conversations about the feasibility of sending Jews en masse to Russia's arctic region, as already imagined in 1941.[95] In February 1942 Heydrich found this to be an "ideal destination," but Hitler seems to have been skeptical.[96] In tune with such a plan was Himmler's intention – shortly after the Wannsee conference – to secure wood for SS construction programs "through allocation of forest concessions in Northern Russia" from the Reich Forestry Office.[97] In early April Hitler rejected the idea of the SS sending their concentration camp inmates to former Soviet prison camps in the Russian arctic, and on May 15 he again dismissed the suggestion of deporting Jews – the "most climate-resilient human on earth" – to Siberia, because that would only strengthen them. Goebbels echoed this assessment two weeks later.[98]

In February, Heydrich and Himmler still envisioned a relatively slow process of destruction (which they imagined taking place in territories that the Germans never actually conquered) instead of the quick and direct killing of all Jews. Some lower-ranking officials shared their view. Karl Jäger, the leader of Einsatzkommando 3, reported on December 1, 1941, that he "regarded the Jewish action by and large as finished, as far as the EK. 3 is concerned" and expected that most of the remaining Lithuanian Jews would be needed as laborers in the long run and, therefore, that they should be sterilized.[99] Around the same time, Einsatzgruppe A also reported: "The Jewish question in the Ostland is to be regarded as solved. Large [numbers of] executions have greatly reduced Jewry, and the remaining Jews have been ghettoized."[100] In June 1942, Arthur Greiser, chief of the Nazi Party and the civil administration in the Wartheland, stated, "I think that we have solved the Jewish Question in a way that Jews and probably Germans would have never imagined"; and like Jäger suggested that surviving Jews should be employed on a large scale as forced labor.[101] These were not the reports of moderates but of some of the most extreme mass murderers of Jews, and yet they considered the "Jewish question" solved without the need for total extermination. The forced labor programs they mentioned did exist: they were not smokescreens or pretext.

[95] See Hitler's quote of July 22, 1941, in Aly 1999, p. 38.
[96] See Witte *et al.* 1999, p. 353 (February 17, 1942) with note 75.
[97] Himmler to Pohl, January 31, 1942, BDC, Sammlung Schumacher, vol. 238.
[98] Picker 1977, pp. 192 (April 5, 1942), 305–6 (May 15, 1942); for Goebbels, see Longerich 2001, pp. 164–5.
[99] Einsatzkommando 3, report, December 1, 1941, in Klee *et al.* 1988, p. 61.
[100] Activity and situation report no. 7 of the Einsatzgruppen of Security Police and SD (November 1–30, 1941) in Klein 1997, p. 248.
[101] Quoted in Epstein 2010, p. 241.

Two accelerations in 1942

For reasons outlined below, in 1942 the measures against Jews were speeded up in two stages occurring in the spring and summer of 1942. Also, their geographic scope was widened. In fact, "acceleration" or "accelerate" became key expressions in important documents. On February 14, Goebbels noted after a conversation with Hitler that the Jews deserved their destruction and that "we must accelerate this process with cold ruthlessness."[102] In late August, General Governor Hans Frank called for an "acceleration" of the Jewish extermination, given the fact that no Jews (except for 300,000 laborers) would receive food any more; meanwhile, the Commander of the Security Police and SD in Volyn demanded to "accelerate" the murder of Jews in order to complete this undertaking within five weeks – pointing to the call of the Reich Commissar for Ukraine, Erich Koch, for "one hundred percent solutions."[103] And on September 24 the Foreign Minister ordered his ministry "to accelerate the evacuation of Jews from the various countries, if possible" – mentioning Denmark, Italy and Germany's allies in southeastern Europe.[104]

In late March 1942 the Security Police still planned to deport just 6,000 Jews from France in that year (and more later).[105] On April 10, 1942, Heydrich told the Slovakian Prime Minister, Vojtech Tuka, that he would organize the deportation of half a million Jews from the German Reich, the Protectorate of Bohemia and Moravia, Slovakia, the Netherlands, Belgium and France. (This would have amounted to virtually all of the Jews of central Europe plus 100,000 from western Europe.) On May 6 he said in Paris that the "death verdict" had been imposed on Europe's Jews and that more advanced and efficient means than gas vans were now available for the completion of the task.[106] His latter remark is recorded in a post-war memoir; however, a week later, Theodor Dannecker, a Paris-based Security Police expert in anti-Jewish policies, defined the aim as the "final solution of the Jewish question with the purpose of the complete destruction of the enemy."[107] Since the mid 1930s the term 'final solution' had been given various meanings (for example, forced emigration); often it had not meant total extermination. Now that it did, it required a special verbal description (like Philipp

[102] Quoted in Broszat 1977, p. 758.
[103] Quoted in Gerlach 1998a, pp. 220, 242.
[104] Luther's note, September 24, 1942, is printed in Steur 1997, p. 210.
[105] Herbert 1996, p. 317.
[106] Longerich 1998a, p. 37; Gerwarth 2011, pp. 316, 322 (quote); Herbert 1996, p. 320.
[107] Quoted in Steur 1997, p. 73.

Bouhler's phrase "a solution to the Jewish question that goes to the ultimate consequence").[108] Around the same time, some politicians, like Robert Ley, head of the German Labor Front, even made public statements about the direct murder of all Jews.[109]

In May the deportation plans for 1942 still had some limits. However, on June 9, the day of Heydrich's funeral (he had been assassinated by Czech agents sent from Britain), Himmler told high-ranking SS officers, "We will be done with the great migration (*Völkerwanderung*) of the Jews within a year; then, none will wander any more. For, now, a clean sweep has to be made."[110] Kurt Daluege, the chief of the German Order Police, had made a similar statement ten days before, although without mentioning a deadline.[111] The plan to murder the European Jews by 1943, developed in the center due in part to Jews allegedly being a security risk, became a guideline for the actions of the SS and police in the following months.[112] However, local and regional interests continued to influence them.

Along with these changes in how Europe's Jews were to be destroyed, Nazi discussions about Jewish labor were also modified. Imminent and quick extermination explains the sudden urgency with which not entirely new ideas for sterilizing those Jews fit for work were proposed to Himmler on June 23, for example, by Viktor Brack, the organizer of the murder of the disabled. Brack wanted to sterilize 2–3 million out of a total of 10 million Jews. This led Eichmann's deputy, Rolf Günther, to request files concerning this matter on July 1, and Himmler to talk to SS doctors on July 7 about the "sterilization of Jewesses" – which they aimed to complete on a large scale. Himmler said of their meeting "that this was about most secret matters." Due to a lack of inexpensive methods for quick mass sterilization, however, these ideas were never put into practice.[113]

On July 28 Himmler mentioned that Hitler had commissioned him to make the occupied Soviet territories "free of Jews," and he claimed for that purpose a free hand for the SS and police to define who was a Jew.[114]

108 Bouhler to Bormann, July 10, 1942, BA 62 Ka 1, Nr. 83, p. 109 ("einer bis in die letzte Konsequenz gehenden Lösung der Judenfrage").

109 See Herf 2006, p. 155; Dörner 2007, pp. 150, 169.

110 Himmler's speech, June 9, 1942, in Smith and Peterson 1974, p. 159.

111 "Ansprache vor Mitgliedern der Protektoratsregierung in Prag," May 29, 1942, BA R 19/382. The typed manuscript called for the "total destruction (*Vernichtung*) of Communism and Jewry." "*Vernichtung*" was replaced in handwriting by the more ambivalent "*Ausschaltung*" (elimination).

112 The most comprehensive and best-documented study of this is Brayard 2004, esp. pp. 31–8. For the security argument, see Friedländer 2006, esp. pp. 375–8.

113 Brack to Himmler, June 23, 1942; "Herbert" to Brandt, July 2, 1942; Brandt's note, July 1942 (sole copy), along with other correspondence, are all in BA NS 19/1583, pp. 16, 34–5, 45.

114 Himmler to Berger, July 28, 1942, BA NS 19/1772, p. 5.

The implementation of a quick extermination campaign also made the removal of other legal and political obstacles necessary, especially in the field of property regulations concerning foreign Jews. On July 30, a meeting between various German ministries and agencies agreed on the so-called 'territoriality principle': a Jew's assets were to be turned over to the state where he resided.[115] Eichmann had already called for such a clarification on July 1 because he recognized that arguments about Jewish assets could lead to complications in foreign policy and delays "that have to be avoided at any costs for the implementation of the RF-SS order" to deport 100,000 Jews from France.[116]

SS officers in the General Government told armament authorities on August 14 that, according to Hermann Göring's "clear and tough" orders, even Jewish workers would not be allowed to live to the end of the war in any German-occupied area.[117] Theodor Dannecker had already concluded in July that "the Jews in the German sphere of influence will face total extermination."[118] But fortunately relatively few steps in this direction could be taken in western Europe in 1942 (see below).

Deportations, mass murders and the construction histories of the annihilation camps developed according to these changes in plans. This was at its clearest and most lethal in the General Government. In the spring of 1942 the regional civil administration and the SS and police planned together to gas those Jews unfit for work (but to exempt people, especially men, between sixteen and thirty-five years of age). The civil administration accorded these plans more urgency in late June. On July 19 Himmler ordered that the only Jews remaining in the General Government by the end of the year should be confined in five large labor camps. This was necessary, he argued, for the "separation of races and peoples necessary for a new order in Europe," for security reasons, and because Jews were a "moral and physical source of infection."[119] In August the civil administration once more called for a speeding up of the process and planned for only 300,000 Jewish workers to survive until 1943. This became the grim reality even though for some time in the fall of 1942 the SS wanted to leave only about 100,000 Jews. Behind these policies were the complex goals of the civil administration, the SS and the military: to save the food that Jews consumed, to provide slightly better rations to non-Jewish Poles, to dry up the widespread black market (thereby reducing the number of absences of non-Jewish Poles from

[115] Foreign Office circular, July 31, 1942, on the basis of an interagency meeting on the previous day, Nuremberg Document NG-424; see also Browning 1978, pp. 96–9; Lipscher 1972, p. 130.

[116] Eichmann's note, July 1, 1942, in Klarsfeld 1977, pp. 70–1; see Wildt 2003, pp. 685–6.

[117] Pohl 1996, p. 233; for the context, see also Gerlach 1998a, pp. 216–17, 222–3.

[118] Quoted in Steur 1997, p. 73.

[119] Himmler to Krüger, July 19, 1942 (copy), BA NS 19/1757, p. 1.

work), and to bring the whole regional economy under control. Tied to this was the desire to contain epidemics and prevent resistance from hungry Polish non-Jews. Such pragmatism reflected anti-Jewish stereotypes and attitudes: i.e., that Jews were black marketeers, dirty people who spread diseases, disorder, and dangerous anti-German sentiments, and, generally speaking, the least deserving of resources. In August, sudden demands from Berlin for large food deliveries to the Reich exacerbated the deadly dynamics. (See Chapter 9.)[120] The figures show dramatic twists. In the General Government about 160,000 Jews were gassed in the first half of 1942 (close to 50,000 per month from mid-March onwards) and 110,000 in July; but from August to October 1942 it was close to 900,000 (or 300,000 per month) plus 200,000 in the last two months of the year combined.[121] Tens of thousands were also shot, especially in the summer.[122] These sudden increases intensified the difficulties that Jews faced in saving themselves and left many of them amazed and paralyzed.

The history of the construction of the extermination sites reflects these shifts in policy: murders at the camp at Bełżec (which had been planned since October) started on March 17; construction of the camp at Sobibór began in February 1942 and that at Treblinka in May. Killings at Sobibór started in early May and in Treblinka, where the Jews of Warsaw were deported, on July 23. In order to provide for a much larger killing capacity than at Chełmno, or those places where disabled people had been murdered, these new sites were built with multiple stationary gas chambers that were fueled with engine exhaust fumes.[123] If Jews were temporarily spared as laborers, they were 'selected' at their place of origin. The rest were crammed into locked freight cars and unloaded at the extermination centers, which weren't really camps, and where almost nobody was sorted out for work. Men and women were separated upon arrival, forced to undress and driven into the gas chambers with unspeakable cruelty, where they suffered an agonizing death. But Bełżec, Sobibór and Treblinka were soon temporarily closed down – despite the mass murder going on elsewhere – in order to build new, larger gas chambers. Bełżec was inactive in May and June, Sobibór between July and September, and Treblinka in September.[124] This demonstrates that the plans had changed and that

120 See Gerlach 1998a, pp. 181–232.

121 Berger 2013, p. 177.

122 Browning 1993, pp. 55–87; Pohl 1993, pp. 130–1.

123 Berger 2013, pp. 47–51, 81; for initial killing capacities see pp. 78, 117. For possible preparations in Sobibór beginning in November 1941 see Schelvis 1998, pp. 37–8; Pohl 1993, p. 106 note 86.

124 Berger 2013, pp. 93, 177 for Bełżec (although she is somewhat contradictory); see also pp. 123, 129, 151; Gerlach 1998a, pp. 202–3, 232. For the beginning of construction and operations, see Berger 2013, pp. 51, 56, 73.

the number of killings was to be greater than had been expected just a few months before. Part of the reason for Bełżec's closure in May was to review experiences with killings by gassing. Treblinka was also closed for a week in late August, through to early September, because so many Jews had been transported from Warsaw in such a short time that masses of corpses had yet to be disposed of. Thousands more died of thirst in the trains that were forced to wait on the sidings for days before unloading.[125]

Parallel events occurred in other regions. German SS and police shot 300,000 Jews in Volyn, Podolia, and southwestern Belarus, in 1942. This campaign, which began in May, was accelerated in response to demands for food from the Reich in late August, as in the General Government, and ended in late October.[126] Tens of thousands of Jews fell victim to murder in what has been described as the "worst month" for the Jews of the Wartheland in the smaller places in August 1942. A deportation wave from Łódź followed in the first half of September.[127] In the camp at Auschwitz, 7,716 Jews arrived in May 1942, 21,496 in June, 41,960 in August and then about 20,000 arrived each month until the end of the year.[128] A lack of food and shelter, a typhus epidemic, and direct killings, all meant that circumstances worsened for those newly arriving Jews who were *not* among the increasing number immediately gassed upon arrival. As a result mortality rates increased. For nine days (not running consecutively) between January 27 and March 28, 1942 – for which figures are available – 129 prisoners (of whom about 17 were Jews) perished in Auschwitz daily. In June the number was 123 prisoners per day, 76 of whom were Jews; in July, it was 133 prisoners of whom 94 were Jews; and in the first 19 days of August, 216 prisoners (of whom 155 were Jews) died each day.[129] In Theresienstadt – the ghetto camp that received controversial 'cases,' elderly Jews from the Reich and Czech Jews – arrivals numbered between 3,600 and 4,600 monthly from January to May 1942, when all arrivals were Czech. When arrivals included Germans and Austrians, the figures rose dramatically: 9,215 in June, 25,078 in July, 13,469 in August and 18,639 in September. The number of deaths rose, due mainly to starvation. In September and October the number shipped out of the overcrowded camp at Theresienstadt to extermination sites rose sharply.[130]

125 See Berger 2013, pp. 38, 55, 119–23; Arad 1987, pp. 72–3, 81–100; Grabitz and Scheffler 1993, pp. 151–76. For breaks in transports going from Warsaw to Treblinka see the day-by-day list in Gutman 1982, p. 212.

126 Gerlach 1998a, pp. 237–45. See also Chapter 9.

127 Krakowski 2007, p. 88 (quote), 107; Unger 1998, p. 126.

128 Orth 1997, p. 48.

129 My calculations are based on Czech 1989, pp. 178–92, 239, 262–3, 281.

130 "Die Bevölkerungsbewegung der jüdischen Siedlung Theresienstadt in der Zeit vom 24.11.1941-31.5.1945," AMV, 305-633-1, pp. 272–3. The population of the ghetto

Auschwitz, however, was not the center of the murder of European Jews in 1942. Up to 175,000 Jews were deported there in 1942 as compared to at least 713,000 to Treblinka and 434,000 to Bełżec.[131] In 1942, about as many western and central European Jews were brought to the district of Lublin (close to 130,000) as to Auschwitz.[132] And Jews were not shipped to Auschwitz because of its large killing facilities; rather, large crematoria with gas chambers were built because of the many arrivals. As the SS construction authority in Auschwitz noted later, "The new construction of the crematorium had to be started immediately in July 1942 due to the situation that the special operations (*Sonderaktionen*) had created."[133]

Other parts of Europe

The first foreign state to deport its Jews to Germany was Slovakia. In November 1941, it, like Romania and Croatia, declared disinterest in its citizens who resided in German-controlled territory.[134] In early 1942, the German government requested 20,000 Jewish workers from Slovakia. The Slovaks agreed and also offered to include women and children. That is to say, Slovakia offered to deport a large part of its Jewish population without pressure from Germany.[135] After eight trains of only able-bodied young men and women were dispatched, the first family transport left on April 11.[136] The Jews were arrested, detained and loaded onto trains by Slovakian authorities. But because of the brutal scenes of Slovakian Hlinka Guards, and others, forcing Jews onto trains, plus information that was coming in about the German murder of Jews in Poland, the deportations became unpopular with Slovak elites – including some leading figures in the regime – and among other sections of the population.[137] By late June, 52,000 Jews had been transported to Germany; but then the pace of deportation slowed. Many of the approximately 30,000 Jews remaining enjoyed the protection of the Slovakian government as laborers, converts and in other capacities. In

camp at Theresienstadt peaked on September 18, 1942, at 58,491; see Hájková 2013, p. 9.

131 See Berger 2013, pp. 177, 254; Witte and Tyas 2001; Hilberg 1994b, p. 86.

132 See Kiełboń 2004, p. 132.

133 Bischoff to WVHA, October 13, 1942, printed in Pressac 1989, p. 198. For the context, see Pressac 1995, pp. 54–9.

134 Browning 1978, pp. 67–8. Romania withdrew this declaration later.

135 Longerich 1998a, pp. 491–2; Browning 1978, p. 94; for preparations for the deportations since January, see Kamenec 2007, pp. 215–17.

136 Lipscher 1979, p. 109.

137 Rothkirchen 1998, pp. 54–6; Lipscher 1979, pp. 130–4.

total, from March to October 1942, 57,752 Jews from Slovakia were sent to German-controlled territory (39,006 to the district of Lublin and 18,746 to Auschwitz).[138] In addition, Slovakia expelled 8,000 Hungarian Jews to Hungary from March to August 1942.[139] Some Slovakian Jews fled to Hungary because it was safer there than in Slovakia at the time.

The deportations from France in 1942, which involved the government of a country of which half was occupied, are among the best documented. In the first six trains from France to Auschwitz, which ran from June to early July 1942, more than 1,000 of the 6,078 deportees were French citizens, mostly from Paris.[140] On May 6 the French Minister of Police, René Bousquet, negotiated with Heydrich and the Higher SS and Police Leader in France, Carl-Albrecht Oberg, that the Vichy government would get authority over the French police forces in the occupied part of France – an important element of French sovereignty. In return the French police would help the Germans by arresting Jews without French citizenship, but no French Jews, in both parts of France.[141]

This paved the way for larger transports. From July 16 onwards, women were included, and after July 20 children (some of whom the Vichy authorities had already offered to transport) and old people were also shipped off.[142] But the Security Police could not fill their trains because the French authorities were not making enough arrests. In northern France and Vichy-controlled territory the German SS and police relied mostly on the French police and gendarmerie for raids on Jews and for their subsequent detention; but French police officers became increasingly hesitant to perform this role as criticism of their brutality, and of the deportations in general, mounted – just as in Slovakia, but in France part of the criticism was public (see Chapter 13). And, as in Slovakia, news of the German extermination of Jews spread. More and more Jews were warned, sometimes by officials, of imminent operations.[143] Many went underground. Consequently, deportation figures plunged in the fall. In response to Eichmann's demand that deportations from France be "swiftly and considerably increased" with "the aim of emptying France of Jews as soon as possible," the Security Police and SD planned, from July 6 onwards,[144] to widen incrementally the

138 Browning 1978, pp. 95–6; Hradská 1996, p. 82.
139 Kallis 2009, p. 249.
140 Zuccotti 1993, pp. 90, 110.
141 Steur 1997, pp. 76–7, 80–1.
142 Adler 1989, p. 47; note by Dannecker, July 21, 1942, printed in Steur 1997, p. 209.
143 Kasten 1993, pp. 97–101; Poznanski 1997, pp. 339, 347–64; Marrus and Paxton 1981, pp. 270–9; for the lack of arrests and detentions in July, see Steur 1997, pp. 77, 83–4.
144 See Meyer 2000, p. 37.

circle of those to be deported. But the increasing passivity of the French police eventually thwarted these plans.[145] Dannecker, Eichmann's deputy in France and one of the most aggressive persecutors, agreed with Eichmann's demand.[146] But the Higher SS and Police Leader in France, Carl-Albrecht Oberg, found Eichmann's goal of deporting 100,000 French Jews in 1942 unrealistic. He also advised Himmler against a planned large-scale annulment of the naturalization of Jews and in general not to act against Vichy's (partial) protection of French Jews.[147] On August 28 Eichmann set as the target the deportation of all stateless Jews by the end of the year, and of all foreign Jews by June 1943.[148] In the end the German authorities deported 41,951 Jews from France in 1942, most of them in the summer, somewhat more than the 40,000 Oberg and Bousquet had agreed to on July 2. Vichy also overfulfilled its quota by providing about 11,000 people from its zone instead of the 10,000 originally agreed. Few deportees, however, were French citizens.[149]

Deportations of Jews from the Netherlands and Belgium developed in waves similar to those in France in 1942. In order to avoid unrest, the German military administration in Belgium (where most Jews were foreigners) decided to target only alien Jews. As in France, large-scale German raids drove many Jews underground early on. In the Netherlands there was no talk of deporting only foreign Jews, but cooperation ran much more smoothly between the German SS and police, the German and Dutch administrations, the Dutch police, Dutch units of volunteers (mostly local fascists) and the Jewish council, which tried to spread undue optimism. As a result, relatively few Dutch Jews went into hiding, and, when deportations to extermination centers resumed in 1943, much larger numbers were deported from the Netherlands than from France or Belgium.[150] Croatian authorities and Ustaše had started brutally killing Jews in 1941 and the murders were intensified during 1942. In response to a German request close to 5,000 were sent to Auschwitz in August 1942, but the majority of Jews in Croatia and Bosnia were killed by Croatians.[151]

[145] Eichmann's note, Paris, July 1, 1942, printed in Steur 1997, p. 206.
[146] Steur 1997, p. 73.
[147] See Lappenküper 2000, pp. 134–5; Eggers 2002, p. 377; for Eichmann's plan dating from June 11, 1942, see also Steur 1997, p. 74.
[148] Rother 2001, p. 94.
[149] Eggers 2002, pp. 182–4, 376–7.
[150] See the comprehensive comparisons by Zeller and Griffioen 1996 and 1997; Griffioen and Zeller 2011; Rauter to Himmler, September 24, 1942, BA NS 19/3364, pp. 100–1. For the police see Mason 1984, p. 327.
[151] Hilberg 1994a, pp. 761, 764.

Himmler and SS negotiators demanded, for some months, that able-bodied men be deported from Slovakia and France.[152] Initially, Slovakian and French Jews arriving at Auschwitz were taken into the camp and those arriving in the district of Lublin placed in various ghettos and camps.[153] Gassing upon arrival started later. Still, due to atrocious treatment at Auschwitz, most of these Jews died within a few months. The first mass 'selection,' following which 1,000 inmates were gassed, took place on May 4. The first transport of Jews (from Slovakia) to undergo 'selection' – after which some of the deportees were killed instantly – arrived on July 4. The same happened with a transport of Dutch Jews on July 17, and with Jews from France on July 19. Between mid-July and early August the percentage of newly arriving Jews who were killed right away rose steeply.[154] In the district of Lublin, direct transports to extermination sites included German Jews from May 14 onwards; and Slovakian Jews from June 1.[155] At other places (like Chełmno and Maly Trostinets, near Minsk), Jews from the Reich were murdered en masse upon arrival, starting in early May.[156]

Unlike in Poland, however, no further accelerations took place in August in most of the other areas of Europe occupied by Germany or allied to it. The total number of Jews deported from France, Belgium and the Netherlands reached almost 100,000 by the end of 1942, just as Heydrich had envisaged in May, but the planned increase for the fall did not materialize – except in the case of Belgium.[157] In late September the German Foreign Ministry intensified its efforts to deport Jews from allied or neutral countries (Hungary, Bulgaria, Denmark and Italy) to Germany,[158] but deportations did not occur from any of these countries in 1942. Separate Security Police negotiations with the Romanian government seemed to be succeeding in early August, prompting Globocnik to lobby for more fuel for the engines that produced the deadly carbon

[152] This was still so according to a note of Dannecker's, June 15, 1942, in Klarsfeld 1989, pp. 379–80.

[153] Czech 1989, pp. 190–234.

[154] See Czech 1989, pp. 199 and note, 206, 209, 241–3, 250–72; see Poznanski 1997, p. 347. There seems to have been no large transport of German and Austrian Jews to Auschwitz before mid-July 1942: see Gottwaldt and Schulle 2005, pp. 393–5.

[155] Kiełboń 2004, pp. 126–7, 131.

[156] Longerich 1998a, p. 488. For several earlier massacres of German Jews in 1942 see Angrick and Klein 2006, pp. 239–44, 338–44; Klein 2009, pp. 452–3.

[157] See Korherr's report to Himmler, March 23, 1943, www.ns-archiv.de/verfolgung/korherr-lang.php (accessed April 26, 2014); for plans for increased deportations see Zeller and Griffioen 1996, p. 50.

[158] Luther to von Weizsäcker, September 24, 1942 (copy), reporting on Ribbentrop's order of the same date, Nuremberg Document NG-5631.

monoxide in Treblinka, Sobibór and Bełżec.[159] But the Romanian government, like others, grew hesitant and postponed these plans in the fall. By contrast, 532 Jews, a large part of the Jewish population, were deported from Norway to Auschwitz (see Chapter 5.)

Conclusion

In this chapter, I have emphasized the partial decentralization of the German mass murder of Jews. This character is also visible in the process of ghettoization. In a classic account, concentration was portrayed as a necessary administrative step for the destruction of the Jews.[160] Organizationally, it was crucial. However, concentration took many different forms in German-controlled Europe. There was no central order to establish ghettos across Europe. Western and central Europe had only two ghettos: one in Amsterdam, the Netherlands, and the other in Theresienstadt, Bohemia. It is not by accident that the death rate for Jews from these countries was higher than in neighboring regions (and the same could be said about Salonica as compared to some other places in Greece). In German-occupied eastern Europe, regional civil or military administrations, at the highest level, issued ghettoization orders, but it was often just local German administrations that set up ghettos or Jewish residential neighborhoods, as was the case in different parts of Poland from 1939 to 1941.[161] Frequently, this didn't happen until 1942, as in the western Ukrainian region of Volyn, southwestern Belarus and parts of northern Poland, and, occasionally, no ghetto was instituted.[162] In some of the districts of the General Government, such as Radom and Kraków, Jews were fenced or walled in, but in the district of Lublin – Odilo Globocnik's field of operation – most Jews did not live in sealed ghettos in early 1942;[163] they were 'only' forbidden to leave their neighborhoods. And yet few went underground (see Chapter 15). In accordance with the localized genesis, general as well as local reasons for ghettos were cited: to separate the ethnicities, to limit the political and moral influence of Jews, to protect non-Jews from disease and hunger,

[159] Globocnik's telegram to Grothmann, September 4, 1942, BA NS 19/3165, p. 287. "Large deliveries from abroad" (*grosse Auslandsanlieferungen*) for "Operation 'Reinhard'" could only mean Romanian Jews at this point.

[160] Hilberg 1994a, pp. 56–7.

[161] See Hilberg 1994a, pp. 231–9; Browning 1986; Seidel 2006, pp. 238–44; for Belarus see Gerlach 1999, pp. 521–33.

[162] For Volyn, see Spector 1990a, pp. 366–7; for Ukraine in general see Pohl 2010, p. 31; for Belarus see Gerlach 1999, p. 532; for Zichenau district see the note about a meeting in the Reich Labor Ministry on November 28, 1941, in Pätzold 1984, p. 323.

[163] Silberklang 2004, p. 144; Browning 2010, p. 55.

to combat the black market, and to supply Germans and non-Jews with better housing.[164]

1942 marked the peak of the murder European Jews. Under German command, more than 3 million Jews were killed in that year.[165] What had emerged from regional contexts and initiatives grew in 1942 into a program of extermination steered, in part, from the center. While regional authorities continued to organize the mass murder of Polish and Soviet Jews, central coordination there did increase and did generate some important impulses in the summer of 1942. By contrast, Berlin directed the deportations from other parts of Europe. But, as the French, Slovakian and Romanian cases show, these transports also depended on the outcome of negotiations with national governments and bureaucracies and on the popular response in occupied or allied countries. Information policy also exhibited a degree of central control. Remarkably, German anti-Jewish propaganda was toned down in 1942, quite in contrast to the second half of 1941 and much of 1943. In 1942, the Ministry of Propaganda issued several instructions to journalists about not reporting measures taken against Jews. That year also saw few anti-Jewish lead stories in the Nazi Party organ, *Völkischer Beobachter*. The exception to this reluctance was the Nazi Party's widely placarded "motto of the week."[166] Whether the radio programming also included occasional exceptions, as one listener's notes suggests, warrants further research.[167] Occasionally, the media made general references – often ambiguous, but occasionally unmistakeable – to the fact that all of the Jews were to be killed.[168] But there was neither an official announcement nor any detailed reporting and, thus, no certainty. The extermination of Jews remained an official secret, but one that actively involved so many Germans that rumors about it became widespread.

[164] Hilberg 1994a, pp. 234–5; Neumann 2010, pp. 125–6; excerpt of a report of the Chief of the Resettlement Department, district of Warsaw (Schön), January 20, 1941, in Berenstein 1961, p. 111.

[165] Among these were at least 1.4 million in the General Government (1.27 million as outlined by Witte and Tyas 2001, not including the victims of mass shootings and hunger; Berger 2013, p. 254, suggests higher figures), about 600,000 in Ukraine not including eastern Galicia (Zabarko 2005, p. 391 is based on figures by Alexander Kruglov), 250,000 in Belarus (Gerlach 1999, pp. 628, 683–728), about 100,000 in Russia plus mainly German, Austrian, Czech and Slovakian Jews, those from the Wartheland and from the Polish parts of the Bialystok and Zichenau districts, and close to 100,000 from western Europe (Korherr's report to Himmler, March 23, 1943, www.ns-archiv.de/verfolgung/korherr-lang.php, accessed April 26, 2014).

[166] Dörner 2007, pp. 166–8; Herf 2006, pp. 281–8; Longerich 2006, pp. 190, 205.

[167] See the diary of Karl Dürkefälden, June 12, 1942, and the end of 1942, Obenaus 1985, pp. 111, 126.

[168] See Dörner 2007; Longerich 2006; Bajohr and Pohl 2006.

5 Extending mass destruction: 1942–45

As described in Chapter 4, Hitler had decided in principle in December 1941 to kill the Jews in Europe, Göring had given the matter urgency in August 1942, and by June 1942 Himmler had adopted a plan to murder all of the Jews within one year, i.e., by the middle of 1943. But none of this meant that annihilation would run automatically or smoothly. Further mass murders required new impulses and institutional support based on the views and interests of German functionaries. They also needed the consent of foreign governments, bureaucracies and, to a certain extent, populations. Moreover, in the second half of World War II, Germany occupied one friendly country after the other in order to prevent them from switching sides, and this brought new Jewish communities under more direct German control. This expanded and prolonged efforts aimed at the extermination of Jews, with greatly varying outcomes.

By the end of 1942, the great majority of Jews within the German sphere of influence had been murdered. About 4.5 million were dead, about 1.1 million lived in German-occupied countries (primarily Poland and France), and some 1.2 million others lived in countries allied with Germany but not occupied (above all, Hungary and Romania).[1] About 3 million Jews perished from May to December 1942, 2 million in the four horrible months from July to October 1942 alone.

This chapter provides a survey of the major mass murders of the second half of World War II, and is based on the assumption that they did not

[1] According to my estimates, to mention only the biggest national or regional groups, close to 2.5 million Jewish non-combatants were killed in Axis-occupied Soviet territory (according to 1945 borders; including Romanian policies of violence), 1.5 million in western and central Poland, and a quarter of a million of those who lived in western and central Europe. Roughly 300,000 were alive in the General Government; 150,000 in western Poland; over 250,000 in France; 100,000 each in the occupied Soviet territories, the area of Białystok and the Netherlands; 700,000 in Hungary (according to 1942 borders); 250,000 in Romania; and 100,000 or so in Italian-controlled areas. Another 300,000 central European Jews had emigrated to destinations outside of continental Europe. See also Browning 1998a, p. 213 note 2.

happen randomly. Rather, the places and times of their occurrence were the result of certain political groups, and their considerations, winning the upper hand over other groups and considerations. The fact that the pace of mass murder clearly slowed after the end of 1942 was also due to a number of political factors. In German-occupied countries without dependent national governments, the German demand for Jewish labor decelerated the destruction. In several countries with a national government, whether under German occupation or not, the readiness of regimes, non-German administrations and local non-state actors to hand over their Jewish compatriots decreased considerably. Such reluctance had already begun to develop between August and November 1942, most notably, and in remarkably parallel fashion, in Romania, Italy, France and Slovakia – but also, to a certain degree, in occupied Poland, though for other reasons.[2] These developments had to do with the almost immediate spread of the news in the period from June to August 1942, that the total extermination of the Jews in Europe had begun.[3] In this context emerged "one of the chief obstacles to the extension of the Final Solution: the reluctance of many of Germany's most important allies to do anything which might be construed as diminishing their own sovereignty."[4]

Destruction: Initiatives and halts

Throughout the late summer and fall of 1942, the mass murder of the Jews of Germany, Austria, Luxembourg, Bohemia and Moravia, Poland and western Ukraine – all areas under direct German control – was in full swing. At the same time, there were substantial deportations of Jews from the German-occupied part of France, the Netherlands, Belgium and from independent Slovakia; and smaller transports from Croatia. Beginning in August 1942, most of the deportees sent to Auschwitz-Birkenau were murdered upon arrival, as were almost all those sent to Sobibór. Starting in July 1942, there was discussion of deporting Jews from mainland Romania to German-occupied Poland, but the plan was shelved by the Romanian government in mid-October and was never implemented. In October 1942, German authorities approached other governments – such as those of Italy, Hungary and Bulgaria – with various degrees of

[2] This chapter focuses on German policies and interaction with foreign authorities. For a discussion of other governments' policies, see Chapter 14.

[3] See Laqueur 1980, esp. pp. 32–9; Penkower 1988, pp. 59–97; for the case of Italy see Steinberg 1992, pp. 81, 89–90, 103.

[4] Mazower 2008, p. 394.

intensity and urgency, in order to lay their hands on these countries' Jewish populations.

Yet these efforts had, by the spring of 1943, led to the deportation of only approximately 11,000 Jews from the Greek and Yugoslav territories that Bulgaria had annexed. Almost simultaneously, the German authorities shipped more than 50,000 Jews from neighboring northern Greece to annihilation camps. Massive deportations from the Netherlands had also resumed. But this was not at all the case in unoccupied fascist Slovakia, where about 35,000 Jews remained, often in forced labor camps, or in north Africa. Deportations from France and Belgium slowed to a trickle[5] because many Jews had gone underground and because most, though not all, local authorities refused to cooperate in arresting Jewish compatriots and had become hesitant even about arresting foreign Jews. A similar situation emerged in Italy, and the areas of France, Yugoslavia, Albania, and Greece it had occupied, after German troops occupied most of these areas in October 1943.[6] The largest populations of Jews in Axis Europe – in Hungary and Romania – were not subject to any deportations to German death camps in 1943, though deaths from starvation and, sometimes, from Romanian brutality, continued in Transnistria. Jews in forced labor battalions in the Hungarian army were also subject to Hungarian atrocities and some German mass shootings. Both of these combined claimed many thousands of lives. Under direct German administration the removal of German, Austrian and Czech Jews, including many of those in Theresienstadt, was largely completed by August 1943. Most of these were murdered at Auschwitz. Repeatedly, the Jews remaining in Polish and Soviet territories occupied by Germany were sorted according to skill or ability to work. Large numbers were killed in the process and the rest were gradually moved to camps. Most of the ghettos were dissolved.

In 1944, sporadic transports of Jews from Germany, Poland, the Netherlands, France, Belgium, Italy and Greece to extermination camps, continued. In the labor camps, Jews continued to be undersupplied and to fall victim to the cruelty of SS camp crews who killed especially those who had become unfit for work. Romania and Bulgaria refused to hand over Jews from their mainland. However, there were massive deportations from two countries that Germany had recently occupied: from Slovakia between August and the fall of 1944; and, most importantly,

[5] Griffioen and Zeller 2011, pp. 899–901; Peschanski 2002, pp. 349, 354; Steur 1997, pp. 90–1.

[6] There were some exceptions in Dalmatia and locally in Greece.

from Hungary mainly between May and July 1944. The approximately 410,000 Hungarian Jews killed out of the 530,000 brought to Greater Germany in 1944 (330,000 of whom were deemed unproductive and immediately killed in Auschwitz) was the largest single group of Jews murdered after the fall of 1942. The intensive cooperation of Hungarian authorities – and parts of its population – contrasted with the general trend in other countries of hesitancy and conditional and limited support for German deportation plans after the fall of 1942. But the organization of mass murder outside Hungary – with the exception of Norway in the fall of 1942 and northern Greece in the spring of 1943 – went less smoothly.

German efforts to overcome foreign reluctance

In most countries with a national government – whether they were occupied by German troops or whether they were unoccupied allies of Germany – the deportation and destruction of Jews remained incomplete.[7] The SS and police had other plans. At first they exempted certain groups for tactical reasons. These exemptions were meant as temporary compromises to address local concerns. Still, the exemptions highlight the need for winning the support of a country's authorities and police, Jewish functionaries and other social agents. In the Netherlands, for example, the Higher SS and Police Leader reported that he intended to later deport 6,000 Jews in childless intermarriages, although he would permit 13,000 persons of mixed heritage to remain. Furthermore, 20,000 Jews in labor service organization had so far not been arrested in order to lure them into a false sense of security – although they were to be deported later. In the end, only 6,000 other forced laborers with special skills would remain in the country. 'Jews' of Protestant faith, unlike those who were Catholic, were exempted from deportation, because Lutheran church leaders had not made their protests against the deportation of Jews in public as the Catholic bishops had.[8] In France, too, the Security Police wanted to proceed in stages, as documents reveal, starting in early July 1942 with the deportation of those Jews whose arrest would arouse the least political resistance. The intention was gradually to include as many other categories as possible.[9] The adviser for Jewish questions of the Security Police and Security

[7] Bloxham 2009, pp. 235, 244–5. Serbia and Greece were counter-examples; the government of the Protectorate of Bohemia and Moravia had little political weight.

[8] Rauter to Himmler, September 24, 1942, BA NS 19/3364, pp. 100–1.

[9] Meyer 2000, p. 37 points to several documents; Eggers 2002, p. 386; Röthke's note, August 15, 1943, in Longerich 1989, p. 252.

Service in France to the French government, Theodor Dannecker, formed an "action commission" which included French representatives of the Commissariat General for Jewish Questions, the police and the administration.[10] But Dannecker and his successor, Heinz Röthke, did not have the full support of their German superiors, and this limited their success. Even the Commander of the Security Police and Security Service in France, Dr Helmut Knochen, judged the support of the French administration and police in favor of conscripting forced laborers for Germany, and in preventing political unrest, more important than to obtain support for the deportation of Jews. This applied even more so to the Higher SS and Police Leader Oberg, and especially to the German military administration.[11] Despite insisting to Laval in August 1943 that "the order of the Führer for the Final Solution of the Jewish question in all of Europe was definitely certain," Röthke resigned himself to the fact that the Vichy government refused to strip further categories of immigrant Jews of their French citizenship – an act that would have widened the circle of those who could be shipped off to the death camps.[12]

In the summer of 1942, German and Romanian authorities planned to deport Jews from certain parts of (or even all of) Romania to Poland. But in September the Romanian government grew hesitant, and on October 13–14 the plans were postponed – indefinitely, as it turned out. Historians have described a complex set of background circumstances that included worsening situations for the Germans on the frontlines, threats and appeals by foreign politicians like US Secretary of State Cordell Hull, the realization that the persecution of Jews might harm Romania's position in anticipated peace negotiations with the Western Allies, and the fact that Germany offered Romania no help in its fight against Hungary to win back northern Transylvania. Several groups and individuals expressed objections against the planned deportations, among them inhabitants of southern Transylvania, intellectuals, an archbishop, the king and queen mother and the leader of the opposition Liberal Party.[13] After October, anti-Jewish propaganda was scaled down and there were so few prospects for a Romanian change of attitude that

[10] Note by Dannecker on the first committee meeting, July 8, 1942, PA AA R100857, pp. 373–6.

[11] See Meyer 2000, pp. 42, 45–6; Eggers 2002, p. 392; Knochen's letters to the RSHA, September 25, 1942 and February 12, 1943, in Klarsfeld 1977, pp. 151, 174.

[12] Röthke, about a conversation with Laval, August 14, 1943, quoted in Meyer 2000, p. 45; for denaturalizations see Zuccotti 1993, p. 178.

[13] Ancel 2011, pp. 486–509; Ancel 1984, pp. 388, 398–9; Deletant 2010, pp. 172–8; Hausleitner 2001a, p. 402; Haas 1994, p. 89. See also Hilberg 1994a, pp. 847–50.

Himmler recalled the Security Police's adviser to the Romanian government on Jewish questions.[14]

Against the background of increasing foreign hesitancy to support German deportations, the deportation of Jews from Norway in November 1942 stood out. During the Wannsee conference, Foreign Office Undersecretary Martin Luther had warned that Germany might encounter resistance against the deportation of Jews in Nordic countries.[15] However, the available evidence suggests that Norway's fascist government co-initiated the deportations (see Chapter 14). On the German side, Reich Commissar Josef Terboven seems to have been reluctant, and there is no evidence that the RSHA played any active role; the Security Police in Oslo, on the other hand, seems to have been a driving force. Between 740 and 761 Jews were deported to Auschwitz, where 97% of them were murdered.[16] The other half of Norway's Jews managed to flee with help from locals. The persecutory effort of the Norwegian government is all the more remarkable in comparison to neighboring (unoccupied) Finland – where the German regime put no pressure on its ally to deport its Jews. In August 1942 Himmler apparently did no more than offer to 'take back' several hundred central European Jewish refugees who had fled to Finland – largely without success.[17] Germany's attempt to deport the Danish Jews in October 1943 largely failed because locals there helped most of them flee to Sweden (see Chapter 13). German pressure on Italy – whose authorities refused to hand over Jews from the mother country, as well as from most Italian-occupied territories – was somewhat stronger, but remained without effect until German troops occupied Italy in September 1943.

Limited German disunity: Homegrown obstacles to the plan for total extermination

In June 1942 Himmler had announced, internally, that the Jews should be destroyed within a year (see Chapter 4). According to a Security Police officer specializing in the persecution of Jews in France, this plan applied to all of German-occupied Europe.[18]

[14] Ancel 2011, pp. 508–9; Himmler to Müller, January 20, 1943, BA NS 19/2859, p. 50.
[15] Minutes of the Wannsee conference on January 20, 1942, in Tuchel 1992, pp. 130–1.
[16] See Abrahamsen 1991, pp. 54, 88–93, 97–105, 115–18, 127–30, 148; BdS Oslo, "Meldungen aus Norwegen," November 14 and 26, 1942, in Ugelvik Larsen 2008, pp. 879 and 941; Hoffmann 2001, p. 270.
[17] Rautkallio 1987, pp. 166, 168, 178.
[18] Röthke's note, September 9, 1942, in Klarsfeld 1977, p. 140.

In order to understand the considerations that influenced the mass destruction of Jews under direct German control, the following contexts should be kept in mind. After 1942, the year of the largest forced mobilization of foreign workers, it became harder for German authorities to find new supplies of labor (see Chapter 8). After the human resources of Soviet urbanites and POWs were exhausted in one way or another, the new targets were western Europeans, Soviet citizens in areas from which German troops were retreating, and people from the countryside – especially in the occupied Soviet territories. This, however, made many young people go underground and helped armed partisan movements spread. In eastern and southeastern Europe, anti-guerrilla warfare, in turn, was used to deport the productive members of populations of entire areas to forced labor camps. German army, SS and police forces killed hundreds of thousands of partisans and people who lived close to their bases. This had a number of consequences for the treatment of Jews. On the one hand, Jews were considered more seriously as forced laborers. As with Soviet POWs previously, but in even more limited ways (a million Soviet POWs perished from 1942 to 1945), there was a switch from destruction to exploitation. On the other hand, Jews were suspected of being participants in active resistance and viewed as potential refugees to the forests (i.e., the partisans), which fueled intentions to kill them. Considerations of food policy no longer spurred large extermination campaigns after the fall of 1942 because Germany's food supply stabilized in 1943; those Jews who were still alive were no big consumption factor, and their access to food in camps was controlled. Indeed, they were starved there. Hunger remained a reality for most Jews in the camps (to which most were transferred in 1943), where starvation contributed to their physical and moral exhaustion and to the periodic murder of those who had become unproductive. In this way, being killed as a 'useless eater' in an occasional 'small' action remained a constant threat for Jews.

Among the German-occupied areas, Ukraine (excluding eastern Galicia) was one where the destruction of Jews was more or less completed by early November 1942. Some 300,000 Jews were shot, mostly between August and October. This was clearly connected to food policies (see Chapter 9). Fewer than 4,000 Jewish forced laborers remained under German control, and most of these were murdered in 1943.[19] On Belarusian territory (according to 1945 borders), a large proportion of Jews fell victim to German massacres in 1942, with only some 60,000 remaining alive by the end of that year and only 16,000 by mid 1943.[20]

[19] Spector 1990a, pp. 186 note 63, 366–7; Gerlach 1998a, pp. 237–45.

[20] Gerlach 1999, pp. 728–9, 733, 736.

At that time several tens of thousands of Jews were still alive in the Baltic countries.

In the General Government, the SS's plans, laid down in August and September 1942, suggested that little more than 100,000 Jews would be left by the end of the year. However, the pace of mass murder then slowed, and 297,314 Jews were still alive by December 31. In the district of Radom, however, only 7% of the former population of 360,000 Jews remained alive.[21] Because major industrial production was relocated to the General Government between April and August 1942, military authorities, private companies and, to a degree, the civil administration, wished to keep more Jewish workers than the SS wanted to allow. By late September a compromise was reached.[22] More Jewish workers were allowed to remain for the time being, but non-Jews were to be trained to replace them gradually. Himmler accepted more production sites employing Jews, but he emphasized that "it is the Führer's wish that also [from] there the Jews shall disappear one day"; he left it unclear when.[23]

On July 19, 1942, Himmler had ordered that all of the Jews in the General Government were either to be murdered or brought to SS camps by December 31. In reality, though, some ghettos continued to exist into 1943. Roughly 161,000 Jews – more than half of those still living in the General Government by late 1942 – were housed in ghettos and SS camps in the district of Galicia. All of the ghettos were dissolved and 140,000 of these Galician Jews were murdered in the first half of 1943, 80,000 of them in the four week period between late May and late June alone. (Thus, at least 21,000 were left.)[24] It was probably not by accident that the regional SS and Police Leader, Fritz Katzmann, sent out his infamous report about the murder of the Galician Jews on June 30, 1943, the date of the second deadline that Himmler had set for extermination.[25] As in Volyn-Podolia and western Belarus, there was little industry in eastern Galicia – except for the oilfields near Drogobycz – but Jews were important for the local economy since most of the local artisans were Jewish.[26] This economic role preserved them for a time, but

[21] In late September 1942 the deportation of 600,000 Jews from the General Government to Operation Reinhard death camps was planned. In reality, slightly more than 400,000 were murdered. See "Protokoll über die in Berlin am 26. und 28. September [1942] abgehaltene Konferenz," printed in Ancel 1984, p. 419; Gerlach 1998a, p. 231 note 188. For Radom, see Seidel 2006, pp. 329–30.

[22] Gerlach 1998a, pp. 225–31.

[23] Himmler to Krüger, Globocnik and others, October 9, 1942, BA NS 19/352, pp. 11–2.

[24] Pohl 1996, pp. 246–65.

[25] SSPF Galizien, "Lösung der Judenfrage im Distrikt Galizien" with cover letter, June 30, 1943, IMG, vol. 37, pp. 391–410.

[26] Ibid., p. 394.

it did not generate sufficiently strong interest later on, especially among the military, in maintaining Jewish workers. In all three areas, regional SS and police organized the mass murders largely in agreement with the civil administrations. The same was true in the separately administered districts of Bialystok and Zichenau when the almost 200,000 Jews there were destroyed, the majority between November 1942 and February 1943. A small number were sorted out for forced labor in Auschwitz, but hardly any among those shipped to Treblinka. The ghetto of Białystok, housing 30,000 Jews who were considered important to the textile industry, existed until August 1943.[27]

The situation in the rest of the General Government and in the Baltic countries was somewhat different. The number of Jews officially listed as alive in the General Government at the end of 1942 was reduced by almost a third by March 1, 1943.[28] However, as some mid-sized industry existed in these regions, the proportion of Jews murdered during the rest of 1943 was smaller. (In the fall of 1942, though, some army officials had expected to lose their 50,000 Jewish workers by early 1943.[29]) Instead, persons deemed to be still productive were transferred to SS camps, or ghettos were converted to such camps. Himmler was infuriated on a visit to Warsaw on January 11, 1943, to see that the ghetto there still existed. The first attempt to 'liquidate' it a week later failed largely because of Jewish resistance. It took the SS three more months – which included preparations for the relocation of industry and workers (mostly textiles and leather goods) – before a second attempt was made, and this led to the Warsaw ghetto uprising of April 19–May 16. The desperate insurgency was put down and the process devastated most of the ghetto area. Still, of the more than 56,000 Jews discovered there afterwards, about 42,000 were taken to SS camps as potential forced laborers instead of being killed instantly.[30] In this way, Jürgen Stroop, the SS and Police Leader in the district of Warsaw, met Himmler's second deadline: but he left many Jews alive.

In fact, leading SS figures in the General Government like Higher SS and Police Leader, Krüger, and the SS and Police Leader in the district of Lublin, Globocnik – director of the Operation Reinhard mass murders – became advocates and organizers of the exploitation

[27] For Zichenau see Grynberg 1984, p. 107; for Bialystok see Gerlach 1999, pp. 723–33.

[28] On March 1, 1943, there were 203,679 Jews according to "Bevölkerungszahlen Generalgouvernement," BA R 52 VI/21.

[29] "Protokoll über die erste Sitzung der Rüstungskommission am 24. Oktober 1942," BA-MA RW 23/2, p. 38.

[30] Scheffler and Grabitz 1993, pp. 14–16; "Es gibt" 1976. In a telegram of May 24, 1943 (copy included in "Es gibt" 1976), Stroop reported that 12,000–13,000 Jews in the ghetto had been killed, as were all of the 6,929 deported to "T II" (Treblinka).

of Jewish labor in 1943 (see Chapter 8). Globocnik also organized the 'liquidation' of the ghetto in Białystok (which was outside the General Government) that was carried out from August 16 to 20, 1943, and brought about 11,000 of its inhabitants to labor camps in his district of Lublin, while a further 17,000–19,000 were killed.[31] In a similar reorganization and murder of the allegedly unproductive by other agents, more than 10,000 Jews were killed in Lithuania in the fall of 1943; 19,000 remained, and at least 7,000 were deported to worksites in Estonia and Latvia.[32]

Himmler seemed to want to encourage his underlings by sending foreign news items concerning the plan to murder all Jews, and concerning the acceleration of their extermination to the RSHA, to Eichmann, or others.[33] On April 9, 1943, Himmler urged the chief of the RSHA, Kaltenbrunner, to "bring as many Jews to the east as humanly possible" and report about his success only to him.[34] Through the RSHA, Himmler affirmed in May 1943 that all Jews – including the frail, armament workers and members of the Reich Association of German Jews – should be deported to the 'east' or Theresienstadt by June 30, 1943.[35] Hitler had energetically reemphasized in another meeting of Nazi Party leaders on May 7 that all of the Jews in Europe were to be exterminated, which triggered activities by others.[36] Three days later, Himmler noted that the Jews in the General Government were to be killed for their cooperation with partisans,[37] which had in fact occurred only sporadically during the Warsaw ghetto uprising. By May 1943, major deportations of Jews from the Netherlands and some from Croatia were resumed. The Foreign Office urged Slovakia to hand over more Jews and Himmler pressed the French government to consent to the surrender of Jews naturalized after 1927, although both efforts were ultimately unsuccessful (for Slovakia, see Chapter 14).[38] In East Upper

31 Gerlach 1999, p. 732.
32 Dieckmann 2011, pp. 1280, 1294–7, 1317.
33 Brandt to Eichmann, October 2, 1942, BA NS 19/2760; Persönlicher Stab Reichsführer-SS to RSHA, December 5, 1942, BA NS 19/217, p. 8; Brandt to RSHA, February 22, 1943, BA NS 19/1577, p. 13.
34 Rückerl 1977, p. 292.
35 Gryglewski 1996, p. 34, with reference to a RSHA circular of May 21, 1943.
36 Notes by Herbert Backe, BAK NL 75/5; for the context, see Gerlach and Aly 2002, pp. 87–8. For Goebbels' stepping up anti-Jewish propaganda on May 8, see Dörner 2007, p. 176; see also Longerich 2010, p. 575 (both with little regard to Hitler's impulse); for the anti-Jewish propaganda offensive in the spring of 1943 see Longerich 2010, pp. 570–8.
37 "Aktennotiz über Bandenbekämpfung," May 10, 1943, BA F 2918, p. 177.
38 Longerich 2001, p. 181.

Silesia, major deportations started in June 1943 and continued until August, while smaller numbers of Jewish workers remained alive in SS camps in the region.[39]

On June 19, Hitler told Himmler that "the evacuation of the Jews has to be carried out in a radical way despite the upheaval it will cause within the next three to four months, and [that it] had to be toughed out."[40] According to Himmler, Hitler thereby acknowledged that he too regarded the obstacles to be great and the task arduous, and he consented to an extension of the deadline. Himmler, exaggerating their number, stressed the urgency of removing the Jews still living in the General Government.[41] On June 21 he ordered that all of the ghettos in Reich Commissariat Ostland be emptied by August 1 and that a certain proportion of their inhabitants be killed, with the rest transferred to concentration camps. This meant not just a new timeframe but giving up the goal of total destruction. Once again, his deadline was missed because the replacement of Jewish workers met with resistance and other difficulties. Himmler's plans were only partially implemented by October 1943. The task he had set was fully completed in the Soviet areas under military occupation, for which Himmler had issued instructions on August 13, 1943, to murder or remove all remaining Jews as Soviet troops were approaching.[42]

Germans (and others) suspected Jews in general of being spies, leftists and revolutionaries, and of supporting armed resistance. In some areas and time periods, such suspicions led various authorities, especially in the military, to support their murder (see Chapter 11). In reality, Jewish uprisings were rare. When they occurred they were usually acts of desperation, a last resort in the face of imminent extermination. They started in 1942 in small towns in western Belarus and Ukraine, where locally they led to the flight of some dozen or a hundred people.[43] Later in the war, Jewish uprisings became bigger and more spectacular, prompting the Germans to use heavy weapons as in Warsaw (in April–May 1943), and Białystok and Glubokoje (both in August 1943). The SS and police announced that they intended to deport most to forced labor – yet not everybody in the ghettos believed this claim, or they resisted anyway.[44] Revolts among

39 Steinbacher 2000, pp. 296, 300–2, 305.
40 Himmler's note, June 19, 1943, BA NS 19/1671, p. 68.
41 Greifelt's note on an appointment with Himmler, May 12, 1943, BA NS 19/2648, p. 135; see Himmler's note on anti-partisan warfare, May 10, 1943, BA F 2918, p. 177.
42 Gerlach 1999, pp. 736–42; Dieckmann 2011, pp. 1248–52, 1268–1321.
43 Ainsztein 1993, pp. 86–90.
44 See Ainsztein 1993, pp. 265–75, 305–61, exaggerating German victim numbers; Gerlach 1999, p. 739.

the Jewish crews in the extermination camps of Treblinka (August 2, 1943) and Sobibór (October 14, 1943) – whose members lived under the constant threat of being replaced through massacres[45] – forced the SS to close down these camps earlier than had been planned; it also led to the shooting, on 3 and 4 November 1943 during the so-called Operation Harvest Festival, of more than 40,000 Jewish forced laborers in the General Government as potential security risks.[46] Still, in the summer of 1944 about 50,000 Jews remained alive – with the support of the heads of the civil administration and the military armament authority – as legal members of the workforce within the General Government.[47] There were repeated manhunts for those who remained in hiding, which resulted in the deaths of tens of thousands. Such manhunts seem to have taken place over several days after many of the deportations.[48] In July and August 1944 – after the civil administration, despite pressure from Himmler, had delayed the destruction of the Łódź ghetto and its workforce for more than a year – the perceived (but unreal) danger of an uprising of the ghetto's inhabitants as Soviet troops were approaching was cited as the reason for deporting the Jews from Łódź – first to the temporarily reopened killing station at Chełmno and then, two days after the Polish national uprising had started in Warsaw on August 3, in larger numbers to Auschwitz.[49] It was in no small degree as a result of the security argument – which was itself connected with old anti-Jewish stereotypes – that Himmler was able to overcome employers' objections in 1943–44 to murdering those Jews remaining in eastern Europe who might still be further exploited.[50]

In Germany, few Jews remained after the deportation of the Jewish armament workers of Berlin in February and March 1943. The last legally living Jews (except for those in mixed marriages) – which included many of the functionaries of Jewish communities – were deported in the second half of June 1943, in accordance with Himmler's deadline.[51] The Ministry of the Interior and the Ministry of Justice tried from January to May 1943 to get a law passed to break up all marriages between Jews and non-Jews. In the end, however, their efforts came to nothing because such a regulation would have stirred up too much unrest among the

45 Ainsztein 1993, pp. 408–11, 423–9.
46 Scheffler and Grabitz 1988, pp. 262–72, 328–33.
47 Karay 2004, pp. 233–40.
48 For the district of Radom, see Seidel 2006, pp. 348–51. For regular manhunts see Browning 1993, pp. 121–32; Klukowski 1993, pp. 219–22 (diary, October 19–28, 1942).
49 Klein 2009, pp. 612–13 (see also pp. 590–611 for interests that the civil administration might have had in dissolving the ghetto); Krakowski 2007, pp. 129–30.
50 See also Pohl 1998, pp. 427–8.
51 Gruner 2004, pp. 58–9.

many non-Jewish relatives affected.[52] The Gestapo succeeded in gradually including so-called 'half-Jews' in forced labor and other measures of persecution, but this did not often lead to their being killed.[53] German authorities also exempted Jews married to non-Jews and persons of mixed Jewish and non-Jewish heritage in other countries, even in eastern Europe, from extermination and certain other methods of persecution.[54] Such people were also protected under other regimes – such as in Croatia and Norway – usually because of the influence of the various churches.[55]

Whether Himmler's extermination deadline of June 30, 1943, also applied to Jews in occupied countries with their own government remained unclear. In any case, as the deadlines could not be met, they were extended. For France, Eichmann had already set the goal in late August 1942 of deporting all stateless Jews by the end of the year, and all of the Jews without French citizenship by the end of June 1943.[56] This implied that it would take longer to ship off Jewish French nationals. The deportation of Jews with third country nationality from France, Germany and elsewhere also ran into difficulties because neutral governments held objections and either did not make clear which of their citizens living abroad they claimed, or they did not bring such people home within the time limits that the German Foreign Office had set in conjunction with the RSHA. The first of these deadlines expired in the spring of 1943.[57] For example, in October 1943 the Turkish government finally showed a heightened interest in Jews with Turkish citizenship not being deported from France, but it did not evacuate many to Turkey.[58] In early October 1943 Himmler seems to have told Nazi leaders that all European Jews could be killed by the end of that year (as Italian representatives had been told before).[59] Fortunately this deadline was also unrealistic.

52 See the documentation in the files BA R 18/5519, pp. 499–521 and R 22/460, pp. 334–47; Meyer 1999, pp. 29–31, 96–100.

53 Meyer 1999, pp. 52–9, 248–51; Hilberg 1994a, pp. 448–9; Adam 1972, pp. 316–33.

54 Account by Benjamin Vinter in *We Survived*, vol. 3, p. 363 (Serbia); Fleischer 1986, p. 687 note 34 (Greece); Sanders 2005, p. 194 (France); Mason 1984, pp. 317–18, Moore 1997, pp. 104, 123–7 and Hilberg 1994a, p. 616 (Netherlands). For the contradictory practice in the occupied Soviet territories, see Arad 2009, pp. 360–70; Grossman and Ehrenburg 1994, pp. 70–1, 73, 236, 338–9, 408, 411, 524–5, 705, 765. See also Essner 2002, pp. 362–5, 370–1, 379–80, 400–44.

55 Gitman 2011, pp. 56, 67 (Croatia); Abrahamsen 1991, p. 108 (Norway); indictment against Bosshammer, StA KG Berlin 1 Js 1/65, April 23, 1971, pp. 256, 371, 373 (Italy).

56 IVJ SA16 Ah/Br., "Tagung beim Reichssicherheitshauptamt am 28.8.1942 über Judenfragen," September 1, 1942, Eichmann trial document 142.

57 See the correspondence in the file PA AA R 100857; Browning 1978, pp. 154–8.

58 See the file PA AA R100857, pp. 250ff.; Guttstadt 2008, pp. 298–305.

59 See Longerich 2010, p. 601; for the Italians, see Steinberg 1992, pp. 126–7; for a French resistance journal reporting about this German objective in June 1943, see Cohen 1993, p. 322.

Persecution in newly occupied territories

From late 1942 German troops occupied a number of countries which were more or less allied to Germany: Vichy France in November 1942; Italy and Italian-occupied areas of France, Yugoslavia, Albania and Greece in September 1943; and Hungary, Slovakia and Croatia in 1944. This constituted a mortal threat to Jews in these areas. And yet in many of these countries the problems of the SS and police in getting hold of persons of Jewish heritage repeated themselves – with one major, terrible exception: Hungary.

In Italy, as in other countries before, cooperation of the local police was crucial to the German Security Police for reasons of manpower and local knowledge.[60] The Security Police tried conducting raids against Jews in Merano, Trieste, Rome, Florence, Genoa and Milan between September and November 1943 but found such operations to be inefficient.[61] Most Jews went underground with the support of local residents. Some crossed the border into Switzerland or joined the partisans. Since the Italian fascist state organs were also slow and sometimes hesitant in registering, arresting and concentrating Jews, and since they also exempted many persons of Jewish heritage, the SS managed to deport no more than 8,000 Jews (18% of the Jewish population, about a tenth of whom survived the German camps).[62] More Jews in Italy were arrested by Italian fascists, the police, the Carabinieri, and the militia than by Germans.[63] In France, as was initially the case in Italy, the Security Police organized one raid after another in 1943–44 – but with only limited success.[64] The outcomes of operations in southern Greece varied. In contrast to the smaller islands – where Jews were easily concentrated if local German military and the local Greek administration cooperated – most Jews in Athens managed to go underground, helped by non-Jews and the anonymity of a large city.[65] In Belgium (which had been occupied since 1940), the arrest of individuals and small groups produced more than half of the total internments and deportations. The other side of this unusually high percentage was that 60% of the Jews in the country were able to escape because manhunts had a more limited capacity to inflict damage than did systematic concentration. The raids scared many

60 See note by Wagner (Foreign Office), December 4, 1943, in Longerich 1989, pp. 332–3.
61 Steur 1997, pp. 116–23; Picciotto Fargion 1989, pp. 258–60.
62 Klinkhammer 1993, pp. 534, 546–7, 549–53. The numbers include Jews from Rhodes and Kos (Italian territories) in the Aegean.
63 Zuccotti 1996, pp. 189–90.
64 Kaspi 1997, pp. 244–50; Meyer 2000, pp. 139–44.
65 Gerlach 2010, pp. 244, 247.

Jews, early enough, to go into hiding.[66] When German troops invaded southern France in November 1942, Hitler ordered Himmler to ship off the Jews "and other enemies" there, but made this contingent upon his (Hitler's) future consultation with French Prime Minister Laval.[67] These examples illustrate that German occupation of a country was no guarantee of persecutors being able to get hold of, deport and murder all of the Jews there present when that country had a national government and when the local bureaucracy and police did not enthusiastically pursue or support such activities.[68]

In March 1944, German troops invaded Hungary in order to prevent that country from switching sides – like Italy had a few months before – and to force it to increase its contributions to the German war effort. From the point of view of German politicians and high officers, this attempt to overcome Hungary's lack of engagement had many links with removing the Hungarian Jews. They had allegedly conspired against the Axis, sabotaged Hungary's military and economy, and favored communist revolution to which Hungary, a country without an internal social policy at a time when Soviet troops were approaching, was perceived as vulnerable.[69] German politicians and the SS were determined to round up the Hungarian Jews, but it was crucial that the Hungarian political right shared these aims and judged the deportation of Jews useful for attaining its own political goals. These goals included limiting inflation, expanding social insurance and distributing consumer goods, all financed by expropriating Jewish assets, delivering minority members but few Magyars to Germany as labor, avoiding aerial attacks, facilitating food exports without sacrifices for Magyars, and, finally, regaining full sovereignty and freedom of foreign policy with a view to avoiding the country's destruction by way of a timely ceasefire but without losing its recently annexed territories.[70] Large-scale deportations started on May 15, 1944, only two months after the German invasion, and 430,000 Hungarian Jews were shipped to Auschwitz within just eight weeks; about 75% were killed immediately upon arrival. Aside from the availability of German mass murder facilities (and the German demand for forced labor), it was the almost frictionless cooperation of Hungary's politicians, bureaucracy and gendarmerie – in fact, their zealousness – that made the concentration

[66] Meinen 2008 (pp. 55, 58–78) identifies the Devisa Protection Squad as one of the most active arrest units.

[67] Himmler's note, December 10, 1942, BA NS 19/2159, p. 3.

[68] According to Griffioen and Zeller 2011 (pp. 1009–10) this explains to a large degree the differences between deportation rates from France, Belgium and the Netherlands.

[69] Gerlach and Aly 2002, pp. 98–110.

[70] Ibid., pp. 149–248, 344–51.

and deportations possible, and popular Hungarian hostility toward Jews (due in part to greed) that in many ways blocked their escape. Only forced laborers working for the Hungarian military, and the Jews of Budapest, enjoyed some protection offered by various Hungarian elites who were aided by diplomats from neutral countries. As a result, about 120,000 Jews survived within Hungary, and slightly more in German hands, while close to half a million perished.[71] But Hungary was neither the first nor the last of Germany's allies to be occupied by it. The explanation for these rapid mass murders lies also with the particularly cynical calculations of Hungarian authorities and the exceptional degree of cooperation they fueled. Under these conditions, the most aggressive German protagonists of anti-Jewish policies became bolder and bolder.

When a large uprising in support of approaching Soviet troops broke out in Slovakia on August 29, 1944, the German military occupied the country. The German Security Police took the opportunity to arrest and deport as many Jews as it could. Of the up to 25,000 Jews in Slovakia, 12,000 were deported, 2,000 were killed in the country, 300 fell as insurgents and 10,000 survived in hiding. Suspected insurgents, democrats and Roma were also shot or deported to German concentration camps. At least 7,336 were shipped to Auschwitz in October and November (the majority after the gassings there had stopped); the rest went to other concentration camps, including Theresienstadt. More than half of the deportees are thought to have survived.[72]

There is no evidence of German extermination efforts against the 100,000–130,000 Jews in Libya and Tunisia – Italian and French colonies, respectively – where German troops operated in 1942–43. This was in contrast to the fact that in the protocol of the Wannsee conference French northern Africa was included in the figures of Jews to be targeted.[73] Measures, which began in November 1942, were largely restricted in Tunisia to German- and Italian-organized forced labor and official plunder; and in Libya to the Italian internment of foreign Jews and those from the region of Cyrenaica.[74] Jews were also subjected to job restrictions, partial expropriation, internment and forced labor under the Vichy-controlled administrations in Algeria, Morocco and Tunisia from 1940 until Allied or Axis occupation in November 1942.[75] Primarily as

[71] Gerlach and Aly 2002, pp. 275–6, 295–6, 306–13, 409–12.
[72] Fatran 2005, pp. 46–50; Hradská 1996, pp. 92, 94; Schmidt-Hartmann 1991, p. 374.
[73] For this point see Friedländer 2006, p. 368.
[74] Abitbol 1983, pp. 126–46; Sebag 1991, pp. 240–5; de Felice 1985, pp. 175, 179–80; Roumani 2008, pp. 28, 31–35; Mallmann and Cüppers 2006, pp. 138, 146, 206 (in part speculative).
[75] Abitbol 1983, pp. 62–79, 99–107; Sebag 1991, esp. pp. 222–7.

a result of the bad living conditions in general, and also to internment, approximately 1,500 Jews died in Tunisia in 1943 and more than 500 in Libya in 1941–42; an unknown number of interned foreign Jews died in Libya and Algeria.[76] This death toll was much lower than in other countries.

Policies that allowed for survival

In November 1944 Himmler's anti-Jewish policy changed, as he wanted to use Jews as bargaining chips in planned secret peace negotiations. The mass gassings in Auschwitz were stopped and the crematoria soon dismantled. In the Auschwitz camps, direct killings by other means were also greatly reduced, and Jewish inmates started to seek transfers to the hospital barracks, which would have meant almost certain death before.[77] However, the exhausting exploitation of concentration camp inmates (and of Hungarian Jews working on fortifications along the Austro-Hungarian border) and the undersupply of necessities continued. In fact it actually worsened. As a result, prisoners – Jews and non-Jews alike – continued to die in large numbers, peaking in March and April 1945. Concentration camp crews also carried on with the murder of weak and sick inmates (including non-Jews) in the beginning of 1945, at which time Auschwitz was liberated by Soviet troops.[78]

Hitler, who thought that prisoners had played a crucial role in the leftist revolution of 1918, had started in 1941 to give Himmler orders to liquidate concentration camp prisoners if the Germans were militarily or politically in a desperate situation, or at least not let them fall into enemy hands.[79] As a result, concentration camps were evacuated when foreign armies approached. In mid 1944 such operations were well planned and organized, and claimed comparatively few victims, although the murderous conditions of camps and forced labor continued.[80] During the evacuations of 1945, in contrast, guards shot many tens of thousands of prisoners because they could no longer walk, or simply to get rid of them.

[76] For rising death figures in Tunisia, see Sebag 1991, p. 254; for Libya see Roumani 2008, pp. 29, 34–5.

[77] Czech 1989, pp. 921 and 936 note; Blatman 2011, pp. 83, 93; Gerlach and Aly 2002, pp. 401–2. See Bauer 1993.

[78] See Blatman 2011 (pp. 130–2) for murders in Ravensbrück, Dachau, Flossenbürg and Mauthausen; see also pp. 131–4, 140, 156, for tens of thousands of prisoners starving in various camps.

[79] Hitler 1982, p. 59 (September 14–15, 1941); Goebbels 1995, diary, May 24, 1942, vol. II, 4, p. 361. For 1945, see Blatman 2011, pp. 153–5.

[80] Blatman 2011, pp. 51–62.

Many guards despised them.[81] Because orders were unclear or contradictory (including some from Himmler to treat Jews with decency), many decisions regarding the specific organization of marches and transports, and about individual murders and massacres, were made by lower-ranking SS officers and SS-enlisted men, some of whom had been transferred to the SS from the army in 1944. Some local Nazi Party functionaries also urged that prisoners be removed from their areas one way or another.[82] Inside the concentration camps and, especially, on the marches, the treatment of Jewish and non-Jewish prisoners differed less and less; for the German authorities they fused into a faceless mass which in turn led to them being regarded by their guards as menacing, dirty, repulsive and useless. In consequence they were killed for no clear political reason or in line with any particular program.[83] Although largely "decentralized,"[84] the process nonetheless killed masses of people. As many as a third of the more than 700,000 concentration camp inmates evacuated between January and May 1945 may have perished.[85] Most non-Jews among these prisoners were Soviet and Polish forced laborers arrested in Germany, and Polish and Soviet civilians arrested in the occupied territories, mostly for resistance, flight or some kind of alleged or real disobedience. POWs held by the army, and prison inmates, were also sent on evacuation marches. Some died of exhaustion and cold, in combination with undernourishment, and Soviet POWs were also shot if unable to go on.[86]

At the end of the Nazi regime in May 1945, about 1.3 million Jews who had been under German or Axis control were still alive; among this number were close to half of those who had been under Axis control at the end of 1942. Some 200,000 had survived 'illegally' in hiding in various countries including Netherlands, Belgium, Germany, Poland, the occupied Soviet territories, Italy, Yugoslavia, Greece, Slovakia and Hungary, where they had usually been helped by local non-state agents. Roughly 300,000 central European Jews under Nazi rule had managed to emigrate by 1941, when the German authorities still permitted it, and many hundreds of thousands of Soviet Jews saved themselves by fleeing eastward

[81] Blatman 2011, pp. 125, 152, 179, 236.
[82] Blatman 2011, pp. 52–7, 80–1, 90, 124–5, 136–7, 144; for persecutors see pp. 367–405.
[83] This is the thesis of Blatman 2011, pp. 10–11, 192–3, 271, 410, 416–18, 426–7. Orth 1999, pp. 272–4 emphasizes the role of regional SS leaders.
[84] Blatman 2011, p. 418, calls it "totally decentralized."
[85] Blatman 2011, pp. 2, 12, argues that at least 35% of inmates did not survive. Considering the figures in Gerlach and Aly 2002, pp. 409–13 the survival rates during 1945 may have been slightly higher.
[86] For prison inmates, see Wachsmann 2004, pp. 325–38; for POWs, see Chapter 9 in this volume.

into the Soviet hinterland or being evacuated from the approaching German armies. Others had survived through their own resourcefulness, but were helped by the policies of German or non-German agencies. Allied armies liberated about 250,000 Jews from SS camps where they had been exploited as forced laborers. Several tens of thousands of Jews had been held as hostages to be traded for money, goods or foreign policy objectives. More than 600,000 Jews had been persecuted but otherwise more or less shielded from deportation by their own national governments, often right-wing authoritarian or fascist regimes. Among these surviving Jews were 250,000 in Romania, 220,000 in France, 120,000 within Greater Hungary, at least 100,000 in Tunisia and Libya, 50,000 in Bulgaria and more than 30,000 in Italy.[87] In France and Slovakia, government obstruction improved one's chances of survival in hiding; in Hungary and Bulgaria the survival chances of Jews were helped by their value as forced laborers. In none of these four countries, or in Romania, did governments always object in principle to the deportation or murder of Jews. In all four, as described above, the influence of elites and, sometimes, popular pressure, forced state leaders to desist from total extermination. This outcome, like the fate of Jews in the last six months of Nazi rule, illustrates once more the main policy objectives that allowed for survival: the emphasizing of national sovereignty and the demand for forced labor under conditions of wartime scarcity.

[87] For survival figures by nation see the contributions in Benz 1991; for the USSR see Arad 2009, p. 525. Marrus 1985 (p. 331) estimated a million survivors outside the Soviet Union.

6 Structures and agents of violence

This chapter deals with the interrelated issues of the organizational structures of German mass violence against Jews and others, and of the people who participated in these processes. It contradicts the popular image that Nazism worked on the basis of strict hierarchies, orders and obedience, and that the extermination of Jews was organized smoothly in a factory-like fashion. In reality, the Nazi system was semi-decentralized and permitted a good deal of flexibility, informal coordination and autonomy, but it also generated some friction because it gave individuals and groups room to pursue their own interests.

A semi-decentralized process

Table 6.1 is telling in several ways. It shows that of the five major German extermination camps[1] three different agencies were in charge and three different technologies used. Four of these camps, or rather killing stations, had a regional function and were run by regional agencies. They were primarily used to kill Jews from the areas where they were located. Virtually everyone who arrived there was murdered, unlike at Auschwitz-Birkenau, where staff sorted out considerable numbers of deportees for forced labor. (Regarding the other killing centers, 'selections' took place at the location of departure before deportation.) The experimental character of the methods of destruction in the beginning is well known. But although the planning of these five killing stations stretched over a year, new technologies or operational procedures for murder introduced at one site did not lead to a change at the others. All of this shows that the killing process was not fully centralized.

[1] Other extermination camps or killing grounds can be mentioned here, such as Majdanek, a concentration camp in Lublin where 100,000 Jews (and others) may have perished, Semlin (Serbia) and Maly Trostinez (Belarus), two camps run by the Security Police and Security Service with tens of thousands of victims each, most of whom were killed in gas vans.

Table 6.1 *Murder of Jews in major German extermination camps*

Camp	Area/responsible agency	Killing technology	Start of planning/ construction	Duration of murder of Jews by gas	Approximate number and origin of Jews killed
Chełmno	Wartheland/HSSPF Wartheland	Gas vans	Exploration for site in July 1941	December 8, 1941 – April 1943 (when destroyed), reactivated April–July 1944	150,000 from Łódź area and deportees from Germany
Bełżec	District of Lublin, General Government/ SSPF Lublin	Engine exhaust in stationary gas chambers	Mid October 1941	March 17, 1942 – December 1942	450,000 from districts of Lublin, Galicia and Kraków/GG
Sobibór	Same	Same as above	Unclear, between fall 1941 and March 1942	May 1942 – October 1943	250,000 from districts of Lublin and Galicia and deportees from Europe
Treblinka	District of Warsaw, General Government/ SSPF Lublin	Same as above	Second half of April 1942	July 22, 1942 – October 1943	800,000 mainly from districts of Warsaw and Radom/GG
Auschwitz-Birkenau	East Upper Silesia/ Inspectorate of Concentration Camps, SS Administrative and Economic Head Office	Prussic acid in stationary gas chambers, crematoria for disposal of bodies	September 24, 1941, as POW camp, large crematoria planned in Oct. 1941; gradual shift to annihilation camp for Jews; huge crematoria planned in July 1942	On a small scale from February 1942, increased in May and July 1942 – October 1944	900,000–1,000,000 from East Upper Silesia and across Europe

Table 6.1 also indicates that about every second murdered Jew was gassed, if one includes the victims of gas vans at other places than Chełmno and murders in other concentration camps than Auschwitz. About 2 million Jews were shot, primarily in the occupied Soviet territories. The existence of gas chambers and gas vans did not stop the mass shootings, which continued through 1942 and into 1943, claiming far more than half a million victims in 1942 alone.[2] Thus, four major technologies for murder existed in 1942. Much has been made of the smoothly working so-called 'industrial' German mass murder that was taking place in extermination camps,[3] but this picture is somewhat misleading given that half of the murdered Jews did not perish in gas chambers, that three of the five major annihilation centers listed above had no crematorium, that some of the five consisted for the most part of wooden buildings, and that the crematoria in Auschwitz were often out of order due to their sloppy construction.[4] Many of the shootings in 1941–42 were carried out not only by the Security Police and Security Service (controlled by the RSHA but not Eichmann, who is often portrayed as the chief organizer of extermination) but also by units of the Order Police, the Waffen-SS and, in some cases, the army. So in fact even more agencies were involved than those mentioned in Table 6.1.

In 1942–44, the Security Police and Security Service tried, in what was called 'Operation 1005,' to eliminate all traces of the murders by exhuming mass graves and burning the remains of the victims (including non-Jewish ones). This attempt to limit the possible spread of knowledge about the killings failed, as the operation quickly became known among the local population and German functionaries.[5] What is more, the incineration squads overlooked many mass graves because so many units and agencies had produced so many graves – another illustration of the fact that extermination was not a fully centralized operation or that it can be considered as a single operation only to a degree. Therefore, after the German retreat, Soviet and Polish investigators found unburned bodies in many mass graves. As a former Security Service officer who had defected to Switzerland, reported in 1944 about the German exhumatio, "This plan was in part carried out, but for another part it was

[2] These included 300,000 in western Ukraine, more than 200,000 in Belarus, and an unknown number in the General Government. See Spector 1990b, p. 186; Pohl 2000, pp. 148–9, 162; Gerlach 1999, pp. 628, 733.

[3] See, for example, Traverso 2003, pp. 43–6.

[4] On the faulty design and sloppy construction of the gas chambers see Pressac 1989, pp. 224, 227, 236, 252–3. For no crematoria see Berger 2013, pp. 190–213. For the late erection of crematoria at Chełmno during the short time when the camp was reopened in 1944 see Krakowski 2007, p. 132.

[5] See Pohl 1996, p. 381; Pohl 2010, p. 54; Gerlach 1999, p. 773; Hoffmann 2008.

not known any more where the graves were located."[6] As for the mobile Einsatzgruppen and their stationary successors the Security Police and the SD, there was so much confusion about the extent of their killings that the RSHA ordered on July 1, 1942, new reports of all the figures on past massacres – reports which had to list the different victim groups separately and which could not include murders that "cannot be counted toward the accomplishments of one's own work."[7] While this order can be read as an attempt at central organization, Operation 1005 illustrates the failure of such attempts.

That the mass murders were not fully centralized is confirmed by other facts. None of the five major death camps was under the command of the RSHA or notorious figures like Heydrich or Eichmann. But they were all run by the SS and police. As has been shown, Heydrich's efforts, including those at the Wannsee conference, to centralize anti-Jewish policies under the RSHA, had only limited success[8] (see Chapter 4). Beginning in the fall of 1941, Adolf Eichmann, who led the RSHA's unit for anti-Jewish measures, managed to exert influence and coordinate the deportation of about a million Jews from large areas of Europe to death camps and ghettos,[9] but his coordination did not include the treatment of most of the Jews in Poland and the occupied Soviet territories where the majority of European Jews lived.[10] In these areas the regional Security Police and SD, and the Higher SS and Police Leaders – not Eichmann's unit – coordinated the murder of Jews; while other formations, especially the Order Police, also carried out killings. According to one estimate, Order Police units were involved, usually but not always as assistants of the Security Police and SD, in the slaughter of at least 975,000 Jews in

6 "Militärisch-politische Berichte. Ueber den deutschen Nachrichtendienst," *c.* February 1944, Bundesarchiv Bern, EMD, E27, 9928, vol. 2183, dossier 306, p. 61; also quoted in Haas 1994, p. 165. See Gerlach 1999, p. 774.

7 Müller circular, "Einsatzbefehl Nr. 20, Betr.: Gesamtübersicht über die Sonderbehandlung von Personen," July 4, 1942, BA R 58/3568, pp. 8–9, also printed in Klein 1997, pp. 361–2.

8 A contribution that revises downward Heydrich's often-exaggerated influence is found in Angrick 2013.

9 According to Marrus and Paxton 1982, p. 696, German anti-Jewish "measures in various countries [were] not closely coordinated" until late 1941. Then "European-wide coordination" gradually became a reality (p. 699). This reflects the perspective of scholars focusing on western Europe.

10 This was already noted by Reitlinger 1961, p. 31. See the figures in Wannsee Conference 2009 pp. 254–5. Even the deportations from East Upper Silesia to nearby Auschwitz were organized by the regional Gestapo, instead of Eichmann: Steinbacher 2000, p. 280. Eichmann's transport manager, Novak, estimated that he organized the deportation of 1.7 million people (850,000 to Auschwitz), a figure which included, according to him, many who were deported more than once, and one which thus had to be adjusted downwards: examination of Franz Novak, February 2, 1961, StA KG Berlin 1 JS 1/65, vol. 6, pp. 54–5.

the German-occupied Soviet territories, and the murder or deportation of 555,000 Polish Jews.[11]

There was one man who supervised and coordinated virtually all of the murders of Jews. This was Heinrich Himmler, the head of the SS and police. He claimed, for example, to have made the decision to murder not only Jewish men but also women and children (apparently this pertained to Soviet Jews in the summer of 1941, for no other such decision is known.)[12] Still, his central supervision was probably quite lax because it was exercised, literally, by just one man, a man who devoted most of his working hours to political issues other than the persecution of Jews. The scholarly scrutiny of Himmler's role has found no indication that he had any central staff specializing in anti-Jewish policies outside the RSHA.[13] Eichmann did not fill this void. Himmler had asked Eichmann to submit an "Action and situation report 1942 about the final solution of the European Jewish question," but became very dissatisfied with the results.[14] Heydrich might have become Himmler's central coordinator, but his attempts to acquire competence and elaborate an overall plan were terminated by his assassination in May 1942.[15]

Of importance similar or greater to Eichmann's unit in the RSHA in terms of Jewish victim numbers – about 1.5 million – was Odilo Globocnik's staff for Operation Reinhard (or 'Reinhardt') in the General Government, the running of the extermination camps in Bełżec, Sobibór and Treblinka. Although in some documents Auschwitz-Birkenau figures as "station 2 of Operation Reinhard," and there were a number of administrative relations,[16] in practice the activities of Globocnik and his team only occasionally extended beyond the General Government. The core members of Operation Reinhard's personnel, who were directed by Hermann Höfle, were dispatched by a central Nazi Party agency outside the SS: the so-called Chancellery of the Führer (which was Hitler's chancellery in his capacity as Chairman of the Nazi Party).[17] It is not

[11] Curilla 2006, pp. 835–6.

[12] Himmler's speech to the highest Nazi Party leaders, October 6, 1943, BA NS 19/4010, p. 175.

[13] I know of nobody in the *Persönlichen Stab Reichsführer-SS* who specialized in anti-Jewish policies. See Breitman 1992; Longerich 2008. For Himmler's daily schedule in the decisive years 1941–42, see Witte *et al.* 1999. For Eichmann's areas of competence, see Cesarani 2007.

[14] Friedländer 2006, p. 508; for details about the content of this report see the indictment, StA KG Berlin 1 Js 1/65, April 23, 1971, pp. 426–7, 429–30.

[15] See Gerlach 1998a, pp. 142–5, for evidence that Heydrich never submitted the overall plan for the so-called 'final solution' to the Jewish question that Göring had requested.

[16] Report on Pohl's visit to Auschwitz, September 23, 1942 ("Station 2 der Aktion Reinhard"), CChIDK 502-1-19; see also Perz and Sandkühler 1999, pp. 283–316.

[17] Rückerl 1997, pp. 61, 72–5; see also Berger 2013.

exactly clear when Operation Reinhard officially started; it seems it was mentioned in a document dated May 24, 1942, while the secrecy form that every staff member had to sign was dated July 18, 1942.[18]

For a long time, historians exaggerated the number of people murdered at Auschwitz, thereby underlining what they took to be the centrally organized character of the destruction.[19] But Auschwitz was not central to the murder of European Jews until 1943, the year *after* the greatest destruction. About 175,000 Jews arrived there in 1942, and by the first quarter of 1943 still only a minority of victims came from countries outside Germany, Poland and the Czech lands. About half of Auschwitz's Jewish victims (close to 1 million) arrived only in 1944 when the camp surpassed Treblinka and Bełżec in terms of victim numbers.[20] The fact that Jews from the Greater German Reich were deported in sizable numbers to Minsk for their annihilation until October 1942, in line with a 1941 concession of the Reich Ministry for the Occupied Eastern Territories, is another illustration that at that time Auschwitz was not the one central location for the murder of Jews.[21] By 1944 it was. Huge crematoria were operational by the second quarter of 1943. Historians have taken plans to relocate these crematoria (and Jewish forced laborers) to other concentration camps – Mauthausen and Gross-Rosen – after the end of mass gassings at Auschwitz in November 1944 as possible schemes to continue the mass extermination. Fortunately this did not materialize in the same way as it had at Auschwitz.[22]

"The destruction of the Jews was not centralized. No agency had been set up to deal with Jewish affairs and no fund was set aside for the destruction process," as Raul Hilberg concluded. However, he assumed that there was a tacit national agreement: "All components of German organized life were drawn into this undertaking [...]; and every stratum of society was represented in the envelopment of the victims."[23] There is plenty of evidence for the partially decentralized character of the murder of European Jews. It extended, until late 1942, to the melting down of

[18] The form is in BA R 102 II/31 ("Einsatz Reinhardt"); for May see Pohl 1993, pp. 129–30.

[19] Kárný 1987, p. 145 ("*Millionen*"/"millions"); Geiss 1988, p. 293 (2.5 million); Dawidowicz 1987, p. 191 (2 million).

[20] Hilberg 1994b, pp. 86, 89; see Bloxham 2009, pp. 234–5.

[21] See Gerlach 1999, pp. 751–61; for transports from Vienna to various destinations in 1942, see Botz 1975, pp. 113–14.

[22] Perz and Freund 2004, pp. 58–70; Neumann 2010, p. 58; note of a Sonderkommando member from Auschwitz, November 25, 1944, in Pressac 1989, p. 363; account by Edita Armut Kašikovič in *We Survived*, vol. 3, p. 112; Oleksy 1995, p. 124.

[23] Hilberg 1992b, p. 20. The quotations highlight the ambivalence of Hilberg's arguments on this matter; Hilberg also tended to describe the destruction of the Jews as a monolithic process which implied central steering (see Hilberg 1992a, pp. 33–8; Jasch 2012, p. 4 note 8.)

precious metals stolen from Jews, as well as to ideology. "Scientific anti-Semitism" was also never fully developed and was "shaped by improvization at almost every step along the way," according to Alan Steinweis, who adds that there was a "decentralized institutional structure of Jewish studies in Nazi Germany."[24] Such structures and their terrible efficiency raise many questions.

Responsibility beyond the SS and police

When 1,943 Jews were deported from the areas of Düsseldorf and Aachen in July 1942, organizers in the city of Essen included, in addition to the Gestapo, the police headquarters, the Order Police, the labor office, the registry office, the local revenue office, the housing office, various local banks and railway offices and, at the collection point in Düsseldorf, the criminal police, a local court, thirteen bailiffs, the regional civil administration, the personnel at the central train station, the railway police, the Waffen-SS, the regional tax authority and the Commerzbank, a private financial institution.[25] On a national level numerous official agencies shaped anti-Jewish policies.[26]

However, this widespread participation was not just a matter of organization. Although the SS and police carried out most of the German mass killings of Jews, this does not necessarily mean that they shaped the policies by which such murders took place. A number of other agencies and institutions participated in these decisions, decisions that were undertaken in the broader context of occupation policy (96% of the victims were neither German nor Austrian). Before taking a brief look at these other agencies, I turn to the similarly diverse organizations responsible for the misery and mass death of non-Jewish victim groups.

Soviet POWs were the second largest victim group of German policies. Most of them died in the custody of the German military. Again, there was no single central agency in charge; in this case, there were two – the POW department of the Allgemeine Wehrmachtsamt (General Military Office) at the Supreme Command of the German Armed Forces for camps in Greater Germany and in territories under a German civilian administration;[27] and for the territories under German military administration,[28]

[24] Banken 2009, pp. 742–3. The quotations are from Steinweis 2006, pp. 10, 14.
[25] Zimmermann 1995, pp. 369–70.
[26] Adam 1972, pp. 97–108.
[27] Examples include all of the annexed territories, the General Government, the Reich Commissariats of Ukraine and Ostland, Norway, and the Netherlands.
[28] Examples include Belgium, most of France, Serbia, Greece and the eastern half of the occupied Soviet territories.

the Department of War administration of the Quartermaster-General of Ground Forces within the Supreme Command of Ground Forces.[29] Below each of these two head offices there was a hierarchical apparatus that gave relative autonomy to the POW camp authorities. In addition, other agencies influenced the fate of Soviet POWs: central and regional food and agriculture authorities and certain military supply offices – namely quartermasters – co-determined their starvation rations; railway authorities were responsible for the conditions of their transport; military units in the rear, who guarded prisoners while on the march, often shot those who were unable to walk any further; all sorts of military units and private firms who employed them and often mistreated them horribly; and some SS and police units, and the military Secret Field Police identified and murdered political suspects among their ranks. In the Reich, Nazi Party officers on all levels also influenced the treatment of Soviet POWs.[30]

SS and police units caused roughly half of the deaths in German anti-guerrilla warfare; army units in the rear caused the other half. Military administrations, or civil administrations in territories where they were in charge, and agricultural and transport administrations in particular, influenced the design of these operations. With their small central staff, the efforts of the SS and police in 1943 to centralize their part of anti-partisan warfare were not very effective. Local non-Germans were instrumental in anti-partisan warfare just as they were in the camps for Soviet POWs and in the murder units and extermination camps that targeted Jews (where Soviet citizens also played major roles).[31] To mention another major program of mass violence, there was also no single authority in charge of bringing about 12 million forced laborers to Germany (let alone for organizing forced labor inside the occupied countries). From 1942 onwards, the men of the Plenipotentiary for Labor Deployment Fritz Sauckel competed with local German labor authorities in to organize conscription. The fate of forced laborers in Germany was determined by labor authorities, employers, local administrations and police.[32]

Raul Hilberg has connected the absence of central planning for German occupation policies and the murder of Jews: "There was never a map that showed how a German Europe would look like after a victorious war, and there was no blueprint to outline the destruction of the European

[29] See Streit 1991, pp. 67–80.

[30] See Streit 1991.

[31] See Gerlach 1999 (pp. 859–1054) for Belarus; Scholder 2002 for Yugoslavia; Mazower 2001 for Greece.

[32] See Herbert 1985 and Eikel 2005 for labor conscription in Ukraine.

Jews."[33] German occupation policies differed so much and were so uncoordinated that Jan Gross even refused to construct a typology of German occupation systems because the Germans "lacked a systematic plan for governing the countries they conquered."[34] Consequently, the typologies that other scholars have offered differ widely.[35] There was no German "authority that designed, coordinated and regulated the entire occupation policy" in Europe, except for Hitler.[36] The two politicians who came closest to him in conceptualizing and coordinating German occupation policies were Werner Best (chief of the German military administration unit in occupied France in 1940–42 and the German Plenipotentiary in Denmark in 1942–45); and Wilhelm Stuckart (State Secretary in the Reich Ministry of the Interior and coordinator for the annexed territories). Neither of them was able to systematize occupation policies or had much impact on these policies. Best himself recommended tactical pragmatism in each territory.[37]

Responsibility for violence against Jews was often shared. Historians have explored the influence of German diplomats and military authorities in some detail.[38] Another example is the General Government, where the civil administration implemented ghettoization and food and health policies that claimed tens of thousands of lives. The formal transfer of Jewish affairs to the SS and police on June 3, 1942,[39] did not end the civil administration's work and influence in that field.[40] When deporting and murdering Jews, the SS and police often responded to the civil administration's wishes and demands (see Chapters 9 and 10)[41] and often took their requests for labor exemptions into account despite gradually emerging differences concerning this point. The SS and police did interfere

33 Hilberg 1992b, p. 10.

34 Gross 1979, p. 32.

35 They are summed up in Röhr 1997, pp. 11–45.

36 Röhr 1997, p. 25. Röhr denies, however, that there was chaos (pp. 11–45).

37 See Herbert 1996, pp. 271–84, 290–5; Jasch 2012, esp. pp. 137–50; See also Stuckart to Himmler, March 19, 1943, BA NS 19/3776, pp. 3–4.

38 For the diplomats' influence, see Kletzin 1996, pp. 221–4 (concerning France) and, in general, Browning 1978; for the military, see Verbrechen 2002, pp. 91–185; Oldenburg 2004, pp. 167–8, 206.

39 Pohl 1993, pp. 124–5. The Reich Commissar for the Netherlands, Seyss-Inquart, gave a similar assurance to his HSSPF: Rauter to Himmler, October 7, 1942, BA NS 19/1558, pp. 9–10.

40 A similar point can be made for the Reich Ministry for the Interior after Göring had charged Heydrich with coordinating anti-Jewish policies in 1939 and 1941, with Himmler claiming the authority for Jewish questions in November 1941. See Jasch 2012, pp. 282–3, 297–302, 314–15.

41 See, for example, the recommendation (on request) to deport 19,735 Jews in Kreishauptmann Lublin-Land, *Amt für Innere Verwaltung* to the Governor of Lublin district, May 19, 1942, in Berenstein *et al.* 1962, p. 277; see also Musial 1999, pp. 239, 246.

in policy issues, but they did not simply sideline the civil administration politically.[42] In the end it was General Governor Hans Frank – who had insisted that the police could not be anything other than the enforcement arm of his government[43] – who remained in office, unlike his SS rivals. The Higher SS and Police Leader, Friedrich-Wilhelm Krüger, the Commander of the Security Police and SD, Eberhard Schöngarth, and Odilo Globocnik, SS and Police Leader in Lublin and organizer of the death camps of Operation Reinhard, were all sacked. In neighboring Wartheland, the strong influence of the civil administration concerning anti-Jewish policies is even less in doubt. Arthur Greiser, its head, thanked Himmler for having "approved" the murder of 100,000 Jews in his area and later wrote to Himmler to say that Hitler had told him (Greiser) concerning the Jews, "I should deal with them at my own discretion."[44] If the SS and police simply did what other authorities wanted, or what these influenced them to do so, the term 'perpetrator' is problematic because it may connote that those who actually did the killing, or their officers, made their decisions about mass killings independently. Autonomy of action and a system favoring participation did not, for the most part, mean that a single agency (like the SS and police) could ignore all of the others involved or indeed broader policy issues. This system required cooperation.

The persecutors

What was striking about German persecutors of Jews was their diversity. The violence cannot be attributed to people of a single social background, a single type of education or career, one kind of life experience, or one age cohort.[45] Some were highly educated. Among the upper level functionaries in the RSHA, two-thirds had earned a university degree and one-third a doctorate.[46] The leaders of the Operation Units and

[42] The HSSPF, Krüger, and the Military Commander in the General Government, Gienanth, both complained to an inspector from Berlin, with some exaggeration, that Krüger "is not independent and has no power" ("*ist nicht selbständig und hat nichts zu sagen*"). Kommandeur des OKW-Stabes z.b.V., Sonderbeauftragter des Führers, Bericht Nr. 5, August 21, 1942, BA NS 6/794, p. 20.

[43] General Governor, official diary, April 21, 1942, BA R 52 II/191, pp. 60–1. Rosenberg, as Minister for the Occupied Eastern Territories, argued in the same vein: "*Zuständigkeitsabgrenzung auf dem Gebiet der Judenfrage in den besetzten Ostgebieten,*" May 6, 1942, BA R 43II/684a, p. 155; note by Wetzel (RMO), June 4, 1942, BA R 6/74, p. 123.

[44] First quotation: Greiser to Himmler, May 1, 1942; second quotation in Greiser to Himmler, November 21, 1942 – both in BA NS 19/1585, pp. 1–2 and 18, respectively.

[45] See Hilberg 1992a, pp. 33, 64, 80; Paul 2002, p. 62; Welzer 2005, p. 43.

[46] Gerwarth 2011, p. 207; see also Dams and Stolle 2008, p. 59.

Operation Squads, which shot hundreds of thousands of people, mostly Jews, in the Soviet Union, were, likewise, usually well educated and included an opera singer and a professor of international law.[47] By contrast, many of the men who worked in Eichmann's group for anti-Jewish policies – from 1938 onwards – were laborers, tradesmen or clerks who had enjoyed little success in their previous careers.[48] Of the ten so-called "Jewish advisers" of the Security Police and SD in foreign countries, six were trained in commercial occupations, two were jurists and two were without professions.[49] Over the course of World War II the Gestapo was replenished with diverse groups of SS reservists, professionals, members of the Hitler Youth and conscripts, and this led to both deprofessionalization and a changing social make-up.[50] Among the staff who carried out the mass gassings of first the disabled, and then Jews in German extermination camps in Poland, were medical doctors, police officers, and former workers and craftsmen working side by side.[51]

The picture is similar for functionaries involved in violence against other groups. Nearly half of the leading personnel in the Reich Ministry for the Occupied Eastern Territories had earned a doctorate. The same was true of the ninety highest officials in the German civil administration in Warsaw, and it was a similar picture among high-ranking economic officers in the German military in the occupied Soviet territories.[52] By contrast, ranking SS officers in the concentration camps usually had a lower-middle-class background and no higher education.[53] There is some evidence that the younger military guards serving in Soviet POW camps were more brutal than the older ones who served later on.[54] But the men in the army units in the rear who committed mass atrocities during the course of anti-guerrilla warfare, who shipped off forced laborers, and who occasionally hunted Jews, were, on average, thirty-five to forty years old; they were married and had children. Their commanding officers were decades older.[55]

Nor were German persecutors uniform in ideological terms. SS and police officers and the higher strata of the civil administrations were hardened Nazis among whom were many 'old fighters' for the Nazi Party.[56] Ideologically conscious SS economic officers could be

[47] See Wilhelm in Krausnick and Wilhelm 1981, pp. 281–3.
[48] Safrian 1997, pp. 49–56.
[49] Steur 1997, pp. 158–9.
[50] Lotfi 2000, pp. 96–7, 117.
[51] See Berger 2013, p. 302; Klee 1986, pp. 159–63.
[52] Zellhuber 2006, p. 167; Gross 1979, p. 54; Terry 2005, p. 44.
[53] Orth 2000, pp. 87–90.
[54] Borgsen and Volland 1991, p. 82.
[55] Gerlach 1999, pp. 222–3.
[56] For example, see Gerlach 1999, pp. 223–5.

pragmatic at the same time, identifying with their tasks and pursuing what they found best for German society (some pursued this more than they did personal gain).[57] Demonstrating "a propensity to theoretical discussions and philosophical considerations," SS personnel at Treblinka apparently lectured Jewish prisoners on the meaning of the annihilation for the future of Germany.[58] Yet the leaders of the Haupttreuhandstelle Ost, which administered the expropriation and redistribution of Polish and Jewish property in occupied Poland, are said to have been "not at all staunch supporters of Nazism."[59] Research in the 1990s revealed that many persecutors were not Nazis, i.e. they were not members of the Nazi Party. This was true for the majority of the enlisted men in reserve police battalions and for the German military. But although they were neither ideological elites nor specially trained killers,[60] they still carried out many atrocities against Jews and other groups. Not all of these misdeeds should be attributed to Nazi indoctrination.[61] Less than 23% of a sample of staff at the Auschwitz concentration camp were members of the Nazi Party (who might be expected to share a special ideological affinity), while more than 38% of those arriving in 1944 were not in the SS either, but rather were transferred from the military.[62] It seems, therefore, that the outlook of the Nazis, and others, coincided. The political views of German generals, for example, overlapped or were at least compatible with those of the Nazi leadership.[63] The same can even be said of members of the opposition movement involved in the coup attempt against Hitler in 1944, many of whom were conservative aristocrats. Some of them either consented to, or participated in, mass violence against Jews, Soviet POWs and rural populations during the course of anti-partisan warfare and in line with anti-Jewish laws.[64]

[57] Allen 2002, pp. 1–18, 90–1, 159.

[58] Wassili Grossman, "Treblinka," in Grossman and Ehrenburg 1994, p. 848; Willenberg 2009, p. 106.

[59] Rosenkötter 2003, p. 91.

[60] For the Order Police see Browning 1993, pp. 48, 164. A third of Order Police *officers* were not members of the Nazi Party: "Schematische Darstellung über die Zusammensetzung des Offz.-Korps der Schutzpolizei und Gendarmerie," February 1942, BA 7.01, Nr. 4071, p. 67 and reverse side. For the military see the various contributions in Heer and Naumann 1995.

[61] Westermann 2005 (pp. 92–123, 239) documents such indoctrination largely for the officers corps, but he also points to what he calls "building a martial identity" (pp. 58–91). When the Nazis took power in 1933, very few of the former men and officers in what became the Order Police had been purged (pp. 36–7); Dams and Stolle 2008, p. 17.

[62] Strzelecki 1994, pp. 280, 283.

[63] Ogorreck 1992, p. 238 note 1.

[64] Gerlach 2000, pp. 127–45; Gerlach 1999, pp. 1104–26. For a general study of the growing overlap between the ideas of German aristocrats and the Nazis, see Malinowski 2003.

Perpetrators were even more diverse if one takes violence against more victim groups into account. Labor officials, as well as public and private employers, organized the recruitment and merciless treatment of forced laborers. The police and gendarmerie, storm troopers, factory security forces, labor office functionaries, military reservists and civilians were all involved in hunting down escaped forced laborers in Germany.[65] Murderous food policies and agricultural planning for anti-guerrilla warfare were determined by civil and military functionaries and military supply officers. In the occupied territories many representatives of these groups also dealt with Jews, but this was only one part of their broader responsibilities. Likewise, in the SS and police – including the Operation Units – few men were exclusively in charge of Jewish affairs.[66]

Although German persecutors came from all walks of life, support for persecution and mass murder was not unanimous. Compared to the persecutors, the documented number of German rescuers was small, but they too were from a "broad spectrum of differing social origins, religious beliefs, political affiliations, and occupations" such that the "search for a single, overarching explanation [for their actions] is in fact misconceived."[67] Hitler accused the middle class, in particular, of opposing the deportation of German Jews.[68] Protestant leaders primarily opposed, although not publicly, imminent steps against persons of so-called 'mixed blood' and the treatment of Jewish partners in mixed marriages as Jews. In contrast, Catholic bishops publicly protested against the murder of the disabled; however, they also welcomed Germany's invasion of the Soviet Union.[69] This highlights the fact that few protestors raised objections against every sort of mass violence. No method has yet been found for reliably estimating the numbers of those who supported and opposed persecution.[70]

There was a multitude of German persecutors; accordingly, the motives for their actions differed widely. They also mixed in various ways "anti-Semitic bigotry, vengeful anticommunism, organic nationalism," material gain, career ambitions, "enjoyment of their own power,"

65 On this point see Lotfi 2000, p. 187.

66 See Hilberg 1992a, p. 37; for Operation Unit D see Angrick 2003, esp. p. 8; see Herbert 1996 and Wildt 2003 on various SS and police officers; and Lifton 1986 on Nazi physicians.

67 Frank 2003, pp. 224, 229.

68 Picker 1977, pp. 305–6 (May 15, 1942). In that instance Hitler implied that the Jews would be killed.

69 Cardinal Bertram, letters to the Reich Ministry of Justice, November 11, 1942, March 2, 1943, and January 29, 1944, BA R 22/4009, pp. 26–9, 35–6; see Gellately 2002, p. 151.

70 See, for example, Bankier 1996; Longerich 2006; Dörner 2007.

and constraints by hierarchies and pressure for conformity, as Michael Mann wrote to describe non-Germans cooperating with the Nazis.[71]

The idea that the murder of Jews was based on a division of labor is problematic, because it can lead to the misunderstanding that the process had a monolithic structure.[72] The German state, bureaucracy and organization remain important. But Nazi German violence was not based on factory-like organization.[73] In fact, the demarcation of competences among different authorities and agencies of the state, and the Party, was left systematically unclear.[74] However, the polycentric political structures under Nazi rule did not lead to paralyzing chaos.[75] On the contrary, their efficiency in the field of violence was terrifying. There were armed formations whose members carried out mass murder under orders; but the thrust of the violence owed much to a system and a philosophy that was open to participation.

Persecutors' autonomous decision-making

Research in the 1990s concerning German persecutors showed how many acted on their own initiative, or at least not thoughtlessly. Here are some glaring examples. Bavarian labor official Count von Spreti boasted of his "first class performance" in having filled three deportation trains per week with laborers for Germany from the town of Uman, Ukraine, in June 1942. He reported that he despised violence but that he had decided to have the parents of labor conscription evaders taken hostage.[76] Hanns Martin Schleyer, an occupation officer in Prague (and later President of the Employers' Association in the FRG), wrote in 1942 that the "readiness to seek tasks instead of waiting for them [to be assigned to us] was instilled in us during our time of struggle [before 1933]."[77] German agricultural officers deployed to the occupied Soviet territories were told by their boss:

> Have no fear to make decisions. One who does not do anything makes no mistakes [...] I demand from you genuine leadership [...] Set yourself high, even seemingly unattainable targets [...]. You are totally on your own, therefore [you

[71] Mann 2005, pp. 313–14.
[72] As Browning 1978 (pp. 9–10) already argued, criticizing Raul Hilberg.
[73] The image of the factory of destruction evokes, inter alia, a strict command structure. For that image, see for example Wassili Grossman, "Treblinka," in Grossman and Ehrenburg 1994, p. 840.
[74] An early account by a protagonist is Dietrich 1955, pp. 125–36.
[75] See Aly 1993, p. 634.
[76] Hansch-Singh 1991, pp. 205, 209 (quote), 216, 218.
[77] Quoted in Aly 2005, p. 13 (my own translation, C.G.).

should send] no complaints and cries for help to [your] superiors. Help yourself, then God will help you![78]

The case of Paul Raab is exemplary. Raab was a low-ranking labor administrator in the German civil administration of Vasilkov, a rural district near Kiev, Ukraine. His actions became a matter of inquiry at the Eastern Ministry after an army officer complained that Raab had had several houses of local labor conscription evaders burned down. Raab responded in a brisk tone, one which few people today would use when writing to their superiors; he had indeed done what he was accused of, but he had done so because it was necessary to intimidate people in order to ensure that he could deport 31,000 forced laborers from this district to Germany, an action that was "definitely important for the war effort." Raab emphasized that he had performed this task "conscientiously" (*gewissenhaft*), although it had been "displeasing" (*unangenehm*) to him. However, responsibility for the conscription of forced laborers in the district of Vasilkov was his, and therefore "the choice of the means with which I carried out this task had to be left to me," based on a general authorization by his superiors in Ukraine. They had consented to his measures, Raab wrote in summary, "because of their success."[79] Here a young civil servant (who had probably no more than three or four German underlings) sternly insisted on his freedom to make decisions about violence within the limits of his general instructions on the basis of efficiency and "success."[80]

Earlier notions that most Germans involved in mass violence simply obeyed orders – notions that were based on assumptions about either the alleged German national character (of obedience) or the fear to refuse to carry out orders – are now outdated. In reality, Article 47 of the German Military Law Book (which also applied to attached police battalions and certain other persecutory units) stated that enlisted men were legally responsible for their behavior if they carried out an order to commit a criminal deed.[81] This law was valid during the Nazi period, and troops were regularly informed of this. In September 1942 Himmler told Erich Koch, Reich Commissar for Ukraine, that he preferred subordinates in

[78] Herbert Backe, "12 Gebote [für das Ver]halten im Osten und die Behandlung [der Russen]," June 1, 1941, IMG, vol. 39, pp. 367–71.

[79] Raul Raab to RMO, June 7, 1944, IMG, vol. 25, pp. 313–16.

[80] Roth 2009 (p. 426) finds this approach typical for county chiefs in the German civil administration in the General Government.

[81] However, this paragraph did not apply, for example, to the extermination camp guards: Rückerl 1977, p. 124. Hitler's basic order on the conduct of troops of May 13, 1941 (see Ueberschär and Wette 1991, pp. 252–3) overruled the validity of this article for the occupied Soviet territories by restricting the military prosecution of crimes by German troops more or less to individual actions (see also Welzer 2005, p. 100).

the SS who were not merely yes-men.[82] It was also "typical for Heydrich's management style repeatedly to demand from his men to have initiative and make their own decisions."[83] Such practices could draw their ideological justification from general principles of education that Hitler had laid out: young men should be instilled with "the joy of determination and willpower" and self-confidence; they "must not only learn to obey, but must thereby acquire a basis for commanding later"; and education needed to cultivate the "joy of responsibility," "courage for action," and "the strength for an independent decision."[84]

What emerged from such ideas was a culture in which orders were often formulated vaguely so that soldiers and lower-ranking officers were left room to make their own determinations. This sort of autonomy was practiced in various degrees in the German army, although it did not make orders and obedience totally irrelevant.[85] It was also known from previous German colonial wars,[86] and from the early days of the Nazi movement. In 1939 the Supreme Nazi Party Court recognized vague orders and the freedom for their recipients to interpret them as a general principle of the Party. The context of this ruling was the violence of the pogrom of November 1938.[87]

Organizational necessities reinforced such ideas. Agricultural officers or gendarmes were often, as they were in the occupied Soviet territories, the only Germans within a dozen kilometers. Without phone or wire communications, central control over them had to be loose, and the room left for them to make their own decisions, wide.[88] The more countries Nazi Germany occupied, the fewer available occupation troops, police and administration staff there were. For example, in August 1941 little more than 700 Germans worked as military administrators in Serbia and there were fewer than 3,000 of them in France; just over 3,000 Germans were civil administrators in the Netherlands; and even in the annexed Polish territories not all civil service positions could be filled by Germans.[89] While serving as Reich Protector in Bohemia and Moravia, Heydrich planned to cut German administrative personnel in the area drastically

[82] See Blood 2006, p. 80, and Meindl 2007, p. 365.
[83] Gerwarth 2011, p. 171.
[84] Hitler 1999 [1925–27], pp. 408 (first quote), 411, 414 (second quote), 416–17 (for the remaining quotes).
[85] See the comprehensive study by Sigg 2011, esp. p. 448; see also Rass 2005, pp. 86–7; Knox 2007, p. 75.
[86] Kuss 2011, pp. 414–15.
[87] See Longerich 2001, p. 24.
[88] See also Zellhuber 2006, p. 202.
[89] Schlarp 1986, p. 113; Marrus and Paxton 1982, p. 690; MadR 43, January 22, 1940, vol. 3, p. 672; Mazower 2008, pp. 238, 448–9.

(from 14,100 to 1,800 men).[90] The same problem affected the manpower available for the murder of Jews and mass violence against other groups. In March 1937 the Gestapo employed 6,500 people, and in September 1941 it was close to 15,000. But within Germany their numbers had stagnated. In 1944 three-quarters of all German Gestapo officers served abroad.[91] The German Security Police in France had grown from 20 to 200 men between 1940 and 1942, but when Helmut Knochen, the Commander of the Security Police and the SD in France, asked for 250 more men in July 1943 (in order to hunt for Jews, among other reasons), he received only four because more were not at Berlin's disposal. In December 1943 there were a total of 2,200 Gestapo personnel in France, but only a quarter of them belonged to the criminal police, which was crucial for carrying out searches; most of the rest had little training (and little numeric support by Order Police forces).[92] As one author concluded: "The ostensible German omnipotence was a bluff, as the French increasingly understood." Without assistance from the French gendarmerie, the German police organs were "virtually blind."[93] A similar argument has been made about the 2,000 Security Police and SD in the General Government – the center of the extermination of Jews – in November 1942. The ranks of these units were subsequently replenished with Polish officers.[94] The Chancellery of the Führer dispatched just ninety-two men to the SS and Police Leader in Lublin for the annihilation camps of Operation Reinhard.[95]

On top of freedom of initiative for German forces and functionaries on the ground, this shortage of manpower also required the cooperation of locals in every occupied country, a parallel to mechanisms that operated during European overseas colonialism.[96] *Aufsichtsverwaltung*, the principle that local staff (supervised by Germans) manned at least local administrations, was a reality in all German-occupied states. And it applied to policing and to anti-Jewish policies.[97] In France, as in Copenhagen, the German Security Police relied on autochthonous police for anti-Jewish action.[98] It has been claimed that this participation

90 Gerwarth 2011, p. 286.
91 Dams and Stolle 2008, p. 46; see also Kohlhaas 1995, pp. 221–5; Wildt 2003, p. 284.
92 Müller to Knochen, July 2, 1943, in Klarsfeld 1977, p. 204; Kasten 1993, pp. 97–101, 109, 125–58, 170. For the Order Police see Kletzin 1996, p. 242.
93 Kasten 1993, pp. 19 (second quote), 213 (first quote).
94 Borodziej 1999, pp. 34–5. In November 1942 there were 12,000 Germans of the Order Police in the General Government; in May 1943 the number was 19,000, and in 1944 it was 40,000.
95 Rückerl 1977, pp. 117–18. See also Chapter 10.
96 For colonialism see Robinson 1972, pp. 137–9.
97 For France see Meyer 2000, pp. 13–29. Most scholars apply the term '*Aufsichtsverwaltung*' only to certain occupied western European countries.
98 See Wildt 2003, p. 521; Herbert 1996, p. 367.

by locals "determined" in part the "character of colonial rule" overseas and its content,[99] and the same claim can be made for German rule across Europe.

The system of vague instructions, empowerment, and freedom of action left Germans room for individual initiative beyond their orders. It was not uncommon for men to participate in mass violence during their free time.[100] In Poland and Transnistria, German militias massacred thousands of Jews and others, albeit under SS and police command.[101] Anti-Jewish riots in which non-Nazi civilians participated were quite common in Germany from 1933 to 1938 (see Chapter 3) – although not afterwards – and riots were uncommon against non-Jews. State and party authorities could manipulate but not totally control this violence.[102] In a post-war inquiry, 30% of German Jewish men and 11% of Jewish women who had survived stated that German civilians had beaten them – more than had been beaten by officials.[103] A petition writer offered, in June of 1941, his "idea or invention for sending this [Jewish] brood quietly to kingdom come" and added that it could also be used to deal with Poles, Czechs and Serbs "or the intelligentsia of these peoples." A lady advised the Foreign Office where to house the Jews of Budapest to make sure "that the enemies with their [aerial] terror attacks strike the *right* people."[104] But generally speaking, German participation in mass violence functioned through, rather than circumventing, state apparatuses, and the agents of violence were usually functionaries of the state or the Nazi Party.

The roots of cruelty

Daniel Goldhagen correctly reminded scholars in 1995 that the brutality of many German persecutors of Jews was striking and had been neglected in research. He argued that this cruelty largely served no goal "save the

99 Robinson 1972, p. 139, see also p. 137.
100 See SS Cavalry Brigade, daily order, November 10, 1941, citing an order by the Commander of Rear Army Area Center against private participation of troops in mass executions, BA-MA RS 3–8/42; on October 18, 1941, the same commander forbade the private entry of German troops into Jewish ghettos, BA-MA RS 4/3.
101 For Poland see Jansen and Weckbecker 1992, pp. 8, 111–59 (however, the SS stopped what may have been the attempt of a new type of murderous mass militia: pp. 198–201); Schenk 2000, pp. 156–61. For Transnistria see Angrick 2003, pp. 285–8.
102 See Wildt 2007, pp. 277–81.
103 See Johnson and Reuband 2005, pp. 277–80.
104 Letter from Ulm (railroad station manager in Imst, Tyrolia) to the Reich Chancellery, June 13, 1941, BA 7.01, Nr. 4112, p. 383; letter of Marianne Siebrasse, May 4, 1944, PA AA R 99449 (emphasis in the original). Herbert Klein, son of the head of the Jewish community in Nürnberg, says that after the Nazi defeat he found the floor in the office building of the journal *Stürmer* covered with papers, including many letters like those I just cited: Johnson and Reuband 2005, p. 106.

satisfaction and pleasure of the perpetrators."[105] There is plenty of evidence of insults, public humiliation, beatings and torture of Jews – and others.[106] No act of mass destruction was free from brutality, nor were the events in the extermination camps.[107] Just imagine the noise during such events! Often they took place in eastern Europe, but Jews were also beaten, gold crowns broken out of their mouths, and some mistreated to the point of death during strip searches before they were deported from Nuremberg in 1941–42.[108] The causes of cruelty are controversial. Most scholars agree that only a minority of German persecutors can be correctly described as clinically sadistic.[109] Many, but not all, think that the impulse for brutality originated from "collective fears and emotions of hatred" rather than from individuals' "psyche[s]."[110] Christopher Browning sees brutality increasing with the rise in the numerical disparity between German persecutors and their victims on the ground.[111] According to Raul Hilberg, the brutal acts of Germans were usually signs of their impatience.[112] Impatience certainly played a role. However, it can be expressed in different ways, and what was manifested in these cases was the peculiar impatience with supposedly inferior people. Germans who participated often spent a good deal of time engaged in acts of cruelty and mockery[113] that made no contribution to the war effort or even, arguably, to the destruction of the Jews. Delight in abusing people did play a role. The evidence suggests, however, that there was more than one cause for this cruelty.[114]

Brutality did serve certain organizational goals. The phenomenon of learned helplessness illuminates this fact.[115] According to this concept,

105 Goldhagen 1997, pp. 15–22, 388 (quote).

106 For the example of Lublin see Fritz Cuhorst, report, *c.* December 1939, in Mallmann *et al.* 2003, p. 14; for Slonim, Belarus, see interrogation of Alfred Metzner, September 18, 1947, StA Hamburg 147 Js 29/67, Sonderband A, p. 32; for the actions of Theodor Dannecker, see Steur 1997, pp. 154–8. For cruel treatment of Soviet POWs, see Chapter 9, note 44.

107 This is made clear by the descriptions in Krakowski 2007; for whippings of camp inmates (as opposed to those who arrived to be immediately gassed) in Sobibór, see also Schelvis 1998, pp. 105–7. When Himmler visited this camp, truncheons and whips were concealed because Himmler opposed their use (p. 111; former perpetrators said the same after the war: Sereny 1980, p. 224).

108 Banken 2009, pp. 385–7.

109 Hilberg 1992a, pp. 67–9; Browning 1998b, p. 151.

110 Ingrao 2012, p. 255; see Welzer 2005, pp. 262–3.

111 Browning 1993, p. 95.

112 Hilberg 1992a, p. 67.

113 See, for example, Hilberg 1992a, pp. 67–9.

114 For different functions of cruelty see Berger 2013, pp. 340–6; Młynarczyk 2007, pp. 163–9, 172.

115 For the concept of learned helplessness see Peterson *et al.* 1993. I am very grateful to Brett Wieviora, a former student of the University of Pittsburgh, for having pointed me to the use of this concept in this context.

individuals sometimes stop struggling for a way out of a threatening situation – or even for survival – after having been systematically discouraged by repeated exposure to overwhelming physical harm. With regard to Nazi violence, this phenomenon has not often been applied to explaining the behavior of victims of mass shootings. Explanations in terms of "psychic freezing" – a physically debilitating reaction of alarm – have been offered: in their shock, victims may have thought that "life after death must be better than this current horror."[116] Such approaches intended to explain how thousands of Jews could be massacred by just a dozen shooters aided by a dozen to a few hundred Germans and their auxiliaries, without chaos or attempts at mass flight.[117] Jews also did not resist because they saw no place left for them to hide (see Chapter 15). In many places, Jews, and also Roma, were rushed to the sites of mass shootings by being beaten with truncheons and whips. Excessive beatings were intended to overcome their resistance and to instil fear in them.[118] This helped to maintain order, which was for the persecutors both an organizational and a psychological need. It also sped up the process.[119] Insofar as it created order and, through it, allowed the process to appear legitimate, brutality was an instrument for justifying the murders.[120] The victims were often too numbed by cruelty and intimidation to break through the thin lines of the persecutors. In the words of one participant in massacres in northern Ukraine, "On the way to the execution site, the victims were totally worn down by various ways of mistreatment."[121] In other places beatings and starvation lasted days. As survivor Leyb Koniuchovsky observed, Lithuanian police "were 'ripening' the Jews so that they would 'die without resistance.'"[122]

However, as in the early days of Treblinka, brutality sometimes also replaced the clear organizational structures of murder.[123] When the ghettos were emptied and Jews were massacred en masse, it was often a far

116 Turan and Dutton 2010, pp. 10–12, for massacres see pp. 8–10, quotes p. 12. For examples citing Jewish survivors see Kassow 2010, p. 494 (on Treblinka); Grossman and Ehrenburg 1994, p. 70 (on Berdichev, Ukraine).

117 For a handful of mass flights on such occasions in eastern Poland in 1942, which often occurred before the start of a planned execution, see Levin 1979, pp. 133–49.

118 For Jews, see, for example, Haase and Oleschinski 1995, p. 37; Alvensleben to Brandt, March 4, 1943, in Longerich 1989, p. 165; for Roma see Holler 2009, p. 56; for overcoming resistance (by Lithuanian militias at Pasvalys on August 26, 1941) see Levinson 2006, p. 113.

119 Welzer 2005, pp. 139, 147, 154, 167.

120 This point was also made by Kühne 2006, p. 152.

121 Interview by Swiss authorities of a twenty-five-year-old Austrian-born NCO who deserted from the German military, end of February 1942, quoted in Haas 1994, p. 140 ("*durch allerlei Misshandlungen* [...] *total mürbe gemacht*").

122 Quoted in Bankier 2011, p. 102, see also p. 136.

123 Berger 2013, pp. 118–19.

from orderly process; these events could be messy and chaotic. Numerous victims were left crying, some escaped, many were left half-dead, while a few shouted for help for days afterwards.[124]

Brutality, humiliation and exposing Jews to degrading living conditions seem also to have served another purpose. Non-Jewish Germans and Jews, or at least assimilated Jews, resembled each other. Both were often from a middle-class background and dressed (when not in service) similarly; and many Jews spoke German or Yiddish, which includes many elements of German. The forms of violence employed were meant to create mental and emotional distance between persecutors and victims. As Theodor Clausen, who commanded a police company in 1941, later described the scene just before a massacre in Riga,

> [Jews were driven forward] as one chases pigs to load them [onto a wagon] or to [bring them to] the slaughter on a ramp. With clubs and kicks and loud noises and with a pistol in hand, the Jews were forced to the execution pit.[125]

Jews were often forced to undress before being shot or gassed – not necessarily to make the killing impersonal[126] but in order to strip them of the hallmarks of civilized society or of their middle-class status.[127] For Franz Stangl, Commandant of Treblinka, Jews were inhuman flesh; for Gustav Münzberger "those naked ones" (*diese Nackten*).[128] The same effect was brought about when, as in the Warsaw ghetto, Jews had to walk around in tatters, for this made victims appear ugly, uniform and, perhaps, ridiculous. For the many Germans who were streaming into the ghettos to watch Jews – mostly in disgust,[129] or gaping at the massacres[130] – this created distance.

People who kill need a moral framework for it. The mass murders were designed to create or reinforce such a framework. In fact, there was more than one such framework. Another, which was in conflict with the one I just mentioned, was in play whenever Himmler, as well as low-level persecutors, emphasized that the work of mass killing was a severe psychological strain. In essence they portrayed these murders as rationally justified albeit against human nature. This attitude also allowed

[124] Grossman and Ehrenburg 1994, pp. 132–3, 444–5, 995–7.
[125] Interrogation of Theodor Clausen, 1963, quoted in Angrick and Klein 2006, p. 88.
[126] For a different interpretation see Welzer 2005, p. 262.
[127] See Mosse 1990, p. 258. In addition, forcing Jews to undress before execution enabled the German authorities to reuse their clothes.
[128] Sereny 1980, pp. 223–4, 250 (quote).
[129] Harvey 2003, p. 131 (Łódź ghetto); Lehnstaedt 2008, pp. 87–8 (Warsaw); one of the few sympathetic accounts of the Warsaw ghetto is found in Blättler 1945, pp. 26–34, 82–5.
[130] Welzer 2005, pp. 133–4; telegram from Müller (RSHA) to the Einsatzgruppen, August 30, 1941, BA R 70 SU/32.

authorities to be supportive and caring in response to the many executors who suffered nervous breakdowns.[131]

Why does this book not analyze methods of violence or killing in more detail? The comparison of violence against a variety of groups suggests caution for the following reasons. First, a wide array of forms of violence were applied to the same group (for example, the Jews in Ukraine[132]). Second, the same method of violence was used against different groups (for example, disabled people, Jews, Soviet POWs, Roma and Polish and Soviet political opponents were all gassed). Third, the same unit or individual might use various methods of violence.[133] Also, inasmuch as people other than those in the killing units determined who was to be killed or deported, and when, the ways in which the killings occurred do not explain the events. All this implies that the methods of violence employed do not necessarily say much about the relationship between perpetrator and victim, and do little to explain why an act of violence took place.[134]

The semi-decentralized character of German violence against Jews and other groups increased its efficiency by leaving room for participation. Many, from almost all walks of life and from most agencies – although not everybody – joined in. The fact that many acted with brutality does not always indicate that they acted under their own initiative, but it does show that they appropriated violence.

131 Himmler to Berger, July 28, 1942, BA NS 19/1772, p. 5; for Himmler's speech at Heydrich's funeral see Gerwarth 2011, p. 246; other examples are in Wildt 2003, pp. 530, 576; for a physician at Auschwitz, see the diary entries of Johann Kremer for September 5 and 12 and for October 18, 1942, in Klee *et al.* 1988, pp. 234, 237–8; for a newspaper article on the "elimination of the Jews" in 1943, see Dörner 2007, p. 179; on anti-partisan warfare see a letter from Knut L. to his mother dated February 19, 1943, in Kilian 2005, p. 272; for the many nervous breakdowns see Welzer 2005, pp. 163 and 291 note 363.

132 See Zabarko 2014, p. 385.

133 See the units mentioned in Chapter 1; for an individual, see the diary of Johann Kremer (August 8–November 24, 1942) in Klee *et al.* 1988, pp. 231–42.

134 Some sociologists and anthropologists hold the opposite view. For example, see von Trotha 1997, esp. pp. 19–20, 24, 26, 35. Attempts to "read" the manifestations and methods of German violence as messages have had relatively limited results. An example is Ingrao 2012, pp. 241–314.

Part II

Logics of persecution

7 Racism and anti-Jewish thought

Nazi ideology is often given a major or overriding importance in explaining the murder of the European Jews.[1] Many scholars see racism and anti-Jewish attitudes at the core of this ideology. Some historians argue that anti-Jewish ideas were necessary or a precondition for extermination but not sufficient to explain it.[2] Some have portrayed hatred of Jews as being at the center of Nazi ideology, in contrast to those who put anti-Judaism in a broader context of racism and social utopias.[3] In fact, "anti-Semitism," though important, does not explain "eugenics, pro-natalism, killing the disabled, militarism, expansionism, or Nazi racial policies aimed at Gypsies, blacks, Slavs, or the 'asocial.' "[4] This chapter takes a closer look at the sometimes surprising inner workings of Nazi and German racist thought in order to locate anti-Jewish sentiments therein and explain differences between racial theory and political practice.

Racism as a form of ascribing a common ancestry to groups, assuming qualitative differences, and justifying social hierarchies among them on that basis, has been known in many cultures and for thousands of years.[5] European 'scientific' racism evolved in the seventeenth century – first as a legitimation of European superiority over non-European peoples, supplemented in the nineteenth century by the idea that large human collectives within Europe differed biologically.[6] In the second half of the 1800s, some degree of racist thought became common among European thinkers.[7] This way of thinking influenced the spread of nationalism in Europe (and beyond), generating something that has been called

1 For example, see Bauer 2001, p. 24.
2 Volkov 1990, p. 57; Holz 2001, pp. 360–3.
3 For the first version see Melson 1992, p. 206, and Bauer 2001, p. 67; for the second view see Pohl 2003, pp. 3–9, and Scheffler 1985, pp. 31–4.
4 Weikart 2009, p. 15.
5 Poliakov 1974, pp. 3, 5; Geiss 1988, pp. 16, 27, 49, 54.
6 Geiss 1988, pp. 15–17, 141–50, 160–2; Weikart 2004, pp. 103–22.
7 Poliakov 1974, pp. 174–5, 230; Geiss 1988, pp. 203, 208–10.

"ethnopolitics,"[8] and certain aspects of such racism have been portrayed as "rebellion against modernity."[9] Racial thinking seemed to provide orientation during a time of social upheaval that was being brought about by industrial capitalism and moral crisis.[10]

According to Nazi-German racists, race membership determined everyday and political life. They explained history as a sequence of struggles among races, for example, over land for sustenance. Increasingly, races were assumed to be of different values, as were the people who belonged to them. Racists ascribed certain mentalities, character traits, patterns of behavior and cultural achievements to each race, usually putting their own race first. In Germany, people of the 'Nordic' race were supposed to be of the highest quality.[11] One German didactical book hierarchically ordered the races as follows: white people over people of color; among whites, Aryans over Jews; and among Aryans, the "Nordic" races over the eastern ones.[12] Accordingly, within Europe Scandinavians (excepting Finns), Dutch, Flemish and the British, respectively, were supposed to have had the greatest amount of influences from the 'Nordic' race and so were called 'Germanic' peoples (an expression that did not belong to race terminology). Racists also correlated with certain races certain bodily features – such as the form of the face, the shape of the skull, skin pigmentation, the color and texture of the hair, eye color, height, the shape of the pelvis, the gaze, posture, style of walking, arm movements, gestures and ways of speaking, but also susceptibility to disease and, possibly, blood type. Such musings concentrated on the features of males, whether they concerned characteristics of Jews or others.[13] Racism stimulated policies that fostered one's own stock by pro-natalist and eugenic programs to improve its own quality while sterilizing or destroying inferior individuals. Territorial expansion was also meant to improve the 'race' by improving its living conditions at the expense of so-called inferior races or peoples with whom one's own people should not mix.[14] Since the eighteenth century there had been a strong intellectual current in

[8] See the interpretation of Bloxham 2009.

[9] Stern 1965, p. 13.

[10] For the notion of a general social, political, intellectual and spiritual crisis, see Rosenberg 1939, pp. 1, 637.

[11] See, for instance, Harten *et al.* 2006, p. 7.

[12] Ibid., p. 15. Many experts and politicians would have disagreed with the final level, seeing a greater variety of races that could be subsumed under 'Aryan'; others thought that the notion of the 'Aryan' was no racial concept at all.

[13] Günther 1937 [1922], pp. 8, 11, 174–8, 185–6; a large part of this book discussed only physical characteristics (pp. 38–157). Regarding Jews see Günther 1930, pp. 209–76; Steinweis 2006, pp. 34–8; Breitenfellner 1998, p. 119 note 19.

[14] Weikart 2009, pp. 8–9.

Europe according to which inferior or uncivilized races would die out in the course of the conquest of the world by the superior white race or races. The former were held to have no right to stand in the way of the latter, who would exploit the resources of their lands for the benefit of all mankind and for its progress.[15] But these discussions made little reference to Jews, at least not until the Nazi takeover.[16]

There were considerable differences among the strands of racist thought. While many believed that race was a matter of biology, inheritance and 'blood,' others held that it was constituted by inheritable common mental dispositions or attitudes, combined with a subjective sense of belonging. In this view the anti-Jewish struggle was above all a spiritual one.[17] During the Nazi period, Nazi ideologist Alfred Rosenberg was the most important representative of this view, although other influential figures also held it, thus requiring compromises when it came to formulating racial ideology.[18]

Racists also thought that social and economic phenomena had their roots in human biology. For Hitler, economic inequality within a nation was natural because of hereditary racial inequality; on the other hand, a thriving economy served to strengthen the population.[19] But the idea that class was based on race was a very old and widespread one; conquests in Asia, Europe and Africa often produced caste-like systems in which the nobility, warriors and clergy tried to remain apart from, and above, other social groups. In France this had led to the theory that the French comprised two nations of which the social elite could trace its roots back to the invading Franks of the early Middle Ages, whereas the lower classes allegedly descended from the Gauls.[20] A similar theory held that people of the 'Nordic' race had once conquered Germany and subjugated the inferior races living there.[21] Race scholar Hans Günther argued that almost every social hierarchy – even those within large businesses – could be explained by racial difference.[22]

Of course there was a dearth of evidence for the existence of races beyond the fact that some people looked a bit different to others. DNA

[15] Grosse 2000, pp. 99–102; van Laak 2005, p. 108.
[16] Weikart 2004, pp. 183–206.
[17] Saller 1961, pp. 36, 79 (on Ludwig Schemann and Fritz Lenz); Stern 1965, pp. 91–2 (on Paul de Lagarde).
[18] Koonz 2006, p. 404; on Rosenberg see Piper 2005, p. 207; Kroll 1998, p. 106. For Hitler's conclusions concerning Jewish religion see Hitler 1999 [1925–27], pp. 306–7.
[19] Weikart 2009, pp. 109, 111, 160; Hitler 1999 [1925–27], p. 339.
[20] Geiss 1988, pp. 16, 49, 53; Holz 2001, pp. 317–18; Kallis 2009, p. 60; Rosenberg 1939, pp. 28, 31.
[21] Harten *et al.* 2006, p. 13.
[22] Günther 1937 [1922], pp. 198–200, 432.

analysis was not available (and, to be sure, it would not have revealed significant differences among ethnic collectives sufficient to confirm the existence of distinct races). What race scholars took instead as evidence to support their theories were stereotypes about the character, behavior and history of ethnicities, now interpreted as characterizing 'races.'[23] There was a circular logic at play: stereotypes were taken to prove that people were influenced by a certain 'race,' and race or certain bodily features were in turn related to some mental characteristics. In this process, the old stereotypes were not subject to revision; rather they were reconfirmed and taken to be lawlike.[24]

Jews in the framework of racist thought

For modern racists, Jews were a race or people of extra European origin. As aliens, they did not belong to the group of European peoples.[25] Already, at the beginning of the nineteenth century, it was argued that Jews could not be integrated and exerted a bad influence on the state, society and culture.[26] With reference to the widespread claim to represent an 'anti-Semitism' of reason,[27] some race scholars held that conflicts between Germans and Jews resulted not from Jewish inferiority but from Jewish otherness. Such specialists could find agreement with Zionists over the idea that a spatial separation was necessary.[28] By contrast, State Secretary Wilhelm Stuckart, who was usually more guarded in his statements, insisted in a 1942 book: "The destruction of the Jews (*Judenvernichtung*) is thus justified not because of their otherness (*Andersartigkeit*) but because of the different quality (*Anderswertigkeit*) of Jewry."[29]

Race scholars alleged that Jews united in themselves the "passion," "hatred" and "cruelty" of the oriental pastoralists, with the "skillfulness, adaptability, cleverness and imperiousness" of the western Asian state founders, and a fanaticism as evidenced in monotheism. One theorist,

[23] See Günther 1937 [1922], pp. 190–243 on the "mental characteristics" of the races in Germany. In Günther 1930, writing about Jews, this part came interestingly before dealing with bodily feature (pp. 20–135), unlike in Günther 1937 [1922].

[24] See also Burleigh 1988, p. 9.

[25] Lösch 1997, p. 282; Saller 1961, pp. 66–8.

[26] Hortzitz 1988, pp. 1–2.

[27] Herbert 1996, pp. 204–13; Rupnow 2006, p. 582; for Hitler see Hilberg 1992a, p. 17.

[28] Steinweis 2006, pp. 39–40 (on Günther); Günther 1937 [1922], p. 449; Günther 1930, pp. 324, 333–43. Some Zionists and Jewish scholars regarded Jews as a race: Niewyk 1980, pp. 129–32; Mosse 1990, pp. 156–9.

[29] Wilhelm Stuckart and Leopold Schiedermair, *Rassen- und Erbpflege in der Gesetzgebung des Dritten Reiches* (Leipzig, 1942), p. 12, quoted in Herbert 1996, p. 286.

however, wrote that "the Jews are, on average, intellectually more gifted than the average of the German population" and ascribed to Jews a "sense of family, a strong cohesion and mutual helpfulness," sobriety, and the willpower, self-confidence, entrepreneurial energy and a "downright master spirit" similar to the Germanic people.[30] Jewish religion and alleged rituals were cited to explain the purported Jewish will to dominate the world and a supposed lack of creativity.[31] Hitler argued that Jews lacked any "idealistic attitude" or spirit of self-sacrifice beyond the immediate family and that they embodied the pure "egoism of the individual" – which their religious teachings displayed. Therefore, they were unable to create culture or build a territorial state.[32] Nazi ideologues also propagated the myth that Jews were responsible for a large proportion of ordinary crime – for example, pickpocketing – and the international drug trade. More sober racists stated that Jews were overrepresented among perpetrators of some kinds of crime, like fraud, but not others such as murder, assault and vandalism. This, too, was explained by the Jewish racial 'character.'[33]

Aside from religious anti-Judaism – the traditional image of 'the Jew' as the murderer of Christ or of Christian children for Jewish rituals – envy and economic prejudice determined traditional anti-Jewish stereotypes, which were themselves updated in the 1930s and 1940s. According to such views, trade and money-lending were parasitic in character, finance capital and large corporations were inspired or led by Jews, and Jewish wealth was gained illegitimately. So-called social anti-Semitism had helped to mobilize workers and small craftsmen against Jews since the late nineteenth century.[34] But the image of 'the Jew' as a cheater, exploiter and parasite was already common in Germany before 1870, and this was combined with notions of Jews being alien or intruders with references to blood and impurity.[35] In 1911, Werner Sombart praised the Jews as creators of capitalism, which he endorsed.[36] For Hitler, the supposed Jewish quest for economic power was fundamental and intertwined with their supposed struggle for political domination.[37] This

[30] Saller 1961, pp. 66–71 (on Fischer and Lenz).
[31] SS-Sturmbannführer Zapp, "Das Judentum" (*c.* January 1941), BA NS 31/252, pp. 1–3.
[32] Hitler 1999 [1925–27], pp. 301–2, 306–7, quote p. 301. Rosenberg's arguments (1939, pp. 265, 362–5) were similar.
[33] Westermann 2005, p. 47 (on Daluege); Müller 2005, p. 88; Günther 1930, pp. 276–80; Steinweis 2006, pp. 138–42.
[34] See Libionka 2004 for Poland. Regarding social anti-Semitism see Aly 2011, pp. 119, 126–36. For Kant's view that Jews were traders and swindlers see Poliakov 1974, p. 172.
[35] See the illuminating linguistic study by Hortzitz 1988, esp. pp. 1–2, 120, 140–3, 148–53, 168–72, 177–81, 184–96, 211–14, 262–73.
[36] Poliakov 1974, p. 286.
[37] Hitler 1999 [1925–27], pp. 309–26.

points to the importance that Nazis assigned to economic reasons for persecuting Jews and shows that anti-Jewish attitudes and economic life (and social life in general) were closely linked for those who were hostile to Jews. In one of his earliest speeches, "Why are we anti-Semites?", Hitler explained this in terms of the concept of labor in order to demonstrate the allegedly destructive character of Jews as well as the 'Jewish' idea of Marxism.[38] Economic anti-Judaism played a big role in other countries too.[39]

According to Hitler, the races fairly sought to kill or subjugate each other in the struggle for land, whereas Jewry, devoid of a state-building capacity and lacking their own land, undertook their "life struggle" through other, quasi unfair means: economic power and parasitism, cunning and ideologies meant to undermine other races and nations. Among their destructive ideas for achieving world domination (allegedly by conspiracy) were equal rights, liberalism, (financial) capitalism and communism; Jews attacked traditional customs, ethics, marriage and the existing elites and nations.[40] Nazi propaganda also listed materialism, individualism, revolution and bourgeois democracy among Jewish-inspired ideas; earlier Jew-haters included aspects of modernity such as urban life.[41] Rosenberg developed the clearest idea why "raceless universalism" ought to be rejected: given the premise that every culture was based on race, culture was bound to communities of blood; of necessity, then, any universal idea was derived from racial mixing and, thus, to be dismissed.[42] According to Hitler, all existing culture was of Aryan origin.[43]

The growing popularity – in many countries – of the idea that Jews were traitors to the nation has been linked to the rise of the nation state.[44] It seemed logical to racists that if Jews did not belong biologically to a nation, then they would either be indifferent toward, and unreliable in pursuit of, that nation's concerns or actively try to undermine it since nationalism was against Jewish interests. This conclusion was in harmony with older claims that many Jews were spies or revolutionaries. Hitler argued that Jews wanted to defile any people, racially, and denationalize it. In part they did so by migrating from country to country. In the time of German anti-Jewish violence, the idea that Jews were alien to

[38] A comprehensive analysis can be found in Holz 2001, pp. 367–94.
[39] For Romania after 1945 see Glass 2001, p. 157.
[40] Hitler 1961, pp. 220–3; see also Jäckel 1997, pp. 102–6. See also Hitler 1999 [1925–27], p. 304.
[41] See Saller 1961, pp. 129–30; Stern 1965, esp. pp. 13, 185; Hitler 1961 [1928], p. 62.
[42] Rosenberg 1939, esp. pp. 33 (quote), 70–1, 120.
[43] Hitler 1999 [1925–27], pp. 290–2.
[44] Almog 1990, esp. p. 86; Holz 2001.

their nation led to views such as the one that reprisals in France should be directed only against Jews and alleged agents of the Soviet Union (e.g., communists) in order to counter British propaganda claims that a *French* resistance existed.[45] The idea that communism was inspired by Jews was widespread. The Jewish backgrounds of revolutionary leaders in Soviet Russia, Hungary, Germany and Austria seemed to be evidence of this. Nazis thought communism was the final stage of a Jewish plot to dominate the world. Working-class internationalism seemed to be directed not only against the 'natural' system of nation states but, at the same time, against private property and, thus, the essence of the internal social order of states.[46]

Such ways of thinking were also developed, even in smaller countries, far beyond the mere adoption or parroting of German ideas.[47] These lines of thinking included the belief that Jews manipulated international politics and certain governments, especially the Soviet Union and the USA but also the United Kingdom and France.[48] Moreover, there was supposed to be a Jewish world conspiracy or "Jewish international" that had united capitalists and communists. The best known such invention, "The Protocols of the Elders of Zion," found an eager reception shortly after World War I, when the belief in the political power of Jews was at its peak.[49] If propaganda against Jews persisted in a certain area after most of them had been killed, it was as a result of the assumption that Jews were still behind Soviet communism, exerted influence in enemy countries, and were behind the military efforts against Germany. Continuing propaganda either served to remind Germans and its subjugated people of these supposed facts, or it was addressed to foreigners in enemy countries.[50] According to these views the destruction of the Jews was a "world

[45] Holz 2001, p. 406 (on Hitler); Kletzin 1996, p. 238 (on the German envoy in France, Otto Abetz).

[46] Nova 1986, pp. 103–24 (on Rosenberg); Hitler 1982, p. 279 (February 17, 1942); Almog 1990, pp. 49, 79–81.

[47] Witt 2012, esp. pp. 323–7, 425–44, on Slovakia; Libionka 2004, pp. 15–35, on the Polish clergy.

[48] Hitler's Reichstag speech, December 11, 1941, in Verhandlungen des Reichstags 1986, p. 104; article by Seibert, *Völkischer Beobachter*, November 12, 1941, BA NS 22/567, p. 1.

[49] Kroll 1998, pp. 300–1; article by Seibert, *Völkischer Beobachter*, November 12, 1941, BA NS 22/567, p. 1. See Battenberg 1990, pp. 233–7; Almog 1990, p. 99. For the Jewish world conspiracy in general see Meyer zu Uptrup 2003; Friedländer 1998, pp. 182–4; Friedländer 2006, p. 586. For earlier comments on internationally operating Jewish organizations like B'nai Brith or the Alliance Israélite in the nineteenth century as an international conspiracy see Stern 1965, p. 92; Geiss 1988, p. 232.

[50] This is obvious from material such as Himmler to Kaltenbrunner, May 19, 1943, in Berenstein *et al.* 1961, pp. 357–8; *Deutscher Wochendienst*, anti-Jewish special, May 21, 1943, in Mathieu 1981, esp. the facsimile after p. 294; on German-controlled anti-Jewish propaganda in the Crimea see Tyaglyy 2004, esp. pp. 430, 432, 437, 442; for Orel see Herzstein 1989, esp. pp. 36–7, 48. Tyaglyy's interpretation of his material (pp. 441–4) differs from mine.

problem," as Goebbels wrote in 1943, not "naive revenge schemes" but a matter of survival.[51] It has been generally observed that most German press articles about Jews during World War II concerned enemy countries.[52] Nazis also thought it necessary to continue serious, interdisciplinary research about Jews in order to 'enlighten' people on the issue. To this end, enormous amounts of plundered material were collected, a museum was founded in Prague and a library established at the Institute for Research on the Jewish Question in Frankfurt to make it accessible. In 1943 the library's organizers called it the largest collection of books specializing in Jewish studies in the world, which, with over half a million volumes, it actually may have been at that time.[53]

Jews were sometimes supposed to be so powerful and so opposed to the vital interests of others that they were portrayed as a "counter-race."[54] This implied that they were enemies of every other race and sought to undermine and topple the governments of every state.[55] Other scholars argue that, given the supposed racial inferiority of the lower strata of their own country's population and the people of neighboring countries, German racists did not really need the Jew as a bogeyman.[56] Hitler sometimes stated that phenomena of degeneration like overpopulation, urbanization, the lack of racial pride and declining cultural values were not caused by Jews but were used by them after they emerged.[57] In *Mein Kampf* he demanded "extreme and brutal" measures against criminals and the sterilization of disabled people. On the other hand, he said that the world was heading toward a decisive battle between Aryans and Jews in which Germany would be the crucial battleground.[58] In any case, it is important to note that German racists concerned themselves with race problems unrelated to Jews, which are not accounted for in a simple "binary formula" of Germans versus Jews;[59] and that they imagined the

[51] Press article by Goebbels, May 9, 1943, quoted in StA KG Berlin 1 Js 1/65, indictment, April 23, 1971, p. 409.

[52] Gellately 2002, pp. 205–6.

[53] See Rupnow 2000; Piper 2005, p. 479. For the serious (though, of course, not unbiased) character of Jewish studies under Nazism see Rupnow 2006, esp. pp. 542, 575; Harten *et al.* 2006, pp. 29–31.

[54] See Schulle 2001, p. 67, on Hitler; Rosenberg 1939, p. 464. Günther 1930 (p. 206) rejected the concept of "counter-race" since he did not consider Jews to be a race.

[55] Harten *et al.* 2006, p. 267.

[56] Essner 1995, p. 204.

[57] Hitler 1961 [1928], pp. 62, 66, 129.

[58] Hitler 1999 [1925–27], pp. 427, 623.

[59] Traverso 2003 (pp. 138, 145) advocates such a formula. Note the scarce material presented where Poliakov 1974 (pp. 272–7) depicted "[r]acial [m]anichaeism," especially when it comes specifically to "Aryans" versus Jews. For the concept of racial manichaeism in historiography see Geiss 1988, p. 56.

struggle against Jews to take place in a world ridden also by other conflicts. For racists, even murdering all of the Jews would not necessarily achieve racial purity or redemption.[60] For a politician like Wilhelm Frick, the Nazi takeover in 1933 was thus just the beginning of a complex process of ethnic, or 'racial,' renewal.[61] For Himmler, the extermination of the Jews was not "his final political goal" but the "point of departure for much more comprehensive plans to create a bloody 'new order' on the European continent."[62] It may be true that for Germans with an anti-Jewish outlook in the late nineteenth century, action against Jews promised to solve all of society's problems,[63] but this no longer applied to the Nazi Party in and after 1933. It is essential to understand that the Nazis were successful only because they were *not* monothematic. They became attractive to a variety of population groups as they developed policies for a wide range of social issues reaching from a viable farming sector to economic recovery, public health and tourism. It was because they pushed such policy issues that they were able to celebrate election victories in 1932–33 when Nazi anti-Jewish propaganda was reduced. After 1933 they tried to put into practice all of these policies, which were connected with their biologistic views but far from limited to the Jewish issue.

Contrary to the common view, but also to some of Hitler's speeches, many Nazi racists believed that Jews were not a race at all but rather a mixture of races, though an 'alien' one. In Germany, this idea came about in the 1880s. From around 1920 to 1921 (shortly before Hitler wrote *Mein Kampf*), this was the dominant view among German race scientists.[64] The Nazi Party's Racial Policy Office cited this notion in December 1941 to justify the mandatory marking of Jews in Germany with a yellow star, their complex racial mix making many of them otherwise not easy to recognize.[65] Other influential scholars defended the position that Jews did constitute a race because they had amalgamated their mix of Oriental, West Asian, Inner Asian, Negroid, Hamitic, Western, Eastern, Nordic, and Eastern Baltic races into a new cohesive formulation.[66]

60 For the concept of redemptive anti-Semitism see Friedländer 1998, pp. 73–112.
61 Koonz 2007, p. 103.
62 Longerich 2008, p. 770.
63 Rürup 1975, p. 91.
64 Lösch 1997, p. 280; Günther 1930, pp. 11, 13, 281–3; Essner 2002, p. 43; Ehrenreich 2007, p. 3.
65 Saller 1961, p. 129.
66 See Saller 1961 (pp. 66–8) about Eugen Fischer (1938). According to Günther 1930 (pp. 203–6), Jews had not fused again into a race following many racial influences upon them throughout history (see pp. 191, 228).

One consequence of the assumption that Jews were enormously influential, intelligent, and, in some ways, superior[67] – which was expressed already before 1850 – was the idea that an anti-Jewish attitude was a matter of self-defense,[68] which lent that attitude a special air of urgency and aggressiveness. Some racists argued that Germany's prospects for racial salvation were not good.[69] Thus, they imagined that the struggle against the Jews was a fight for existence, or at least crucial in the fight against racial decline.[70] This theory was emphasized at important points during World War II – which had allegedly been imposed on Germany by Jews – and during the mass destruction of Jews. In November 1943, Himmler declared: "We had the moral right, we had the duty before our people to kill this people that wanted to kill us."[71] He continued that German individuals had no right to plunder Jewish possessions, for, he argued, that would be a victory for the Jewish spirit.[72] Here he was borrowing from the concept of a racial spirit. It was not only Himmler's belief that Jewish influence reached beyond the physical existence of Jews. Jews had allegedly developed many concepts – such as liberalism, communism, internationalism and universal human rights – that would not be automatically destroyed if all of them were killed. In the summer of 1942 such thinking even led SS journalist Gunter d'Alquen, unsuccessfully, to demand the nationalization of the retail trade in Germany because, he argued, it was usually "inferior" people who had the "trader's instinct," which was mentally alien to, and inappropriate for, Germans.[73]

Because Jews were blamed for many of modernity's different evils, "anti-Semitism" has been called a "cultural code"; that is, a *chiffre* for anti-modern sentiments. Shulamit Volkov sees a "common pattern of values and norms" in the desire of many Germans by the late nineteenth century for a "recreation of a folk community in harmony and justice." This desire was usually combined with fierce nationalism, expansionism, militarism, economic protectionism and, increasingly, with the rejection of bourgeois democracy, trade unions and urban life.[74]

67 For Gobineau's and Nietzsche's (temporary) ideas of Jewish superiority see Poliakov 1974, pp. 235–6, 300. Geiss 1988 (p. 169) regarded Gobineau's view as less enthusiastic.

68 Almog 1990, pp. 25 (about Marr and Wagner), 99; Battenberg 1990 (on Fichte); Piper 2005, pp. 64, 66, 72 (on Rosenberg).

69 Saller 1961, p. 75 (on Fritz Lenz).

70 Steinweis 2006, pp. 69, 73.

71 Himmler's speech to high-ranking SS officers, November 4, 1943, IMG, vol. 29, p. 146. See Hitler's declaration, December 19, 1941, BA-MA RS 3/6–7, p. 275; Stuckart's rationale for the murder of Jews from Berlin on December 19, 1941, according to Lösener: Jasch 2012, pp. 362–3, see also pp. 400–1.

72 Himmler's speech, November 4, 1943, IMG, vol. 29, p. 146.

73 Ingrao 2012, pp. 167–8.

74 Volkov 1990, pp. 20 (quotes), 22–3, 32, 50–1, 64. See also Jochmann 1988a, pp. 52, 83–4.

Anti-Jewish sentiments were part of this attitude, but the hatred of Jews became important as an emblem for the rejection of all of these notions. "Anti-Semitism" literally rejected not Jews but "Semitism" – i.e., certain alleged principles and character traits of 'Semites.'[75] Thinking that Jews were responsible for liberalism, capitalism, freemasonry and socialism was not restricted to Nazis; it was, for example, also common among European Catholic clergy from the late nineteenth to the mid-twentieth century.[76] Among Nazis and others opposed to Jews there was not a single, separate line of thought called anti-Semitism isolated from (and in contradiction to) all other issues of culture, politics, society and economics. On the contrary, if anti-Jewish sentiments functioned as a cultural code, then their very essence was their intimate and inextricable connection with what Nazis and other Jew-haters saw as real life.[77] Realizing this is fundamental to understanding why the organizers and executors of mass murder could later link violence against Jews to political, social, economic and cultural interests.

Contrary to Marxism (despite all its schisms), however, Nazism never generated "a uniform world view" with a theoretically sound basis or a strict doctrine.[78] This is not surprising, for "if heredity alone enabled a man to act as an Aryan should, education and indoctrination could, in logic, achieve very little."[79] As the Nazi mentor Alfred Rosenberg commented, "The new world view is no dogma, but an inner attitude," and as SS-Obersturmführer Georg Wolff, an SD officer in occupied Oslo, put it, "A world view can neither be learned nor taught, it must rather be experienced."[80] In Nazi pedagogy, abstract learning counted for little compared to a holistic understanding of one's experience, including one's own action.[81] Nonetheless, there was a substantial amount of ideological indoctrination in SS, police and army units.[82] For the general audience there were training courses, exhibitions, information sheets, propaganda plays, films, and slide shows, presentations in schools, calendars and

75 Volkov 1990, pp. 21, 27 (quote), 28.

76 Schlemmer and Woller 2005, p. 171 (for Italy); Libionka 2004 (for Poland); Volkov 1990, p. 65 (for France).

77 Pulzer 1966 (p. 24) also makes this argument. See excerpts of a radio program with Nazi ideologue Walter Frank, January 11 and 13, 1939, in Pätzold 1984, p. 213.

78 Rupnow 2006, pp. 579–80.

79 Cecil 1972, p. 145.

80 Rosenberg, "Weltanschauliche Thesen," July 1939, quoted in Zellhuber 2006, p. 19 note 63 (a similar quote from 1940 is in Westermann 2005, p. 108); Wolff's report about the political situation in Norway in 1941 can be found in Ugelvik Larsen 2008, p. 566. See also Rosenberg 1939, p. 78.

81 See Neumann 2010, pp. 24–5, 28, 186; Nyssen 1979.

82 Matthäus *et al.* 2003; Westermann 2005, pp. 92–123; Rass 2003, pp. 307–30.

radio programs.[83] But it would be strange for us to think that *what* was taught – i.e., ideology – was static or unchangeable. In many regards, what is called Nazi ideology was in reality subject to change, tactical alterations and obstacles. It was also incoherent, contradictory, vague and flexible, and thus compatible with popular ethnic stereotypes.

Racial mixing everywhere – and its consequences

In the 1920s, when Nazism emerged, and in the 1930s, when it came to power, knowledge of historical migrations, intermarriages and sexual mixing resulted in the view that there were no longer any pure races. The population of each nation was supposed to be a racial mixture, as were most individuals.[84] This meant that there was neither a German nor an Aryan race and no Jewish race either, as most German race scholars agreed.[85] According to this view the Germans and the Jews were peoples, not races. The political implications of this sort of racial thinking were profound and complex.

Racial mixing was supposed to have accelerated in the nineteenth century, particularly in cities.[86] The assumptions and terminology varied somewhat, but most argued that the German people consisted of the so-called Nordic, Western (also dubbed Mediterranean), Eastern, Falian, Eastern Baltic, and Dinarian races.[87] The view that all nations were of mixed race was not entirely unchallenged; some Italian race scholars held, contrary to Mussolini, that there was an Italian race (which included elements of most of the historic ethnicities in the country except for the Jewish one). With this they wanted to counter the concept of the Nordic race, which put Italians in a bad light.[88] In Sweden the view that there was a "Swedish race" was popular, although it lacked a contemporary anthropological basis.[89] Similarly, some German scholars who assumed that historical and environmental influences constantly reshaped races, postulated the existence of a German race; but they were silenced in the early years of Nazi rule.[90] On October 24, 1934, the Nazi Party's Racial Policy Office announced as the official Party line that no German race

83 Harten *et al.* 2006, pp. 43–4 (on Thuringia).
84 See Günther 1937 [1922], pp. 17, 261; Saller 1961, p. 42.
85 Essner 1995, pp. 204, 221; Conte and Essner 1995, pp. 70, 93.
86 Günther 1937 [1922], p. 423.
87 Günther 1937 [1922], pp. 22–5; Seidler and Rett 1982, pp. 49–58.
88 See Saller 1961, p. 94; Schlemmer and Woller 2005, p. 180; Kallis 2009, pp. 68–70; Michaelis 1978, pp. 152–3, 171, 181, 324–30. For Mussolini see Saller 1961, p. 13.
89 Frykman 2000, pp. 220, 224.
90 Saller 1961, pp. 38, 45; Schulle 2001, pp. 149–50.

existed and that the Germans were a "racial mixture."[91] If there *was* a doctrine in Nazi racism, this was it. Regarding Jews, accordingly, the official comment on the Nuremberg racial laws by Wilhelm Stuckart and Hans Globke stated that there was no Jewish race, and, so, this term did not appear in these laws.[92] Thus, this was more than a matter of theory only; it had practical implications. And, it was propagated: a contemporary photograph shows the leading Nazi ideologist Alfred Rosenberg at a Hitler Youth meeting sitting in front of a poster featuring portrait photographs under the caption: "Images of German races."[93]

Influential figures in racist thought – for example Joseph Arthur de Gobineau, Friedrich Nietzsche and Friedrich Ratzel – had voiced relatively early the opinion that there were no pure races. Houston Stewart Chamberlain had argued that most peoples, including Slavs and Jews, were racial mixes.[94] Moreover, these mixtures were not supposed to be favorable even in countries of the north. In Norway and Sweden, countries whose populations were supposed to be of a relatively pure and valuable racial nature, racists thought that there were few people of "one hundred percent Nordic race."[95] Hans Günther asserted in 1920 that only 6% of all Germans were purely of Nordic race, although Nordic blood was supposed to make up half of the German mix; and a German publication during Nazism stated that no more than 40% of German military officers during World War I had been of the "Nordic race."[96]

Important Nazi leaders agreed that the German people were a racial mixture. Reich Minister of the Interior Wilhelm Frick and his State Secretary, Wilhelm Stuckart, publicly said so. Himmler had believed this since 1924. Otto Ohlendorf, a former commander of an Einsatzgruppe, also held this opinion.[97] Hitler, too, stated at different points in time that Germans, Americans and also Jews were racial mixtures and occasionally displayed a working knowledge of then current racist theory;[98] but his statements on the subject were contradictory. In February 1945

[91] Quoted in Saller 1961, pp. 84–5.

[92] Steinweis 2006, p. 44; Essner 1995, p. 221.

[93] Printed in Cecil 1972, plates prior to p. 134 ("Bilder deutscher Rassen").

[94] For Nietzsche, see Poliakov 1974, pp. 71–2; for Gobineau see Poliakov 1974, pp. 236–7 and Kallis 2009, p. 60; for Chamberlain see Poliakov 1974, p. 316 and Schaller 2002, pp. 96, 98–9; for Ratzel see Smith 1986, p. 152.

[95] Abrahamsen 1991, p. 50, citing Dr Jon Alfred Mjoen.

[96] Hermann Römpp, *Vererbungslehre und Rassenkunde für Jedermann* (Stuttgart, 1933), pp. 23, 26, cited in Neumann 2010, p. 31; for Günther see Harten *et al.* 2006, p. 11.

[97] For Frick (1934) see Neliba 1992, p. 225; for Stuckart see Jasch 2012, p. 42; for Himmler see Ackermann 1970, p. 36; for Ohlendorf see Ingrao 2012, p. 168.

[98] Weikart 2009, pp. 65 (for 1944), 144; for 1944 see also Steinert 1970, p. 601; Hitler 1961 [1928], for example, pp. 124, 126, 131, 220; Conte and Essner 1995, p. 106 (August 1933); Hitler 1982, p. 293 (February 22, 1942).

he seems to have admitted to Bormann that the Jews were not a race "from the genetic point of view" but rather "a racially and spiritually cohesive group."[99] In reference to racial mixing he told the head of the Nazi Party's Office for Race Policy in September 1935 that "no completely satisfying solution" existed for the so-called Jewish problem.[100] In *Mein Kampf*, Hitler did not clarify whether Jews were of mixed race, but described Jews alternately as a "people" and a "race."[101] The same was true for his speeches and other public utterances.[102] SS men were taught that Jews were a racial mix that included some Nordic blood.[103] General Governor Hans Frank said publicly that Jews were a race mix (of Asian origin) – as Roland Freisler had already argued in 1933.[104] It was Rosenberg, the second chief Party ideologue, arguing on the basis of supposed psychological characteristics rather than biology, who classified Jews unambiguously as a race, not as a people.[105]

Unsurprisingly, race scholars felt compelled to admit that "we don't know much yet about [the] effects of racial mixing," but they usually assumed that when Europeans received the blood of members of supposedly inferior non-European races through intermixing, it led to cultural decline.[106] To some scientists, only mixes among more or less European races were acceptable. Eugen Fischer, for example, argued in February 1933 that persons of mixed but related racial heritage, or from "mixed zones," could achieve great cultural and moral accomplishments. By contrast, Hitler argued that intra-European mixing also led to decline.[107] Hitler, like Gobineau, thought that racial mixing was a ubiquitous fact that threatened the existence of mankind. For Hitler it was precisely the racially heterogeneous nature of the German people – its "blood-related disrupted condition due to [its] superior and inferior racial elements," even beyond the influences of Jewish or African genes – that had problematic consequences for the

99 Genoud, n.d. However, the authenticity of this material is a matter of controversy.

100 Quoted in Koonz 2007, p. 185.

101 "Race": Hitler 1999 [1925–27], pp. 150, 232, 307, 315, 661; "people": Hitler 1999 [1925–27], pp. 56, 300; for "race" and "people" on the same page see pp. 301, 306.

102 For "race" see Domarus 1962–63, pp. 249 (March 28, 1933), 729 (September 19, 1937), 1867 (April 26, 1942); for "people" see also pp. 537 (September 15, 1935), 2237 ("political testament," April 29, 1945); for both see pp. 1056–7 (January 30, 1939).

103 Ackermann 1970, pp. 159–60 note 13.

104 General Governor's log, January 21, 1941, in Präg and Jacobmeyer 1975, p. 330. For Freisler see Essner 2002, p. 97.

105 Rosenberg 1939, pp. 464–5, see also p. 637.

106 Eugen Fischer, *Die Rehebother Bastards und das Bastardisierungsproblem beim Menschen* (Jena, 1913), cited in Gründer 1999, p. 292; Lösch 1997, pp. 67, 72.

107 Lösch 1997, pp. 231–3; for a similar view of the economist and sociologist Werner Sombart see Harten *et al.* 2006, p. 217. See Hitler 1999 [1925–27], pp. 285–6, 289.

German national character and was responsible for the "extraordinary extremes [...] in the life of our people." Already in *Mein Kampf*, he had stated that the fact that Germans were a racial mix had led to a lack of inner cohesion and their failure to form a unified nation state as well as to "hyper-individualism." These divisions had, at least, preserved many purely "Nordic" individuals.[108] But in practice, intermarriage and mixing between Germans of the different 'related' races, which were supposed to be prevalent in Germany, encountered no obstacle in Nazi Germany. Purist objections remained marginal.[109] Still, when Hitler propagated the German 'people's community,' he did so on the assumption that it did not exist and thus needed to be created.[110] Inner differences also implied that the German people were not necessarily united in fighting the Jews.

The idea of Aryanism and inner contradictions of racial thought

Leading racist scholars like Hans Günther rejected the idea that there was an Aryan race. For them, 'Aryan' was a term that belonged to linguistics.[111] As a result, the term 'Aryan' was neither used in the Nuremberg racial laws nor in many other relevant Nazi laws starting in the second half of 1933.[112] Historically, the European idea of Aryanism had emerged from structural similarities between Indian and European languages that were discovered in the late eighteenth century. Through much of the nineteenth century, the theory of an Indo-Germanic language spurred imaginings that there were also relations of blood among most European and Indian peoples; and some, such as the Iranians, who were in between. This 'Aryan' family of people was supposed to exclude, for example, 'Semites' like Arabs and Jews and 'Asian' peoples like Turks, Hungarians or Sami (Lapps).[113] The Aryan myth had been in decline since the late nineteenth century,[114] but, on a popular level, ideas persisted that

108 Hitler 1961 [1928], p. 126; Hitler 1999 [1925–27], pp. 395–7. On another occasion, however, Hitler stated that Germany was racially relatively homogenous, a claim used to justify Germany's future expansion: Hossbach's protocol of a meeting between Hitler and military leaders on November 5, 1937, IMG, vol. 25, pp. 403–4. For Gobineau see Poliakov 1974, pp. 236–7.

109 See Seidler and Rett 1982, pp. 65–75.

110 For differing views on the existence of a people's community see Bajohr and Wildt 2009; Gailus and Nolzen 2011.

111 Günther 1937 [1922], p. 358; Günther 1930, p. 14; see Poliakov 1974 (pp. 213–14) for the linguist Max Müller's view in 1872.

112 Rürup 1975, p. 112; Ehrenreich 2007, pp. 9–10, 166.

113 See Poliakov 1974.

114 Poliakov 1974, p. 327.

relatively close relations existed among certain (European) races, and so did the (often non-official) use of the term 'Aryan.' Hitler used the term in his book, *Mein Kampf*, without defining it or reflecting on it. In his later speeches he talked about "Aryan peoples," "Aryan peoples and races" and "European-Aryan peoples" interchangeably.[115]

Explications of who was supposed to be Aryan, if that concept was used, differed slightly. Addressing the diplomatic corps in 1934, Minister of the Interior Frick stated that all "non-Jewish members of all European peoples" were Aryan. Poles were defined as Aryan, but "gypsies" and "Negroes" were not.[116] The view that Poles were Aryans can be found in documents of occupation authorities, and non-Jewish Poles were told as much.[117] The former applied to Slavs in general – Russians, Ukrainians, Belorussians and Serbs – whom earlier theorists also considered Aryan.[118]

The fact that 'Aryan' was a popular buzzword, but expressed no definite concept, is underlined by racists' widely varying and ambivalent assessments of Slavs.[119] Slavs, of course, were not supposed to be a race.[120] Even important Nazi politicians-cum-ideologues did not agree on how to evaluate them: Himmler, who wanted Germany to lead a struggle against Asia, advocated radical policies against Slavs and racial screenings of them, but he also had Slavic (and Asiatic) ethnicities recruited into the Waffen-SS; whereas Rosenberg viewed certain Slavic peoples as potential allies who should be allowed a separate, appropriate, segregated and dependent development.[121] Erich Koch had praised the "young peoples of the East" prior to 1933, even proposing "racial mixing" between Prussians and Slavs, and he saw positive aspects of Soviet society as late as 1939–41, before turning to brutal racist oppression as the Reich Commissar for Ukraine.[122] Like Hitler, many Nazi leaders had said little (and little negative) about Slavs in their early writings.[123] The general view in Germany was that the Slavs were a mixture of races.

115 Hitler 1999 [1925–27], esp. pp. 640, 644; Domarus 1962–63, pp. 1828–9 (January 30, 1942), 1844 (February 24, 1942), 1920 (September 30, 1942).

116 Neliba 1992, p. 224; Kundrus 2009, p. 111. For a different view see Kallis 2009, pp. 81–2.

117 Governor of Warsaw district, bimonthly report, October 15, 1942, AIPN NTN 53, p. 138; diary of Zygmunt Klukowski, December 20, 1939 and April 23, 1942, in Klukowski 1993, pp. 62, 193.

118 Anderson 2000, p. 347; Essner 1995, p. 210 (Freisler 1934); Manoschek 1993, p. 36 (for Serbs). For theorists see Saller 1961 (Schemann); Holz 2001, p. 321 (Gobineau); Geiss 1988, p. 173 (Chamberlain).

119 See, for instance, Connelly 1999, pp. 20, 28.

120 Günther 1937 [1922], pp. 5–6.

121 Kroll 1998, pp. 117–18, 164–5, 193, 214, 222–6; see also Piper 2005, pp. 49–51.

122 Fuhrer and Schön 2010, p. 63 (quotes), 74.

123 Broszat 1965, p. 12; Connelly 1999, p. 3.

The Polish people were supposed to consist of the same races as the Germans, although in a different mixture. Russians were said to have also incorporated Mongol blood.[124] Anti-Slav prejudices were old and widespread in Germany but they were also displayed, for example, by Italian diplomats.[125] Yet some scholars argue that in German academia views hostile to Slavs were only infrequently expressed. Apparently, no general Nazi guidelines for Slavic philology or eastern European history existed.[126] In a 1944 propaganda brochure entitled "What are we fighting for?" the Supreme Command of the Ground Forces omitted explicit anti-Slavic arguments, listing Jews, Bolshevism, the USA and England as Germany's main enemies.[127]

Given all these inconsistencies, old prejudices – also cultivated by intellectuals – influenced German policies strongly. According to these attitudes, Slavs were uncultured, stupid, alcoholic, disorderly and undisciplined. During the Weimar Republic they were also portrayed as treacherous, brutal and revengeful.[128] In Germany after 1939, when large numbers of Polish forced laborers were used, Poles were portrayed as lazy, undisciplined, envious, hateful, revengeful, and as only pretending to be subservient, and their country was described as pre-industrial.[129] Even to writer Heinrich Böll, an admirer of Russian literature, Russia appeared "sad and vast and demonic, the country without fences."[130] Racists held that Slavs were incapable of sustained state-building and of bringing order to environments. On the one hand, the old stereotypes allowed for the publication shortly after the German-Soviet non-aggression treaty in 1939 of a relatively respectful brochure on Soviet Russia that described the Russians' national character as natural, friendly, pious, down-to-earth, passionate, adaptable, and ambitious though non-achieving; but on the other hand it did emphasize some negative elements of prejudice by adding that Russians were also passive, melancholic and devoid of individual personalities.[131] And even

124 Banse 1939, pp. 8, 12, 15; Blatman 2011, p. 74. Only a few race experts saw 'Mongoloid' traces also among Poles (Harten *et al.* 2006, p. 281), Günther 1937 [1922], pp. 162–3, also among Germans.

125 Burgwyn 2005, p. 7; for the popular view in Germany see Furber 2004, pp. 549–50; Connelly 1999, pp. 20, 23.

126 Schaller 2002, pp. 16, 20, 66, 109, 286, 289.

127 Lieb 2007, p. 136.

128 Borejsza 1989, pp. 57–8; Burleigh 1988, pp. 3–4; von Zitzewitz 1992, pp. 25, 31, 52–5. However, the same author (pp. 37–9, 182–4, 225) argues that before World War I the German image of the Pole shifted to the positive in some periods.

129 Hansch-Singh 1991, pp. 129–32.

130 Letter from Heinrich to Annemarie Böll, November 6, 1943, in Böll 2001, p. 942.

131 Banse 1939, pp. 15–28. See also Rosenberg 1939, pp. 113, 206–14, on the Russians.

during the ongoing German war against Poland in 1939, Hitler publicly praised the bravery of Polish soldiers.[132] Thus, Aryanism and, so, racist thinking itself, to a degree had room for such contradictory evaluations. Nevertheless, after 1943 calls for treating the Slavs well, and the 'Europe versus Bolshevism' propaganda, were rarely justified by reference to Slavs' positive 'racial' value.

German anti-Slavic racism was also the basis for extreme forms of racist dehumanization.[133] For it was not only Bolsheviks, commissars and Jews against whom the concept of the "subhuman" was employed, but also the Soviet people collectively.[134] To be sure, this term was also applied to German criminals and people of supposedly low intelligence as well as 'Negroes' and 'Mongoloids.'[135]

Disunity between racist concepts feeding into contradictions between policies and racism

For a number of reasons, not all policies in Nazi Germany could be reconciled with racist thought. One was theoretical; 'experts' on race could not agree on many aspects of their subject, their political influence was limited, and political mechanisms as well as Nazi thinking worked against the development of rigid dogma. Also, political necessities often overrode racist ideas; or the latter, facilitated by the often-flexible character of prevailing ideas, turned out to be malleable when conditions required it. And, sometimes, finding racist thinking unconvincing, relevant groups of the population acted against it.

Not even leading Nazi politician-ideologues, who all hated Jews, agreed on the reasons why. This disagreement stemmed from their different conceptions of race. Hitler considered the main problem with the Jews to be a biologically founded inability to create culture and a territorial state, which made them embark on special strategies to subjugate landed peoples by introducing or manipulating certain ideas. By contrast, Rosenberg deduced Jewish inferiority from their religion, their lack of any metaphysical characteristics and their arrogance at being, as they believed, God's chosen people; for R. Walther Darré, history was a struggle between farming and nomadic races, of which Jews were only one

[132] See Schenk 2000, p. 137.
[133] For Himmler's views see Ackermann 1970, pp. 206–22.
[134] MadR 199, July 3, 1941, p. 2473; Müller 2005, pp. 50–2; for the SS brochure "Der Untermensch" of 1942, 4 million copies of which were distributed, see Gerlach 1999, pp. 100–1.
[135] See the undated propaganda sketches "The Menace of the Subhuman" in Burleigh and Wippermann 1991, p. 169; Saller 1961, pp. 109–14.

but one that helped bring about financial and trade capitalism; perhaps Himmler concentrated more on the perceived fight between Europe and Asia than on the Jews; for Goebbels, who may have lacked any systematic ideas of race or the forces that determined history, Jews had to be opposed as the force behind bourgeois ideas and practices and enemy powers (including, for him, communism).[136]

The German institutes for Jewish research were scattered, marginal and in conflict with each other.[137] In 1934, Rudolf Hess, Hitler's deputy as head of the Nazi Party, commissioned Walter Gross to found the Racial Policy Office of the Nazi Party in order to "standardize and popularize Nazi racial thinking"; but Gross failed to achieve the first of these two goals. This repeated the failure of the Committee of Experts for Population and Racial Policy, established by Frick in June 1933 and which included Himmler, R. Walther Darré, Reich Health Leader Gerhard Wagner, the racial expert Fritz Lenz and others. The debates in what Claudia Koonz has characterized as a conceptual crisis in Nazi racial policies ended in part inconclusively.[138] The compromises among different factions on, for example, what role the so-called Nordic race played and whether inherited features were automatically racial features, as Günther argued, remained partial and fragile.[139]

Contrary to authors who assert that racial research was directly and seamlessly put into effect through Nazi policies, Koonz argues that scholarship provided the idea and "rationale" for persecution and killings but not a clear framework, and this left room for the actions of officials and the general public.[140] Indeed, the absence of a rigorous racist doctrine facilitated changes and turns in racist-inspired policies. Before 1933, Nazis had made few statements about Poland, and from 1934 to 1939, when Germany was allied with Poland, anti-Polish research and propaganda were almost non-existent. But these flourished during the tensions of 1939 and the following war and occupation. Nazi propaganda then fell back on old stereotypes. Such reversals had a long tradition

[136] Kroll 1998, pp. 48–53, 118–23, 164–6, 214, 259, 282, 293–4, 300–1; see also Hitler 1961, pp. 220–3; Rosenberg 1939, pp. 362–5, 463. For Goebbels see also Longerich 2010, pp. 570–8, 686. For differences among notorious nineteenth-century German Jew-haters, see Volkov 1990, p. 61.

[137] See Steinweis 2006, pp. 10–14; Schiefelbein n.d.

[138] Koonz 2006, pp. 402–10; Rost 1992, p. 47; for the committee, see Burleigh and Wippermann 1991, p. 57.

[139] Essner 1995, esp. p. 204; see also Saller 1961, esp. pp. 50, 55, and Steinweis 2006, p. 157, who sees, however, "consensus [among scholars] when it came to the substance and direction of Nazi anti-Jewish policies."

[140] Koonz 2006, pp. 419 (quote), 422. For the first view see Burleigh and Wippermann 1991, pp. 50–6.

in German-Polish relations.[141] When it seemed opportune, a racial expert like Hans Günther could still state in 1940 that 80% of the Poles were closely related racially to the Germans, thereby confirming the policy in Danzig-West Prussia, where, in contrast to neighboring Wartheland, the regional line was to assimilate most locals.[142] There were similar twists in the views of the people of German-occupied Greece. They were first identified with the supposedly noble ancient Greeks, but after the famine of 1941–42 and the partisan uprising they were described as the corrupt, miserable, cultureless and untrustworthy descendants of Slavs.[143] Given its Arab and African influences, some Germans had long considered the Italian 'racial mix' problematic, but it was only after Italy withdrew from the war in 1943 that the treatment of Italians changed from favorable to hostile.[144] Up to 1944, when they were German allies, Slovaks, Bulgarians and Romanians were treated cordially; afterwards, prisoners from these countries received harsh treatment as treacherous Slavs (which was a questionable label for Romanians).[145] The Nazi attitude to Arabs remained inconsistent[146] though, to be sure, each response was largely a matter of national or ethnic stereotyping rather than the so-called racial value of individuals or families. Similar developments can be observed in other countries; for example, with Romanian politicians' sudden acceptance, around 1940, that there was a 'Roma problem.'[147]

Similarly, anti-Jewish agitation, which was strong in some periods, was for various reasons scaled down during others, for example around 1922–23. In Hitler's unpublished book manuscript of 1928, the "Jewish question" played a relatively small role.[148] In 1930–32, and also during 1933, his first year in power, Hitler emphasized topics other than explicit hatred of Jews (the Versailles peace treaty, the 'treacherous' revolution of November 1918, international capital, Marxism, the middle-class parties) in order to win new party members and convince voters – though Jews were indirectly connected to these topics for him. He did practice Jew-baiting when speaking before Nazi audiences or small store owners (workers seemed to be less receptive), and in at least one phase in 1932 Nazi propaganda against Jews

141 Borejsza 1989, pp. 60–6; von Zitzewitz 1992, esp. pp. 37–9, 52–5, 225; Jockheck 2006, pp. 45–59, 66–7.
142 Harten *et al.* 2006, p. 142.
143 Fleischer 1999, pp. 151–224.
144 Schreiber 1996, pp. 22–9; but see Morandi 2004, p. 149.
145 Speckner 2003, p. 223.
146 Mallmann and Cüppers 2006, pp. 43, 101, 106.
147 Achim 2004, pp. 163–6.
148 Gerhard Weinberg's introduction to Hitler 1961 [1928], p. 34; Meyer zu Uptrup 2003, pp. 29–30.

was frequent.[149] The fact that Nazi anti-Jewish propaganda was largely in the background in the late 1920s and early 1930s was neither a matter of chance nor merely tactical, but rather a logical consequence of the fact that the Party had developed a comprehensive political program that it promoted to win Germans over. Of about 2,000 German movies made from 1933 to 1939, it seems that three were openly anti-Jewish and newsreels did not contain much about the Jewish issue.[150] Most importantly, Hitler apparently did not publically threaten death to Jews as a collective before 1939 and did not do so at all between 1920 and 1939, according to one scholar.[151] Preaching hostility against Jews was probably not central to Hitler's electoral victories before he came to power and not central to the experience of non-Jewish Germans under his rule: at least not until 1938. This casts doubt on the view that Jew-baiting was important for distracting the masses from social problems. Men who became Nazi leaders, and later important figures in the extermination of Jews – such as Himmler, Göring and Hans Frank – reportedly did not join the Party out of hatred of Jews.[152] The same may also have been true of many of the Nazi rank and file who joined the Party before 1933, for, according to an inquiry in 1933, 60% – especially younger, rural and less educated male members – made "no reference whatsoever to indicate that they harbored anti-Semitic feelings."[153] Himmler had held comprehensive anti-Jewish views since 1922 but, unlike Heydrich, hardly mentioned Jews in his speeches before 1938.[154] Throughout much of his political career, Arthur Greiser – who later directed the mass murder of the Jews in the Wartheland – picked on Poles more than he did on Jews.[155]

But even in periods of strong, open hostility, Jews were not necessarily a frequent topic. In the SD's reports about public opinion in Germany during World War II, especially before June 1941 but even afterwards, Jews were rarely mentioned.[156] During the war, eighty-four

[149] Winkler 1981, p. 286; Longerich 2001, p. 40; but see Niewyk 1980, p. 54. For 1933 see Friedländer 1998, p. 69; for anti-Jewish propaganda in general in 1933 see Longerich 2006, p. 67.

[150] Koonz 2007, p. 12.

[151] Herf 2006, p. 3.

[152] Traverso 1999, p. 13.

[153] Abel 1966 [1938], p. 164, see also p. 161. The less well educated and younger Nazis were precisely those who would expect to be less (and not more) concerned about concealing a hatred of Jews for tactical reasons when in contact with a foreign research team. According to the study, racism beyond anti-Jewish sentiments held even less appeal (p. 155).

[154] Longerich 2008, pp. 224, 226.

[155] Epstein 2010, pp. 57, 62, 105, 166.

[156] MadR, vol. 1, pp. 1–17, esp. 1–7; see Mommsen and Obst 1988, p. 406.

issues (slightly more than 4%) of the Nazi's leading newspaper, *Völkischer Beobachter*, carried anti-Jewish accusations on its front page. Jeffrey Herf concludes from this: "Anti-Jewish propaganda was no everyday occurrence."[157] The same can be said about racism more generally: of about a hundred books published by the Nazi Party's Eher Press in 1933–34, only three had "race" in the title.[158] In speeches during the 1920s and 1930s, Hitler hardly ever talked about the East. And scholarly research interest in Russian history, having been marginal since 1933, suddenly grew only with the German attack on the Soviet Union in 1941. The same can be said about interest before 1940 in Polish history.[159]

Beyond rhetoric, a number of German policies concerning Jews and others clearly contradicted the mainstream of racial theory. Among them was the policy – motivated by the labor demand of the German war economy – of importing to Germany millions of Slav forced laborers, and, in 1944, several hundreds of thousands of Jewish forced laborers (although their contact and mixing with Germans was undesirable). In reference to the former, Göring declared in January 1941 that "concerns based on population and racial policy currently have to take a back seat."[160] Even the most radical of the regional-administration leaders in terms of Germanization and ethnic separation – Arthur Greiser in German-annexed Wartheland – stated internally that no one should speak publicly of a "solution to the Polish question" (though one was desired) because such talk could reduce the willingness of the Polish population to work, thus revising his earlier arguments that the danger from Poles weighed more than their labor. Low-level functionaries shared his view. On the basis of similar arguments, Germanization policy in the Protectorate of Bohemia and Moravia was slowed down; the Higher SS and Police Leader Karl-Hermann Frank supported this deceleration in late 1940.[161]

Economic considerations were not the only ones that could stand in the way of racial policies. In the sequel meeting to the Wannsee conference, participants stated that "a total biological solution to the problem of cross-breeds would only be achieved with a sterilization of all Jewish half-castes"; but most agreed that sterilization was not a solution for political reasons and because it would require too much legal effort.[162] In

157 Herf 2006, pp. 162, 281–8. Herf is not known for underplaying the importance of anti-Jewish propaganda.
158 Koonz 2006, p. 407.
159 Kroll 1998, p. 93; Camphausen 1990, pp. 246, 390, 397–8; for Poland see Guth 2009.
160 Göring's order of January 29, 1941, quoted in Lang 1996, p. 69; see Aly 1999, p. 161.
161 Quoted in Hansch-Singh 1991, p. 276; see Rutherford 2007, pp. 194–207; Roth 2009, pp. 8, 33; for Bohemia and Moravia see Oprach 2006, p. 51.
162 Protocol of the meeting on March 6, 1942, PA AA R 100857, pp. 99, 101.

November 1941 Hitler had pleaded for, as Goebbels summarized, a "resolute policy against the Jews, which, however, does not create unnecessary difficulties for us."[163] Occasionally, Hitler personally exempted, at least partially, certain persons considered as Jews from persecution; something by law he alone could do.[164] As SD agents reported, Germans who had attended political lectures cited contradictions between Nazi principles and actual policies, including "the establishment of the Protectorate [of Bohemia and Moravia], the annexation of ethnically alien territories, [and] the immigration of foreign workers."[165]

Poles and Czechs were both considered to be Slavs, 'racially' not very different;[166] but Poles suffered much more from German violence than Czechs did because Czech industry was of crucial importance to the German war effort.[167] The treatment and death rates of Polish and Soviet POWs differed in the extreme, although in 'racial' terms there was not much of a difference between them. Moreover, racist hierarchies cannot explain why, beginning in 1942, Soviet POWs from the Caucasus were treated better than the others.[168] Likewise, there was no racist rationale for the fact that in 1941 Serb soldiers had to remain German war prisoners whereas other Yugoslav nationalities (who were also Slavs) were released. In part, older anti-Serb sentiments were at work here.[169] The numbers of people expelled from different German-annexed French territories varied widely – 2% from Alsace as opposed to 15% from Lorraine – because of alternative political strategies, not 'racial' differences.[170] When the Supreme Command of the German Armed Forces ordered, finally, that (most) Soviet POWs should be fed sufficiently, it stated that this policy was "pragmatic [*zweckbedingt*] and does not change the [...] political [and] ideological attitude toward the Soviets *per se*." A month later, employers stated that hostile feelings toward Soviet POWs were understandable, but that in "total war, such emotional aspects cannot play a role."[171] Generally, many long-term goals of racial policy were deferred and then never fully implemented.

[163] Goebbels diary, November 21, 1941, quoted in Broszat 1977, p. 752.
[164] See Steiner and von Cornberg 1998.
[165] MadR 262, February 23, 1942, vol. 9, p. 3360.
[166] See Hans Frank during a General Government meeting, December 9, 1942, BA R 52 II/243, p. 15 (reverse side).
[167] For this argument see Teichova 1997, p. 96.
[168] Overmans 2005, p. 807.
[169] Overmans 2005, p. 781.
[170] These figures are in Jäckel 1966, pp. 230–1.
[171] OKW order, December 18, 1941, quoted in Keller 2011, pp. 247–8. The second quote can be found on p. 347.

It was not really true, then, that "National Socialism is nothing but applied biology," as Hess famously said.[172] But while not alone in determining German policies and the actions of individuals, racism did contribute significantly to shaping them. And since racism and anti-Jewish attitudes did not exist in a vacuum, but rather were thought of as linked to political, social, economic and cultural issues, they could be connected intellectually.[173] What is more, special forms of racist practices emerged from the combination of ideological and pragmatic considerations. For example, bringing millions of Polish and Soviet workers to Germany contradicted racist thinking; but their subordination and segregation in Germany reinforced ethnic hierarchies and helped many Germans to feel superior as an everyday experience. On December 7, 1942, the RSHA ordered that foreigners in Germany be treated according to the following hierarchy: A (best) for Italians; B for Germanic peoples (Flemish, Danes, Dutch, Norwegians); C for "members of non-Germanic peoples with whom we are allied or with whom we have ties because of their cultural or European [strategic] (*gesamteuropäischen*) importance"; and D for Poles, Soviets, Serbs, Czechs and Slovenes. This ordering combined racist ethnic stereotyping with cultural, military and other strategic considerations. In reality, however, such a hierarchy of treatment was not feasible.[174] Still, death rates could reflect such a mesh of different influences, including (popular) racism: in the large concentration sub-camp of Ebensee, where an average of 30.2% of the inmates died, the mortality rate among Italian prisoners reached 53.6% after Italy had fallen out of German favor by ending their alliance in September 1943. This figure surpassed that of Hungarian Jews (45.1%), all Jews (38.5%), Poles (36%) and Soviets; Soviet political prisoners died in a higher proportion (53.7%) than any other group, but Soviet civilians died at a much lower rate.[175]

Ethnic stereotypes instead of racial examinations

Supposing that humans were of different 'racial values' that varied from clan to clan within a people, then blanket judgments about a people or ethnicity would be of little use. Rather, one would expect that a policy based on such scientific racism would prescribe that people be

172 Hess said this in 1934 but borrowed the phrase from the race scientist Fritz Lenz, who coined it in 1931: quoted in Kühl 1994, p. 36.
173 A similar thought can be found in Kallis 2005, p. 6.
174 Herbert 1985, p. 189.
175 Freund 1998, pp. 878–9.

assessed on the basis of comprehensive racial examinations and their treatment dependent on the results. By and large, this did not happen. In total, about 4 million people underwent racial screening by the SS, of whom 2.5 million were either German SS members, their brides, or ethnic Germans – most of them living in annexed western Poland, primarily in the Wartheland – and 1.3–1.5 million non-Germans.[176] Many of these assessments were superficial.[177] Examinations aimed largely at finding people of supposed German heritage or Nordic blood outside of Germany;[178] they did not serve to exclude foreigners of high 'racial value' from violence. Most Jews, forced laborers, concentration camp inmates and Soviet POWs were not racially screened.[179]

Of course, screenings were also hampered by the fact that biologists of the Nazi era had no effective test for verifying that a person belonged to a specific race. Neither blood type, odor, toe or fingerprint pattern, skull size or shape, or the shape of the nose, reliably confirmed racial identity, and experts told the Justice Ministry that a breakthrough was not expected for years.[180] As a result, race specialists found they could determine the race to which an individual (or rather, a clan) belonged only through interpreting a complex combination of various bodily features, which required enormous effort (in addition to being arbitrary).[181] From this, the Minister of Justice concluded that there was no other way to determine who was of alien blood (for example, Jewish) "than to work on the basis of genealogy," in the way of a "coarse bricolage," although scientists might find that to be "cruelly primitive."[182] One rationale for not having physicians or anthropologists racially screen all Jews was the assumption that in earlier times members of the Jewish religion were also of Jewish biological extraction, because before emancipation Jews had avoided intermarriage and reproduction with non-Jews.[183] For example,

[176] These estimates are found in Heinemann 2003, pp. 600–2. In general, Heinemann does not tend to underplay the influence of the SS race experts.

[177] Leniger 2006, pp. 149, 163–71 (but see p. 185).

[178] Likewise, genealogical research in the German-occupied Soviet territories by the civil administration was limited to people considered to be ethnically German: memo about a meeting between Mayer and Kinkelin, September 2, 1942, BA R 39/830.

[179] For Soviet POWs, see Burleigh 1988, p. 224. Schafft 2004 (pp. 115–47) seems to suggest the contrary but gives no evidence.

[180] Koonz 2006, p. 408; Essner 1995, p. 211.

[181] See Schmuhl 2005, pp. 44, 308, 445–6; see Günther 1937 [1922], p. 249 for why it was necessary to examine clans.

[182] Gürtner, during a May 1934 meeting, quoted in Essner 1995, p. 211; see Essner 2002, p. 102.

[183] Seidler and Rett 1982 (pp. 112–13) refer to a 1939 publication co-authored by Stuckart. But Günther 1930 (pp. 196–7, 228) disputed the claim that Jews had lived entirely without mixing with others between 1000 and 1800.

the participants of the Wannsee conference, where mass destruction and delineating Jews from persons of mixed blood and others were discussed, do not seem to have talked about racial examinations.[184]

Following Eugen Fischer's studies on racial mixing in German Southwest Africa in the early 1900s, ancestral research through parish registers became the basis of race research.[185] It seems that the churches – including among the Protestants the Confessing Church – readily cooperated for the most part with inquiries; as did 2,000 private clubs for ancestral research.[186] Parish registers were also available in occupied countries, including the Soviet Union, and Soviet non-Jews married to Jews were often exempted, together with their children, from German persecution if the non-Jewish partner agreed to a divorce.[187]

Given their laborious character, a lack of capacity also made anthropological-medical examinations exceptional. They required too much time (for measuring bodily features), money and material (for example, photographs),[188] and there were too few experts considered fit to conduct them. For instance, in 1937 hardly more than a hundred cases per month could be handled countrywide.[189] By 1939 anthropologists and race biologists were demanding the creation of more institutes and scholarly positions because of the strain under which the required number of expert reports put them, but in 1942 there were too few qualified candidates even to fill the open professorships in race biology and genetics.[190] And, most of the biological ancestral examinations conducted inside Germany (not to mention the occupied countries) were not intended to discover Jews; they were concerned with unrelated questions of paternity.[191] After 1939 the SS acquired a larger, but still insufficient, capacity. Five to seven existing commissions (which at one time included up to eighty racial testers) could politically, medically and racially screen about 1,000 ethnic Germans per day, and a few more by 1941. This low capacity contributed to a delay in the realization of the desired settlement policy.[192]

184 The protocol of the meeting of January 20, 1942, can be found in Tuchel 1992, pp. 122–36.
185 Essner 1995, p. 203.
186 For the churches, see Gailus 2008, pp. 8–18; for the clubs see Schulle 2001, p. 109.
187 Dr Speer, report of September 2, 1942, BA R 39/760; for German practice see Chapter 5.
188 Seidler and Rett 1982, pp. 175–6, 192–4.
189 Schulle 2001, p. 214.
190 Lilienthal 1992, p. 76; MadR 312, p. 4143 (August 27, 1942).
191 Seidler and Rett 1982, pp. 175–6; Lilienthal 1992, p. 78; Schmuhl 2005, pp. 268–9.
192 Leniger 2006, pp. 167–72, 193, 227–8; Heinemann 2003, p. 199.

Since August 1934 the Reich Hereditary Authority had held a monopoly on clarifying the ancestry of German citizens, which it did mostly through archival genealogical research. But this also required so much effort and so many documents that the activities of this office remained limited. For example, each 'special ancestry certificate' that every Nazi Party member theoretically required, needed one working day to process.[193] With a maximum staff of just 165 persons (due to financial constraints) and an annual budget markedly smaller than a million Reichsmark, projects like a country-wide kinship card index, a card index of all Nazi Party members (let alone the screening of all party functionaries as originally planned) and the photocopying of all available German parish registers – relevant for hunting for Jews – could not be finished. With the Authority's six photocopiers, the latter enterprise would have taken 266 years.[194] In March 1941, German authorities were ordered to stop checking if civil servants were of "German blood" for the duration of the war. By law, every couple intending to wed needed a genealogical certificate of marriage suitability, but there was not enough personnel for that either.[195] Around 1938 the overflow of documents led some local authorities to destroy ancestral documentation. And the Reich Ministry of Finance rejected plans to create county Kinship Offices.[196] All of this indicates that Nazi Germany invested little in 'racial' proofs.

Many, though not all, of the Reich Heredity Authority's operations were related to checking on Jewish heritage, but only upon request. More than half of the requests from 1935 – after the Nuremberg racial laws – up to 1939, were by persons who challenged their 'racial' status.[197] From September 1933 until 1942, the Reich Hereditary Authority examined about 140,000 cases and found 24,000 persons of "alien blood" or mixed-blood of the "first degree" (mostly so-called half-Jews), usually on the basis of genealogical research and not physical examination. This means that, at most, the ancestry of 15% of deported German Jews was checked genealogically. Remarkably, Hans Ehlich, a RSHA advocate of planning the violent ethnic restructuring of eastern Europe, found it imaginable in the context of the war-related streamlining of public

193 Schulle 2001, pp. 88, 161, 196, 201.
194 Schulle 2001, pp. 41, 177, 217, 227; for staff numbers, see pp. 168, 200; for the budget see Ehrenreich 2007, p. 82.
195 Schulle 2001, pp. 256–7. For civil servants see the letter of the Reich Ministry of the Interior, April 24, 1941, BA 15.01, Nr. 27448, p. 88. Kallis 2005 (p. 15) argues that racial standards for marriages were also lowered during the war to increase the number of births.
196 Schulle 2001, pp. 275–8.
197 Schulle 2001, pp. 83, 161–3, 169–70, 181. Other cases included nationalizations.

offices to reduce the work of the Reich Hereditary Authority further than it had been already "given that the percentage of persons of alien blood found within nine years is relatively low."[198] Indeed, the Reich Hereditary Authority ceased operating in September 1943.[199]

Except for some of the deportations from annexed western Poland, most foreign forced laborers were not sent to Germany on the basis of racial screenings. Adhering to the ideas of Hans Günther, whose *Race Study of the German People* Himmler often gave to people as a present, the Reichsführer-SS championed ideas about racial mixing and locating Nordic blood throughout Europe (including abducting people to Germany)[200] – but he could put little of this into practice. Although he desired race examinations for Poles, and although SS officers found it equally desirable (calling it "the basis of our considerations" about individuals in Poland's ethnic "mush"),[201] Himmler had to concede that it was unrealistic: "I cannot screen one million people in four weeks."[202] So Poles received blanket treatment. Besides the lack of technical and financial capacity, political reasons also limited racial screenings of non-Germans especially. Examinations were often veiled,[203] and conducted without informing test subjects, in order to avoid political resistance. In the end scientific racism could not be put fully into effect.

Unlike Jews, a large proportion of Germany's Sinti and Roma (18,904 or two-thirds by September 1942) were racially examined as legally required since 1938. Later, the results became one of the criteria for deportation to Auschwitz. However, there were also political, social and economic considerations (persons who had held a steady job for a long time, worked in the armament industry or were married to non-gypsy Germans or foreigners could be exempted). And the number of those exempted as 'pure' Roma (e.g., Aryans) – that is, on 'racial' grounds – was kept low as a result of the protest of the Nazi Party Chancellery that ordinary people and party members would not understand such reasoning. Again, popular conceptions were given priority over race theory. Foreign Sinti and Roma, in almost every case, were persecuted without racial screening. The distinction that was sometimes made between sedentary Roma, who were to be left alive, and nomadic Roma, who were to

198 Memo by Ehlich, "Betr.: Reichssippenamt," January 25, 1943, BA RW 42, Nr. 4, folder 2.

199 Schulle 2001, pp. 371–3.

200 Ackermann 1970, pp. 206–9, 217, 226, 299.

201 For the desirability see Roth 1997, pp. 67–8; Schaller 2002 p. 124. For Hitler's ideas of racial "sifting" see Hitler 1982, pp. 90, 265 (October 17, 1941, February 4, 1942).

202 Himmler said this in a speech on February 29, 1940, quoted in Herbert 1985, p. 75.

203 Leniger 2006, pp. 167, 171.

be killed, had no racial rationale.[204] It was an exception to the pattern of mass shooting as practiced against any group, when, during a German massacre of Roma in Alexandrovka, near Smolensk in Russia, a number of persons who claimed to be ethnic Russians were given spontaneous, superficial 'racial' examinations (of their hair color, upper body, etc.) and some were spared on the basis of the results.[205]

'Racial' examinations remained limited in Nazi Germany, and those that were conducted did not aim at a general racial unmixing of peoples. Thus, the targets of violence were not determined through a consistent application of racial theory, for that would have required different treatment for the members of each 'clan,' which would have first necessitated the determination of 'racial' identities through elaborate screenings. Less meticulously, nationalities and ethnicities were treated as entities and usually subjected to the collective denial of rights and violence. Race – as Hitler understood it at least since 1928 – did not determine whether or not a Jew or Slav was killed, or whether a person was deported for forced labor to Germany.[206] Nazi violence was no straight implementation of contemporary scientific racism, or of the racist thinking of the highest Nazi leaders. One can make the argument that "racism is a syncretic and cumulative phenomenon, encompassing both scientific theories, surviving religious beliefs, social stereotypes, and persistent cultural prejudices."[207] However, it may be illuminating to differentiate among these factors. What most influenced violent action was a crude, popular racism, rather than a scientific one.[208] This underscores the fact that there is a racist tendency in nationalism and xenophobia, not just in Nazism but generally.[209]

Imperialist mindsets and racial chauvinism

Popular racism was particularly evident in the occupied countries, where it was intertwined with German imperialist policies and co-determined

204 Fings 2006, pp. 308–22; see also Seidler and Rett 1982, p. 111. For the sedentary-nomadic dichotomy see Zimmermann 1996, pp. 259–76.

205 Holler 2009, pp. 56–7.

206 There were some exceptions in German-annexed western Poland.

207 Kallis 2009, p. 55; for a similar remark see Trubeta 2003, pp. 501–2.

208 See also Ehrenreich 2007, pp. xvi, 174. For an opposite opinion see Bauer 2001, p. 49. For Mark Roseman's view that "biological thinking was not a pre-requisite for genocide" for Germans, but that a "rather generalized sense of ethnicity" was important, see Giltner 2010, p. 165.

209 See also Kallis 2009, p. 95. Unlike Geiss 1988, I prefer to talk of racism inclusively instead of distinguishing racism and xenophobia (p. 28) or speaking of "proto-racism" and "quasi-racism" (p. 78).

imperialist practices. (For these practices, see Chapters 8 to 11 and for the practices of other Axis countries, Chapter 14). German imperialist thought is of interest here because the occupied countries were where most of the Jews under German authority lived, and the specific functions of a territory within the German sphere of control also influenced the way that Jews were treated there.

In Germany there were two traditions of imperialist thinking. One aimed at *Weltpolitik*, which implied the exploitation of local colonial subjects, and the other, which sought *Lebensraum* (living space), involved settler colonialism and included a tendency toward removing all of the other people living in a territory that was in line with ideas of racial purity and legitimized by the view that an industrializing country with strong population growth had a natural right to more territory. The former tradition was mainly supported by the commercial bourgeoisie, the latter by elites like industrialists and the owners of large estates who sought popular, lower-middle-class support.[210] In the 1930s and 1940s the *Lebensraum* vision, which had usually focused on expansion eastward, was influenced by theories of the necessary division of the world into continental spheres of influence that had been developed since the late nineteenth century. This *Grossraum* concept influenced Richard Coudenhove-Kalergi's Pan-European ideas of the 1920s[211] as well as schemes for a far-reaching German expansion during World War I, and similar non-Nazi plans afterwards.[212]

Nazi leaders tried to combine the concepts of *Lebensraum* and *Weltpolitik*.[213] In Hitler's understanding, "living space," a term incorporating some of the earlier ideas of the All German League, included the idea of a closed settlement of Germans through which the 'racial' regeneration of the Germans could be stopped and an apocalyptic battle against Jewry and Bolshevism could take place, but also a strategically important supplementary area whose raw materials and markets could be exploited.[214] In Hitler's eyes, acquiring a large enough market was a precondition for Germany to develop large industries like the USA.[215] The fact that Hitler advocated in *Mein Kampf* an eastern expansion with

210 Smith 1986, esp. pp. 21, 29, 37, 57, 84, 89, 101–2.
211 Van Laak 2005, pp. 54–5, 63, 126; Stern 1965, pp. 97–9.
212 See, for example, Smith 1986, pp. 172, 178; for the post-war period see Böhler 2006, p. 27; Zellhuber 2006, pp. 21–9.
213 Smith 1986, pp. 242–5, 254; Lower 2005, pp. 23–5.
214 Kroll 1998, pp. 62, 94; see also Lange 1965, pp. 426, 428; Smith 1986, pp. 146–54, 220; the founding appeal of the General German League (later the All German League) in 1891 can be found in Gründer 1999, p. 237.
215 Tooze 2007, pp. 29–30.

a focus on Soviet territories – stating that "we break off the colonial and commercial policy of the pre-War period and shift to the soil policy of the future"[216] –might seem to suggest that he wanted to pursue settler colonialism exclusively. But Hitler also argued in his book that high cultural achievements (in a wide sense) were impossible without "using lower human beings" in a so-called 'racial' sense.[217] In other words, in a new empire, Germans would have to coexist with so-called lower races because they needed their labor (despite the danger that Hitler saw in the potential for crossbreeding, which would lower what he regarded as the Germans' racial value). In 1937, before Germany had significantly expanded, Hitler pointed to Japan and Italy, who had. In these countries too, "economic misery [was] the driving force" for imperialism. Hitler stated that an "age of economic empires" had come. Neither trade agreements nor armament booms could provide a secure economic basis in the long run. Restricted to its present territory, Germany could not be self-sufficient. Only territorial expansion within Europe, he told military leaders, could solve Germany's two major problems: food and raw materials.[218] The importance of food independence could make German and Japanese actions appear as a calculated "contemporary solution to the problems caused by industrialization" and "the global market in food."[219] In order to be able to exploit many of the world's countries, Hitler had already proposed in the 1920s that industrial nations refrain from industrial investment in those countries – which resembles the policy of de-industrialization that he later advocated for the occupied Soviet territories.[220] But food and settlement were not the only *economic* motives for expansion. Consequently, political measures varied and sometimes contradicted each other.

Hitler's views on imperialism were already multifaceted; in addition, German elites differed substantially over what territorial expansion was about. Rosenberg argued that Germany should combine its policy of eastern expansion and *Weltpolitik*.[221] Leaving aside other elites, such as military and business leaders, some within the Nazi Party, like Göring, pursued the traditional aims of German imperialism in central

[216] Hitler 1999 [1925–27], pp. 138, 140, 641–67, quote p. 654.

[217] Hitler 1999 [1925–27], p. 294; see also Lower 2005, pp. 24–5. Zellhuber 2006 (pp. 27–30) is an example of a scholar who sees Hitler's aims in German settlement only.

[218] Hossbach's protocol of a meeting between Hitler and military leaders on November 5, 1937, IMG, vol. 25, pp. 404–5; see also Hitler 1961 [1928], pp. 102–3.

[219] This point is overstated in the formidable Collingham 2011, pp. 2, 16–17, 32, 64, quotes pp. 32 and 64.

[220] Hitler 1961 [1928], p. 60 and note.

[221] Furber and Lower 2008, p. 385.

Europe; others, such as Goebbels, regarded new colonies as a means to increase German wealth and power; and still others, like Himmler, concentrated on agrarian settlement in the East in order to create a human wall against Asian invasions.[222] German ideas of dominance over eastern Europe, especially the Soviet territories, already varied before the actual occupation.[223] But one purist who insisted on closed German settlement in the East (instead of 'islands' of settlement sprinkled over the map), felt compelled to leave his job in the SS's settlement planning authority due to the resulting isolation he experienced.[224] By contrast, the Minister for Food and Agriculture, Darré, was skeptical about far-reaching colonialism and endorsed colonial settlement in the East only in the distant future – after inner colonization within Germany.[225] In 1933 the German Propaganda Ministry advised against publishing propaganda on the issue of colonies because there was no agreement, "no clarity yet,"[226] and there never was. As a result, Nazi leaders' visions ranged from calling the Soviet territories Germany's India and likening their populations to 'Negroes' (both of which point to economic colonialism); to likening the conquered Soviet territory to North America (a settler colony) and its inhabitants to the decimated North American 'Indians' (an older German tradition).[227] To be sure, Hitler admired British indirect rule for what he viewed as its racial separation, which he considered to be the source of Britain's colonial success.[228] In the 1920s, accordingly, Hitler had demanded that after a German conquest of their country the Poles be either segregated or removed, and in 1941 he envisioned Ukrainians living separately from their German rulers.[229] As previously mentioned, Germany also tried indirect rule to different degrees – including Jewish self-administration in ghettos during World War II (see Chapter 6). For example, Edmund Veesenmayer, the leading German politician involved in bringing about the deportation of half a million Hungarian Jews with the help of Hungarian state organs, "was a

[222] Hildebrand 1973, pp. 19–29; see also Kroll 1998, pp. 222, 299.
[223] Zellhuber 2006, pp. 21–9.
[224] See the correspondence from the first half of 1942 in BA Film 3342, pp. 403–29.
[225] Kroll 1998, pp. 117–18, 164–5, 183, 192–4, 214, 222–6; Piper 2005, pp. 49–51; but see Tooze 2007, pp. 237–8.
[226] Confidential circular, December 4, 1933, in Gründer 1999, pp. 336–7 (quote p. 337).
[227] Lower 2005, pp. 19, 109–10. For India see Kay 2006, p. 80; Hitler 1982, p. 91 (October 17, 1941); Goebbels diary, vol. II, 2, p. 499 (December 13, 1941). German nationalists had likened Poland to the North American West, and Poles to Indians in the mid-nineteenth century: Thum 2013, p. 48.
[228] Kroll 1998, p. 78.
[229] Hitler 1961 [1928], p. 81; Hitler 1982, p. 63 (September 17–18, 1941).

student and admirer of government by indirect rule, such as the British used it in their overseas colonies."[230]

Before the beginning of World War II, Nazi settlement fantasies concentrated, following Hitler's lead, on the Soviet Union. Poland, the first country east of Germany, played a minor role in these considerations; if mentioned at all, it was supposed to be eliminated as a state.[231] By 1928, Hitler had declared that he wanted Germany to acquire half a million square kilometers in the east; this demand could have been largely satisfied by occupying Poland. Simultaneously, he stated that Germany should take this land from the Soviet Union which, again, might be taken to imply that Germany intended to acquire land for closed settlement (from the Soviet Union) and other land where locals would be exploited (from Poland).[232] When expansion actually took place during World War II, the need to coexist with subjugated people led to demands that Germans deployed in Poland learn Polish; and to Himmler's order to SS and police personnel in the occupied Soviet territories to learn Russian. The civil administration demanded the same from its employees.[233]

It has to be taken into account that there was virtually no annexed or occupied territory where the majority of the population did not reject German rule.[234] Under these conditions, a more or less open treatment of locals as colonized people aroused anger and resistance.[235] Policies that were acceptable to many Europeans when pursued against people of color were considered inappropriate against Europeans – as the British had already learned from public opinion hostile to their treatment of the Boers during the Boer War in 1899–1902. As Aimé Césaire has put it, what the "Christian bourgeois" "cannot forgive Hitler [for] is not [...] the crime against man as such, it is the crime against the white man."[236] Although the philosopher Carl Schmitt tried to justify colonization inside Europe, many German politicians criticized a too overt colonial attitude toward eastern European subjects.[237] And other German politicians including Heydrich, who considered certain occupation methods such as

[230] Tomasevich 2001, p. 68.
[231] Zellhuber 2006, p. 44 (on Rosenberg in 1927); Connelly 1999, p. 3 (on Hitler).
[232] Hitler 1961 [1928], p. 102, see also p. 81.
[233] MadR 69, March 27, 1940, vol. 4, p. 920; for Himmler and the civil administration see Gerlach 1999, p. 171.
[234] This included Norway, the Netherlands, Bohemia and Moravia, Alsace-Lorraine and Luxembourg; exceptions were Austria and the Sudeten area. See innumerable reports in MadR.
[235] Furber 2004, pp. 569–77.
[236] Quote: Césaire 1972, p. 14. For the Boer War see Cecil 1972, p. 70.
[237] Furber and Lower 2005, p. 373; Dallin 1958, pp. 142, 148, 599.

executing hostages appropriate in eastern Europe, did not find them suitable for France.[238] German nationalism was not so different from that of other countries in Europe, but as a result of Germany's economic and political power, its restricted colonial possessions overseas, and its geopolitical location, its imperialism was especially aggressive inside Europe.

Leading Nazi politicians and organizers of destruction linked the murder of Jews to the creation of a new order in Germany's eastern empire. To begin with, they thought that Germany had lost its overseas colonies because a Jewish conspiracy had manipulated the Entente powers.[239] In his order to the Higher SS and Police Leader in the General Government to kill most of the Jews in Poland, Himmler, aside from citing security and health concerns, stated: "These measures are necessary for the ethnic separation of races and peoples,[240] [which is] needed for a new order in Europe."[241] When Globocnik prepared a report about his activities regarding Jews, he explained its name, "folder 3," by the fact that this was "only one part of the entire population system (*Bevölkerungsordnung*)."[242]

In the eyes of German racists, it also made sense to eliminate the Jews because Germans could then replace them as elites (Jews were considered to be illegitimate elites anyway). This was also thought to be true in places other than the Soviet Union where, it was assumed, Jews were in control because the Slavic elites had been incapable of state-building.[243] A functionary in the German Foreign Office envisioned this on a large scale for the Madagascar resettlement scheme: "The leading principle is, so to speak, to replace the Jewish economic influence in Europe in one blow with the German [influence]."[244] The race scholar Fritz Lenz had once likened Germans to Jews in that both tried to be masters and, like the Jew, the Germanic man "prefers to leave the physical labor to others."[245] Destroying the existing elites and intelligentsia would enable

238 Borodziej 1999, p. 17 notes 95 and 96 (on Heydrich and Otto von Stülpnagel); Kasten 1993, p. 27; Herbert 1996, p. 320.

239 Essner 2002, p. 290.

240 This can be read as another reflection of the ambiguity as to whether Jews were a race or a people.

241 Himmler to Krüger, July 19, 1942 (copy), BA NS 19/1757, p. 1.

242 SSPF Lublin to Himmler, cover letter, June 3, 1942 (copy), BA NS 19/1755, p. 2; see also, from the same source, Meine to Greifelt, July 15, 1942, p. 3. The folder itself has not been found.

243 Hitler 1999 [1925–27], p. 158.

244 Rademacher, "Gedanken über die Gründung einer intereuropäischen Bank für die Verwertung des Judenvermögens in Europa," August 12, 1940, PA AA R 100857, p. 228.

245 Saller 1961, p. 71, quoting Fritz Lenz, *Die nordische Rasse*, vol. II. No page number is mentioned.

bourgeois colonizers to feel superior in terms of lifestyle, values and knowledge to the locals who were thought to lack middle-class characteristics.[246] And the resulting disgust toward the poor, shabby, dirty and childlike locals[247] might confirm settlers' feelings of being on a civilizing mission of bringing progress to the conquered land.[248] Bringing German women to the German-annexed Polish territories to work as social workers was one element of this fantasy, which aimed at creating the "bourgeois domesticity"[249] that other ethnicities were denied. A similar kind of racist arrangement had already served as a basis of social order in German and others' colonies after 1880 when the turning away from the assimilation of colonial subjects functioned as a new way to integrate colonies into bourgeois-industrial societies.[250] "The idea of racial superiority obviously rationalized exploitation of 'inferiors' for economic and political gain."[251]

In some countries, however, non-Jewish elites were allowed to maintain their positions. In Bohemia and Moravia, for instance, Germans, by and large, usurped only the elite positions of Jewish businessmen, not those of non-Jewish Czechs.[252] Moreover, in as much as locals were allowed to take over substantial amounts of Jewish property (such as housing and businesses, as described in Chapter 10), German exploitation and domination remained predominantly indirect as, for example, through payments for (alleged) occupation costs. Even where German appropriation was comprehensive and exploitation direct, as in Poland, large efforts were made to valorize countries through modernization and economic rationalization. This was also the case in central Poland where no major German settlement took place. Murdering almost all of the Jews and resettling millions of non-Jews facilitated this valorization.[253] Whether Germans brought progress to the *people*, or, where locals were removed, only to the land, both were compatible with German self-images of fulfilling a civilizing mission.

The idea that masses of people had to die, or entire peoples be extinguished in the process of developing an area even where this was not

246 This process also ensued, for example, after the British conquest of Bengal in the eighteenth century and the French colonization of Algeria from 1830. Both cases involved substantial population losses.

247 Müller 2005, pp. 74–9; Böhler 2006, esp. p. 37; Shepherd 2004, p. 135. For Italian troops' similar views of the Soviets, see Schlemmer 2005, pp. 43–4.

248 Kletzin 2000, p. 115; Orlowski 1996, pp. 339–46.

249 Harvey 2003, p. 7.

250 See Grosse 2000, pp. 10–11, 19, 27–9.

251 Ehrenreich 2007, p. xii.

252 Balcar and Kučera 2010, pp. 78, 90.

253 Aly and Heim 1991, esp. pp. 185, 474, 477.

desired, was not new.[254] The phenomenon was known from the colonial context and the cases of the indigenous peoples of North America, Australia, New Zealand and Africa had been discussed internationally since the eighteenth century.[255] These were seldom merely hypothetical considerations. In many colonial areas – Central America and the Caribbean, North America, Patagonia, Australia and New Zealand, Bengal, Ceylon, Algeria, Congo, Ivory Coast, Sudan, Tahiti and New Caledonia – the majority of the population perished as a result of colonial conquest and transformation. None of these were German colonies, but population losses in German Southwest Africa and German East Africa in the period of 1904–08 had also been enormous. Some of the other cases also dated back just a few decades.[256] What has become known as Social Darwinism (although some of the events cited preceded Darwin's publications) was directed against certain categories of unproductive people portrayed as a burden, and it grew in importance in parallel with the emergence of the social welfare state. (Both primarily addressed the new lower classes.) Social Darwinism was, thus, increasingly applied within Europe – in Germany verbally by the 1920s, even by some social democrats.[257] Such links among imperialist and exterminatory lines of thought during the period of European overseas colonialism do not, *per se*, explain mass murder.[258] But they do point to similar attitudes and constellations in overseas colonialism and Nazi expansion. For example, there were marriage prohibitions in colonies, but such laws did not exist in all German colonies before 1914, inter-racial sex was nowhere outlawed, and the number of intermarriages with people of color – especially involving Germans – was very low.[259] Furthermore, the early anti-guerrilla warfare from 1939 to 1941 drew linguistically and conceptually, to some degree, from modes of counterinsurgency developed during German colonialism.[260]

Why was imperialism popular, and how popular was it?

How Germans other than elites thought about imperialism is difficult to establish. In general, explanations of why imperialism has enjoyed

254 See also Traverso 1999, pp. 51–3; Traverso 2003, p. 21; Zimmerer 2005, pp. 197–219.
255 Grosse 2000, pp. 99–102; Weikart 2004, pp. 183–206.
256 Traverso 2003, pp. 66–71.
257 See Weikart 2004; Poliakov 1974, p. 172; Harten *et al.* 2006, p. 7.
258 Furber and Lower 2008 (p. 374) argue for this conclusion against Traverso and Zimmerer.
259 See the contributions in Becker 2004; for intermarriages see Grosse 2000, pp. 150–1.
260 Blood 2006, pp. 55–8; Böhler 2006, p. 156.

popular support concentrate on two issues: government manipulation through the media and expectations of economic gains. Others have cited national security, great-power prestige and the urge of workers to raise their social positions indirectly through the subjugation of others (so-called social imperialism).[261] I find these explanations insufficient and incomplete. As theoreticians' interests focused on systems, instead of actors, some of them concluded that imperialism had a limited number of beneficiaries[262] – but this questionable, too. The present section does not fill these gaps in scholarship, but it tries to provide some additional insights for the case of Nazi Germany.

In the late nineteenth century, German colonialism drew support, as is indicated by membership in the All German League, largely from aristocrats and bourgeoisie. The membership of the Ostmarkenverein, which was devoted to supporting eastern settlement, was primarily teachers and pastors.[263] Especially after the beginning of the economic turmoil of 1873, business circles wanted government support for investments abroad.[264] Only after Germany had *lost* its colonies as a result of World War I and the Treaty of Versailles did colonialism enjoy a mass popularity in Germany, which drew from various social groups; a petition for the return of Germany's former colonial possessions garnered 4 million signatures by mid 1919 with even social democrats in agreement.[265] Behind the fact that the provisions of Versailles were rejected by a large majority of Germans was the sentiment that Germany, an important European power, deserved more territory than was left to it. In the 1920s the debate among bourgeois elites over whether Germany needed colonies or not centered on perceived German overpopulation and the need for raw materials and markets. (The interests of the people to be colonized played no role.)[266] Political thinkers too deemed popular support important though in different ways. Paul Rohrbach and, to a degree, Max Weber thought that colonial expansion would reduce social disunity within Germany; Arthur Moeller van den Bruck argued it would increase

261 Mommsen 1987, pp. 16, 19; "The New Imperialism," available at www.suu.edu/faculty/ping/pdf/TheNew Imperialism.pdf (accessed January 20, 2009); Kiernan 1995, p. 167; Stern 1965, p. 274; a variation on social imperialism is provided in Mason 1978, pp. 299–322.

262 See Etherington 1984, esp. pp. 63–4, 71, 77, 181, 189, 256, 271.

263 Van Laak 2005, p. 73; Thum 2006, p. 183. But there was broader support for the Navy League.

264 Smith 1986, pp. 7, 34, 57.

265 Van Laak 2005, pp. 96, 107, 109; Smith 1986, pp. 37, 214–16; Battenberg 1990, p. 237; Leniger 2006, p. 25.

266 See Gründer 1999 (pp. 327–31) with opinions by Konrad Adenauer, Albert Einstein, Thomas Mann and others.

the wealth of German workers.[267] After 1873 and 1918, German imperialist desires had followed from socioeconomic crisis; the same occurred, with some delay, after the crisis of 1932–33.

A country's conquests often make many of its citizens proud. Germany's bloodless expansions from 1935 to 1939 greatly increased Hitler's popularity.[268] The SD reported later that many Germans considered the conquered Soviet territories as replacements for the lost colonies.[269] Popular interest in lectures and articles on colonial topics, and then in Soviet life, increased during the war.[270] However, some considered the Soviet territories as unsuitable for German settlement because the landscape was too alien and adverse, or at least required large-scale reforestation.[271] This opinion was partly the result of popular belief that eastern Europe was culturally inferior and dirty. Often enough, such traditional stereotypes – expressions of a general, popular racism – were, under certain conditions, sufficient to set off German mass violence against a population as in Poland in 1939 where official propaganda reverted to old prejudices.[272]

However, racist stereotypes were neither unchangeable nor unchallenged. The popular image of the Soviet citizen shows such changes. As the SS's Security Service reported, in the first months of the war against the USSR, German soldiers and civilians at home found that Nazi depictions of the Soviets were confirmed, and they often regarded the Soviet people as a subhuman and soulless mass. According to the report, many called for the killing of Soviet POWs or stated that they should be given minimal amounts of food.[273] In early 1942 half a million people visited the anti-Soviet exhibition, "The Soviet Paradise," over a four-week period.[274] But news from the front, newsreel images and the appearance of Soviet male and female forced laborers changed these views. Pictures of large industrial plants demonstrated the existence of a Soviet intelligentsia, so Bolsheviks and Jews could not have killed them all. And Soviet cities demonstrated the communists' achievements, so the Soviet system had some merits. Soviet forced laborers were viewed as disciplined, clean, decent and often pious; they had a sense of family

[267] Smith 1986, pp. 158, 162; Stern 1965, p. 274.
[268] Steinert 1970, pp. 76–82.
[269] MadR 211, August 14, 1941, vol. 7, p. 2644.
[270] MadR 62, 165, 186, 215, March 6, 1940, February 24, May 15 and August 28, 1941, vol. 3, p. 846, vol. 6, p. 2036, vol. 7, p. 2304, and vol. 8, p. 2701, respectively.
[271] Schmuhl 2005, p. 455; Gerlach 1999, p. 112; MadR 204, July 21, 1941, vol. 7, p. 2546.
[272] See Rossino 2003, esp. pp. 121–5, 203–15; Jockheck 2006, esp. pp. 42, 66–7; Blachetta 1939, pp. 8, 20, 22, 30; Blättler 1945, p. 121.
[273] MadR 205, 210, July 24, August 11, 1941, vol. 7, pp. 2563–4, 2632; and see Chapter 9.
[274] Gerwarth 2011, p. 291.

and displayed intelligence and technical and linguistic knowledge; and they should be fed better (as men said) and were pitied (purportedly by women). Soviet housemaids appeared diligent and honest. The morale of Soviet soldiers, even in hopeless situations, indicated courage and Bolshevik patriotism, and it even earned political commissars and Stalin some respect. To some Germans, the Soviets, like the Japanese, seemed alien but praiseworthy.[275] For some time the SD reported this trend without alarmism or misgivings. After the Battle of Stalingrad, however, they warned that Soviet forced laborers had become defiant, they were threatening revenge after the war, and women were wastefully decorating their rooms. During this period the German image of Soviet POWs, whom they mostly saw from afar, continued to deteriorate.[276] However, according to the SD's reports, complaints about lazy, obstinate civilian forced laborers, who crowded trains and stores and received too much food and money, were largely aimed at Poles, Greeks, Italians and western Europeans rather than Soviets.[277] Nevertheless, the treatment of Soviet civilian forced laborers did not improve much in 1942–43, and this emphasized their otherness.

Military men can generally be expected to be nationalists, and, therefore, to be attracted to imperialism. But analyses of German soldiers' war letters are largely consistent with the swings in attitude reported above. Although always reporting about dirt, vermin and the lack of culture in the Soviet territories, the letters contained relatively few derogatory blanket statements about the Soviet people, except in the first months of the campaign. Increasingly, soldiers differentiated between Soviet holders of power and ordinary people. In none of a sample of 739 letters was the expression 'subhuman' used. Jews were rarely mentioned in the same sample.[278] What remained influential was the appeal of fighting

[275] MadR 243, December 4, 1941, vol. 8, p. 3065; 288, June 1, and 301, July 20, 1942, vol. 10, pp. 3800–1 and 3979; 302, 309 and 320, July 23, August 17, and September 25, 1942, vol. 11, pp. 3987–8, 4084–6 and 4235–6; 340, 349, December 3, 1942 and January 11, 1943, vol. 12, pp. 4532, 4663–6; 376, April 15, 1943, vol. 13, pp. 5128–36; SD reports, July 26, 1943, ibid., vol. 14, pp. 5532–4; February 7, 1944, vol. 16, p. 6304.

[276] MadR 362, February 25, 1943, vol. 12, pp. 4848–50; SD reports, September 2, 1943, ibid., vol. 14, pp. 5702–10; October 7, 1943, vol. 15, pp. 5861–7; January 6, 1944, vol. 16, pp. 6221–2.

[277] MadR 154, January 16, 1941, vol. 7, p. 1913; 282, 287, May 7 and 28, 1942, vol. 10, pp. 3715–16, 3760–3; 309, August 17, 1942, vol. 11, pp. 4090–1; 336, 358, November 19, 1942 and February 11, 1943, vol. 12, pp. 4489–90, 4795–6; 381, May 6, 1943, vol. 13, pp. 5224–32; SD report, July 1, 1943, ibid., vol. 14, pp. 5418–21. For disagreement among Germans on these matters, see ibid., vol. 13, pp. 5067–70.

[278] Humburg 1998, pp. 95–145 (but negative comments are mentioned on pp. 179, 181, 224–5), 147–8, 152–4, 193–7, 201–4, for Jews see 197–203. Not entirely different is the assessment in Latzel 1998, pp. 145–56, 371.

communism and the image of a half-Asian, threateningly expansionist Russia. But the stereotype of the subhuman was strong enough to be successfully reactivated by German propaganda, which pointed to atrocities the Soviets committed while invading Germany in 1945.[279] Previously, it may have had a point if a German intellectual expected that their practice of occupation had turned millions of German soldiers into a political base of support for imperialism.[280] While some Germans became concerned or even ashamed of imperialism, for others, *l'appetit venait en mangeant.*

According to SD reports, those involved in the attempted coup against Hitler in 1944, most of whom were conservative elites, also had contradictory attitudes concerning imperialism: they condemned (in mid 1944) the killing of the commissars, the starving of Soviet POWs, hunts for forced laborers, and antagonist policies in the German-occupied territories in general; they advocated a system of free nation states in Europe but seemingly did not want to return many annexed areas; and some mused about the return of former overseas colonies to Germany.[281] With some variations, the same people expressed their shame about Germany's destruction of the Jews, but some did not want to lift all of the legal restrictions on Jews (namely, their status as foreigners and their being banned from public office, and, according to some, also their removal from the economy).[282]

Some other hints at the essence of popular German racism can be found in interviews with German troops of various backgrounds captured by western Allied armies. These soldiers usually displayed a strong nationalism, were convinced that it was their duty to fight for their country, and wanted to reverse the humiliation of the Versailles treaty; they felt threatened by Bolshevism, thought that defeat would bring Germany's destruction, and believed that Jews were responsible for the war.[283] However, as with the conspirators against Hitler, there was no consensus on many points.

Racist chauvinism – which also tended to make arguments about communities of inheritance and, thus, biology – represented a major popular input to the persecution and murder of European Jews and others.

[279] For the image in scholarship of Russia as a threat see Camphausen 1990, pp. 356, 361–2, 367–74. For 1945 see Blatman 2011, pp. 75–9. Müller 2005 (pp. 50–2) sees residues of the subhuman stereotype existing throughout the period 1942–45.

[280] See Kletzin 2000, p. 43.

[281] Spiegelbild 1961, pp. 34, 110, 126–7, 133–4, 227, 236–7, 250–2, 411; see also Heinemann 2004, pp. 777–89.

[282] Spiegelbild 1961, pp. 110, 134, 149, 230, 257, 449–50.

[283] Zagovec 2005, pp. 330–1.

This "ordinary racism," which could be directed against Jews, Slavs and Italians, was, as Gerhard Schreiber argues, not a trait of the Nazis alone.[284] Other authors have called this the German "everyday nationalism."[285]

As for Jews, some authors have concluded, on the basis of German secret reports on public opinion, that Nazi anti-Jewish propaganda was not very effective – although traditional negative stereotypes about Jews were widespread, that support of, or disagreement with, anti-Jewish measures depended on the personal interests of individual Germans – and that attacks by Germans against Jews were not necessarily the result of having been persuaded by racial anti-Semitism.[286] Again, these conclusions point to the importance of popular racism; although, on the other hand, it is far from true that all Nazi Party members expressed anti-Jewish sentiments, at least not by 1933.[287] For the participants in imperialism and mass violence, racist chauvinism more than acceptance of race biology – which had no coherent doctrine anyway – was one determinant of their actions.

284 Schreiber 1996, p. 75.

285 Müller 2005, p. 75, with reference to Humburg 1998, pp. 91, 193–5. See also Latzel 1998, pp. 371–2.

286 Bankier 1996, esp. pp. 71, 80, 84.

287 Abel 1966 [1938], p. 164.

8 Forced labor, German violence and Jews

Many scholars have argued that the murder of Jews in Europe defied all economic logic, violated Nazi economic interests and contradicted their war effort. Blanket statements about, for example, the "fundamentally anti-economic character of the [Nazi] genocide"[1] are popular but untenable. Others have offered arbitrary and contradictory interpretations about what had primacy – the war economy or racist ideology. This shows how problematic it is to ask simplistic either/or questions in this context.[2] It is more fruitful not to take economics and ideology as opposites. There were complex interrelationships between the two.

This chapter deals with the labor factor in relation to Jewish and other forced labor. But it is important to understand that economic considerations related to the killing of Jews were not about labor alone. Further chapters will treat the connections between food, housing, settlement, finance and transportation policies and the persecution and extermination of Jews. They will show that some economic factors tended to spur the murder of Jews in crucial ways, while others, such as labor and transportation, were obstacles to it. Contradictions between economic interests and the destruction of Jews were more limited than is often assumed. And severe contradictions emerged between different German economic interests (e.g., labor versus food, labor versus housing and transportation versus housing). The fundamental situation underlying all these issues was scarcity. Modern economies in major wars are economies not of surplus but of want, shortages and restraints. Moreover, the debate has so far centered on the logic of national economies, but some things that did not make sense for a national economy were in harmony with individual gain.

This chapter starts with a sketch of the German labor supply, the forced labor program and the situation of forced laborers as the context for the

[1] Traverso 1999, p. 58. See also Attali 2010, p. 461; Arendt 1986 (1955), pp. 738, 866–7, 918, 940; Claussen 1994, pp. 72–3.

[2] See Steinbacher 2000, pp. 105, 140–1, 264.

development and conditions of, and the restrictions on, the forced labor of Jews. It deals with the geographic distribution of labor and the evolution of forced labor in general, and Jewish labor in particular, because these were closely related.

In the Reich: The forced labor program

In early November 1941 Hitler stated: "The area that works for us now includes more than 250 million people, but the area indirectly at our disposal has more than 350 million human beings."[3] These figures were more or less realistic, and about 250 million people remained under German rule until the fall of 1944.[4] Given that German experts assumed that 40% of a population could be realistically employed, a population of 250 million implied a labor force of 100 million. Although this may seem like a lot, it was much less than Germany's war enemies could command, and many of these people lacked the skills or were wrongly located to be productive. Within the German sphere of influence in Europe and northern Africa there were about 7 million Jews by 1941, i.e., a workforce of 2.8 million, most of whom lived in eastern Europe in regions not slated for major industrial exploitation. Some 5–5.5 million Jews came under direct German control. Thus, the Jewish labor potential was, although not insignificant, a relatively minor factor in the general labor picture – less than 3% of the total workforce. In certain countries the proportion of workers among the Jewish population was less than 40%: in Germany this was because most young Jewish men had emigrated; in the occupied Soviet territories it was because many young men had been drafted into the Red Army or evacuated eastward.

Nazi labor policy had started out with restrictions on foreign labor. In part this was the result of racist motivations, but it was mostly down to ordinary xenophobia.[5] Internationally, the inter-war period was characterized by new immigration quotas, stricter passport controls and travel permit regulations restricting cross-border and, at times, domestic migration. (There was also an increased use of coercive labor in the colonies.) The need to bring Germans back into employment had become urgent at the time when the Nazis came to power. Unemployment had plagued the Weimar Republic; even in 1929 – a relatively prosperous

[3] Quoted in Elsner and Lehmann 1988, p. 189.

[4] Germany occupied southern France in November 1942, lost Ukraine and southern Russia by the fall of 1943, but at the same time occupied most of Italy, further parts of Greece and Yugoslavia, and, in 1944, Hungary, Slovakia and Croatia.

[5] Elsner and Lehmann 1988, pp. 156–7.

time – only 17.9 million people were employed in Germany compared to the 13.1 million on the eve of 1933, 21.4 million by 1937, 22.7 million at the beginning of 1941, and 24 million by early 1942.[6] Given mass unemployment, in the initial years of the Nazi era Jews were squeezed out of jobs and out of the country, as were some foreigners – although economic recovery increased the overall employment of foreign workers from 1933 onwards. As the need for labor increased, especially after 1936, the German government concluded agreements with other countries to supply workers, but by 1938 Germany had less than half a million foreign workers – most of them Czechoslovaks, Poles and Austrians working predominantly in agriculture.[7] Hard currency problems restricted the import of voluntary foreign labor because workers wanted to send part of their income home to their families. By as late as 1942, difficulties with these money transfers led Italy's government to reduce markedly the number of Italian workers in Germany.[8] During the war, the German government overcame its hard currency problem by force: it imposed on occupied countries the obligation to pay money transfers to workers' families. German civil servants invented so many wage 'deductions' for Polish and Soviet workers that next to nothing was paid to them or their families, and the German state budget received billions of marks on the wages.[9] In other words, occupation and force were first of all a financial necessity, which later became profitable.

Because of the increasing labor demand in 1938–39, Jews came to be regarded as a labor pool to be mobilized. Previously, forced labor had not been an important element of their persecution in Germany. But after the pogrom of November 1938, Jews were pressed into work gangs in various economic sectors. However, as members of the Jewish communities were predominantly over-aged and female, the number of German Jewish forced laborers in the Old Reich and Austria was only 33,000 in May 1939, and peaked at around 50,000 in 1941 (0.2% of the workforce). More than half of these Jewish workers were used in Berlin.[10]

Labor legislation in general soon became more draconian because German leaders could no longer afford to offer enough economic incentives to German workers to induce them to work for the desired armament effort. So they resorted to force.[11] Certain groups of Germans could

[6] Kranig 1986, p. 26.
[7] Elsner and Lehmann 1988, p. 164; for the legislation see Kranig 1986, pp. 38–9; for employment figures of foreigners see Herbert 1985, pp. 49, 58.
[8] Elsner and Lehmann 1988, p. 157; Lang 1996, pp. 27, 39, 77, 80; Raspin 1986, pp. 287, 296.
[9] Aly 2006a, pp. 156–64.
[10] Gruner 1997, pp. 15, 40–52, 92, 339, 349.
[11] Mason 1978, pp. 214–22, 239–40, 313–19; Tooze 2007, pp. 306–8.

be assigned certain jobs by the government or obliged to work in certain organizations: 1.5 million fell under one of these regimes in 1939, and the number rose to 2.7 million by 1941. In case of emergency, all fit male citizens could be forced to work, and the movement between jobs was restricted in wartime.[12] Later a 56-hour workweek became mandatory for Germans; in certain industries it was 72 hours.[13] In order to intimidate other workers, the persecution of 'asocials' (i.e., social deviants, the unproductive and so-called work-shy people) was intensified in 1938–39. More than 10,000 were sent to concentration camps for forced labor in the spring of 1938.[14] During the same period, the more than 100,000 prison inmates in Germany were also discovered as a labor resource. The kind of labor they did changed too – from making paper bags, weaving mats and recycling string, to work largely outside prisons in agriculture, construction, transportation and industry.[15] In 1939–40, so-called labor education camps – run by the Gestapo – were introduced as another instrument of intimidation. The regime there was "usually harsher than in a concentration camp" (Kaltenbrunner), and inmates' incarceration was limited to eight weeks to prevent too many deaths. Only a minority were political prisoners. Many companies were in close contact with the Gestapo in this matter and denounced their undesirable German workers.[16] But from 1941, most inmates were foreigners, especially eastern Europeans, some of whom did not survive their stay.[17]

Foreign workers were brought to Germany from the beginning of the war in 1939, despite racist objections against importing Poles, and more especially Soviets.[18] Their number may have cumulatively reached 13–14 million (Soviets and Poles were the largest groups) according to new calculations that confirm earlier east German and Polish estimates.[19] Only some hundreds of thousands of them participated willingly.[20] Especially in the earlier years, some western Europeans were able to return legally; others did so illegally. By the end of 1941 there were

12 Kranig 1986, pp. 30–1, 38–41; Eichholtz 2001, pp. 3–4.

13 MadR vol. 13, p. 5281 (May 24, 1943) and vol. 17, pp. 6582–3 (June 8, 1944).

14 Ayaß 1988.

15 Wachsmann 2004, pp. 96–9.

16 Lotfi 2000, esp. pp. 11, 85–90, 96, 115, 122, 226 (quote).

17 Lotfi 2000, pp. 193–210, 250–60.

18 Herbert 1985, esp. pp. 75, 135, 139.

19 Spoerer 2001, pp. 221–3 (whose data appear slightly inflated). For Polish and GDR estimates see Hansch-Singh 1991, p. 201; Elsner and Lehmann 1988, pp. 200–1. Herbert 1985, pp. 7–8, estimated 10 million.

20 This rate was higher among western Europeans, especially before 1943. For French workers see Brulligny 2007, pp. 13–14; for Polish workers see Gross 1979, p. 79 and Roth 2009, pp. 121–5. However, many who went voluntarily were prevented by force from leaving again or were treated in a way that justifies calling them forced laborers.

3.5 million foreign workers (civilians and POWs) in Germany; by the end of 1942 it was 5.6 million; by the end of 1943 the number had risen to 7.3 million and by the end of 1944 it was 8.2 million (to which should be added the bulk of the 700,000 concentration camp inmates).[21] With these methods it was possible to keep employment in German agriculture in the second half of the war at or above pre-war levels, and to raise the level of employment in German industry despite the millions of men being drafted into the military.[22] From mid 1941 onwards, foreigners were also increasingly used in industry.

This meant that the authorities and firms had little demand for German Jewish workers and could replace those they already had. This was also relatively easy because Jews were usually employed as unskilled labor (rather than in their former jobs). Even among the Jewish armament workers, who became a matter of conflict in 1941–43, few had worked at such jobs five years before.[23] German Jews were one (small) group available for the labor market; they fitted easily into the emerging war production system in which the organization of labor created many unskilled, heavy jobs for forced laborers, and it was just as easy to replace them. Early in the Nazi era the mass flight of Jews made many jobs, and many attractive ones at that, available; on the other hand it caused a brain drain. Jewish forced labor became an issue in Germany only when labor became scarce, but by that time the remaining Jewish population was over-aged. Other sources of labor meant that it was a long time before the government found it necessary to import Jewish workers from abroad. Thus, Hitler rejected plans to import tens of thousands of Jews in the spring of 1941 and the fall of 1942.[24] Only in 1944 when the labor situation was tight, were tens of thousands of Jews from concentration camps in the East, and close to 200,000 Jews from Greater Hungary, brought to Germany as forced labor, contradicting the old Nazi goal – which had been more or less achieved in 1943 – of ridding Germany of Jews.[25]

The treatment of foreign forced laborers

Different groups of forced laborers were treated differently. The hierarchies of their treatment were shaped by state-prescribed and popular

[21] Spoerer 2001, p. 89
[22] Corni and Gies 1997, p. 448.
[23] Gruner 1997, pp. 116–33, 161–78.
[24] See Herbert 1993, pp. 207, 222–3. For another plan see Maurer (WVHA) to Höss, September 4, 1943, in Longerich 1989, p. 287.
[25] Orth 1999, pp. 271–2; Gerlach and Aly 2002, pp. 158–71, 375–414; Herbert 1993, p. 231; Bloxham 2001, p. 50.

racism, but these were not the only determinants. Considerations of foreign policy, the political system of workers' countries of origin, older traditions of foreign labor (and their racist notes), the institutions overseeing workers, and their labor assignments were also influential. Laborers from countries allied with Germany (who were often recruited in accord with inter-state contracts) were at the top: that is, Italians, Croats, Bulgarians, Romanians, Slovaks, Spaniards and Hungarians (who were not necessarily members of what – from the Nazi point of view – was a racial elite). Second came people from 'Germanic' or western European occupied countries like Norwegians, Danes, Dutch, Belgians and French (and sometimes Czechs and Greeks are put in this category as well as Anglo-American POWs). Treatment of Serbs, Italian Military Internees (after 1943) and, especially, Poles was worse; it was worse still for Soviet civilians. Jews and Sinti and Roma were at the bottom of the hierarchy. To be a POW sometimes meant a bit of protection, but Soviet POWs had a much harder time than Soviet civilians. To be a concentration camp prisoner was still worse. Due to popular pressure, however, these differences, especially at the top of the hierarchy, did not all hold at all times and places. Treatment and food in agricultural work was usually better than in factories, which were still preferable to road construction or mining.[26] For example, Poles were predominantly used in agriculture, Italians were employed more than others in construction, as had been the case in the late nineteenth century, and most western Europeans and Soviets worked in industry.[27]

Polish and Soviet forced laborers in particular suffered brutal treatment in Germany. They worked long hours and had no rights. They were underfed, often exhausted, housed in barracks (Soviet civilian forced workers were interned in camps behind barbed wire), received insufficient medical treatment and were barred from public air raid shelters, a measure which by itself claimed tens of thousands of lives. Many had to wear wooden clogs, even in winter. Contemporary reports document, and memories recall, frequent verbal abuse, beatings, cruelty and occasional shootings – not only by German police but also by guards in camps and at worksites, although survivors also testify to vastly different treatment by different persons. The perspective of German workers is best characterized not by solidarity or help, despite occasional gestures, but by "disinterest and a kind of indifferent, matter-of-fact attitude." Like many overseers of Jewish laborers, those of Polish and Ukrainian

[26] This paragraph draws from Spoerer 2001, pp. 91–2; Herbert 1985, pp. 98–102, 189; Lang 1996, pp. 7–10; Hansch-Singh 1991, pp. 129–32.

[27] Spoerer 2001, p. 225.

workers in Germany used whips.[28] Up to a million of the forced laborers were children.[29] After March 1940 Polish forced workers were compelled to wear a distinctive marking in public, the first such group to have to do so in the Old Reich. Given the long-term physical and mental stress, many women stopped menstruating, as was also the case with female concentration camp inmates.[30] Soviet forced laborers who died were often buried in Jewish cemeteries.[31] In 1945 forced workers in many regions of the Reich were also sent on evacuation marches, handed over to the police, and some arrested as security threats and shot.[32]

German conscription methods, after the initial flow of volunteers had dried up, were also violent. One method was arbitrary encirclement of crowds in markets, cinemas, churches and at railway stations, not infrequently criticized as slave hunts. This method was primarily used in the occupied Soviet territories, but by late 1944 it was even being employed in the Netherlands.[33] Other measures included imposing delivery quotas on local authorities, the mandatory conscription of certain cohorts from the spring of 1943 onwards, the so-called combing out of unnecessary persons at certain workplaces, and the evacuation of entire populations from areas near partisan bases or frontline regions from where the German military was about to retreat.[34] In Ukraine, conscription was more intense in areas that were under military rather than civil administration.[35] Considerable pressure was put on potential conscripts. They had their identity cards confiscated, which made life in their homeland virtually impossible. They and their parents were sometimes threatened with execution. Parents were arrested, families' livestock was confiscated, and the homes of evaders were burned down.[36] Autochthonous functionaries

[28] "Aufzeichnungen über die Lage der Ostarbeiter in Deutschland," August 16, 1943, in Pagenstecher *et al.* 2008, pp. 220–31; whips are mentioned by more than a quarter of the respondents in Berliner Geschichtswerkstatt 2000, pp. 45, 53, 59, 60, 67, 94, 105. For survivors' reports see Schwarze 2005; Berliner Geschichtswerkstatt 2000. For the German perspective see Herbert 1989, p. 352.

[29] 550,000 of those deported for labor from the USSR to Germany were less than sixteen years old according to data from a survivors' association: Schwarze 2005, p. 55.

[30] "Aufzeichnungen über die Lage der Ostarbeiter in Deutschland," August 16, 1943, in Pagenstecher *et al.* 2008, p. 217.

[31] K. Hoffmann 2001, p. 127; Schäfer 2000, p. 51.

[32] Schwarze 2005, p. 288; Herbert 1985, pp. 336–9; Eichholtz 2001, pp. 19–21.

[33] For the "slave hunts," see Penter 2004, p. 74; for the Netherlands see K. Hoffmann 2001, p. 63.

[34] For Belarus see Gerlach 1999, pp. 467–76; most methods were also applied, for example, to Italy: Klinkhammer 1993, pp. 185–6, 209–38, 506–11; for France see Zielinski 1995a, pp. 140–8; Lieb 2007, pp. 46, 206, 281, 302.

[35] Penter 2004, p. 72.

[36] Labor office Spittal to recruitment commission Minsk, August 5, 1942, and General Commissioner in Minsk, Aso, citation for Vera Dubrownik, May 13, 1943; Ermacenko

were often deeply involved in the process, which led to societal tensions as in Ukraine.[37]

The treatment of forced laborers in the Reich resulted in hundreds of thousands of deaths, primarily after laborers had been transferred to concentration camps or by aerial bombing. Estimates of the number of Polish forced workers who died in Germany range from 20,000 to 137,000 (the latter figure includes 1–6% of the POWs).[38] Losses among Soviet civilians forced to work in Germany may have been around 50,000 (2%) though a considerable number of the 150,000–200,000 who were deported back to Soviet territory as unfit also died.[39] Tens of thousands of western Europeans perished, too.[40] A total of 250,000–300,000 foreign forced laborers may have died,[41] which is striking given that most of them were between fifteen and thirty years old, a cohort for which the number of naturally occurring deaths is close to zero. At the same time, mortality rates for even eastern European civilian forced workers were far below those for Jewish forced laborers, concentration camp inmates and Soviet POWs. However, those Eastern Europeans who survived often spent the rest of their lives impoverished because (inter alia) they could not make up for the interruptions in their education and suffered from bad health (both was also true for Ukrainian Jewish survivors).[42]

Given the terrible living and working conditions, what German authorities called 'breaches of the labor contract' (e.g., flight, refusal to work, sabotage) became a mass phenomenon. The German response was even fiercer repression. Employers or foremen reported many forced laborers – especially Soviets and Poles but also others – to the police for slow work or recalcitrant behavior. Soviets especially tended to be severely punished; French and Czech workers less so.[43] Masses fled from their camps and

instruction, November 18, 1942, all in "Ostarbeiter," pp. 96, 116–18, 136; Hansch-Singh 1991, pp. 216, 218; Paul Raab to RMO, June 7, 1944, in IMG, vol. 25, pp. 313–16.

[37] Eikel 2005, pp. 427–32.

[38] Spoerer 2001, p. 221; Dollmann and Eckelmann 2000, p. 18. Pohl 2003, p. 61, gives a minimum of 150,000 Polish and Soviet civilian forced laborers (combined) who died.

[39] Gerlach 1999, pp. 478–9; Spoerer 2001 (pp. 227–8) assumes that another 120,000 died inside concentration camps. Both authors use inter alia data from Pavel Polian.

[40] Lagrou 2002 (p. 319) estimates 20,000 French civilian workers instead of the official figure of 40,000. Pohl 2003 (p. 61) mentions 10,000–20,000 French and 8,500 Dutch workers deceased, Spoerer 2001 (p. 221) 5,000 French and 10,000 Italians.

[41] For contradictory and partially overstated figures see Spoerer and Fleischhacker 2002, pp. 184–7.

[42] See, for instance, the accounts in Berliner Geschichtswerkstatt 2000; Schwarze 2005. For Ukrainian Jewish survivors see Zabarko 2005. Surviving Italian Jews fared better in terms of education: Sabatello 1989, pp. 81–4, 91.

[43] Herbert 1985, pp. 303–4; Hammermann 2002, p. 483; Freund 2000, pp. 121, 124. For reasons why people were denounced see Schäfer 2000, pp. 234–5; see also Brulligny 2007, p. 21.

assigned employers as early as 1941;[44] Soviets and Poles just tried to find forced labor in Germany with less inhumane conditions. In 1941 more than 4,600 foreign workers were arrested per month; from May to August 1942 it was close to 20,000; the monthly figure was more than 29,000 from January to September 1943 (about 1% monthly in the third quarter of the year), and it rose to 31,000 in the first half of 1944.[45] In 1943, escapes numbered more than 30,000 per month on average; in some regions, 1–1.5% of all foreign workers, and probably more than 10,000 POWs, fled each month during 1944.[46] In fact, hunting down foreign workers on the run became the main business of the Gestapo and the German gendarmerie in the second half of World War II, greatly overtaxing their personnel[47] and limiting their ability for other repressive action. Despite Himmler's orders to intern all captured Soviet and Polish forced laborers in concentration camps, the punishment for those caught differed widely from fines to eight weeks in one of the Gestapo's "labor education camp[s]" to, rarely (especially for women), long-term imprisonment in a concentration camp.[48] Nonetheless, Poles made up 44% of the inmates at Mauthausen in March 1943 and 57% in Buchenwald in July, many of whom were probably arrested forced laborers.[49] Data for French forced laborers interned in concentration camps in Germany suggest that 85% were punished for 'breach of labor contract,' but far from all who fled from their workplaces were taken to concentration camps.[50] Still, many of the growing number of concentration camp inmates were former Polish or Soviet forced workers and Soviet POWs, as the trend toward increasingly young inmates illustrates.[51] Surprisingly, 91% of the more than 25,000 Soviet forced laborers detained in the Dachau concentration camp managed to survive.[52] Yet in mid 1944, concentration camp internment of

[44] Lotfi 2000, pp. 71, 109–10; Bräutigam 1996, p. 20 (Poles, French, Dutch in 1940–41); Hansch-Singh 1991, pp. 106–7 (Poles, 1941); K. Hoffmann 2001, p. 67 (Dutch workers, 1941); Lang 1996, p. 61 (Italians, 1941); Zielinski 1995a, p. 87 (French laborers).

[45] Elsner and Lehmann 1988, p. 210; Herbert 1985, pp. 299–304.

[46] Herbert 1985, p. 310; Freund 2000, p. 114; for POWs see Overmans 2005, p. 859.

[47] Herbert 1985, p. 305; Hansch-Singh 1991, pp. 106–7; Lotfi 2000, pp. 11, 96.

[48] Lotfi 2000, pp. 180–4, 236; Buggeln 2012, pp. 46, 141; examples in Garstecki 1998, pp. 79, 82–3, 86–7 and Berliner Geschichtswerkstatt 2000; statistics for North Westphalia, February–May 1944, in Schwarze 2005, p. 267; K. Hoffmann 2001, p. 65.

[49] Herbert 1993, p. 227.

[50] Brulligny 2007, pp. 11, 18, 21, 35; Arnaud and Fabréguet 2000 (p. 434) offer much lower figures of slightly over 1,000 French civilian forced laborers brought to concentration camps in 1943–45.

[51] In December 1944, 36.6% of all prisoners in Buchenwald were less than twenty years old, and another 27.6% were aged between twenty and thirty years of age: Stein 1998, pp. 179, 185.

[52] Zarusky 2007, pp. 105, 127. A similar picture emerges from Ebensee, a sub-camp of Mauthausen: Freund 1998, pp. 879–81.

forced laborers was so extensive that the Armament Minister, Speer, tried to gain access to inmates as a labor pool.[53]

German and Austrian employers, or other private individuals, reported virtually all of these hundreds of thousands of recaptured foreign workers to the police. This means that foreign workers were by far the largest group of people denounced inside Nazi Germany, a fact scarcely reflected in the scholarship on denunciations – which concentrates on Germans reporting each other and the denunciation of Jews (which was relatively infrequent, given their low numbers in Germany) and, if dealing with forced laborers, on the much rarer charge of forbidden contact, especially sexual contact.[54] Accordingly, findings that few Germans were ready to denounce others, or that denunciations tended to come from socially lower placed persons,[55] are based on what is a small minority of cases. They do not apply to Germans reporting forced laborers to the police. These informers came from all walks of life; many wanted to enforce the subordination of foreigners, but often acted in the heat of the moment. So many informers were employers or staff managers of large companies that the Gestapo started to think that they reported forced laborers too easily.[56] Thousands of police officers, storm troopers, factory security guards, labor officials and soldiers participated in manhunts for escaped conscripts; as did civilians, beginning in 1943, for the posted reward.[57]

Nobody in Germany could say that he did not know about non-Jewish forced labor. Forming up to a third of the German labor force, forced workers were nearly everywhere. According to estimates, there were 30,000 forced labor camps across the Reich: almost 1,000 in Berlin, 560 in Hamburg, 300 in Essen and 131 in Munich. Oldenburg, a town of 100,000 people, had 40 camps for civilians, 11 for POWs, 5 with the railways and 3 Gestapo camps.[58] And forced laborers worked almost everywhere. German Protestant churches employed about 15,000.[59] Private firms ran most camps; foreign workers were also housed in farms, in

53 Lotfi 2000, p. 236.

54 For the latter, see Gellately 2002, pp. 219–54; Abke 2003, pp. 151–82, but see also pp. 174–5, 178–9, 283.

55 Diewald-Kenkmann 1995, pp. 124–5, 138. More differentiated is Abke 2003, esp. pp. 314–19, 361–2; for reluctance to denunciate see Dörner 1998, p. 108.

56 Abke 2003, pp. 319, 354, 358, 360; Hansch-Singh 1991, pp. 113–16; K. Hoffmann 2001, pp. 167–82, 258–9; for managers and foremen see Hammermann 2002, pp. 290–308; for the last point see Lotfi 2000, pp. 129–31.

57 Lotfi 2000, p. 187.

58 Herbert 1991, p. 12; Kubatzki 2001b; Demps 1986, pp. 70–159; Morandi 2004, pp. 160–1; Kubatzki 2001a, p. 92; K. Hoffmann 2001, pp. 101–6; Schäfer 2000, pp. 70–92.

59 Hermle and Thierfelder 2008, pp. 522–3.

basements, in idle or producing factories, in office buildings, in dancing halls and restaurants, in bars, in business premises, in derelict houses, barns and other farming buildings, in coal yards, sports fields, in meadows, in public parks, [...] in garden-plot colonies [...] and on railway station premises.[60]

Government pressure also increased on German employees. They too were sometimes sent to labor education camps (though less frequently than foreigners, especially eastern Europeans, were); they too were threatened by aerial attacks (although they had easier access to air raid shelters) and some were shot for abandoning their jobs or fleeing air raid prone cities.[61] New regulations in 1942–44 restricted the freedom to change one's job (a severe restriction since changing jobs was the chief strategy to protect oneself against employer harassment after unions were banned), stiffened the penalty for slow work and absences, and mandated employment for more people including – in the end – mothers of small children.[62]

Labor resources and forced labor: In occupied countries

The overwhelming majority of Jews under German rule lived outside Germany. The conditions and distribution of labor in their home region or country was much more important to their fate than what happened in Germany. In many occupied countries, including the occupied Soviet territories, France, Belgium and the Czech lands, 3–4% of the civilian population was deported to Germany as forced labor by the fall of 1943. In Poland, the ratio was close to 7%; in the Wartheland it was 12%.[63] Including POWs, 13 million forced laborers were shipped to Germany, which meant that 5% of the close to 250 million Europeans who lived (at different times) in German-occupied areas – or 13% of the continent's workforce – were conscripted. This also had severe consequences *within* these countries.

Conflicts emerged between using foreign labor in occupied countries and in the Reich, but the former largely had priority – as German orders and instructions document and the figures attest. For instance, priority for local use was stated for France in 1940 and again in the fall of 1943, and far more laborers worked for German interests in France in

60 Quote: Kubatzki 2001a, pp. 92–3; see Bräutigam 1996, pp. 13–14.

61 Gauleiter Hildebrandt report on air raids on Rostock (excerpt), *c.* May 1942, BA NS 6/339, p. 101; for the labor education camps see Lotfi 2000, esp. pp. 12–13, 43–63, 131–3.

62 Kranig 1986, p. 32; Hammermann 2002, pp. 128–31.

63 Liberman 1996, p. 45 (some percentages he offers need revision); Steinbacher 2000, p. 141; Madajczyk 1988, p. 246.

1944 than in Germany.[64] The same applied to the occupied Soviet territories: close to 22 million people were employed by the end of 1942 while a total of 3 million laborers were deported to Greater Germany.[65] In Greece, workers for strategically important projects – such as mining, construction and roads – were much more important for German administrators than conscripting labor for Germany.[66] One must add that the German army, especially at the Eastern Front, press-ganged many hundreds of thousands of POWs and civilians and worked them to the point of exhaustion. To use forced workers at the front was viewed as a military necessity after the losses that the German troops suffered in 1941.[67] Other workers were also forced to move within the occupied territories and/or kept in camps, often under horrendous conditions. In the district of Radom (General Government) alone, there were at least 140 forced labor camps.[68]

Conscription for forced labor in the Reich caused local resistance and was one of the most important factors in strengthening the partisan movements in a number of countries.[69] In general, it alienated much of the population from the Germans (people sometimes likened forced labor deportations to those to Siberia, or to the treatment of Jews[70]) and especially affected families who tried to hide their younger members. Protests among elites, and popular demonstrations – both peaceful and violent – broke out in Greece.[71] But, the deportations of Jews brought no such manifestation of discontent, and while the French police conspired to obstruct the deportation of forced laborers, sabotage against the deportation of Jews, although it existed, was less widespread.[72] Certain specific forms of recruitment induced young people to flee, go underground and join resistance groups. This most often happened when the Germans conscripted entire cohorts of young people (often those born

64 Elsner and Lehmann 1988, p. 187; Marguairaz 1991, pp. 125–7; Zielinski 1995a, p. 280.

65 Penter 2004, pp. 71–2; Gerlach 1999, pp. 480–2; Eikel 2005 (esp. pp. 424, 426) sees no clear priority for either side.

66 Mazower 2001, pp. 214–17.

67 Terry 2005, pp. 75–93; Gerlach 1999, p. 831; Streit 1991, pp. 239–43; Herbert 1985, p. 256; Rass 2003, pp. 360–78.

68 For Belarus see Gerlach 1999, pp. 480–97; for Ukraine see Eikel 2005, pp. 21–9; Zielinski 1995a, pp. 164, 188; for Radom see Seidel 2006, p. 384.

69 For the Soviet territories, see Shepherd 2004, pp. 152, 175; Spoerer 2001, p. 75; for France, the Netherlands and Norway, see Mazower 2008, pp. 491–3.

70 Situation report by Commissar General Leyser (Shitomir) to Rosenberg, June 17, 1943, IMG, vol, 25, p. 320.

71 Letters by Maria J. and Anna K. in Schwarze 2005, pp. 139, 254 (Ukraine); for demonstrations in March and August 1943 in Greece: Loulos 1999, p. 149; Loulos 1994, p. 412; Fleischer 1986, p. 167.

72 Kasten 1993, pp. 166, 168.

in 1919–25) for labor to Germany since such measures had to be publicly announced – thereby giving young people time to react. In many countries this started in the spring of 1943[73] at a time when the situation at the fronts had moved against the Germans (after the Battle of Stalingrad and the Allied invasion of north Africa), which also spurred the resistance struggle.

Jewish labor: The selection principle

Like Germany from the late 1930s onward, many Axis countries engaged in the practice of driving Jews out of their jobs, or at least out of attractive jobs in the professions, commerce, finance, the universities, the media, the arts and the civil service, and then collecting them into forced labor units (see Chapters 3, 12 and 14). One of the distinctive facets of the German practice was the sorting out of those not fit for work and murdering them.

The year 1942 saw the most intense labor economization in the German-ruled parts of Europe. That year also yielded the largest levels of deportation, in total as well as for the occupied Soviet territories, the Netherlands and Belgium, and of foreign forced laborers to Germany where they replaced Germans drafted into the military.[74] Labor deportations also reached their maximum in the General Government, but there, as in much of German-controlled Europe, the destruction of Jews was simultaneously at its peak. The principle of separating Jews who could be exploited further from those who were unproductive and, thus, slated for destruction, emerged in concentration camps in mid 1941, in the occupied Soviet territories in August 1941, in some German-annexed Polish territories in late 1941. It was also practiced in central Poland, especially from May 1942.[75] The procedure was known already at the time as *Selektion* (selection), a word borrowed from evolutionary biology although not used with any Darwinian connotation of preserving the strongest Jewish individuals for the future.[76] Inherent in the selection principle was not only the idea that Jews who could not work

[73] Gerlach 1999, pp. 471–2; Hill 2005, pp. 150–3. In Greece, German-Italian regulations to make work, including abroad, mandatory, triggered the resistance: Mazower 2001, p. 223.

[74] Herbert 1985, pp. 180–1, 258; Spoerer 2001, p. 89; for the Netherlands and Belgium see Elsner and Lehmann 1988, p. 197; Hirschfeld 1984, p. 140.

[75] For the Wartheland see undated note (November or December 1941) mentioning plans to "expel" all Jews unfit for labor before March 1942, BA R 22/2057, p. 208 and reverse side; for East Upper Silesia see Steinbacher 2000, p. 277. For concentration camps see Allen 2002, p. 127.

[76] The etymology of the term '*Selektion*,' as sketched here, appears unclear.

did not matter but, worse, that they should be actively exterminated. After mid 1941, German functionaries debated whether to kill Jewish workers,[77] but hardly ever about other Jews. The selection principle was not entirely new; decisions about the life and death of disabled people had been made according to labor ability; and the same principle applied to Soviet POWs in the fall of 1941 (see Chapters 3 and 9).

The most widely known selections took place in Auschwitz, where they were performed by SS doctors and other officers. But sorting according to labor ability or usefulness was carried out elsewhere thousands of times, frequently by labor officials[78] – and those deemed unproductive were killed. In 1944 this system was replaced by treating Jews summarily according to age and gender.[79] In death camps such as Chełmno, Bełżec, Sobibór and Treblinka, there was virtually no sorting of newly arriving prisoners because the selection had taken place at the transports' points of origin before the trains had departed.[80] SS organizers had recommended this procedure at the inception of the mass murder program, either because they themselves or officials in the civil administration thought it necessary to maintain a Jewish workforce.[81] In many cities, towns and camps, there was more than one selection, and many survivors have reported undergoing more than one. The 'selections' have been described as their most traumatic experiences due to the threat to one's own life and the loss of relatives and friends whom one could not protect.[82]

The direct confrontation with an official, who could send a line of people in this or that direction, to death or temporary survival through forced labor, took other, less dramatic forms: the handing out of certificates whose bearers had jobs important to the Germans (or local authorities) and the creation of two or three ghettos in one city in which people were grouped according to their usefulness. These practices spread from the German-occupied Soviet territories, where they had begun in 1941,

[77] See, for example, Generalkommissar Shitomir, situation report for May, June 3, 1942, BA R 6/310, pp. 17, 21.

[78] For example, see Steinbacher 2000, pp. 277–8, 281; Gerlach 1999, p. 666.

[79] Lifton 1986, pp. 176, 180–92.

[80] The concentration camp in Lublin (Majdanek) served as a selection site for some of those deported to Bełżec and Sobibór; for example for deportees from Hanau, Kassel and Merseburg in late May 1942: Wannsee Conference 2009, p. 276.

[81] See memo by Reuter of the civil administration in Lublin district, March 17, 1942, quoting Hermann Höfle, Globocnik's deputy, as organizer of the gassings of Jews (based on a meeting on the previous day, a day before gassings in Bełżec started); and for the civil administration's claim of exempting workers note Abt. Bevölkerungswesen und Fürsorge, March 19, 1942, BA R 102II/29. The first document is printed in Berenstein *et al.* 1957, pp. 280–1.

[82] Browning 2010, pp. 94–100; Gerlach and Aly 2002, pp. 285–9.

to other areas.[83] For some time, Jewish workers could claim their spouses and two direct relatives as dependents to be exempted from being taken away. As the downside of temporary exemptions was the immediate murder of the unproductive, scholars have concluded that 'selections' for labor purposes were a process that accelerated and intensified, rather than impeded, the mass murder of Jews.[84]

It is also important to examine changes in selection criteria. Often, certain age groups were exempted from deportation in order to put them to work.[85] Slovak Jews were ostensibly brought to Germany for labor beginning in March 1942, and none of those on the first trains were murdered immediately. Weeks later, Himmler wanted to concentrate Jews, including women, from western and southeastern Europe (especially Romania) as forced labor in Auschwitz.[86] No Jewish inmate in the first transports from France to Auschwitz in late June 1942 was killed upon arrival. Regular selections in Auschwitz started on July 4 with a train from Slovakia.[87] Between July 19 and August 3, 12.2% of the incoming French Jews were murdered at once, but the figure rose to about 85% after August 9.[88] This corresponded somewhat to changes in selection criteria: up to mid-June only people between 16 and 40 years old were to be deported (which pointed to a forced labor scheme); but during July the range was extended first to those between 15 and 50, then 15 and 60, and finally included children.[89] Of prisoners transported from France, 1% of those aged 15 or younger, 9% of those over 51, 41% of those between 16 and 40 and 28% of those between 41 and 51 were not killed upon arrival in Auschwitz. Women had a much lower chance than men.[90]

By contrast, some sources say that there were special periods when nobody was sorted out for forced labor among new arrivals at Auschwitz, but it is not easy to identify them. In a report on his visit to Poland in May 1943, SS-Sturmbannführer Franke-Griksch, noting that 500,000 Jews had been killed so far in Auschwitz and calling it an "accomplishment

[83] For Belarus see Gerlach 1999, p. 666.

[84] Most notably, see Steinbacher 2000; see also Bloxham 2009, p. 217.

[85] Armament Command Warsaw, war diary, July 22, 1942, and monthly report for July, BA-MA RW 23/19, p. 5 reverse side and 6 reverse side (sixteen to thirty-eight years); Müller (RSHA) to Jäger (KdS Litauen), May 18, 1942, in Mendelsohn 1993, p. 196.

[86] Note Dannecker, "Weitere Judentransporte aus Frankreich," June 15, 1942, in Hilberg 1981, p. 167.

[87] Czech 1989, pp. 241–3.

[88] Mariot and Zalc 2010, pp. 183–4, 195; for July 4 see Steinbacher 2000, p. 278.

[89] Steur 1997, pp. 74, 82–3.

[90] Mariot and Zalc 2010, p. 198. The data are for all inmates on deportation trains in which there were Jews from the area of Lens, France.

of this 'resettlement action,'" remarked: "The resettlement operation of the earlier practiced kind is being completely rejected because one cannot afford routinely to destroy important labor resources."[91] Possibly this alluded to practices in August 1942; there were relatively few deportation trains whose passengers were all immediately killed but a larger number where the quota was above 90%.[92] In mid-September 1942, Himmler again told Pohl that "Jews fit for labor who are destined for migration to the East will have to interrupt their journey and work for the armament industry." These Jews would be "primarily siphoned off from the migration eastward at Auschwitz";[93] that is, they should not be immediately killed. Even in late July there were plans to sort Jews fit for labor out from arriving trains; as was the case, for example, with the Romanian Jews.[94]

In general, 20–25% of the Jews deported to Auschwitz were tentatively kept alive for forced labor. This meant the extermination of not only those perceived as unproductive but also a part of those 40% of a normal population that German functionaries assumed to be fit for work. These stricter standards reflected hatred and disdain, of women especially. Less than 14% of the Jews deported from the Bialystok district to Auschwitz in early 1943 were exempted from immediate killing. Some 11–22% – men aged 18–40 and women aged 18–33 – of the Jews arriving at the same time from Theresienstadt were not immediately killed.[95] Of the Greek Jews, 20–23% of those arriving at Auschwitz were temporarily exempted for forced labor. Among the approximately 430,000 Hungarian Jews sent to Auschwitz from May to July 1944, a quarter were selected for labor; as were 28% of the 67,000 Jews shipped from Łódź in August 1944 and 28% of the Dutch Jews deported to Auschwitz.[96]

The selection principle was applied to Jews with particular ruthlessness, but there were other victims among whom were non-Jewish prisoners in concentration camps, especially from 1942 onwards. In late 1941 Soviet POWs were selected for labor, and those found unfit left to die, and from the population of Belarus affected by anti-guerrilla operations conducted by the SS, police and military, with the cooperation of the

[91] Fragment of a memo about a trip to the General Government, May 4–16, 1943, which is, however, only available as a post-war copy: printed in Pressac 1989, p. 238.

[92] See Czech 1989, pp. 274, 293–7, 313–33, 337–493.

[93] Himmler to Pohl, September 16, 1942, BA NS 19/14, p. 132.

[94] Telegram from envoy Rintelen to Unterstaatssekretär Luther, August 19, 1942, quoting RSHA to Himmler, July 26, 1942, Nuremberg Dokument NG-3559.

[95] Bitterberg 1995, p. 50; report of Schwarz to WVHA, February 20, 1943, quoted in indictment, StA Kammergericht Berlin 1 Js 1/65, April 23, 1971, pp. 477–8, about transports arriving January 21–7.

[96] Mazower 2001, p. 256; see, for example, Steinbacher 2000, p. 301. For the Hungarians see Gerlach and Aly 2002, pp. 274–96; for Łódź see Klein 2009, p. 622; for the Dutch see Mason 1984, p. 336.

civil administration the able-bodied were deported and the others murdered on the spot in some areas (see Chapters 9 and 11).

Shifting and replacing labor contingents

Increasingly, German authorities and enterprises treated foreigners as a mass without rights that could be used, substituted or transferred at will, no matter the suffering caused, for the sake of the war effort. This affected Jews in various ways. One of these was that foreign governments, aware of Germany's brutal treatment of laborers, tried to avoid or delay sending citizens of their dominant ethnicities, or minimize their number, and instead placed Jews at the Germans' disposal thereby replicating the ruthless German practice of group substitution (see Chapter 14).

Jewish laborers were sometimes murdered without preparations for their replacement having been made. Usually, however, such arrangements were made as in Belarus, where non-Jews were trained for the specific jobs for which they would have to substitute for Jews.[97] The same applied to a central feature of the German war effort – the armament industry in Berlin. In the fall of 1941, at the beginning of the large-scale deportations of Jews, the slightly more than 50,000 workers nationwide who were among the over-aged Jewish minority did not play a major role in terms of the national economy or the workforce. But in some places, especially Berlin, many administrators viewed Jewish workers as irreplaceable.[98] After initial conflicts, Eichmann and the OKW agreed on October 23, 1941, that deportations needed the consent of labor offices and Armament Inspectorates.[99] Goebbels, who was also the Nazi Party leader in the capital, had demanded that Berlin's Jews be deported and replaced by other laborers – arguing that, given the 240,000 foreign forced workers in Berlin, the city's 40,000 Jews (of whom 17,000 were employed as workers) were expendable.[100] The background to his demand was that the number of foreign civilian workers in Berlin had risen dramatically from 19,000 on January 1, 1941 to 68,480 by late April 1941, to 105,000 by January 1, 1942. After adding POWs to the figures, the numbers are 110,203 by April 1941 and 178,560 by January 1942.[101] Hitler first agreed with Goebbels on May

[97] Gerlach 1999, pp. 666–8.
[98] Even Heydrich: Goebbels 1996b, p. 309 (diary, November 18, 1941). See Gruner 2001, p. 64; Gruner 1997, pp. 279–304. For the following paragraph see also Bräutigam 2003, pp. 26–9.
[99] Herbert 1993, p. 216; Kwiet 1991, p. 401.
[100] See Kwiet 1991, p. 403; Goebbels 1995b, p. 606 (diary, September 30, 1942).
[101] Kubatzki 2001a, p. 98 (civilians only); Bräutigam 2003, pp. 30–1.

29, 1942, and urged the Armament Minister, Speer, to replace Jewish labor.[102] Actually, in November 1942 Sauckel ordered that the so-called Berlin armament Jews, and other Jewish workers, be replaced by Poles from the General Government – beginning with unqualified workers; in January Hitler wanted to conscript additional forced laborers in France and the Netherlands for that purpose.[103] In fact, Berlin's Jewish workers were deported in February and March 1943 and replaced largely by Poles from the region of Zamosc who were expelled to make room for a settlement project for ethnic Germans. In some cases, the very same train that first carried 1,000 Poles from Zamosc to Berlin then took an equal number of Jews from Berlin to Auschwitz and arrived empty back in Zamosc where it was used to deport 1,000 'useless' ethnic Polish civilians to Auschwitz.[104] By deporting other groups to Berlin, the authorities could largely avoid the decrease in productivity in Berlin's industrial sector that the murder of the city's Jews would have otherwise caused. The number of foreign civilian forced laborers in Berlin rose to 327,378 by August 1, 1943, more than triple the figure of seventeen months earlier, to more than 400,000 when POWs are included. And it later rose even further.[105] A similar development can be observed in the region surrounding Berlin where the initial Jewish population was much smaller,[106] and in the industrial region of Upper Silesia to where especially Soviet and British POWs were shipped as laborers in much larger numbers than the Jewish workers deported to their deaths.[107] On the other hand, Berlin's import of forced labor, which exceeded the number of deported Jews by far, did not make up for the loss of German labor in the first half of the war.[108]

Initially Goebbels had suggested to Hitler replacing Jewish workers in Berlin with Soviet POWs.[109] (It is somewhat remarkable that Goebbels considered the latter to be less risky in terms of sabotage, political influence and inter-racial contact.) Yet given the mass death of the prisoners, this plan came to nothing and was abandoned in the spring of 1942. Ideas for replacing other groups of foreign workers in Germany with Soviet POWs also had to be dropped for the same reason (see Chapter 4).[110]

[102] Gruner 1997, pp. 299–300; Gruner 2001, p. 65.

[103] Plenipotentiary for Labor Deployment circular, November 26, 1942, IMG, vol. 37, p. 496; Gellately 2002, p. 202.

[104] Aly and Heim 1991, pp. 436–7.

[105] Kubatzki 2001a, p. 98; Bräutigam 2003, pp. 30–1.

[106] Bräutigam 1996, pp. 10, 13.

[107] See Steinbacher 2000, pp. 286–301, with Sulik 1991, pp. 113–18.

[108] Demps 1986, pp. 15–16.

[109] Goebbels 1996, p. 533 (diary, December 18, 1941).

[110] Goebbels 1996, p. 484 (diary, December 12, 1941); Keller 2011, p. 346; Borgsen and Volland 1991, p. 142.

Instead, Soviet civilians were pressed into forced labor in place of Soviet POWs.[111]

Temporarily, replacement also worked the other way round with Jews substituting for other groups. In the second half of 1941 they supplanted Soviet POWs at many worksites in Lithuania and in road building projects in eastern Galicia.[112] The Auschwitz II (Birkenau) camp was established in the fall of 1941 for Soviet POWs, but only about 10,000 arrived, and these soon died.[113] Afterwards, in the spring and summer of 1942, Jews replaced Soviet prisoners as the planned labor force in Auschwitz, although later that summer this plan was supplanted by one for their mass extermination by gas. In the summer of 1944 the so-called 'gypsy camp' in Auschwitz was dissolved and its inmates either killed or sent to other camps to make room for Jews from Hungary and Łódź who were destined for forced labor.[114]

In the second half of 1942, the shifting of groups for forced labor reached certain limits. In western Ukraine the last 250,000 Jews were murdered in the period from August to October (see Chapters 4 and 9), while the number of laborers conscripted in Ukraine – Germany's preeminent source of labor – dropped drastically in August and September.[115] At the same time, however, enough workers were available for at least 200,000 to be sent by force from northern to southern Ukraine to gather in the harvest.[116] From the spring of 1943 the numbers of workers sent to Germany – also in western Europe – picked up again due to the new conscription methods, which, however, triggered the resistance mentioned above.[117]

Skilled labor was often the first to be in short supply even when German experts thought that labor was generally available. This temporarily saved the lives of many western Ukrainian Jews, primarily in Volyn and Podolia, until the summer of 1942 and into 1943 in the district of Galicia. In both areas artisans were vital to the local economy.[118] General Governor Hans Frank expressed his doubts in September 1940 that

[111] Statement by labor plenipotentiary Mansfeld, February 20, 1942, in Keller 2011, p. 431.

[112] Dieckmann 2005, p. 232; Pohl 1996, p. 169.

[113] Keller 2011, pp. 407–11; Pohl to Himmler, September 16, 1942, BA NS 19/14, p. 132.

[114] Gerlach and Aly 2002, pp. 156, 293; Zimmermann 1996, pp. 340–1.

[115] Eikel 2005, pp. 405–6, 413–14; for a similar development in Belarus see Gerlach 1999, p. 460.

[116] See Gerlach 1995, pp. 35, 57.

[117] For 1943 see Buggeln 2012, p. 76; for recruitments in western Europe see Herbert 1985, p. 252.

[118] For Ukraine see Eikel 2005, p. 411; see also SSPF Galizien, "Lösung der Judenfrage im Distrikt Galizien" with cover letter, June 30, 1943, IMG, vol. 37, pp. 391–410.

Poles would ever be able to replace Jewish craftsmen due to what he saw as their lack of natural "energy" and "ability."[119] But German economists found factories more important in the longer run than small workshops, which made Jews expendable.

Labor policy in the General Government and the Jews

With close to 2 million Jews, central Poland, administered through the German General Government, exemplifies the connections between labor policies and the fate of Jews. From the point of view of the German civil administration, the majority of Polish Jews were 'unfit for work' and hardly any functionary advocated their continued existence. Different economic interests were in conflict: delivering food and Polish forced laborers to Germany and producing industrial goods, mainly for the German army, within the General Government. And many tens of thousands of skilled Jewish workers seemed irreplaceable in industrial production.

Poland had been a traditional source of seasonal labor in German agriculture since the nineteenth century. During World War II the Nazi regime greatly expanded this role. The State Secretary for Food and Agriculture, Backe, said in December 1939 that he expected Poland to deliver "workers and workers and workers."[120] In fact, more than 1.2 million were sent by 1944, two-thirds of whom worked in German agriculture. At the end of 1941 the civil administration judged the "labor reserves" to be exhausted. But from May 1942 onwards, Berlin demanded even more workers than before. Some 565,000 were deported to Germany by the end of 1941 with another 398,000 sent in 1942 – more than in any other single year – peaking in the second half of 1942, simultaneously with the mass murder of the Jews. (More than half of the labor deportees of 1942 were from the district of Galicia.) In 1943 and 1944, forced recruitments decreased considerably.[121] In 1942 the civil administration presumed that there were still large reserves of superfluous labor among non-Jewish Poles in the allegedly overpopulated countryside.[122]

The civil administration of the General Government planned in the spring of 1942 to murder about 60%, and in late August 80% (or

[119] Hilberg 1994a, p. 272.
[120] Quoted in Elsner and Lehmann 1988, p. 185; see Broszat 1965, pp. 25.
[121] Madajczyk 1988, p. 246; Herbert 1985, pp. 87, 271; for Galicia, see Broszat 1965, p. 103; Roth 2009, p. 137.
[122] General Governor, log, April 15, 1942, BA R 52II/191, p. 35; Aly and Heim 1991, pp. 91–124.

1.2 million) of the Jews and keep the rest alive as workers.[123] But Jews formed a considerable part of the urban workforce, and, at the same time, Jewish labor was actually expanded (as it was simultaneously in East Upper Silesia).[124] This meant a culmination in the use of the selection principle.

By July 1941 Hans Frank still viewed many Jews in the General Government as idle and unproductive and suggested sending them eastward, including to the marshy area of Polesye, which he wished to bring under his authority.[125] In January 1942 there were no more than 27,000 Jews in the Warsaw ghetto, with a population of 400,000, working for German purposes; as compared to 67,650 seeking employment.[126] But from April 1942 the plan of the army and civil administration was to replace non-Jewish Poles who were to be deported to Germany, with Jewish workers. In this context, factories for the war effort – much of it in the textile and leather industries – were even relocated from Germany to the General Government.[127] Accordingly, the civil administration's labor department ordered on May 9 the registration of all Jewish workers. On the same day, it struck an agreement to replace 100,000 non-Jews working in industry with Jews.[128] In June the head of this department, Frauendorfer, demanded to keep the Jewish workers for the duration of the war. As the civil administration argued, 800,000 civilians and 400,000 POWs from the General Government were already in the Reich.[129] The SS interfered. After June 25, Jewish work deployments required the approval of the local SS and police representatives, and in mid-August the SS cancelled the earlier agreement to expand Jewish labor.[130] The ensuing struggle between the SS and the military was fought out between Himmler and Keitel in September and October; on September 22, Sauckel and

[123] Gerlach 1998a, pp. 181–3, 220.

[124] Steinbacher 2000, p. 274.

[125] Frank to Lammers, July 19, 1941 (copy), BA R 6/21, p. 136 reverse side.

[126] Governor, district of Warsaw, January report, February 10, 1942, AIPN NTN 53, p. 23.

[127] Military Commander in the General Government, *Oberquartiermeister*, war diary, entries on May 8, June 20 and July 16, 1942, BA-MA RH 53-23/80; *Rüstungskommando* Krakau, war diary, surveys for third and fourth quarter 1942, BA-MA RW 23/10, pp. 9, 39–40; General Government, government meeting July 13, 1942, BA R 52II/242, pp. 60, 69 reverse side. See Spoerer 2001, p. 53. Pohl 1996 (pp. 133, 182) suggests that Jewish labor played a big role in the planning of the civil administration in October 1941, at least for the district of Galicia.

[128] Pohl 1993, pp. 120, 123; letter by General von Gienanth, September 18, 1942, BA NS 19/352, p. 2.

[129] Minutes, 7. *Hauptabteilungsleitersitzung*, June 22, 1942, BAR 52II/243, p. 61; General Governor, log, August 18, 1942, BA R 52II/195, p. 8 (about a meeting between Frank and Sauckel).

[130] Qu. 2, "Judeneinsatz," August 15, 1942, BA-MA RH 53-23/87, pp. 47–50. See Frauendorfer circular, June 25, 1942, BA R 52II/255, p. 35.

Armament Minister Speer extracted from Hitler a decision to preserve the Jewish skilled workers in the General Government. The military authorities kept the existing Jewish workforce but agreed, as a compromise, not to expand it.[131] This entailed keeping 300,000 Jews alive for the time being, as the civil administration had wanted, and not only the 100,000 that the civil administration's labor offices regarded as skilled Jewish workers, as the SS and police had assumed for some weeks.[132] Some major employers still received additional Jewish workers.[133]

When up to 320,000 Jews were deported from Warsaw between July and September, it was reportedly impossible to replace them with non-Jews – tens of thousands of whom were instead conscripted for labor in Germany. In fact, in September 1942 there were two types of massive raids in Warsaw: in the ghetto for deportees to Treblinka, and outside it for deportees to Germany.[134] However, contrary to the complaints of the armament administration, the overall number of workers in the firms under its control actually grew during the peak period of the murder of the Warsaw Jews. The reason is that the SS and police agreed to exempt Jewish workers between sixteen and thirty-eight years old.[135] In the district of Galicia, the SS and police were even more careful not to deport Jewish employees of the military. Both coordinated their actions, and the SS and Police Leaders stamped the identity cards of Jews fit for work, "for example in the age group of 16 to 35 years."[136] By October 1942 Himmler and the Supreme Command of the Armed Forces had agreed to shift Jewish laborers into SS camps and replace them with non-Jews gradually, so as not to harm military production. As the army reported in December, this program ran "smoothly."[137]

131 Pohl 1993, p. 160; *Wehrkreisbefehlshaber im Generalgouvernement*, O.Qu./Qu.2 to OKW/WFSt, September 18, 1942, BA-MA RH 53-23/87, pp. 116–18.

132 Figures in Pohl 1993, p. 117; see also p. 91.

133 General Governor, log, meeting between Frank and Gerteis on September 22, 1942, BA R 52II/196, p. 17 reverse side for the railways; for the district of Radom see Karay 2004, p. 232; Wenzel 2007, pp. 194–5.

134 For the latter, see Roth 2009, p. 138.

135 *Oberfeldkommandantur* [OFK] 379, monthly report for August 16–September 15, September 22, 1942, BA-MA RH 53-23/39, p. 42; Governor of District of Warsaw, report for September and October, October 15, 1942, AIPN NTN 53, p. 137. *Rüstungskommando Warschau*, lists of "W-Betriebe" and "A-Betriebe" for the end of each month, July 31–October 31, 1942, BA-MA RW 23/19, pp. 8–9, 13–14, 19–20, 39–40, and log, July 22, 1942, ibid., p. 5 reverse side.

136 OFK 365, monthly report for July 16–August 15, 1942, August 17, 1942, BA-MA RH 53-23/38, p. 92; *Rüstungskommando Lemberg*, reports for third and fourth quarter 1942 and report, January 5, 1943, BA-MA RW 23/13, pp. 4, 7, 8. Quote in *Militärbefehlshaber im Generalgouvernement*, OQu/Qu.2 to OFK Lemberg, August 8, 1942, BA-MA RH 53-23/87, p. 27.

137 Documentation in BA-MA RH 53-23/87, pp. 160–93; quote from Qu.2, December 1, 1942, ibid., p. 264.

Jewish workers were supposed to train their non-Jewish replacements before being deported to their deaths. One has to add that military authorities often exaggerated the number of Jews they employed. In three of the five districts, there were in reality fewer than 10,000 Jewish workers; altogether, there were 50,000 in August 1942, and 22,000 by September 1943.[138] In December 1942 General Governor Hans Frank, himself an advocate of the murder of *most* of the Jews in his area, criticized the order that "*all* Jews are slated for destruction" – which came "from a higher level" – and expressed hope that the order to extract all Jews from armament works would be revised.[139]

Some German officials from both the SS and the army thought in 1942 that the extermination of Jews could even *ease* the labor situation. For companies in the General Government had 20–30% more workers on their books than was actually necessary because of the high absence rates of employees who spent one to two days weekly procuring food on the black market for their families. The mass murder of Jews, they argued, would rapidly reduce demand, and, so, prices, on the black market and thus improve the official rations supplied directly to non-Jewish workers; as a result, absence rates of non-Jews would drop, factories would no longer need to engage extra workers and the supply of labor would rise.[140] To be sure, there was no agreement on this view. But it was a radical version of the opinion that the mass murder of Jews could be reconciled with the German war effort. According to this perception, non-Jews, not Jews, were Poland's major resource, and it would be worthwhile to improve their mood and work motivation by feeding them better (see Chapter 9).

The consequences of Jewish unskilled labor deployment

If people – whether Jews or non-Jews – were recklessly shifted around, replaced and shipped over long distances, this had to do with the design of the German forced labor system. Especially from 1942 onwards, the system demanded largely unskilled or semi-skilled labor. Workers were hastily pressed into service and swiftly transported in large groups to industrial sites where production was organized around a core of

[138] Military Commander in the General Government, *Oberquartiermeister*, war diary, August 19 and 21, 1942, BA-MA RH 53-23/80; "Vierteljährlicher Überblick des Rüstungsinspekteurs," third quarter 1942, BA-MA RW 23/1, p. 13; Budrass 2004, p. 61.

[139] General Government, government meeting, December 9, 1942, BA R 52II/243, p. 16 and reverse side (my emphasis, C.G.).

[140] Gerlach 1998a, pp. 173, 226–7.

experienced skilled workers supplemented by a large number of manual laborers. The latter were active in transportation, basic assembly, digging, construction, cleaning, and, for non-Jews, also agriculture and mining. Entrepreneurs often asked labor offices for workers without specifying any necessary skills.[141] This organization of labor also led to worsening working conditions.

This system meant that Jews could easily be put to work when no other, or better, labor was available.[142] They were also easily replaced. Just like inside the Reich, German authorities viewed Jews as a reserve of cheap unskilled labor readily available for temporary jobs, easily mobilized when an exceptionally large number of workers were needed, and driven by fear and brutality to a high level of performance.[143] Accordingly, many Jewish survivors relate being coerced into work outside their field of qualification and frequent worksite changes.[144] These changes, together with the large number of firms and institutions (including Gestapo offices) that employed Jews, indicate that Jews were used as stopgaps. In some areas, such as Lithuania, local non-Germans were among the employers.[145]

It is not surprising that Jews were used as unskilled workers, given that their typical forms of expertise were not often in demand. Before World War II many of them had been intellectuals or white-collar workers in trade, finance, civil service and the free professions. Under the Nazi regime, German occupation, and other Axis governments, they were forced out of these jobs for the benefit of non-Jews. During the war, some of these economic sectors, such as trade, were also downsized. Of course Jews were not lazier than other people, but many of them were not trained for the kinds of manual labor demanded of them, especially in 1941–43.

[141] Eichholtz 1985 (pp. 295–306) describes this system for inside wartime Germany; Herbert 1989 (p. 330) as a longer term tendency. Further examples for unskilled labor deployment can be found in Eggers 2002 (pp. 135, 137) for Jews in France; Hammermann 2002 (pp. 183, 199–207) for Italian Military Internees; Keller 2011 (pp. 154, 171, 329–36) for Soviet POWs.

[142] For example, thousands of Hungarian Jews were brought to the large copper mine of Bor in German-occupied Serbia because many other workers had fled Allied bombings, intimidation by partisans and low wages. Schmider 2002, p. 562; Braham 1977a, pp. 50–8.

[143] Governor, district of Warsaw, bimonthly report, October 15, 1942, IfZ Fb 95/64; Pohl 1996 (p. 133) for eastern Galicia; Browning 2010 (p. 38) for Wierzbnik, district of Radom.

[144] Gerlach 1999 (pp. 661–2) for Belarus; Fogel 2007 (pp. 131–7) for Zemun, Serbia; Angrick and Klein 2006 (pp. 123–4) for Riga – for a contemporary count see also p. 128.

[145] Warsaw Jewish Council, labor department, list of worksites, May 26, 1942, in Hilberg 1981, p. 157; Tauber 2008, pp. 111–12.

Many Germans, not just those in the SS, took pleasure in forcing Jews, and particularly those from the middle class, to do manual labor such as cleaning streets and toilets, clearing rubble and removing snow. These were public, discriminatory, humiliating acts which were frequently combined with arbitrary mistreatment or punishment. For instance, in German-occupied Poland in 1939, such treatment was imposed in order to signal that Jews had lost their allegedly high position in the social hierarchy.[146] Local Lithuanian measures after the German invasion of 1941 were similar.[147]

The SS and police as organizers of forced labor

Forced labor of Jews that the SS and police organized is often associated with concentration camps. This took place especially after 1943, but before that time the SS and police used Jewish labor predominantly in other camp complexes. The SS started to organize it late in 1939, in Poland. Previously, it had pursued a strategy of punitive labor in concentration camps – which had little economic significance. Labor was part of an effort to compel political or social conformity by breaking the will of inmates through brutality. Jews temporarily incarcerated in these camps were also subjected to punitive labor. (Jews were eligible for release until May 1940, and many were set free.)[148] The first large SS projects for Jewish labor, primarily organized by Globocnik in the district of Lublin in the General Government, were in part shaped by this practice of punitive labor. Up to 70,000 Jews (also brought in from other districts) were set to work under sufferance of severe, sometimes lethal, mistreatment – building more or less useless fortifications, but also in road building and land amelioration which were administered by the civil administration.[149] Under SS-Oberführer Albrecht Schmelt, a second system of SS-administered camps existed from 1940 to 1943 in the German-annexed Polish industrial region of East Upper Silesia. Up to 50,000 Jews were put to work there (and in neighboring territories) in an economically more conscious way than in the Lublin area, mostly in factories and building roads, though later also constructing armament works. However, they were worked to exhaustion, and as early as November 1941, even before Globocnik, Schmelt introduced selections,

[146] For Poland in 1939 see Böhler 2006, pp. 191–3; for Tunisia in 1943 see Abitbol 1983, p. 137.

[147] Bankier 2011, pp. 58–72.

[148] Generalstaatsanwaltschaft Kammergericht Berlin 1 Js 7/65, indictment against Fritz Wöhrn *et al.* July 10, 1968, p. 209.

[149] Pohl 1998, pp. 416–17; for the conditions there see Klausch 1993, pp. 46–58.

as a result of which the unfit were sent to Auschwitz. From May to August 1942, Schmelt's organization also selected at least 38,000 Jews from ghettos in the region, while 20,000 others were sent to Auschwitz where most were killed.[150] The civil administration in East Upper Silesia, unlike that in the General Government, seems to have come to doubt the value of Jewish skilled labor before the SS, in the fall of 1942.[151]

Two other camp complexes for Jewish labor existed in the district of Galicia, in the General Government, and in western Ukraine. They were linked by a project – the so-called highway IV, an important military supply route – on which about 25,000 Jews, but even more non-Jews of different categories, worked. However, conditions were worst for Jews and Soviet POWs. Many from the latter two categories were worked to death or the exhausted were sorted out and shot. Workers were guarded by the SS but driven to work by employees of private companies working with the Organisation Todt – true forced labor specialists who also 'used up' Jewish workers in other areas.[152] At the road's western end the camps were located in the district of Galicia, but the regional SS and Police Leader also kept prisoners, up to 50,000 at one time, for other projects. In all five districts of the General Government combined, there were up to 120,000 Jews at one time (a peak that was reached in the period from March to May 1943) and more than 200,000 Jews at different points in time who were kept in SS labor camps to carry out a variety of jobs. The treatment of prisoners varied greatly from camp to camp, as well as within a single camp under different commandants and according to the type of work done. For example, conditions were somewhat better for factory workers. Few women, not to mention children, had the chance to get into these camps. (Some Jews, hoping for survival, bought their way in.)[153] The SS and Police Leaders for each district, and the camp commandants under them, had a great deal of autonomy in their treatment of prisoners.[154]

During the course of 1943, Jews from dissolved ghettos and other types of SS-organized camps were transferred to concentration camps (or such ghettos and camps were declared sub-units of concentration camps). This is why many survivors remembered a stay in a

[150] Steinbacher 2000, pp. 130, 138–53, 275, 277–8, 287–90, 293, 305.

[151] Steinbacher 2000, p. 294.

[152] Kaienburg 1996, pp. 13–39; Lower 2005, pp. 62, 143–50; Pohl 1998, pp. 417–18. For Belarus see Gerlach 1999, pp. 662–3.

[153] Pohl 1996, pp. 331–55; Pohl 1998, pp. 415–38, esp. 415, 421–2, 424 (additional camps were organized by the civilian water management and agricultural administrations); Wenzel 2007. For changes within a single camp see Browning 2010, pp. 125–67, 255.

[154] Pohl 1998, p. 426.

concentration camp and, consequently, why these camps grabbed the public attention of future generations. Still, this was atypical: only a minority of Jews were ever imprisoned in concentration camps. For those who were, it was often a turn for the worse, even compared to other SS camps, because by 1942–43 concentration camps usually had a killing infrastructure and routine, and there were regular 'selections' according to labor ability. Transfer to a concentration camp was life-threatening as long as labor was carried out within the camps themselves – since the concentration camp administration never really developed concepts for organizing labor productively. For a prisoner it was therefore vital to be assigned to an external worksite and, if possible, a sub-camp. The chances of this were low until, during the course of 1944, concentration camp prisoners were used in armament works in sizable numbers.[155]

The often-cited expression 'extermination through labor' did not apply to a general program of murder for camp prisoners, or even Jews. It was contemporarily used only to refer to the transfer of about 20,000 inmates of German prisons (certain Poles, criminals, Jews and others) to concentration camps from October 1942 to April 1943. Most of these perished within a short time.[156]

For many, the transfer to a concentration camp did not mean immediate death. The problem for them was a process of physical erosion through hard labor, malnutrition, lack of other supplies and mistreatment – increasingly combined with selections for labor ability. This system was not necessarily designed to kill inmates[157] – though it often did, usually after months of suffering – but, importantly, it was not designed to keep them alive either. When Himmler wanted to gather Jewish hostages with American relatives in late 1942, he felt it necessary to announce explicitly that in the camps "they shall work, but under conditions [that ensure] that they remain healthy and alive."[158] In one of the first instructions about economic activities in concentration camps, on April 30, 1942, the chief of the SS Main Economic and Administrative Office, Oswald Pohl, wrote: "This use [of labor] must be exhausting in a true sense in order to achieve a maximal output."[159] (The document did not mention Jews, who were a minority of the prisoners in concentration

155 Herbert 1991, pp. 13–14; Bloxham 2001, pp. 38–42; Schulte 2001, pp. 217, 226–7; Buggeln 2012, pp. 18, 20, 23.

156 Wachsmann 2004, pp. 279–301; see also Kaienburg 1996, p. 14 note 5; Bloxham 2001, p. 45.

157 See Buggeln 2012, pp. 162, 164; Kárný 1987 (esp. p. 152) has an opposite view.

158 Himmler to Müller, December 10, 1942, quoted in Longerich 2001, p. 180.

159 Printed in IMG, vol. 38, pp. 365–7, quote p. 366.

camps at the time, and the productive labor of prisoners had no quantitative significance before 1943.)

At the Wannsee conference of January 1942, which provided a vision rather than a clear plan, Heydrich envisioned large-scale Jewish forced labor with a high mortality rate – and murder for those who would survive it.[160] But not every SS leader shared this view. SS-Standartenführer Karl Jäger, listing the daily totals of the shooting of 137,346 Jews that he had organized largely in Lithuania, recommended sterilizing the remaining Jewish men and women and murdering Jewish women who became pregnant – since these groups were needed in the longer run for labor.[161] Heydrich and Jäger differed in their outlook, but neither thought that *all* Jews would be *worked* to death, and nor did Himmler when he wrote, in October 1942, that Jewish forced laborers in the General Government, even if kept in SS camps, "shall disappear one day according to the wish of the Führer."[162]

What did working Jews to exhaustion mean? Of a small sample of Jews from Lens, France, selected for labor in Auschwitz in 1942, 24% were dead after one month; another 20% of the original number died in the second month; 24% perished in the third; 16% died in the fourth month; and only 7% were still alive after six months.[163] Auschwitz was one of the worst camps, and mid 1942 was one of the worst periods for inmates in any concentration camp – but generally speaking many prisoners survived for less than a year. From the spring of 1943 to the fall of 1944, death rates in concentration camps were actually brought down considerably precisely in order to exploit prisoners more efficiently; they reached a second peak in early 1945 due to overcrowding, ruthless treatment and decreasing labor demand.[164] In the end, only 3% of French Jews deported to concentration or extermination camps, and about 5% of Dutch and Belgian Jews – mostly those deported in 1943–44 to camps other than Auschwitz – survived.[165] Of about 1,400 Jews sent to Auschwitz from the Starachowice labor camp in July 1944, about half survived; and of about 200,000 Hungarian Jews deported to

[160] Protocol of Wannsee conference on January 20, 1942, in Tuchel 1992, pp. 128–9.
[161] Einsatzkommando 3, "Gesamtaufstellung der im Bereich des EK. 3 bis zum 1. Dez. 1941 durchgeführten Exekutionen," December 1, 1941, in Klee *et al.* 1988, pp. 52–62, quote p. 61.
[162] Himmler, October 9, 1942, quoted in Friedländer 2006, p. 524.
[163] Mariot and Zalc 2010, p. 204, also with similar data for other French and Slovak Jews who arrived in the spring of 1942.
[164] See the data in Buggeln 2012, pp. 61–5, 68–71, 73, 152–4; Pingel 1978, pp. 133, 182–5; Fabréguet 1998, pp. 202, 205.
[165] Klarsfeld 1982, pp. i–ii; Griffioen and Zeller 2011, pp. 892, 896, 898.

German-controlled areas in 1944, about 63% survived.[166] In many concentration camps conditions resulted in mortality rates of 25–40% of all prisoners, and out of a total of 2 million deaths (Jews and non-Jews) in concentration camps, approximately 1 million occurred in the orbit of the Auschwitz concentration camp system.[167] The overall death rate among all concentration camp prisoners may have exceeded 60%. It was around 75% among all inmates if one includes those shipped to Auschwitz and killed immediately, i.e., if one includes those who never actually became *prisoners*.[168] Important reasons why the strategy of survival through labor[169] worked for so few people were the selection principle and the fact that even those few who were selected for labor mostly ended up in concentration camps.

The treatment of Jewish forced laborers often corresponded with the kind of work they did. Road building was especially brutal, and work on fortifications was, perhaps, even worse – as was the case on the Austro-Hungarian border, for example, where tens of thousands of Jewish workers died in late 1944 and early 1945.[170] (Non-Jews also suffered greatly at these sites; for example, the German military worked many Soviet POWs and, to a lesser degree, civilians, to death on fortifications on the Eastern Front.[171]) The treatment of Jews who were skilled artisans or factory workers tended to be better than for unskilled laborers. At some sites, beatings of the former were forbidden. Occasionally, Jewish prisoners of different labor qualifications were housed separately.[172] However, private companies did not always try to preserve Jewish workers. Their interest in profit could correspond with either relatively good or ruthless treatment of workers,[173] including selections and outright murder by foremen or plant security guards.[174] Jews were often burdened with the most degrading or exhausting work. Many perished

166 Browning 2010, pp. 259–60; Gerlach and Aly 2002, p. 409.

167 Pohl 2003, p. 141; Grabowski 2008, pp. 111, 113, 145, 161, 173, 201, 218, 236, 242–3, 252, 265–6, 317; Orth 1999, pp. 345–9.

168 This is based on the following estimates and assumptions: 400,000–500,000 prisoners were liberated in 1945; perhaps 200,000 were released from 1933 to 1945, and 1.3 million died. About 700,000 Jews were murdered in Auschwitz upon arrival and thus never became prisoners of that camp.

169 Trunk 1972, pp. 400–13; Corni 2002, pp. 234–42, 246–51.

170 See Szita 1999.

171 For northern Slovenia to the Adria see Williams 2005, p. 198; for West Prussia in the fall of 1944 see Schenk 2000, p. 250; for the front area on Soviet soil, see Rass 2003, pp. 360–78.

172 Wenzel 2007, p. 196; Buggeln 2012, p. 157, 159; Allen 2002, p. 227; Pingel 1978, p. 184. See also Pohl 1998, p. 424.

173 Bloxham 2001, pp. 45–8.

174 Examples in Wenzel 2007, pp. 203–4.

not from the useless, purely punitive work often mentioned,[175] but from ruthless exploitation of a special sort, deeply ingrained with racism.[176]

SS and police functionaries did give labor issues consideration. For example, Rudolf Höss, during his time as commandant at the Auschwitz concentration camp, was a member of the Gauarbeitskammer (the regional corporate authority for labor issues) for Upper Silesia. When in late 1944 he was in Austria to take custody of Hungarian Jews marched to the Hungarian-Austrian border, his official position was "Chief of Jewish [Labor] Deployment" of the region of Niederdonau, and he stated that he was interested only in Jews fit to work; whereas he wanted to send the others back.[177] Himmler was also conscious of labor problems, but he clearly preferred non-Jewish labor. In 1940 he told a group of senior SS leaders, referring to Polish forced laborers: "It would be better if we would not have them [inside Germany] – we know that – but we need them." When in late July 1943 Hitler suggested sending Italian military personnel home in the event of Italy's pulling out of the war, Himmler insisted that they should be detained and used as labor.[178]

A remarkable number of senior SS and police officers developed an interest in maintaining a limited number of Jews as forced laborers for war production, despite the fact that this would prevent their extermination. This was true of all of the leading figures in the General Government – Krüger, the Higher and SS Leader, Katzmann, the SS and Police Leader in the district of Galicia, his colleague in the district of Lublin and chief organizer of the Operation Reinhard annihilation camps, Globocnik, and the Commander of the Security Police and SD in the General Government, Schöngarth, who was a participant of the Wannsee conference. This despite the fact that they had all been driving forces for mass murder. It was also true ofWilhelm Altenloh and Herbert Zimmermann, the consecutive Commanders of the Security Police and SD in the district of Bialystok. Globocnik, who had workers from the destroyed ghettos of Warsaw, Białystok and other cities transferred to his camps in the district of Lublin, expressed regret that his so-called development work with Jewish forced labor had ended when their deaths were ordered by Himmler.[179] In order to circumvent the resistance of

175 Goldhagen 1997, pp. 293–316.

176 Herbert 1993, pp. 235–6.

177 See Steinbacher 2000, p. 236; telegram Veesenmayer, November 21, 1944, PA AA R 100894, pp. 112–13.

178 Hammermann 2002, p. 28; quote: Herbert 1985, p. 75.

179 Grabitz and Scheffler 1993, pp. 318–28, 334; Pohl 1996, p. 264; Rückerl 1977, pp. 130–1; Schelvis 1998, p. 147. For Bialystok see Gerlach 1999, pp. 731–2; for an

these officers, as well as SS camp personnel, Himmler transferred them to other posts and on several occasions brought in SS and police forces from other regions specifically to carry out the murders of Jewish workers; as was the case, for example, during Operation Harvest Festival, the murder of 40,000 Jews in the General Government on November 3–4, 1943; and twice for massacres and deportations to empty the ghetto in Białystok in 1943.[180] Operation Harvest Festival was not the end of the camps in the General Government either. In early 1944 there were between 70,000 and perhaps as many as 100,000 Jewish workers, who were treated less brutally than was typical earlier.[181]

Conclusion

According to one estimate, 2.4 million able-bodied Jews, and 2.4 million able-bodied non-Jews, were killed by Germans.[182] This means that the death rate for Jews was proportionally much higher. For Jews, labor considerations played a smaller role in survival than it did for any other large victim group.[183] Soviet POWs experienced a turn in the winter 1941–42 – from destruction to exploitation via forced labor – although this change for the better was relative; another million Soviet POWs, or almost 30%, died between the spring of 1942 and 1945 (see Chapter 9). The process was more complex for Jews as the intensification of their use as labor was combined with intensified mass murder – not temporarily, as was the case for Soviet POWs from November 1941 to about January 1942, but continuously. This and the transfer of Jews to camps under SS control in 1943 made the strategy of many Jewish councils – trying to ensure the survival of as many Jews as possible by making them irreplaceable as workers – obsolete (see Chapter 15). In 1944–45, the fate of the members of many victim groups converged when they joined the growing population in the concentration camps.[184] These camps were among the best options available for Jews; for other inmates they were usually the worst. Jews were worst affected, but it would be incorrect to say that their labor ability played no role in their fate under the Germans. Consequently, a few hundreds of thousands managed to survive through forced labor.

example at highway IV see Eikel 2005, pp. 423–4. For Gutman 1982 (pp. 328–33) Himmler also moved toward favoring forced labor.

180 Grabitz and Scheffler 1993, p. 329; Hilberg 1995, p. 43; Gerlach 1999, pp. 730–2.

181 Pohl 1998, p. 429.

182 Tooze 2007, pp. 601–2. The latter figure is a low estimate.

183 The work of Sinti and Roma may have appeared even less valuable to German authorities.

184 Bloxham 2001, p. 50.

9 Hunger policies and mass murder

Food was a scarce commodity of major political importance during World War II. Unlike in the European Union of today, there were no large European grain surpluses, butter mountains and wine lakes. Instead, Europe – and especially its chief industrial powers, Germany and Great Britain – depended on large overseas imports. However, Germany, her allies, and the countries she occupied, had these deliveries cut off from late 1939 by the British naval blockade. This resembled the situation in World War I, which is why German leaders – and especially Hitler – worried about it. They believed Germany had lost that war because of a breakdown of morale and political willpower in 1918, and that famine (which was supposed to have claimed the lives of 300,000 Germans) had played a crucial role in this collapse, as well as mobilizing proletarians for the 1918–19 revolution. They wished to prevent a repeat of this at all costs.[1] Nazi leaders blamed hunger in Europe from 1939 to 1945 on the Allied blockade, which was allegedly inspired by Jews who were, thus, responsible for the fact that Aryan children starved to death, as Hitler wrote in his testament.[2] Before the war, Hitler had already emphasized that territorial expansion was necessary for German food autarchy.[3] In *Mein Kampf* he had portrayed starvation as a crucial personal experience and a great threat to the German nation and its culture.[4]

The potential for increasing domestic food production to replace lost imports was low. Food production markedly decreased in most countries, as one would expect, due to a lack of agricultural inputs. The supply of labor fell as the military recruited men from the countryside; less machinery could be used because of the lack of fuel and the military's

1 Corni and Gies 1997, pp. 401–5; Kay 2006, p. 40.
2 Longerich 2001, p. 192; see also Rosenberg speech, February 22, 1941, BA NS 8/63, pp. 73–4.
3 Hossbach protocol on a high-level meeting, November 5, 1937, IMG, vol. 25, pp. 404–6. See Wildt 2003, p. 420.
4 Hitler 1999 [1925–27], pp. 20–1, 27, 131, 133, 177, 233; see Jäckel 1997 [1969], p. 91.

requisitioning of tractors; horses were also requisitioned; less mineral fertilizer was available since it was produced from phosphate and nitrogen, which were needed for making ammunition; and natural fertilizer was scarce because the lack of imported feed grains and forage meant that the number of livestock had to be reduced as pasture was converted to cropland.[5] The move from animals to grain for human consumption, and from grain to potatoes or sugar beet (which were more calorie-efficient), could only remedy the problem in part. Thus, human consumption needed to be reduced, which raised the issue of food distribution and who should get more and who should get less.

Food shortages had a major impact on the life of Europeans especially in the eastern half of the continent, to which we will soon turn, but also in the occupied west. Rising death rates were the greatest factor in the multidimensional process causing a declining rise, or a loss, in population. Europeans noticed their weight losses in private, and remembered them years later, but it was also a matter of public debate, as in France where many urban workers lost 4–14 kg.[6] For POWs, other prisoners and camp inmates, weight losses were particularly drastic.[7] Death rates in western and central Europe were already elevated in the period 1935–38, before the start of World War II, probably as a result of the economic crisis and deteriorating public healthcare.[8] These conditions worsened during the war. In large Italian cities, infant mortality, especially from tuberculosis, increased sharply in the period 1941–43 (and in 1943 in particular).[9] The crude death rate in Belgium, France and the Netherlands rose early in the war, especially in 1940 and 1941; it either remained steady or dropped until 1944 and then rose strongly in 1945. In an average war year, two out of every 1,000 Belgians, or 16,000 in total, more than usual, died; and perhaps 100,000 Dutch died before the famine of 1944–45.[10] In more than half of the French *departements* that were predominantly rural, mortality dropped during the German occupation as agriculturalists

[5] For Germany see Corni and Gies 1997, pp. 423–68, 477–8.

[6] Kistenmacher 1959, pp. 30–1; Cépède 1961, pp. 407–8; Lafont 1987, p. 80; see also Trienekens 1985 (pp. 431–5) for the Netherlands.

[7] Lang 1996, p. 94 (Italian Military Internees with Krupp company, 1943–44); interview with Herbert Grunewald in Johnson and Reuband 2005, p. 99 (Jewish Auschwitz survivor, 1943); letter of Anna Grigorewna T. in Schwarze 2005, p. 70 (forced worker with farmers near Münster).

[8] For Germany, Britain, Denmark and the Netherlands, see Baten and Wagner 2003, esp. p. 103.

[9] Raspin 1986, p. 307.

[10] For Belgium, see figures in Brandt *et al.* 1953, p. 473; for food availability see pp. 466–70; for the Netherlands see Trienekens 1985, esp. pp. 389, 431–3, and Kleman and Kudryashov 2012, p. 374; for France see Sauvy 1978, p. 190.

benefited from favorable black-market conditions. Conditions for urban workers, by contrast, were very harsh, particularly in the area of Paris and on the Mediterranean coast. In 1941, 100,000 miners in northern France went on strike in protest against hunger.[11] Outright famine killed about 300,000 people in Greece in 1941–43, 20,000 in the Netherlands in 1944–45, and an unknown number in French Algeria in 1942.[12]

Food may appear to be an unremarkable, even banal, subject, but it is the essence of life and a common means to express social hierarchies and cultural and ethnic difference. During the war, varying rations assigned to different groups determined different qualities of life and chances of survival. The hierarchy of consumers became a powerful driving force for the murder of millions of people – Jews and others – by starvation or other means, with the intention of excluding them from the food balance. Food had a major impact on German occupation policy.[13] In a global perspective, extraction of resources by occupiers, mass detention, decreasing food production and interrupted economic relations led to a worldwide wave of famines, especially in occupied countries and colonies. According to one high-end estimate, 20 million people around the globe died from starvation and related diseases during World War II.[14] This would mean that one in three of the war's victims succumbed to hunger. Issues surrounding food were also very influential upon German policies. Famine raged in a number of countries under German or Axis control. German leaders even tried to create a giant famine in the USSR. This chapter outlines this policy and its consequences for Soviet Jews. Nonetheless, in late 1941 and early 1942, political and military authorities came to the conclusion that famine among entire civilian populations was counterproductive and ought to be stopped. This chapter explains why German authorities first destroyed millions of Soviet POWs through systematic starvation but why most Jews then were *not* starved to death – although the refusal to feed them contributed heavily to their extermination, as I will show for occupied Poland in 1942 – and why some Jews died of hunger nonetheless.

The starvation policy of 1941

In eastern Europe, the impact of German food policies was more severe. This was especially so after Germany's reserve of 6–8 million tons of

[11] Cépède 1961, pp. 403–6, 415; Kistenmacher 1959, pp. 30–1, 125–6; Delacor 1994, pp. 14, 20, 25; see also Sanders 2005, pp. 150–5. For the strike see Zielinski 1995a, p. 78.
[12] Hionidou 2006, pp. 2, 158; Trienekens 1985, pp. 398–407; Hirschfeld 1984, p. 37; Thomas 1998, p. 242.
[13] See Volkmann 1984, pp. 9–74.
[14] Collingham 2011, p. 1.

grain was used up by the winter of 1940–41.[15] Occupying one country after another had not helped the situation, since most of them, even Poland (excluding eastern Galicia) and France, were normally net food importers. Belgium, Norway, Finland and, for some time, the Czech lands, also had to receive German food deliveries during the war to cover part of their deficits.[16]

Germans still had enough to eat, but the dwindling reserves made Germany's ability to continue fighting the war questionable in the minds of politicians. As a result, they cut meat rations in Germany in April 1941, and before their attack in June on the Soviet Union, food and agriculture experts together with military strategists developed a scheme to starve part of the Soviet populace within a year. "Umpteen of millions of people will without doubt starve to death when we extract from the country what we need" read a note from a meeting of state secretaries and military generals on May 2.[17] Two population groups became the main targets: urban dwellers and the inhabitants of the supposed food deficit areas in Belarus and northern and central Russia, which were to be cordoned off in so that "the industry as well as [a] large part of the people die off." Simply lowering the food ration of every Soviet citizen would not suffice because it would be impossible to confiscate produce before it went on the black market.[18] Hitler, Göring and other leading politicians approved the general outline of the policy. This was the origin of talk during this phase among SS and military officers about reducing the Soviet population by 30 million people.[19]

Aside from the overall German food supply, military strategy fueled the scheme. The logistical challenge of the planned invasion of the USSR was enormous. The campaign was supposed to engage the Soviet army, which was numerically at least on a par with the Germans, as far west as possible, and thus required speed. It was planned to conquer an area up to 2,000 km deep and 1,600 km wide. For reasons of transport efficiency, the necessary supplies could only be guaranteed via the railways (not the

15 Corni and Gies 1997, p. 406; material in file BA R 14/128.

16 Volkmann 1984, esp. pp. 19–21, 31–8, 42; Brandt *et al.* 1953, esp. pp. 273, 366–7, 447, 467, 517; Cépède 1961, p. 33; Kistenmacher 1959, p. 42; OKW, WiRü Amt, "Kriegswirtschaftlicher Lagebericht" Nr. 21, June 10, 1941, BA-MA RW 19/177, p. 19; Goebbels diary, October 23, 1941, Goebbels 1996, vol. II 2, p. 161.

17 "Aktennotiz über Ergebnis der heutigen Besprechung mit den Staatssekretären über Barbarossa," May 2, 1941 in IMG, vol. 31, p. 84.

18 Wirtschaftsstab Ost, Gruppe La, "Wirtschaftspolitische Richtlinien für die Wirtschaftsorganisation Ost, Gruppe Landwirtschaft," May 23, 1941, IMG, vol. 36, pp. 135–57, quote on p. 156.

19 For the starvation policy see Aly and Heim 1991, pp. 365–93; Gerlach 1999, pp. 46–76; Dieckmann 2011, pp. 192–222; Kay 2006.

roads), but there existed too few west–east railway lines. This lack of transportation capacity implied that the rear shipments from Germany had to be reserved for troops, weaponry and ammunition and omit all that was expendable: especially food. Food procured from the occupied Soviet territories would primarily serve to feed the eastern armies, not the German homeland. This way of thinking linked the starvation policy directly to military operations and the success or failure of the fight against a deadly enemy. It could therefore be seen as being in the interests of the army, and this was what earned the scheme the support of many military officers. The Quartermaster General of the German ground forces, Major-General Eduard Wagner, who was in charge of military supplies, occupation policy and POWs, played a key role.[20]

This starvation policy, one of the biggest mass murder plans in human history, was designed earlier than any specific plans to kill European Jews, and was intended to kill far more people. Although deeply rooted in pragmatic considerations, it was broadly compatible with important elements of Nazi thinking: racist contempt and enslavement of Slavs, the destruction of communism and long-term intentions to win land for German settlers in the east. Thus the hunger policy was based on military necessity, but none free of ideology. For Hitler, war was the moving principle of history as races struggled for territory to secure their livelihoods – a philosophy he summarized in a 1928 speech as the "fight for the daily bread." As early as 1922 he had announced his intention to "take possession of the grain areas of Poland and Ukraine." Goebbels added – in an article dated May 31, 1942 – that the war against the USSR was also fought "for grain and bread, for a well laid breakfast, lunch and dinner table, a war for the material preconditions for solving the social question."[21] In the short run, however, exploiting the agricultural sector and settling Germans were potentially conflicting aims. Neither in terms of racism nor settlement was there any reason why Ukrainians should be treated much better (relatively speaking) than Russians or Belarusians, which shows how much weight economic issues carried.

The hunger scheme went far beyond Jews. They were automatically among its targets because they were a significant portion of the urban population of the western Soviet Union, which was to be wiped out. In effect, then, the starvation policy also aimed at killing most of the Soviet Jews. If cities and industry vanished, it would also be a blow to the communism which was politically rooted there. Jews were also

[20] Gerlach 1999, pp. 66–76, 150–6; Dieckmann 2011, pp. 184–92, 209–22.

[21] The first quote is from Kroll 1998, p. 61; the second and third quotes are from Corni and Gies 1997, pp. 451, 500.

generally suspected of strongly supporting the communist regime, fighting Nazi rule and black marketeering – three activities that could endanger German objectives.

After Germany had invaded the Soviet Union, troops and civil and military administrations tried to carry this across-the-board starvation policy into effect. But soon there were disagreements. Military commanders objected that the army needed a supply of indigenous labor in the cities, that they did not have enough troops to suppress the widespread unrest that might arise due to hunger, prevent urban dwellers from getting supplies from the countryside, and that epidemics among the population would be disastrous for the German army. By the late summer and early fall of 1941 these concerns led to a transition from the initial utopian design of the hunger policy to manageable mass murder programs targeting specific groups for swift destruction either by hunger (Soviet POWs) or direct killings (especially Jews).[22] Food rations for urbanites were introduced, but they were so small that millions went hungry and many left the cities for the countryside.

Historians have described how considerations about food policy impacted upon the murder of Soviet Jews in different areas. In Lithuania, the supply problems of Army Group North were already so large by July 1941 that there was pressure on the local administrations (from the German civil administration) to reduce the number of food recipients and of so-called useless eaters among the Jews. This led to the practice of shooting women and children by mid-August 1941, and explains in part the fact that more than 80% of Lithuania's Jews were murdered by 1941.[23] In Belarus, the mass murder of Jews peaked in October and November 1941. It went much further in the eastern half that was under German military administration – where close to 90% were killed in 1941 – than under the German civil administration in the west where a quarter or less of the population perished that year. A number of factors explain this, including the Army Group Center's endangered supplies, a particularly serious food situation and food denial policy, and a low demand for industrial labor in the severely destroyed cities and towns of the east. Army squads hunted the countryside for non-locals, among them hunger refugees from the cities and Jews, as suspected potential partisans. The personnel of the civil administration were much more Nazified than those of the military, and yet the military cooperated more than the civil administration did with the SS and police in the murder of Jews – or pressed them for it – in order to secure their own food supplies for

[22] Gerlach 1999, pp. 1132–9.
[23] Dieckmann 2000, pp. 251–64.

military operations and to suppress resistance.[24] Similar arguments have been made about Ukraine.[25] Jewish workers and civil servants seemed to become superfluous in large areas slated for de-industrialization and de-Sovietization. As in the western parts of Belarus and Ukraine (and parts of Poland until 1939) – where there was another economic structure dominated by small-scale craftsmanship – more Jewish labor was needed and the majority of the Jewish communities were retained for the time being.[26]

There were also specific connections. In many places – including Kiev and Kharkov –civil, or especially military, administrations demanded massacres of Jews because of food crises or the health risk posed by starving Jews. SS and police units were told before executions that shooting Jews was preferable to having them starve. Some units protested against having to kill people who the military was starving.[27]

German policy was quite systematic and managed in the occupied Soviet territories by an elaborate agricultural administration of more than 20,000 German and at least half a million local employees. The agricultural administration organized food procurement and distribution, but it was also responsible for obtaining machinery and other agricultural inputs from Germany, and for carrying out measures like the agrarian reform of 1942–43 that partially dissolved Soviet collective farms and affected about 2 million farm families. Romania undertook similar measures in Transnistria. The importance of food is also reflected in the fact that about half of the entire German administrative apparatus in the Soviet Union was dedicated to agriculture.[28]

Despite the change of policy in the summer and fall of 1941, great numbers of Soviet citizens died of starvation as a result of German policies. The largest group (aside from the 3 million Soviet POWs, who I will discuss below) was the civilian population of the besieged city of Leningrad where between 600,000 and 1.3 million people (which was fewer than

[24] Gerlach 1999, pp. 574–606.

[25] Boll and Safrian 2000, pp. 256–64; Pohl 2000, pp. 143–8; for the Crimea see Angrick 2003, p. 336.

[26] Dean 2000, pp. 38, 53.

[27] Pohl 2000, p. 147 (Kiev, Kharkov); Oldenburg 2004, pp. 167–8 (Zimferopol, Crimea, December 1941); Hasenclever 2006, p. 213 (Field Commandant 197, Priluki, Ukraine, April 20, 1942); Gerlach 1999, pp. 596–7 (Vitebsk, October 1941); Gerlach 1999, pp. 622–3 (Slonim, Belarus, November 1941); Neitzel 2005, pp. 304–5 (Riga); Levinson 2006, p. 100 (Kretinga, Lithuania); Keller 2011, p. 138 (Heydrich's complaint about the military sending half-dead Soviet POWs, among them Jews, to concentration camps within the Reich, November 9, 1941).

[28] Gerlach 1995, esp. pp. 11, 25–33; for Transnistria see Dallin 1998, pp. 96, 100; Hausleitner 2003, p. 93.

German strategists intended) died – mostly in 1941–42, of hunger and cold. The fight for survival led to criminality and corruption among the inhabitants, including theft, armed robbery, embezzlement, ration card fraud, patronage systems, black marketeering and cannibalism – even among close relatives.[29] Many managed to flee other large Soviet cities that were under German occupation, so figures on death from starvation in these places were much lower: 11,000 in Kharkov in the first eight months of 1942; an unknown number in Kiev and 9,500 in Pushkin, a suburb of Leningrad under German control. One author estimates that 200,000 Soviet civilians died of starvation in the area of Army Group Center alone.[30] If more urban dwellers – especially from smaller towns – survived than many Germans had expected, it was because the population had access to the black market, scoured the fields, and relied on family and friends in the countryside.[31] Another vulnerable group were refugees and those subject to forced resettlement, especially when being put into camps. In 1943–44, the Germans evacuated close to 2.5 million Soviets – who were often marched and held in camps under brutal conditions. Partial data suggest that 30,000 evacuees may have died in Alytus, Lithuania, 9,000 near Ozarichi, and 6,000 near Baranovichi, Belarus.[32]

During three years of occupation, Germans confiscated large quantities of food in the Soviet Union, including more than 9 million tons of grain. This alone equaled the estimated pre-war consumption of 12 million Soviet citizens over three years. "[T]he fact that Germany could pass through World War II without a food catastrophe was due in part to the utilization of the agricultural resources of the occupied Soviet territories."[33] Many Germans believed that Germany needed land in eastern Europe to feed itself. A sufficient number of German soldiers took pity on the Soviet population that commanders found it necessary to issue and widely distribute orders against such mercy and to point out that food given to Soviet citizens would not be available to the German homeland.[34] This thinking became so influential that officers later warned of "the earlier adopted attitude that we had too many people in this area

[29] See Ganzenmüller 2005, pp. 13–53, 68–9, 237–78.

[30] Hilberg 1992a, p. 223; Berkhoff 2004, pp. 164–86; Ganzenmüller 2005, p. 74 with note 281; see Pohl 2011, pp. 191–3, 199. For the 200,000 figure see Terry 2005, pp. 201, 260.

[31] Oldenburg 2004, pp. 103–4 (Crimea); see also Kunz 2005, pp. 141–3, 155; Gerlach 1999, pp. 284–9 (Belarus).

[32] Dieckmann 2011, pp. 1388–91; Rass 2003, pp. 386–402; Terry 2005, pp. 243–59; Gerlach 1999, pp. 1092–6.

[33] Brandt *et al.* 1953, pp. 129–30, quote on p. 146.

[34] Furber 2004, pp. 549–50; Ganzenmüller 2005, pp. 73–8; order by Colonel General von Reichenau, 6th Army, October 10, 1941, in Müller 1982, p. 111; Instructions for all front newspapers, November 1, 1941, in Reinhardt 1972, p. 92 note 289.

and that their destruction was a blessing for Germandom."[35] As the rest of this chapter will show, policies matching this attitude led to mass murder, especially of Soviet POWs and Jews.

Soviet prisoners of war

With about 3 million deaths out of approximately 5.7 million people (a mortality rate of more than 50%), Soviet POWs were the second largest group of victims of German rule.[36] Most of them died from hunger and undersupply of other goods (which is why I discuss their fate in this chapter). Many features of the treatment of Soviet POWs either resemble that of Jews, or were connected with policies against Jews. To give just a few examples, the first experiments, in late 1941, in Auschwitz of gassing people with prussic acid were carried out on hundreds of Soviet POWs (together with a smaller number of other camp inmates including Jews).[37] Soviet POWs were apparently also the first prisoners in Auschwitz to be tattooed with numbers.[38] When Soviet POWs started to die en masse on German soil in the summer and fall of 1941, local authorities ordered many of them to be buried in Jewish cemeteries.[39] Himmler considered the mass sterilization of not only Jews but also of Soviet POWs on the advice of a physicist in 1942.[40] The SS and German military also conducted medical experiments on Soviet POWs who had been transferred to concentration camps, as they did on other camp inmates.[41] SS-Sonderkommando 1005 exhumed and incinerated the remains of tens of thousands of Soviet POWs in addition to those of murdered Jews (and non-Jewish Poles) in order to destroy the evidence.[42] And, not unlike concentration camp inmates (including Jews), those Soviet prisoners who were still alive in early 1945 were sent on evacuation marches during which those no longer able to walk were shot. The rationale for the evacuations were similar: fear of uprisings and the

35 RMO representative with the staff of Army Group North, memo, December 1942, Nuremberg Document PS-1381.

36 Streit 1991, p. 21; for the number of Soviet POWs, see the recent calculations by Otto *et al.* 2008, esp. pp. 592, 595.

37 Hałgas 1987, p. 169.

38 Ibid.; Otto 1998, pp. 190–1; see also Datner 1964, pp. 92–4.

39 Schäfer 2000, p. 51 (Ulm, Tübingen); Hoffmann 2001, p. 127 (Oldenburg); Keller 2011, p. 313.

40 Pokorny to Himmler, October 1941, and Himmler to Pohl, March 10, 1942, BA NS 19/1583, pp. 5–7.

41 Otto 1998, pp. 76–81; Datner 1964, pp. 322–35.

42 For Belarus see Spector 1990b, pp. 165–6; see also Gerlach 1999, p. 774; for western Poland, see Hoffmann 2008, pp. 393, 400–3.

refusal to surrender any prisoner to the enemy. Anecdotal evidence suggests that the risk of being shot during the marches was higher for Soviets than for other POWs and higher still for concentration camp inmates (including Jews).[43]

As with Jews, the murder of Soviet POWs was carried out with hatred and brutality. Direct mass killings claimed the lives of hundreds of thousands of POWs, as described below. Camp guards, the troops accompanying them on marches, and employers alike committed unspeakable cruelties against Soviet prisoners. Such maltreatment was already practiced by so many Germans in 1941 that it may have become a model for others. Survivors' memories describe beatings and torture in some detail. These, together with hunger and hard labor, were cited as reasons for attempted escape. There are also German accounts of horrendous mistreatment.[44] Unfortunately, few POW accounts were ever published, and even worse, there has been next to no research based on those that were.[45] One effect of this is that the mistreatment of Soviet POWs is hardly known today. There are no analyses of camp society, or of the inmates' psychology and their relation to the endurance of these prisoners; no studies of long-term consequences; and hardly any works on the relationships between guards, prisoners and nearby residents. In brief, there has been no research on the victims as personalities. Unlike other POWs, they did not have post-war associations that lobbied for them.[46] Just how devastating the impact of German captivity must have been is illustrated by the fact that, despite the enormous casualty rate and traumatic experiences of Soviet troops serving on the frontlines, by the late 1990s only 1% of former Soviet POWs were still alive, compared to about 5% of all war veterans.[47]

[43] Speckner 2003, pp. 190–6 ("in almost all parts of the Reich"), 208; Datner 1964, pp. 209–12; Lauerwald 1996, pp. 76–88; survivor letters in *Ich werde* 2007, for example pp. 121, 204, 224, 236, 239–40, 241.

[44] Examples in *Ich werde* 2007, pp. 44–5, 56, 61, 68, 70, 76, 90, 100–2, 127–8, 138–9, 148–50, 154, 163, 169, 172, 175–6, 182, 188–9, 198, 203–4, 206–7, 211–12, 229 (mistreatment, often fatal, is mentioned in twenty-three of sixty survivors' letters in that volume); Keller 1994, pp. 46, 49; Keller 2011, pp. 118–21; Obenaus 1985, p. 106; Speckner 2003, pp. 131–2; Reese 2003, p. 48. See ZStL V 319 AR 327/77, esp. interrogations of L.B.S. and W.T.N., January 28, 1975 (vol. 3, pp. 533, 544–5), P.J.K., August 30, 1944, and August 21, 1975, W.M.R., January 10, 1975 and Karl Langut, December 24, 1945 (vol. 2, pp. 285, 338, 419) on the camps in Krichev, Mogilev and Bobruisk.

[45] This is also true for the Soviet Union and the post-Soviet era: Erin 2004, esp. p. 54. See also Keller 2011, pp. 37–9.

[46] Keller 2011, p. 37; for one exception in post-Soviet Armenia: *Ich werde* 2007, p. 244.

[47] Sergej Osipov, Deputy Chairman of the Commission for POWs, Interned and Missing, with the President of the Russian Federation, gave, according to Zeidler and Schmidt 1999 (p. 29), 10% as the percentage of military personnel still alive, but this was based

Such treatment had one of its roots in the racist and political attitudes toward Soviet POWs. Most of them were Slavs, some were central Asians, and, thus, they belonged to groups widely regarded as low in culture, and inferior. Importantly, due to the flight of Soviet functionaries as the Germans approached, the POWs were almost the only representatives of the Soviet state to fall into German hands. Therefore, they were associated with communism and a demonized regime purportedly masterminded by Jews. In 1941 and especially in 1942, German propaganda in print and newsreels portrayed Soviet POWs as subhuman beasts and murderers.[48]

These attitudes contributed to the low number of Soviet prisoners taken by the Germans. There is abundant evidence of German units shooting Soviet troops who surrendered, particularly in the summer of 1941 but also later.[49] The strongest evidence is the unusually low ratio, about 1:1.5, of prisoners taken to Red Army soldiers who died on the battlefield.[50] This may in part be testament to the particularly stiff resistance of Soviet troops – which may itself have been in response to rumors and propaganda about the appalling treatment meted out to those who surrendered to the Germans, German revenge against Soviet breaches of the laws of warfare, the harsh laws in the USSR against surrender, and the fact that Soviet commanders often wasted their troops in frontal assaults. Yet the ratio is also due to the Germans' widespread refusal to take prisoners.

The intention since even before the German invasion on June 22, 1941, to feed Soviet POWs inadequately, in keeping with the starvation policy, is well documented.[51] The plan was for most of the prisoners to remain in Soviet territory, which was slated for mass starvation. Transports westwards were supposed to be organized largely on foot to keep the railways free for troops.[52] Improvised camps were hurriedly erected in the occupied territories as well as in the Reich; many had no buildings at all even into the very cold winter of 1941.[53] Due to temporary shortages and

on 1 million survivors and the unrealistic assumption that there were only 10 million Soviet combatants. See also Polian 2005b, p. 139.

48 Obenaus 1985, pp. 103–4 (August 1941); Borgsen and Volland 1991, p. 125 (February 1942).

49 Gerlach 1999, pp. 774–81, 878–9; Datner 1964, p. 17; Stein 1978, pp. 119–20, 245; Rass 2003, pp. 335–8; Lieb 2007, p. 162.

50 The ratio is computed on the basis of 5.7 million prisoners and 8.6 million fallen. The latter is a lower end figure.

51 Streit 1991, p. 79.

52 Gerlach 1998a, pp. 23–4; Keller 2011, p. 158; until April 1941 there were plans to bring more POWs to Germany: Keller 2011, pp. 56, 58, 62.

53 Keller 2011, pp. 92–103; Streit 1991, pp. 171–7; Osterloh 1997, p. 37. But this was so for the Polish POWs in the winter of 1939–40 (Overmans 2005, p. 744) who survived in the main because they received enough to eat.

disorganization – but also to the fact that rations were intentionally meager and deliveries to German troops took priority – prisoners received little or nothing to eat, and what they did get was often buckwheat and millet, which German troops were not used to. Tens of thousands died of malnutrition, but a number of factors kept the mortality rate much below that reached in the fall.[54] The human body can withstand weeks of hunger, the prisoners had often been adequately fed *before* capture, and their numbers tripled in September and October.

A crucial factor in the fall's increased mortality, however, was that after discussions among leading politicians (including Göring and Goebbels) and high functionaries in charge of food and military supplies, the latter agreed to reduce food rations – especially for non-working prisoners – by 27% as measured in calories, and 46% in terms of the amount of protein, on October 21, shortly before the onset of the cold season. Not only did the size of rations differ greatly between those who worked and those who could not, but in many places the latter were also separated from the former in special sectors or separate camps and left there to perish.[55] At a meeting on November 13 of the chiefs of staff of all the German armies and army groups on the Eastern Front, Quartermaster-General Wagner stated in a discussion about the possibilities of feeding Soviet POWs reasonably, "Prisoners of war in the prisoner camps who do not work have to starve to death." Even working POWs, Wagner said, should be fed with army supplies only in exceptional cases because the provisioning of German troops had absolute priority.[56] This turn of events in the fall marked a second stage of the hunger policy. While the overall starvation plan for large sections of the Soviet population had to be given up at this point, the strategy was intensified for the Soviet POWs, a group for which one could realistically force the unproductive to starve to death. This was seen as a necessity of war, since the problems of supplying German troops on the Eastern Front had become even graver than foreseen.

As a result, 300,000–500,000 prisoners died each month between October 1941 and January 1942,[57] one of the highest rates of human destruction in history. A comparable rate would be reached for the

[54] Gerlach 1998a, pp. 33–4 versus Streit 1991, pp. 130–2, 187–9. Inside the Reich, 19,000 Soviet POWs had perished by early November 1941 (fewer than by direct killing, which is not included in this number), but 200,000 awaited death through starvation, as was reported: Keller 2011, p. 265.

[55] Gerlach 1998a, pp. 36–41; Keller 2011, p. 434.

[56] Chief of Staff, 18th Army, "Merkpunkte aus der Chefbesprechung in Orscha am 13.11.41," Nuremberg Document NOKW-1535.

[57] These figures are based on data in Streit 1991, pp. 130–7.

murder of the Jews in July–October 1942. This implied 10,000–16,000 deaths per day – 300–400 per day for many POW camps. Death rates were especially high in the General Government, in the area of operations of Army Group Center during the Battle of Moscow, and the Reich Commissariat Ostland.[58] Since the policy that supplies for the captives had to come from the occupied Soviet territories only after the needs of German troops had been met was always in effect, prisoners mostly received only watery soup and a little bread made from ersatz ingredients, which was hard to digest, another factor in many deaths. Such food contained hardly any fat, protein or vitamins.[59] Although dysentery and typhoid broke out, most fatalities by far were caused by hunger, and, increasingly, hunger in combination with cold since in many camps there was no heating and not even enough buildings.[60] Gruesome mass graves became necessary in the camps, including those located inside Germany.[61] Other concentration camp inmates were amazed to discover that Soviet POWs arriving in the fall of 1941 got far less food than they did, and they tried to help them.[62]

A large number of Soviet POWs were starved to death as part of the plan to defeat the USSR in a single giant push. The function of this starvation plan was to give the push as much thrust as possible. These POWs were a large labor force, but that was of secondary importance as long as Germany seemed to need no new major armament effort. In the fall of 1941, however, it gradually became clear that such an effort would be necessary since victory over the Soviet Union could not be expected by the end of the year. By late October and early November 1941, only weeks after the food supplies for non-working prisoners had been reduced, Hitler and Göring ordered that Soviets be transported to Germany en masse to work in German industries.[63] Much of the period during which the number of Soviet POW deaths were at their greatest came after the issue of orders to use them as forced labor. This was the result of a number of factors. The military's orders to keep prisoners alive remained ambivalent until December, for until then there was still an attempt being made to treat the fit markedly different from the unfit. However, the former were also underfed and forced to do hard labor, and guards tended to treat both groups with equal brutality. Also, food administrators refused to provide the necessary resources. Additionally,

58 Gerlach 1998a, p. 45.
59 Streit 1991, pp. 137–62; survivors' accounts in *Ich werde* 2007.
60 Streit 1991, pp. 171–7, 180; Gerlach 1998a, pp. 49–50; Keller 2011, pp. 265, 287–97.
61 Keller 1994, p. 46.
62 Hałgas 1987, p. 169 (Auschwitz); Keller 2011, p. 418 (Neuengamme).
63 Herbert 1985, pp. 137–49; Streit 1991, pp. 201–8.

since it had been decided in early November not only to bring large numbers of Soviet POWs but also Soviet *civilians* to Germany, the latter constituted the larger workforce.[64] Right through until the end of the war, troops at or near the front tried to reserve a large number of Soviet POWs as laborers, servants, and, later, also as auxiliary forces. At no point before 1945 were the majority of Soviet POWs inside Germany.[65]

There is an old debate about the extent to which the mass death of Soviet POWs was due to policies or to circumstances.[66] While it is obvious that not every German officer, soldier and functionary unanimously wanted to destroy POWs, there is enough evidence to conclude that many of them saw this as either their duty, or desirable. Officers in a casino in Riga talked about their mission to starve and freeze POWs to death.[67] As some observers reported with regret, the opinion was widespread, especially, but not only, in leading officers' circles, that it was in Germany's interest for as many Soviets as possible, and especially POWs, to starve to death.[68] On March 27, 1942, the Chief of Prisoner Affairs in the OKW, Major General von Graevenitz, said in reference to an order from Hitler to keep POWs fit for work, "The formulation [that] the Russian was a beast, he had to perish, thus had to disappear," which documents indirectly that he believed that this destructive attitude was widespread.[69] It has been argued that there could not have been any intention to starve hundreds of thousands of Soviet POWs to death because about half of them (that is, those who came under OKW's command) were meticulously registered individually.[70] But then the existence, deportation and seized belongings of many Jews who were killed were also meticulously documented, despite their impending murders.

German leaders knew about the mass deaths of Soviet POWs. When Raoul Wallenberg attended a banquet in Berlin in the winter of 1941–42, people talked about the 10–20 million Soviets who would die of hunger, inter alia in the famine in Leningrad.[71] Göring more or less boasted

[64] Gerlach 1998a, pp. 52–5; Gerlach 1999, pp. 816–17, 823–9; Keller 2011, pp. 240, 244, 247–8, 251; Streit 1991, pp. 208–16.

[65] Streit 1991, pp. 239–44; Gerlach 1999, pp. 830–4; Keller 2011, pp. 158, 220, 503–6.

[66] Streit 1991, pp. 187–9.

[67] Recollections by Helmut Paulsen in Schröder 1992, p. 706; see Neitzel 2005, p. 261 (recollections by Lieutenant Paul Seyfarth, wire-tapped in British captivity in September 1944).

[68] Army Group Center, Ib, to Quartermaster General, December 7, 1941, BA-MA RH 19 II/127, p. 228–9; in retrospect: Vegesack 1965, p. 237; see another example in Overmans *et al.* 2012, pp. 296–7.

[69] Quoted in Keller 2011, p. 349.

[70] Otto *et al.* 2008, pp. 595–6.

[71] Bankier 1996, pp. 106–7.

to the Italian Foreign Minister about Soviet prisoners starving and eating each other. Goebbels, informed by Backe, anticipated mass deaths among Soviet POWs and intended to tell Hitler that it was necessary. On December, 14 Rosenberg also informed Hitler that 2,500 Soviet POWs died each day in Reich Commissariat Ukraine and that "one has to assume that not many will remain [alive]."[72] Hitler also announced in a public speech on November 8 that the enemy would starve to death in Leningrad. If anything, these leaders could have expected only *slightly* different data on mortality and survival. Beyond the politicians, army generals not directly involved thought that a million or more prisoners, or about one third of them, had died.[73]

Aside from policy makers, debates about the responsibility for the mass death of Soviet POWs have centered around German military camp administrations, camp guards and guard units on marches and transports. Their attitudes and behavior cannot be simplified to a single case, and, sometimes, an individual's acts were contradictory. Accordingly, some scholars have argued that camp commandants of good will who made serious efforts to improve matters could not do much to save the prisoners given the existing supply system and the prevailing ideology.[74] Others have observed "widespread indifference" on the part of those responsible toward Soviet POWs dying en masse.[75] The "irritating synchronism between war of extermination and labor deployment" has been explained as a result of the interplay between the different interests and goals of different German institutions, among which the German military "behaved inconsistently."[76] But the military was certainly not a monolith; it consisted of different groups and factions with conflicting goals. The losses among Soviet prisoners were so great, and the measures taken by camp administrators were such that many historians locate part of the responsibility with them.[77]

I estimate the total number of deaths among Soviet POWs at about 3 million (52–53% of 5.7 million in total).[78] The bulk of these perished in

[72] Rosenberg's note, December 16, 1941, about a meeting with Hitler on December 14 in IMG, vol. 27, p. 272. Göring: Ciano 1946 (November 25, 1941); Goebbels 1996 (II, 2), pp. 132, 161, 484 (October 17, October 23 and December 12, 1941); see Otto 1998, p. 197 (Himmler, January 23, 1942).

[73] For wire-tapped conversations see Neitzel 2005, pp. 255, 271. For Hitler see Piper 2005, p. 544.

[74] See, for example, Hartmann 2001. Schulte 2000 (pp. 318–19) called these cases exceptional.

[75] Otto *et al.* 2008, p. 595.

[76] Keller 2011, p. 429.

[77] Streit 1991, pp. 137–80, 187–9; Gerlach 1999, pp. 802–13.

[78] Since the early 1980s, serious scholarship has placed the figure between 2.5 and 3.3 million (Streit 1991, p. 21). Due to slight downward revisions for some camps or

eastern Europe: possibly 1.3 million in Ukraine, 700,000 in Belarus and 400,000–600,000 in Poland.[79] Most of the total, about 2 million, had died by January 1942, which is more than 60% of the prisoners taken by that time; the percentage was even higher for some groups.[80] By comparison, about 900,000 Jews had been murdered in Europe by January 1942. Mortality among the approximately 30,000 Soviet POWs in SS concentration camps was even higher than in army camps (even without counting prisoners transferred to SS camps for immediate execution as political suspects): about 80% had starved to death or were killed by February 1942.[81] This also exceeded the death rate for other groups of concentration camp inmates by this point.[82] Similar incredible mortality rates also occurred in the POW camps of Waffen-SS units in the occupied Soviet territories.[83] But the vast majority of Soviet POWs died not at the hands of the SS but in army custody. A million Soviet POWs, or 27% of 3.7 million prisoners, perished at the hands of the German army and SS in the thirty-nine months between February 1942 and April 1945.[84] Death rates among Polish and Soviet *civilian* forced laborers inside Germany were well below 10%. This means that Soviet POWs were at all times treated far worse than these civilians.

As with almost any population under famine conditions, the competitive struggle for survival differentiated Soviet POWs. The theft of food was frequent and a few resorted to cannibalism. Prisoners competed for the 'best' jobs. Some secured better treatment by acting as camp 'police' or reporting fellow prisoners or denouncing Jews, political commissars, communists and officers.[85] More than half a million joined German units (Army, Waffen-SS or other SS or police forces), not necessarily out of conviction but for survival, even if only for a little while. After 1942 many Soviet POWs achieved a low level of social integration by establishing relations with Germans at their workplaces, attracting pity or selling hand-made trinkets or toys to Germans in the area.[86] We know relatively

territories (Germany, Belarus) Streit's figure of 3.3 million needs to be somewhat reduced. See Zeidler and Schmidt 1999, pp. 35–7. Soviet and later Russian overall estimates differ widely and are unconvincing: see Erin 2004, pp. 42–6.

79 Kumanev 1991, p. 66 (official figure for Ukraine); Gerlach 1999, pp. 856–7; Datner 1964, pp. 228–35.

80 Gerlach 1998a, pp. 42–5; Streit 1991, pp. 131–7, 245. Keller 2011 (pp. 320–3) estimates that 1.6–1.8 million died before February 1, 1942.

81 Keller 2011, pp. 419–23; Datner 1964, pp. 286–321; Steinbacher 2000, p. 239; Otto 1998, pp. 192–3; Brandhuber 1961, pp. 5–46.

82 Snyder 2010a, p. 183.

83 Cüppers 2005, pp. 233–8.

84 Streit 1991, pp. 244–9.

85 Dawletschin 2005, pp. 61–5

86 Speckner 2005, p. 346; Osterloh 1997, pp. 127–8; Borgsen and Volland 1991, p. 140; account by Emmanuil Sossin in *Ich werde* 2007, pp. 195–7.

little about the general solidarity among Soviet prisoners. Many historians have viewed the officers among Soviet POWs as being particularly targeted, considering that many were executed[87] – but this view may have been the result of misinterpretation. Judging from data on those former Soviet POWs in German hands who returned to the Soviet Union, officers and non-commissioned officers had a much higher survival rate than ordinary soldiers. Among 1,826 million returnees, 20.8% were officers (379,666) and 10.7% were sergeants.[88] If it is true that 400,000 Soviet officers were captured,[89] almost all would have survived. While this seems unlikely, they probably made up less than 20% of total troop strength. Thus it seems that Soviet officers in German captivity – very few of whom disclosed their status to the Germans – wielded considerable power within prisoners' communities and commanded social capital that, undesirably for the Germans, gave them much better chances for survival than the rank and file. There seems to be no research on this subject, but this raises questions about prisoner society and German power inside the camps.[90]

Direct killing of Soviet POWs and popular knowledge of their fate

Among the several groups of Soviet POWs especially targeted for direct killing were Jews, political officers, military officers (though less systematically) and Asian-looking individuals. In accord with Hitler's order, German frontline army units murdered captured political officers (commissars) in 1941–42 (up to 10,000 – such killings were reported by at least 85% of all frontline divisions); as did Security Police and SD in the rear or inside Germany, where some 38,000 prisoners (7–8%) were sorted, most as commissars or Jews, in 1941–42.[91]

[87] For example, see Gerlach 1999, p. 836; Streit 1991, p. 257.

[88] Data are from Polian 2005b, p. 129; Polian 2007, p. 38; the conclusions are mine.

[89] Pohl 2011 (p. 232) assumes a much lower number of returnees than cited above.

[90] For better housing (initially) for officers, see Dawletschin 2005, pp. 83–5, 87–8, 113, 130–3. Until April 1942 about 0.5% of the Soviet POWs (15,681) were registered as officers: Römer 2008, pp. 423–7. Contrary to many assumptions, only a minority of former Soviet POWs in German hands was severely oppressed by Soviet authorities after their return. Several hundred thousand were interned by the NKVD, transferred to special settlements or military labor battalions, or shot: Polian 2005a, pp. 129–31. If former POWs from liberated German camps were remobilized into the Soviet army, this was dangerous but not an oppressive act.

[91] See Römer 2008, esp. pp. 359, 367, 405; Otto 1998, esp. p. 268; Keller 2011, pp. 111, 114, 135; Streit 1991, pp. 88–9; Gerlach 1999, pp. 834–7.

Often army troops, Security Police or commissions from the Eastern Ministry conducted screenings during which they checked for all of the mentioned groups simultaneously. Jews were often separated and soon shot, sometimes after periods of torture.[92] Sometimes, German troops formed Jews into separate columns when marching POWs, granted Jews only half of the starvation rations given to others, and compelled them to exclaim that they deserved such treatment because they were responsible for starting the war.[93] Until 1944, prisoners thought to be Jews were separated from the others and tortured. The evidence for this consisted of bruises, broken bones, ruptured eardrums and injuries from electric shock treatment.[94] According to most current estimates, a total of 80,000–85,000 Jewish-Soviet military personnel (1.5–1.8% of Soviet troops were Jewish) fell into German hands, of whom between 4,457 and 20,000 (5.5–25%) survived. Most Jews were revealed by medical examinations; others were denounced by fellow prisoners; still others came under suspicion because of their facial features. Those who survived managed to assume another identity or pretended to be civilians and were assigned to the civilian forced labor program.[95] Although registered as Jews in their units and sometimes the target of hostile reproaches or jokes before capture, their survival rate seems to indicate that Soviet-Jewish POWs did find some protection among their fellow prisoners.[96] If 15,000 of them (18%) survived, this was a lower survival rate than for all Soviet POWs taken together; but their survival rate, remarkably, was higher (or at least not lower) than for Jewish civilians in the German-occupied Soviet territories.

Yet the largest group of Soviet prisoners who were directly murdered were not singled out on political grounds. Army guards killed probably hundreds of thousands on marches because they could no longer walk; at stations because they did not enter or leave railroad cars fast enough; or in camps and at worksites because they were too weak to work; or simply threw them, half-alive, onto piles of corpses. Others froze to death or just expired during marches and transports.[97] Thus, the largest number of direct killings of Soviet POWs followed the logic of labor and of

[92] Arad 2009, pp. 376–81; Gerlach 1999, pp. 834–43.

[93] Letter by Dmitrij Sacharowitsch Woloschin in *Ich werde* 2007, pp. 220–1.

[94] Nikolaj Scheklakow, statement of May 30, 1945, in Drieschner and Schulz 2006, p. 181.

[95] Polian 2005a, pp. 502–5 (15,000–20,000 survivors); Maksudov 1993, p. 211 (70,000 killed; this would imply 10,000–15,000 survivors); Arad 2009, p. 381 (4,457 survivors); Levin 1992, p. 235. Krakowski's estimate (1992, p. 227) of "only a handful" survivors has been disproven.

[96] Anecdotal evidence is based on survivors' accounts: Levin 1992, pp. 236, 239–40.

[97] Streit 1991, pp. 162–71; Gerlach 1999, pp. 843–8; Reinhardt 1972, p. 91; Schäfer 2000, p. 44.

food (combined with political prejudice, racist views and military 'necessity'): murder the weak and exhausted who are no longer exploitable. Consideration was also given as to which Soviet POWs required too much time and too much food to recover; the latter were removed from the other prisoners and left to starve on minimal provisions. Wounded Soviet POWs received similar treatment and were often shot.[98] Thus, a life-and-death selection process according to labor ability was already functioning for Soviet POWs, and Soviet Jews, in 1941, before it was applied to Jews in most of Poland and many other areas of Europe. Still, most Soviet POWs selected for destruction were separated from the rest of the camp population and starved to death on short rations of food and other goods.

After 1945, many Germans claimed that they had not known about the murder of Jews, which had happened far away. They could hardly have overlooked the huge number of foreign forced laborers in their country, but the fate of these may not have appeared deadly. But Soviet POWs were dying in huge numbers in camps *inside* Germany by 1941[99] – a fact that was widely known and was occurring before most of the Jews had been deported and killed. We have no reports about German guards being traumatized from watching these mass deaths. Large numbers of Germans went to Soviet POW camps in 1941 to see the prisoners; most looked on in disdain since they did not regard them as human; but others felt pity.[100] Observers noticed that the prisoners lived in self-dug pits because most camps had no buildings prior to the first winter.[101] A photograph of freezing Soviet POWs being transported in open cattle cars was on the cover of the widely distributed military magazine *Die Wehrmacht* in early November 1941.[102] Residents observed that many POWs had died on the trains to Germany; that others were beaten; that many died of hunger; and that some ate grass, leaves and bark from trees. Children found corpses, some naked, lying in the streets after having been shot or collapsed on a march. Photographs went from hand to hand to convince those who did not believe the stories about the situation.[103] Employers and co-workers noticed that prisoners were so

98 Datner 1964 (p. 350) on an OKW order, July 24, 1941; Streit 1991, pp. 183–7.

99 Keller 2011 (p. 436) estimates at least 227,000 had died in Germany by mid 1942. See also ibid., p. 83, and Streit 1991, p. 135.

100 Letter by Wladimir Margewskij in *Ich werde* 2007, p. 241; Borgsen and Volland 1991, p. 116; notes by Karl Dürkefälden for August 1941 in Obenaus 1985, p. 103; Keller 1994, p. 40; Osterloh 1997, p. 126; Otto 1998, p. 178.

101 Keller 2011, pp. 92–103; Keller 1994, p. 40.

102 Osterloh 1997, p. 28.

103 Keller 1994, pp. 39–41, 46; Borgsen and Volland 1991, pp. 122, 138, 143–5. For weak prisoners shot upon arrival near Zeithain, Saxony, see Osterloh 1997, p. 30.

weak that they collapsed from even light work.[104] Near Bremen, prisoners could be heard several kilometers away shouting for food. This went on far days. Christians living in the vicinity knew enough about the mass death of prisoners to protest against Soviets being buried in the same cemetery as Germans.[105] It was also known that Soviet POWs were shot, and some knew that selected groups were deported to concentration camps to be murdered. The population living near the camp at Gross-Rosen, in Silesia, talked so much about the systematic shooting of Soviet POWs that the murderers switched the method of killing to lethal injection.[106] A German woman who asked a guard why they were not given more food heard him respond: "Then we would have nothing ourselves." Officials encouraged such thinking.[107] At first more people took pity on prisoners (which alarmed some German authorities), sometimes even aiding those who had escaped – although this changed after the Nazi press warned of the outbreak of epidemics in the camps in the winter of 1941–42. Residents' initial occasional help – throwing potatoes to prisoners, for example – gave way to passivity or verbal abuse as guards' treatment grew worse.[108] POW camps were often located in rural areas, perhaps to hide them from sight, but already in 1941 prisoners working in small groups could be seen at hundreds of places, where many of them died.[109] In brief, this mass destruction was already happening inside Germany in 1941; simultaneously with the beginning of the deportation of Jews. It was no secret.

Moreover, the Security Service persistently reported to decision-makers from as early as day two of the war that many Germans were worried about the possibility that food supplies for Soviet POWs would decrease their own rations. Citizens were repeatedly calling for the destruction of Soviet POWs for this very reason, they claimed.[110] If these reports are remotely accurate, many Germans were demanding a starvation policy from the very start.

[104] Keller 2011, pp. 203–8.

[105] Borgsen and Volland 1991, p. 114 (Bremen); burials: Drieschner and Schulz 2006, p. 15 (Fürstenberg); Borgsen and Volland 1991, p. 162 (Bremervörde).

[106] Notes by Karl Dürkefälden for August 1941 in Obenaus 1985, p. 103; Keller 1994, p. 37; Keller 2011, pp. 12, 121–2; Otto 1998, p. 93.

[107] Notes by Karl Dürkefälden, February 20, 1942, in Obenaus 1985, p. 107; see Keller 1994, p. 44; Schäfer 2000, p. 104.

[108] Keller 1994, pp. 40–3, 47, 49; Borgsen and Volland 1991, p. 160; Osterloh 1997, pp. 127–8.

[109] Osterloh 1997, pp. 22, 80–2; Keller 2011, pp. 488–98; see Otto 1998, pp. 36–9, 176, 193.

[110] MadR vol. 7, pp. 2428 (June 23, 1941), 2515 (July 14), 2563 (July 24), 2632 (August 11), 2651 (August 14); vol. 8, pp. 2704 (August 18, 1941), 2797 (September 25), 2809

The treatment of other prisoners of war

Many of the war's other POWs suffered under similar conditions – including hunger and the denial of food – to the Soviet POWs in German hands. Yet there were also significant differences, and the death rates for most groups were lower. Of the approximately 35 million POWs in World War II, about 5 million (14%) – or more, depending on the unknown number of Chinese POWs held by the Japanese who died – did not survive captivity.[111] To be a POW in World War II was more life-threatening than in World War I when about 750,000 out of 6.6–8.4 million prisoners (approximately 10%) perished. During World War I the highest prisoner losses occurred in countries where the food situation was most grave, state structures the least sophisticated, and the political conflict between combatants the most charged: that is, Russia, Romania, the Ottoman Empire and Bulgaria (but also along the Austro-Italian front).[112] At that time Germany usually treated their captives properly, and their chances of survival were very high.[113] World War II involved much higher prisoner numbers, more supply problems, politically motivated denial of food, hard labor, direct violence and higher death rates. Much of this resembles the suffering of captured Africans and Chinese during Germany's colonial wars *before* World War I.[114]

Still, in World War II the German military again treated prisoners, except those from the USSR, largely according to the international laws of war. The Germans held close to 5 million non-Soviet POWs.[115] Prisoners from many nations were released after a brief captivity, and Hitler publicly lauded those from certain nations (Norwegians, Greeks and also Poles) for their bravery. The German army released groups of Soviet and Yugoslav prisoners on the grounds of their ethnicity and many French, Polish and Italian POWs because the German leadership preferred to use such people as civilian forced laborers. Mortality rates were low: 2–4% for Poles, 1–2.8% for French, about 1% for British and US prisoners, 2–2.5% for Belgians, 2–3% for Dutch and 3–6% for Yugoslavs.

(September 29), 2824–5 (October 2), 2855 (October 9, 1941), which related to reports about Germans satisfied that the conquest of Ukraine would ease their food situation (pp. 2643, 2659, 2687, 2727, 3019).

111 MacKenzie 1994, p. 487.

112 See Kramer 2010, pp. 75–90.

113 But this was not true for Romanians in German hands: Kramer 2010, p. 77; see Datner 1964, p. 226 (4.8% overall mortality).

114 Kuss 2011, pp. 96–101, 122–3, 352–3.

115 Overmans 2005, p. 853.

Only the fate of Italian Military Internees after 1943 bears some resemblance to that of Soviet POWs, with mass shootings, beatings, denial of proper POW status and hard labor. However, the Italians sustained much lower mortality rates (40–50,000, or 6–7%, died).[116]

Many of Germany's Jewish POWs who were not Soviets did benefit from the protection of international law. Jews among British and US, but also French and Yugoslav POWs, received largely the same treatment as non-Jews (despite occasional harrassment) – and usually survived.[117] While Jews among Polish POWs were involuntarily released in 1939–40 and, stripped of their POW status, mostly murdered along with other Jewish civilians in the coming years, Jewish prisoners from Yugoslavia could choose between release and continued captivity – and virtually all of those who decided to remain POWs survived.[118] If POW camps provided relative security for Jews, the principle of reciprocity was an important reason: the German military feared reprisals against German POWs in Allied hands. Still, this can hardly explain the treatment of Jewish POWs from Yugoslavia, a country that did not field an army capable of taking German prisoners after April 1941. Appearing to adhere to the rule of law was apparently of so much propagandistic value for German military authorities that this consideration of foreign policy overrode murderous government policies against Jews.

By contrast, Soviet troops in Finnish POW camps suffered much the same treatment as those in German camps: more than 18,000 out of 64,000 (28%) died, mostly of hunger, largely in the first half of 1942. Political officers and communists were segregated and some sent to Germany. Necessities were in short supply and beatings were frequent, and many Soviet prisoners tried to flee. About 1,000 were executed.[119] Some 5,000 of the approximately 91,000 Soviet POWs in Romanian hands died, a fairly low percentage. There do, however, seem to have been

[116] Overmans 2005, esp. pp. 755, 772, 775, 779, 785, 799, 836. For Hitler on Polish troops' bravery see Schenk 2000, p. 137. See also Datner 1964, pp. 21–31. For Italian Military Internees see Hammermann 2005, esp. pp. 443, 455; Lang 1996, pp. 95–7.

[117] Overmans 2005, pp. 748–9, 766, 780–1, 871. For Yugoslavs see also Pavlowitch 2008, p. 21; Romano and Kadelburg 1977, p. 689; a few survivors' accounts can be found in *We Survived*, vol. 2, pp. 503–19; for French-Jewish POWs see also Durand 1999, p. 73; Lieb 2007, p. 195; estimates of 10,000–60,000 French-Jewish POWs are found in Kaspi 1997, p. 21; Adler 1989, p. 6. For the 1,700 Jews from Palestine captured along with British troops in Greece, see Mallmann and Cüppers 2006, p. 171.

[118] Overmans 2005, pp. 746–9, 766, 780; for the arrival of POWs in Warsaw and Lublin see Datner 1964, pp. 102–3, and Lauerwald 1996, pp. 24–5.

[119] "POW Camps 1939–1944," www.geocities.com/finmilpge/fmp_pow_camps.html?200919 (accessed May 19, 2009); Silvennoinen 2008, pp. 178–80, 219–20; Overmans 2005, p. 821.

some direct killings.[120] As for the more than 11,000 Soviet POWs interned in Switzerland after they fled there from German captivity, there are reports that they were housed in separate camps, of workdays of between nine and eleven hours, insufficient food, and even some killings.[121]

The fate of POWs in Soviet captivity resembled that of Soviet POWs in German hands in many ways. According to official Soviet figures, about 518,000 Europeans (15%) died, but scholars from the nations of origin of these POWs estimate mortality rates of about 30–35% with the total number of deaths approaching 1.5 million.[122] Italian POWs suffered the highest mortality rate: 56.5% according to Soviet records, 85.6% according to Italian data. As with Soviet POWs in German internment, Italians suffered the highest death rates in the beginning; their biggest problems were a lack of food combined with cold, hard labor, insufficient shelter and unsanitary conditions. There were many assaults on Italian soldiers, not backed up by any Soviet official orders, right after they had been taken prisoner and during transport to internment camps.[123] The fate of Germans, Romanians, Hungarians and Japanese in Soviet captivity shared similar features.[124] For all of the prisoners in Soviet hands, 1943 was by far the most lethal year. The Soviet government, however, tried to bring down the number of deaths by reorganizing the camps and the system of forced labor.[125]

Similar general patterns of high death rates as a result of hunger, hard labor, mistreatment and execution, sometimes tied to racism, can be seen elsewhere: for the Republican soldiers captured by Franco's Nationalist forces in the Spanish Civil War, who were not recognized as POWs; for German POWs captured in southeastern Europe; for British, Australian and US POWs but most especially for Chinese and Filipino POWs in Japanese hands.[126] Very few Japanese were taken prisoner by the US military before 1945; many fought to the death, but many were also massacred while surrendering. Racism on both sides has been cited as a partial explanation for the low captivity figures.[127]

[120] See Pohl 2011, p. 242; Şiperco 1997, pp. 36–54 (thanks to Vladimir Solonari for pointing me to this publication); Overmans 2005, p. 821; Ancel 2011, p. 647 note 31.

[121] Erin 2004, p. 38.

[122] The Soviet figures are summarized in Karner 1995, p. 79.

[123] Giusti 2003, esp. pp. 33–44, 66, 77–92, 96; Müller 2007, esp. pp. 86–7; for contradictory evidence about the treatment see Schlemmer 2005, pp. 44–6.

[124] Karner 1995, pp. 11–14, 38–42, 58–9, 79, 178; Hilger 2000, pp. 56–62, 103–18; Zeidler and Schmidt 1999, p. 9; Stark 1999, pp. 410, 413; Stark 2005, pp. 109–12; Nimmo 1988, esp. pp. 13, 25, 43–5, 115–18.

[125] Karner 1995, pp. 61–78, 90. For a different view see Zeidler and Schmidt 1999, p. 14.

[126] Gerlach 2005b, pp. 46–7; Overmans 1999, p. 252; MacKenzie 1994, pp. 515–16.

[127] Dower 1986, esp. pp. 60–71.

The fate of POWs in World War II reflects the paramount importance of the food supply, or undersupply, for survival. However, the lack of food was not merely an abstract necessity brought about by a general scarcity that produced equally distributed suffering. Rather, hierarchies of supply were created for political reasons and reduced the chances of survival for some groups. Indifferent acceptance of unequal suffering was one factor in the resulting mass deaths of POWs at the hands of the Germans in 1941–42 and at the hands of the Soviets during a general famine and the difficult military situation of 1942–43. The popular racism behind this acceptance also resulted in hard labor for exhausted prisoners, and abuse and mistreatment by guards who often treated them worse as they became weaker, sicker and appeared more ragged. Guards sometimes assigned labor, withheld food and worsened the conditions of transport as punishments. Direct and structural violence were connected. Many hate crimes against captured soldiers occurred between their surrender and their registration in large POW camps.[128] But political issues other than racism were involved. If, for example, the Germans had used violence only according to a racist hierarchy, then how can one explain why half of the non-Jewish Soviet POWs died while virtually all of the Jews among the British, American, French and Yugoslav POWs survived?

Other inmates of total institutions

Soviet POWs were especially exposed to hunger because they were tightly confined in total institutions[129] whose organizers were unwilling to provide them sufficient supplies and, in particular, enough food. The point is that, closely guarded in camp and at their workplaces, most of them were unable to find additional provisions and, thus, almost entirely depended on their rations. As we will see, their situation was even worse than that of Jews in most of the ghettos. How did the inmates of other total institutions fare?

As is well known, about 70,000 inmates of German mental institutions, who were unfit for work, were killed, largely by gas, from 1939 to 1941. This was in accord with Nazi racist thinking combined with the idea that the victims were "useless eaters."[130] Some 40,000 Polish and Soviet mental

[128] Karner 1995, pp. 11–14, 38–42, 58, 178; see Streit 1991.

[129] For the concept, see Goffman 1961, pp. 1–124.

[130] Interrogation of Viktor Brack, 12 October 1946, Nuremberg Document NO-426, with reference to Hitler; for Christian Wirth's utterances (later commander in Treblinka), see Sereny 1980, p. 53.

patients were shot by German units in the same period. The fact that the total excess mortality of psychiatric patients under German control was around 220,000 – half of whom died from hunger – and that the number had risen especially in 1942 and 1944, in parallel with the concentration camps, when hunger was often combined with the use of intentionally lethal doses of medication, is less known. Few mental hospitals were exempt. Racist thinking and considerations of utility were intertwined as doctors and hospital authorities were unwilling to commit resources of food and money to humans who they considered to be inferior. Shouts of "hunger, hunger!" resounded in German clinics.[131] Some doctors at first refused to hand patients over to be gassed, only later to administrate to their slow deaths themselves. The fact that outright killings continued in the picturesque Bavarian town of Kaufbeuren for several weeks in 1945 during the US occupation, and that more than 60,000 mental patients starved to death in German clinics during World War I,[132] shows that Nazism was, unfortunately, not the only problem in German history.

Starvation in French psychiatric institutions was almost the same. The *extermination douce* killed at least 40,000, reaching its peak in the winter of 1941–42, earlier than in Germany. Neglect by Vichy authorities and weary, indifferent staff have been cited in explanation. Being old, male, a long-term patient, an evacuee or someone who did not receive food parcels increased a patient's risk of dying.[133] As in Germany (where an end to the centralized mass murder of patients was forced in 1941), public protests in 1942 ended the practice; but in France, unlike Germany, some doctors were among the protesters in a debate that involved the medical profession and managed to bring the number of hunger deaths down.[134]

In German prisons, nutrition deteriorated, especially from 1942 onwards, although it seems to have been better than in the worst phases of World War I. Still, prisoners were losing weight and many were unfit for work. Up to 20,000 people may have died from hunger and diseases brought about by food deficiency. Given a prison population in the second half of the war of usually more than 120,000 inmates, with considerable turnover, this mortality rate was probably less than one in ten prisoners. The majority of inmates were foreigners from eastern Europe and, thus, not highly regarded, but they fared markedly better in terms of hunger than

131 See the comprehensive study by Faulstich 1998 and excerpt of memo by Pastor Paul Braune, July 9, 1940, in Hermle and Thierfelder 2008, pp. 634–6, quote p. 634.
132 Faulstich 1998, pp. 25–68, 342, 651–2.
133 Faulstich 1998, pp. 374–7; Lafont 1987, esp. p. 40–1, 60–8, 110, 124, 127, 215–16.
134 Lafont 1987, pp. 130–50.

those in Soviet POW camps, the concentration camps and mental institutions.[135] In some German-run prisons in occupied Poland and the Soviet Union, hundreds of detainees starved to death.[136] In German-besieged Leningrad, hardly any prison inmates survived under Soviet authority.[137] But in French prisons and asylums also, cases of tuberculosis increased sharply – as did the mortality rate, just as it did in prisons in Athens.[138] In 1940–42, about 3,000 out of 100,000 inmates (3%) in camps run by the Vichy government in France died of hunger, lack of other supplies and related diseases. Among the dead were roughly 1,000 Jews (5% of Jewish inmates, mostly German deportees) and 300 Sinti and Roma (a mortality rate of 10%). Jews interned in Italian camps in Yugoslavia received more food than Slovenes, the contrast being most visible in the camp at Rab. Up to 7,000 Slovenes died here; at the same time, want, but no deaths, among Jews was reported. Rations in Italy were very small, but this does not fully explain the apparent food hierarchy – Italian military leaders apparently wanted to collectively punish Slovenes.[139]

Food policy and the murder of two million Polish Jews

Mass destruction, partially caused by food policy, had become a reality – most notably for Soviet POWs – in 1941. At that time the Polish population was not yet much affected. In 1939 German authorities divided Poland administratively: the western territories were annexed and the rest remained occupied as the General Government. In economic terms, the annexed Polish areas were to provide settlement space, workers and food for Germany – "grain, grain and grain again, 'a grain factory,'" as Arthur Greiser, a regional leader, summed up Hitler's and Göring's expressed expectations in February 1941.[140] Yet this was after Germany's reserves had dwindled: in December 1939, even according to Backe (a politician responsible for food and agriculture), Poland was to deliver "a bit of bread and grain" but mainly "workers and workers and workers" (to be employed in German agriculture).[141]

135 The data for prisons are from Wachsmann 2004, esp. pp. 238–41, 248; for foreigners see pp. 225, 269. 272.
136 Chodakiewicz 2004, p. 404 (Lublin).
137 Reznikova 2000, pp. 139–40; Ganzenmüller 2005, p. 279.
138 Sanders 2001, pp. 158–60; Hionidou 2006, p. 224.
139 Peschanski 2002, pp. 142–6; Peschanski 2010, pp. 39, 61–5, 69, 72; Eggers 2002, pp. 259, 276, 312, 450–61; Klarsfeld 1982, p. i; for Yugoslavia see Burgwyn 2005, pp. 193, 249, 254, 288–9, 373 note 988; for Italy see Raspin 1986, pp. 302, 305, 354–5.
140 Quoted in Aly 1999, p. 150; see Rutherford 2007, p. 127.
141 Quoted in Elsner and Lehmann 1988, p. 185.

The General Government, by contrast, could hardly feed its own population.[142] It was indirectly exploited by denying it food deliveries from outside and forcing it to export small amounts of agricultural products to Germany. In early 1941 the situation worsened as a result of the immense concentration of German troops staged for the impending campaign against the USSR. In the summer of 1941 the non-Jewish population received food rations of about 600 calories per day, Jews about 200 calories. During the course of that year, more than 40,000 inmates of the Warsaw ghetto perished from hunger and disease.[143] The situation there came to a head in the fall, when even potato peeling sold for two Złoty a kilogram. In September the civil administration of the General Government, together with the Supreme Command of the German Armed Forces, cut the food rations for Soviet POWs in camps in the General Government. This led to the death of 290,000 men, 85% of prisoners, within six months.[144] Food policy, with the marginal involvement of the SS and police in the decision-making, had also begun to trigger mass murder in the General Government. A Swiss observer in Warsaw noted some starvation among Polish non-Jews but much more in a Soviet POW camp and, especially, in the Jewish ghetto.[145]

For the 2 million Jews in the General Government, German persecution had brought deprivation of their rights and property, and ghettoization, by 1941. Procuring food developed into one of the biggest problems for Polish Jews, and hunger became a key experience. Neither Jews nor non-Jews could live on the official rations so everybody in the cities and towns had to participate in the black market to survive. Jews were even more dependent on the black market than non-Jews but they had less access to it. They received less food officially, had fewer opportunities to earn money, saw their money and other assets dwindle, and they were not allowed to move about freely – most of them being squeezed into ghettos under awful conditions. They had no choice other than to break the occupiers' laws by leaving the ghettos and smuggling food in.

From the point of view of German authorities, mass hunger had several negative effects. The productivity of workers decreased and the black market that hunger perpetuated caused mass absences

[142] The following account in this section draws from Gerlach 1998a, pp. 167–257; later largely confirmed by Browning 2000, pp. 76, 134–5; Tooze 2007, pp. 619–33; Collingham 2011, pp. 204–13.

[143] Berenstein 1961, pp. 136, 138.

[144] Streit 1991, p. 189; Musial 1999, pp. 198–9; General Governor, log, September 23, 1941, BA R 52II/184, p. 70; for the potato peeling see undated report of Dr Biehl (fall 1941), BA R 52 VI/8, pp. 1–6.

[145] Blättler 1945, pp. 12, 13, 26–34, 52–3, 59 (observations *c.* January 1942).

from work as Polish workers went off to procure food or earn money through illegal petty trading. On average, workers were absent one to two days per week –which forced companies to employ 25–30% more workers than they actually needed.[146] Farmers preferred to sell their products profitably on the black market instead of delivering them to the German authorities at low fixed prices. In 1941, German authorities did not know how to remedy this situation quickly. In their view, Jews were the most active participants in the black market as well as being responsible for spreading epidemics. In fact, typhoid fever – originating as it did from Soviet POW camps – spread in, and outside of the ghettos in the second half of 1941. In mid-October, during this crisis, the civil administration insisted on a new order to the police to shoot all Jews found outside the ghetto without a permit.[147] Jews were provided with even fewer resources than the rest of the population in order to slightly alleviate the situation for non-Jews. Resulting hunger and disease forced Jews to enter the black market – which only served to confirm anti-Jewish stereotypes[148] – and the only countermeasures that hostile German occupation authorities could think of to deal with the problem consisted of violence against Jews. Utilitarian and ideological thinking were inseparable, and the consequence was destructive, even without a master plan.[149] Discussing the shooting order, the head of the General Government's health department, Jost Walbaum, stated:

> Of course it would be the best and easiest to provide these people [the Jews] with enough food. But this is not possible due to the general food and war situation [...] there are only two ways: either we doom the Jews to starve or we shoot them. The final effect is the same, but shooting is more daunting [...] We have only the task that these parasites cannot infect the German people, and for this any means are justified.[150]

A development that can be linked to the food situation are the mass shootings in the district of Galicia, which also began in October 1941. These took place in Lvov and the southern part of the district, exactly where a flood had struck causing a famine that exceeded the silent hunger in the rest of the General Government. The mass killings – praised in

[146] Gerlach 1998a, pp. 173, 227.
[147] Ibid., pp. 174–6.
[148] See, for example, SSPF Galizien, "Lösung der Judenfrage im Distrikt Galizien," June 30, 1943, IMG, vol. 37, p. 392; diary of Jürgen Flick, March 22, 1941, on a tram ride through the Warsaw ghetto, in Glees 1995, p. 64.
[149] See Pohl 1996, p. 122.
[150] Quoted in Gerlach 1998a, pp. 176–7.

contemporary documents as a way of tackling the black market – were resumed in the same areas in the spring of 1942.[151]

The cynical hope of General Governor Hans Frank to deport all Polish Jews eastward, in the short run, faded on October 13 after his meeting with Rosenberg, the Minister of the Eastern Occupied Territories. On the same day, Himmler commissioned Globocnik to erect the first extermination camp in the General Government, which was designed with a limited killing capacity and located at Bełżec. Documents from the winter of 1941–42 outline a process of mass murder that was slow in comparison to what would follow. When Frank informed his administration on December 16 that he had been told in Berlin to murder the Jews in the General Government, instead of shipping them to the Soviet territories, he emphasized that they were "useless eaters" who had to be killed – although he added that he did not know how to proceed (see Chapter 4). This did not trigger the immediate construction of more extermination centers, but at the Wannsee conference, State Secretary of the General Government, Josef Bühler, urged that the Polish Jews be killed faster than the RSHA intended – arguing that the project involved no labor concerns and only minor transportation problems and that "the Jew represents an imminent danger by spreading epidemics and permanently causing economic disorder through his persistent activities on the black market. Out of 2.5 million Jews that come into question, the majority is unfit for work anyway."[152] Thus Bühler insisted that this kind of economization through mass murder – to prevent starvation-induced epidemics – would ease the situation in general. The first murders in the gas chambers at Bełżec started in March 1942, targeting Jews from the districts of Lublin and Galicia. They were designed to kill people unfit for work – about 60% of the population, excluding those aged between sixteen and thirty-five years old. The destruction of most of the Jewish community of Lublin – which reportedly eased the black market situation – served as a pilot program and seemed to prove that this kind of mass murder could be carried out in the entire General Government. In April, the site for the Treblinka death camp was chosen, and in May gassings started in Sobibór. Simultaneously, all Jewish workers in the General Government were registered and forced labor was intensified for Jews.[153]

151 Gerlach 1998a, pp. 185–6; for the famine see also Losacker in police meeting, June 18, 1942, BA 52 II/235, p. 71.

152 Gerlach 1998a, pp. 177–84; quotes in Frank's speech, December 16, 1941, BA R 52 II/241, p. 76 and reverse side; protocol of Wannsee conference on January 20, 1942, Tuchel 1992, pp. 135–6.

153 Gerlach 1998a, pp. 181–9.

By mid-July 1942, 160,000 Jews had been gassed or shot. The sudden, terrible expansion of mass murder afterwards owed much to two aspects of economic and food policy: restoring order to the Polish economy and exploiting it for exports to Germany. The German civil administration believed that the seizure of the new harvest would lead either to improvements or economic collapse. Either the small rations for Polish non-Jews of 150 g of bread per day could be raised and, thus, also the political situation eased; or the produce would find its way onto the black market. Facing this alternative, officials of the civil administration, the SS, police and the army in the districts of Galicia, Lublin and Kraków, stated repeatedly that the mass murder of Jews was ameliorating the black market situation. Some civil and military officials even thought that the murder of Jews could improve the labor situation, because if Polish workers did not need to spend so much time working the black market, then fewer workers would have to be employed. In May 1942 the administration of the district of Warsaw – a district that usually depended on food imports – was assigned the highest delivery quotas of all the districts. When it expressed amazement at this decision, Karl Naumann, the chief of the General Government's agriculture department, pointed to the expected reduction in the Warsaw ghetto's population of more than 400,000 people. However, Naumann tried to lower the quota that Berlin had assigned to the General Government, and Backe (who had met with Himmler the previous day) started his reply with the words, "In the G.G. there are still 3.5 million Jews. Poland will be sanitized as early as this year."[154]

On June 18, 1942, this connection was frankly expressed during a governmental session in Kraków on police matters. It was the civil administration – the heads of the three district administrations of Lublin, Kraków and Warsaw, together with State Secretary Bühler – who urged the SS to speed up the mass murder of Jews "unfit for work" in order to combat the black market. The Higher SS and Police Leader, Krüger, defended himself by pointing to the lack of trains while confirming the civil administration's points:

> The problem of evacuation is urging a decision. The current measures have demonstrated that the elimination of Jews results in a drop in black market prices. The success of a best possible seizure of the harvest can only be achieved after the abolition of the black market, which is only possible after the elimination of the Jews.

[154] Chef Wi Z, "Aktenvermerk über die Besprechung bei Staatssekretär Backe am 23.6.1942 mit den landwirtschaftlichen Sachbearbeitern der besetzten Gebiete," copy, June 24, 1942, Nuremberg Document NI-6194; see also Gerlach 1998a, pp. 189–96.

However, the representative of the civil administration of the district of Radom, Alfons Oswald, objected to SS and police plans to start deporting Jews from Radom in six to eight weeks time. Pressing for earlier deportations, he said that in six to eight weeks time they would come "too late for the operation to seize the harvest."[155] For this particular functionary, the food business was not a simple pretext for murdering Jews. If Oswald had been merely a Jew-hater, he could have waited a few weeks. He was a Jew-hater, but one who wanted to solve his most urgent political problem – one that required accelerating the extermination.[156]

The civil administration also took less violent measures for the "action to seize the harvest" – which included the declaration of an overall "harvest state of emergency" on July 11, 1942. The civil administration threatened Polish peasants with the death penalty for withholding agricultural goods, sold industrial goods to farmers to reduce demand for them on the black market, concentrated police manpower on 'protecting' the harvest against 'plunder' by partisans, and isolated Warsaw from the countryside in order to prevent illegal food deliveries. The campaign was concerned with much more than the mass murder of Jews.[157] In fact, it is important to understand that the murder of Jews was intended to enable the Germans to get the Polish population and the circulation of money and goods under control – the central instrument of this control being food rationing. Farmers had been threatened with the death penalty for refusing to work since 1939. The importance of the agricultural sector is illustrated by the fact that 60,000–70,000 ethnic Poles and Ukrainians (and 2,000 Germans) worked in the agricultural administration of the General Government.[158]

Himmler and the Reich's SS and police leadership soon got involved. Events like Heydrich's assassination spurred on the extermination of Jews. After talking, on July 9, with SS and Police Leaders from eastern Europe about anti-partisan warfare, and with Krüger and Globocnik about measures against Jews, Himmler offered to take over responsibility from the military for the seizure of the harvest in Ukraine. The OKW quickly accepted. On July 17 Himmler visited Auschwitz and observed the gassing of Dutch Jewish women. On July 19 he issued

155 General Government, Protocol of meeting on police matters, June 18, 1942, BA R 52II/235, pp. 68–79 reverse side.

156 Nonetheless, Oswald tried to protect one particular Jewish family in August 1942 and had been in trouble with the Nazi Party in the 1930s: Roth 2009, pp. 48, 393, 490.

157 Gerlach 1998a, pp. 200–1; see more generally, also, Seidel 2009, pp. 55–6; Roth 2009, pp. 144, 160.

158 Corni and Gies 1997, p. 449; Chodakiewicz 2004, p. 35 note 65; Brandt *et al.* 1953, p. 10.

the notorious written order to Krüger to kill all of the Jews in the General Government, except for the laborers in certain camps. The order stated that racial policy and segregation, security and the prevention of epidemics made the action necessary. (Jews were "morally and physically a focal point of epidemics.") On the same day he ordered Krüger to support in every way the General Governor's "carrying out the seizure of the harvest" and to assemble laborers for projects within the General Government as well as the German Reich. Strangely, this second order was top secret even though the "action to seize the harvest" had been publicly announced and the conscription of forced laborers was well known. By July, the mass murder of Jews had started in the General Government on a scale previously unknown; and by August 5 it was proceeding in all districts. And yet the program was still limited to people not needed for forced labor, a restriction that, according to some sources, was intended to remain in effect for some time.[159]

Until then, the main task of the civil administration in the General Government had been to improve the situation of Polish non-Jews (in the German interest). But beginning in August 1942, large food deliveries to Germany took priority. By May 1942 it had become clear that much of the German grain crop had been destroyed by the harsh winter. Security Service reports available to German leaders suggest that the food supply was the greatest worry of German citizens and that the matter became the hottest political issue between March and August 1942. Defeatism, criticism of the Nazi regime and black marketeering spread. Citizens were envious of foreign workers' allegedly high food rations, as well as of their own bourgeoisie. People called the harvest a "vital question."[160] His alarming reports had helped Backe, the State Secretary for Food and Agriculture, to succeed his superior, Minister Darré. By late June, however, Backe had been unable to win more than minor concessions (first 85,000 tons, then 150,000 tons) from the General Government for grain deliveries to the Reich because Frank wanted to "sanitize" his area's economy.

Fearing that German bread and meat rations would have to be lowered once again, Backe continued to lobby in Berlin for large-scale General Government deliveries. On the basis on these proposals, Göring imposed much higher export quotas on most of the occupied territories – and on

[159] Gerlach 1998a, pp. 203–7; Himmler to Krüger, July 19, 1942, BA NS 19/1757, p. 1.

[160] See MadR vols. 9–11, pp. 3366, 3435–6, 3348–9, 3470–1, 3496–8, 3543–5, 3566–9, 3592, 3595, 3613–14, 3626–7, 3639, 3697, 3715–16, 3747, 3768, 3772, 3923–4, 3936, 3944–6, 3951, 3966, 3985–6, 3999, 4005 (July 27, 1942/quote), 4032–3, 4042, 4047, 4073, 4106, 4123, 4148, 4232, 4259, 4279, 4291–2, 4351–6 (February–October 1942).

the General Government, the occupied Soviet territories, and France in particular – at a summit meeting on August 6 with all the heads of German civil and military authorities from across Europe. Göring, who claimed that he had been "given general authority by the Führer in an unprecedented extent," threatened to relieve the chief administrators from their posts if they did not meet the new quotas, adding "I don't mind whether your people will collapse from hunger." The threat to the morale and productivity of the *German* people took priority. The General Government was to deliver 600,000 tons of grain, plus potatoes and meat – twelve times the amount demanded the previous year. This much grain was enough to feed 3 million people. Participants in the meeting also explicitly linked food supplies and the murder of Jews, pertaining to Reich Commissariat Ostland.[161]

After their initial disbelief, Frank and Naumann prepared an emergency plan which they presented at an urgent governmental meeting on August 24, 1942. According to Naumann's plan, the delivery quota for Polish farmers would be raised by a quarter and their food allowance reduced by a sixth. The daily food ration for Polish non-Jews was cut to 150 g of bread, then to 100 g after January 1, and finally to none from March to July. Naumann added that 1.2 million Jews would receive no more food – only the 300,000 Jewish laborers working "for the German interest" would be fed, and on slightly increased rations. General Governor Frank predicted serious consequences for public order in early 1943, which had to be accepted because "other peoples have to perish before the German people will starve." He continued: "It is only marginal that we doom 1.2 million Jews to starvation. Of course, if they do not starve this will hopefully lead to an acceleration of the anti-Jewish measures." In other words, most Jews were to be killed as soon as possible to prevent them from provisioning themselves through the black market.[162]

Several meetings between Backe, Hitler, Himmler and Göring in late August and early September 1942 on food policy in the General Government underline its importance. In December Backe again expressed his gratitude to Himmler for the "special and effective help" provided in seizing food in the General Government. Himmler marked Backe's letter "top secret."[163]

Jewish laborers were no longer exempt from being murdered as a result of Göring's and Backe's initiatives. During a meeting on August

161 Gerlach 1998a, pp. 210–17 (quotes pp. 215–16).
162 Gerlach 1998a, pp. 218–20; General Government meeting protocol, August 24, 1942, BA R 52 II/242, pp. 76–82.
163 Gerlach 1998a, pp. 221–2 (quote p. 222).

14, SS representatives told the Armament Inspection of the General Government:

> We must come off the position that the Jew is irreplaceable, according to the opinion of the Reichsmarshall [Göring]. Neither the Armament Inspection nor the other authorities in the General Government will keep their Jews until the end of the war. The given orders were clear and tough. They are not only valid for the General Government, but for all the occupied territories. The reasons behind them must be exceptional.[164]

To doom the Jewish workers to death was new, and it had presumably happened during the meeting on August 6 that Krüger had attended. In the only known copy of the minutes of this conference, an important page containing a remark of Göring's concerning Jews is missing.[165] It is also remarkable that from the point of view of the SS representatives the reasons for total extermination were "exceptional" – that is, beyond their usual understanding of why Jews were to be murdered. Food policy intertwined with ideological motives was given priority over labor policy at this time.

This change in priorities coincided with orders to expand the mass murder of Jews in other parts of Europe (see Chapter 4). By and large, the given scenario also matches the information that a German industrial manager, Eduard Schulte, took to Switzerland, where Gerhard Riegner, the representative of the World Jewish Congress, transmitted it to the Western Allies in July and October of 1942. According to Schulte, a plan to kill all European Jews in the gas chambers in occupied Poland had been discussed in Hitler's headquarters in July 1942. Backe had initiated the plan and Hitler had eventually accepted it, allegedly over the objections of General Governor Frank, because of the German food situation.[166]

As a horrible consequence, more than 750,000 Jews were murdered in the General Government between late July and the end of September 1942. And nearly 400,000, mostly from the district of Radom, were killed in the last three months of 1942. At the end of that year only 297,914 Jews remained. That was – hardly accidentally – almost exactly the "presumed population figure" of Jews anticipated by Naumann and Frank on August 24.[167] Those ten weeks in the summer and fall of 1942 were the peak of mass murder in the General Government. German

[164] Military Commander in the General Government, Qu. 2, note August 15, 1942, BA-MA RH 53-23/87, p. 47.

[165] Meeting protocol, August 6, 1942, in IMG, vol. 39, pp. 401–2; thanks to Jörg Morré for looking up the original for me (GARF Moscow 7445-2-105, pp. 198–9).

[166] See Gerlach 1998a, pp. 254–6.

[167] Gerlach 1998a, pp. 220, 251–2.

food policy can help explain why the extermination reached its apogee at this time, why one deportation wave followed another in the Warsaw ghetto – unexpectedly overtaking victims who thought they would be spared – and why so many people were deported to Treblinka that its murderous operations broke down on August 28 and many victims had to wait for days in the deportation trains where many of them died of thirst. Presumably it was this new policy to kill almost all of the Jews in the General Government that quickly led to the construction of several new gas chambers in Treblinka and Sobibór, beginning in September 1942.[168]

During these terrible months the civil administration reported on the continual drop in black market prices and an easing of the food situation (although policies had changed toward the large-scale extraction and export of resources).[169] Police officers were given the rationale that Jews had to be murdered because they drove prices up on the black market.[170] The new direction even employed the arts as a weapon: beginning in August 1942 the Polish play *Quarantine*, which primarily addressed farmers and workers with the message that Jews spread epidemics, was staged in Warsaw, Kraków, Tarnów and other towns. The Germans awarded the playwright a prize, subsidized admissions and expanded the audience by sending students and public servants to attend.[171] The propaganda topos associating Jews with lice and diseases had been used before, but the propaganda aimed at deterring non-Jews from having contact with, and, specifically, black marketing with Jews, or offering them help, was stepped up in 1942–43.[172]

In a remarkable parallel, food policy also became a driving force for the murder of 300,000 Jews in western Ukraine from August to early November of 1942. In the General Commissariat of Volyn-Podolia, the 330,000 Jews still alive there in the spring of 1942 had been kept so because they were considered important for the local skilled trades – which it was in the interests of the German civil administration and military to maintain. In the mass murders committed from May 1942 to

[168] Arad 1987, pp. 119–24; Pohl 1993, pp. 134–5. For a parallel acceleration of the murder of Jews in the Wartheland in August and September 1942 see Krakowski 2007, pp. 88, 104, 107.

[169] Governor, Warsaw district, bimonthly situation reports, October 15 and December 10, 1942, BA R 52 III/21.

[170] Notes by NCO Cornides, August 31, 1942, in Longerich 1989, p. 216.

[171] Agata Katarzyna Dąbrowska, "The Campaign 'Jews-Lice-Typhus' as an Example of Polish Participation in the Nazi Antisemitic Propaganda," paper presented at the conference "Towards an Integrated Perspective on Nazi Policies of Mass Murder," Oslo, June 21, 2009.

[172] See also Weindling 2000, pp. 2–3, 273, 278, 285.

reduce the number of Jews, the SS and police had shot 60,000 people within three months. As mentioned before, concern about the seizure of the harvest extended to Ukraine; as for the General Government, at first the Reich Commissariat's civil administrators could not believe Göring's impositions on August 6. The situation changed abruptly when Reich Commissar Koch returned from a visit with Hitler on August 28 and declared that immediate and large-scale food exports to Germany – for which Hitler had made him personally responsible – were of major political importance to winning the war. Three days afterwards, the Commander of the Security Police and Security Service for Volyn-Podolia informed his field outposts about "Jewish actions":

> The actions are to be speeded up in a way that they are [...] finished within five weeks. At the conference of the district commissars in Luzk 29 to 31 August 1942 it has been clarified that generally one hundred percent solutions have to be carried out. The district commissars were told by the attending deputy of the Reich Commissar – Regierungspräsident Dargel – that these one hundred percent settlements [*Bereinigungen*] also conform to a strong wish of the Reich Commissar personally.[173]

Again, we observe a sudden acceleration of the mass murders driven by the civil administration in the context of food policy. It included rail transports to improvised death camps where mass shootings took place and claimed 271,000 Jewish lives in September and October of 1942. Destruction was more or less total, unlike in Poland, and the last large-scale massacre, which took place in Pinsk, was carried out under the motto "Ukraine free of Jews." At the same time, large food exports rolled out to the Reich.[174]

The cynical German food policy was a frightening success. In the agricultural year 1942–43, the General Government delivered 504,000 tons of grain and 237,000 tons of potatoes to Germany – far more than in the previous three years combined and almost exactly what Göring had demanded. As railway transport and storage were insufficient, some of the produce was tentatively stored in Polish synagogues. In 1942, which marked the culmination of the murder of Jews in Europe, Germany also recorded her highest import share of grain, meat, fats and oils (as a percentage of total supplies) during World War II. The General Government

[173] Generalkommissar für Wolhynien und Podolien [actually, Commander of Security Police and Security Service in Volyn-Podolia], August 31, 1942, AIPN, Collection of Miscellaneous Files of SS and police units, No. 77. I am indebted to Dieter Pohl who first pointed me to this document.

[174] For the events in western Ukraine see Gerlach 1998a, pp. 237–45; Gerlach 1999, pp. 709–23.

supplied more than 50% of the imports of rye, oats and potatoes (not counting what was supplied to troops in the occupied territories). In August 1942, while Warsaw was isolated from the countryside and the ghetto was being emptied by deportations to Treblinka, Goebbels came to the city in order to ensure vegetable supplies for his Berliners (he was also the regional Party leader of Berlin). The German leadership thus succeeded in stabilizing food supplies for the German population until late 1944 by exploiting Europe's resources, carrying out mass murder and imposing hunger on other peoples. This this was one of the reasons behind popular support at home for Nazi policies, right to the end.[175]

The policy no longer to provide the urban Polish population with bread after early 1943 could not be sustained. Although Reich authorities refused to make major concessions, the regional civil administration and the Higher SS and Police Leader in the General Government decided together not to carry out the plan. As Krüger stated, to do otherwise would have turned 2 million Poles into the arms of the resistance movement, and the black market that would have mushroomed could not have been controlled due to the lack of German police to crack down on it. In the event, a fruitful harvest meant that bread rations for non-Jewish Poles were not cut, and in fact were considerably raised in the autumn of 1943, in spite of continual large-scale exports to Germany.[176] Unlike the case of non-Jews, the Germans thought they could afford the mass murder of Jews. They feared neither the solidarity of an entire population nor unrest. It seemed possible for them to separate from the general population this already isolated, well controlled, oppressed, deprived and nearly helpless group – a group they despised – and annihilate it.

Without the food policy's impact, the dynamics of the summer of 1942 might not have occurred, and the mass murders would have taken longer. That is to say, the face of extermination might have looked different. Also, it was the civil administration that repeatedly urged the SS and police to accelerate the killings, especially at major meetings: the Wannsee conference, the meeting on police matters in June 1942 and the meeting on food policy in August 1942. SS leaders adopted their motives, and this conformity of political goals greatly intensified the destruction. Food policy, of course, was one factor among several. It is not that considerations of food *instead of* anti-Jewish attitudes evolved into a driving force; rather, both were mutually supportive and went hand in hand with remarkable

[175] Brandt *et al.* 1953, p. 610; Gerlach 1998a, pp. 245–6. For the synagogues see General Governor's log, September 17, 1942, Präg and Jacobmeyer 1975, p. 564.
[176] Gerlach 1998a, pp. 246–8; see also Seidel 2009, p. 200.

ease. The food issue mobilized local functionaries, who might otherwise have remained aloof, to support the mass murder of Jews.

Why were all Jews not starved to death?

But, if the intention to murder Jews en masse evolved in connection with the intention to save food, why were they not all quickly starved to death like almost 2 million Soviet POWs had been? The answer is that there existed no capacity for this. The ghettos were not total institutions, which meant that large amounts of food could be smuggled in. Despite all of the forms of persecution of Jews, POWs were held in much stricter isolation and even more closely guarded than Jewish ghetto inmates. Only huge camps would have provided a way to starve most Jews to death, but the SS never came close to having sufficiently large camps to achieve this, or the number of troops at their disposal necessary to guard them, in contrast to the army's POW camps. The SS had no capability to put 4–5 million Jews into camps in September 1942, at a time when the concentration camps held 110,000 inmates (of whom Jews were a minority).[177] Direct forms of killing in extermination stations provided a more manageable and much cheaper method of murder.

There is plenty of evidence that the Polish and Soviet ghettos were far from sealed. Many ghettos were not cordoned off by a wall or fence. In one part of Poland, East Upper Silesia, Jewish neighborhoods only became sealed ghettos between October 1942 and March 1943.[178] There is no doubt either that food was smuggled into most ghettos in sufficiently large amounts to allow most inmates to survive despite the extremely small food rations provided by the German authorities.[179]

Underfed people who were not isolated could spread disease. Ghettos were first presented as a measure for preventing the spread of epidemics, but given the overcrowding and miserable hygienic and medical conditions inside, combined with the many contacts outside, they increasingly appeared as menaces in terms of disease. Pleading first for ghettoization and later for the murder of Jews, German doctors made a significant contribution to the mass murder.[180] The Ministry for the Occupied

[177] For the figure of 110,000 see Orth 1999, p. 165.

[178] Steinbacher 2000, p. 120; for Wartheland see Alberti 2006, pp. 168–71; for Belarus see Gerlach 1999, pp. 529–33.

[179] Paulsson 1998, p. 30.

[180] Hilberg 1992a, pp. 85–6; Dr M. Biehl "Die gegenwärtige Wirtschaftslage im GG," n.d. (fall 1941), BA R 52 VI/8, p. 2; for doctors (regarding Poland) see Browning 1992, pp. 149–60.

Soviet Territories and Reich Commissariat Ostland obliged their civil administrations to prevent the spread of epidemics from Jewish ghettos, which meant providing at least some food supplies to Jews, on the one hand, and spurred calls for extermination, on the other. In the General Government, too, the civil administration did not stop food provisions for Jews completely.[181] Meanwhile, Jewish administrations concealed outbreaks of epidemics in the ghettos from the Germans or admitted only the existence of a few cases.[182]

The demand to kill Jews instead of insufficiently supplying *other* groups is already known from military units.[183] The call for the murder of Jews instead of letting them die of hunger appears in well-known documents, such as the letter of July 16, 1941, from Rolf-Heinz Höppner of the Security Police in the Wartheland to Eichmann. This letter has been taken as one of the origins of the idea of gassing. Höppner reported considerations in the civil administration thus:

> This winter there exists the danger that not all Jews can be fed anymore. It should be seriously considered whether it would not be the most humane solution to finish off the Jews that are unfit for work through some fast acting means. In any case, this would be more agreeable than to let them starve to death.[184]

This policy led to the murder of close to 100,000 Jews by mid 1942, and synchronously, in 1941–42 (and not a year later as in the General Government), the Wartheland greatly increased its food exports to Germany.[185] The starvation policy against the unproductive came about in a complex process that started in 1940 and incrementally led to the idea of killing them.[186]

Because of these policies, most Jews did not die of hunger or related causes. To be sure, undernourishment was for some time a daily, corrupting and weakening reality for most of them. In the Croatian camp of Jasenovac, "the inmates were primarily preoccupied with the thought of food and how to obtain it," and they risked being shot in fighting one another for, say, a piece of bread lying on the ground.[187] The well-known writer Bruno Schulz, from Drogobycz in Eastern Galicia, regretted

181 Gerlach 1999, pp. 674–5; Pohl 1996, p. 114.

182 For example, up to 85% of the typhoid cases in the Warsaw ghetto were concealed: Lenski 1959, pp. 288, 290.

183 339th Infantry Division, situation report, November 5, 1941, BA-MA RH 26–339/5.

184 Quoted in Rückerl 1977, pp. 256–7.

185 For the exports see Brandt *et al.* 1953, pp. 47–8.

186 Klein 2009, pp. 130, 152, 210, 216–20, 290, 294, 320–2. Klein rejects the idea that food policy directly necessitated the murder of Jews in the Wartheland (p. 342).

187 Memories by Cadik-Branco Danon in *We Survived*, vol. 3, p. 158; the quote is from Jewish survivor Ervin Rosenberg, cited in Fogel 2007, p. 140.

his mistake of not stockpiling food when he had the chance, and his thoughts circled around his nagging hunger. Even in Drogobycz, where the situation was especially grave, 'only' 5% of the inmates may have starved to death within eight months. The rate was lower in other ghettos in the region and also in the Polish region of East Upper Silesia.[188]

Although victims of hunger were reported in many ghettos,[189] their numbers reached the thousands (or a high percentage) in only a few places[190] outside the large cities of Warsaw and Łódź, where 16–18% and 25% respectively of the inmates died; and outside Theresienstadt. In Warsaw, where rations were 169–219 calories per day from January to August 1941 (and slightly higher later; actual consumption was 800–1,600 calories), mortality was particularly high between May 1941 and July 1942. Of almost 92,000 recorded deaths, most must be attributed, directly or indirectly, to starvation – as must most of the more than 43,000 deaths in Łódź. In Theresienstadt, 33,600 people died in German confinement from the consequences of undernourishment.[191] In these ghettos the chances of establishing contact with the surrounding population and obtaining food were much less than in smaller places. A fierce struggle for survival ensued among the starving Jews, as it would in virtually any population exposed to famine. The largest groups pushed to the side and left to starve were refugees and returnees who had often lost most of their possessions in the course of their displacement, lacked local knowledge and social networks to fall back on, and could count less on solidarity with local residents. In Warsaw, most of those who died from hunger were forced migrants; 'only' 100,000 people depended on soup kitchens, and these were "bound sooner or later to die of starvation." In the Łódź ghetto, 25% of all inmates – but 37% of foreign deportees – died of hunger and disease.[192] Those least affected by hunger were to be found among those working for the Jewish self-administrations or their families' members[193] – a parallel to officers among POWs in German captivity.

188 Bruno Schulz, undated notes, quoted in Bähr 1961, p. 161; see also Pohl 1996, pp. 119–20; Steinbacher 2000, pp. 154–5; Sinnreich 2004, pp. 187–202.

189 Rautkallio 1987, p. 135 (Tartu, Estonia); Gerlach 1999 (Belarus); Chodakiewicz 2004, p. 360 (rural area of Janow, Poland).

190 Examples can be found in Kunz 2005, pp. 199–200 (Crimea); Gerlach 1999, p. 596 (Vitebsk); see Seidel 2006, p. 277; Trunk 1972, pp. 152–3.

191 For Warsaw see Pilichowski 1982, pp. 205–8; Paulsson 1998, p. 29; Berenstein 1962, pp. 136, 138; Gutman 1982, p. 64; Engelking and Leociak 2009, p. 407. For Łódź see Alberti 2006, pp. 301–13; Sinnreich 2004, pp. 49, 215. See Steinbacher 2000, p. 154. For Theresienstadt see Hajková 2013, Chapter 4. Theresienstadt, nominally a concentration camp, functioned like a ghetto.

192 For Warsaw see Snyder 2010a, p. 146; Lenski 1959, pp. 287–93, quote p. 288; for Łódź see Moser 1966, p. 29.

193 For Łódź see Alberti 2006, p. 188 note 159.

Very many Jews suffered from hunger in German-organized ghettos, but relatively few died of it.[194] Romanian-imposed ghettos, where the number of famine victims may have surpassed 100,000 despite a relatively comfortable general food situation, were a different matter. The Romanians also pursued a policy of preventing epidemics by mass murder – but not everywhere, and many of the ghetto inmates were, as migrants, especially vulnerable to starvation.[195] Locally, German police complained that "the Romanian government exposes the Jews [...] to starving to death because it does not dare to shoot them according to the German model," and called for Germany to intervene with the Romanian government "to solve the Jewish question as it happens in the [German-] occupied East (by shooting)" – obviously to prevent the outbreak of epidemics near a German headquarters.[196] But at the date of this complaint, mass shootings in order to prevent the spread of typhoid – that would claim the lives of 70,000 Jews from the region of Odessa and northern Transnistria – had already been under way for more than three weeks.[197] This did not prevent German officers from continuing to warn that Romanian policies were endangering the lives of ethnic Germans and German troops through epidemics by not murdering all destitute Jews.[198] Under the Germans, 150,000 Jews may have died of hunger and related diseases in ghettos and segregated Jewish neighborhoods across Europe. The risk of dying from hunger and exhaustion was much higher for camp inmates – since they were guarded more closely, they had less chance to procure food to supplement their rations or to receive help from families that were no longer together. I estimate that there were 200,000 Jewish victims of starvation in concentration camps, 100,000 in other camps (primarily labor camps in Poland) and perhaps 50,000 among the Soviet POWs in German captivity – which brings the total of Jewish victims of hunger under German control to approximately half a million.[199] The SS and police did have the capability to starve a large proportion of Jewish camp inmates to death, and they either utilized that capacity (often in combination with exhaustion from forced

194 For example, see Młynarczyk 2007, pp. 215–24.
195 See Deletant 2006, p. 186; for hunger deaths in northern Transnistria see Vynokurova 2010, p. 21. For the food situation among peasants and in cities see Dallin 1998, pp. 86, 105, 111, 114–20, 134–6.
196 Schmitt (Einsatz Eichenhain) to Rattenhuber (Reichssicherheitsdienst), January 14, 1942, quoted in Eikel 2005, p. 421.
197 See Ancel 2011, pp. 342–5, 395–416; Ancel 2007, 264–5, 283–7.
198 See Browning 1978, pp. 92–3 (Eichmann, April 14); Ancel 2011, p. 385 (German civil administration in Nikolayev district, February and March).
199 See higher estimates in Hilberg 1994a, pp. 1292–4; partial estimates for Poland can be found in Pohl 1996, p. 122.

labor) or murdered emaciated prisoners. However, it must be noted that non-Jewish inmates also fell victim to this policy. It is striking that the mortality of Jewish and non-Jewish concentration camp inmates, in both absolute and relative terms, reached its first peak (before the overcrowding of 1944–45) in the second half of 1942 at the same time that the policy of murdering Jews – which was related in part to a perceived need to tackle the food problem – culminated. At that time, 70,000 concentration camp prisoners died from a lack of necessities and exhaustion. Their food rations were cut in January and May 1942. About 10% of the inmate population (excluding deportees to Auschwitz and Maidanek who were immediately killed and so never became prisoners) died each month, and if mortality rates were brought down in the first half of 1943, then that was in part through the murder of the exhausted and emaciated.[200]

Food and survival chances of Jews: The example of western Europe

The lack of food had other consequences for the fate of Jews, as a comparative look at western Europe shows. The low survival rate of Jews in the Netherlands during World War II has often been unfavorably compared with the higher rates in France and Belgium. In searching for an explanation for the difference, scholars have pointed to Germany's more direct rule in the Netherlands and the stronger influence of the SS and police there, the closer cooperation of the Dutch administration and police in registering and arresting Jews, and the fewer and later-emerging opportunities (compared to the two other countries) for Jews in the Netherlands to hide. In the Netherlands, Jews seemed to be better integrated in society, and, thus, they relied on their compatriots for aid more than French and Belgian Jews did.[201] Food plays no role in the explanations that have been offered,[202] but a brief comparison shows the specific difficulties that nourishment posed for Dutch Jews trying to escape persecution.

Anecdotal evidence suggests that it was hard for Jews in hiding, or trying to hide, to secure supplies of food – which meant they had to procure

200 Kárný 1987, pp. 140–5; WVHA, DII to concentration camp commanders, "Ärztliche Tätigkeit in den Konz.-Lagern," December 28, 1942, in Bauche *et al.* 1991, p. 144; Orth 1999, esp. pp. 110–12. For ration cuts see Buggeln 2012, pp. 27–8.

201 Zeller and Griffioen 1996, pp. 31–41.

202 See Zeller and Griffioen 1996 and 1997; Griffioen and Zeller 2011; Moore 2004, pp. 385–95; Moore 2010; Blom 1989, pp. 273–89; Marrus and Paxton 1982, pp. 687–714.

ration stamps in addition to false identity papers and forged population registers that such illegality required.[203] But the Dutch food and agriculture sectors were much better organized and more tightly controlled by the national administration than they were in Belgium and France.[204] From a German perspective, Dutch organization permitted the extraction of more agricultural products than in France and Belgium, where the proportion of food channeled through the black market was markedly higher (already in 1942 when large numbers of Jews began to go into hiding) and public procurement rates were considerably lower.[205] Food rations for the Dutch were accordingly higher. It was still important for Jews living underground in France and Belgium to have forged ration cards,[206] but there was more of a chance, especially in southern France, to get by on black market supplies, in particular when Jews took up jobs in stores or offices. Some among the police and the local population in southern France, however, resented Jewish refugees from the north – arguing that because they did not work they would become active on the black market and that increased demand for food and supplies would drive prices up.[207] The flip side was that Jews became valued customers of French farmers and traders. In many cases this also created human bonds, courtesy of which the latter sometimes also continued to support Jews who were threatened by deportation and who had no money left.[208]

The considerable losses in weight and the previously mentioned rises in mortality in the Netherlands, Belgium and France due to the lack of food suggest that it was very difficult to feed somebody in hiding on one's own ration card. As a result of the higher reliance on markets in France and the different market power of individuals, hunger struck there more unequally. Hardest hit were the urban poor, particularly in the south, and inmates of total institutions (who depended entirely on rations) such as prisons, camps and psychiatric clinics. But what worked against the life chances of some groups opened up opportunities for others. The different food economies in France and Belgium contributed to the existence

[203] Moore 2010, p. 224, see also pp. 245, 252; see Moore 1997, pp. 158–9; Houwink ten Cate 1999, pp. 121, 125–6.

[204] Brandt *et al.* 1953, pp. 371–569; Trienekens 1985, esp. p. 427.

[205] Cépède 1961, pp. 386, 393–4; Kistenmacher 1959, pp. 16, 25–6, 66, 95–103; Sanders 2001, esp. pp. 31, 40, 47, 157, 277; for Belgium see Brandt *et al.* 1953, pp. 455, 546.

[206] Griffioen and Zeller 2011, p. 512; for ration stamp forgeries in general in France see Sanders 2001, pp. 95–105 and Alary 2006, p. 214; for forgeries in Belgium see Brandt 1953, p. 471; Jewish survivor's account from Belgium: interview with Armin Hertz in Johnson and Reuband 2005, pp. 29–30.

[207] Kasten 1993, pp. 95–6; see Kaspi 1997, pp. 166–72.

[208] Pathbreaking is Fogg 2009, pp. 130–7, 140–1, 145–7, 176; this matches the evidence in Marrus and Paxton 1982, pp. 183, 187.

of proportionally more hiding opportunities for Jews in comparison to the Netherlands. The different proportions of people going underground explain many of the disparities in survival rates.[209] Given the overwhelming difficulties in Holland, fewer Dutch Jews seem to have seen a chance to go into hiding. Moreover, supply on the Belgian and French black markets was higher in comparison, and Jews in the Netherlands were more dependent on professional help and larger networks (for forging ration cards and population registers) than in the other countries. These networks emerged later in the Netherlands than elsewhere. Finally, the tight control of the Dutch food sector made hiding in urban environments more difficult in the long run, and this prompted many Jews (and other illegals) to move to rural eastern provinces such as Friesland, Groningen and Drenthe where they were not only further away from the German Security Police and people who might recognize them,[210] but also closer to farms.

Broadly speaking, these comparisons suggest that the significance of the well-oiled Dutch administration extends beyond the police matters that many historians emphasize so much. Yet beyond the actions of state machineries, they also show the importance of the social environment for the life chances of various groups, including Jews under persecution.

Food and destruction

Food policy could work strongly against the life chances of Jews, but this was not the case everywhere in Europe. For example, we have no evidence that the food argument was important in the deportation of Jews from Germany. And it played only a secondary role in the deportation of the Hungarian Jews.[211] To be sure, a precarious food situation for the Greek population and partially related security issues did foster German military support for the deportation of Jews from Rhodes, Crete and Corfu in 1944 – and this has often been put down to purely ideological motivates. Without military support it would not have been possible for groups of fewer than a dozen Security Police agents to arrive on each of these islands and arrange the deportations.[212] On the other hand, food policy may indirectly have helped save the lives of Danish Jews because German decision-makers, including Herbert Backe, did not want to put

209 See Chapter 15 and the data in Griffioen and Zeller 2011, pp. 518, 543, 572.
210 Moore 2010, p. 240.
211 For Hungary, see Gerlach and Aly 2002, pp. 175–86.
212 Safrian 1997, pp. 275–83; Gerlach and Aly 2002, pp. 438–9; Aly 2006a, pp. 267–75; see also Hionidou 2006, p. 34 note 7.

at risk the main German interest in the country – its meat and dairy products –by antagonizing the Danes.[213]

Still, there were two occasions – in the fall and winter of 1941 (in the case of Soviet POWs), and in the summer and fall of 1942 (in the case of the Jews of Poland and western Ukraine) that food policy was in tune with anti-Jewish attitudes and therefore gained priority over labor interests. Each time, it heavily contributed to a hideous acceleration of murder and to the death of almost 2 million human beings. And each time, such murder responded to the reported voice of the German people – the first time directly, the second time indirectly.

Food distribution was also influenced by social conditions and relationships within occupied Europe. In this context, Jews – like migrants, refugees and guerrillas – were drawn into conflicts including those between rural dwellers (who benefited from favorable terms of trade and paid off their debts) and urbanites, especially during famines.[214] Such conflicts were part of a broader crisis. European and north African societies were under stress. A rise in general criminality was part of the background to these social and political conflicts. In Romanian-occupied Transnistria this included graft, bribery, embezzlement and illegal trade as the "primary accumulation" method of wealth for some among the population; and the rise of new elites. But it also included all sorts of denunciations and alcoholism – and a growing number of murders, even among civil servants and the intelligentsia, were also observed.[215] Denmark illustrated how criminality could rise under special conditions. When the Germans deportated or ousted a large proportion of the local police force in September 1944, a steep rise in theft, ration card fraud, robbery, kidnapping and murder followed. Additionally, the boundaries between common and political offenses became increasingly blurred.[216] Unlike in Denmark, Jews elsewhere were especially vulnerable to the kind of desolidarization and brutalization that then became the background against which they were hunted, blackmailed, denounced and desecrated post-mortem, as was the case in Poland.[217] In at least some areas of Poland armed robberies became common from 1940 onwards (again, ordinary crime and political struggle were not easy to distinguish),

213 Nissen 2006, esp. pp. 172, 186–7; Petrow 1974, p. 185; see also Yahil 1983, pp. 73, 117–18.

214 For Yugoslavia see Pavlowitch 2008, pp. 100, 225, 243; for France see Delacor 1994, pp. 14, 20; but Saunders 2001 (p. 27) locates the large-scale profiteers among larger traders, not farmers.

215 Dallin 1998, p. 137.

216 Trolle 1994, esp. pp. 27, 34, 49–50, 67, 79, 106, 163–4, 195.

217 See Gross 2012a.

a situation facilitated by weak policing under German quasi-colonial rule. When Jews went into hiding, they were either assaulted by gangsters or hunted down by farmers who regarded their search for food as criminal.[218] Policies of food denial imposed against Jews – as described in this chapter – were another expression of this desolidarization.

[218] Abundant evidence of banditry can be found in Klukowski 1993; for Jews see esp. pp. 223, 227 (diary, November 4 and 26, 1942).

10 The economics of separation, expropriation, crowding and removal

The impact of settlement policies

Settling Germans throughout large parts of eastern Europe was an important long-term aim for some Nazi racial ideologists, including Hitler. This conflicted with the exploitative or economic imperialism also pursued by some of the same ideologists (see Chapter 7). Some historians have argued that the settlement policy determined the German policies of violence in eastern Europe; they view the displacement of populations and large-scale mass murder against Jews and Slavs as fairly straightforward implementations of an ideological blueprint of Germanization.[1] Given the ideological contradiction just mentioned, German settlement schemes and their effects require evaluation.

This matter is often discussed under the headline '*Generalplan Ost*.' Scholars understand the *Generalplan Ost* as a number of interconnected plans drawn up by a variety of SS authorities, namely the Planning Office of the Reich Commissioner for the Strengthening of Germandom (RKF) – the planning authority in charge – and the Head Office of Reich Security (RSHA). Other authorities such as the German Labor Front and some civil administrations also produced less detailed or less comprehensive plans.[2] A first RKF draft from June 1941 referred to occupied Poland. A later version produced by the RSHA in late 1941 provided for the eastward displacement of 31 million– plus all of the Jews – of the 45 million inhabitants of Poland, the Baltic area, Belarus and northwestern Ukraine to be replaced over thirty years by 4.5 million Germans who would later proliferate.[3] According to an RKF scheme from May 1942, 5.5 million Germanic settlers (including about 700,000

[1] One example is Jäckel 1986.

[2] See, for instance, RMO, "Anweisung an den Reichskommissar des Reichskommissariats Ostland," n.d. (*c.* May 1941), BA R 92/2, p. 17.

[3] This version (on which Alexa Stiller is preparinga publication) is not known but has been reconstructed through a critical comment of Erhard Wetzel (RMO), April 27, 1942, printed in Heiber 1958, pp. 297–324, see esp. 299–300.

Germanized locals, especially from the Baltic countries) were to settle within twenty to twenty-five years in western Poland, large parts of central Poland, two strings of a total of twenty-two small settlement areas in the Baltic and Ukraine, and larger settlement regions in and north of the Crimea as well as around Leningrad.[4] An enhanced RKF "general settlement plan" of December 1942 covered Poland, Bohemia and Moravia, Alsace, Lorraine, Luxembourg, parts of Slovenia and settlements in the Baltic countries. The non-German population was to be reduced by about 25 million to 11 million people within 30 years and replaced, excluding the Baltic area, by 12 million Germanic settlers.[5] All of these plans anticipated the assimilation of various percentages of non-Germans in the settlement areas.

However, few Germans ever settled in these areas. Those who did largely consisted of about 500,000 ethnic Germans who were pulled out of eastern Europe in 1939–41 and mostly placed in German-annexed western Poland.[6] Settlement projects further east remained limited: about 20,000 ethnic Germans were installed in two counties in the area of Lublin, an equal number brought back to Lithuania, and ethnic Germans from Ukraine were concentrated in rural areas near Zaporoshie and Zhitomir – all in 1942 or 1943. In November 1939 Hitler had prohibited Reich Germans from settling in the East as he was worried that soldiers at the front – who were intended to be the majority of settlers – might resent it if the booty had already been divided up behind their back.[7] Thus, essentially only ethnic Germans could settle there until the war was won. Even in many areas with German settlement projects, quite apart from the other occupied Soviet territories or the General Government, settlement policies did not determine general occupation policy.[8] By mid 1942 no more than 73,000 Reich Germans and 131,000 ethnic Germans (1.2% of the population) were resident in the General Government.[9] Hitler's own order in 1942 to remove Russians and other nationalities from the Crimea and settle it with Germans came to nothing.[10] Settlement policy is another area in which Nazi planning should not be examined without paying attention to actual practice. Similarly,

4 *Generalplan Ost*, June 1942, in Madajczyk 1962, pp. 401–42.

5 "Dispositionen und Berechnungsgrundlagen für einen Generalsiedlungsplan," October 29/December 23, 1942, printed in Rössler and Schleiermacher 1993, pp. 96–117.

6 The number of colonizers in annexed Alsace, Lorraine and Slovenia remained low. See Stiller 2009, pp. 70–3. For places of origin see Leniger 2006, p. 89.

7 Müller 1991, p. 87.

8 Lower 2005, p. 178 (Zhitomir); Dieckmann 2011, pp. 786–7 (Lithuania).

9 HSSPF Ost, "Aufstellung eines SS-Oberabschnitts Ost," July 16, 1942, BA NS 33/24, p. 16

10 Kunz 2005, pp. 65–71.

ambitious plans to remove millions of alleged ethnic aliens from their own or annexed territory existed in other countries as well; and in Romania, Hungary and Croatia such plans were not necessarily scaled down even when it became clear that their realization was impossible. (See Chapter 14.)

Generalplan Ost, it should be added, is not to be conflated with the starvation plan of 1941 against sections of the Soviet population (see Chapter 9), as sometimes occurs[11] because of the huge dimensions and geographical overlap of both. They had different, and conflicting, objectives, focused on different populations and areas, were designed by different people at different times and involved substantially different timeframes.[12]

As in most of eastern Europe, the impact of settlement policy on overall German occupation policies was limited, and the link between settlement policy and the persecution of Jews was weak. Important framework orders, such as Himmler's order of July 19, 1942 to Krüger to murder most of the Jews in the General Government, mentioned a new ethnic order as one objective. However, when ten months later Himmler appeared to suggest that to "remove" the remaining "3–400,000" Jews in the General Government would free up space to accommodate ethnic Poles – who would themselves be displaced by the settlement of some additional Germans – it was only rhetoric.[13] Both Himmler and Globocnik were simultaneously in charge of murdering Jews and settling Germans, but these tasks were only loosely connected, as, for example, in arguments that major cities should be emptied of Jews so as to make German settlers feel more comfortable.

To be sure, the connection between German settlement and the destruction of Jews was more important in those annexed territories such as western Poland, where most ethnic Germans resettled. Settling masses of people is expensive, and there was no way to do so during the war other than by

[11] Examples are Snyder 2010a, pp. 160–70; Collingham 2011, pp. 40–8.

[12] The starvation policy, which was developed in the first half of 1941 (the *Generalplan Ost* (GPO) was developed largely between mid 1941 and late 1942), and targeted primarily Soviet urbanites and inhabitants of northern and central Russia and Belarus (whereas the GPO targeted parts of Ukraine and the Baltic area – where many rural dwellers lived – and Poland) and was developed by food and agriculture experts together with economic strategists from the military (the GPO was developed largely by SS officers) in order to secure the short-term food supply for Germany and its eastern armies. The GPO was about implanting German settlers in the long term.

[13] Note about Greifelt's appointment with Himmler, May 12, 1943, BA NS 19/982, p. 135. In reality, fewer than 200,000 Jews in the General Government were still alive ("Bevölkerung im Generalgouvernement," March 1, 1943, BA R 52 VI/21), and as they all lived in camps, little housing space for Poles would be vacated by their 'removal.' See Himmler to Krüger, July 19, 1942, in Röhr 1989, p. 227.

ruthlessly evicting others and expropriating their housing. By 1944 close to a million people were either deported eastward (almost 400,000) or to the Old Reich as forced labor, or displaced within the province, and the proportion of residents regarded as German increased to a quarter of the population.[14] According to one influential study, the inability of Himmler and the SS to find accommodation and livelihoods for ethnic German resettlers created pressure to kill Jews. It proved increasingly difficult to displace ethnic Poles and Jews from western Poland to the General Government – where those who had already been removed eastward had to be accommodated. Failure to implement settlement policies (e.g., the blocking of planned deportations in the spring of 1941) thus led to mass murder.[15] A variation to this argument is that deportations of Jews from central Europe, in the fall of 1941, to the areas of Wartheland and Lublin, were closely connected to the start of mass murder programs in these regions.[16]

Neither argument has found much in the way of confirmation at local level. Even in the Auschwitz area, more than a year separated the failure to displace Poles and the beginning of the mass murder of Jews.[17] The influx of Jewish deportees was of minor importance to the General Government, except in some areas in the district of Lublin,[18] and had less of an impact than the Eastern Ministry's refusal to accept the deportation of the Polish Jews in October 1941. In any case, the 'failure of resettlement' explanation applies only to certain territories, not generally.

It does not even apply to all of western Poland since settlement policies there varied greatly. It was of significance in the Wartheland as the center of (ethnic) German settlement, where few locals were accepted into the *Deutsche Volksliste* Germanization program and large deportations of Poles to the General Government occurred in 1939–41.[19] By contrast, Albert Forster, the Nazi Gauleiter and chief of civil administration of Danzig-West Prussia – which had more self-identified Germans among its population from the start, and relatively few Jews (23,000 in the fall of 1939) – pursued a policy, famously in conflict with Himmler and the regional SS, of Germanizing most Poles.[20] The flip side of this has received less attention. Forster had begun his rule with a much larger scale mass murder of the Polish intelligentsia than had been put into

[14] Rosenkötter 2003, pp. 274–5; Röhr 2002, p. 45.

[15] Aly 1999.

[16] Longerich 2001, pp. 134–5. On a smaller scale, there is evidence that local Jews were killed to make room for Jewish deportees to Minsk and, to a degree, Riga.

[17] Steinbacher 2000, p. 215.

[18] See the excerpts of a report by the head of the department, "Bevölkerungswesen und Fürsorge," of the district of Lublin, Türk, April 7, 1942, in Berenstein 1961, p. 271.

[19] Steinbacher 2000, pp. 97–9; Harvey 2003, p. 79.

[20] Schenk 2000, pp. 205–10; Steinbacher 2000, p. 81; Madajczyk 1988, pp. 479–99.

effect anywhere else (see Chapter 11). This apparently gave him the confidence to assimilate the rest of the ethnic Poles in his area. In East Upper Silesia the regional authorities pursued a very similar policy of large-scale Germanization of Poles – though with many fewer murders of intellectuals and with fewer protests from the SS. One reason for this policy was the especially high demand for labor to run the region's heavy industries, a factor that also slowed the persecution of Jews.[21] German settlement worked hand in hand with forced labor conscription – which is why 12% of the population of the Wartheland was deported for forced labor, compared to only 3.5% in Danzig-West Prussia and East Upper Silesia.[22] Even according to plans drawn up by the SS and regional Nazi Party leaders for western Poland – including the Wartheland – Poles were to remain at least half of the population for the next twenty to thirty years. A lack of German settlers meant the region could not be exploited without Polish labor.[23] Hinting at this latter point, Governor General Hans Frank said publicly: "We cannot deal with this space in a way that we conduct 16 million shots in the neck for 16 million Poles and thus solve the Polish problem."[24] It is evident from all of this that economic and settler imperialism had to be reconciled, and the latter often took the back seat.

Different resettlement programs conflicted with each other, and sometimes the deportation of Jews – like the 300,000 German and Austrian Jews to be shipped to Poland in the nine months after October 1939 – had to be postponed in favor of that of Poles.[25] There is no evidence that Jews were transported with more urgency from western Poland than ethnic Poles in the period 1939–41.[26] Many deportation programs failed because of protests by German civil and military authorities at the planned destinations. Thus, the forced removal of ethnic minorities for settlement purposes did not, in general, take priority over other objectives.

Gaining private living space: Housing shortages and the persecution of Jews

While the impact on the persecution of Jews of policies pertaining to large settlements has sometimes been overestimated, the importance of

[21] Figures can be found in Röhr 2002, p. 51, and Steinbacher 2000, esp. p. 222 note 90.
[22] Steinbacher 2000, p. 141.
[23] Note by von Schauroth, July 8, 1942, BA R 49/985 (asking whether Himmler knew that); *Generalplan Ost*, June 1942, in Madajczyk 1962, p. 436.
[24] Frank spoke at a press conference, April 14, 1942, BA R 52 II/191, p. 18.
[25] This plan is mentioned by Longerich 2001, p. 81; for the Viennese Jews see Moser 1966, p. 18.
[26] However, among the 87,000 deportees from the Wartheland during the so-called First *Nahplan*, many were professionals or owners of small businesses and stores: Steinbacher 2000, p. 97.

housing space has been underestimated. Housing was another scarce commodity before and during World War II. Apartments, especially for the lower strata of urban populations, were tiny and sub-standard, a situation that had the potential to provoke unrest and led to resentment against the bourgeoisie by 1942–43. In Vienna, 72% of all apartments had fewer than two rooms in 1934, and 60% lacked running water.[27] Such housing conditions were the result of widespread deficiencies in the urbanization process since the nineteenth century, but they were aggravated by a severe slowdown in construction during the economic depression of the 1930s, further decreases in the building sector brought about by the war, and, finally, by the loss of housing due to aerial bombardment and fighting on the ground.[28] Neither the German authorities nor those in other European countries could keep their promises to remedy the housing crisis. In this context, seizing Jewish apartments could serve as a substitute for social reform.[29] Raul Hilberg has pointed out that the Germans managed to free up far more than a million apartments in Europe by evicting, squeezing into ghettos and, then, deporting 6 million Jews.[30] This section briefly examines this process.

German house owners and local party organizations had pressed since 1937 for the 'Aryanization' of ownership and the right to evict Jewish tenants. By 1939, however, only public housing cooperatives had come close to this goal, and Göring told the Reich Ministries that real estate should be expropriated only at the end of the 'Aryanization' process.[31] Consequently, among the few deportations that were authorized to start with were those in which emptying apartments played a role.[32] Elsewhere – in Vienna, for example – low-level functionaries' ideas for deporting Jews to camps out of town, or to Poland, had few immediate consequences in 1939.[33] But pressure from Nazi authorities in several regions of Germany had increased by the summer and fall of 1941, while the Security Service reported discontent with the housing situation and popular criticism of the bourgeoisie for occupying excessively large apartments.[34] These authorities sought to evict urban Jews from their apartments and squeeze them into so-called Jew houses, or remove them to remote building complexes out of town. In Hannover, the mayor was

27 Botz 1975, pp. 18, 26.
28 Schildt 1998, pp. 158, 162–3; Führer 1995, pp. 40, 338–9; Botz 1975, pp.14–20, 26; Heiden 1995; Gebel 2000, pp. 242–3, 266–7.
29 Botz 1975 was ground breaking.
30 Hilberg 1992a, p. 236.
31 Führer 1995, pp. 99–104.
32 Toury 1986, p. 432 (evidence for Stettin in January and February 1940).
33 Botz 1975, pp. 84–5, 89–103, 146–62.
34 MadR, vol. 8, pp. 2987–94 (November 13, 1941).

soon ousted from office because he had hesitated to support Gauleiter Hermann Lauterbacher in this effort.[35] In Breslau, deportations to the vicinity of the city, which had been called for since 1940, began in June 1941, and they continued into 1942 even after deportations from Breslau to the East had started.[36] Where Jews could not yet be deported eastward for lack of transportation, in Göttingen for example, they were squeezed together in order to appropriate their apartments for non-Jews. This is one more indication that generating apartment vacancies was not simply a pretext for deportation, but rather was driven by what local politicians at least perceived as considerable popular pressure. In Mainz, for example, citizens reportedly complained that Jews enjoyed much better housing than non-Jews. In Münster, it was the talk of the town in bars that one aim of deporting the Jews was to vacate apartments.[37]

By August 1941 Heydrich's priority was to remove Jews from large cities.[38] An initiative of Hamburg's Nazi leader, Karl Kaufmann, to deport Jewish residents – which he rationalized by citing damage to residences caused by an aerial attack in September – was one of the initiatives that prompted Hitler, around September 16 or 17, 1941, to permit (after some months of hesitation) large-scale deportations of Jews from Greater Germany to the East.[39] In the fall of 1941 Hitler also recommended to the provincial leader of Vienna that he solve the city's housing crisis by removing all of its Jews, and later all of its "ethnic aliens" (such as Czechs), instead of embarking on an unrealistic construction program.[40] The Gestapo also explained to Jewish community leaders in Berlin and Nuremberg that Jews had to be deported to Łódź in order to vacate apartments to alleviate the consequences of aerial bombardments. Similar arguments were reported from Cologne. One of Eichmann's secretaries had worked for Generalbauinspektor Speer's planning authority for the reconstruction of Berlin.[41]

[35] Buchholz 1994, esp. pp. 62–3; see Neliba 1992, p. 337; Dörner 2007, pp. 148–9; for the Sudeten area see Gebel 2000, p. 79; for Vienna see Botz 1975, pp. 89–103, 148.

[36] Gryglewski 1996, pp. 42–55; Jonca 1996, pp. 277–8; Konieczny 1996, pp. 318–20, 330.

[37] Correspondence about "Unterbringung von Judenfamilien in Göttingen," November and December 1941, BA, BDC, Sammlung Schumacher 240 II; see Führer 1995, p. 105. For Münster see Longerich 2006, p. 196.

[38] Eichmann on August 15, 1941, according to Witte 1995, p. 42.

[39] Kaufmann to Görnnert, September 4, 1942, BA 34.01 FC film 375; Bajohr 1995, pp. 291–2.

[40] Transmitted by Bormann to von Schirach, November 2, 1941 (copy), BA R 43 II/598; Botz 1975, pp. 199–200. For exceptional deportations of Viennese Jews to the district of Lublin for the same purpose in early 1941, see Botz 1975, p. 197.

[41] Stoltzfus 1996, p. 163; Longerich 1998a, pp. 700–1; Aly 2006a, pp. 117–18; Hildegard Henschel, "Aus der Arbeit der Jüdischen Gemeinde während der Jahre 1941–1943: Gemeindearbeit und Evakuierung von Berlin 16. Oktober 1941–16. Juni

Some authors have argued that housing needs were an important driving force behind the deportation of German Jews, but more evidence is needed to show that attempts to remove Jews from specific neighborhoods – in order to vacate apartments or facilitate construction related to new city planning – influenced the selection of deportees in the fall of 1941.[42] In any case, Jews were deported in the fall of 1941 from cities exposed to Allied bombardment – like Hamburg, Bremen and Cologne.[43] The Supreme Command of the Armed Forces also advocated this in October 1941.[44] But Jews were also deported from large cities like Berlin, Vienna, Prague, Munich and Breslau, whose severe housing crises had other causes.

Freeing up apartment space continued to be cited as the motive for deporting Jews from Germany and Austria in 1942. At the Wannsee conference on January 20, Heydrich announced that Europe was to be cleared of Jews from West to East but explained that this had to begin in Germany, Austria and the Czech lands "especially because of the housing question and other necessities of social policy."[45] Housing considerations seemed to be important enough to have a major impact on considerations about the sequence of deportations. When the German Commander of the Security Police and Security Service in Prague protested in mid-August 1942 about planned deportations to Theresienstadt –which he regarded as excessive in scale – he argued:

> Although I understand the need to evacuate [Jews living in] the areas under threat of air attacks, I nonetheless must request to temporarily postpone allocations from Vienna and other regions not threatened by aerial attacks until we have created more room by erecting new barracks.[46]

But in the next eight weeks, fifty transports – including six trains from Vienna and one each from Breslau, Königsberg and Dresden (where the housing situation was also problematic, although not due to bombardment) – brought 22,300 inmates to Theresienstadt.[47] The importance of the housing issue and the dynamics it created are highlighted by the fact

1943," *c.* 1949, StA Kammergericht Berlin 1 Js 1/65, vol. 12, file 61; memories by Herbert Klein, son of the former head of the Jewish community in Nuremberg, can be found in Johnson and Reuband 2005, p. 102. Secretary: interrogation of E. F. (Lukasch), September 4, 1968, StA Kammergericht Berlin 1 Js 1/65, vol. 44.

42 Most notable is Willems 2000 (for Berlin); see also Longerich 1998a, p. 700; Gryglewski 1996, pp. 38–57, esp. pp. 56–7 (for Breslau).

43 This is emphasized by Aly 2006a, pp. 117–18, in part with reference to Longerich 1998a, pp. 705–6.

44 Kroener 1999, pp. 817–18.

45 This is from the Wannsee conference protocol facsimile in Tuchel 1992, p. 129.

46 BdS Prag (Böhme) to RSHA (Müller), August 17, 1942, BA D-H M 501, file 3 (AMV 109-4-978).

47 Gottwaldt and Schulle 2005, pp. 310–37. For Vienna's housing situation see Botz 1975, pp. 14–20.

that overcrowding increased the death rate in Theresienstadt in August 1942 and the problem was partially 'solved' by October by deporting close to 8,000 people to Auschwitz and other extermination sites.[48]

There is more evidence of popular pressure from below on German authorities to remove Jews in order to improve housing conditions. In Vienna, thousands of citizens took matters into their own hands and took possession of apartments by forcibly evicting Jews or forcing them to sign fake contracts under duress. According to one estimate, three-quarters of the approximately 65,000 apartments in Vienna that Jews lost to non-Jews in 1938–39 changed hands illegally.[49] While the situation in Vienna may have been unusual, it would be worth examining whether the takeover of Jewish apartments across the German Reich was actually the orderly administrative act that one may imagine it to have been. In some cities in German-occupied or allied countries there is also evidence of widespread squatting in Jewish apartments (see. p. 349).

In some German-occupied territories housing conditions in the 1930s were even worse than they were in Germany and Austria.[50] The creation of ghettos, and their subsequent reduction or elimination through mass murder, were often political means for improving the housing situation of locals who had been affected by the destruction of war and as a way of consolidating Germans neighborhoods – as in Kiev, Kraków and Lublin.[51] Chain resettlements were not infrequent. For example, 62,000 Poles were deported from the Wartheland to Warsaw in 1940–41 to make room for ethnic Germans from Romania; the Poles, meanwhile, were then resettled in Warsaw in the former residences of 72,000 Jews who were, in turn, forced into the ghetto. Poles sometimes received slightly better apartments than they had had before, but Germans were the real beneficiaries.[52] In Simferopol (in the Crimea), Einsatzgruppe D originally planned to murder 14,500 local Jews in March 1942, but actually carried out the executions in December 1941 because of a request by the headquarters of the German 11th Army which was seeking to mitigate the local housing and food crises.[53] In territories designed for immediate German settlement, emptied Jewish apartments were reserved

[48] Hájková 2013, pp. 6–9; for the trains see Gottwaldt and Schulle 2005, pp. 245–6, 256, 397.

[49] Botz 1975, pp. 27, 61, 78.

[50] Marcus 1983, pp. 183, 187; Młynarczyk 2007, p. 25.

[51] Einsatzgruppen der Sicherheitspolizei und des SD, "Tätigkeits- und Lagebericht Nr. 6" for October 1941 in Klein 1997, p. 236 (Kiev); General Government, government meeting protocols, March 11 and June 18, 1942, BA R 52 II/242, p. 34 (Lublin) and R 52 II/235, p. 82 (Kraków).

[52] Aly 2006a, p. 236; Alberti 2006, pp. 154–5; for eastern Galicia see Harvey 2003, pp. 246–7, 252; for Bohemia and Moravia see Oprach 2006, pp. 71–4.

[53] Oldenburg 2004, pp. 167–8.

only for Germans; in Posen in February 1940 6,000 apartments (possibly including some commandeered from Poles) were redistributed to Reich Germans (2,150), local ethnic Germans (2,000) and Baltic German resettlers (1,850).[54]

Wartime destruction did not have much of an impact on the housing situation in German cities in the fall of 1941, when the massive deportations started.[55] It took about four years of aerial bombardment to destroy as many apartments as had been lacking for other reasons before the war.[56] However, it seemed politically more important to support the victims of war than the victims of housing construction mismanagement, and the former were mentioned more often than the latter in discussions about deporting Jews. The resentment of Jews was inextricably linked with the desire to alleviate the real social problem that both groups were part of. Non-Jewish citizens who argued that Jews should not enjoy better housing than they did, and wanted to improve their lots, insisted on a racist hierarchy with overtones that Jews' wealth might have been illegitimately amassed at the cost of non-Jews. However, the Nazi government never dared to introduce a centrally planned redistribution of housing space since it feared alienating the bourgeoisie (although quartering bombed-out residents in the apartments of their fellow citizens became common practice in 1943). This also shows that anti-Jewish actions served as a "substitute for Nazi social policy."[57]

Other arguments, on the basis of the bombardment itself, were also powerful. Jews were said to pull the strings of enemy governments, support the enemy or at least sympathize with the other side and spread its propaganda, and, thus, they shared responsibility for the aerial attacks. This accusation was important enough for Hitler to mention in his political testament of 1945 – in which he reminded readers that Jews were punished for, among other things, the "hundreds of thousands of women and children in the cities burned and bombarded to death."[58] In this context, citizens viewed the deportation of Jews as a form of punishment that would compensate German bombing victims. Other Germans discussed where to house Jews in order to increase their chances of being hit in the bombing raids – such as on the upper floors of urban buildings or in houses located near factories – "so that the enemies with their terror attacks really hit the *right people*," as one German woman advised the German Foreign Office

[54] Rosenkötter 2003, p. 193.
[55] Longerich 1998b, p. 23.
[56] See Führer 1995, pp. 40–1 and 342.
[57] The quote is from the subtitle of Botz 1975; for debates about a planned housing economy see Führer 1995, pp. 338–49.
[58] Adolf Hitler, "Mein politisches Testament," IMG, vol. 41, p. 549.

on planning for a ghetto in Budapest. In fact, such ideas did influence Hungarian plans for ghettoization.[59] Conversely, it was also thought that Jews gave ground signals to enemy bombers and that they should therefore be moved from proximity to certain facilities. In Germany, such rumors were also spread about foreign forced laborers.[60] By 1943, however, some Germans were regretting that the Jews had been deported, for they assumed that the Allies might show more restraint in their aerial assaults if the Jews were still living in German cities. This idea also appeared in a former regional Nazi Party leader's post-war memoir.[61] Many Germans took this connection a step further and, according to agents' reports, regarded the bombing raids as vengeance for the persecution of Jews.[62]

All of these variations were based on the idea that the Jews were fiends who supported enemy bombing. Political prisoners were also linked to bombing raids. In September 1942, Himmler ordered that units of concentration camp inmates (probably including Jews, but more non-Jews) be established for clearing rubble.[63] It was a disdained, repulsive, dangerous and tiring task. In Cologne, SS guards shot exhausted workers in broad daylight.[64] Workers from the general forced labor program were forced to clear rubble and dig graves even earlier, and in greater numbers.[65] This 'punishment,' however, disregarded the fact that foreign laborers themselves were also often the victims of carpet-bombing.[66]

Starting in January 1942, the furniture and household possessions of Jews that had been plundered by the state was used to help bombed-out Germans. They were auctioned off to cover the costs (such as the lost income of the former landlords of Jews) of displacing Jews.[67] In Hamburg and its vicinity alone, people (mostly women) from 30,000 families are estimated to have bought possessions stolen from Jews in

59 Handwritten letter by Marianne Siebrasse to German Foreign Office, May 4, 1944, PA AA R99449 (emphasis in original); see Steinert 1970, p. 260; local Nazi Party group Rossau (Vienna), Karl Ocenasek, October 3, 1939, in Botz 1975, p. 84. (This was years before the first bombs actually hit Vienna.) For ghetto planning in Budapest and considerations about bombing see Cole 2003, pp. 81–9, 115–24.

60 Kochan 1998, p. 32 (concerning Berlin-Rangsdorf).

61 For various examples see Kulka and Jäckel 2004, pp. 515, 540, 542; memoir: Jordan 1971, p. 236.

62 Bajohr and Pohl 2006, pp. 67–8.

63 Himmler to Pohl, September 9, 1942, and other correspondence, BA NS 19/14, esp. p. 11.

64 Gellately 2002, p. 294.

65 Kubatzki 2001a, p. 102; survivors' accounts from Kazimiera Czarnecka, Jerzy Sadecki, Jekaterina Spiridonowa and Sofia Pronko can be found in Berliner Geschichtswerkstatt 2000, pp. 33, 59–60, 103, 119.

66 Fuchslocher 1998, p. 93.

67 Aly 2006a, pp. 125–31; Buchholz 1994, p. 66; report about "Aktion M," IMG, vol. 38, pp. 28–9.

state-organized auctions.[68] The German railway organization, in addition to deporting Jews and employing some as forced laborers, secured 1,576 railroad car loads of furniture taken from Jews for redistribution among its non-Jewish staff whose flats had been destroyed during air raids.[69] Kindergarten teachers in German-annexed areas of Poland gave their students clothing, toys, crockery and cooking pots that had been confiscated from Jews.[70] For those few Jews who returned after the war, the loss of personal belongings, seeing their families' furniture and other goods in the possession of others, the struggle to get their property back, and the inability to "go back to their pre-war accommodation" because others had occupied their homes, intensified their sense of uprootedness.[71] Quite literally, it was difficult to come home.

Expropriation, finance and violence

The financial effects of the persecution and mass murder of Jews had many aspects. Those briefly treated here include: the financing of deportation and extermination, the German trade in the movable and immovable property of Jews, and the redistribution of jobs that Jews had held.

It would be a mistake to assume that it cost the German state huge sums of money to murder Jews and other Europeans. It has long since been established that the destruction was designed to be self-financing.[72] Deported Jews had to pay for their rail transportation, and Jewish organizations had to finance those who could not pay for themselves.[73] In the Protectorate of Bohemia and Moravia, the Gestapo-organized Center for Jewish Emigration assumed control of Jewish assets and financed emigration and deportation by appropriating that wealth.[74] The RSHA did the same with the funds of the Reich Association of German Jews and part of the assets of Jews who were to be deported.[75] As described above, Jewish emigration between 1933 and 1941 was restricted precisely because the German authorities wanted to avoid loss of foreign currency and to make Jewish exits profitable for the state. Essentially, Jews from Greater Germany were forced to leave most of their property within the

68 Bajohr 1998, pp. 332–8, 345.
69 Hilberg 1981, p. 91.
70 Harvey 2003, pp. 254–5.
71 Lewkowicz 2006, pp. 192, 195–6 (quote) for the example of Salonica.
72 Barkai 1988, pp. 194–8.
73 Gryglewski 1996, p. 15 note 65 (Breslau); Guckes 1999, pp. 100, 103, 105 (France).
74 Oprach 2006, pp. 67, 69.
75 Gruner 2000a, p. 142; Zimmermann 1995, pp. 362–3; note by Maedel (Finance Ministry), December 14, 1942, in Longerich 1989, p. 171.

Reich.[76] The Haavara agreement of 1933 between Jewish organizations and the Reich Ministry for Economic Affairs was meant to partially address this problem. According to its terms, the assets of Jews emigrating to Palestine were held by the German state in blocked accounts, and half of the total was returned to emigres upon their arrival in Palestine – this transfer being financed by the sale of German exports to Palestine and other countries in the Near East brokered by Jewish agents.[77] A functionary in the Foreign Office later suggested extending this model to the creation of a new inter-European bank which would finance the deportation of all the Jews of Europe to Madagascar and their settlement there.[78] Later, the Gestapo tried to establish the principle that wealthy Jews should provide the means for poor coreligionists to emigrate. When the SS was deprived of a large part of the assets of German Jews in November 1941, it attempted to finance its operations by imposing special fees on Jews and by deporting the wealthy ones first.[79]

The income generated by the annihilation centers far exceeded their costs because Jews were robbed of the possessions that they brought with them. Globocnik's administration, which managed the camps of the Lublin-based Operation Reinhard – namely, Bełżec, Sobibór and Treblinka, where at least 1.6 million Jews were murdered – reported proceeds of over 178.7 million Reichsmark, mostly in bills, valuables and clothing.[80] (But note that this average of about 110 Reichsmark per human life was relatively small compared to the 1.1 billion Reichsmark that German and Austrian Jews were forced to pay following the nationwide pogroms of November 1938.[81]) Construction costs were much lower than 178 million Reichsmark since all newly erected buildings in the three centers were made of wood, except for those housing the gas chambers and the quarters of the German guards. Globocnik claimed costs of 11.89 million Reichsmark, 40% of it for rail transport.[82] These were not "enormous, costly extermination factories"[83] but small killing

[76] Heim 1999, pp. 107–38.
[77] Oprach 2006, p. 91.
[78] Rademacher, "Gedanken über die Gründung einer intereuropäischen Bank für die Verwertung des Judenvermögens in Europa," August 12, 1940, PA AA R 100857, p. 228.
[79] Gryglewski 1996, pp. 16–18. For similar efforts in the Netherlands to finance internment camps, see the material in BA R 2/12158, pp. 170ff.; see Michman 1986, pp. 163–5.
[80] "Vorläufiger Abschlussbericht der Kasse Aktion 'Reinhardt' Lublin per 15. Dezember 1943," IMG, vol. 34, p. 81–2. This report likely excluded Majdanek, which, as a concentration camp, was under a different administration.
[81] For the sum, see Aly 2006a, pp. 46–8.
[82] Excerpts from Globocnik's report, January 5, 1944, can be found in Berenstein 1961, pp. 421–2; see Rückerl 1977, pp. 133–4, 162–6 (Sobibór).
[83] Arendt 1986 (1955), p. 918.

stations with a few hundred inmates each. In Sobibór, Jews were killed with engine exhausts, but the gas chambers required just four canisters of fuel per day.[84] The labor costs for these three annihilation centers were also low. The largest, Treblinka, employed at most 43 German SS guards at one point in time; on average, 18 Germans worked at Sobibór. Bełżec, Sobibór and Treblinka combined employed fewer than 1,000 'Ukrainian' auxiliaries and fewer than 3,000 temporarily spared Jewish prisoners.[85] The German team responsible for Chełmno numbered 85. A maximum of 29 German SS officers and 120–150 Czech gendarmes worked at Theresienstadt.[86] The staff at Auschwitz and other concentration camps (40,000 in 1944) was much larger,[87] as was the investment in construction. By contrast, General Governor Hans Frank had rejected, in January 1940, a proposal by Heydrich to invest 90 million Reichsmark in the construction of four new giant forced labor camps for Jews.[88] The murderers at Bełżec, Sobibór and Treblinka were proud of their cheap and efficient operations; the SS at Auschwitz found their operation more elaborate and reliable, though much more expensive.[89]

These arguments also apply, with some modifications, to other elements of anti-Jewish policies. Personnel costs are difficult to establish since few Germans outside of the killing centers of Chełmno, Bełżec, Sobibór and Treblinka were employed full time to implement anti-Jewish policies only. Payrolls were kept down by measures such as self-administration in ghettos and camps, and employing non-German auxiliaries. Auschwitz and Majdanek were large camps that required more investment in construction. The largest one, in Auschwitz, was the result of an expansion in 1942–43 that included massive crematoria and cost 13.7 million Reichsmark.[90] Yet that was still much less than the value of property confiscated from arriving Jews. One author estimates that the SS made a profit of 1,231 Reichsmark per prisoner in Auschwitz if one compares the value of their labor, valuables and belongings to the incineration costs.[91]

Several months after Jews were squeezed into large ghettos, as in Warsaw and Łódź, the communities were stripped of most of their money

[84] Schelvis 1998, p. 126.
[85] Berger 2013, pp. 138, 218, 224–5; Schelvis 1998, p. 295; see Rückerl 1977, pp. 206–7.
[86] Greiser to Himmler, March 19, 1943, in Longerich 1989, p. 351; Hájková 2013, pp. 3, 43.
[87] Bauche 1991, p. 99.
[88] See Herbert 1993, pp. 208–9.
[89] Berger 2013, pp. 96–9.
[90] See Freund *et al.* 1993, esp. pp. 195–9.
[91] Strzelecki 1994, p. 262.

and required public subsidies. German civil administrations had various ways to economize here: starvation rations, forced labor and later murder of the unproductive.[92] In fact, this economizing seems to have been so effective that public funding for the Warsaw ghetto was never provided. The civil administration reported this while calling for Warsaw to be "liberated from the burden of the Jews unfit for labor soon."[93] Mass deportations to Treblinka started five weeks later. The civil administration did list substantial losses of 155.9 million Złoty (78 million Reichsmark) after most of the Warsaw ghetto was emptied through deportations, but these consisted largely of building damage caused by an earlier lack of maintenance, plus unpaid rents.[94]

As all this indicates, the expulsion and murder of Jews produced financial gains, not losses. Finance was a factor pushing for, not an obstacle to, persecution. Booty collected in the extermination centers was only a fraction of the total. The questions that remain concern the type of proceeds generated, the beneficiaries, whether confiscating assets was a causal factor in the mass murders, and if it was, through what mechanisms.

Direct plunder was just one aspect of the looting of Jewish assets. After the German annexation of Austria, a variety of persons confiscated or appropriated Jewish-owned businesses and the possessions of Jews and political opponents.[95] During later occupations, Jews and non-Jews were plundered more evenly. In the first months of the German occupation of western Poland, it was especially middle-ranking German officials – such as district administrators, Nazi Party county chiefs, mayors, police authorities and military officers, but also Reich German and ethnic German individuals – who appropriated or requisitioned the property of locals in "tens of thousands of cases."[96] After the German conquest a giant wave of plundering spread throughout the occupied Soviet Union (as had occurred earlier in Poland). Jews were frequent victims[97] but the population in general was greatly affected. Soldiers searched apartments for food, clothing, shoes and valuables, and there was also a good

92 Heim and Aly 1987, pp. 19–29, 70–9; Browning 1986, pp. 343–68; Rosenkötter 2003, pp. 226–7.

93 Amtschef Dr Hummel, Warsaw district administration, statement during the government meeting of the General Government, June 18, 1942, BA R 52 II/235, p. 75 reverse side.

94 Governor, Warsaw district, report for August and September, October 15, 1942, BA R 52 III/21.

95 Bajohr 2001, p. 32.

96 Rosenkötter 2003, pp. 103, 134 (quote: Winkler, Haupttreuhandstelle Ost, to Göring, February 5, 1941); Alberti 2006, pp. 105–18.

97 See Grossman and Ehrenburg 1994, pp. 43, 68–9, 84, 128, 675; Pohl 2011, p. 250. See Gutman 1982, pp. 9–10; Młynarczyk 2007, pp. 129–30.

deal of vandalism.[98] A local joke was that one could catch a German soldier by staking a goose in the open because one would soon appear and try to take it. Allegedly, some Red Army soldiers successfully tested the hypothesis in September 1941.[99] It was the same in Yugoslavia and Greece, where German soldiers, often in small gangs, looted everything from food to watches, jewelry and furniture.[100] German divisions from the Eastern Front, sent to France for rest and recreation, brought with them their habit of pillaging – as evidenced by the complaints of the German occupation authorities.[101] But even close to the Eastern Front lines, soldiers rooted through the ruins of houses, assuming that Soviet citizens had buried valuables there.[102] Deep in the hinterland, Germans, often in search of food or alcohol, continued to rob and extort the population.[103] The same was true in occupied Greece: the First Mountain Division's record included stealing, open plunder, assaults on hotels and other facilities, sexual exploitation and gang attacks on locals, but also (as in Warsaw) selling German army property.[104] As the population frequently complained, apartment searches were often accompanied by plundering, whether by the German Security Police, the city police (Schutzpolizei), the Belarusian Schutzmannschaft in Brest, Belarus, or the German Criminal Police in Kattowitz, East Upper Silesia.[105] German soldiers seem to have removed gold teeth from the corpses of Soviet POWs in at least one camp.[106] Inside Germany, and as early as 1941, men of the Reich Labor Service, and, in Aachen, perhaps even soldiers, occasionally went on pillaging missions following air raids.[107]

The mass looting in occupied countries – mostly carried out by Germans in an official function – contradicts the image of the disciplined

[98] Angrick 2005, p. 119 (Kharkov, Ukraine); memories of Raissa Stepiko in Berliner Geschichtswerkstatt 2000, p. 82 (Belgorod, Ukraine); Gerlach 1999, pp. 376–7 (Belarus).

[99] Beevor 2007, p. 46.

[100] Yugoslavia: memories of Julije Kemenj and Rukula Bencion in *We Survived*, vol. 3, pp. 385, 438. Greece: Mazower 2001, pp. 23–4; Fleischer 1986, pp. 76–9; Matkovski 1959, pp. 208–9.

[101] Lieb 2007, pp. 38–9.

[102] Letter by Harry Mielert, March 29, 1943, in Bähr 1961, p. 370.

[103] Generalstaatsanwaltschaft Königsberg, report, May 29, 1943, in Tilitzki 1991, p. 242.

[104] Mazower 2001, pp. 215–18; see Feldkommandantur 1042 (Peloponnese), report of December 31, 1943, in Seckendorf 1992, p. 295. For Warsaw see Klukowski 1993, p. 170 (September 3, 1941).

[105] *Gebietskommissar* Brest-Litowsk, October 18, 1944, BA R 6/87, p. 69; Steinbacher 2000, pp. 311–2.

[106] Dawletschin 2005, p. 197.

[107] Schlegelberger to Lammers, August 12, 1941, BA R 43 II/668, p. 8, see pp. 9–17, 38, 42–72, 88–102.

German military and a bureaucracy running like clockwork. Rather, it shows an anarchic struggle for personal enrichment that undermined the efficiency of state-organized exploitation.[108] Often this struggle went hand in hand with murder. However, the pillage was so widespread that its victims included many more than just Jews.

This went beyond the non-violent, unequal exchange, highlighted in a recent study, in which exchange rates with local currencies set artificially low allowed German soldiers, functionaries and private individuals to buy up everything of value in occupied countries.[109] It was an extremely widespread phenomenon for Germans to trade items on the black market that their relatives had sent them for this purpose – acquiring in exchange everything from meat and eggs to furs. Facilitated by some German authorities, the practice also permeated the SS on Soviet territory even though some of its officers did not approve.[110] Many of the inhabitants of occupied countries – such as, for example, Jews from the Łódź ghetto – sold their property out of destitution. In 1940–41, German authorities purchased their belongings – furs, carpets, porcelain, glassware, jewelry and watches – and sold them in public stores.[111]

One might call the previously described looting as 'violent corruption,' but that classification is not meant to suggest that other forms of corruption played no role. A lack of control, no rule of law, the perpetual claim that actions carried out in conquered countries were a means to greater German ends, power, a master's attitude and an almost unchallengeable impunity made corruption a mass phenomenon in the occupied countries.[112] The situation was especially bad in the General Government and in the German-occupied Soviet territories. German SS, army and civil administrators robbed Jews and non-Jews of their valuables.[113] Next to Hermann Göring, the most corrupt man in the Third Reich seems to have been Erich Koch – head of the civil administrations in East Prussia, Białystok and the Zichenau districts in Poland, and Reich Commissariat of Ukraine.[114] Eichmann's collaborator Alois Brunner, and others in Salonica, enjoyed the good life with the finest furniture, tableware and food, and they sexually

108 Bajohr 2001, pp. 133, 193–4.
109 Aly 2006a, pp. 94–117, 134–55; see also Lower 2005, p. 46.
110 Higher SS and Police Leader Russia-Center and White Ruthenia, order, August 16, 1943, CChIDK 1323-2-225, p. 13.
111 Alberti 2006, pp. 217–23, 273.
112 Bajohr 2001, esp. pp. 13–14, 76.
113 Pohl 1996, pp. 302–4; Borodziej 1999, pp. 56–7; Banken 2009, pp. 448–56. For the Soviet territories see Zellhuber 2006, pp. 199–204.
114 Fuhrer and Schön 2010, pp. 83–104.

abused local women when organizing the deportation of the city's Jewish community.[115] SS men in annihilation centers kept a sizable part of the gold of murdered Jews and others for themselves.[116] Odilo Globocnik, who had already been under Nazi Party and SS investigation for severe corruption when he was in Austria in 1938, took possession of the property of the Jews whose killing he had organized in Lublin, enjoyed their clothing and carpets, and savored their exquisite food, beverages and cigars during lavish parties.[117] Rarely was this sort of behavior punished, although a prosection did take place in the case of the chief of the Gestapo's Jewish affairs office in Breslau, and also against German officials in the town and concentration camp of Auschwitz. However, the prosecution at Auschwitz related only to a small part of the officials' embezzlement, black marketeering and extortion, which was perpetuated against both Jews and ethnic Germans.[118] Managers of many SS organizations maintained illicit funds, including the staff of Operation Reinhard and Higher SS and Police Leaders. The fact that many police institutions were stealing or embezzling money illustrates the general decline of law and order.[119] By the time the still existing Reich Accounting Office in Potsdam called for a thorough audit of the finances of the Central Office for Jewish Emigration in Prague on July 31, 1945, and an investigation into the accounts for the "transports of Jews" and the "economy of Jewish camps," Stalin, Truman and Attlee were two weeks into the Potsdam Conference that was discussing the future of Europe.[120] It was a bit late now to be tackling SS corruption.

The many individuals who engaged in plundering activities, black marketeering and the other forms of corruption mentioned so far appear not to have been satisfied with the potential benefits of official policies – to which we now turn. The plunder of Jewish property, and obliging German Jews to pay a huge atonement payment, were important in 1938–39 both in terms of preparing Germany for war and keeping the social peace (among non-Jews). (See Chapter 3.) All Jewish possessions were judged to have been illicitly acquired.[121] The German state, as did German-allied states also, sought to channel the redistribution of most of the Jewish property through public hands. This was then usually sold, not given away free. Usually the civil or

115 Safrian 1997, pp. 240–1.
116 Banken 2009, pp. 612, 630–9.
117 Rieger 2007, pp. 37, 43, 63, 78–9, 121–2, 138–9.
118 Gryglewski 1996, p. 17; Steinbacher 2000, pp. 171–5; Zürcher 2004, p. 180.
119 See Weinert 1993, pp. 131–59.
120 "Beiträge zur Denkschrift," July 31, 1945, BA R 2301/8420, p. 18. A first audit had taken place in 1941, see Weinert 1993, pp. 129–30.
121 For example, see Alberti 2006, p. 159.

military administration, not the SS, was in charge. The proceeds were used to help balance the state's overstretched budget and thereby check inflation.[122] However, in Germany and other countries, the practice of confiscation was different: the proceeds derived from property sequestrated from Jews and non-Jews were often less than half of the value of the assets. In western Poland this revenue was mostly realized through the sale of large firms, while aspiring small business owners were strongly subsidized.[123]

In 1940 it was still possible for the German Foreign Ministry to make this naive proposal: "The guiding principle is to substitute quasi in one stroke the Jewish economic influence in Europe with the German one, without economic interruptions in the economies of the different countries, by closing down the big Jewish companies."[124] But it was only in annexed areas and in countries rendered powerless by the German occupation – Poland, the Soviet Union, Bohemia and Moravia – that all, or virtually all, Jewish property fell into German hands. For the other occupied and allied countries, the "territoriality principle" was accepted in July 1942, according to which Jewish assets fell to the state from whose territory their former owners, irrespective of citizenship, were deported.[125] To some degree, it applied even to occupied Serbia.[126] In Germany and much of occupied Europe, this principle lightened the social burden of the costs of war and, thus, prevented (more) unrest among the population. This was a goal of preeminent political importance. In occupied countries, Jewish assets helped finance the enormous occupation tributes that Germany imposed every month. In the Netherlands, 10% of the occupation costs were financed through 1.5 billion Reichsmark worth of property seized from Jews who represented just 1.8% of the population.[127] By contrast, public proceeds from Jewish property in the German-occupied Soviet territories were as little as perhaps 20 million Reichsmark.[128] Götz Aly has shown that considerations of public finance,

[122] Aly 2006a, esp. pp. 42–9, 194–6, 221.

[123] For the example of Haupttreuhandstelle Ost, see Rosenkötter 2003, pp. 278, 281–4. By the spring of 1942, the HTO owned property worth 6–7 billion Reichsmark; by March 1945, 3.16 billion Reichsmark was left, including real estate, whereas the proceeds of the sales that had taken place of items (that should have yielded 3–4 billion Reichsmark) amounted to 1.45 billion Reichsmark.

[124] Rademacher, "Gedanken über die Gründung einer intereuropäischen Bank für die Verwertung des Judenvermögens in Europa," August 12, 1940, PA AA R 100857, p. 228.

[125] Foreign Office circular, July 31, 1942, on the basis of an interagency meeting on the previous day, Nuremberg Document NG-424. This rule was later repeatedly challenged or breached by German and foreign agents, but it did become the general line of action.

[126] Schlarp 1986, pp. 295–300.

[127] Aly 2006a, pp. 75–93, 210.

[128] For Belarus and Reich Commissariat Ostland, see Gerlach 1999, pp. 682–3; for Reich Commissariat Ukraine, see RMO, financial report for 1942, December 1942, appendix 2, BA R 43 II/689, p. 233 reverse side. This excludes Bialystok and eastern Galicia.

combating inflation and substituting social policy were important factors in the deportation and mass murder of Hungarian and Greek Jews.[129] An important aspect of the earlier justification for the murder of the mentally disabled had also been to cut the food and heating costs involved in looking after them. According to one contemporary calculation, the murder of about 70,000 patients would save 885.4 million Reichsmark over ten years. For years before, Nazi propaganda had emphasized how much money the disabled cost the state.[130] By contrast, mass sterilizations were a burden on the state budget in the short run (and were therefore reduced during the war).[131]

The largest assets confiscated from Jews were real estate and businesses; the value of bank accounts was usually less, while cash, jewelry and movable property were of relatively minor importance.[132] Real estate and businesses could be counted toward the state budget even if they remained unsold. Most Jewish firms were not sold; they were administered by public trustees who usually tried to put something away for themselves. These persons were obvious beneficiaries. Many, however, did not wait for public authorization – they seized businesses by force at the beginning of the occupation. In Austria, many of these illegal appropriators were soon ousted.[133] However, many stores – and sometimes also artisans' workshops – were closed down in various countries under German control since German experts believed that general business conditions were unhealthy, especially for the retail trade. This measure created benefits, primarily, for the remaining shopowners and trustees. Industrial enterprises were less affected.[134] In occupied Poland, such liquidations had huge consequences: from the fall of 1939 through to October 1, 1943, 74% of 195,000 stores (112,100 of which were Jewish-owned) were liquidated in the General Government. Only 25,000 of the former Jewish shops remained in business by the fall of 1941; and none were left a year later.[135] So, most Jewish stores were closed down, and Jewish-owned shops constituted the majority of those stores that

129 Gerlach and Aly 2002, pp. 186–239; Aly 2006a, pp. 244–64.

130 Kanzlei des Führers to Reinhardt (Treasury Ministry), March 7, 1941, BA 7.01, Nr. 3586, p. 48; Hilberg 1992a, pp. 82–3; Rost 1992, pp. 55, 60–1.

131 Bock 1986, p. 106.

132 This was also the case in Italy. See Collotti 2006, pp. 206–7. For Romania see Ancel 2007, p. 351.

133 Rosenkötter 2003, pp. 7, 22, 24, 92; Genschel 1966, p. 163.

134 Aly and Heim 1991, pp. 22–32; for Vienna see Rosenkötter 2003, pp. 100, 155, and Genschel 1966, pp. 207, 251 note 9; for the Netherlands, Belgium and France (which was an exception) see Hilberg 1994a, pp. 602–3, 635, 654. See also Lipscher 1979, p. 67 for Slovakia.

135 "Der Handel im Generalgouvernement," n.d., BA R 52 VI/21.

were shut down. In annexed Poland, 100,000 of 130,000 stores were liquidated; the others (all of which were handed over to Germans) generated "enormous business."[136] In general, German confiscations hit Polish Jews harder than non-Jews (who also often kept their agricultural land). There is a debate about whether big business, smaller firms or the government inside Germany benefited most from the expropriation of Jewish business assets.[137] The fact is they all did to varying degrees.

An equally important incentive for displacing Jews was the fact that many of them held down attractive jobs that German non-Jews wanted for themselves(for similar tendencies in other countries, see Chapters 12 and 13). This fact was deliberately incorporated into a policy facilitating social ascent. As Hitler pointed out in a 1944 speech, his anti-Jewish policies had resulted in the vacation of "hundreds of thousands of jobs," and that as a result "hundreds of thousands of children of proletarians and farmers will be able to rise into these positions in the future." He had already mentioned this in his infamous speech on January 30, 1939.[138] And he had already announced his interest in creating such effects – by eliminating Jews from "cultural and intellectual life" – during a discussion with doctors held shortly after he had come to power.[139] For example, in Germany after 1933, 1,500 professors, 4,000 lawyers and 3,000 physicians lost their jobs for political reasons, or, as was the case for the largest number, by virtue of their Jewish extraction.[140] German functionaries also argued that removing Jews would free up jobs for locals in the occupied countries.[141] German lawyers, in turn, hoped for jobs in occupation administrations abroad, although they were often disappointed in this respect.[142]

Clothing may have been less valuable than other items, but it was symbolically important, and confiscated Jewish clothing was distributed as charity to alleviate some of the hardship of the needy. For example, 60–70% of the belongings of Jews from Bochum went to the local welfare office.[143] Proceeds from the sale of goods expropriated from Jews were used to help

136 Rosenkötter 2003, pp. 199 (quote), 203.
137 For the first version, see *Sicherheitshauptamt*, situation report for 1938, MadR, vol. 1, p. 172, 182; van Laak 2003, pp. 290, 294. For the second version, see Bajohr 1998, pp. 245, 315–23, esp. p. 316. For the third opinion, see Tooze 2007, pp. 325–8.
138 Hitler's speech, May 26, 1944, quoted in Bajohr and Pohl 2006, p. 74; see Weikart 2009, pp. 193–4; Domarus 1963, p. 1057 (January 30, 1939).
139 Hitler's speech, April 6, 1933, quoted in Longerich 2001, p. 46; see also Kroll 1998, pp. 42, 91.
140 Koonz 2006, p. 409; Conze *et al.* 2010, p. 51.
141 See Meyer 2000, p. 38, for France.
142 See MadR, vol. 5, p. 1421 (July 25, 1940).
143 Deposition of Wilhelm Werner, August 7, 1951, in Schneider 2010, pp. 60–1.

both SS families and Waffen-SS divisions. From German-occupied Belarus and west central Russia, the Higher SS and Police Leader repeatedly sent to Himmler huge amounts of children's socks and gloves, as well as ladies' stockings, taken from murdered Jews and the victims of anti-partisan warfare. Himmler, in turn, donated them to SS women's homes and as Christmas presents to SS families.[144] On Christmas Day 1942, 235,000 ethnic Germans in Poland received suitcases containing a dress or a suit, a coat, and other clothing taken from murdered Jews.[145] Less attractive clothing was handed out to non-Jewish inhabitants of occupied countries; for example, Globocnik gave 25,000 suits, coats and boots "from [the] Jewish action" to workers in the mines and the power station of Zaporoshie, Ukraine, in response to a direct request from the army.[146] Alternatively, clothing could be put on the market in times of scarcity, as occurred weeks after the deportation of the Jews from Salonica when some of their clothes were sold in the Peloponnese.[147] Similarly, furniture confiscated from Jews was often distributed according to an ethnic hierarchy. Some locals, however, went so far as to petition German (or other) authorities for certain pieces of their neighbors' furniture.[148]

The expropriation of Jewish possessions was meant to reduce inflation (they were probably also used to this end in Romania[149]), but in none of the countries concerned, including Germany, was inflation prevented and in fact hyperinflation plagued Hungary and Greece. This indicates that the organized looting of Jewish property was, for many, mitigation against the war-related *reduction* in living standards rather than a means of *raising* livings standards. Even for Germany, the costs of the war exceeded everything that could be squeezed out of the occupied countries – of which Jewish property was only a part. While occupation tributes may have been higher than actual German military expenses, and while gains were made from industrial occupied countries,[150] revenues did not offset costs in the two financially most important regions – the

[144] Gerlach 1999, p. 1076; see also Steinbacher 2000, p. 153 (for East Upper Silesia); Turner to Meyszner, August 29, 1942, and Meyszner to Himmler, September 4, 1942, BA NS 19/1672, pp. 14, 38 (the HSSPF in Serbia ordered the SS "Prinz Eugen" division to return a large sum of such money).

[145] Berger 2013, p. 186.

[146] Himmler approved. Telegram from Krüger to Himmler with handwritten note, October 9, 1942, Nuremberg Document NO-2095.

[147] Mazower 2001, p. 55; for Romanian-occupied Odessa see Dallin 1998, p. 115.

[148] Rosenkötter 2003, p. 168; for a large-scale project to provide air raid-afflicted Germans with the furniture and household items of Dutch Jews, see Aly 2006a, pp. 117–31.

[149] Jean Ancel estimates that expropriated Jewish assets covered between a quarter and a third of Romania's war costs. Ancel 2007, pp. 249, 362, for the context see pp. 225–51.

[150] Aly 2006a, esp. pp. 75–93; Liberman 1996.

occupied Soviet territories and Germany itself. Few managed to profit from Jewish property in the long run, and the benefits of confiscation were unevenly spread. For these reasons the term "booty community"[151] may be misleading. But the public and private desire for this property did help propel the persecution and extermination of Jews. And historical agents did not pursue *either* nationalist (and racist) ideas *or* their own personal gains and careers – there was a logical connection between *both* these goals, and profiteers were often fervent nationalists.[152]

Deporting Jews on trains: Undermining the German war effort?

The most frequent argument used to illustrate the putative irrationality of the mass murder of Jews (aside from the issue of Jewish labor, for which see Chapter 7) cites transportation. Deporting Jews to their deaths by train, it is argued, was damaging to the German war effort because it diverted scarce resources from military operations.[153] The argument is supposed to prove that ideological doctrine took priority over economic reasoning. While there were some conflicts of interest over transportation, a closer look reveals that such conflicts were limited and partial, and that in actual fact military necessity often forced the postponement of deportation transports or stopped them altogether.[154]

The railways were the backbone of transportation for the German economy, military and society. Jews were deported on special trains – usually in passenger cars inside the German Reich and west of it, and in cattle cars east of Germany – not included in regular circulation and timetables. However, the number of these deportation trains was very low compared to all rail transport. For example, in April 1942 there were 37 deportation trains of Jews in the German Reich, which represented about 1.05% of all *special* trains that month (or 0.005% of the at least 750,000 trains in 1942). The number of trains that transported Jews to extermination camps over the *entire period* of the destruction of the Jews (approximately 2,000) compares to the 20,000 train movements *per day* in the German-controlled area.[155]

Moreover, if one considers transportation by itself, supplying the close to half a million people in the Warsaw ghetto with minimal rations

[151] The term is used by Bajohr 2001, p. 15, with some reservation.
[152] Mann 2005, p. 239.
[153] For example, Arendt 1986 (1955), p. 918.
[154] See also the considerations in Pätzold and Schwarz 1994, pp. 86–114.
[155] Plenipotentiary for the Four Year Plan, Transportation Department, "Tätigkeitsbericht" for April 1942, May 18, 1942, BA R 26IV/vorl. 47; the total number of trains is

required 73 railroad cars per day. The deportation of 400,000 Jews from Warsaw about 80 km to Treblinka – where they were killed in 1942–43 – required about 80 trains of 50 wagons each, or about as many railroad cars as were required to the supply the ghetto for two months.[156] It is an inhumane thought, but the murder of these men, women and children can actually be viewed as saving, not wasting, rail capacity.

Contrary to some assertions,[157] Jewish deportation trains did *not* have the highest priority – this was given to military transport. The Security Police repeatedly interrupted or postponed the deportation of Jews because of transportation stoppages; that is, short-term bans on non-military rail traffic. Some of these stoppages fell during periods of massive deportation from the General Government of Poland – as occurred in the second half of June, and the first half of September 1942. (These times were used to build new gas chambers in Sobibór and Treblinka, respectively.)[158] Even in late July 1942, the most intense period of deportation, Himmler had to beg the State Secretary in the Reich Ministry for Transport for more trains.[159] The plans for deporting Jews took into account that work on the tracks between Lublin and Cholm in October 1942 would make deportation to Sobibór impossible, and reduce the number that could be brought to Bełżec. After the work was completed, new transports would depend on the availability of cattle cars.[160] Another ban on low priority transport (such as deportations of Jews) in the General Government was in effect from December 15, 1942 to January 15, 1943, during the Battle of Stalingrad.[161] This halt in rail

according to Pätzold and Schwarz 1994, pp. 104–5. Similar considerations are mentioned in Hilberg 1981, p. 61; Mierzejewski 2001, pp. 35–6.

156 Thanks to Götz Aly, who first pointed me to this. For the railroad cars needed for supplies, see Reichskuratorium für Wirtschaftlichkeit, Dienststelle Generalgouvernement, "Die Wirtschaftsbilanz des jüdischen Wohnbezirks in Warschau," March 1941, in Heim and Aly 1991, pp. 132–3. This calculation was based on higher food rations than were actually provided to Jews during most of 1941–42. (See also pp. 114–15, and Engelking and Leociak 2009, pp. xiv, 407). However, as the actual average consumption (including that from smuggling: see Engelking and Leociak 2009, p. 407) was higher than the rations anticipated in the previously cited report, and because this food had to get to Warsaw, supplying the ghetto did require the railroad capacity mentioned above.

157 For example, see Dawidowicz 1987, pp. 181–3.

158 General Government, "Polizeisitzung," June 18, 1942, BA R 52 II/235, p. 78R (two weeks), and see Browning 1998a, p. 132; war diary of the Military Commander in the General Government, Chief Quartermaster, September 2, 1942 (two weeks), BA-MA RH 53-23/80. For Treblinka and Sobibór see Arad 1987, pp. 119–24; Schelvis 1998, p. 59; for June 1942 see Hilberg 1981, p. 82.

159 Correspondence Ganzenmüller-Wolff, July 28 and August 13, 1942, BA NS 19/2655, pp. 58, 64; Pätzold and Schwarz 1994, p. 92.

160 Protocol of a railway conference on September 26 and 28, 1942, Eichmann trial doc. 1373.

161 Pohl 1996, p. 241; Hilberg 1981, p. 86.

traffic also delayed the deportation of 45,000 Jews from the Bialystok district to Majdanek and Auschwitz.[162] The absence of deportations of Jews from France between November 1942 and March 1943 was partly because the Reichsbahn couldn't provide any trains between November and January. A railroad bottleneck was also the reason why 1,000 "young communists and Jews" arrested in France in December 1941 could not be deported to the East before March 1942.[163]

Such difficulties had hampered deportations from Germany from the outset. A lack of trains was among the reasons for the lull in deportations of Jews from Austria to the Lublin area in late 1939, and, again, in March 1941.[164] Expulsions of non-Jewish and Jewish Poles to make room for ethnic German resettlers were stopped in March 1941 at the request of the military – which needed the railways for its deployments for the invasion of the Soviet Union.[165] When Army Group Center suffered a transportation crisis during the Battle of Moscow in November 1941, the military had Jewish deportations from the Reich to the Minsk ghetto temporarily stopped after only the seventh train had been dispatched. (The remaining eighteen were resumed in May 1942.)[166] Speer informed Rosenberg on January 26, 1942, that deportation of Jews had been "temporarily stopped until about April for technical reasons of railway transportation."[167] In December and January, transports were also limited for the sake of German soldiers and civilians traveling home for Christmas and then back again.[168] Finally, and with Himmler's consent, construction of the Lublin (Majdanek) concentration camp in the first half of 1942 took longer than planned because the Reich Ministry of Transport postponed the trains that should have been carrying the necessary building supplies.[169]

Although their numbers were relatively small, trains carrying Jews from central Europe to the East, or for deportations within Poland, tended to interfere with military transportation – especially in 1942 when the deportations of Jews were at their peak and the situation at the Eastern

[162] Müller to Himmler, December 16, 1942, in IMG, vol. 27, pp. 251–3.
[163] See note BdS Paris IV J SA 16, "Tagung beim Reichssicherheitshauptamt am 28.8.1942 über Judenfragen," September 1, 1942, Eichmann trial doc. 142; for 1941–42 see Seeger 1996, p. 128.
[164] Moser 1966, pp. 18, 24.
[165] Ogorreck 1992, p. 258; Hilberg 1981, p. 82.
[166] Gerlach 1999, pp. 752–3, 758; Reinhardt 1972, pp. 57, 116–20, 153–60.
[167] Speer is quoted in Adler 1974, p. 193. See also Hilberg 1981, pp. 82, 141; facsimile of Eichmann to Stapo(leit)stellen, January 31, 1942, in Wannsee Conference 2009, p. 229.
[168] Seeger 1996, p. 128.
[169] Kleinmann to Himmler, March 7, and Himmler to Reich Transport Ministry, April 14, 1942, BA NS 19/3625, pp. 7, 19–21.

Front appeared critical. For example, in March 1942 the rail transport situation in the General Government was labeled "disastrous,"[170] and yet, some deportation trains started to arrive from the West. By early December 1942, transports in the General Government for militarily relevant economic purposes were jammed. (This led to the ban on low priority transports from December 15 onwards.)[171] However, the number of Jews to be deported from France in 1942 was reduced from 100,000 to 40,000 due to limited train availability and the priority given to the deportation of French non-Jewish civilian workers to Germany.[172] German experts noted with some satisfaction that the Slovaks provided the trains necessary for the deportation of their Jews.[173]

Transports in other directions conflicted less with military or economic necessities. This included the deportations from Greece (which ran until late August 1944) and from Hungary in 1944. Both of these are often cited, incorrectly, to demonstrate that the murder of Jews had priority over economic concerns.[174] Transportation officials' records present another picture. In the case of Greece, there was a transportation bottleneck, but it affected supply trains *to* Greece; while returning trains (which could be filled with Jews) often ran empty.[175] As for Hungary, the transport situation for most of the period of the deportations from May to early July 1944 was relatively unproblematic, as was the situation in Germany and, until mid-June, at the Eastern Front. Trains were routed through Slovakia – somewhat west of the direct path to Auschwitz, through Galicia – in order not to interfere with frontline operations in western Ukraine. After the massive German retreat from Romania, Greece and southern Yugoslavia had begun in late August 1944, new deportations of Jews from Hungary could, for the most part, only be carried out on foot because no trains were available, as Eichmann and Novak confirmed.[176]

Another indication that Jewish deportation transports had low priority with railway administrations is that they were slow. This was because they usually had to give way to military and regular trains.[177] Countless

[170] General Government, government meeting, March 11, 1942, BA R 52 II/242, p. 17 and reverse page.
[171] Protocol, "3. Sitzung der Rüstungskommission," December 2, 1942, BA-MA RW 23/2, pp. 57–62.
[172] Eggers 2002, p. 377.
[173] See Kamenec 2007, p. 194.
[174] An example is Traverso 1999, pp. 58–9.
[175] Aly 2006a, p. 270; Dr Karl Pfauter, "Die Verkehrslage Griechenlands während der deutschen Besatzungszeit 1941–1944," PA AA R27320, pp. 247–8.
[176] Gerlach and Aly 2002, pp. 271–4, 364.
[177] See Hilberg 1981, pp. 54, 81, 135; Mierzejewski 2001, p. 36; Guckes 1999, pp. 69, 77, 80.

survivors have reported that the trains on which they travelled took excruciatingly long periods of time and made many long stops.[178] Many of the trains from Greater Germany to the ghettos, labor camps or annihilation centers in eastern Europe between 1941 and 1943 took more than a day. (They often took two to three days if they were bound for German-occupied Poland, and two to five days when headed for Soviet territory.)[179] In 1944 it took most Jewish transport trains from Greater Hungary three days to arrive at Auschwitz.[180] Although this reflected disregard for the needs of the passengers, many of whom died en route, it was not because the transport organizers wanted to torture deportees; the slow schedule was due, rather, to the low priority of deportation trains (the same priority that, for technical reasons, most special trains had).

Of course, the closed cattle cars used outside western and central Europe (where passenger cars were typical) shows the same disregard. Passenger cars were largely reserved for people considered worthy of them. Closed cattle cars had already been utilized to transport Polish forced laborers to Germany,[181] and Soviet POWs were shipped in open cattle cars with lethal consequences as a result of the cold, until November 1941. However, the cattle cars on some Jewish transports, especially within the General Government, were especially crowded.[182]

This was just one example of how seemingly banal interests spurred the persecution and murder of Jews, and brutality against them, but also of how these interests were connected with ideas about Jewish inferiority. As shown previously for labor and food policies, German authorities often saw few contradictions between concerns of settlement, housing, property, jobs and transportation, on the one hand, and the murder of Jews, on the other; or they tried to minimize such contradictions.

178 A few examples are printed in Pätzold and Schwarz 1994, pp. 175–229.
179 See Gottwaldt and Schulle 2005.
180 Gerlach and Aly 2002, p. 286.
181 Spoerer 2001, p. 49.
182 Report 7./Pol. 24, "Judenumsiedlung," September 14, 1942, in Hilberg 1981, pp. 194–7, describes a train journey from Kolomea to Bełżec, with 8,205 people on board (180–200 per car), from which hundreds fled.

11 Fighting resistance and the persecution of Jews

During World War II, more than 200 million people in seventeen nations came under German occupation.[1] Germany conquered these countries for a mixture of intertwined political, strategic and economic reasons. Control over them served military functions, but it was also a precondition for exploitation.[2] Because of geographic overextension and the concentration of troops at the fronts, the Germans were usually only able to deploy relatively weak military and police forces to the occupied areas.[3] This resulted in the German view that one needed to rely, first, on indigenous forces and, second, on fear-inducing violence. For this they developed systematic strategies that went far beyond aimless reprisals. Nonetheless, armed resistance movements and guerrilla warfare sprang up in many areas. Across Europe, German repression led to the deaths of about a million people (most of whom were not Jews), often unarmed civilians, primarily in rural areas.[4]

In comparison to work about the impact of repression on the countryside, there has been little systematic research on German methods of terror for suppressing urban resistance. Though it is clear that thousands

[1] This is not counting countries where there were sizable deployments of German troops but no occupation regime: such as Finland, Romania, Bulgaria and Italian Libya.

[2] For Yugoslavia see Burgwyn 2005, pp. 35, 43; Pavlowitch 2008, pp. 28, 40, 49, and for the economic success p. 68.

[3] For the occupied Soviet territories see Gerlach 1999, pp. 214–18; for France see Lieb 2007, pp. 56, 61, 98.

[4] See Gerlach 1999, p. 957 (340,000 died in Belarus); I estimate 300,000 deaths in the rest of the German-occupied Soviet territories, up to 100,000 in Greece, 200,000 in Yugoslavia (see Schmider 2002, pp. 317, 331–2: 49,000 dead reported from September 1943 to January 1944, and Shelach 1992, p. 170: 23,000 killed in October 1941). In France there were 20,000–45,000 killed (Lieb 2007, pp. 412–13), in Italy under German occupation, probably 45,000–50,000 (Klinkhammer 1993, pp. 573–4; Longhi 2010, p. 113; only 10,000 were killed according to Gentile 2001, p. 534; 37,000 out of 46,000 died in German camps: Pohl 2003, p. 132), in Slovakia 25,000 died (Müller 2007, p. 105), in Poland 20,000 rural dwellers died (Pohl 2003, p. 121, is consistent with the partial figures for the Lublin district in Chodakiewicz 2004, p. 368). The figure in Albania was comparatively low: Fischer 1999, p. 268.

were detained,[5] deported to German camps and often murdered,[6] numbers specifically for urban victims of terror have not been clearly delineated from other forms of persecution (such as forced labor conscription), and nor are the patterns of urban violence entirely clear.

The fate of Jews was connected in many ways to the persecution of resistance fighters and those suspected of supporting them. Blaming partisan activity on Jews prompted many efforts to kill them, but guerrilla warfare also created spaces where it was possible for Jews to survive. In order to understand these links it is necessary in this chapter to explain, phase by phase, who the partisans were, what their activities consisted of, and which repressive strategies and for which areas Germans developed. These conflicts were not always binary. Other Axis governments killed hundreds of thousands in this context (see Chapter 14). As a result of the German practice of indirect rule, partisan warfare included an element of domestic conflict from the start, and, given deepening social tensions, it often ended in civil war. The end of this chapter discusses the influence of partisan war on the survival chances of Jews. The connection that German politicians and functionaries saw between Jews and insurgency was important, but not their only reason by far for killing Jews.[7]

The association of Jews with resistance fighters and partisans had to do with older, widespread prejudices about Jews as unreliable, rumormongers, saboteurs, spies, agitators, defeatists, insurgents and communists (see Chapter 7). Accordingly, when Jews within Germany were forced, in September 1941, to wear an identifying mark, Goebbels believed this would avert the hazard of Jewish "grousers and scaremongers."[8] Hitler's remarks on December 18, 1941, to Himmler – who then jotted down "Jewish question./ to be exterminated as partisans" – were probably also a general sort of accusation intended to justify collective extermination.[9] Later Hitler called Jews the "phone cable" of the partisans.[10] In the fall of

5 For France see Lieb 2007, pp. 67, 306.

6 For deportations of non-Jews from Warsaw to Auschwitz, and killings in that city, see Engelking and Leociak 2009, pp. xv-xvi; for towns in the region of Zamosc see Klukowski 1993.

7 Friedländer 2006 (esp. pp. 265, 586) strongly emphasizes the influence of ideas concerning the potential Jewish threat.

8 Goebbels 1996, vol. 1, p. 265.

9 CChIDK 1372-5-23, p. 334, facsimile in Witte *et al.* 1999, p. 293. The assumption that the remark was a specific instruction related to the occupied Soviet territories (Longerich 2001, p. 187) is inconsistent with the fact that in most German-occupied Soviet areas – including partisan strongholds – the mass murder of Jews was not resumed for six months. See pp. 81 and 93 of this volume.

10 Hitler 1982, p. 377 (August 30, 1942).

1941, and again in the spring of 1942, Hitler ordered Himmler to shoot all former opposition leaders, criminals and concentration camp prisoners (who, at these times, were mostly non-Jews) in the case of a revolt in Germany.[11] Concentration camp personnel were told in July 1943 that prisoners were dangerous because they could endanger national unity and cause an insurgency like the one at the end of World War I.[12] In the fall of 1942, Himmler told Mussolini that the Jews were being "taken away" from Germany and all its occupied countries as saboteurs and spies, and he found that the Italian leader approved when he added that many Soviet Jews, including women and children, were shot for such reasons.[13] A few weeks earlier, Foreign Minister Ribbentrop had rationalized his push for deportations from other European countries by saying, "it is certain that the Jews agitate against us everywhere and have to be held responsible for acts of sabotage and assassination attempts."[14] Later, Himmler would repeatedly argue that the earlier annihilation of the Jews had prevented a moral breakdown in Germany now that it was under pressure from Allied bombings and from Soviet armies on the Polish border.[15]

It was not only Germans who identified Jews with hostile nations. In Poland, the Baltic countries and Bessarabia, many residents associated them with the Soviets; in Slovakia and large parts of Romania, with Hungary; in Hungary, many suspected the Jews of Transylvania to have sympathies for Romania; and in the Czech lands and northern Bukovina, Jews were seen as being linked to the Germans.[16] During the Slovakian national uprising of 1944 the fascist press portrayed the Jews as Soviet allies.[17]

Jews were members of most national partisan movements. In several countries (e.g., Yugoslavia, Bulgaria, Slovakia and Lithuania), Jews formed a larger percentage of partisans than their percentage of the total population; in Ukraine and Belarus (with the exception of the Volyn region) there was the opposite trend. In some areas (like Italy and Volyn) Jews constituted a relatively large proportion of partisans in the beginning, although their relative numbers decreased over time.[18] But it is

[11] Wachsmann 2004, pp. 213–14; Goebbels 1995, vol. 4, p. 361; Hitler 1982, p. 59 (September 14–15, 1941).

[12] Allen 2002, p. 179.

[13] Himmler's report about his meeting with Mussolini on October 11, 1942, can be found in BA NS 19/2410, pp. 6–7.

[14] Luther's note of September 24, 1942, from which this is quoted, is printed in Steur 1997, p. 210.

[15] Himmler 1974, pp. 169, 200–5.

[16] Case 2006, p. 19.

[17] Kamenec 2007, p. 330.

[18] Longhi 2010, esp. pp. 145, 150, 152, 154–92 (Italy); Gitman 2011, pp. 167–8; Tomasevich 2001, p. 605 (Yugoslavia); Lewkowicz 2006, p. 165; Bowman 2002, p. 18;

important to understand that in every country, even partisan strongholds like Belarus and Yugoslavia, only a small fraction of the population – well below 10% – joined the armed resistance. And only small minorities of Jews became guerrillas, which is why this chapter does not concentrate on this aspect.

Four phases of anti-partisan warfare

Many of the arguments just cited referred to Germany, where the Nazis never faced an uprising. Things were different in the occupied countries, to which we now turn. In the first phase, from 1938 to mid 1941, however, armed resistance was virtually non-existent in German-occupied Europe. During the first eighteen months of the German occupation of France, for example, not a single German was killed by a Frenchman, and only one French civilian was executed, according to one account.[19] This calm had much to do with the German-Soviet alliance and the USSR's urging that communists in other countries should not rise against the Nazis. In the absence of uprisings, German authorities in annexed territories mainly pursued preemptive policies of intimidation and expulsion, which affected Jews to varying degrees.

In the areas that Germany incorporated first (Austria and the Czech lands), acts against Jews were not rationalized in terms of an alleged Jewish threat to German rule. A different picture emerged in the regions of Poland that Germany annexed. After the end of military operations and the subsequent execution of thousands of Polish troops, suspected *francs-tireurs* and hostages in reprisal,[20] a combined policy of mass executions of members of the Polish intelligentsia (broadly understood), on the one hand, and mass expulsions from western to central Poland, on the other, was adopted in differing intensity according to region. The policy was intended to prevent resistance to German incorporation by neutralizing the Polish leadership.[21] In the *Gau* of Danzig-Westpreussen, Nazi authorities under Albert Forster mobilized SS units and local militias to conduct the large-scale mass murder of aristocrats, leading members of various political parties, priests, academics, mentally disabled persons and other groups. Between 30,000 and 50,000 people were killed; 87,000

Bowman 2006, pp. xxii, 12–15 (Greece); Spector 1993, p. 140 (Ukraine – Jews made up 1.1% of the fighters known by name); Spector 1990a, pp. 322–3, 337 (Volyn); Gerlach 1999, p. 745 (Belarus); Zizas 2005, p. 328 (Lithuania); Chary 1972, p. 48 (Bulgaria); Lipscher 1979, pp. 175–6 (Slovakia).

19 Pryce-Jones 1991, p. 26.

20 Rossino 2003; Böhler 2006.

21 Borodziej 1999, pp. 81–2.

others were expelled. In the other annexed areas of Poland the number of murders was smaller, though still horrific. According to estimates, 10,000 were killed in the Wartheland, 4,000 in the Zichenau district and 2,000 in Silesia.[22] But the number of deportees by late 1940 was as large in some territories as in Danzig-West Prussia (81,000 from East Upper Silesia), or larger (at least 236,000 from Wartheland).[23] (Preemptive killings of intellectuals, but comparatively few, also took place in the General Government.[24]) Among the 60,000–80,000 Polish civilians murdered by early 1940, 7,000 may have been Jews,[25] which represented a little more than the overall Jewish proportion of the population. Although the number of Jews among those deported eastward by the spring of 1941 is unknown, the total constituted a minority, and most Jews remained in western Poland. The situation in Alsace and Lorraine, which Germany annexed from France in the summer of 1940, was different. Mass murder did not begin immediately, but French nationalists, criminals, Roma and all of the Jews were expelled en masse.[26] However, repression was limited in most occupied countries, and preemptive strikes against resistance in most of the annexed regions did not primarily target Jews until the summer of 1941.

A second phase of armed resistance began in that summer when the situation changed fundamentally. Communist parties abandoned their reservations after Germany attacked the Soviet Union and called on their compatriots – for example in Yugoslavia and France – to rise up against the German occupiers.[27] There was an important new theater of guerrilla war in the German-occupied Soviet territories, although the resistance began slowly because Soviet authorities and the Communist Party had not prepared for it. In the USSR and other countries, communists and soldiers who found themselves behind the German lines, together with small numbers of people fleeing from racial persecution, formed the core of the new partisan movements.[28] Partisan strongholds were located in

[22] Ibid., p. 29; for the Wartheland see also Alberti 2006, p. 85; for Zichenau see Röhr 1994b, p. 43; for figures in Danzig-Westpreussen see Schenk 2000, pp. 172, 291; for Forster's aims see pp. 129, 143, 147, 150; for SS policies and organizing the Volksschutz militia see pp. 156–63; see also pp. 164–76. See also Madajczyk 1988, pp. 14–15.

[23] Steinbacher 2000, pp. 97–9, 119–20, 132–3, 135–6.

[24] Some 4,000 were killed in the spring of 1940, and thousands were put in camps by 1942: Pohl 2003, p. 49.

[25] Schenk 2000, p. 172; Pohl 2003, p. 49 (60,000). For Jewish victims see Rossino 2003, p. 234.

[26] See p. 63.

[27] Delacor 2000a, p. 19; Pavlowitch 2008, pp. 37–9, 54–9, 75–8.

[28] Bonwetsch 1985, esp. pp. 104, 115; Shelach 1992, p. 164; Wiesinger 2008, p. 40. Loulos 1994, p. 400; Longhi 2010 (p. 109) sees a broader base for the Greek and Italian partisans.

Belarus, Yugoslavia and Greece. In later years the percentage of communists within the resistance movement would decrease as more rural dwellers and youths joined.[29]

To stamp out the still-weak partisan movements, German forces intensified their anti-resistance measures, although some of the new tactics had, in fact, been designed before Germany's attack on the Soviet Union. Since exploitation of the occupied Soviet areas called for a small number of rear units to carry out the starvation of millions, the army pressed for large SS and police formations and the use of massive violence.[30] A variety of measures were combined. Hostages were shot or hanged in response to partisan attacks – to instil terror in the populace. The members of certain groups (in particular members of a loosely defined Jewish intelligentsia and communist functionaries), especially in the cities, collectively suspected of being opponents, were preventively detained or killed. Collective reprisals for acts of sabotage were taken against entire villages when the perpetrators could not be found. (However, this was rarely applied in 1941, in contrast to later years.[31]) And, as travelers and non-locals were especially suspected of supporting guerrillas or being former enemy soldiers, 'wanderers' on country roads and those living far from their home towns were arrested during large-scale raids and killed by the thousands, especially from September 1941 onwards.[32] The number of victims ran high, and it increased during the fall of 1941. German forces in Serbia killed 11,522 purported insurgents and 21,809 hostages – including 7,000 Jews and members of the Belgrade intelligentsia – between August and early December; and more than 59,000 alleged partisans were killed in the rear area of Army Group Center in Belarus and western central Russia by late 1941.[33]

In this way, different groups – including communists, Roma, black marketeers, refugees from cities and Jews – became the focus of German efforts to combat resistance. Camps were set up immediately after the German invasion, and all men of working age were interned for days or weeks in order to screen not only Red Army soldiers but all male Soviets who were suspect in any way. SS and Secret Field Police shot thousands

[29] See Kalinin, pp. 395–7; arrest figures for France in 1943 are found in Kasten 1993, pp. 180, 214.

[30] Dieckmann 2011, pp. 209–22.

[31] Anderson 1995, pp. 300–3; Gerlach 1999, pp. 871–2; but for Crete in May–June 1941 see von Xylander 1989, esp. pp. 32–3.

[32] Boll and Safrian 1995, pp. 285–8; Gerlach 1999, pp. 873, 877–83.

[33] Pavlowitch 2008, p. 67 note 18 (Serbia); see Shelach 1992 (23,200 persons, including 4,200 Jews, were shot in Serbia in October 1941 alone); Schmider 2002, pp. 70–80; Burgwyn 2005, p. 75. For Army Group Center killings see Gerlach 1999, p. 875.

of inmates, but most of the detainees, including most of the Jews, were then released.[34] There were mass arrests of communists in France (where the Vichy government seized more than 10,000 in 1941) for deportation to German-occupied Russia.[35] Those arrested formed a large percentage of the hostages killed in several countries. Some 8,000 were killed, largely in 1941, in Estonia alone.[36] On September 16, the Supreme Command of the Armed Forces issued an order stating that it should be assumed that communists were behind every uprising and that a hundred locals should be executed in reprisal for every German killed.[37] Although many communists were involved in armed insurgencies, as mentioned before, most who were executed had fallen victim to blanket internment rather than having had their personal responsibility proven. By contrast, the link of Jews or Roma to the partisans was largely a product of the German imagination. Traditional prejudices against Roma as unreliable, anti-social or spies worked against them, and many – especially those who were living on the road – were shot either immediately or taken as hostages.[38]

In accordance with the conceptualization sketched out above, Jews also became targets as refugees and as members of a group chosen for preemptive decimation. After all, the Jews were supposed to have inspired communism. The connections between Jews and partisans were regarded as tight. "Where the partisan is, is the Jew, and where the Jew is, is the partisan," was one of the quintessential lessons that SS officers taught at an officers' course in anti-partisan warfare, organized by the Commander of the Rear Area of Army Group Center together with the SS in late September 1941. The course's highlight was a demonstration search of a village that included the real-life execution of about thirty Jews and non-Jews.[39] One should distinguish two levels of argument here. On the one hand, everybody knew that many partisans were not Jewish. Jews among them were often refugees who had little other option but to join them, as one German unit insightfully reported, "because of the partially conducted mass shootings" against Jewish communities.[40] In Serbia and Croatia, there were relatively many Jews among the

[34] Gerlach 1999, pp. 503–14.
[35] Le Secrétaire Général de la Vice-Présidence Conseil, communiqué, December 10, 1941, in Delacor 2000a, pp. 105–6; Hirschfeld 1984, p. 111 (Netherlands, June 1941); Witt 2012 (Slovakia, June 1941, 1,100).
[36] Müller 2007, p. 159; see also Rautkallio 1987, p. 135.
[37] Keitel's order, September 16, 1941, in Ueberschär and Wette 1991, pp. 305–6.
[38] Zimmermann 1996, pp. 248–66; see also Holler 2009; Fings 1992, pp. 31–4.
[39] Krausnick and Wilhelm 1981, p. 248; Gerlach 1999, pp. 643–4, 882.
[40] 339th Infantry Division, situation report, November 5, 1941, BA-MA RH 26–339/5.

early insurgents, and, as survivors noted, many of them were arrested or executed in the first months not as Jews but as opponents.[41] On the other hand, Jews were collectively seen as instigators and supporters of resistance, and, therefore, either Jewish communities were massacred (in the occupied Soviet territories) or Jews were killed en masse after being taken as hostages (in Serbia[42]). The annihilation of Jewish communities was justified by accusations that members had supported partisans and aided (probably imagined) parachutists, supported attacks on railway lines and spread rumors and anti-German propaganda.[43] The main line of argument cited the 'Jew-as-partisan-helper.' Dissenting voices – even within the Einsatzgruppen – who argued that killing Jews was but a distractive side-show in the ongoing effort to crush the resistance, had little effect.[44]

German occupation forces in France drew slightly different links between Jews and armed resistance. There were few underground groups and also few single acts of sabotage or assault. Again, communists formed the core of France's weak resistance movement, but few Jews participated. Jews identified or caught as resisters were taken as proof of a significant Jewish contribution.[45] A different history defined the French context. While German troops in eastern Europe acted much more brutally than they had in World War I, the German military in Belgium and France wished to appear *softer* than it had in the previous war in order to avoid repetition of the excesses of the fall of 1914, when thousands of civilians were shot as alleged irregulars.[46] Accordingly, and contrary to demands from Berlin, Military Commanders in the fall of 1941 tried to keep the number of hostages who were shot, down, so as not to alienate the French public. (See Chapter 4; by October, 600 hostages, most of them communists, had nonetheless been executed.) They also faced strong opposition from the Vichy authorities, who were happy to *arrest* thousands of communists but disapproved of their execution.[47] In lieu of that, they suggested

41 Speech by Edo Neufeld, December 1943, and recollections of Magda Simin in *we survived*, vol. 3, pp. 169, 301.
42 Shelach 1992, pp. 164–70; Manoschek 1993.
43 Headland 1992, pp. 62, 75–6, 80, 213–15.
44 Lozowick 1987, pp. 234–5.
45 Lieb 2007, p. 25.
46 Scheck 2008, pp. 64–5; Lieb 2007, p. 15; for Norway see Petrow 1974, p. 119.
47 Pétain even wanted to offer himself to the Germans as a hostage and planned a dramatic radio speech about this. See the documents in Delacor 2000a, pp. 142–3, 148, 150, 202,

deporting Jewish (and communist) hostages from France, among other measures, in order to deter acts of resistance. In December 1941, Hitler consented to deporting 1,000 Jews eastward (which was carried out in March 1942). Today, historians view this as having opened the door to the larger deportation of Jews from France.[48] For reasons of political convenience, French Jews replaced non-Jews, and even communists to a degree, as scapegoats. (Still, the desire to avoid French unrest prompted the German military to resist Security Police demands to deport the remaining 40,000 Jews from Paris in 1944.[49] This time the security argument worked the other way.)

German oppression carried out in the fall of 1941 was successful in several areas of Europe – in that it sharply reduced guerrilla activities for months, or even years. This was the case in Serbia, northwestern Russia and, to a degree, France. (Bulgarian oppression was also effective in the Greek territories they occupied.[50]) These successes may have been attributed in part to the violent methods used against Jews and, thus, may have reinforced the stereotype that Jews were leftist instigators. By the spring of 1942, however, partisan forces in other areas had grown stronger and more socially diverse – they were better organized, had shifted the focus of their activities to the countryside, and the connection between Jews and guerrillas became less plausible.

The army, SS and police developed new strategies to combat partisans in rural areas based on their sense that the guerrillas were less of a military than a political threat. The partisans began to influence the local population and prevent them from delivering agricultural goods to the Germans, while parts of the population supplied the partisans with food, shelter, information and manpower. Slowly, more men from the farming sector joined the resistance. To strip the insurgents of such support networks, the new German strategy (which the Hungarians and Italians also used, as I discuss in Chapter 14) mainly targeted rural population living near the partisans' bases, more than the partisans themselves. In addition, since communities that did not deliver produce

216. Mazower 2008 (p. 249) offers lower victim numbers. Sections of the French police started to refuse to arrest communists in 1942 out of fear that they might be shot as hostages: Kasten 1993, pp. 68, 76.

[48] Herbert 1996, pp. 298–314; Lieb 2007, pp. 27–9; see the various documents in Delacor 2000a, pp. 107, 117, 142–3, 201, 242, 253–4, 271.

[49] But 1,300 Jews were deported from Paris to Auschwitz in the summer of 1944: Lieb 2007, p. 410.

[50] Strugar 1969, p. 21; Pavlowitch 2008, pp. 63, 66, 121; Schmider 2002, pp. 74–84, 113, 142, 192; German military commander in France, Situation report for October and

to the Germans were of little economic value to them, villages were torched, civilians were shot in their houses, on the run and on the edges of hastily dug pits, and rural communities were assembled in barns or stables and burned alive. Others were chased away or resettled by force. A single large operation, requiring several thousand troops, could lead to the deaths of many thousands of people. This new strategy was first employed in Yugoslavia and some of the occupied areas of the Soviet Union, especially Belarus.[51] Many people became targets almost out of the blue and died – not after detention and deportation, but in or close to their villages and sometimes in their own homes.[52] The burning of villages may have provided sadistic pleasure, but it also served to prevent survivors from escaping, destroyed the evidence, and denied partisans shelter.[53] In the more exploitable regions (agriculturally speaking) – like northern Ukraine and central Poland – civil administrations, but also the SS and police, rejected such destructive tactics.[54] This is to say that such operations were not just the work of the police and the military – civil administrations and, therefore, political and economic interests, were involved in the process. Large-scale operations were not conducted in Greece before March 1943 because the partisans, including the communists, focused their attention on Italian forces and mostly refrained from attacking Germans.[55]

These strategies did not add to the pressure for exterminating Jews in the larger cities, but they did lead German authorities to dissolve ghettos in small towns located near partisan areas. They reasoned, not unrealistically, that the general threat of death would increase the likelihood that Jews, and especially young men, would flee into the woods where many would join the partisans. During this so-called liquidation of the marginal ghettos, from September 1942 to March 1943, Jewish

November 1941 (excerpt) in Delacor 2000a, p. 146; Hill 2005, esp. pp. 82–9, 114; Fleischer 1986, p. 71.

51 Gerlach 1999, pp. 884–1010; Schmider 2002, pp. 149–52, 198, 207; Pavlowitch 2008, pp. 121–2. For Italian troops already in Montenegro in 1941, and then in 1942, see Burgwyn 2005, pp. 93, 111–13, 137–8, 154, 182. On German mass resettlements in western Russia see Terry 2005, pp. 218–22.

52 According to Yugoslav census results, 74.4% of Serbs, 89.5% of Montenegrins and 95.6% of the Muslims killed did not die in "concentration camps": Cvetković 2008, p. 366.

53 See Heer 1995, pp. 119–22; Gerlach 1999, pp. 966–9; wire from "Berta" to Schutzmannschaft battalions 276–279, February 18, 1943, in Vernichtungskrieg 1996, p. 174.

54 Gerlach 1999, pp. 933–43, 989–91; Borodziej 1999, p. 169.

55 Fleischer 1986, pp. 182–3.

communities – especially in western Belarus – were wiped out during anti-guerrilla operations. At least 16,000 Jews, which includes a relatively small numbers of refugees captured in the woods, were killed as part of these actions. German forces pursued Jewish partisans and refugees with a special zeal that led to a higher death rate for Jews than for non-Jews; and Jews, like Roma, were shot on sight and reported as so-called 'bandit helpers.' Nevertheless, it is important to note that the great majority of the victims of anti-guerrilla operations during this period were unarmed, non-Jewish, rural civilians. In other words, the operations were not simply a pretext to kill Jews.[56] Rather, genuine concerns about partisan activities – and their potential political influence – led to brutal German strategies that Jews also found themselves caught up in.

In 1943 anti-partisan warfare became linked with labor recruitment in the countryside. When entire cohorts were ordered to report for German labor duty, young people went into hiding, and this increased insurgents' numbers and popular support in a number of countries. This has been correctly called an "important, often decisive factor" in the evolution of partisan bands into mass movements.[57] In 1943 the focus of large-scale anti-partisan operations became the depopulation of entire areas, sometimes as large as counties, combined with the deportation of all those considered fit for work. Since the conscription of forced labor became an important aspect of anti-guerrilla warfare, the selection principle (see Chapter 8) was introduced to remote rural areas, accompanied by destruction of greater intensity. (In Belarus, 63% of the hundreds of burned villages were torched in 1943.[58]) Single operations could produce 12,000 or more victims.[59] 'Large operations' (so-called) and the destruction of villages spread to some areas of western Europe and Greece following the redeployment of German units and officers westward, and southward, from the occupied Soviet territories and Yugoslavia.[60] The

[56] Hilberg stated this in 1994a, pp. 389, 402; however, see Gerlach 1999, pp. 743–6, 913, 957; see also Haberer 2001 Part I, pp. 20–1, and Part II, p. 212.

[57] Mazower 2001, pp. 113, 120; quote: Herbert 1991b, p. 16.

[58] Romanovski *et al.* 1984, pp. 46–7. For Greece see Nessou 2009, pp. 204–31; Mazower 2001, pp. 155–89; for Yugoslavia see Burgwyn 2005, p. 196.

[59] See Schmider 2002 (pp. 253–4, 280–3) for operations "Weiss I and II" and "Schwarz" in Bosnia and Montenegro, June 1943; see Gerlach 1999 (pp. 943–51) for operations "Hornung" and "Kottbus" in Belarus.

[60] For France see Martin 1999, pp. 88–9; Lieb 2007, pp. 38–9, 162; Kasten 1993, pp. 32, 34; for Italy see Klinkhammer 1993, pp. 423, 446–52, 486; for Greece and Albania see Meyer 2008, pp. pp. 113–27, 159–224, 567–82; BA, BDC, SS officer file of Walter Schimana; generally see Gerlach 1999, pp. 951–3.

criteria for murder shifted in July and August 1943. Keitel ordered that armed partisans be treated as POWs[61] and that the rest of the population be conscripted into forced labor; however, those recognized as Jews were still usually killed. In the Balkans, all men of working age were to be deported. In early 1944 the policy was applied to French areas that had been evacuated to prevent an uprising during the imminent Allied invasion; the policy was intensified after the invasion, when the surging partisan movement became a direct threat to the German rear; and after mid 1944 it was applied in Italy to partisans, suspected partisans and men born between 1914 and 1927. In 1944 the mass deportation of civilians from partisan areas became more systematic in Greece.[62] In certain places in Italy, captured male civilians who were considered unfit for labor were added to the pool of hostages to be shot in the case of a partisan attack.[63] A similar sorting process began after the nationalistic Warsaw uprising of 1944: probably 170,000–180,000 people (mostly civilians) were killed, and 600,000 residents evacuated, when the city was destroyed. The fit and able (about 70,000 of them) were sent to work in Greater Germany, 60,000 others were transported to concentration camps, and the aged and sick were sent to remote places in the countryside.[64]

Several aspects of these developments are remarkable. The selection of laborers in the Belarusian forests in 1943–44 resembled the selections in Auschwitz. By international standards, large-scale massacres and deportations from areas located close to partisan activity, and the pursuit of economic interests, were not unusual aspects of anti-guerrilla warfare in the twentieth century; but the fact that more women and children than men were directly killed in Belarus in 1943–44 was.[65] Thus, the criteria for selection for execution had shifted to those *least likely* to be partisans. Many victims were burned alive in large buildings. The large-scale raids of 1943–44 affected Jews in several ways.

[61] Colonel General Löhr, order, August 10, 1943, in Seckendorf 1992, pp. 244–5; for the implementation by German troops in Croatia see Pavlowitch 2008, p. 201; Schmider 2002, pp. 336–7; see also p. 283; Overmans 2005, p. 783. Some of them later had to wear special marks in German POW camps: Speckner 2003, p. 57.

[62] Colonel General Löhr, order, August 10, 1943, in Seckendorf 1992, pp. 244–5; Lappenküper 2000, p. 139; Lieb 2007, pp. 275, 281, 302; Klinkhammer 1993, pp. 460, 466; Hadziiossif 1991, pp. 228–9.

[63] Gentile 2001, pp. 543–4.

[64] Röhr 1994b, pp. 52, 54 (216,000 dead); Pohl 2003, p. 121; memories of Alexandra Remiszewska in Berliner Geschichtswerkstatt 2000, p. 37.

[65] See Gerlach 2010, pp. 222, 448 note 287; Gerlach 1999, pp. 1001–3.

One effect was the risk that German forces (and their auxiliaries) might discover their hiding places during such raids. This happened especially in the forests on the Belarusian-Lithuanian border, during the Slovak national uprising, and during the repression of Warsaw's nationalist uprising in 1944 – the latter two events cost the lives of 7,000–8,000 and 5,000 Jews, respectively.[66] Jews were able to survive the uprisings if they were able to hide their identity. The situation was different in the Jewish ghetto uprisings in Warsaw and Białystok between April and August 1943. These revolts belong in this context not only because they occurred in parallel with large-scale anti-guerrilla operations-cum-forced labor conscription, but also because a large percentage of the inhabitants were deported to forced labor instead of being killed immediately. The SS and police, together with the civil administration, had been planning such deportations before starting to 'liquidate' these ghettos – which triggered defensive uprisings. About 42,000 out of 56,000 Jews from Warsaw, and 11,000 out of 30,000 Jews from Białystok, survived – for the time being.[67] In both cases, the policy of conscripting residents of known insurgency hotspots into forced labor was also applied to Jews.

Desperate Jewish uprisings to resist ghetto liquidations, as in Warsaw in 1943, in some death camps, and among units assigned to the burning of corpses,[68] once again reinforced the image of Jews as resisters and potential revolutionaries. The same may have been true for the alleged or real Jewish uprisings that broke out at the approach of Allied troops – as in Algiers in November 1942, and in Jassy, Romania, in 1944, both of which confirmed Hitler's worries.[69]

Fear of uprisings and the deportation of Jews from western Europe

Similar patterns of thought as those during the suppression of resistance in the Soviet Union, Yugoslavia and France in 1941, and in the occupied Soviet territories in 1942, generated support for the deportation of Jews

[66] Ainsztein 1993, pp. 119–20, 147–8 (Kowel, Ukraine); Tec 1996, pp. 177–202; Paulsson 2002, p. 168 (4,500 Jews were killed during the Warsaw uprising, 900 afterwards after being revealed in German camps).

[67] Hrádská 1996, pp. 92–4; Scheffler and Grabitz 1993, pp. 15–16; Gerlach 1999, p. 732.

[68] Hoffmann 2008, pp. 102–3, 114–15, 246.

[69] Roberts 2006, pp. 63–88 (85% of the 350–400 insurgents in Algiers were Jews); telegram, Ribbentrop, November 23, 1944, PA AA 100894, p. 116.

in other German-occupied areas and at later periods. German authorities often believed that resistance and unrest had foreign, and especially British or Soviet, support; and that Jews aided such foreign interests as spies and by spreading defeatist rumors. Thus, deporting Jews was intended to intimidate the population, weaken opposition to German rule and eliminate supporters of possible enemy attacks. This was also true for areas rarely considered in this context. In the fall of 1942 the German Military Commander, Nikolaus von Falkenhorst, and the civilian Reich Commissar, Josef Terboven, as well as Hitler, expected the British to invade Norway. (They were taken in by Allied diversionary tactics intended to deflect attention away from the upcoming landing in north Africa.) Between October 6 and 12, Falkenhorst and Terboven declared a so-called civilian state of emergency in northern Norway. Hundreds of people, including all of the region's Jews, were arrested. At least eighty-four people, including ten hostages and one Jewish man, were shot. After crushing the British-supplied armed underground in southern Norway between April and June, the Germans then managed to do the same in northern Norway between October and December 1942.[70] Mass arrests of Jews in Oslo had already started in September 1942; they were intensified after a group of Jews shot a Norwegian police officer while escaping to Sweden.[71] The Norwegian government and police organized all of these arrests. In fact, some evidence suggests that Terboven's German civil administration was not keen on having the Norwegian Jews deported and that the initiative came from the fascist Norwegian government together with the German Security Police in Norway.[72] The Norwegian government wanted to counter British threats to its (weak) rule; it arrested Jews on the basis of its law for the confinement of people suspected of activities against the state; and in late 1942, Prime Minister Quisling, alluding to the security risk that Jews allegedly posed, justified the deportations with the claim that Jews, an "internationally destructive element," were behind the English war effort.[73]

The German attempt to deport the Jews of Denmark occurred in the same context of combating a resistance movement that was inspired,

[70] Petrow 1974, pp. 131–7; Petrick 1998, p. 178.
[71] Petrow 1974, pp. 115–17.
[72] See Chapter 5, note 16.
[73] Petrow 1974, p. 116 (quote); Abrahamsen 1991, esp. pp. 34–5, 73; Hoffmann 2001, pp. 268, 270; BdS Oslo, "Meldungen aus Norwegen," November 26, 1942, in Ugelvik Larsen 2008, p. 941.

supplied and also enforced by Britain. To be sure, though, this movement was stronger than in Norway, and the Danish government, while cooperating to a certain point, never agreed to abide by any German anti-Jewish policies. In August 1943 a wave of strikes, demonstrations and sabotage swept through Denmark.[74] When the German military declared a state of emergency, and disarmed and dissolved the Danish army and navy and started to arrest its officers, the Danish government resigned.[75] In this case, the pressure to deport Jews came from Berlin, and especially from Hitler and Ribbentrop. Goebbels, too, argued that the Danish Jews ought to be removed because they were allegedly responsible for the rise in partisan activity.[76] The German plenipotentiary, SS-Gruppenführer Werner Best, and the Military Commander in Copenhagen, Hermann von Hanneken, had tried to dissuade the central leadership from undertaking such a move, but given the prevailing political crisis they gave in to pressure in September 1943. For Best, it may have been a tactical move to strengthen his political position. Both German civilian and military representatives swiftly changed their minds again, returning once more to the view that deporting the Jews would further arouse Danish opposition to occupation and create more problems than it would solve. They settled instead for letting the Jews get away instead of deporting them, and organized patrols, searches and arrests only half-heartedly. This allowed most Jews to escape to Sweden, supported by a Danish mass rescue movement and public protests (see Chapter 13).[77] Best himself stated publicly that the Danish Jews had to be deported (or driven into exile) because of their moral and material support for the resistance movement; but he admitted to authorities in Berlin that he lacked specific evidence for this, although he also stated that Jews were no longer in a position to poison the political atmosphere in Denmark.[78] Gestapo agents (most of whom were new to the country) seem to have believed in such a connection, for they mistreated the Jewish residents of a retirement home in Copenhagen, questioning the pensioners "about their knowledge of sabotage operations."[79]

Danish Jews' support for the underground movement was probably minor, but German repression from late August 1943 onwards,

[74] For the increasing number of acts of sabotage in 1943, particularly in August, see Petrow 1974, p. 186; see Herbert 1996, pp. 248–59.

[75] Petrick 1998, pp. 182–3.

[76] Longerich 2001, p. 173; Goebbels 1994, pp. 46, 51, 61–2, 98–9 (diary October 3, 4, 6 and 13, 1943).

[77] See Petrow 1974, pp. 185–228, 307–13; Hilberg 1994a, pp. 586–96.

[78] Hilberg 1994a, p. 596; Petrow 1974, p. 213.

[79] Petrow 1974, p. 212.

as well as the fact that the resistance movement seems to have focused its energies in September and October on rescuing Jews, apparently brought the number of public actions and acts of sabotage down for a while. While the German attempt in Denmark to deport Jews tended to unite the nation against its occupiers, such tactics proved more divisive, and more successful, in Norway, and, at least in 1944, in Greece (see Chapter 13).

In Greece, the deportation of Jews depended on German military support because the small units of the Security Police were not able to carry it out. Army officers assisted the Security Police, as in Corfu, Crete and Rhodes, for a number of reasons. As in Norway, one of these was the fear that Jews would aid the British in their expected landing and the partisans operating in coordination with them. Again, military officers considered Jews a hostile group and suspected them of militarily important espionage. Army units initiated the arrests and concentration of Jews, and participated in their deportation.[80] The Jews from the aforementioned islands were deported in 1944 and either died in the transport ship was that was sunk en route, or in German extermination camps.

The presumed connection between Jews and the enemy, whomever that may have been, was powerful enough to influence British authorities, though with less murderous consequences, on the island of Mauritius in the Indian Ocean. Here about 1,500 Austrian, Czech, Polish and German Jews had been stranded since late 1940. When Japanese submarines torpedoed ships in the area in August 1943, these Jews were detained because British officers believed it possible that they would cooperate with the Japanese.[81] In the same year, one of the arguments made by British government officials in parliament for not letting more Jews enter Palestine was that German spies were among the refugees.[82]

'Security' considerations did not always play a major role in German violence against Jews. In the General Government of Poland, for example, Jewish support for partisans was not frequently cited as a

[80] See Safrian 1997, pp. 273, 275–83; Gerlach and Aly 2002, pp. 438–9; for British secret and commando operations on Crete during the entire time of the German occupation, and partisan operations, see von Xylander 1989, pp. 50, 66–74, 82, 98, 102, 120–4. By contrast, the German commander on Zakynthos island successfully opposed the deportation of the 275 local Jews, arguing that they were poor and had strong family ties to local non-Jews: Fleischer 1986, p. 366.

[81] As on German-occupied Greek islands, the tense food situation was also cited as a reason for the measure, and food rations were reduced: Zwergbaum 1960, pp. 215, 252.

[82] Penkower 1988, pp. 56–7. Again, the tense food situation was also cited.

reason to murder Jews in 1942. But German police officers participating locally in the deportations were apparently told that one reason why the Jews had to be murdered was that they were spying for the Soviets.[83] The reasons Himmler gave Krüger in his order of July 19, 1942, to kill most of the Polish Jews, included only a general reference, without much emphasis, to the "security" of the German Reich. After the fall of 1942, the security argument for murdering Polish Jews – employed primarily by Himmler – became more influential.[84] Similarly, when around the same time the Security Police rationalized the deportation of Jews from France, they placed it generally "in the framework of the general solution to the Jewish question and for the security of the occupation troops in the occupied French territories."[85] Nevertheless, the fact remains that in important regions during different phases, mass violence against Jews was considered necessary for preventing, or fighting, political resistance. This argument opened the door to further persecution. The SS and police were not alone in linking Jews to unrest and partisan activities; other authorities and occupation forces adopted such thinking as well. In addition to Nazi Party members, this notion appealed, especially, to many military officers and rank and file, and, thus, broadened support for massacres and deportations. German soldiers abhorred no one more than a partisan. It was not a coincidence that Serbia and the eastern section of Germany's occupied Soviet territories, where the mass murder of Jews went especially far in 1941, were then under military administration. Such murderous actions would have been impossible without the military's initiative or consent, or its guidelines and manpower.

A tendency toward civil war

Aspects of the partisan war other than German strategies and operations greatly affected Jews as well. Some of these aspects had to do with complex inner conflicts breaking out among the societies they were living in. Especially in the last years of World War II, these led to several outright civil wars in countries under German (and Italian) occupation. These were fought over different visions of what society and nation should be after the

83 Notes by the German NCO Cornides, Cholm, August 31, 1942, in Longerich 1989, p. 216.

84 Printed in Röhr 1989, p. 227; see Himmler to Krüger, telegram, November 17, 1942, BA NS 19/1433, p. 32 and Chapter 5.

85 Memo of Dr Siegert, "Kosten bei der Evakuierung der Juden aus Frankreich," August 17, 1942, BA R 2/12158.

foreign occupation and the global conflict. Often, more than two, or even three, parties fought each other, which underlines how fragmented some populations were.

First, German policies involved many local officials. Local police in eastern Europe provided guard services, gathered information and conducted many of the small raids, searches and arrests of insurgents and others – such as Jews and forced labor evaders.[86] Many locals also served in mobile auxiliary units under German military, SS or police command, and took part in large anti-guerrilla operations. Local administrations kept their populations under control via various registry methods, organized the seizure of agricultural products, and forced labor recruitment.[87] Knowing that German occupation could not work without the indigenous apparatus, partisans – as guerrillas in other contexts have done – often focused their attacks primarily on local police and administrators.[88] Fighting among locals was rancorous. Thus, Nicolai Vasilevich Mogilny, a partisan in Belarus during World War II, told me, and quite against the dominant national narrative: "It was a fratricidal war."[89]

Second, the lives of civilians were tightly restricted. Carrying ID cards and work passes at all times became compulsory.[90] There were curfews, off-limits areas, limited mail and phone services, prohibitions against using motor vehicles and bicycles, and restrictions on rail travel. Leaving the county required an official permit, and there were many checkpoints. Everyone had to be registered with the local authorities, and in many areas a list of all of a house's residents had to be posted at its front entrance. Elders in every building and local mayors were held responsible for their accuracy. Hosting strangers was forbidden and severely punished. In some places the police or army compelled local residents to wear identity necklaces, and they introduced forgery-proof identity cards that bore the holder's fingerprints.[91] Some of these measures resembled those that a number of colonial powers had undertaken in Africa.[92] They

86 See Dean 2000; Chiari 1998, pp. 160–94.

87 Chiari 1998, esp. pp. 123–59.

88 For example, lecture by von Schenckendorff (Commander Rear Area of Army Group Center), June 2, 1942, BA R 6/217, p. 2; Kasten 1993, pp. 171–8 (for France); see also Gerlach 2010, pp. 193–200.

89 Interview, June 21, 2001.

90 Chodakiewicz 2004, pp. 110, 125 note 23.

91 See Gerlach 1999 (pp. 218–22) for Belarus; Hionidou 2006 (pp. 148–57) for Greece.

92 For identity documentation see Gründer 1999, p. 155 note 6 (German Southwest Africa, 1907); Elkins 2005, p. 16 (a little metal box, containing ID, fingerprints and one's employment history, had to be worn around the neck in British Kenya, *c.* 1910).

created an atmosphere of suspicion and distrust. People became insecure and no longer knew whom they could rely on. Draconian German punishment spread fear.

Third, foreign civilians were sometimes given a more active role: the Germans facilitated the establishment of local militias when it wasn't possible to establish an adequate police force. Such was the case in Serbia, Bosnia, Greece, and also during the first months of the German occupation of Lithuania and western Ukraine. Although some Germans wanted to induce civil war,[93] these militias were a non-German initiative; they were tied to a place, pursued their own local interests, and often refused to obey any central command.[94] A large majority of the Ustashe in Croatia started out as anarchistic "wild" groups.[95]

The transitions to civil war were rapid. In Yugoslavia, divided by occupation and ad hoc state-building, radical Croatian Ustashe, communist partisans, nationalistic Serbian Chetniks, Bosnian-Muslim militias, Slovene home guards and Serb- and Kosovar-Albanian militias fought each other as well as German, Italian, Bulgarian and Hungarian occupation forces.[96] For example, the town of Foča changed hands ten times; Ustashe killed Serbs, Chetniks killed Muslims (whereas most Catholic Croats fled) and communists killed Chetniks, well-off farmers and gendarmes.[97] German and Italian observers estimated that 200,000–600,000 people – predominantly Serbs – were killed by Croatian forces alone.[98] Ana Šomlo, a Jewish refugee, hid in the mountains with her family for two months after the Germans had retreated from Serbia because they mistook fighting between communists and Chetniks for the German frontline.[99]

In Volyn in western Ukraine (later also in the neighboring region of eastern Galicia and, to a degree, around Lublin), tensions between Ukrainian and Polish nationalists simmered in 1942 and exploded into armed conflict in 1943. As Soviet partisans entered the region by the summer of 1943, and with the existence of different Ukrainian factions, this was another multipolar fight. Units of Ukrainian nationalists

93 Turner to Himmler, situation report, February 16, 1942, BA NS 19/1730; von Herwarth 1982, p. 242.
94 Burgwyn 2005, pp. 59, 140, 144, 173–5.
95 Pavlowitch 2008, p. 29.
96 See Burgwyn 2005, p. 110; on some of the origins, see Pavlowitch 2008, pp. 37–9.
97 Pavlowitch 2008, p. 115.
98 Trifković 2008, pp. 52, 57, 62–3.
99 *We Survived*, vol. 3, p. 412.

attacked Polish villages, mostly in the summer of 1943, killing many inhabitants and forcing an estimated 350,000 to flee. Polish partisans fought back. In eastern Galicia, Ukrainian attacks reached their greatest intensity in early 1944; tens of thousands, predominantly Poles, died; a further 35,000 fled. One Ukrainian historian claims that, beginning in 1942, Poles killed 2,000 Ukrainians in the district of Lublin, which also led to a mass flight. According to Polish scholars, 80,000 Poles (40,000–50,000 in Volyn) and 20,000 Ukrainians may have been killed in these regions.[100] In the district of Lublin this conflict was in part sparked by the German resettlement of Ukrainians in forcibly vacated 'Polish' villages in late 1942 and early 1943, and was then exacerbated by incoming Polish refugees from the East.[101] The conflicts in south-eastern Lithuania and western Belarus were less lethal. In the formerly Polish area of Lithuania, around German-occupied Vilnius, Lithuanian nationalists challenged Polish dominance. Lithuanian police pressed for the persecution of the Polish intelligentsia, during the course of which 1,000 people may have been killed.[102] In Belarus, auxiliary police officers and mayors who professed to be Belarusian persecuted Poles and became targets of the nationalistic Polish Home Army. Hundreds may have died even before the conflict intensified, in 1943, when pro-Soviet partisans arrived in the region and the three groups fought each other, as they did in Lithuania. In September 1943, Polish Home Army units were ordered to attack all Soviet and Jewish partisan units.[103] Aside from their ethnic and political aspects (e.g., the conflict over communism), both struggles had a class dimension. Many Poles were from elite groups – administrators in the towns and estate owners in the countryside – while most Ukrainians, Lithuanians and Belarusians were small farmers or farmworkers.

Historians have described some of the contemporary conflicts in other countries as civil wars, although this is sometimes a matter of controversy. The guerrilla war in Italy has been portrayed as a struggle between insurgents and local fascists.[104] Well-known post-war memoirs

[100] Snyder 1999, esp. pp. 99–100, 96 note 21; Prusin 2003, pp. 527–34; Spector 1990a, pp. 250–71; Pohl 1996, p. 376; Prusin 2010, pp. 197–9; Ther 2011, p. 142; Kosyk 1993, p. 381; Wnuk n.d., p. 7.

[101] Conte and Essner 1995, pp. 309–17; Poprzeczny 2004, pp. 191, 222, 320–3.

[102] See Wardzyńska 1993; Prusin 2010, pp. 184–7; Brakel 2009, pp. 323–32.

[103] Chiari 1998, pp. 270–302; for September 1943 see Cholawski 1982, p. 162.

[104] Pavone 1992, esp. pp. 221–5. See Mazower 2008 (pp. 502–7) on France, Belgium and Italy.

portray this picture, but partisans' statements during the war also point in this direction; against this backdrop, the German army sometimes negotiated non-aggression agreements with the partisans, who then would only target fascists.[105] But the Italian anti-fascist insurgency was not homogeneous. Among the partisan groups were communists, monarchists and others. The term 'civil war' applies less controversially to Poland where historians refer to the struggle between the nationalistic, underground, Home Army, and the extreme right-wing National Armed Forces – both of whom attacked the People's Guard, a clandestine communist group. Several thousand people were killed in these skirmishes.[106] Underground forces also targeted those who cooperated with the Germans. In the General Government, more than 1,000 alleged informers for the German police were killed in 1943 alone.[107] In Albania, skirmishes between the conservative, nationalist National Front and the communist-dominated National Liberation Movement started in March 1943 and intensified after the German occupation in September 1943. Albanian losses in the civil war and those inflicted by occupation forces were lower than in neighboring countries.[108] In Kosovo, which was annexed by Albania while under Italian and German occupation, the overall death rate was higher. While ethnic Albanian and Serb gangs fought each other (and tens of thousands of Serbs fled the region), the largest proportion of those killed were monarchists and former members of two local Waffen-SS divisions. Some 40% of Kosovo's few Jews were also murdered after having been arrested by the Waffen-SS's "Handschar" division in 1943.[109]

In summary, the civil wars during World War II were usually fought among multiple groups. Often, these were armed formations of political parties, which suggests that pre-war divisions and militant rhetoric were aggravated by the stress of war. One important confrontation was between communists and conservatives. The latter group had varying and volatile relationships with the Germans. Sometimes proponents of a multi-ethnic state were pitted against separatists, but nationalism was pervasive and even the communists were often fiercely nationalistic. Important ethnic divisions were often tied to class conflict. That these civil wars had deep autochthonous roots is also illustrated by the fact that

[105] Cervi 1956; Klinkhammer 1993, p. 476.
[106] Pramowska 2010; see also Borodziej 1999, p. 169.
[107] Madajczyk 1994, p. 148.
[108] 26,500 people (2.5% of the population) were killed or died of famine: Fischer 1999, pp. 198, 268. Yugoslavia and Greece lost about 4% of their populations.
[109] These data are found in Antonijević 2008, pp. 414–15. General population losses seem to have been higher than 3%.

some continued after the end of German occupation and of World War II itself; as, for example, was the case in Greece and western Ukraine. In each of these areas the post-war conflict claimed at least 100,000 lives, in Poland at least 10,000.[110]

The prejudices of participants in the civil wars – and it became less and less clear who did not participate – often associated Jews with one or another side. They were suspected of leftist leanings and as agents of social discord. Many civil wars were about defining the nation, and right-wing nationalists did not see Jews as a reliable part of their nations. Jews were also drawn into rural–urban tensions. Farmers were sometimes suspicious to urban refugees (and partisans), since rural dwellers tended to profit from conditions of hunger in urban centers and tended to support ruling right-wing regimes; but the suspicion cut both ways.[111] This reflected a broader social crisis in which material deprivation led to migration, the loosening of family bonds,[112] and a meltdown of solidarity among the general populace; in response to which people sought protection via membership of tight-knit, allegedly natural, communities, of which Jews were often supposed to have no part.

Anti-partisan warfare and civil war created for Jews a reality of raids, roadblocks and spying; a situation in which it was more difficult to hide than it would have been had they been the only persecuted group. Hundreds of Jews were arrested and handed over to the Germans or killed by the Polish Home Army in Lithuania and Belarus in 1943–44; thousands in Volyn fell victim to the nationalistic Ukrainian People's Army in 1943.[113] Many more Jews gave up on going into hiding and stayed put. In this context, it is intriguing that Polish–Ukrainian violence over control of the area started in the counties of Cholm and Hrubieszów in the district of Lublin in 1942, at the time when the death camps of Sobibór and Bełżec were in operation there, and continued into 1944.[114] This reduced the survival chances of Jewish refugees even further; in fact, the survival rates for Jews in some civil war areas were especially low. In Volyn and western Belarus the Jewish survival rate was lower than

[110] See Weiner 2001, pp. 172–3; Gerlach 2010, pp. 180, 455; Michlic 2006, p. 202.

[111] For France see Lynch 2012, pp. 233–42; Sanders 2001, p. 296.

[112] Bićanić 1944, pp. 44–5.

[113] Dieckmann 2011, pp. 1464, 1469, 1482–3; Eckman and Lazar 1977, pp. 85–90; for Volyn see Snyder 2010b, pp. 98–103; Spector 1990a, p. 256. Some of the Ukranian Insurgent Army (UPA) had participated in the summer 1941 pogroms and as auxiliary police in the German mass killings of Jews in 1941–42: Spector 1990a, p. 269.

[114] For the civil war in these areas, see Chapter 14, note 100; Kosyk 1993, p. 381; Wnuk n.d., p. 7. According to Pohl 1996 (pp. 376–7) relatively few Jews were killed in civil war violence in this region. But see Conte and Essner 1995, p. 319.

it was in Lithuania – even though Belarusians had a reputation of tolerance toward Jews, and Lithuanians were reputedly extremely hostile toward them.[115] But in some cases Jews found niches for survival by, for example, becoming members of, or getting protection from, large-scale illegal movements operating in the Serbian, Bosnian and Greek mountains. In the forests of Belarus, and in Volyn, they were supported by communist partisans, Polish villagers and the Home Army, respectively – all of whom they had helped in the struggle against Ukrainian nationalists. Sometimes these groups retaliated against murderers of Jews.[116] In general, however, German preemptive violence against potential resisters, and their subsequent measures against real insurgencies, strongly fueled the murder of Jews – including Jewish refugees. The violence among different groups of locals that was facilitated by German counterinsurgency efforts often became another threat to the lives of Jews.

[115] Of the Jews from Volyn, just 1.7% survived on German-occupied territory (Spector 1990a, p. 332); of the Jews from Belarus, 3.5% survived (estimated on the basis of Gerlach 1999, pp. 740–5); and of the Jews from Lithuania, 4% (based on Dieckmann 2011, p. 1538).

[116] Spector 1990a, pp. 250–1, 259–61, 263–4, 266–7; for retaliation see pp. 267, 296, 302, 308, 310.

Part III

The European dimension

On November 25, 1941, the largest political show of force of Hitler's international coalition took place in Berlin. High representatives of thirteen member states of the Anti-Comintern Pact – Germany, Italy, Japan, Hungary, Manchukuo, Spain, Bulgaria, Nanking China, Croatia, Denmark, Finland, Romania and Slovakia – met to demonstrate their participation in the fight against the Communist International and also their mutual political support in general. The last seven signed the revised treaty on that day.[1] The German press called the meeting a "world sensation."[2] But what a strange coalition it was! Despite their official condemnation of communism, these states varied considerably in their political systems and economies as well as their involvement in World War II. Denmark, an occupied and neutral country according to the Danish Foreign Minister, Erik Scavenius, had outlawed the Communist Party but would not declare war on any state (including the USSR) because the population would not support that. Franco's regime in Spain, which had come to power in what it portrayed as a largely anti-communist civil war, argued that it had to remain neutral in World War II because of the devastation it had already suffered. Finland's Foreign Minister, Rolf Witting, was happy that his country fought against the USSR but did not commit itself to declaring war on Great Britain. By contrast, Bulgaria did so in December 1941 while at the same time refusing to declare war on the Soviet Union, despite its fiercely anti-communist government, because of its historic cultural ties with Russia. Hungary and Romania, which both had troops on the Eastern Front, also had troops amassed along their common border and within weeks would come close to armed hostilities against each other;

[1] See the revised treaty and documents of meetings with the German leadership in ADAP, vol. XIII, 2, pp. 671–729; for speeches by the European accession countries' representatives, see www.forost.ungarisches-institut.de/pdf/19411125-1.pdf (accessed July 12, 2012).

[2] *Das 12-Uhr Blatt*, November 25, 1941, facsimile of front page available at www.dhm.de/lemo/html/nazi/aussenpolitik/antikomintern/index.html (accessed July 12, 2012).

and Romania's Antonescu conspired against Hungary during the meeting in Berlin.[3] And the Japanese representative, Ambassador General Nagisa Oshima, did not even reveal (either openly or in secret talks) that his country would attack the USA within two weeks,[4] let alone the fact that Japan would not invade the Soviet Union. Of the thirteen member states of the Anti-Comintern Pact in late 1941, only seven entered the war with the USSR.

This episode shows that national interests, rather than the interests of Germany or other partner states, determined the core policies of these countries. This challenges the idea that the governments of countries such as Bulgaria or occupied Denmark were mere German puppets; recent insights about the frustration and relative lack of success of official German advisers in Slovakia point in the same direction.[5] Still, Germany's allies were very important to her because they provided, for instance, about a million troops (compared to 3 million German ones) on the Eastern Front in 1941, and 2 million in 1942.[6] The meeting of November 1941 also demonstrates that however manipulated public opinion was, certain attitudes among the population did matter to these regimes. We will see that this also applied to policies and actions against Jews.

Some European countries were occupied by other Axis powers; others were not. Some of these occupied countries had national governments (Vichy France, Denmark, Greece, Norway from 1942, and the particularly weak regimes in Serbia, Albania and the "Protectorate of Bohemia and Moravia"); others did not (as, for example, the occupied Soviet and Polish territories). Some countries were belligerents, others neutral (including Sweden, Switzerland and Turkey). Some were ruled, strictly speaking, by fascist parties (Italy, Croatia, Slovakia and occupied Norway), others by authoritarian right-wing regimes (Hungary until October 1944, Romania and Bulgaria); while others still had somewhat functioning parliaments or even social democrats in their government coalitions (Denmark and Finland). Even when a regime was controlled by one ruling party, it was often divided by fierce political conflict, as was the society it governed. These conflicts were often going on behind the scenes, but sometimes resulted in fierce and open struggles. Because of these differences from country to country, and within societies, the title of this part of the book is not intended to suggest any unified, collective European stance or responsibility.

[3] Cornelius 2011, p. 184; Ancel 1992, p. 203. In mid 1942, they were close to war with each other: Cohen 1987, p. 181.

[4] However, German diplomats came to consider a Japanese attack more likely between November 18 and 27, 1941 (Martin 1969, pp. 34–7).

[5] See Tönsmeyer 2003; see also Fein 1979, p. 102 and Korb 2013, pp. 438, 443 on Croatia.

[6] Müller 2007, p. 293.

For all their differences, the countries allied with and most of those occupied by Germany to a large extent shared certain political features. These included ardent nationalism, a biological or organic understanding of the people or own ethnic group (which often led to one-party states, restricted political discourse and behind-the-doors decision-making), a corporate understanding of society (which the Holy See also supported)[7], a sanctification of family and farming, state-controlled paramilitary organizations, administrative centralization, disempowerment of the legislature and courts, the curtailing of civil rights, press censorship, state control of labor unions and the outlawing of strikes and leftist parties while denying or downplaying class differences.[8] Many of these features stiffened later in the war due to martial law. Thus, many actors in these countries, especially many politicians and intellectuals, shared certain ideas about a new order in society and politics – one in which Jews seemed not to belong. However, many of these countries – even some, like Romania and Hungary, with their mass killing of Jews – were not governed by fascists in the narrow sense of the term. (More precisely, Hungary was not fascist until October 1944.) On the other hand, the hyper-nationalism of most of these regimes meant that they tended to come into conflict with neighboring countries and this prevented close and lasting alliances. Consequently, a Mussolini-inspired international conference of fascist parties in 1934 led nowhere, not even to a second meeting.[9]

In socioeconomic terms, continental Europe included some industrial countries (like Germany, and some with hard currencies, unlike Germany) such as France, the Netherlands, Belgium, Denmark, Sweden, Switzerland and the Czech lands; but most, and particularly in the eastern half of Europe, had little industry, a largely rural and poorly educated population, small towns and deficient infrastructure.

Right-wing authoritarianism and pseudo-organic nationalism were responses to the perception that the nation was in crisis. There were three important notions of crisis. One was the long-term upheaval caused by industrialization, urbanization and secularization – "the great world crisis that our civilization inevitably undergoes," as Norwegian fascist Prime Minister Quisling called it.[10] Second, the world economic crisis of the 1930s seemed to endanger farmers and the middle class, generate social conflict and discredit liberalism while middle- and upper-class leaders

[7] Witt 2012, p. 127.

[8] See Mazower 2000, esp. pp. 13–32; for an interesting observation regarding Slovakia see Nedelsky 2001; for Vichy France see Lemkin 1944, pp. 178–82 and Kletzin 1996, pp. 29–39; for unions in countries occupied by Germany see Petrick 1995.

[9] Cohen *et al.* 1992, p. 88.

[10] Quisling was quoted on April 8, 1942 in *Fritt Folk*, quoted in BdS Oslo, "Meldungen aus Norwegen," April 26, 1942 (Larsen 2008, p. 610).

regarded communism as a threat (and all the more for its successes). And third, the global war produced deprivation, economies of shortage, government intervention and public rationing of commodities in all of these countries. Many who saw their nations in crisis called for a rebuilding of society and values.[11] In many countries this led to demands for national unity and what was called a "new order" – although this order usually was not clearly defined.

In a speech on December 16, 1941, shortly after the Anti-Comintern Pact meeting and several states' declarations of war against the USA, Reinhard Heydrich depicted the global situation as that of two worlds in confrontation: "Against the world of Jewry, of Bolshevism, of unscrupulous profit, of egoism, stands a unified Europe."[12] In reality, even Axis Europe was less than unified, and that also applied to anti-Jewish policies. There seems to be no methodology for comparative assessment of anti-Jewish attitudes (i.e., to measure "anti-Semitism"), despite occasional claims that they were more intense in one country than in another (in France, say, compared to Germany before World War I[13]). It is frequently held that anti-Jewish sentiments were stronger in several eastern and southeastern European countries (such as Poland, Romania and Hungary) than in Scandinavia, Italy, Bulgaria and the Netherlands; while the situation in the Soviet Union, Croatia and France remains unclear.[14] As for the most popular forms of hostility toward Jews, it appears less promising to search for a single dominant form for each country (such as racial "anti-Semitism" in Germany, or the religious version in parts of Poland) than to recognize that different strands coexisted and were everywhere enmeshed. I cannot offer in this part of my book a comprehensive analysis of anti-Jewish thinking across dozens of countries over extended time periods. Instead, I concentrate on actions taken against Jews, and those occasionally taken in their favor, particularly legislation and other official policies as well as activities by other social agents, and interpret these in terms of the underlying ideas that motivated them.

[11] For Vichy France see Peschanski 2010, p. 31.

[12] Reinhard Heydrich, "Die Wirtschaft als massgeblicher Faktor der staatlichen und politischen Neuordnung Böhmens und Mährens im Reich," BA D-H R 63/279, p. 11. See Heydrich's notes for the address in AMV 114-6-1, p. 74, reverse side. The motif of "two worlds" is also in Göring's speech delivered in the Reichstag immediately after Hitler had declared war on the USA on December 11, 1941 (*Verhandlungen*, p. 106).

[13] Dreyfus 1981, p. 246.

[14] Brustein and King 2004a, p. 36, judge the work of sociologists – excluding Fein 1979 – similarly, but offer no convincing yardstick for the assessment. But see the ranking in Fein 1979, p. 39; Déak 2010, p. 225.

12 Legislation against Jews in Europe: A comparison

Researchers have equipped us with a solid inventory of anti-Jewish legislation in Europe during the 1930s and 1940s. However, few analyses across national boundaries exist. This demonstrates, once again, how much the history of the persecution of European Jews consists of separate *national* histories – which serve, first of all, to create national identities. Accordingly, there is a debate for virtually every country about the degree to which anti-Jewish laws and regulations depended on German rule or political influence, Nazi ideas, or had indigenous origins. Indeed, these discussions dominate the field.

Just a handful of works – a few articles and short book sections – attempt a comprehensive analysis of anti-Jewish legislation outside Germany. Their authors likewise either take German regulations as a yardstick – as, for example, did Raul Hilberg, who emphasized, however, that the intensity and form of persecution by non-German governments differed according to their various and shifting interests[1] – or they assess the extent of German influence as being either small (like Asher Cohen), or large (like Randolph Braham).[2] Donald Bloxham puts the persecution of Jews outside Germany within what he calls an ethno-political context of other violence.[3] All of these authors note that the economic aspects of such legislation were important, but treat them relatively briefly. The entire debate focuses on countries that were either occupied by Germany, depended on it politically, or were otherwise ruled by right-wing authoritarian or fascist regimes: Vichy France and Norway; Slovakia, Croatia, Hungary and Romania; Bulgaria and Italy.

1 Hilberg 1992a, esp. pp. 90–3.

2 Cohen 1987, pp. 163–98; Cohen 1988, pp. 45–59; Braham 1992, pp. 125–43; Jelinek 1989. Lipscher 1972 assumed that all Axis states followed the same pattern by copying German policies against Jews.

3 Bloxham 2009, pp. 110–23. There are very few other studies (usually just short book chapters or a few pages) that compare anti-Jewish legislation and policies across Europe. Some are restricted regarding time or space; as, for example, Sarfatti 1994, pp. 81–9, 124–6, which deals only with 1938, and Cohen 1987, which discusses only three countries. Maifreda 2001 focuses on economic aspects.

In my view, a comparative analysis should take into account countries that are often left aside in this context, as well as aspects (especially xenophobia) that have not received much attention. This leads to a number of new conclusions. My objective here is, in part, a generalizing and, in part, a variation-finding comparison of government actions, which I shall approach in three different ways: by country, according to historical phases, and, finally, according to various themes that are set out in the content of legislation.

This chapter is restricted to legal regulations of non-German states, broadly understood. German-occupied territories without their own governments are not considered here. I will deal with mere executive measures and orders in later chapters; alongside boycotts, pogroms and other action taken by non-state protagonists. However, I do not aim at purely legal considerations here, and complete coverage of every relevant law is impossible. And, of course, there was a difference between legal constructions and practice. For instance, Hungary's laws against Jews were not completely implemented.[4] On the other hand, this chapter will show that several countries passed laws that, though not mentioning Jews at all, were intended to apply mostly or only to them. Some states – the Soviet Union, Denmark, Greece, and, from 1939 to 1940, France – had laws against inciting anti-Jewish attitudes. For Denmark this was the case even while under German occupation.[5]

Countries

Where else, other than the countries already mentioned, were anti-Jewish laws and regulations adopted? Unsurprisingly, this occurred, first of all, under other right-wing authoritarian regimes. Franco's Spain restricted the entry of foreign Jews and made re-entry more difficult for Jews with Spanish citizenship. This began after the end of the civil war in March 1939. Before this date people fled from Spain rather than to it. Synagogues closed during the civil war were not reopened after it. The basis for these anti-Jewish measures has been described as "more a diffuse resentment than part of a consistent world view."[6] Croatia's legal persecution of Jews, which started immediately after the state was founded in April 1941, has often been described; less well-known is that already in October 1940 the predecessor state of Yugoslavia had largely excluded Jews from the food trade and adopted restrictions of the percentage of Jewish students at universities,

4 Don 1997, esp. pp. 59–60.

5 See Petrow 1974, p. 197; Zuccotti 1993, p. 27; Fein 1979, p. 372 note 38.

6 Grüttner 2001, pp. 112–16, quote p. 118.

high schools and middle schools – a regulation that was implemented at once. Foreign Jews were no longer allowed to attend such educational facilities at all. Reportedly, the Yugoslav state ordered foreign Jews to leave the country. These measures, together with others such as introducing a uniform state-controlled labor organization and instituting additional rights for the German minority, were taken as ideological concessions – a substitute for an alliance – at a time when Yugoslavia still rejected a foreign policy rapprochement with Germany.[7] In fascist Austria, Chancellor Kurt Schuschnigg prevented a planned ban of kosher slaughtering in 1937. Yet several legal regulations affected Jews indirectly. The Trade Law of 1934 prohibited traders from visiting customers, strengthened the role of mandatory associations, and restricted sales on instalment – thereby damaging the business of Jewish merchants originating from eastern Europe. A law concerning social insurance, also dating from 1934, resulted in many Jews losing their jobs. All bar two of the fifty-eight medical doctors fired in accordance with a new law against social democrats in public service were Jews. In addition, restrictions of the number of foreign Jews at the University of Graz and the Technical University of Vienna had already been in effect since 1923, during the first Austrian republic.[8]

Other nationalist authoritarian regimes should be mentioned here. Lithuania passed legal measures to eliminate Jews from the country's important trade in wood and flax; and from the transportation business. Language tests in Lithuanian served to keep many Jews from studying at the University of Kaunas.[9] In Poland, besides fervent anti-Jewish propaganda and violence, legislation against Jews went further than in Lithuania. When large numbers of civil servants were dismissed in 1919 to reduce the size of the public administration, Jews were disproportionately affected. From 1937, Jewish university students had to sit on special so-called ghetto benches. A 1938 law virtually closed the legal profession to Jews, and the number of Jewish students in other disciplines – especially political science – also dropped off. Since 1937, there were legal restrictions on kosher slaughtering, and from 1936 Jews were no longer allowed to work in the dairy industries.[10] A March 1938 decree served notice that tens of thousands of Jewish Poles living abroad would be

[7] The text of these laws can be found in Freidenreich 1979, pp. 239–42. For the political context see Pavlowitch 2008, pp. 9–11; Wuescht 1969, p. 135; Wuescht 1975, p. 10; Olshausen 1973, pp. 31–2. For the expulsion order see Rother 2001, p. 151. According to Opfer 2005 (p. 275) Yugoslavia also outlawed some Jewish organizations in 1940.

[8] Maderegger 1973, pp. 167, 230–2; Königseder 2001, pp. 82–3; Melichar 2005, p. 159.

[9] Dieckmann 2011, pp. 102,104.

[10] Mahler 1944, pp. 301–6, 312–17; Melzer 1997, pp. 21, 75–6, 81–7, 91; Farmer *et al.* 1985, p. 39; Rothschild 1974, p. 41.

stripped of their citizenship within months. This provoked Nazi Germany to expel 17,000 Polish Jews in October 1938 – shortly before the deadline expired – but in some places the Polish authorities prevented them entering. By July 1939, thousands of Polish Jews were still trapped in camps on the Polish side of the German-Polish border.[11]

From February 1939, the royal dictatorship of Albania allowed the entry of only those foreign Jews with valid passports and visas and the equivalent of 250 gold francs. Under Italian rule, Jews were to have been expelled from Albania from 1940 onwards – although this was rarely implemented.[12] Since 1938, Turkey, too, had impeded the entry of foreign Jews and, like Spain, the return of Turkish citizens of Jewish faith. The Turkish authorities went even further than the Spanish ones by stripping Jewish citizens living abroad – primarily in France – of their citizenship. This move likely cost the lives of far more than the 2,000 Jewish Turks who the Germans consequently deported from France. A 1938 law expelling foreign Jews was soon abrogated. However, the free professions in Turkey had been largely restricted to Muslims since 1932, and between 1932 and 1934 'foreigners' – among them hundreds of Jews – were dismissed from the civil service. The pogroms that led to the flight of virtually all of the Jews from Thrace in the summer of 1934 (see p. 342) followed on from a law that allowed for the compulsory resettlement of minorities in the national interest. Moreover, regulations that had been introduced in World War I regarding the conscription of non-Muslim men aged between twenty-five and forty-five into army labor battalions were reactivated in 1941. In 1942 the Turkish Republic also imposed a special tax on the property of non-Muslims (ten times higher than the property tax for Muslims) in order to finance the country's armament policy and to counter war-related economic problems. This ruined many Jewish businesses, and up to 2,000 men (who were unwilling to pay the tax) were interned in camps.[13] However, despite the measures outlined above, Albania and Turkey are sometimes presented as savior nations.

Civil democracies, too, did not shy away from legal measures against Jews. These mostly concerned immigration. Like the USA, Japan, South Africa and several Latin American countries, Poland, Hungary, Italy, France (as early as 1935), Britain, Belgium and Sweden also restricted

[11] Melzer 1997, pp. 91, 123–5.

[12] Kotani 1995, pp. 43–6.

[13] Guttstadt 2008, pp. 189–90, 199–208, 228–32, 279–84, 298–407; Pekesen 2012, pp. 143–5, 175–7, 227–34; Shaw 1993, pp. 26, 35, 39–41, 58; Bayraktor 2006. For Spain see Rother 2001, pp. 143, 150–62, 175, 184.

the entry of foreign Jews.[14] Many countries, such as Denmark, granted Jewish foreigners only tourist visas in order to prevent them from seeking employment and staying in the country. Above all, it was the wave of refugees from German-annexed Austria in 1938 that first prompted the authorities in a variety of states, like Finland, to refuse entry to Jewish refugees.[15] This was particularly true for Switzerland. It was only under the pressure of the Swiss, and to a lesser degree the Swedish authorities that in the fall of 1938 Germany began to mark the passports of German Jews with a "J." (This was not in the Nazi government's interest since it did not facilitate its plans for the emigration of Jews from Germany.)[16] In August 1942, in response to a wave of Jewish refugees from France after the Germans had started mass deportations from there to extermination camps, the Swiss government further tightened immigration by declaring most entries illegal and sending back even those whose lives and health were in danger, including refugees who were being persecuted explicitly on racial grounds. In total, the Swiss authorities rejected at least 24,000 refugees at the border, among them many Jews. Such rejections occurred especially at critical periods (Jews arriving from France in August 1942 and from Italy in September 1943). But the Swiss *did* accept a total of 21,000 Jews during World War II. In addition, 14,500 of the 24,100 immigration requests filed at Swiss diplomatic offices were rejected.[17] Switzerland had a longer tradition of official hostility against foreign Jews: since 1926 the mandatory waiting period for naturalization was longer for eastern European Jews than it was for other immigrant groups, and from 1941 the quota for Jews gaining Swiss citizenship was tiny – just twelve people per year. From November 1941, Swiss women who were married to foreigners lost their Swiss citizenship, which could prove fatal for Jewesses when abroad.[18] Since 1933, refugees had been prohibited from seeking employment in Switzerland, a regulation that often affected Jews. After 1940, the prohibition against employment was

[14] Jobst 1939, pp. 207–25; Strauss 1987, pp. 216–28; Weingarten 1981, pp. 190–203; Picard 1997, pp. 158–60; for France see also Caron 1999, p. 126; for Japan see Kaneko 2008, pp. 25–6, 37–8.

[15] Wagner 2001, pp. 289–90; Hösch 2001, p. 245; Yahil 1983, pp. 19–20.

[16] Unabhängige Expertenkommission Schweiz 1999, pp. 77–88; Levine 2000, esp. pp. 219–20. I do not agree with Kvist's (2000, pp. 199–211) fine distinction, according to which there were no anti-Jewish laws in Sweden although Jews had fewer rights here than other refugees did.

[17] Picard 1997, pp. 146, 324, 415–19; Unabhängige Expertenkommission Schweiz 1999, pp. 20–3, 89–90, 133–4, 152–3, 278. Aside from Jewish civilians, Switzerland admitted close to 104,000 foreign military and 44,000 civilian refugees, more than 66,000 border refugees, and 60,000 schoolchildren over short time periods.

[18] Arlettaz and Arlettaz 1998, p. 382; Picard 1997, pp. 68, 209–10; Unabhängige Expertenkommission Schweiz 1999, p. 301.

combined with requirements for compulsory work, which resulted in thousands of refugees, including many Jews, performing forced labor. A tax on returning Swiss citizens that was introduced in 1944 primarily targeted Jews.[19]

Legal measures enacted by earlier democratic civil governments became a blueprint for successor authoritarian regimes. After the Munich Agreement cemented Germany's annexation of the Sudeten border areas in October 1938, Czecho-Slovakia (as the state was then called) dismissed Jewish civil servants, curbed immigration, expelled Jews who had immigrated after 1914, planned to erect camps for the internment of allegedly work-shy people and outlawed kosher slaughtering.[20] The constitution of Czechoslovakia was nullified, most political parties including the Communist Party were banned, parliament was disempowered and press censorship extended.[21] In March 1939, in the first days after the German occupation of Prague, the still-existing Czech government under Rudolf Beran barred Jewish doctors and attorneys from practice, removed Jews from the public health service and high managerial positions in private enterprises and social associations, and marked appropriate stores as 'Aryan.' Later, an uneven power struggle developed between the German Reichsprotektor and the Czech government of the German Protectorate of Bohemia and Moravia over the question of for whose benefit Jews were to be expropriated. (Hitler had at first said that this should be left to the Czechs.) The Czech press conducted a lively debate about this topic.[22] The Third French Republic interned (among enemy aliens) many central European Jews in 1939; and, in April 1940, prohibited nomads, mostly Roma, from traveling through the country on security grounds.[23] This made it easier for Vichy France and the Germans to control these groups. In fact, of the approximately 600,000 civilians interned on French territory between 1938 and 1946, about a quarter were held in Vichy camps, more than were held in German-controlled camps.[24] This meant that nearly three-quarters were held in camps run by the French Third and

[19] Picard 1997, pp. 85–100, 151, 163; Unabhängige Expertenkommission Schweiz 1999, pp. 172–3.

[20] Urban 1939, p. 73; Milotova 1996, p. 178 note 44; Gruner 2010, p. 144–5. For the background see Milotova 2002, pp. 79, 100.

[21] Rothschild 1974, p. 133; Oprach 2006, p. 35.

[22] Milotova 2002, pp. 75–115; Kárný 1998, pp. 7–22; Gruner 2005, pp. 33, 36–7; Urban 1939, p. 74; Kokoška 1997, pp. 37, 48 note 12; Milotova 1996, pp. 167–8. See also Lemkin 1944, pp. 138, 149. Less than 10% of trustees were Czech, and they worked only in small enterprises (Oprach 2006, p. 60 note 242).

[23] Mariot and Zalc 2010, p. 73; Peschanski 2010, pp. 21, 27, 39, 72, 103–6.

[24] By late 1940, fewer than 1,000 people were in German-controlled camps; compared to 50,000 in Vichy camps (Peschanski 2010, pp. 31, 73).

Fourth Republics,[25] foreshadowing the atrocious mass internment that would cost the lives of hundreds of thousands during the French war in Algeria in 1954–62.

In the countries more often cited for their legal persecution of Jews, somewhat different patterns are recognizable. I shall deal with them when covering themes of legislation. Countries commonly adopted many anti-Jewish laws – 350 in Slovakia, more than 150 in France, at least 315 in the German-occupied Protectorate of Bohemia and Moravia[26] – all of which took years to pass. The focus was either at first xenophobic and economic, with politico-racist elements – such as bans on intermarriages, marking Jews with badges or placing restrictions on their movement – added later; or both sorts of measures were taken at about the same time. Italy was an example of the latter.[27]

Thus, many countries in Europe and beyond – not only those under German rule or political dominance, but also those with different political systems – adopted anti-Jewish laws and regulations. Unlikely states – such as Poland, Turkey and Switzerland – had enacted quite extensive legislation against Jews. Anti-Jewish regulations also existed in countries that are sometimes celebrated for their protection for Jews – as, for example, Albania, Turkey, Denmark and Bulgaria.

Phases of anti-Jewish legislation

Legislation against Jews accelerated during certain time periods. Four major anti-Jewish laws were passed in Hungary from 1938 to 1942; to which more legal measures were added after Germany occupied that country in 1944. The most important laws in Italy came into effect in 1938–39 and 1943. In Vichy, France, most regulations originated between 1940 and 1942;[28] in Bulgaria, it was from 1940 to 1943. Romania had started earlier, in late 1937 under the Goga government, and the legislative process continued until 1943. In Croatia, most anti-Jewish laws and regulations were passed in 1941–42; likewise in Slovakia it was from 1939 to 1942, soon after the Slovakian state was founded. Romania, Hungary, Italy and Bulgaria passed their first anti-Jewish laws before they were at war. The same applies to countries like Poland.

[25] Peschanski 2002, p. 475. Among those interned were foreign citizens (above all, Spaniards), nomads (especially Roma), communists, Jews, and former representatives of the Vichy regime. However, neither German POWs in French captivity, French POWs in German hands, nor French civilians held inside Nazi Germany (who were mainly forced laborers) appear in these statistics.

[26] Fatran 2001, p. 85; CDJC 1982; Oprach 2006, p. 58.

[27] Voigt 1987, p. 5.

[28] Texts are in CDJC 1982; important Italian laws of 1938 in Sarfatti 1994, pp. 185–97.

Anti-Jewish legislation in Europe accumulated between 1938 and 1942. This was significantly later than in Germany. The fact that laws against Jews were not adopted en masse in the middle of the 1930s seems to indicate that, insofar as they were linked to developments in Germany, they were not the result of German ideas alone; rather, they also required strong German political power. Accordingly, Emil Schumburg, an official in the German Foreign Office, commented in January 1939: "Simultaneously with the state system in Central Europe created in Versailles to suppress Germany, Jewish power in Vienna and Prague collapsed [too]." These developments he put in the same context with anti-Jewish laws in Italy, Romania, Hungary and Poland.[29] Little anti-Jewish legislation was added between 1943 and 1945 when German power was weakening. On the other hand, anti-Jewish sentiments were also a homegrown problem; hostile propaganda against Jews in countries such as Poland, Yugoslavia, Lithuania, France and Austria was on the rise from the mid 1930s. Apparently, such popular attitudes needed a certain amount of time before they could produce a legislative effect.

While the short-lived administration of Prime Minister Octavian Goga in Romania in 1937 has been called "the second openly anti-Jewish regime in Europe,"[30] legal measures against Jews were taken earlier by the Romanian and other governments – some even before the Nazis came to power in Germany, although very few before 1930. Sure enough, most of these laws targeted Jews only implicitly, as was the case in Turkey, Austria and Switzerland (or Italy[31]); in Poland, however, explicitly anti-Jewish regulations had already been adopted in 1936–37. With the exception of Romania, countries that became allies of Germany rarely enacted laws against Jews before 1938 (although Hungary's law restricting the number of Jewish students was passed in 1920[32]).

Still, even during the decline of German might in the second half of World War II, there were several new restrictions against Jews imposed in Romania (against the return of Jews from Transnistria[33]), and in Bulgaria, Hungary and Switzerland (requiring compulsory labor for Jewish and other refugees). If (in contrast to, say, Poland and Bulgaria) the restoration of equal rights for Jews following the reconquest of a country by

[29] "Die Judenfrage als Faktor der Aussenpolitik im Jahre 1938," PA AA R 100857, p. 235, reverse side.

[30] Ahonen *et al.* 2008, p. 54.

[31] In March 1935 a law prohibited foreigners from practicing medicine in Italy (Voigt 1987, p. 15). For Romania in 1934–36, see Ancel 2007, p. 37.

[32] This Hungarian law was less strictly applied after 1928: Gerlach and Aly 2002, pp. 38–9.

[33] According to Decree-Law No. 698 of September 19, 1942 (found in Lemkin 1944, p. 567), this was punishable by death.

the Allies took months (as in Badoglio's Italy), or a year (as in French Algeria),[34] this can hardly be attributed to the political influence of the Nazis. While anti-Jewish laws were annulled in French Tunisia immediately after its conquest by the Allies, the fact remains that the property of Italian Jews was confiscated and 200 Jewish lawyers, physicians and dignitaries were detained in a camp.[35] In many countries – such as Hungary, Greece, Italy, France and Poland – the property of surviving Jewish citizens was never even close to being fully restored after the war; this was a result of the private initiative of profiteers, but they were aided and abetted by official regulations.[36] In Italy it took about ninety laws and forty-four years, until 1987, to repeal all fascist anti-Jewish policies.[37]

Themes

From a thematic perspective, regulations of a religious nature, or pertaining to racial ideology in a more narrow sense, did not necessarily form the centerpiece of the anti-Jewish laws in Europe. As far as religion is concerned, the most important measures were laws against kosher slaughter, which were adopted in Norway in 1929, in Sweden and Poland in 1937 and in Czecho-Slovakia, as well as in Italy and Romania, in 1939; in Switzerland, this practice had already been prohibited by referendum in 1893.[38] In Norway, hostility against Jews had strong religious roots. In Spain, circumcisions and Jewish weddings and funerals were prohibited, and synagogues and Jewish cemeteries were closed during World War II.[39] Between May and August 1941, the Croatian state tried to control the forced conversion, mainly of the Orthodox but also of Jews, to Catholicism; it essentially gave up on regulating the former by mid 1942.[40]

Legislation that points to a specifically racist ideology includes regulations which defined who was a Jew, prohibited marriages and sexual

[34] Picard 1997, p. 187; Michaelis 1978, p. 342; Roberts 2006, pp. 79–82; Abitbol 1983, pp. 173, 196. For Poland see Dobroszycki 1994, p. 6; for Bulgaria see Opfer 2005, p. 280. The reenactment of the Crémieux decree for Jews in Algeria in 1943 differentiated them from the inferior legal position of Muslims.

[35] Abitbol 1983, pp. 167–8.

[36] Braham 1994, pp. 1311–3; Gerlach and Aly 2002, pp. 210–11; Gerlach 2010, p. 245; see Chapter 13.

[37] Longhi 2010, p. 199 note 16. For the incompleteness of restitution, see Collotti 2006, pp. 209–10.

[38] Lerner and Rabello 2006–07, pp. 14–15; Sarfatti 2006, p. 140; for Poland see Chapter 12, note 10, and for Czecho-Slovakia, see Chapter 12, note 20, above.

[39] Abrahamsen 1991, pp. 37–44; Rother 2001, pp. 58–9.

[40] Biondich 2005, esp. pp. 82–3, 96, 109–10.

relations between Jews and non-Jews, and required the marking of Jews with signs or badges. For Raul Hilberg these were essential steps in what he described as the process of destruction.[41] However, only Italy, Hungary, Bulgaria, Vichy France, German-occupied Norway, Croatia and Slovakia introduced relevant definitions – most of which differed from one another and from the one adopted by Germany. Romania used a variety of definitions depending upon a particular anti-Jewish law's subject. Definitions of 'Jew,' where they existed, were sometimes based upon religious affiliation (as was even the case for the radical Croatian government). The definitions were often too restrictive for the taste of German observers – who tended to complain about alleged deficiencies in the anti-Jewish laws of other countries in general, especially with regard to far-reaching exemptions in the definition of a Jew.[42] Slovakia and Hungary (in 1941) and Bulgaria (in 1942) tightened their definitions. Individual exemptions, which were usually granted by the head of state or government (including in Germany, where Hitler also did this), might include qualified people from the professions, businesspeople (who were needed, maybe only temporarily, to prevent damage to the national economy), skilled workers, Jewish community leaders, military veterans, artists, scholars and former members of right-wing parties.[43] In rare cases the definition of 'Jew' in other countries extended further than in Germany, as was the case in Hungary (even before the German occupation), Croatia, Bulgaria after 1942, and German-occupied Norway.[44] Marriage and sexual contact between Jews and non-Jews was outlawed in a few countries, including Italy, Croatia, Romania, Hungary, Bulgaria and Norway. Jews were legally compelled to wear a mark (often a yellow star) in even fewer states: Slovakia, Croatia, and, from 1944, Hungary. Bulgaria passed such a law but never implemented it outside the annexed territories. In some provinces of Romania, Jews were forced to wear the yellow star for some time; in France, this was the case only in the German-occupied part, and it was not at all the case in fascist Italy.[45] In the German Reich, regulations coercing Jews to wear a yellow

[41] Hilberg 1994a, pp. 56–7, 165–7.
[42] Hilberg 1992a, pp. 90–3; Miller 1975, p. 95.
[43] Gitman 2011, p. 68 (Croatia); Gerlach and Aly 2002, p. 241 (Hungary); Hausleitner 2001a, p. 396 (Romania); Mann 2005, p. 294 (Slovakia); for Germany see Steiner and von Cornberg 1998.
[44] Gerlach and Aly 2002, p. 49; Hilberg 1994a, p. 757; Larsen *et al.* 2008, pp. 949–50; Chary 1972, p. 54.
[45] Hilberg 1992a, p. 92; Kletzin 1996, p. 225; Lavi 1960, pp. 280–1, 288; for marriages in Bulgaria see Opfer 2005, p. 276. According to a speech by Edo Neufeld in December 1943, the Croatian government retracted the marking of Jews following protests by the Catholic clergy (*We Survived*, vol. 3, p. 172).

star first came about in the annexed Polish territories (and the General Government) in late 1939;[46] the measure was introduced in the Old Reich only in September 1941.

The existence of a specialized central authority for measures against Jews can also be read as a sign of a coherent, racist policy. However, such institutions were established only in Vichy France and Bulgaria, and even these did not remain free from competition by other authorities. The authority of the French Commissariat-General on Jewish Questions was, in fact, limited – focusing on proposing and preparing legal measures against Jews (including police measures for implementing them) and dealing with the property of Jews, a central preoccupation.[47] Croatia and Romania founded public agencies that specialized in administering and redistributing the property of Jews; in Slovakia, its responsibilities included forced labor.[48] One should not forget that Nazi Germany itself had no *central* public institution for implementing anti-Jewish policy.[49] As is the case in Germany, the diverse structures that were operating suggest that a variety of agencies pursued – in a sometimes cooperative and in a sometimes competitive manner – policies against Jews, though without strict centralization.

Instead of concentrating on matters of racial ideology in a stricter sense, anti-Jewish legislation targeted two other areas: immigration and economic aspects. As mentioned above, many countries closed their borders to Jewish refugees to the greatest extent that they could, especially in 1938–39 in response to the mass expulsions of Jews from German-annexed Austria and Nazi Germany itself. These included, to varying degrees, Sweden, Denmark, Turkey, Switzerland, Italy, Albania, France, Great Britain, Belgium and Spain, among others. In the fall of 1938, the Czechoslovak authorities expelled masses of German refugees (most of them Jewish), sometimes by violent means, and only a small proportion of the 100,000 Austrian applicants (many of whom were Jewish) had been permitted entry within five months of the Anschluss.[50] Much of the legislation against Jews targeted Jewish immigrants; and in countries like Italy in 1938 and Bulgaria in 1939 (where especially Jews from Greece and Turkey were driven out) their expulsion was

[46] Steinbacher 2000, p. 166.

[47] See Law of March 29, 1941, and the internal division given in Commissariat Général aux Questions Juives, Personel du Commissariat, October 21, 1941, in CDJC 1982, pp. 39, 91. The German ambassador described the Commissariat's task similarly (Abitbol 1983, p. 60).

[48] Steur 1997, pp. 49–52, 70; Hilberg 1994a, p. 797; Chary 1972, pp. 54–5; *The Power of Civil Society* 2005, p. 100; Deletant 2006, p. 106; Braham 1992, p. 133.

[49] This is contrary to Lipscher 1972, p. 126.

[50] Oprach 2006, p. 88; Gedye 1942, pp. 349, 489–91; Rother 2001, pp. 44, 109–10.

stipulated.[51] Such xenophobia led to the organization, and the failure, of the international conference on Jewish refugees from Germany, held in Evian in July 1938: the USA would not commit to permitting the immigration of large numbers of Jews, southeastern European countries closed their borders almost completely to Jews, and France and Britain made no clear commitment.[52] The transnational wave of nationalism, the walling off of each country against foreigners (to a large degree caused by the global economic crisis), could not be overcome by an international resolution.

The violence in Palestine from 1936 to 1939 can be placed in this context, although it was not about anti-Jewish legislation. Many of the Jews expelled from, or rejected in, Europe, sought refuge in British Palestine, but the immigration of more than 160,000 Jews in 1933–36 raised fears of land-seizure among local Muslims. In the violent clashes of 1936–39, 547 Jews were killed, and several times as many Muslims, including almost 500 by Muslim hands. Responding to the bloody protests in May 1939, Britain restricted Jewish immigration to Palestine in May 1939 to 15,000 persons annually for the following five years.[53]

In many countries, alien Jews were especially unwelcome compared to other foreigners. On the one hand, imposing restrictions on the entry of Jews was meant to deny them access to economic activities in the host country; on the other hand, it was intended to eliminate them as economic rivals of local businesspeople. Professional and business associations' many interventions with the state authorities to these ends testify to their active role. Labor unions also demanded restrictions on the entry of foreign Jews (see Chapter 13). For example, union pressure led French authorities to deny many Jewish refugees work permits between 1932 and 1936 (although the wave of xenophobia also affected non-Jews).[54] More often, however, keeping Jews out was justified by the alleged German displeasure it would cause (for which there was rarely cited any evidence) and the fear that foreign Jews might become a burden to public welfare. As late as the fall of 1940 these considerations, among others, led the Vichy government to reject the idea of a further deportation of all German, Austrian and Czech Jews to France.[55]

[51] Voigt 1987, pp. 26–31; Toscano 1995, p. xxxviii; Picard 1997, pp. 184–5; Miller 1975, p. 94; Opfer 2005, pp. 273–4; Guttstadt 2008, p. 282 note 40.
[52] Weingarten 1981, p. 63; Oprach 2006, p. 88.
[53] These figures are from Mallmann and Cüppers 2006, pp. 21, 25, 32–5, 39; see Marrus 1985, p. 152.
[54] Eggers 2002, pp. 23–5; Marrus and Paxton 1981, p. 57.
[55] See the report by Abetz to German Foreign Office, October 23, 1940, quoted in Klarsfeld 1992, p. 273.

There was a strong note of cultural rejection against eastern European Jews in particular, who allegedly could not be integrated and, therefore, would have a negative influence on the life of the host country. For example, there is the view that by the 1930s two Jewries existed in France – with Jewish immigrants not living in the same neighborhoods, speaking the same language, belonging to the same class or performing the same economic activities as Jewish Frenchmen. (The same view, although a little less pronounced, also seems to have been expressed in Italy.[56]) Still, once Jews had acquired French citizenship, they were relatively safe; despite German pressure in 1942–43, relatively few Jews lost their citizenship.[57] By contrast, between 1937 and 1939 the Romanian state stripped about 35% of Romanian Jews (who had recently immigrated from Russia) of their citizenship[58] although this did not lead to their deportation in 1941–42 if they resided in the Old Kingdom. But legal measures went beyond 'eastern' Jews and often targeted Jewish refugees from central Europe – a social 'problem' for which, of course, the German state and German and Austrian societies were responsible in the first place.

To be sure, other elements played a role in the rejection of foreign Jews, among them alleged security concerns. Such ideas led to the internment of German and Austrian Jews (among other enemy aliens) in the French Republic in 1940, the internment of foreign Jews (among other alien civilians, above all Slovenes) in fascist Italy in 1942–43, and, in the USSR in 1940–41, the gulag internment, under much harsher conditions, of Jews – especially those from central Europe and those from Poland who had been located in the former Polish areas annexed by the Soviet Union and who, instead of accepting Soviet citizenship, had declared their wish to return to their home country or to another state. During Soviet internment, Jews were held along with other persons who were deemed unreliable – such as 'bourgeois elements,' party activists, Polish settlers and state representatives, and members of the clergy.[59] In the USSR, too, xenophobia and suspicions about the Jews became fused together, although the Soviet government was unusual in urging foreign Jews to take up Soviet citizenship quickly. In other ways, the Soviet Union reacted much like other states: it accepted Jews, 150,000–200,000 according to one estimate, but then sent thousands of them back to Germany, rejected

[56] Dreyfus 1981, p. 244; for Italy see the interview with Augusto Segre in Caracciolo 1995, p. 111.

[57] About 9,000 Jews naturalized after 1927 lost their French citizenship (Mariot and Zalc 2010, p. 123).

[58] Hausleitner 2003, p. 84; Hausleitner 2001a, p. 332; Ancel 2011, p. 94.

[59] For France Chapter 12, note 23; for Italy see Chapter 14, note 99; for the Soviet Union see Moser 1966, pp. 17–18; Polian 2008, esp. pp. 16–17.

others at the border, and, in February 1940, refused a request by the German Security Police to receive German Jews en masse.[60]

Still, restrictions concerning foreign Jews usually had an economic emphasis; this was also true of legislation against Jews in general, including that which applied to Jewish citizens. Usually the focus was not, first and foremost, on expropriations. Rather, restrictions on the number or percentage of Jewish high school or university students, especially in law and medicine, formed the point of departure.[61] In the inter-war period, the percentage of Jewish students was usually much higher than their percentage of the population. Sanctioned in part by the state, professional associations of medical doctors, lawyers, engineers and journalists expelled Jews, notably in southeastern Europe. Professional associations and students pressured governments to such ends, sometimes for months or years, until the state gave in.[62] (One should not forget that in the USA, especially in the 1930s and 1940s, universities like Columbia and Harvard also restricted the number of Jewish students.[63]) The next step was usually to prohibit Jews from working as lawyers, physicians, and, with slight variations, other professionals.[64]

Other legal restrictions (like some of those already mentioned for Poland, Turkey and Czecho-Slovakia) aimed at removing Jews from the civil service and squeezing them out of certain industries and, especially, trade. This too served the interests of non-Jewish competitors. For example, in 1938 the first major anti-Jewish law in Hungary, "Concerning the More Effective Safeguarding of a Balanced Economic and Social System," restricted the number of Jews in the professions; the 1939 act, "Concerning the Restriction of the Participation of Jews in Public and Economic Life," tightened the earlier provisions and excluded Jews from the civil service, while marriages between Jews and non-Jews were outlawed only two years later.[65] Italy banned Jews from the civil service in 1938; a citizens' committee in Vilnius, Lithuania, fired all Jews and communists from the city administration on June 26, 1941, a day before German troops arrived.[66] Romania began in 1937–38 by disallowing Jews in trade in rural areas, in addition to stripping many

[60] Polian 2008, esp. pp. 1, 15.
[61] For Slovakia see Fatran 2001, 72–5, 79–80.
[62] For Poland see Melzer 1997, pp. 71–80, 90–1. For the percentage of Jewish students in a number of countries over the period 1926–30 see Melson 1992, p. 88.
[63] See, for example, Wechsler 1984, esp. pp. 649–56.
[64] Examples from France and French Tunisia can be found in Sebag 1991, p. 227. A list of twenty-seven French anti-Jewish regulations in Tunisia in the period 1940–42 (in Sabille 1954, pp. 163–5) shows a strong economic emphasis.
[65] Rothschild 1974, pp. 197–8.
[66] Voigt 1987, p. 5; Zuccotti 1996, p. 36; Brandišauskas 2003, p. 55.

Jews of their citizenship. In 1940–41, Romanian restrictions expropriated Jewish rural, and later urban, real estate, and barred Jews from state schools and many professions; but they did permit many individuals to continue their activities in industry and commerce.[67] An almost total expropriation (except for synagogues and cemeteries) – which began in September 1941 – applied only to re-annexed Bessarabia and Bukovina.[68] The French government trumped the Germans in 1941 by outlawing more economic activities for Jews than the German military administration had.[69]

Outside Germany and the German-administered territories special taxes on Jews were hardly ever imposed before 1941–42 (when they were introduced in Bulgaria and Slovakia, and Romania forced her Jews to sign a special bond).[70] The expropriation of Jewish property, especially, came late (France and Croatia were exceptions[71]). In Germany, similarly, most of these things happened in 1938–39, almost six years after the Nazis came to power. As in France and Croatia, the bulk of expropriations in Slovakia and (incomplete ones) in Romania occurred in 1941. In Hungary, expropriations outside of agriculture and forestry (where, partially as a substitute for land reform, they were implemented in 1940–43) took place only in 1944. In the same year, the Italian Jews were expropriated.[72] In Bulgaria, some property was taken from Jews in 1941–42, while in Bulgarian-occupied Macedonia stores and workshops owned by Jews were confiscated only in February and March 1943 against a backdrop of Jewish deportations.[73] If 'Aryanization' was delayed – despite a widespread propaganda message that all Jewish property was illegitimate because it had been derived from exploiting or cheating the ethnically dominant population[74] – then even fascist governments (like the German

[67] For 1937–38 see Hausleitner 2001a, pp. 328–9; for legislation in October 1940 and March 1941 see Deletant 2006, pp. 105–6; Lavi 1960, pp. 271, 277; Ancel 2007, pp. 40–68, 73, 117.

[68] Deletant 2006, p. 107.

[69] Compare "Loi de 2 juin 1941 remplaçant la loi de 3 Octobre 1940 portant statut des Juifs" to "Dritte Verordnung über Massnahmen gegen Juden," April 26, 1941, in CDJC 1982, pp. 41–4, 50–1.

[70] Miller 1975, p. 96; Lipscher 1972, pp. 125–6.

[71] For Croatian regulations between April and November 1941, directly after the state was founded, see Trifković 2008, p. 52; Braham 1992, p. 133; Gitman 2011, pp. 68–9; for France see Dreyfus 2007.

[72] Toscano 1995, p. xl; Collotti 2006, p. 201. See Tönsmeyer 2003, pp. 141–2; Fatran 2001, pp. 81–8; Gerlach and Aly 2002, pp. 61–73; Cornelius 2011, pp. 161–2. For Romania see Ancel 2007.

[73] Miller 1975, p. 96; Opfer 2005, p. 278; see the account by Avram Sadikario from Bitola in *We Survived*, vol. 3, p. 42.

[74] Examples from Germany, Norway, the Czech lands and Slovakia can be found in Alberti 2006, p. 159; Abrahamsen 1991, p. 134; Oprach 2006, p. 42; Kamenec 2003, p. 309.

one) usually hesitated for years to expropriate Jews so as not to damage the national economy.

Expropriated businesses were either taken over by public trustees for a lengthy time period or sold to non-Jews; in several countries, however, most former Jewish-owned stores and businesses were liquidated, as was the case in areas under German administration.[75] In Romania, Ion Antonescu insisted – in anticipation of the negative reaction that international capital would have against such takeovers at future peace negotiations – that the Romanization of Jewish property had to be legalized, even if to do so required a clause for the compensation of the Jewish owners.[76]

In occupied countries (as opposed to unoccupied allies), some expropriation laws that were enacted by national governments were meant to ensure that businesses taken from Jews would benefit local non-Jews rather than Germans. Such competitive thinking was behind legislation in Norway, where the initiative was largely successful, and in the first days of the Protectorate of Bohemia and Moravia, in March 1939, where this attempt failed.[77] The expropriation of Jewish businesses formed a large part of the legislation of 1941–42, and followed on swiftly from Vichy France's first measures (the definition of who was Jewish, and provisions for the internment of foreign Jews). The unusually rapid passage of expropriation laws (by international standards) was apparently triggered by competition with the Germans.[78]

The sequence in which legal measures were taken also suggest certain priorities. After Norway was granted its own government under Vidkun Quisling and the fascist Nasjonal Samling Party in early 1942, its first move was to reinstate a regulation according to which no Jew was allowed to immigrate (February); it then passed a law in October facilitating the confiscation of Jewish property by the Norwegian state, followed in November by another requiring the compulsory registration of Jews (which also defined who was a Jew). Marriages between Jews and non-Jews were outlawed only in December, by which time many had already been deported to Germany and most of the others

[75] For Slovakia see Aly 2006a, p. 226; for France see Mariot and Zalc 2010, p. 143; for Germany see Aly and Heim 1991, pp. 22–32; for German-occupied Belgium see Hilberg 1994a, p. 635. Many also occurred in the Bulgarian-annexed territories (Schechtman 1946, p. 418).

[76] Benyamin 1997, p. 6.

[77] For the Czech lands see Kárný 1982; for Norway see below.

[78] See the French laws about the status of Jews (October 3, 1940) and refugees of the Jewish race (October 4, 1940) and the Chief of German Military Administration, Second decree about measures against Jews (October 18, 1940); the French Law creating a

had fled to Sweden.[79] Fascist Italy first moved against foreign Jews in September 1938 and then, in November, simultaneously prohibited civil marriages between so-called Aryans and non-Aryans (including Africans) – and banned Jews, in particular, from public service and public educational facilities, all of which was combined with the exclusion from economic life.[80]

Most of these measures were for the benefit of the middle class. Although this sometimes included the petty bourgeoisie,[81] laws more often pertained to the jobs and businesses of the elite, the intelligentsia and the bourgeoisie. It was the organizations with which these groups were connected that were energetically pushing to have legal regulations adopted. Statements by Romanian and Hungarian political leaders confirm that it was their aim to placate these groups.[82] One has to bear in mind that at that time a very low percentage of people had the chance to study at a university, obtain a qualified professional position, become an entrepreneur or even become a civil servant. By contrast, the pattern of anti-Jewish legislation represented little in the way of an economic redistribution in favor of blue-collar workers, or the rural population (except for expropriations in the agricultural and forestry sectors in Romania, Hungary and Slovakia[83]). Only when the personal possessions of Jews were distributed as consumer goods did some of the "benefits" of expropriation reach the lower classes.

Going as far as passing a deportation law, as was the case in Slovakia, was quite exceptional.[84] Additionally, no non-German government adopted a systematic ghettoization policy against Jews (and nor did Germany herself). To be sure, Slovakia (1942), Bulgaria (1943), Vichy France (for the most part, 1942), Romania (1941) and Hungary (1944) adopted regulations for the partial concentration, in part in camps, of their Jewish populations. In French Morocco, a law in August 1941 led to the expulsion of the Jews from European neighborhoods.[85] A step taken relatively late in the war, the concentration of Jews often served to

Commissariat-General for Jewish questions (March 29, 1941) already strongly emphasized expropriations (CDJC 1982, pp. 19–25, 39ff.). See Dreyfus 2007.

79 Hoffmann 2001, p. 270; German SD reports of 1942 can be found in Larsen 2008, pp. 879, 928, 949–50.

80 Voigt 1987, pp. 5, 15, 26–31; see also Sarfatti 1994, esp. pp. 190–4.

81 Rothschild 1974 (p. 178) for instance, made this argument for Hungary.

82 Benyamin 1997, pp. 5–6 ("strengthening an agrarian and urban elite," Romanian Deputy Prime Minister Mihai Antonescu, March 21, 1941); Benyamin 2001, p. 140; Ungváry 2005a, p. 44 (concerning a bill planned by Hungarian Prime Minister Imrédy in 1937).

83 Gerlach and Aly 2002, pp. 61–71; Deletant 2006, pp. 105–7; Fatran 2001, pp. 80, 83.

84 For the context see Kamenec 2007, pp. 213, 237–40, 287; Lipscher 1979, pp. 111–12.

85 Abitbol 1983, p. 189.

clear urban apartments during times of aerial bombardment but it also addressed the effects of limited residential construction since the onset of the economic crisis of the 1930s.[86] On the other hand, internment was often connected with forced labor that was imposed on Jews – a policy that was expanded toward the end of the war (see Chapter 13) – after they had been disbarred from working in their original occupations. Legislation prescribing forced labor (in many countries also for minorities other than Jews) came into effect in Italy, Vichy France, Slovakia and Romania; Turkey adopted such measures in 1941–42, Hungary increased theirs in 1942 (and even more extensively in 1944), and they reached their widest extension in Bulgaria in 1943. In Switzerland, too, forced labor reached its peak late: in 1945.[87]

If one considers the anti-Jewish regulations in each country as a whole, one can roughly distinguish two patterns. In some countries, racist regulations were adopted simultaneously with, or only shortly after, those that had an economic and xenophobic emphasis (as in Italy, France, Norway, Slovakia, Croatia – and also Germany). In other states, legal measures of a xenophobic and economic character clearly came first (as in Romania, Hungary and Bulgaria), or, alternatively, there were no distinctly racist steps taken at all (as in Poland, Yugoslavia, Czechoslovakia, Turkey and Switzerland). It has also been argued that in several countries, following an initial phase in 1938–39, legislation against Jews in 1940–41 became more racist in a strict sense.[88] Unquestionably, any distinction between 'economic,' 'xenophobic' and 'racist' is, to a point, artificial: racism in a general sense (as described in Chapter 7) was inherent in xenophobia and economic-group-disadvantaging – no country instituted 'purely' racist legal measures against Jews that did not also include provisions that revealed the pursuit of strong material interests.

Conclusion

Anti-Jewish laws and regulations in Europe were far from uniform. They differed from Germany, and they differed among, and also within, countries. In one country, rights for Jews could be differentiated according to sub-groups and regions. For example, the legal status of Jews in

[86] Hilberg 1992a, pp. 91–2.

[87] Hilberg 1992a, p. 91; for Hungary, see Cornelius 2011, p. 109; for Italy, see Collotti 2006, pp. 113–17 (for the growing labor demand in 1942, see Raspin 1986, p. 296); for Bulgaria, see Opfer 2005, p. 280; for Switzerland and Turkey, see pp. 390–1. In France, there were about 15,000 Jewish forced laborers in a militarized organization by July 1941 (Mariot and Zalc 2010, p. 100).

[88] Cohen 1988, p. 54.

areas (re-)annexed by Romania was even lower than that of Jews in the Romanian mainland.[89] In terms of groups, definitions of Jews often excluded people of Jewish heritage who were Christians, and there were other far-reaching exemptions. The rights of foreign Jews were curtailed even further, and often earlier, rendering those who fled from their own country especially vulnerable. Anti-Jewish propaganda tended to depict Jews (including local ones) as alien to society, but beyond the rhetoric legislation often differentiated between locally born Jews and recent immigrants. The claim that states such as Vichy France and Bulgaria protected Jews, relatively speaking, by granting them citizenship, can be turned on its head: in many countries, including these ones, there was a longer tradition of discrimination against recent Jewish immigrants.[90]

All of this shows that a German influence existed, but was limited. One can say that the Nazis set the agenda. The laws against Jews in Hungary in 1938–39 can be viewed as reflecting German power and Hungarian gratitude for territorial gains made with German help. Slovakia's first anti-Jewish legislation in 1939 – and its subsequent tightening in 1941 – as well as Hungary's in 1944, were in part the result of German influence and the German occupation, respectively. The Polish Justice Minister, Witold Grabowski, considered the possibility of using the Nuremberg laws as a model in 1937. Yet some Hungarian and Italian economic measures against Jews preceded similar German steps. There was also a secret Polish government delegation studying Hungary's anti-Jewish regulations, and the Poles were also interested in replicating measures taken by Goga's Romania and Sweden's ban of kosher slaughter.[91] The Slovakian regime modeled its first anti-Jewish legislation on Hungarian measures; in contrast, it viewed Romania's radical policies under Goga as a cautionary example. Vichy France imitated some Italian laws against Jews, and the Bulgarian authorities adopted ideas from Romanian, Hungarian and French legislation.[92] And there were remarkable similarities between certain legal measures in Bulgaria and Turkey. Aside from any German model, therefore, it can be said that different states influenced each other in their anti-Jewish legislation. But this was mainly driven by national

[89] According to a law in Romania from August 1940, Jews in recently annexed territories had fewer rights than Jews in the mainland even before the (re-)annexations of 1941 (Hausleitner 2001a, p. 341).

[90] For example, for France there is a debate about the role of xenophobia. See Caron 1999; for Jews' portrayal as alien in general, see Birnbaum 1992, pp. 99–146. Others argue that Vichy France's first anti-Jewish regulations were primarily xenophobic and became more overtly racist only in 1942 (Dreyfus 1981, p. 247).

[91] Braham 1992, pp. 29–31; Tönsmeyer 2003, pp. 63, 140; Melzer 1997, pp. 89–90. For non-German measures prior to German ones, see Maifreda 2001, p. 278.

[92] Lipscher 1979, pp. 34, 38; Sarraute and Tager 1982, p. 7; Pavunovski 2001, p. 114.

political parties and interest groups, and based on concepts about the development of a national economy – the productivity of which was supposedly blocked by Jews – and ideas about national interests.[93] Thus, such policies were all the more deeply rooted. Sometimes laws against Jews (often adopted under non-fascist governments) were even explicitly justified in order to take the wind out of the sails of homegrown fascists.[94]

As they were rooted in nationally defined interests, anti-Jewish laws were not necessarily in accordance with the German cause. In 1938–39, restrictions on the immigration of Jewish refugees in many European countries (and beyond) thwarted attempts by the Security Police, the Foreign Office, and others, to force as many Jews out of Greater Germany as possible as a 'solution' to the German 'Jewish problem.' Accordingly, Hitler, Rosenberg, and also the State Secretary in the Foreign Office, Ernst von Weizsäcker, made threatening prophecies about the future destruction of the Jews if no outlet could be found for them.[95] Actual violence swiftly followed. The attempt by the Polish authorities in 1938 to strip Polish Jews living abroad – mainly in Germany and France – of their citizenship, led to the German attempt to expel 17,000 Polish Jews before the law came into force (and these people, who would become stateless, could not have entered any other country). The fact that many of them became trapped at the German-Polish border prompted the son of two of those affected, Hershel Grynszpan, to assassinate a German consular agent in Paris, an act that in turn served as the pretext for the nationwide pogrom in Germany on November 9–10, 1938.[96] At the same time, Hitler and other propagandists could state with satisfaction that Jewish immigration led to increased hostility against Jews in many countries. Another example of interests in other countries colliding with Germany's concerns the confiscation of Jewish property. A supposedly weak government (such as that in Vichy France), and even an extremely weak one (such as Norway's) could successfully claim the property of Jews for their own nationals, obstructing in part the interests of German individuals and companies. Yet there were German financial experts and occupation functionaries for whom it made sense to mitigate the financial burden of the German occupation through such means.[97] An

[93] Ther 2011, p. 165. These ideas were then adopted by Nazi thinkers in their thoughts concerning the development of eastern Europe (Aly and Heim 1991, pp. 82–104).

[94] See Cohen 1992 (p.104) for Hungary, Romania and Vichy France.

[95] Mommsen 1997; "Die Judenfrage als Faktor der Aussenpolitik im Jahre 1938," PA AA R100857, p. 237; for v. Weizsäcker see quote from Stucki's letter to Motta, November 15, 1938, in Unabhängige Expertenkommission Schweiz 1999, p. 86.

[96] See Melzer 1997, pp. 121–4; Milton 1984; Obst 1991, pp. 46–7.

[97] This argument is developed in Aly 2006a.

interagency German conference in July 1942 decided that the property of deported Jews was to accrue to the state from which the owners were deported.[98] Thus, German authorities handed the property of Jews over to the Greek state even though the Greek government made no such demand, as far as is known.[99] Again, there existed relevant competing interests on the German side.

To be sure, history cannot be deduced merely through an examination of laws and regulations, not least because there is often a gap between intention and actual practice. As has already been indicated, some laws were not enforced while others that did not even specifically mention Jews were used to target them. And not all persecution resulted from government action. For example, despite similar regulations restricting Jewish entry and immigration, different countries allowed entry to vastly differing numbers of Jews (although, for the most part, national authorities urged Jews to use their country for transit only): Italy let in more than 120,000, Yugoslavia 55,000, Spain 40,000, Switzerland 21,000 (while sending back up to 24,000), Turkey more than 13,000 (mostly after June 1944) and Sweden about 2,000 by 1942. Finland usually kept the number at, or below, 200; the same was true for Norway. By 1939, the London-based Council for German Jewry estimated that there were 12,000 Jewish refugees in Belgium, 10,000 in Switzerland, 5,000 in all of Scandinavia and more than 20,000 in the Netherlands.[100] It is this difference between law and practice that warrants further examination of actual policies, action and non-state agents in the chapters that follow.

[98] Lipscher 1972, p. 130, citing a German Foreign Office circular of July 30, 1942.

[99] Nessou 2009, pp. 287–8.

[100] Unabhängige Expertenkommission Schweiz 1999, pp. 44 note 39, 104, 278; Picard 1997, p. 415; Freidenreich 1979, p. 188; Guttstadt 2008, p. 256; Kvist 2000; Rautkallio 1987, p. 90; for Finland see ibid., pp. 53–4, 74–85, 108; for Norway see Abrahamsen 1991, pp. 3–4; for Italy see Voigt 1987, p. 12.

13 Divided societies: Popular input to the persecution of Jews

There was a complex interrelationship between official policies and the activities of non-state actors, whether in Germany or elsewhere. Citizens were affected by government propaganda, but they also, in turn, tried to influence government policies in their own interest. A clear-cut distinction between official and private contributions is not usually possible; state functionaries and citizens cooperated in too many ways. What ordinary people did was influenced not only by the state but also by their social situations, the ideas and actions of enemies and allies from other countries, and deep-rooted attitudes (against Jews and toward diverse related political issues).

A very common question in this context – often the first – is how anti-Semitic the population of a particular country was. There are a number of reasons why this will not be central to this chapter. First, there is no convincing way of measuring anti-Jewish attitudes. With one notable exception (see below), we lack contemporary opinion surveys, let alone a series of them over time. Retrospective polls after World War II about anti-Jewish attitudes before 1945 cannot be trusted as the moral frameworks had changed radically. Second, answers to the question 'How anti-Semitic was a country?' are usually speculative, vague and overly sweeping[1] – in part because their bases are national frameworks. Resembling outdated and unscientific inquiries about 'national character,' they ignore vast differences among groups (and individuals) within countries. In fact, one important insight is that a great deal of diversity existed. To be sure, it is not enough to state this fact, for ubiquitous contradictions do not account for the very different outcomes in terms of the persecution and survival of Jews. Yet, third, it may be somewhat comforting that popular attitudes toward Jews among the population of a country, though they did matter, were only one factor determining this outcome. Romania is supposed to have been a strongly anti-Semitic country, but survival rates for Jews were higher there than in Croatia,

[1] See Fein 1979, p. 39.

Slovakia and Hungary. Many scholars assess anti-Jewish attitudes in France as being stronger than in Norway, Greece or the Netherlands, and yet the survival rate was much higher in France. This may underline how questionable judgments about a national level of Jew hatred are, but it also indicates that attitudes did not necessarily lead to related action.

On the basis of these considerations, this chapter will concentrate on the actions, rather than mental outlooks, of non-state players. It will cover propaganda against Jews, anti-Jewish lobbying with governments by different social groups, direct action against Jews by non-state protagonists, aid for them and differences in actions toward Jews within relevant large groups (e.g., Christian churches and opposing armed factions).

Lobbying: Eliminating Jewish competitors

When governments restricted the higher education and professional and business activities of Jews, it was often in response to public pressure. The authorities were usually urged to take such steps by groups whose members wanted benefits for their own careers or enterprises. One example is organizations of university students. Universities were hotbeds of the extreme right in many countries. In 1938 the main demand of right-wing Romanian students was to limit the number of Jewish fellow students.[2] In Poland in 1935–36, students tended to take violent action that spread from university campuses to city streets until the Polish government gave in to their demands for establishing "ghetto benches" by 1937, and the Warsaw Bar Association and the Warsaw Dental Academy forced Jews to complete their degrees in segregated courses.[3] Students in Budapest forced their Jewish colleagues to wear distinctive marks in 1941.[4] However, success often took years. In Zagreb and Bosnia, students had called for restrictions on the number of Jewish students in 1920;[5] they were introduced only twenty years later. In fascist Austria, the demand by fraternities – which had already banned non-'Aryans' from their organizations – for such restrictions (especially in law and medicine) failed until Austria lost her independence to Germany.[6]

Next to students, it was business or professional associations who most often made similar demands, though they tended to avoid direct violence, preferring to use their political influence. Economic rivalries between people defining themselves as non-Jews, and Jews, increased

[2] Hausleitner 2001a, p. 311. [3] Melzer 1997, pp. 71–80.
[4] Nagy-Talavera 2001, p. 258.
[5] Gitman 2011, p. 11; Freidenreich 1979, p. 183.
[6] Maderegger 1973, p. 156.

tremendously during the Great Depression of the 1930s: for instance, in Poland.[7] This fertilized the ground for anti-Jewish demands. A common means to give weight to such demands were boycotts of Jewish businesses like those organized by the Trade Association (Gewerbebund) in fascist Austria.[8] In Poland this led to riots and pogrom-like outbreaks (and, occasionally, counter-violence), which peaked in 1936–37, destroying hundreds of Jewish businesses.[9] For example, József Haracsek, President of the Baross Association (of Christian merchants) and a member of the Arrow Cross Party, prepared lists of Jews from Nagybánya and forwarded them to the Hungarian Army's forced labor service in 1942, helped with the concentration of Jews and the search for hidden valuables in 1944, and, after the deportation of Jews, participated in distributing "among various Hungarian Fascists" the shops and practices of Jews removed from economic life.[10] When Austrian Jews tried to flee to Finland in August 1938, it was the associations of potential competitors – craftsmen, tailors, textile retailers and jewelers – who protested against granting residence permits to foreign Jews.[11]

In many of the professions, the job situation also became more tense during the economic crisis. Around 1937, several organizations in the free professions in Poland (architects, engineers, university assistants, and, regionally, also jurists, economists, banking officials and veterinarians) excluded Jewish members including converts to Catholicism. On the initiative of the lawyers, the legal career was virtually barred to Jews by several regulations in 1937–38. However, there were conflicts within some professional organizations, such as the lawyers' and the medical association, which split into two.[12] Similar tendencies, including partially successful pressure on the government, can be observed in the Czech lawyers' and doctors' organizations from October 1938 to the first months of 1939.[13] The same was reported about various business associations and white-collar employees, and academics and artists pushed Jewish colleagues out of their jobs.[14] In 1930s France, professional and student

[7] See Prusin 2010, p. 118.
[8] Maderegger 1973, p. 167.
[9] Melzer 1997, pp. 53–70.
[10] Judgment of the People's Tribunal of Kolozsvár (Cluj), May 31, 1946, in Braham 1983, p. 116.
[11] Rautkallio 1987, pp. 71–2.
[12] Mahler 1944, pp. 312–13, 318–22, 330–1; Melzer 1997, p. 90.
[13] Milotová 2002, p. 100; Kokoška 1997, pp. 36–7, 48 note 12; Oprach 2006, p. 36. Czech doctors and lawyers called for the government, among other things, to define who was a Jew.
[14] *Sicherheitshauptamt* report for the first quarter of 1939, MadR vol. 2, p. 225; Rothkirchen 2005, pp. 87–94.

associations lobbied with some success against Jewish immigrants.[15] Asked for advice by the authorities in Switzerland, professional associations, most notably the Swiss Writers' Organization, recommended barring many immigrant colleagues from employment, professional activity or even entry into the country; Jewish emigres were even more affected than non-Jewish refugees.[16] In Romania, the professional organizations grew much more united in their hostility: starting with the bar association of Bucharest, which accepted no new Jewish members from 1935 onwards, Jewish advocates, engineers, architects, journalists, writers and doctors had been expelled from their professional organizations by October 1940. In the summer of 1941 the teachers' and medical doctors' associations succeeded in having Jewish private schools and hospitals closed, and Jewish students and doctors removed from other institutions.[17] Four months before the German occupier's first anti-Jewish steps, the Chamber of Commerce in Liège, Belgium, stated in June 1940 that it had initiated and in part already achieved the liquidation of thirty companies of Polish Jews who had fled from the city.[18] The Lithuanian Red Cross went still further, distributing leaflets during the wave of deadly pogroms in the summer of 1941 stating, "We do not help Jews." Polish (and not only German) doctors refused to help with transportation when the German administration forced bedridden patients to move into the Łódź ghetto in the icy February of 1940.[19]

Professional organizations of engineers, doctors and lawyers in Hungary – for example doctors in Budapest – made sure that their Jewish colleagues were drafted into the Hungarian Army's forced labor service in 1942; and later, in 1944, that they were deported to German-controlled areas. As a result, the death rates among these groups were higher than among the rest of the Jewish population. The picture wasn't uniformly this terrible. The Chamber of Lawyers obstructed anti-Jewish legislation until 1941, and non-Jews – often professing to be on the political right – served as straw men in firms formally given to non-Jews that continued to operate under Jewish management. In northern Transylvania, several professional organizations – arguing that their Jewish colleagues had promoted the Hungarian cause when the area had belonged to Romania – made their regional deputies in the Hungarian parliament move to lift restrictions against Jews in

15 Caron 1999, pp. 8, 16, 23–5, 28–32, 234–8.

16 Unabhängige Expertenkommission Schweiz 1999, p. 172; Schulz 2012, pp. 250–4.

17 Lavi 1960, p. 271; Hausleitner 2001a, pp. 328, 394; Ancel 2011, pp. 79–81, 103.

18 Rozenblum 2003, p. 21.

19 Diary of Dr Elena Buivydaite-Kutorgiene, July 7, 1941, in Grossman and Ehrenburg 1994, p. 639; see also Alberti 2006, p. 157.

medicine, law, journalism, theatre and film.[20] Similarly, the unions of Bulgarian lawyers, doctors and writers opposed the anti-Jewish Law for the Defence of the Nation in 1941, and numerous cultural, professional and business organizations in Greece appealed to Prime Minister Logothetopoulos to protest against the German racial persecution of Jews shortly before the deportations from Salonica began. But one author insists that the elites in that city did not participate in this protest.[21]

Whatever the behavior of professional organizations, the deaths of Jews created job opportunities. In Yugoslavia, murdered Jews represented 20% of all dead businessmen and 22% of all the deceased in the professions.[22] As the German administration in the General Government intended temporarily to replace Jews in trade with non-Jewish Poles, German-inspired trade and artisan cooperatives sprouted like mushrooms in 1940–42 and were manned by Polish non-Jews who wished to strengthen their "market position" for the period after an Allied victory.[23] Superseding Jewish merchants and artisans was the declared intention of western Ukrainian nationalists in the summer and fall of 1941, when first pogroms – and then German mass murders of Jews – raged in the region.[24]

In some countries, workers' unions also pleaded for the rejection of Jewish refugees or expelled Jewish members. As one example, Swiss labor unionist Robert Grimm, a leader of the famous nationwide general strike of November 1918, expressed concerns in September 1943 that refugees from Italy (many of whom were Jews fleeing from the threat of death) would create unemployment in the country. Finland's social democrats rejected the immigration of Jews in 1938. Alternatively, the authorities argued on behalf of workers, among others, that Jewish immigration should be restricted.[25] Under the German-Italian occupation of Tunisia in 1942–43, Muslim employees of the local streetcar company demanded that their Jewish colleagues be fired because they wanted to take over their better jobs.[26] Such envy went especially far in Budapest, where in 1944 "Catholic prostitutes" demanded in a letter to the Hungarian

[20] Kovács 1994 is groundbreaking; see also Kádár and Vági 2005, pp. 66–7.

[21] Miller 1975, p. 96; Hoppe 1979, pp. 94–5, 220 note 13; Pavunovski 2001, p. 103; letter to Logothetopoulos, March 23, 1943, in Clogg 2002a, pp. 104–6; but see Mazower 2004, pp. 440–1. For protests by professional organizations against planned deportations in Denmark, see Petrow 1974, p. 214.

[22] The figures are from Cvetković 2008, p. 368.

[23] Chodakiewicz 2004, p. 87. However, many farmers rejected the cooperatives as instruments for their exploitation by the Germans (Madajczyk 1994, pp. 137–8).

[24] Spector 1990a, p. 239.

[25] Lavi 1960, p. 271 (Romania); Rautkallio 1987, pp. 75–7 (Finland); Unabhängige Expertenkommission Schweiz 1999, pp. 49, 54; Arlettaz and Arlettaz 1998, p. 347, see also pp. 330–4; Mächler 1998, pp. 370, 382; Wagner 2001, p. 289.

[26] Sebag 1991, p. 245.

Minister of Justice, István Antal, the removal (i.e., deportation) of their Jewish colleagues.[27] All in all, however, commercial, intellectual and professional elites had a much stronger influence on anti-Jewish measures than workers' or farmers' organizations.

Pogroms and plunder

The lower strata of societies had relatively little leverage for advancing their interests. Frustrated by the economic success of Jews and those who managed to take over their positions or businesses, they turned to direct action – including several forms of violence. But while economic aspects are striking if one looks at the actions, their motives cannot be reduced to that.

The period of the Iron Guard's rule in Romania from September 1940 to January 1941 (a time of national crisis following territorial losses characterized by near-chaos and high inflation) is a case in point. Not counting the larger massacres organized by the Iron Guard in November and January (i.e., in small actions), there were cases of torture, maltreatment, public castration and drowning and other forms of murder of Jews. Synagogues, too, were attacked. But the main thrust in a number of instances was against Jewish property: 88 private Jewish homes were vandalized and 65 cases of wanton destruction were registered, compared to 260 forcible occupations of property, 1,081 confiscations, 1,162 cases of property acquisition by forced sale, and 323 kidnappings of Jews. In the Legion's uprising from January 21 to 23, 1941, many stores run by Jews were looted; this was in addition to the rapes, the burning of synagogues, torture and killings. In total, 118 Jews (plus 256 other civilians and 21 members of the military) died, according to official reports; the number of Jews was 630 according to the Jewish communities.[28]

Several waves of violence against Jews can be identified. They occurred in times of crisis and upheaval. One swept through parts of eastern Europe at the end of World War I. In Poland and Ukraine, where tens of thousands of Jews were killed, the violence was mostly for plunder but also included forms familiar to observers of Nazi German behavior in World War II: beards were cut, Jews were forced to do "gymnastics" and synagogues were broken into and religious artefacts stolen.[29] The white terror in Hungary produced many more victims than the red one did; a

[27] Nagy-Talavera 2001, p. 283 note 43.
[28] Nagy-Talavera 2001, pp. 439–42 with note 32, 448, 453–5 with note 99; Ancel 2011, pp. 157–63.
[29] See Prusin 2010, p. 94.

large number of the 5,000–6,000 dead were Jews, and there were many cases of torture, rape and castration.[30] During the Greek-Turkish conflict of 1918–22, Jews were attacked and robbed by both sides – which caused the Jewish population of Istanbul, Izmir and Edirne to drop by half (mostly by flight).[31] In Yugoslavia there were many anti-Jewish incidents in 1918–19, including attacks on Jewish property, synagogues and graveyards. According to hostile propaganda, Jews had enriched themselves during World War I at the expense of peasants[32] (although one could argue, rather, that peasants had profited at the expense of urbanites). Similar attacks spread through Czechoslovakia, especially in the Slovak regions that had been briefly occupied by troops of the Hungarian Soviet Republic.[33]

Economic crises triggered more riots against Jews before and during World War II. In June and July 1934, large-scale pogroms, fanned by racist propaganda inspired by Germany and obviously, though secretly, favored by local, and possibly central, Turkish authorities, led to the expulsion of between 3,000 and 10,000 Jews (and Bulgarians) from Turkish Thrace. Gangs attacked Jewish stores and people, marauding and raping women in one town after another. No Jews were killed. Jewish businesses were taken over by locals, and Muslim refugees from Crete and other areas were settled in this strategically important region to bolster the nation state.[34] In August 1934, twenty-three Jews and three Muslims were killed in a pogrom in Constantine, French Algeria. Riots against Jews occurred in Salonica and Kastoria in Greece in June 1931 and 1934, respectively.[35] The peak of pogroms during the economic depression in Poland, starting around 1933, was reached in 1936–37; these also involved picketing and boycotts of Jewish businesses, and attacks on them. Thus, the position of the Polish government in supporting boycotts and other economic actions against Jews – but condemning violence – was ambivalent at best.[36] In September 1938, a pogrom in the center of Sofia, Bulgaria, destroyed many stores; in November, violent crowds moved against Jews in Bratislava, Czecho-Slovakia.[37] Still more severe were the pogroms in Romania from 1937 to early 1941.

Already by the early years of World War II, we observe riots against Jews – though minor compared to the events of 1941 – in several eastern

[30] Rothschild 1974, p. 153.
[31] Pekesen 2012, p. 142.
[32] Vulesica 2008, pp. 135–8.
[33] Witt 2012, p. 104.
[34] Pekesen 2012, pp. 41–52; Bayraktor 2006.
[35] Abitbol 1983, p. 18; Plaut 1996, p. 35.
[36] Melzer 1997, pp. 21, 44–7, 53–70, 158; Libionka 2004, pp. 23–6; Mendelsohn 1983, p. 74.
[37] Chary 1972, p. 35; Gedye 1942, p. 500.

European countries. Aside from Romania, they happened in Bulgaria in the second half of 1939 but were less intense than those in the period from the 1880s to the 1900s, and the government suppressed them.[38] Likewise, the local extreme rightist organization, Vlajka (Banner) in German-occupied Bohemia and Moravia organized riots against Jews, which were stopped by the Czech police, in several cities in the second half of 1939. Already by February 1939, after the Munich Agreement in still-independent Czecho-Slovakia, there were bomb attacks on stores owned by Jews in Prague, Pilsen and Hradec Králové; and in March Germans and radical Czechs together burned down a synagogue.[39] In September 1939, the month of the Polish defeat, some lethal pogroms took place in a number of northeastern Polish towns.[40] In the spring of 1940, youth gangs – fed with the ideas of Polish Jew-haters, and tolerated, filmed and photographed by Germans – attacked Jews, looted stores and smashed shop windows in German-occupied Warsaw and neighboring towns.[41] No Germans were present to film the assaults and plundering of Jewish stores in French Tunisia in the months after the French defeat of June 1940. (There were also small riots against Jews in mainland France, such as occurred in Toulouse.) In August and September a spate of attacks on Jews by Europeans and Arabs followed in several cities and towns in French Morocco. At a riot in Gabès, Tunisia, in May 1941, at least seven Jews were killed. In 1941 there were also repeated anti-Jewish riots in regions of Libya under Italian and British control.[42] After British forces had occupied Iraq following a brief war in the same month, at least 110 Jews (including 28 women) were killed and 586 stores and 911 dwellings looted in a nine-day pogrom.[43] In 1941, or possibly later, a crowd of Albanian rural dwellers entered the town of Priština, Kosovo, and harassed and plundered Serbs and Jews.[44] Italian fascists attacked Jews and their stores and synagogues in several towns in 1941–43.[45] Another pogrom took place in Casablanca, French Morocco – which was under Allied occupation – in early 1943, around the time when Roosevelt and Churchill met there for a conference; and another pogrom occurred not far away in Sefrou on July 30, 1944.[46]

[38] Chary 1972, pp. 32–5; for the wave of 1898–1905 see Troebst 1995, pp. 113–15.
[39] Brandes 2006, p. 457; Urban 1939, p. 73; Gruner 2005, p. 33.
[40] Bauer 2013, p. 73.
[41] Friedrich 2003, pp. 138–42; Gutman 1982, pp. 27–8; Paulsson 1998, p. 35.
[42] Abitbol 1983, p. 43; Mallmann and Cüppers 2006, p. 48. For Libya see de Felice 1985, pp. 179 and 359 notes 26–7; for mainland France see Kletzin 1996, p. 221; for Morocco see Thomas 1998, p. 239. See Friedländer 2006 (p. 288) for Belgium.
[43] Mallmann and Cüppers 2006, pp. 83–4.
[44] Memories by Albert Ruben in *We survived*, vol. 3, p. 140.
[45] Burgwyn 2005, pp. 123–4; Schlemmer and Woller 2005, pp. 185–6; Sarfatti 2006, pp. 158–9.
[46] Abitbol 1983, pp. 154–5.

The worst wave of pogroms after 1920, claiming perhaps 50,000 lives, swept through an area from Latvia to the Black Sea in the summer of 1941. Most of them occurred in places that the Soviet Union had annexed from Poland, Romania and the Baltic states between 1939 and 1940.[47] The epicenters lay in Lithuania, the region of Białystok in northeastern Poland, eastern Galicia, northern Volyn, Bessarabia and Bukovina. The pogroms took place after the Germans had attacked the USSR, either just before the German or Romanian troops arrived, or shortly afterwards.[48] While there has been considerable debate as to how much these anti-Jewish riots were staged by the Germans (or Romanians),[49] they are generally viewed as genuine acts of Jew-hatred. Usually they were carried out by one ethnic group that was, or wished to become, dominant: Lithuanians (not Poles) in Lithuania, Poles (not Belarusians) in the area of Białystok, Ukrainians (not Poles) in Galicia and Volyn, and Romanians and Ukrainians in Bukovina.[50] Some Lithuanian gangs intended to terrorize Jews in order to chase them out of the country; others did not want to allow Jews to flee to security in the Soviet Union where they would not be able to kill them.[51] If there were markedly fewer, and less lethal, pogroms in some regions (like western Belarus),[52] this has been explained by desires for revenge for Soviet violence (e.g., mass deportations and the massacre of political prisoners) running stronger elsewhere. Through the notion of 'Jewish Bolshevism,' Jews were collectively associated with communist atrocities.[53] It must be added that Soviet repression had been strong in all of the focal points of the pogroms because nationalist, anti-communist movements had been strong there in the first place.[54] By contrast, Belarus was known for its weak nationalism. Nationalism was a key driving force for the anti-Jewish massacres. And despite all their anti-communist and nationalist motivations, these pogroms were no exception in that they too

[47] One major exception was Iaşi, Romania, in which up to 10,000 Jews were killed: Ancel 2011, pp. 445–56; Ioanid 2000, pp. 63–90.

[48] An overview can be found in Prusin 2010, pp. 150–60; for discussion by region see Pohl 1996, pp. 54–67 (eastern Galicia); Spector 1990a, pp. 64–9, 238, 246 (Volyn); Dieckmann 2011, pp. 313–79 (Lithuania); Solonari 2007b and Geissbühler 2013 (Bukovina and Bessarabia); Angrick and Klein 2006, pp. 79–86 (Riga).

[49] See works cited in the previous note; for the case of Jedwabne see Gross 2001; see also Dmitrów *et al.* 2004; for the Romanian part see Shapiro 1997, pp. 140–1; Heinen 2001, pp. 44–5.

[50] For Bukovina see Hausleitner 2001a, p. 385.

[51] Levinson 2006, pp. 34, 167–9.

[52] Zbikowski 1993, pp. 173–9.

[53] For example, see Pohl 1996, pp. 54–67.

[54] This is also true for the Jedwabne area (Gross 2001, pp. 38, 219 note 9) and northeastern Romania (Rothschild 1974, p. 295).

involved widespread plunder and claims of freeing commerce from alien control.[55]

The area of Janow, near Lublin, in the General Government of Poland, lies outside the pogrom belt. Between 275 and 500 Jews were killed by Poles (and 15,000–17,000 by Germans) during the German occupation there from September 1939 to July 1944; among the former, at least 100 were killed by "bandits," i.e., criminal gangs, 75 by communists, 50 by anti-communist nationalists, and another 50 by locals cooperating with the Germans. At least 14 more Jews were murdered from August 1944 to 1947.[56] The facts from this one county suggest that pogroms – spectacularly large events involving violent crowds and vivid in the memories of Jews and non-Jews alike – may, in many areas, have led to fewer victims than the strings of small-scale attacks by gangs or other groups, although such small attacks have been much less well remembered and researched. For example, in the area of Zamość in the General Government, peasants drove Jews (both local residents and those in hiding) from the land by either driving them to the towns or killing them on their own, as was reported in November 1942.[57] Many did it for booty, and also tortured Jewish refugees. Non-Jews killed each other for loot.[58] The terrible effect of all of this, beyond the direct victims, was to create the impression among Jews that they had nowhere to hide, and this encouraged them, not only in Poland but also in the German-occupied parts of the Soviet Union, to stay put and hope that the German persecution might not claim their or their families' lives. Attacks like those in Janow county were made possible by the existence of small, unofficial groups of armed men ready to use violence (often also in political conflicts among groups). It was not only Polish officials who participated in the hunt for Jews and the massacres and deportations of them in 1942; private individuals also took part in German anti-Jewish massacres – as the Polish underground press complained – some even before the large German extermination campaigns.[59]

Pogroms occurred in several distinct phases, and in many countries, although there are relatively few reports of crowd or gang violence against Jews from western Europe. These riots demonstrated a variety of aspects, as shown by their specific targets and actions. Non-Jews directed their anger toward places of economic activity (shops and markets, for

55 See Mann 2005, (p. 289) for Volyn and Galicia; see Solonari 2007b for Bukovina and Bessarabia; see Levinson 2006 (p. 102) for Lithuania.
56 Chodakiewicz 2004, pp. 359, 361.
57 Kosmala 2001, p. 321.
58 Gross 2012a, pp. 21, 25, 50–63; Engelking 2012, p. 70.
59 Friedrich 2006, pp. 215, 217, 220; Młynarczyk 2007, pp. 241, 304–9, 313–14.

example), religious practice (like synagogues and cemeteries) and – though somewhat less frequently – private life (e.g., when attacking private dwellings and raping women), and their aggression was directed against habits perceived as 'Jewish' (for example, by cutting beards). Jews were also attacked for their assumed political orientation (mostly as leftists and, except in mid 1941, more as the result of gang, rather than crowd, violence). Sometimes pogroms were concentrated in, or were limited to, border regions with a high percentage of Jews among the population.[60]

Still, citizens' collective and individual acts against Jews again and again included plunder and robbery. In the Romanian-ruled district of Moghilev, in Transnistria, Ukrainian gangs "attacked the convoys of Jews [deported by Romanians, C.G.], robbing, killing, and sometimes taking their clothing and leaving hundreds of naked Jews to freeze to death." After massacres in Transnistria, Ukrainians dug among the corpses at night for gold and treasure. Romanian gendarmes and civil servants, meanwhile, went after the living by blackmailing the Jewish survivors.[61] Blackmail probably provided state officials better opportunities to advance their private interests than it did private agents. Still, there was some cooperation: Romanian troops, together with the general population, plundered Jewish homes and stores in Herţa in the summer of 1941, and civilians dragged Jewish girls out of their homes and handed them over to Romanian soldiers to rape.[62] Romanian guards of deportation convoys sometimes shot the best-dressed Jews and 'sold' their corpses to neighboring peasants, who sold or used the clothes.[63] Romanian soldiers, gendarmes and police, as well as German officials, had better chances to get money or valuables from Jews in Chişinău (in Moldova) in 1941; they robbed them, bought the possessions that Jews were forced by looming deportation to sell cheaply, or ransacked their homes afterwards, for whatever was left behind.[64] Armed formations had more weapons at their disposal than civilians, as was the case for the Romanian soldiers who killed about 200 Jews in Storozynets, Bukovina, while looting the town in early July 1941.[65] In Bessarabia, the furniture of deported Jews was distributed among military and civilian officials. Soldiers who were not

[60] This applies to Turkish Thrace in 1934 and northeastern Romania (Moldova, Bessarabia and Bukowina) in 1941. In Italy, anti-Jewish laws are reputed to have been popular only in the area of Trieste where 4% of the population, far more than elsewhere, was Jewish. See Pekesen 2012, p. 219; Brustein and King 2004b, pp. 695–6; Mann 2005, p. 310.

[61] Benyamin 1997, pp. 101 (quote), 120.

[62] Heinen 2001 (pp. 44–5) also mentions other towns in Moldavia and Bukovina.

[63] Ioanid 2001, pp. 82, 85.

[64] Shapiro 1997, pp. 173–4.

[65] Hausleitner 2001a, p. 385.

part of the escorts, as well as peasants, attacked and looted Jews being driven through the villages, sometimes with the complicity of the guards; but they probably didn't often find very much because gendarmes regularly beat, robbed, raped and killed the Jews in the deportation columns they 'guarded.' Still, cart drivers managed to charge enormous prices for their services, and some stole deportees' baggage.[66]

Plunder and chaos became so widespread that the regional authorities in Romanian re-annexed Bessarabia, as in German-annexed Wartheland, imposed the death penalty for looting (in November 1939 and September 1941, respectively).[67] State control over the appropriation of the possessions of Jews and non-Jews, especially in annexed territories, became an illusion also because administrative and police personnel often worked for their own gain as well instead of merely implementing government policies.[68] Bulgarians called merchants and professionals moving into Thrace and Macedonia at the time "usurers" and "profiteers," whereas in Romania in 1941 the Bukovina was nicknamed "California," and the people who went there were called "gold-rushers." Similarly, a German functionary criticized the "gold digger attitude" of Reich Germans coming to annexed East Upper Silesia.[69]

Popular zeal for robbing Jews could already be observed at the beginning of World War II. When Viennese Jews were deported by the German Security Police to the area of Nisko/San in Poland, and forced to move toward the Soviet demarcation line in October 1939, they were "repeatedly attacked by the rural population and robbed."[70] This was a frequent experience for Polish Jews.[71] By October 1942 the press agency of the illegal Polish Home Army critically reported "cases of collective plunder en masse of formerly Jewish property" by Poles.[72]

As the Romanian example shows, however, private, lower-class individuals among the non-Jews were at a disadvantage when Jewish property was distributed. Those driven more by their own misery (which was often exacerbated by the war) than by the desire for social advancement benefited relatively little. In this sense, social mobility

66 Ioanid 2001, pp. 81–3; Shapiro 1997, p. 175. All of these events resemble very closely the treatment of Armenian deportees of the Ottoman Empire in 1915–16; see Gerlach 2010, pp. 96–115.

67 Alberti 2006, p. 115; Ioanid 2000, p. 143.

68 See Gerlach 2012, pp. 145–7.

69 Kotzageorgi 1996, pp. 147–8; see also Kotzageorgi and Kazamias 1994, p. 97; Hausleitner 2001a, p. 399; Weber 2004, pp. 39–40. For East Upper Silesia see Steinbacher 2000, p. 137.

70 Survivor report by Ernst Kohn, 1946, cited in Moser 1966, pp. 17–18.

71 See Klukowski 1993, pp. 29, 39, 69 (diary, September 20 and October 10, 1939, January 11, 1940).

72 Friedrich 2003, p. 134. See also Klukowski 1993, p. 192 (diary, April 13, 1942).

had limits. In Slovakia, the secret service reported in June 1943 in this context that ordinary people "have not received anything so far and are convinced that they will not get anything [in the future] either."[73] In Bulgaria, where state authorities attempted to organize an 'orderly' official plunder of Jewish assets in annexed Macedonia and Thrace, officials misappropriated much for their own personal benefit.[74] At other times, the booty went to the bourgeoisie. In the city of Salonica, some neighborhoods where Jews had formerly resided were leveled as contractors searched for valuables hidden in the walls of buildings – rather than using the dwellings for housing Greek refugees from the Bulgarian-occupied north.[75] Usually, there was no lack of people who were ready to take over Jewish businesses; Belgian citizens and Hungarian lawyers in 1944 were exceptions.[76] When the household effects and clothing of Jews were auctioned off, as Lithuanian authorities, acting autonomously, did at the beginning of the German occupation,[77] the better off were again in a better position to get the best items. In the German-occupied Polish and Soviet territories, Germans and ethnic Germans received the most attractive Jewish movable possessions; Poles and Belorussians could buy the rest cheaply.[78] By contrast, the town population in Southern Bukovina (which Romania conquered in June 1941) was able to plunder the houses of deported Jews – sometimes taking even windows, doors and metal roofs – when there was no police interference.[79]

Only certain types of action (which also depended on the locality) remained open to the lower strata of society. Many of these were illegal, especially under German rule, and risked severe punishment. In German-occupied Volyn (Ukraine, formerly eastern Poland), the population robbed Jews even after the 'liquidation' of all of the ghettos; locals charged Jewish refugees exorbitant prices for food; Ukrainian policemen demanded gold and jewelry for even a glass of water; locals hid Jews in return for payment, and hired them as cheap labor; and Christians holding Jewish property for safe keeping murdered the owners or denounced them to the Germans.[80] When Soviet troops pillaged Budapest after

73 Cited in Kamenec 2003, p. 317; see ibid., pp. 307–18.
74 Plaut 1996, p. 57.
75 Mazower 2001, p. 247; but see Matarasso 2002 (p. 142) for Greek refugees getting shelter.
76 Aly 2006a, p. 204; Kovács 1994.
77 Valentinas Brandišauskas, "The Position of the Lithuanian Catholic Church on the restitution of Jewish property," in Levinson 2006, p. 240 (Rokiškis, June 27 to August 20, 1941).
78 Alberti 2006, p. 111; Gerlach 1999, pp. 679–80.
79 Hausleitner 2001a, p. 383.
80 Spector 1990a, pp. 239–41. For farmers near Treblinka demanding gold for water from Jews in deportation trains, see Gross 2012a, pp. 34–5.

capturing it in 1945, many of the city's inhabitants joined in the looting of primarily (but not only) Jewish homes.[81]

Collective rioting, in the form of pogroms, was another illegal activity that enabled the lower strata of the local population to get a share of the booty. Yet another was squatting in the apartments and houses formerly inhabited by Jews. This was a mass phenomenon in Hungary in 1944, but it also happened en masse in Romanian-reoccupied Czernovits, in Salonica, Greece, and in Romanian-occupied Odessa, where the squatters were ethnic Germans.[82] Blackmailing Jews was equally common. According to estimates, there were 1,000–4,000 Christian professional blackmailers, commonly known as *szmalcownicy* (bacon hunters), who preyed in gangs on perhaps 50,000 Jews hidden in Warsaw between 1942 and 1944: either by extorting money from them or, less often, denouncing them to the Germans for reward. Some of these were killed by the Polish resistance. According to Gunnar Paulsson, almost all of Warsaw's surviving Jews reported having been discovered by police or private blackmailers. Some gangs compiled elaborate lists of Jews in hiding, as well as their personal data.[83] The *szmalcownicy* belonged to all strata of society, including civil servants, teachers, merchants and students, as well as lumpenproletariat.[84] In Slovakia, blackmail was common among the fascist Hlinka Guard.[85]

Locals without official functions or connections often had to settle for the leftovers. This was the case for the Polish population living in villages close to extermination camps, who acquired gold, valuables and money through trade with camp guards or the latter's relationships with local women or girls. Some of the neighboring population later turned to prospecting for gold and diamonds by digging among the bodies and ashes of the Jews murdered at the Bełżec extermination camp, after the Germans had left it. In several places in Poland (and, decades later, at the sites of massacres or military battles in the Soviet Union), this activity continued after the war. The area of Treblinka became known as the "Polish Colorado."[86]

81 Cornelius 2011, pp. 375–6.

82 Gerlach and Aly 2002, pp. 202–3; Deletant 2006, p. 165; Molho 2002, esp. pp. 222–4; Völkl 1996, pp. 117–18.

83 Friedrich 2003, p. 135; Friedrich 2006, pp. 218–19; Paulson 1998, pp. 23, 25; Paulsson 2002, pp. 148–52, and for limits to denunciations pp. 143–4. There are many examples in Śliwowska 1999. For the lists, see the recollections by Maximilian T. in Schoenfeld 1985, p. 241.

84 Gross 2012a, pp. 92–5.

85 Mann 2005, p. 294.

86 Rieger 2007, p. 116; Rückerl 1977, p. 144; Gross 2012a, pp. 20–33; quote: Gross 2006, p. 41; for Auschwitz see Friedler *et al.* 2002, p. 309. For the USSR see Tumarkin 1994, pp. 159–61; Merridale 2000, p. 328.

World War II and the years immediately before it witnessed great social mobility. While Jews were squeezed out of elite positions, and while some other traditional elites (such as the clergy in parts of eastern Europe) also came under attack, other groups rose. Such developments were stimulated by government policies as a way of fostering a loyal elite, and especially a national bourgeoisie. Often this took place in the form of a chaotic struggle. For some time at least, as was the case in Poland, a post in a German-controlled local administration could serve as the basis for enriching oneself, shielding someone from forced labor deportation and, to some degree, for protecting oneself from persecution by the German police.[87] In the Romanian- (and German-) occupied Soviet territories, former low-level managers and technicians were among these nouveau riches.[88] Some extracted resources from Jews. Of course there were also ethnic elites favored by the occupier.[89] Many Jews, especially those from Bessarabia but also locals, starved to death in Transnistria in 1941–42; at the same time, a stratum of non-Jewish "new rich" – many of whom benefited from selling the possessions of Jews and Soviet evacuees – came into being.[90] Problems (from a state perspective) became visible when, as was quite common, incompetent people serving as public trustees for former Jewish-owned businesses quickly ruined them or failed to pay the agreed price or their debts.[91] Social mobility did not work out as planned (inasmuch as it was planned in the first place).

Propaganda, denunciations and agreeing with violence against Jews

Anti-Jewish agitation played on a variety of themes and originated from diverse actors. In German-invaded Lithuania, the focus of nationalists' propaganda against Jews shifted from their alleged support for Bolshevism to their supposed economic exploitation and their reputed fundamental difference from non-Jews.[92] Unofficial propaganda in early post-World War II Poland also linked Jews to Bolshevism (the ideology of the Soviet arch-enemy); the same thing occurred in wartime Finland but reportedly with much less success except within the Finnish Security Police. But Christian anti-Judaism also played a public role as, for example,

87 Chodakiewicz 2004, pp. 72–3, 80.
88 Dallin 1998, pp. 121–2.
89 Ibid., p. 197 (Romanians, Germans, Italians, Moldovans); Chodakiewicz 2004, p. 68 (ethnic and Reich Germans).
90 Dallin 1998, pp. 114–22, esp. p. 115.
91 For Croatia see Gitman 2011, pp. 68–9; for Slovakia see Kamenec 2003, pp. 311–16.
92 Levinson 2006, pp. 225–7.

in Sweden.[93] As in Finland, Jews became central to the Swiss public discourse of hostility to foreign immigration even though they were a small proportion of the immigrant population. The same happened in France, which received the largest number of central European refugees. Xenophobic themes were an important element in the rejection of Jews elsewhere in western Europe and in the industrialized Czech lands, although humanitarian voices were also strong there.[94] In mid 1930s Poland, hostility toward Jewish compatriots (usually charged with ideas about rich and impure Jews) in resorts on the Baltic Sea was so great that some of the latter preferred to go to the beach in the Nazi-ruled independent city of Danzig.[95] Where anti-Jewish sentiments were relatively weak, they have been attributed to the propaganda of small radical groups some of which admired the German Nazis.[96] Where anti-Jewish attitudes were strong and pervasive, either the Christian churches and local militias[97] or political parties played a major role in spreading them.[98] Some of this propaganda had undeniable success: the exhibition "The Jew in France" presented by the Institute for the Study of Jewish Questions in Paris sold 300,000 tickets within a few days in September 1941.[99]

Reporting Jews to the authorities was taking anti-Jewish action much further. In large parts of the German- and Romanian-occupied Soviet territories, denunciation of Jews was a mass phenomenon – as the cases of Odessa, Transnistria in general, and the region of Kiev suggest, where the German SD was flooded with reports.[100] After the October 1942 massacre in Pinsk, Poles looting in the ghetto pointed Germans to hiding Jews, who were then shot.[101] Lithuanians also reported Red Army soldiers hiding en masse to the Germans.[102] Comparison of the memoirs of surviving Jews from Yugoslavia, where reporting seems to have been much less common,[103] illustrates how inescapable denunciations were

93 Pramowska 2010, pp. 159–76; Silvennoinen 2008, pp. 157–8; Hösch 2001, pp. 242–3; for Croatia from 1942 see Pavlowitch 2008 (p. 135), who makes the same connection to alien (Serb) interests.

94 Kury 2003, esp. p. 132; Rautkallio 1987, p. 66; Marrus and Paxton 1981, pp. 34–71, 364; Katz 1973, pp. 105–32; Milotova 1996, pp. 160–1, 178 note 47.

95 Epstein 2010, p. 105.

96 For Turkey see Guttstadt 2008, pp. 189–91; Pekesen 2012, pp. 193–202; for France (as one aspect) see Cohen 1992, pp. 108–12; Kingston 1991, pp. 60–86.

97 Maderegger 1973, pp. 121–4, 129–51 (on Austria); Birnbaum 1992, pp. 179, 190 (on France).

98 Melzer 1997, pp. 22–37 (on Poland); Horváth 2008, pp. 129–32 (on Hungary).

99 Birnbaum 1992, p. 87; Kaspi 1997 (p. 107) gives even higher numbers.

100 Dallin 1998, pp. 209–10 (Odessa); Prusin 2007, p. 7 (Kiev).

101 Interview with Adam Grolsch in Johnson and Reuband 2005, p. 232.

102 Dieckmann 2005, pp. 252–4.

103 See *We Survived*, vols 2 and 3 (with a total of ninety-seven survivors' accounts).

for Jews in the Soviet lands, unlike in some other countries. This hostility is illuminated by the fact that the (very low) survival chances of Soviet Jews in German camps for Soviet POWs were at least as high as they were among civilians in the German-occupied Soviet territories.[104] Yet also in German-occupied Poland, reports about denunciations had a "threatening dimension." In Hungary there were reportedly tens of thousands of denunciations; and allegedly even millions, against all sorts of groups, in France.[105]

Across all countries, from Lithuania to France, janitors in particular seem to have been particularly prone to denouncing Jews in hiding; some of them did so almost proudly.[106] Scholars emphasize envy (for example, of apartments or furniture) as one driving force.[107] From the perspective of the state, denunciation may be the "possibility to give room for [social] participation intentionally without putting the state monopoly of violence in question."[108] From another perspective, denunciation – especially under Nazi German rule – can be regarded as a form of violence in itself. Although perhaps less harsh than outright murder, it was still often lethal. The experiences of Polish-Jewish child survivors, especially in rural Poland, show that they were less often immediately reported to the police or German authorities than they were verbally abused or the subjects of malicious gossip. What endangered their existence were rumors and irresponsible talk.[109] As Stephanie Abke has demonstrated for the German rural area of Stade, such practices served to negotiate local relations of power, ensure conformity to role expectations and reproduce imagined systems of order and values. In order to shape local opinion, this aggressive gossip needed to be widespread,[110] and this made it a deadly threat for Jews after 1941 since it often set the police apparatus into motion. Even when it didn't, Jews (and others in hiding) often felt compelled to flee.

The impact of publicly expressed sympathy for violence against Jews was less immediate than that of gossip, but equally grave in its

[104] See the data on survival rates in Chapters 9 and 15.

[105] Gerlach and Aly 2002, p. 133 (Hungary); Abke 2003, p. 11 (France); quote: Madajczyk 1994, p. 146 ("bedrohliche Dimension").

[106] Pryce-Jones 1991, pp. 38–41 (but see Moore 2010, pp. 113–14 with a more positive assessment); Zabarko 2005, pp. 190–1, 213–14, Prusin 2007, p. 7, and Grossman and Ehrenburg 1994, p. 50 (Kiev); ibid., pp. 629–31 (Kaunas); Mallmann *et al.* 2003, p. 89 (Latvia).

[107] Pryce-Jones 1991, pp. 38–41.

[108] Reemtsma 2008, p. 180.

[109] Based on the accounts in Hochberg-Mariańska 1996.

[110] Abke 2003, pp. 16, 19–20, 118, 147, 334–42, 362. Like Abke, I think that a clear delineation between denunciation and the spreading of rumors makes little sense.

consequences since it helped create a hostile atmosphere in which Jews did not know where to turn for safety. In several places in Lithuania, Jews seeking refuge in the summer of 1941 had to return to their homes because the population refused to help or to tolerate them, and even killed some of them.[111] In several countries, crowds cheered the torture or execution of Jews or scorned the victims.[112] Asher Cohen has called the deportations from Hungary in 1944 a "widespread social phenomenon in which many Hungarians took part, while others looked on and failed to react."[113]

Growing hostility against Jews after the war

The fact that observers in several countries noted an increase in anti-Jewish attitudes following liberation from German or Axis regimes indicates once again the local roots of hatred. Across the board, this is to be explained in terms of segments of the non-Jewish population defending the jobs and social positions, or the dwellings and possessions, they had acquired by replacing Jews.[114] The best-known case is Poland, where non-Jews had taken up the "social space" of Jews and refused to give up their newly won positions to returning survivors. The rise in hostility went far beyond the emblematic July 1946 pogrom in Kielce.[115] Some 600–3,000 Polish Jews were killed in riots and small-scale attacks (the motivations for which were often, but not always, robbery as, for example, when taking place on trains) between 1944 and 1947.[116] Already in the second half of 1943, after the vast majority of Polish Jewry had been murdered in German annihilation camps, there was a lively debate in the Polish underground press over who should own former Jewish property in the future. The fear was raised that many Jews might have survived and would return to reclaim their belongings or jobs. Members of the Polish underground emphasized in August 1943 that Polish non-Jews should be considered to have irreversibly replaced Jews in urban places.[117] Most

111 Levinson 2006, pp. 100, 104, 114.

112 Diary of Dr Elena Buivydaite-Kutorgiene, June 25, 1941, in Grossman and Ehrenburg 1994, pp. 432–3 (Kaunas, Lithuania); see the memories of *Lajčo* Klajn in *We Survived*, vol. 3, p. 325 (Kápolnásuyék, Hungary, October 1944); Fleischer 1986, p. 366 (Corfu, Greece, June 1944).

113 Cohen 1987, p. 183.

114 Ther 2011 (p. 166) emphasizes this point with reference to pogroms in Kielce, Kraków and Bratislava.

115 Gross 2006, esp. pp. 39–40 (quote), 47.

116 1,500–3,000, according to Israeli historians, 600–2,000 according to Polish scholars: Kosmala 2001, p. 313, see also pp. 314–18; Paulsson 1998, p. 35 (1,300 deaths 1945–47).

117 Friedrich 2006, pp. 240–3; Friedländer 2006, p. 562; see also Michlic 2006, pp. 153–64.

of the post-war pogroms occurred in central Poland (for example, in Kielce) where the number of Jewish returnees was relatively small; in fact, most returning survivors went to western Poland (e.g., Silesia and Łódż) where there were few assaults recorded.[118] Anti-Jewish propaganda and rumors, which were often voiced during the course of post-war pogroms, came in a mix of well-known motifs such as the high concentration of Jews in commerce and finance, the claim that Jewish returnees (who were often in bad physical shape) without employment were parasites, the alleged bloodletting of Polish children by Jewish doctors, and also the linkage of anti-Jewish inclinations to anti-German and anti-Ukrainian (or, in Ukraine, anti-Polish and anti-Russian) sentiments.[119] The fact that many Poles rejected the new communist rule after 1944 and linked Jews to communism played an important role, as did propaganda about alleged ritual murders carried out by Jews.[120] But Jews seem to have been attacked in other places and for other reasons, and in numbers that were perhaps even greater, than those who were non-Jewish leftist victims of right-wing violence.[121] Tens of thousands of Jews fled Poland, many to camps in Germany where they did not fear being murdered as they did in Poland in 1946–47.[122] Many non-Jews who had helped rescue Jews kept it a secret out of fear of revenge and robbery.[123]

In Romania, resentment against Jews was on the increase after 1944 as Jews regained their full civil rights; their property, it seemed, was about to be returned to them and the political left (with which Jews were associated) dominated the government. Rumor had it that many alien Jews disloyal to Romania had entered the country; Jews were judged to be impeding the formation of a national middle class by their unfair practices. In reality, no political party, including the communists, dared to fully restitute Jewish property out of fear of alienating the public and, then, losing influence. This resembles the course of events in Hungary, Yugoslavia and Greece, where occupants of former Jewish properties (houses and businesses) founded their own association to defend their 'rights' and less than 10% of former Jewish-owned real estate was returned. Many Jews were not welcomed by their former neighbors in Greece, although the same would be true for exiles returning after the

[118] For Jewish population figures after 1944 see Dobroszycki 1994, pp. 69–90.
[119] Pramowska 2010, pp. 168–74; for Ukraine see Weiner 2001, p. 271.
[120] Tokarska-Bakir 2012, pp. 207–13.
[121] Kosmala 2001, p. 329; for the number of non-Jewish victims see Pramowska 2010, p. 159.
[122] Gross 2006, pp. 34–5, 42–3.
[123] Ibid., pp. ix-xii, 45.

Greek civil war decades later.[124] After March 1938, 60,000–70,000 apartments belonging to Jews were taken over by Austrian non-Jews; little wonder that 46% of Austrians resented the return of Jewish survivors in 1946.[125] But there were also cases in western Europe, as in Lens, France, where non-Jews managed to retain Jewish property for a long period of time, even though, as in Greece, there were no pogroms.[126] Even during the occupation, French custodians of former Jewish businesses that had been expropriated (a local study suggests that most of them, and most of the buyers of Jewish businesses, were neighbors in the same towns) also formed an association to defend their interests in case the real owners returned one day.[127] Even in Dnjepropetrovsk and Kiev, Ukraine, where there had been no pogroms in 1941 and social inequality was low (but the scarcity of goods extreme), riots broke out in 1945 when Jewish survivors returned from service in the military or from civilian evacuation and demanded their furniture, belongings and their dwellings back. An infusion of Nazi Jew-hatred and the accusation that Jews had not contributed to the military struggle against fascism were also influential.[128]

A brief survey of sympathy, help, protest and protection

Of course, far from all Europeans took action against Jews after or during World War II. Many did not hold anti-Jewish attitudes either. Societies were divided over the issue; no unified community of Jew-haters existed. For example, according to Michele Sarfatti there was a "clear-cut confrontation" among Italians about the treatment of Jews.[129] Before we turn to these divisions, an overview of the agents and forms of pro-Jewish action is in order.

German sources reported that pity for the fate of the Jews was expressed among populations from Latvia to Greece and Slovakia, where the deportation of Jews was unpopular and German violence against Jews and Soviets caused an increasing number of Slovaks to desert from the military.[130] In Lithuania, a petition to stop the massacres circulated (though the metropolitan archbishop refused to sign it).[131] In the Czech

124 Glass 2001, pp. 154–63; Braham 1994, pp. 1306–7; Goldstein 2004, p. 67; Gerlach 2010, p. 245; Spengler-Axiopoulos 2011.

125 Bailer-Galanda 2002, p. 886.

126 Mariot and Zalc 2010, pp. 225–6.

127 Pryce-Jones 1991, p. 32; for the area of Lens see Mariot and Zalc 2010, pp. 138, 144.

128 Lower 2005, p. 207; Weiner 2001, pp. 191–4, 376–7.

129 Sarfatti 2006, p. 209.

130 SS- und Polizeistandortführer Libau, January 3, 1942, in Klee *et al.* 1988, p. 129; reports of Italian Consul General in Salonica, Zamboni, October 22, 1942, February 20 and 28, 1943, in Carpi 1999, pp. 126–7, 130, 137; Mann 2005, p. 432.

131 Levinson 2006, p. 235.

lands there were short-lived manifestations of solidarity with Jews after they were forcibly marked with a yellow star in September 1941; the same was true in Belgium and France in June 1942.[132]

Sometimes, though not always, such sympathy was driven by the fear that the non-Jewish majority was next in line.[133] In August 1944, people deported from the area of Pskov, Russia, to forced labor in Germany, cried when compelled to enter a bathhouse because they feared being gassed. Similarly, in the spring of 1942 a rumor that unproductive people would be sorted out and gassed to death (a truly remarkable rumor at this early point in time) spread panic among the passengers, and especially the children, of a train carrying forced laborers from northern Russia upon its arrival in Danzig. It seems that this was not the only case.[134] After Jews and the disabled had been killed in the Crimea, there were rumors in March 1942 that Slavic civilians over fifty years old would be shot and soap made out of them.[135] In the Polish underground press, considerations of this kind surfaced in the form of an accusation: Polish police and labor office employees were now blamed for hunting non-Jewish Poles, just as they had earlier hunted for Jews.[136]

In Bulgaria, interventions by politicians and other elites (also in parliament), as well as public demonstrations in protest against the planned deportation of Bulgarian Jews (some of whom had already been detained) in March 1943, moved the government to withdraw its consent to the German initiative. Close to 50,000 Jews were saved. However, there was no such movement for solidarity with the Jews in Bulgarian-occupied Macedonia and Thrace, so virtually all of the Jews in these places were deported and murdered weeks later.[137] Apparently, these Jews had less influential advocates, and thus attracted less sympathy in Sofia. And when the Tsar ordered two months later that the Jews of Sofia be concentrated in the countryside, neither a demonstration in front of his palace nor a written appeal presented by sixty-three emissaries were successful in getting him to rescind the order.[138] In neighboring Greece at about the same time – that

132 Milotova 1996, p. 171; Rozenblum 2003, p. 32; Adler 1993, pp. 180–1.

133 Dallin 1998, p. 210 (Odessa); Hershkovitz 2001, p. 310 (Dutch underground newspaper *Het parool*, July 1942); Sebag 1991, p. 245 (communist underground newspaper on forced labor in Tunisia, December 1942).

134 Letters by Sofia I. and Antonija A. (from the early 2000s) in Schwarze 2005, pp. 30, 58; see Vegesack 1965, p. 94.

135 Oldenburg 2004, p. 88. The claim that soap was made from the bodies of murdered Jews was based on anti-Nazi propaganda, but never proven. A similar anti-German propaganda theme, without reference to Jews, existed already in World War I.

136 Friedrich 2006, p. 215.

137 Steur 1997, pp. 100–11.

138 Miller 1975, p. 104; Hoppe 1979, p. 139; Chary 1972, pp. 142–52. This deportation intensified anti-Jewish persecution and should not be seen as merely having served to protect them from the Germans.

is, in March and August of 1943 – leftists led large and sometimes violent demonstrations against deportations of forced laborers to Germany; the simultaneous deportation of Jews was not the focus of the demonstrators (although the Communist Party in Athens called for sympathy with Jews as innocent victims of fascism, described their racist persecution as "absurd," and offered to hide Jewish children and welcome young men as partisans).[139] A March 1943 appeal by Greek cultural, religious, professional and business leaders to Prime Minister Logothetopoulos – in protest against the persecution (and impending deportation) of the Jews – was to no avail, and within two weeks Logothetopoulos was forced to resign, although he did send the protest letters to the German plenipotentiary, Altenburg.[140] Sermons in Greek Orthodox churches to raise public awareness, lessons to school children, and an appeal by an association of disabled veterans and civilian victims of war, did not help either.[141] In France, the German military commander reported that protests from among all strata of the population (including the high clergy, politicians and even a general) against arrests and the deportation of Jews grew in waves from early 1942, culminating in August and September. They are reputed to have contributed to the Vichy government's (and the police cadres') withdrawal of most their support.[142] After that, the German SS and police refrained from pressing the issue strongly.

The success of several protests was based on the involvement of civil society: in Romania in September 1942 against planned mass deportations of Jews from the country's core territory to Germany, in Slovakia around the same time against the deportation of the last quarter of the Jewish population (especially elites and forced workers), and in Hungary in June and July 1944 against a spread of the deportations to the capital, Budapest, and against the members of the forced labor service. But, as in Bulgaria, these successes depended mainly on the political influence of elites.[143] Whether in Romania, Slovakia or Hungary, these elites were responding to foreign pressure (among other motives). This, and the fact that large parts of the Jewish population had already been deported and murdered, indicates that this late-emerging opposition to the persecution of Jews was not a principled one. But if manifestations of opposition

139 Loulos 1999, p. 149; proclamation by the communist organization of Athens, fall 1943, in Clogg 2002a, p. 107.

140 Printed in Clogg 2002a, pp. 104–6; see also Bowman 2006, pp. 77–8; Rozen 2005, p. 127.

141 Yacoel 2002, p. 105.

142 See Thalmann 1999, p. 73; Cohen 1987, pp. 176–8; Adler 1993, pp. 181–3; Kasten 1993, pp. 99–101. For elites see Kaspi 1997, pp. 241–4.

143 For Romania see Ioanid 2000, pp. 228–9, 242–8; Baum 2011, pp. 546–7. A protest in Romania in January 1942 was unsuccessful: Solonari 2010, p. 231. For Bulgaria see Chary 1972, pp. 37, 90, 95–100.

were to be successful, then it was generally of little use for non-state actors to address German authorities; one had to put pressure on one's own government.

While the events in Bulgaria, Romania, Hungary and Slovakia centered around political influence with the national governments, the rescue of almost all of the Danish Jews was based on broad popular action. From the beginning of the German occupation, the Danish government had consistently rejected all anti-Jewish measures and declared them politically unacceptable to both it and to the Danish people. But by late August 1943 the Danish cabinet ceased to be a factor since it had by then stepped down in protest at German repression against increasingly frequent acts of protest and sabotage against the occupiers. When, shortly afterwards, the German occupation forces moved to detain and then deport the Jews, thousands of Danes cooperated in a swiftly improvised collective action to warn and hide Jews and then ship them to Sweden. Organizations of almost every profession – jurists, lawyers, police officers, teachers, engineers and government officials – as well as the Supreme Court, various labor unions and the Union of Danish Youth voiced their protests. Saving the lives of Jews became a symbol for national freedom; their flight was facilitated by German toleration that was in turn a response to Danish opposition (see Chapter 11).[144] The explicit political will of the Danish government to protect the nations' Jewish minority, in addition to the efforts of individuals, together with the Danish Red Cross, led to the fact that only 474 Jews were detained and deported to Theresienstadt – where they were interned under preferential conditions, supplied with food parcels through the Red Cross, and never deported onwards. Some 416 of these 474 survived. Other Danes in German concentration camps also received relatively favorable treatment; 90% survived.[145]

This resembled events in Norway. When a large number of Norwegian Jews were arrested, the German Security Police reported growing dissent among the local population (including even parts of the fascist Nasjonal Samling) and massive protests from the Christian churches (as well as other elites and professional associations); taken together, this widespread opposition represented the "greatest commotion since [the start of] the occupation period."[146] As in Denmark, a spontaneous wave of protest among ordinary Norwegians took the form of hiding Jews and helping them across the Swedish border. Although just as improvised

[144] Petrow 1974, pp. 198–227; Yahil 1983, pp. 233–82.

[145] Petrow 1974, pp. 307–13; Schulze 2007, pp. 61–72; Yahil 1983, pp. 287–8, 292, 372.

[146] BdS Oslo, "Meldungen aus Norwegen," November 14 and December 15, 1942, in Larsen 2008, pp. 875, 879–80 (quote), 941; see also Abrahamsen 1991, pp. 76–8, 104–5, 132, 142.

as the Danish escape operation (although it used routes that thousands of non-Jews had used before), it was less extensive – the 'largest' organization helping Jews to flee operated just two trucks[147] – and, unlike in Denmark, it faced many fellow citizens as persecutors, including police officers, a hundred taxi drivers and other non-functionaries who helped during the deportations.[148] This explains the smaller success rate: about 1,000 people, or 50% of the Jews, were rescued compared to the 6,000, or 90%, in Denmark (who had an overall survival rate of 99%).

In Norway, the fate of the Jews caused the greatest upheaval during the occupation. In many other countries it was different. This is illustrated by the anti-German strikes in the Netherlands. In February 1941, workers went on strike in reaction to anti-Jewish policies and the erection of a ghetto in Amsterdam; in April and May 1943 they went on strike in protest against conscription for forced labor in Germany; and in the fall of 1944, strikes were in support of the Allied advance. Luxembourgers went on strike in early September 1941 – at the same time as Jews were being marked with the yellow star – in protest against compulsory service in the German military.[149]

The existence of large rescue organizations – Jewish and non-Jewish – increased the chances for comparatively large groups of Jews to survive. In early 1944, before the Polish nationalist uprising, it is estimated that among 17,000 Jews hidden in Warsaw half were supported by the Jewish National Committee, the Polish Council to Help Jews (Zegota), the leftist Bund, and other political parties. The position of those living underground who were not covered by such organizations, or living in regions where they did not operate, was more difficult.[150] Aid organizations in France rescued many Jews; the Jewish Colonization Association, HICEM, helped 24,000 Jews to emigrate from France between the fall of 1941 and 1943.[151] The fact that there were no large and experienced organizations to support Jews in hiding until 1942 (and a weak political left) has been cited as one reason why so few Jews went underground and survived in the Netherlands as compared to Belgium and France. From 1943, underground organizations provided aid for the Dutch Jews.[152]

The social make-up of rescuers and helpers is less clear than that of persecutors. In France and Belgium, help has been attributed, aside from Jewish resistance, chiefly to political leftists as well as to nationalists and

[147] Abrahamsen 1991, pp. 15–21, 137; Lorenz 2007, pp. 217, 220.
[148] Hoffmann 2001, p. 270; Lorenz 2007, pp. 217, 221.
[149] Wielenga 2009, p. 259; Quadflieg 2009, pp. 176, 179.
[150] Paulsson 1998, pp. 27–8; Steinbacher 2000, pp. 307–8 (East Upper Silesia).
[151] Thalmann 1999, p. 267.
[152] Moore 2003, pp. 298, 302; Moore 2001, pp. 282, 285; Flim 2001, p. 297.

devout Christians.[153] The general picture beyond these countries is similar in political terms but unclear regarding social groups. In a sea of fierce Jew-haters in Lithuania, at least 2,500 people, among which were many from the urban intelligentsia, gave aid to Jews.[154] The image of Italy as a nation of Jew-helpers is under debate; Renzo de Felice argues that Jews found shelter and hospitality especially among rural dwellers.[155]

The German authorities threatened eastern Europeans who aided Jews with the death penalty.[156] A debate is ongoing as to how many executions of helpers were actually carried out.[157] The risk to non-Jews lending support to Jews seems to have been smaller in central and western Europe. In Italy, such help was not outlawed.[158]

Between anti-Jewish zeal, protest and protection: Christian churches and guerrilla fighters

The Christian churches are – beyond religious interests – of special importance for the study of social behavior during the persecution of Jews and others. When labor unions, political parties and associations had been dissolved, and the press intimidated by censorship, the Christian churches remained as one of few organized structures. This was all the more important at "a time when the entire country was becoming increasingly socially fragmented," as Bob Moore observed of the Netherlands[159] but was a situation which applied to all of the other societies involved as well.

However, the churches turned out to be fragmented, too. (This also applies to the German churches, at least in theological terms.[160]) To begin with, there was no common international position. The Vatican, not to mention the possibility of an international ecumenical movement, failed to clearly and officially condemn (or condone) the persecution and destruction of Jews, or any other groups for that matter. This left Christians on their own, but, in most countries, no church, whether

153 Maxwell 1998, p. 18.
154 Levinson 2006, pp. 273, 276.
155 Knox 2007, pp. 53–92; de Felice 1995, pp. xix-xx.
156 See General Government decree, October 15, 1941, in Berenstein 1961, pp. 128–9; see also Chodakiewicz 2004, pp. 151–2. For Norway see Moore 2010, pp. 77, 80.
157 Weiner 2001 (p. 282) sees a radical practice in Ukraine, Młynarczyk 2007 (pp. 311, 317) in Poland. See also Seidel 2006, p. 351. Paulsson 2002 (p. 129) calculates that the Germans executed 'only' 700 of 160,000 helpers of Jews in Poland (0.5%).
158 See Königseder 1996 (p. 200) for Austria; Hilberg 1992a (pp. 232, 336 note 50) and Houwink ten Cate 1999 (pp. 105, 123) for the Netherlands; Longhi 2010, p. 97.
159 Moore 2001, p. 279.
160 This is very obvious in Hermle and Thierfelder 2008.

Catholic, Lutheran or Orthodox, officially took a stance on the persecution of Jews.[161] Christians, including those at the highest levels of Church hierarchies, were divided on the issue, which resulted in a great variety of action and prevented any canonical agreement. To a degree, not to take a stance reflected Christian political opportunism, which served the self-protection of the Church as an institution (just as for other individuals and groups self-protection proved more important than the rescuing Jews, or others). Churches were not effective as political organizations, but some were as charities. In Lithuania, for example, such disagreements resulted in the metropolitan archbishop, Juozapas Skvireckis, and others, supporting the mass murder of Jews in 1941; while 143 Lithuanian priests of various denominations and ethnicities offered Jews safe havens or encouraged others to do so during the war.[162] Thus, the churches and their active membership mirrored the deep disunity in society as a whole.

By far the strongest measures that churches took concerned the protection of people who had converted from Judaism to Christianity.[163] But even here there was no complete agreement. As Jews tried – by conversion – to escape the acute threat of deportation or death, several church organizations tried to bar their way into their communities by insisting that such conversions had to be an act of true faith and, thus, the result of a longer process.[164] This insistence led to the death of many Jews who found themselves unable to convert. The Slovak churches, especially those of non-Catholic denominations, and the exarch of Bulgaria's Orthodox Church, set a different example.[165]

In many countries, strong anti-Jewish propaganda came from the churches. This included Croatia in the 1930s, where Catholics were very influential within the radical Ustasha movement; and Bosnia, where Muslim clerics also joined in the chorus.[166] As in many countries, Catholic anti-Judaism in Switzerland, Poland and Italy was linked to strong anti-socialist tendencies and the rejection of modern society; it was also influenced by racist notions.[167] Church representatives, far from being

161 Moore 2001, p. 281 (Netherlands). For Switzerland see Altermatt 1998, pp. 480–1.

162 Levinson 2006, pp. 231–41, 273.

163 See *The Power of Civil Society* (Bulgaria); Herczl 1993 (Hungary); Adler 1993, pp. 177–8.

164 For Hungary see Gerlach and Aly 2002, p. 313; for Archbishop Alojzije Stepinac of Zagreb, who later changed his position in favor of conversions, see Gitman 2011, pp. 93–126 (although her account is fairly uncritical); Pavlowitch 2008, pp. 35–6, 178–9.

165 See the numbers in Hradská 1996, p. 83; Miller 1975, pp. 96, 104; for Greece see Safrian 1997, p. 270.

166 Gitman 2011, pp. 12–13, 18–19.

167 Ries 1998, pp. 49, 51; Altermatt 1998, p. 485. For Polish Catholics see Michlic 2006, pp. 88, 98–9; for German Christians see Niewyk 1980, pp. 55–61; for Italian Catholicism see Bernardini 1989, pp. 219–20, 223.

traditionalist, often interwove Christian anti-Judaism with economic, cultural, xenophobic and anti-communist or anti-liberal arguments against Jews, even if they rejected explicitly racist statements. The Catholic press in northeastern Poland (a region notorious for the pogrom in Jedwabne) spread many anti-Jewish stereotypes linked to a perceived decay of culture and of Christian values, economic issues and an alleged threat to the nation. How active the Catholic clergy was in inciting pogroms in northeastern Poland is contested, but the ratio of priests who were hiding Jewish children was lower here than elsewhere in Poland.[168] In a broader sense, Catholic intellectuals formed a strong current within right-wing radicalism in inter-war Europe, and anti-Jewish sentiments were a part of this.[169] Radical Christian propaganda against Jews continued even during the mass murders, more so in Volyn, western Ukraine, than in neighboring eastern Galicia. Still, some priests in Volyn were among the most active, relatively speaking, of the few who tried to rescue Jews, and the small Baptist minority in the region managed to save several hundred Jews.[170] As one of the most radical figures at the other extreme, Father András Kun headed an Arrow Cross death squad kidnapping and murdering Jews in Budapest in the winter of 1944–45, and gave the order for executions with the words "In the name of God – fire!"[171]

Most interventions on behalf of Jews remained unofficial and hidden from the public. In Slovakia, interventions by the Papal Nuncio, and pressure from the national Catholic episcopate, contributed strongly to the stopping of deportations by the summer of 1942.[172] Similarly, the threats of Hungarian church leaders to issue a pastoral letter, together with a Papal intervention, helped end the deportations from Hungary in early July 1944.[173] In Bulgaria the positions of church leaders were somewhat divided, at least until the general question of the deportation of all Jews was discussed in March 1943.[174] Strong protests by Greek bishops on behalf of Jews could not prevent the deportations from Salonica, but at least they did prevent those from the small island of Zante.[175] Not untypical was the change in attitude of the mainstream of the Catholic Church in France from accepting the first laws against Jews to different degrees of criticism, some of which may have moved Prime Minister

[168] Libionka 2004, pp. 15–35.
[169] Conway 1997, pp. 8–9, 52–3, 56–7, 82–4.
[170] Spector 1990a, pp. 243–4, 248–9.
[171] Quoted in Braham 1994, p. 976.
[172] Memo from Luther to von Ribbentrop, August 21, 1942, PA AA R 100857, p. 119.
[173] Gerlach and Aly 2002, pp. 325, 330–2, 339–40.
[174] See *The Power of Civil Society*.
[175] Rozen 2005, pp. 127–8.

Laval to rescind a 1943 law stripping Jews naturalized after 1927 of their citizenship.[176]

Christian opinions about violence against groups *other* than Jews were often equally divided. In Croatia, some Catholic Church leaders, even in 1943, justified the persecution of Serbs that had cost hundreds of thousands of lives over the previous two years.[177] By contrast, many imams and Islamic cultural organizations in Bosnia and Herzegovina helped save Muslim Roma from deportation through their consistent interventions (just as Muslim Tatars saved 30% of Roma in the German-occupied Crimea from being shot).[178] The Catholic Church in the Croatian state organized 100,000–240,000 conversions, especially of the understandably frightened Orthodox Christians (who were persecuted as Serbs); but also of several thousand Jews.[179]

Traditionally, European Jews had found support among the political left. Many guerrilla fighters were leftists, and most partisans waged their insurgencies out of opposition to the Germans or other regimes that persecuted Jews. Guerrilla groups potentially provided a refuge for Jews. On the other hand, partisans were from diverse social backgrounds, and, therefore, the question of how guerrillas responded is interesting. Again, events in the Ukrainian region of Volyn may be representative of much of the experience of Jewish Soviet underground fighters, for there were anti-Jewish tendencies among pro-Soviet partisans. Some units did not accept Jews and criticized them for being passive, unarmed or for having surrendered their wealth to the Germans; in other cases they were accepted but were more severely punished in case of wrongdoing than other members. Pro-Soviet partisans killed some Jews. The situation improved, however, in early 1943 when the partisan movement became stronger, was put under centralized control, and discipline tightened. But, this was too late for many of the Jews who fled in the fall of 1942.[180] In the same region, Ukrainian nationalist partisans, with few exceptions, hunted down Jews and killed thousands; the behavior of Polish nationalist guerrillas was more ambivalent, ranging from the murder of Jews to tolerating them (even as temporary allies in the fight against Ukrainian nationalists) to – rarely – accepting Jews as members of their units.[181]

176 Adler 1993, pp. 178–83; for varying positions within French Catholicism see p. 188.
177 Pavlowitch 2008, pp. 178–9.
178 Biondich 2002, pp. 36–9; see Fings 1992, pp. 30, 114–16; for the Crimea see Holler 2009, pp. 90–5.
179 Biondich 2005 does not, however, pay much attention to Jews.
180 Spector 1990a, pp. 282, 284, 288–91, 294, 302, 306, 317, 352–3; see Brakel 2009, pp. 364–5.
181 Spector 1990a, pp. 250–71; similarly for the area of Radom: Młynarczyk 2007, pp. 319–33.

Among pro-Soviet guerrillas in Lithuania there were few assaults against Jews, and some of these were punished. For Lithuanian Jewish partisans, the greater threats were Polish nationalist underground fighters and Lithuanian farmers. But some of the units that fled to neighboring Belarus were disarmed by pro-Soviet guerrillas, dissolved, and their members thereby endangered; whereas the Soviet partisan movement helped protect large groups of Jewish refugees.[182] The Belorussian partisans, who sometimes rejected Jews, cited, among other things, the fear of espionage – a fear that played on an old anti-Jewish stereotype. Many partisans in Belarus refused to admit that they were Jews.[183] Among Italian partisans, by contrast, there purportedly were no anti-Jewish attitudes.[184] None of the collected memoirs of Jewish survivors from Yugoslavia mentions either anti-Jewish attitudes among the leftist partisans or anybody having felt compelled to disguise his or her Jewish identity.[185] Yugoslav partisans had many Jews in their ranks and protected at least 5,000 others, helping many to escape to Italy, when fascism collapsed in the fall of 1943, or elsewhere.[186] When the Jews of Salonica were under the acute threat of deportation, Greek leftist partisans sent out emissaries calling on Jews to join them (and some did).[187] Right-wing insurgent groups or militias in Yugoslavia and Greece were less welcoming to Jews; Serb Chetniks were very dangerous. This shows that partisans, too, were divided in their responses to the plight of Jews, which was a side-show to their primary focus.

Societies shaped by inner conflict

As described in Chapter 11, severe divisions, sometimes even civil war, characterized European societies during World War II. One of the areas of contention was the treatment of Jews, as we can see by looking at the churches. We can also see this in the workings of governments: civil servants by no means merely implemented government policies. Even police officers acted in radically different ways in respect to Jews.[188] However, in no society (including Germany) was killing or saving Jews the main

[182] Dieckmann 2011, pp. 1464, 1469–70, 1482–3; Levin 1985, pp. 114, 131, 180–6, 243–5.

[183] Gerlach 1999, p. 747; Linkow 1956, pp. 462–6.

[184] Longhi 2010, p. 120.

[185] *We Survived*, vols 2 and 3; a possible exception can be found in vol. 3, pp. 23–4.

[186] Gitman 2011, pp. xvii, 160–8.

[187] Report by Italian Consul-General, March 20, 1943, in Carpi 1999, p. 140; Safrian 1997, p. 271.

[188] For Greek police officers see Loulos 1994, p. 408; see also Safrian 1997, p. 270. In Norway, some police officers warned Jews while others eagerly arrested them (Petrick 1998, p. 179). In Switzerland, many police officers at the borders let Jewish refugees

issue of conflict. The Danish Jews were fortunate and unusual in that their rescue became a symbol for national self-assertion.[189] During the occupation, the deportation of Jews in 1942 seemed to a large part of the Norwegian population to be the worst German crime, but this was no longer so after the war when the wartime persecution of Jews contradicted the fiction of a nation that had stood united against the Germans.[190] Just how divided the populace was is illustrated by the fact that in a 1947 opinion poll 32% of Norwegian men and 22% of women surveyed said that it was wrong for Norway to have accepted 600 displaced Jewish people.[191]

Evidence that there were deep disagreements over anti-Jewish policies, as well as indifference, can also be found in the only known contemporary opinion survey, which was conducted by the French Commissariat Général aux Questions Juives in the first four months of 1943.[192] The survey was not representative: it included few women or rural dwellers. Additionally, some respondents may have given answers that they thought were expected. Nevertheless, it served as a supposedly scientific basis for further anti-Jewish policies. Asked, "Do you like Jews?", 51.4% responded "no," 12.1% (including 23% of women) "yes" and 36.5% were indifferent. Workers had the lowest negative response rate (43.45%), and the highest income group polled was the most indifferent. Students (81.48%) and farmers (62.02%) showed the greatest dislike of Jews. But Vichy's anti-Jewish measures provoked more negative responses and less indifference: 51.2% of respondents supported them (as many as self-expressed Jew-haters), 30.1% (including 48% of the lowest income group) were opposed, and 17% expressed no opinion. Somewhat contradictorily, 66.32% approved of further measures, especially expulsions and the denial of civil rights. Asked to give their reasons, self-identified Jew-haters replied that Jews were exploiters, a cause of France's misfortunes, and unable to assimilate. Sympathizers stated that anti-Jewish measures were fascist and German-inspired, that Jews had good qualities, and that Jews were human beings – a reason that the indifferent also gave. Since those without a clear position also often stated

pass, against their orders; while some tortured, abused and robbed them – also against orders (Unabhängige Expertenkommission Schweiz 1999, pp. 108–32, 148–9).

189 Wagner 2001, p. 293.

190 Lorenz 2007, pp. 217–19, 222.

191 Figures are from Abrahamsen 1991, p. 153.

192 The following details are from Adler 1993, pp. 184–7. Of the 3,150 people surveyed, only 10% were women. 967 were blue-collar workers, 707 white-collar workers, 468 shopkeepers, 430 from the professions, 158 farmers and 81 students. They lived in nine towns in the former Vichy zone. See also Poznanski 1997, pp. 454–6; for a skeptical view see Poliakov 1953.

that there was no reason to persecute Jews, many of them were perhaps not so indifferent after all. I think that the results of this poll, conducted six months after the French administration had greatly reduced its support for deportations, encouraged the central French authorities to desist from further measures for fear that the arrest (or worse) of Jews would be rejected or even obstructed by many of its citizens.[193]

The deep discord among citizens over how to deal with Jews explains why in many countries stories of rescue and of persecution coexist, to the extent that there is a split in the historiography.[194] They can coexist without even attacking each other too much because one can find evidence for both sides.[195] Yet what seems to be lacking so far are analytical frameworks that integrate both phenomena. As societies were split concerning action toward Jews, entire countries are not useful units of analysis; similarly, judgmental types of account that try to construct national profiles of anti-Semitism are equally unhelpful.

This is not to say, of course, that responses were either black or white, in favor of persecution or of rescue. Large proportions of the population remained indifferent and passive with regard to the fate of Jews. For example, most French worried more about POWs in German hands, orphans, food, clothing, jobs and the danger of being shipped to Germany as forced laborers than they did about Jews.[196] However, inaction is hard to quantify and not easily explained. Even among helpers of children there were "darker and possibly less altruistic elements of rescue," as Bob Moore has pointed out – such as those who demanded more money for sheltering children than the actual cost incurred, tried to convert them, or saw a chance for adoption without administrative procedures.[197] In Denmark there were bitter recriminations against rescuers who had demanded money from, or even blackmailed, Jews on the run; and against wealthy Jews who had not donated funds to finance the escape of poor coreligionists.[198] Trying to count only those whose purely altruistic actions endangered their own lives, as the Israeli memorial authority Yad Vashem does, may lead to the painting of an erroneous picture of western Europe. Some 75% of all Jews in the Netherlands were killed, 40% in Belgium and 25% in France – and yet by January 2011

[193] For a March 1942 warning by the Commissariat that "Aryans become the accomplices of Jews," and that anti-Jewish measures needed to be "accepted by the masses," see Adler 1993, p. 180.

[194] As Longhi 2010 (pp. 39–40) observed for Italy.

[195] An example is Golczewski 1996.

[196] Zuccotti 1993, pp. 62, 144.

[197] Moore 2003, pp. 294 (quote), pp. 304–5. For adoptions in Poland see Dobroszycki 1994, pp. 16–17.

[198] Petrow 1974, pp. 223–5.

Yad Vashem had listed 5,108 Dutch "Righteous among the Nations," more than in France (3,331) and Belgium (1,584) combined.[199] The figures for survival rates show that Jews (including foreigners) in France must have found more help than they did in the Netherlands. But it is difficult to quantify. And it is true that some countries, or regions, provided a more receptive environment than others.

Concluding, European societies were divided over how to act toward Jews during World War II. Struggles between persecutors and rescuers, and between hatred and sympathy, reflect the complexity of these conflicts – as does the contradictory behavior and ambivalent motives of many non-Jews. However, when facing armed occupiers, or their own right-wing authoritarian regimes, it was much harder for civilians to make an impact in favor of Jews than it was to harm them.

[199] Griffioen and Zeller 2011, pp. 517, 543, 572.

14 Beyond legislation: Non-German policies of violence

In many countries, the persecution of Jews did not stop at legal measures. However, the intensity of anti-Jewish violence differed widely. Three countries conducted mass murders of Jews. In several waves (the worst of which was in 1942), about three-quarters of the 40,000 Jews in the state of Croatia were either massacred by their compatriots or, to a lesser extent, deported to German-run death camps. Most of the rest survived underground; a few thousand belonged to government-protected groups.[1] In 1941–42, largely, Romanians killed or let die at least 250,000 Jews,[2] primarily those deported from Bessarabia and Bukovina to Transnistria and local Soviet Jews from occupied Transnistria, but the Romanian government refused to surrender as many Jews from the Old Kingdom to Germany, and they survived the war. For some time, the Hungarian government refused to allow Jews to be deported to Germany until the German invasion in March 1944, when the Sztójay government cooperated closely in the deportation of more than 400,000 Jews to Germany, and the Arrow Cross regime handed over another 76,000. About 250,000 Jews from Greater Hungary survived, half inside the country in the Budapest ghettos and the forced labor service, and the other half in German camps. Hungarian authorities deported at least 16,000 Jews without Hungarian citizenship to the former Soviet territories of Galicia and Volyn in the summer of 1941, whereupon German and Hungarian forces soon shot them; more than 20,000 Jews may have died in the army's Labor Battalions between 1942 and 1943, and Arrow Cross squads killed many thousands in Budapest in late 1944.

Other governments which did not themselves organize the mass destruction of Jews did, however, acquiesce to it; some (like Slovakia)

[1] See Gitman 2011. In Zagreb, a Jewish community was allowed to continue charity work for the entire war (Freidenreich 1979, p. 196).

[2] See Ancel 2011 (pp. 555–6, 559) for even higher figures on killings.

even offered to deport their Jews to Germany, or (as was the case in Hungary and Bulgaria) sometimes urged Germany to deport Jews more quickly.[3] Non-German police or gendarmerie often made arrests. In this way, 80% of the Slovakian Jews were deported in 1942, and most of them killed, while the rest were kept in Slovakia as forced laborers – although many of these were killed in the wake of the Slovakian national uprising in August and September 1944. The fascist Norwegian government had about half of the country's approximately 2,000 Jewish inhabitants (all they could lay hands on) deported in 1942; the rest escaped to Sweden. Vichy France cooperated in the deportation of roughly 75,000 of its Jewish population of 300,000, surrendering primarily foreign Jews. Some 3,000–4,000 Jews (and 5,000–16,000 Spanish refugees) died in French internment camps, mostly from hunger.[4] Bulgaria rejected the deportation of about 50,000 Jews from its mainland but agreed to hand over more than 11,000 from its annexed territories in Thrace and Macedonia. Some 166 Jews perished during their two weeks of Bulgarian internment in Skopje prior to deportation.[5] Although Italy interned foreign Jews in 1940, and more than 500 Jews of the Cyrenaica region of Italian Libya died in Italian internment in 1942–43,[6] the country largely refused to surrender the Jewish inhabitants of its own territory and also of Italian-occupied areas in Greece, Yugoslavia, Albania, France and north Africa. After large parts of Italy were occupied by Germany in September 1943, some authorities and fascist organizations did cooperate locally in the arrest of Jews; more than 7,000 were then murdered by the Germans. Unlike Albania's administration, the authorities in Serbia, Greece and the Reich Protectorate of Bohemia and Moravia were too weak to prevent German forces from shooting or deporting their Jews. Finland largely rejected moves against their own small Jewish minority, but it handed over some foreign refugees and at least seventy-four Jews from among its Soviet POWs, to Germany. The Danish government refused to cooperate in the deportation of any local Jews, which contributed to the fact that 90% were able to escape to Sweden in 1943. Among the neutral countries it was Turkey which did the least to rescue its subjects living in the German sphere of influence (mostly in France), with the result of about 2,000 deaths.[7] These starkly different outcomes resulted from a

[3] For Slovakia see Longerich 1998a, pp. 491–2; Browning 1978, p. 94; for Hungary see Gerlach and Aly 2002, esp. pp. 257–60; for Bulgaria see Steur 1997, pp. 104–07; see also Chary 1972, pp. 80, 123–4; Safrian 1997, pp. 225–60.

[4] Eggers 2002, pp. 15, 208; Peschanski 2002, pp. 144, 146.

[5] Steur 1997, pp. 94–112, 217–18; Opfer 2005, p. 279.

[6] For Libya see Roumani 2008, pp. 31, 34–5; de Felice 1985, pp. 179–80.

[7] For Finland see Förster 2005, p. 96; for Turkey see Guttstadt 2008, pp. 298–407.

number of intertwined factors. I discuss some of the most important in this chapter.

Mass murder programs and zealous police forces

Although anti-Jewish attitudes were strong throughout Romania and popular violence had flared in different areas of the country, mass murder was concentrated in the regions bordering the Soviet Union and those that Romania occupied. Economic persecution was also most far-reaching there. In the summer of 1940, the USSR had forced Romania to cede Bessarabia and northern Bukovina, and the myth persisted that Jews had attacked Romanian soldiers as they hastily withdrew (though some Jews did celebrate the arrival of the Soviets and insulted Romanian troops). When Romania joined Germany in her invasion of the USSR in June 1941, Romanian authorities intended to 'punish' the Jews in Bukovina and Bessarabia for their alleged behavior of the year before.[8]

This resulted in massacres– in some areas from the first days of the invasion – by the military, police and gendarmerie, but also by crowds or gangs of civilians acting independently or with the armed forces. The German Einsatzgruppe D also shot several thousand Jews in the region. During the summer, the Romanian administration concentrated the Jews from small towns, and in the fall the Jews from Bessarabia and the majority of those from northern Bukovina – as well as Southern Bukovina – were deported to Transnistria, the Moldovan-Ukrainian territory conquered by Romanian troops. Many, especially among the Bessarabian Jews, succumbed on the march to murder, robbery or the unbearable conditions. Given the insufficient housing, food and heating, many of those deported – according to one estimate 30–50% – died in the winter of 1941–42.[9] Romanian forces and ethnic German militias murdered tens of thousands. Starvation and killing continued at a lower intensity throughout much of 1942 and 1943. By the end of the war, 75% of the Bessarabian and 17% of the Bukovinian Jews deported were no longer alive. About 45,000–60,000 Jews from Bessarabia and Bukovina were murdered in the summer of 1941 and 120,000–150,000 were deported – of which 90,000 died and 36,000–38,000 survived; another 15,000 among those allowed to stay in Chernovtsy, mostly to keep the economy running, survived.[10]

[8] For Jews insulting Romanian troops see Ancel 2011, pp. 74–5.

[9] Deletant 2006, pp. 130, 186.

[10] See Geissbühler 2013, p. 150; Arad 2009, pp. 345–6; Hilberg 1994a, pp. 824–40; Ioanid 2001, pp. 91, 95–6. See also Deletant 2006, pp. 145, 314–15 notes 4 and 5; Ahonen *et al.* 2008, pp. 58–9; Ioanid 1997, pp. 96–8.

In addition, most of the local Jews from Transnistria who had not been able to evacuate prior to the arrival of Romanian troops suffered the same conditions. Of the up to 90,000 Jews remaining in Odessa, thousands were shot by a German Einsatzkommando on October 16. In the days after October 22, 1941, Romanian troops massacred about 25,000 Jews (and non-Jews) in revenge for a bomb attack on high-ranking Romanian officers, and in the following weeks up to 30,000 were deported to Bogdanovka and other places in the countryside near Golta, where many Jews from other towns in Transnistria were also brought, and most were shot between December 1941 and February 1942.[11] The Romanians had herded up to 30,000 Jews into a ghetto by early November, and between January 12 and February 23, 1942, they deported close to 20,000 – mainly women, children and elderly people– to Berezovka, where many died from want and typhus, and ethnic German Volksschutz militias shot the rest between the spring and the end of 1943. A small ghetto of artisans remained in Odessa. The death toll among Transnistrian Jews may have reached 160,000, while 10,000–12,000 survived.[12]

Some of the factors that led to this outcome have been identified: the link between anti-communist thinking and the Jews of the region; the desire among the leadership to "purify" and stabilize some regions by expelling the Jews; the free hand given to members of the executive forces and the population to plunder, torture and kill, and the willingness of many of them to do so; and the unwillingness to commit resources to Jews, who were regarded as inferior. However, the decision-making process for the massacres in the winter 1941–42, and in general, remains unclear. Even though high-ranking politicians expressed their will to kill masses of Jews, local circumstances still determined, in part, who was shot and who was not.[13]

From the spring of 1942 to the end of the year, minor deportations not only from Bukovina (over 4,000 people), but also from southern Romania, to Transnistria continued.[14] This encouraged the Germans to believe that Romania would consent to deporting the approximately 250,000 Jews that remained there to German camps. By end of July, Eichmann was

[11] For the murder and other deaths of Jews deported to Bogdanovka from Transnistria and elsewhere see Ancel 1997, pp. 107–20. For non-Jews killed in Odessa before and after October 22, see Dallin 1998, p. 74.

[12] For this paragraph see Litani 1967, pp. 137–45, 151–2; Arad 2009, pp. 241–8, 520. Other estimates range from 130,000 to 170,000 killed (Deletant 2006, p. 314 note 3).

[13] See Ancel 1997, pp. 108, 116–17 (Ion Antonescu's speech of December 16, 1941); see note by SS-Hauptsturmführer Richter, October 17, 1941, Nuremberg Document PS-3319. For the motivation in general see also Benyamin 1997, pp. 10–11; Shapiro 1997, pp. 140–2.

[14] Hausleitner 2001b, p. 18; Ioanid 2001, pp. 95–6; Hilberg 1994a, p. 849.

planning to start deportations to the district of Lublin from around September 10; by late September he arranged for trains with the German railways.[15] Antonescu said these deportations should begin in southern Transylvania.[16] But the Romanian government shelved their plans in mid-October. This decision was influenced by the protests of US Secretary of State Cordell Hull, the Papal Nuntius and the Swiss and Swedish embassies – but also by those of the Romanian King's mother and an archbishop, as well as the head of the National Liberal Party, Dinu Bratianu, who called for "immediately ending a persecution that throws us back for several centuries." Others argued that the deportations would make Romania look like Germany's vassal and that it would make the country appear to lack sovereignty.[17] The situation at the Eastern Front around Stalingrad may also have contributed to the change of mind.[18]

Except for Germany, Romania was the state that destroyed the most Jews in terms of absolute numbers, although in relative terms Croatia had the most lethal anti-Jewish policy. This led to the deaths of at least 75% of the state's 38,000 Jews[19] (and those of 300,000–400,000 others). Croat forces had already started killing the first Jews in May 1941 (before the German attack on the USSR) and the government began to confine Jews in camps in July. Murders reached their first peak in the summer. According to the accounts of historians, and the state's leader, Pavelić, most of the Jews were already dead in 1941.[20] However, statistical data suggest that 50% of those who perished in Croatia proper, 59% of the Jews in the Jasenovac camp and 75% of those killed in Bosnia and Herzegovina (which was part of the Independent State of Croatia), died in 1942.[21] This can be explained in part by deaths from hunger and cold and killings in the internment camps in the winter of 1941–42. In the summer of 1942, Croatian forces again stepped up their violence against Jews while reducing that against Serbs – as German representatives had advised – and the Ustashe assumed responsibility for the Interior

15 CdS (Eichmann) to Himmler, July 26, 1942, quoted in v. Rintelen to Luther, August 19, 1942, Nuremberg Document NG-3559; "Protokoll über die am 26. und 28. September [1942] abgehaltene Konferenz" in Ancel 1984, p. 419; for the German plans see ibid., pp. 381–420; Hilberg 1994a, pp. 845–50.
16 Memo from Luther to von Ribbentrop, August 21, 1942, PA AA R 100857, p. 125; see also Benyamin 2001, p. 148.
17 Ancel 1984, pp. 388, 398–9; Hausleitner 2001a, p. 402; Haas 1994, p. 89; Baum 2011, p. 536.
18 See Chapter 4, note 13.
19 Gitman 2011, p. xxiv.
20 Hilberg 1994a, pp. 758–61; Pavlowitch 2008, p. 32; Korb 2013, pp. 109, 202–4, 271–4, 278–92, 381–5.
21 Based on partial data from a 1964 census presented in Cvetković 2008, pp. 362–3; for Jasenovac see Mihovilović and Smreka 2006, pp. 218–19.

Ministry's camps where many Jews were still detained.[22] Some 4,927 Jews were deported to Auschwitz in August 1942, and Ustasha forces massacred the Jews they were able to capture in Bosnia, Herzegovina and Dalmatia after the Italians had handed over to them some control in certain areas in June 1942.[23] The Croatian extermination of Jews comprised several pushes – as well as local waves of consequent arrests – by a variety of actors, especially members of the politically radical Ustasha. Most of the Jews were then killed in camps. The persecution continued in this way until the end of the war, with at least 2,000 more Jews killed in 1945.[24]

Although Slovakian authorities did not pursue their own program of mass murder of Jews, they seem to have initiated the deportation of the majority of the nation's Jews to German-occupied Poland. From March to October 1942, 57,752 were deported on 38 trains to Lublin and on 19 trains to Auschwitz. According to an official count, about 22,000 people regarded as Jews – including 8,000 Christians – still existed in the country in March 1943. Because of the influence of the domestic Catholic Church and the Vatican, but also out of motives of domestic policy, Slovakia's leader, Tiso, saw fit to prevent further deportations from Slovakia. They were stopped altogether in October 1942, but the council of ministers had already decided on August 11 to defer removals until the end of the war. Attempts by the extreme right of the government party to have more Jews deported in 1943 failed, for the most part, and Tiso subsequently disempowered some rightist leaders.[25] During their suppression of the Slovakian national uprising, which started in late August 1944, the Germans made their own effort to get hold of these remaining Jews: they killed about 2,300 and deported a further 8,800 (see Chapter 5).

The parallels in the turns toward either canceling deportations (by the Romanian government) or discontinuing them (by the Slovak regime) between August and October/November 1942 is remarkable. The reasons were similar. During the same months the French authorities also grew much more reluctant to assist with deportations, likewise influenced by protests that were in part public ones (see Chapter 4 and p. 357); and those in the Italian leadership who opposed deportations from Italian-occupied territories won out over anti-Jewish radicals and persuaded a wavering Mussolini to their way of thinking. Aside from

22 Pavlowitch 2008, pp. 135–6; Ther 2011, p. 146; for Jasenovac see Goldstein 2006, p. 120.
23 Hilberg 1994a, pp. 761, 764; Burgwyn 2005, p. 164.
24 Cvetković 2008, p. 362.
25 Hradská 1996, pp. 82–8; Tönsmeyer 2003, pp. 150–1.

humanitarian motives, which played a role for some military officers, this opposition was also intended to demonstrate Italy's strength in occupied Yugoslavia and its reliability to the Serbian Cetniks, who sided with Rome.[26] In all of these cases, the spread of the news that the Germans had started to systematically exterminate Jews – and negative developments in the Axis's military situation – formed the background to these decisions.

In countries under German occupation, the German persecutors usually depended on autochthonous administrative and executive forces. Local knowledge was necessary, especially for arrests (see Chapter 6). However, the actions of administrators and police personnel could vary greatly from country to country, within a nation, and also over time.

In many countries, the national police, working under Germany's orders, helped to detain Jews with almost no reservations. This was the case in the German-occupied Soviet territories where new police staff were selected according to their likely reliability and their anti-Soviet attitudes. Many of those in the western territories that had been recently annexed by the Soviet Union were peasants with traditional values seeking "economic improvement and social advancement." During the early months of the German invasion, irregulars served as German auxiliaries during the mass shootings.[27] The number of Jews shot in 1941 by Lithuanian and Latvian squads under German command is not known.[28] Local administrations in the occupied Soviet territories registered Jews; some established ghettos and interned them.[29] Nevertheless, a large and expensive German police force was required.[30] In Norway, the Norwegian police handled all the arrests and detentions of Jews, as well as their transportation to German ships for deportation; 30% of the force and 60% of its officers (the highest proportion of all the professions) were members of the fascist Nasjonal Samling Party.[31] In the Netherlands, according to estimates, up to 90% of the police force participated eagerly in the arrests of Jews, although only a small minority

[26] See Knox 2007; Burgwyn 2005, pp. 164, 187, 189–95; Steinberg 1992, pp. 17, 81–116.

[27] Hilberg 1992a, p. 112 (for Ukraine); for the police staff see Prusin 2010, p. 171; Dean 2000, pp. 64–72.

[28] According to Mann 2005 (p. 283), the unit of Latvians led by Viktor Arajs – which was under the command of the German Security Police and SD – killed 26,000 Latvians (including 22,000 Jews). It was also involved in killings in Belarus.

[29] Pohl 2010, p. 55.

[30] In 1943 there were more than 26,000 German Order Police in the occupied Soviet territories under civilian (RMO) administration, costing over 212 million Reichsmark. See Bracht (RMI) to RMO, July 31, 1943, and further documents, BA R 2/12158, pp. 93, 124–33, 154.

[31] Abrahamsen 1991, pp. 76, 104–5, 117, 132; for the Norwegian bureaucracy see ibid., p. 78.

were fascists. Beginning in the spring of 1943, however, obstruction from the police became somewhat more common as local resistance – particularly against forced labor conscription – spread.[32]

Soviet auxiliaries were also used, under direct German command, in extermination and labor camps. Usually recruited from among desperate Soviet POWs, many of them underwent training in the SS camp at Trawniki near Lublin, in the General Government, before being deployed to Bełżec, Sobibór, Treblinka, Auschwitz-Birkenau and Majdanek. In these extermination centers, they formed the majority of the camp guards.[33] It is impossible to quantify how many people they, as distinct from Germans, killed. Their story underlines how much support for the persecution of Jews, and others, the Germans found among Soviet citizens. It also demonstrates how drastic the divisions were among Soviet citizens, since, of course, most Soviet POWs did not become SS auxiliaries and remained fiercely opposed to the Nazi regime.

Where the Germans could not rely on the national police apparatus and attempted to arrest Jews on their own, their success was usually limited because of a lack of personnel and information. In Italy, only 6,806 of about 40,000 Jews were apprehended after the German occupation in September 1943. As far as we know, 2,444 of these arrests were conducted by German SS and police alone, 1,951 by Italians alone, and 332 by joint German-Italian squads. Soldiers, *carabinieri*, police and even camp guards are mentioned among those who committed "acts of decency."[34] In France, the German Security Police was increasingly left to its own devices because after the first large internments and deportations of July and August 1942 – which were conducted entirely by French police (supported by right-wing youth groups and bus drivers) – public opinion shifted, leading the Vichy government to withdraw much of its support. In turn, the readiness of French gendarmes and police to participate dropped sharply; only in some regions did it remain intact.[35]

Although Belgian laws prohibited it, and although they were under orders from Brussels not to obey German commands, some elements of the administration and police in Antwerp assisted in the German effort by arresting Jews in the fall of 1942.[36] Still, local police arrested only 4,300 Jews (17% of all those detained in Belgium). This contrasts

32 Hirschfeld 1984, pp. 112–16.
33 See Black 2004.
34 Longhi 2010, p. 85 note 56; Steur 1997, pp. 116, 120, 122; quoted from Rechnitz Koffler and Koffler 1995, p. xxviii.
35 Adler 1993, pp. 172, 181–2; Zuccotti 1993, pp. 145–56; Kasten 1993, pp. 97–101, 109, 125–58; Kasten 2000, pp. 113–18; Pryce-Jones 1991, pp. 35–6.
36 Brachfeld 2005, pp. 41–58; Meinen 2008, p. 56.

with 24% in the Netherlands and 61% in France.[37] However, these figures tell only part of the story. Dutch police contributed indirectly, but significantly, to a very high proportion of arrests; whereas in France a much higher percentage of Jews could escape than in the Netherlands (75% versus 25% at best), a difference explained in part by the obvious obstructionism of large segments of the French police and civil service.

Still, non-German police, especially – but not only – in western Europe, cooperated more in arresting Jews, especially at the beginning of the process in 1942, than they did in sending people to compulsory labor in their homelands or in Germany in the spring and summer of 1943. This is true for Norway (where the Germans arrested 470 obstructive police officers), the Netherlands and for France.[38] In France, and to a lesser degree in the Netherlands, there was a learning process that also made police officers more reluctant to search for Jews. The fact that non-German police and gendarmerie became less reliable over time may also be explained, in part, by the fact that their numbers were greatly expanded (as were the numbers serving in many other administrations) during the period of war and occupation: the new personnel may have been less dependable from a German point of view.[39]

When loyal police forces weren't sufficient, it remained an option to permit, or encourage, the emergence of local paramilitaries. Unable to control and penetrate large areas of occupied Yugoslavia, Germans and Italians favored such local militias,[40] which, as each of them was pitted against other armed groups of other ethnicities and political orientations, greatly increased the number of victims, also among Jews to a degree, in what amounted to a civil war (see Chapter 11).

Ethno-religious homogenization policies

Several European governments officially announced that they wanted more or less all of the Jews within their borders to emigrate. As this included regimes like Bulgaria and Hungary under the Kállay administration, which would not allow the deportation of their Jews to German-controlled areas, this has often been interpreted as delaying tactics – but it may have had serious, long-term policy objectives. For

[37] Griffioen and Zeller 2011, p. 1007.

[38] Observation by Kasten 1993, pp. 166, 168; see also Petrick 1998, pp. 52–3, 182; Hirschfeld 1984, pp. 112–16.

[39] Kasten 1993, pp. 42, 46, 51–2 (France); Petrick 1998, p. 51 (Norway); Gerlach 1999, pp. 204–5 (Belarus); Thalmann 1999, p. 41 (for the general administration in Vichy France); Engelking and Leociak 2009, p. 33 (for Warsaw's municipal administration).

[40] This comes from my reading of Schmider 2002.

example, the Bulgarian Foreign Minister, Ivan Popov, had suggested such a general emigration policy – even beyond his own country – to his German colleague Ribbentrop and to Hitler in November 1941, and Hitler offered some rhetorical support for the idea. Hungary and Romania had already stated in the spring of 1941 that their goal was expulsion. Norway's leading fascist, Vidkun Quisling, also advocated an international, or at least continental, 'solution' to the Jewish problem.[41] However, in reaction to Popov's proposal, the German Foreign Office stated that Italy, Hungary and Spain objected to a (desirable) European treaty for the common treatment of Jews; for that, Germany could, at best, count on Croatia, Romania, Slovakia and Bulgaria, and finding an agreement even with these states would not be easy.[42] This said, the Italian government's anti-Jewish policy – in place since 1938 – drove Jews out of the country intentionally and lowered the living standard of those that remained: 15,000, including 90% of the foreign and 10% of the national Jews, emigrated within three years.[43] Transitions could be fluent. Vidkun Quisling stated in March 1941 that Jews should be isolated from the rest of the population and resettled by force to a territory of their own, but he rejected killing or sterilizing them; yet, by the fall of 1942 he would consent to, and maybe even pushed for, their deportation to Germany, probably knowing that this would meant their death.[44] Visions of a future scheme for the continent-wide expulsion of European Jews – they were never more than visions – drew upon the ideas of anti-Jewish activists in the 1930s (regarding Madagascar or other territories) and the belief that this project could be part of future peace treaties.[45] Earlier, in the period 1936–39, the Polish government had (unsuccessfully) sought international support for resettling its Jews.[46]

Regimes had long lacked the opportunity to drive Jews out of their country. Some, like the Nazis in Germany, thought that the moment

[41] Note by v. Rintelen about the Ribbentrop-Popov meeting, November 26, 1941, in ADAP XIII, 2, p. 689; see also Chary 1972, pp. 50–1; Conze *et al.* 2010, pp. 185–6. For Quisling see Jansen 1997, p. 379; for Hungary see Gerlach and Aly 2002, pp. 34, 73, 81–2; for Romania see Solonari 2010, p. 137.

[42] Memo from Unterstaatssekretär Luther (English translation), December 4, 1941, and from Legationsrat Roediger, December 31, 1941, Nuremberg Documents NG-4667 and NG-4669. The German embassy in Paris still pursued the idea of a European statute or policy against Jews in 1942–43 (Thalmann 1999, p. 110).

[43] Longhi 2010, pp. 51–2, 59; Schlemmer and Woller 2005, p. 188. However, several thousand other Jews entered Italy within the same period.

[44] Hoffmann 2001, pp. 268–71.

[45] On August 3, 1940, Hitler told the German envoy in France – Abetz – that peace treaties should include a clause requiring countries to resettle their Jews outside Europe (Klarsfeld 1992, p. 271).

[46] Melzer 1997, pp. 131–43.

had come in the summer of 1941 with the multilateral invasions of Yugoslavia and the Soviet Union.[47] In the former, Italian, Hungarian and Bulgarian forces participated along with Germany; in the latter, Romanian, Finnish, Hungarian and Italian troops, among others, fought. What followed in both cases had to do with large-scale schemes of ethnic homogenization which elites in countries with sizable minorities pursued with the goal of creating a stable nation state, the expulsion of elites regarded as disloyal from newly occupied regions (or, in Croatia's case, by leaders of a new state), and the suppression of resistance. Legal discrimination against these national minorities often differed from that against Jews: instead of restrictions in commercial activities, university education and work in the free professions, other minorities lost the right to schooling in their own language and had part of their agricultural land expropriated. Still, when it came to expelling the members of a minority, the primary targets were urban elites, as was the case with Jews. Although ethnic homogenization plans were generally larger than the expulsions that were actually carried out, their implementation did involve hundreds of thousands of people. Germany wanted to evict 260,000 Slovenes and Serbs from Slovenia to Serbia and the Italian-occupied part of Slovenia – the actual number may have been 50,000–60,000, of which 20,000 may have entered the Italian-annexed part of Slovenia. Intermittently, the Croatian government offered to receive 175,000 Slovenes if Croatia in turn could expel 200,000 Serbs to Serbia. Up to 200,000 Serbs were either expelled to Serbia or fled there, many until October 1941. (They too had their businesses expropriated.)[48] Croatia seems to have brought back 70,000 Croatians from the rest of Yugoslavia by November 1941.[49] Hungary removed Serbs (especially those who had settled after 1918 – of which 48,000 were registered) from the Voivodina, although the number was probably 'only' 30,000–60,000 instead of the 150,000 once planned. The German Military Commander in Serbia intervened to stop both the Croatian and Hungarian moves, arguing that they politically destabilized Serbia.[50] Estimates about the number of Serbs expelled from Bulgarian-occupied Macedonia range from 43,000 to 120,000.[51] By May 1941, Serbia

[47] See also Korb 2013, pp. 169, 177–82, 204–5; for reference to Soviet territory see Bloxham 2009, pp. 113, 115.

[48] See Olshausen 1973 (pp. 225–6) for the Military Commander; Pavlowitch 2008, pp. 33, 85–6; Burgwyn 2005, p. 72; Tomasevich 2001, pp. 86–90; 392–7; Ther 2011 (p. 144) for a relevant interstate agreement.

[49] Schechtman 1946, p. 440.

[50] Olshausen 1973, pp. 226–7; Ahonen *et al.* 2008, p. 52; Pavlowitch 2008 p. 84; Tomasevich 2001, p. 170; see also Lea Ljubratic's recollections in *We Survived*, vol. 3, p. 331.

[51] Schechtman 1946, pp. 417.

already hosted 180,000 refugees from the Hungarian, Bulgarian and Croatian zones of Yugoslavia and Kosovo; by 1945, 70,000–100,000 may have been forced out of Kosovo. (Expulsions in Kosovo began under German occupation in April 1941 and resumed, after the Italians had halted them, in September 1943 when the Germans had once again occupied the region.)[52] Some 100,000 Greeks were also soon driven out of Bulgarian-occupied Macedonia and Thrace.[53]

Previous resettlements from 1939 to early 1941 had affected nearly 500,000 ethnic Germans, but also other groups.[54] To mention just the largest, at least 50,000 Czechs were forced out of Slovakia – largely in 1939 – while beginning in the same year, 100,000 Slovaks and Czechs fled from the southern part of Slovakia, which had been awarded to Hungary, and Slovakia expelled 7,500 foreign Jews to the same region (where many got trapped at the border as Hungary tried to send them back). Approximately 200,000 Muslims left Bulgaria and Romania for Turkey from 1936 to 1939; from 1940 to 1943, 220,000 Romanians fled to Romania from northern Transylvania, which had been awarded to Hungary (Hungarians massacred hundreds of Romanians in the process); and 190,000 Hungarians (including some Jews) left southern Transylvania for Hungary.[55] Some of these were compensated with the apartments, businesses or land of Jews. Estimates of the number of expulsions across borders in southeastern Europe from 1939 to 1943 exceed 2 million.[56] Flight movements and evacuations in 1941 were even larger and certainly impressed contemporaries. Some 8 million people fled within France in 1940 – as the Germans advanced – and 10 million or more people fled eastward as the Germans attacked the western parts of the Soviet Union. These included industrial workers, civil servants, local representatives of the Soviet government and – as, for example in Karelia, Bessarabia and Bukovina – recent immigrants who had settled following Soviet annexation in 1940.[57]

[52] Pavlowitch 2008, pp. 52, 72. Pohl 2003 (p. 53) estimates 240,000 were expelled to Serbia in 1941. According to Opfer 2005 (p. 264), 26,450 Serbs were expelled from Bulgarian Macedonia to Serbia in the summer of 1941. Wuescht 1969, pp. 60–1 (by September 30, 1942, 260,000 refugees were registered in Serbia – including about 109,000 from Croatia, 99,000 from Macedonia and 23,000 from Voivodina). See Schechtman 1946, pp. 417, 441 (217,175 refugees by November 1944; some estimates were higher). For Kosovo until 1945 see Fischer 1999, pp. 87, 238; Ther 2011, pp. 157–8.

[53] Kotzageorgi 1996, pp. 141–2.

[54] See Schechtman 1946; ibid. pp. 406, 409 (for population exchanges between Romania and Bulgaria in 1940–41); Ther 2011, pp. 112–17.

[55] Ther 2011, pp. 110, 150–4; Stark 2001, pp. 625–29. For Slovak Jews see Niznansky 1998, p. 29; Kamenec 2007, pp. 42–3; Lipscher 1979, p. 18.

[56] Ther 2011, p. 160.

[57] Lagrange 1977, p. 49; Friedländer 2006, p. 136; Segbers 1987, pp. 167, 179, 183.

It was in this invasion context that Romanian and Hungarian authorities also deported Jews to the newly occupied Soviet territories in 1941. In Hungary, Army Chief of Staff, Henrik Werth, and other officers, planned to enlarge the country to its pre-World War I borders, or even beyond, and then remove up to 8 million ethnic Romanians, Slovaks, Jews and possibly Germans replacing them with 1.2 million Magyar emigres. However, Prime Minister László Bárdossy opposed the plan – which would have meant a strong Hungarian expeditionary force fighting the Soviet Union – and sacked Werth in September 1941.[58] At about the same time as Werth's dismissal and the German massacre at Kamenets-Podolsk of more than 23,000 Jews – most of whom had been deported from Hungary at the end of August 1941, though some were local[59] – the Hungarian expulsions of Serbs from the Voivodina were also stopped.[60] On July 29, Romanian troops in the area of Iampol (Yampil) started sending Jews across the Dniester River into German-occupied territory. By late August, the Germans had deported 27,500 back (many were rejected or shot by Romanian troops) after having shot thousands.[61] Some scholars have concluded that Hitler had told Antonescu on June 13, 1941, that the Jews should be dumped into the Soviet Union but had misunderstood that this could start immediately.[62] The Romanians stopped sending Jews into German-occupied territories and ended up deporting them – mostly from Bukovina but also from Bessarabia – to Transnistria. In this context it is remarkable that the Croatian government did not attempt to expel Jews to Serbia in 1941 (as it tried with Serbs); this may indicate that Zagreb saw Serbs as the more urgent political threat.[63]

By late August 1941 the events at Kamenets-Podolsk and Iampol had made it clear to non-German governments that large-scale expulsions of Jews to the Soviet Union were not possible. In fact, German military authorities resisted any major expulsions, including those of non-Jews. By 1943, only the Bulgarians and Albanians continued – displacing Greeks, Serbs and Macedonians to Greece and Serbia.[64] The situation was similar for German authorities. The deportation of Polish

[58] Horváth 2008, pp. 135–8; Stark 2001, p. 622.
[59] Braham 1973; Angrick 2003, pp. 196, 203–4.
[60] Wuescht 1975, p. 15.
[61] Angrick 2003, pp. 193–203; Ioanid 2000, pp. 116–22; Ancel 2011, pp. 235–7.
[62] Longerich 2001, p. 93.
[63] Korb 2013 (pp. 177–82) argues that the Croatian government turned to the mass murder of Jews and Roma because they could not be expelled, as many Serbs were. One should add that Croatians began to massacre Serbs in 1941 simultaneously with the start of deportations.
[64] Opfer 2005, p. 265.

non-Jews and Jews from western Poland to the General Government was halted in the spring of 1941 and Frank and Rosenberg extended the cessation in October 1941; the military's resistance limited the deportation of central European Jews to the occupied Soviet territories and the General Government, and except for German-annexed territories – primarily those in Poland – the settlement of ethnic Germans was limited to certain parts of Lithuania, the area of Lublin and some population movements within certain areas of Ukraine. (German settlement in Slovenia, Alsace, Lorraine and Bohemia also remained limited.)

As in the German case, other governments drafted huge resettlement schemes – especially after expulsions had largely come to a halt – that closely resembled the *Generalplan Ost*, though with few practical results. Plans in Croatia envisioned the removal of up to 2 million Serbs, Jews and Roma (a third of the population). In Romania, the head of the statistical office, Sabin Manuilă, had a plan in October 1941 to get rid of 3.5 million Hungarians, Ukrainians, Russians, Jews, Serbs and others. (Ion Antonescu had similar ideas, and the scheme was modified in late 1943.) And, although the huge Hungarian resettlement plan mentioned above was not official policy, elite representatives of political parties, the Church and academia continued to support it, as did Regent Horthy, long after mid 1941.[65] Bulgaria's final plans are not known. And, as in the German case, the halt of expulsions had already by the summer of 1941 resulted in the mass murder of Jews by Romanian, Croatian and Hungarian forces.

Several European regimes looked for other ways to rid their countries of Jews. In light of war-related transportation problems and the lack of receptive countries, simply declaring that Jews without citizenship had to leave the country (which I discuss below) was not promising. Both before and after the war, immigration restrictions targeting Jews led to unrealistic demands for colonial aggrandizement. In 1936, the Polish government called for its own colonies in South America or Africa to resettle Polish Jews and developed an interest in Madagascar (as did the Germans later). And, shortly before being replaced as Prime Minister in France in April 1942, François Darlan – who had pursued the Madagascar plan until August 1941 – informed the German Foreign

[65] Achim 2001, p. 617; Solonari 2007a; Ahonen *et al.* 2008, pp. 57–8; Benyamin 2001, p. 147; see Deletant 2006, pp. 142–3; see Schechtman 1946, p. 446 for plans publicized in December 1943 to deport part of the Russian and Ukrainian population of 1.8 million from Transnistria to Romania and replace them with Romanians; Horváth 2008, pp. 135–8; Gerlach and Aly 2002, pp. 427–33.

Ministry that he intended to resettle a large number of Jews from France to Algeria.[66] In fact, foreign Jews were deported from France to north Africa on ten ships (five of which carried a total of 1,944 Jewish passengers) from March to June 1942. By late October 1942, 4,000 Jews (of foreign, French and north African origins) were held in camps in French north Africa; most were forced to work in coal mines or on the never-finished Trans-Saharan railway – where some died from the poor conditions.[67] At some point before September 1943, the commander of the Italian police in the Italian-occupied zone of France, Guido Lospinoso (known for his refusal to surrender Jews to the Germans), also mentioned a plan to send 30,000–40,000 Jews from the zone to Italy, and, then, to Italian colonies in Africa[68] (but by May 1943 no such colonies were left). Spain brought 3,500 stateless Jews to its north African possessions.[69] As most of such outlets remained blocked during World War II, the demands of local elites and the broader population increased pressures on the Jewish population of European countries – with a variety of outcomes from moderate persecution to partial deportation to German camps to mass destruction by own forces.

One aspect of homogenization policies was that the persecution of Jews in territories recently incorporated by states developed much more quickly, or was more intense than in states' own mainlands.[70] This was true in various ways of Romanian policies in Bukovina, Bessarabia and Transnistria, Bulgarian policies in Macedonia and Thrace, Hungarian policies in Upper Hungary, Carpatho-Ukraine and northern Transylvania, Soviet policies in the west in 1939–41, as well as German policies in the Wartheland. These countries were not occupying most of these regions for the first time, and their regimes wanted to avoid 'errors' of earlier unsuccessful integration policies. In particular, they all targeted those elites whom they considered to have alien ethnic backgrounds: civil servants, members of the professions, the intelligentsia, business owners, aristocrats, recent immigrants and the clergy. Many of these lost their jobs or commercial property. Some were killed, many incarcerated, and even more expelled. Such policies also

[66] Melzer 1997, pp. 131–2; Thalmann 1999, p. 267; Brechtken 2000, p. 489. Vichy France lost Madagascar to British troops after a dogged battle between May and November 1942 (Overy 1995, pp. 135–7).

[67] Abitbol 1983, pp. 99–107 (20,000 European Jews went to French north Africa in 1940–42, most only in transit); Roberts 2006, p. 66.

[68] Interview with Father Pierre Marie-Benoît can be found in Caracciolo 1995, p. 38. Already the *Dichiarazione sulla razza del Gran Consiglio del Fascismo* (October 6–7, 1938) had mentioned the possibility of settling European Jews in Italian-colonized Ethiopia (Collotti 2006, p. 190).

[69] Rother 2001, pp. 64, 127–8.

[70] For this paragraph see Gerlach 2012.

engulfed Jews. Among the elites in the professions, the intelligentsia and the business community were many Jews. Many Jews had not resisted the previous takeovers of these territories by foreign powers and had not defended Romanian, Hungarian, Bulgarian or German culture. So, they were perceived as politically unreliable. Regimes wanted to bring in ethnically desirable settlers in order to stabilize their rule in the newly acquired areas, but lacked the means to finance their housing and employment. They needed to expropriate and remove Jews to realize even a fraction of the overly ambitious settlement policies. Also, the new immigrants themselves, as well as previous settlers and occupation troops and functionaries, turned against the despised Jews for their own gain. Jews in general tended to come under suspicion and persecution. The eviction, flight and deportation for forced labor of members of other undesirable groups also went beyond the elites, although Jews were the worst affected. German policies and practice for the incorporation of territories – including racist tendencies – did not differ much from those of other countries, who themselves were not merely imitating German measures, but, rather, were dictated by their own national interests.

National interests and foreign policy

Foreign policy in European countries served prevailing nationalism. To many states, World War II and the months preceding it posed a threat, an opportunity, or both. Some states (like Slovakia and Croatia) were founded; others (like Germany, Italy, Hungary and Bulgaria) expanded their size; still others (for example, Slovakia, Romania and France) lost territory; and many experienced the presence of foreign troops or occupation administrations. Within this entire context, how a country dealt with Jews could become a bargaining chip in negotiations over other issues with Germany or other great powers; but it could also be important symbolically in underlining one's own sovereignty or a matter of one's relations with small neighboring states.

To be sure, German authorities often exerted pressure for deportations – as they did beginning in mid 1942 on the governments of Romania, Hungary, Bulgaria, Slovakia, Croatia, Italy and France. The governments of Greece, Serbia and Bohemia and Moravia were apparently not even consulted. In January 1943 the list of tasks for the German Foreign Office's Division D III with regard to "Jewish questions" abroad included fostering anti-Jewish propaganda, influencing foreign governments' treatment of Jews, settling questions about Jewish property, and, more generally, questions of economic and legal character and the denaturalization and "removal" of Jews.[71] By contrast, there is no evidence that German

[71] "Geschäftsverteilungsplan des Auswärtigen Amtes," January 15, 1943, BA RW 42, Nr. 3.

authorities ever pressured the Finnish government (or any neutral, unoccupied country) to surrender their Jews.[72] When carrying out deportations in an occupied country, the German Security Police exempted Jews of other nationalities when they had not yet been cleared for such treatment. For example, in Salonica, Jews with Spanish, Italian, Bulgarian and Turkish citizenship were exempted in 1943.[73] An employee of the German embassy in Budapest, Horst Grell, checked the citizenship of perhaps 200,000 people to ensure that nobody of an exempted nationality was deported from Hungary to Auschwitz in 1944.[74] It has been argued that the harsher anti-Jewish regulations in Mussolini's Republic of Salò in Italy in late 1943 also underscored national sovereignty.[75] The attempt to intern all of the Jews in Italy was undermined by the late timing of the necessary police decree of November 1943, which allowed many Jews to go underground; as well as by the obstruction of local authorities.[76]

Asher Cohen wrote: "We do not know of any case in which the government of the client state strongly resisted the deportations and failed. Thus it appears that the bulk of responsibility for the fate of Jews in those countries should fall on the national governments."[77] If there was a government that resisted *and failed*, it was Greece's.[78] It should be added that the only government to agree to the total deportation of its Jewish community was Norway's. No other regime completely gave in to German demands, which supports my claim that national politics played a major role in decisions about the treatment of Jews.

It was obvious that a readiness to hand over Jews would please the German leadership. And pleasing them could have certain advantages for foreign policy. In May 1942 the German allies Romania, Croatia and Slovakia "virtually reconstituted the Little Entente," an inter-war alliance directed against Hungary. (Although Hungary was also a German ally, the other three viewed it as a threat to their territorial possessions.[79]) Questions that are deserving of further research are whether these countries wished to gain German support through their anti-Jewish policies, and whether that is the reason why Slovakia, in contrast to Hungary, was by this time already deporting Jews en masse to camps in German-controlled Poland, why Croatia began deportations in August

[72] For Finland see Rautkallio 1987, pp. 163–9, 178, 259.
[73] Plaut 1996, p. 61.
[74] Interrogation of Horst Grell, August 31, 1949, ZStL 502 AR-Z 150/59, vol. 7, p. 123.
[75] Steur 1997, pp. 123–4; Picciotto Fargion 1989, p. 285.
[76] StA GKammergericht Berlin 1 Js 1/65, Indictment of April 23, 1971, pp. 263–8.
[77] Cohen 1987, p. 195.
[78] At some point, each of the three Greek Prime Ministers under German occupation protested against the deportation of Jews (Fleischer 1986, p. 367).
[79] Rothschild 1974, p. 186.

1942, and why Romania declared its readiness to do so in July (although these trains would never roll). In addition, as mentioned above, Croatia's government used its sovereignty over areas close to the Adriatic that it had regained from Italy in June 1942 to intensify the persecution of Jews.

Protecting what were seen as national interests in foreign policy could also work the other way. Several countries refused to deport Jews to German-controlled areas once the Allies seemed to be getting the upper hand against the Axis in the war. Many historians view the Romanian government's relatively sudden refusal in the fall of 1942 to carry out deportations that were already planned, as based on such considerations; the same applied to the regime's critics.[80] Among other things, the Romanian and Hungarian governments took the potential support of the Allies over Transylvania into account when designing their policies against Jews.[81] Beginning as early as November 1941, Romania's leader, Ion Antonescu, repeatedly voiced his concern that the Allies, or international capital, might penalize Romania for its anti-Jewish policies, and that Romania would be forced to compromise at peace negotiations. He wanted to protect Romanians from such consequences.[82] In March 1943, forty-two Bulgarian members of parliament argued similarly: to surrender the country's Jews to Germany would weaken Bulgaria's future position in "international relations."[83] Others see similar factors at work when the Italians stiffened their resistance to surrendering Jews who lived in certain territories they occupied – for example in Croatia – to the Germans.[84] Slovakia also stopped deportations in the fall of 1942. After the Allies had invaded French north Africa in November 1942, the cooperation of the French government and police in the deportations of Jews also decreased markedly – although the administration and police continued to give their support in some regions.[85]

Hungary's foreign policy was linked in even more twisted ways with the treatment of Jews. After Germany occupied the country in March 1944, the government under Döme Sztójay, who had been a Hungarian diplomat in Berlin for seventeen years, pursued a policy of large-scale deportation of Jews in order (inter alia) to convince the Germans of the country's political reliability so that it could regain its national sovereignty (and possibly exit the war). By early July, Regent Miklós Horthy, supported by the State Secretary in the Foreign Ministry, Mihály Arnóthy-Jungerth,

80 See Ancel 2011, pp. 478–89; Ancel 1992, p. 205; Deletant 2010, pp. 172–8.
81 Case 2006, pp. 31, 33.
82 Benyamin 1997, pp. 6–7.
83 Almog 1990, p. 128.
84 Knox 2007, esp. pp. 56–71, 82–88.
85 Kasten 2000, pp. 113–14, 117–18.

prevented the deportation of Jews from Budapest because of pressure from the USA, the Vatican and Sweden, among other reasons. In August and September 1944, the Hungarian Foreign Ministry suggested additional trainloads of Jews to Germany in order to obtain Hitler's approval for sending humanitarian transports of Jews to Switzerland, and, thus, please the Western Allies. Finally, Horthy's successor, Ferenc Szálasi, halted deportation marches in late 1944 in order to gain international recognition for his fascist regime.[86] In these ways, the international distribution of power and shifting foreign policy interests were an important variable for anti-Jewish policies.

Protection and the lack of it

Despite the persecution of Jews by their own regimes in most non-European countries, the existence of a national government, or lack of one, made a difference. In the German-occupied Soviet territories and in Poland, where no national governments existed, Jews had the least protection. By contrast, the government of Italy (until September 1943), and those of Denmark, Finland, Bulgaria and Hungary (until March 1944) prevented Jews holding their citizenship from being deported or killed by Germans, and largely protected them from homegrown violence. To some extent the same was true for the regimes in France and Romania, and, to a still lesser degree, those in Slovakia and Hungary (after June 1944), as well as the local administrations in Belgium and Albania. In addition to demonstrating national sovereignty, such behavior was also an expression of cultural ties.[87] In practice, protection sometimes continued even after Jews were stripped of their citizenship, as was the case in Bulgaria and Italy.[88] Diplomats also intervened to exempt hundreds of their nations' Jewish individuals living in territories under German control from anti-Jewish regulations. On the other hand, several governments – those of Slovakia, Croatia and Romania in November 1941; Bulgaria and Norway in 1942 and Hungary in 1944 – allowed the Germans to treat their Jewish citizens residing in German-controlled areas like other Jews (which facilitated stripping them of their rights, their deportation and their subsequent killing).[89]

[86] Gerlach and Aly 2002, esp. pp. 239–48, 361–4; Cornelius 2011, p. 338.

[87] See also Bloxham 2009, p. 236.

[88] Miller 1975, p. 101; Longhi 2010, p. 83. To a very limited extent, this could also be said about Croatia. See Pavlowitch 2008, p. 31; Gitman 2011.

[89] Browning 1978, pp. 67–8; Oren 1968, p. 95; Steur 1997, p. 94; Braham 1977b. About 3,300 Romanian Jews were thusly deported by the Germans from France before the Romanian government revised their policy in April 1943 and demanded protection of their Jewish citizens (Ioanid 1997, pp. 225–8). Turkey and Switzerland stripped

Alien Jews were more vulnerable to deportation than the local Jewish population. Non-German governments were more ready to hand foreigners over, and the Germans – aware that foreign Jews had been singled out early for legal discrimination in many countries – played on this inclination, hoping it would open the door for later permission to deport Jews who held national citizenship. The best-known case of this is the Vichy government of France. France stepped up its internment of foreign Jews in late 1940.[90] When the German Security Police wanted the Vichy regime's help in deporting Jews in the spring and summer of 1942, it offered to respect their national sovereignty by deporting only Jews without French citizenship and even to extend the French government's authority over the police to German-occupied France. In 1942, the French government and police consented also to the deportation of foreign Jewish children and those from the unoccupied zone. Eichmann's representative, Dannecker, was removed for pressing too hard for the deportation of Jews with French citizenship.[91] Accordingly, the approximately 76,000 Jews deported from France – most of whom were murdered – included 52,000 foreigners and 16,000 more who had either been naturalized or were descendants of naturalized Jews.[92] This has been called the "deportation of the poor Jewish immigrant population from Eastern Europe."[93] Although Belgian authorities cooperated even less than the French ones (for example, they did not agree to the deportation of children or running their own detention camps as Vichy France did, and Belgian police participated in fewer raids), the Germans still met somewhat less resistance in deporting foreigners than Jewish Belgian citizens. The military administration urged from the beginning that the latter group be exempt, although they softened their stance later.[94]

Some Italian authorities, namely those in the military, protected even foreign Jews in Italian-occupied countries – Yugoslavia, Greece and the small occupied zone in France – from murder and deportation. Thousands of Jews fled from German-occupied regions to those controlled by Italy.[95] Still, some Italian officers and units did allow Croatian Ustasha forces to deport thousands of Jews in 1941–42, and some Italian troops also moved against Jews in the Soviet Union – for example delivering them to the German Security Police for execution.[96]

certain groups of their Jewish nationals abroad of their citizenship (Guttstadt 2008, pp. 279–407; Unabhängige Expertenkommission Schweiz 1999, p. 301).

[90] Steur 1997, pp. 52–3, 57.

[91] Steur 1997, pp. 76–86, 209.

[92] Klarsfeld 1982, p. i; Meyer 2000, p. 34.

[93] Delacor 2000b, p. 497.

[94] Meinen 2008, p. 56; Mariot and Zalc 2010, p. 183; Hilberg 1994a, pp. 638–41.

[95] Zuccotti 1996, pp. 74–100; Burgwyn 2005, pp. 186–93; Gitman 2011, pp. 128–46.

[96] Burgwyn 2005, pp. 194–5; Schlemmer 2005, p. 36.

In Italy, too, foreign Jews (40% of whom were from France) ran double the risk of being killed than Jewish nationals; for those remaining in the fascist zone of the country after January 1944 it was four to six times greater the risk than it was for local Jews.[97] Part of this difference can be explained by the fact that roughly half of the Italian Jews were protected because they belonged to so-called 'mixed' families – which included Christians, World War I veterans or former fascists (the German Security Police often respected this),[98] whereas foreign Jews were usually not; xenophobia and less developed social ties account for the rest of the difference (see also Chapter 15). Apparently the protection of foreign Jews by authorities and society in general was not as great. By mid 1943, fascist Italy had also interned foreign Jews, registering them as "civilian war internees."[99] The contrast with Albania, in no way a dominant power in international politics, is striking: despite measures against Jewish immigration having been in place since early 1939 – before the Italian occupation of 1939–43 – despite increasing numbers of internees during 1940–43, and despite varying treatment in camps, the authorities protected not only local Jews but also 1,600 foreign Jewish refugees right to the end. This support, however, did not extend to the 281 Jews, including locals, in Albanian-annexed Kosovo.[100] The offer of the exiled King Zog of Albania in mid 1943 to settle 200,000 foreign Jews in his country after World War II, tactical as it may have been, was exceptional.[101] The Bulgarian government, which had evicted thousands of foreign Jews in 1939–40, appeared to the Germans to be more inclined in 1943 to hand over foreign Jews than it did local ones[102] – but in the end it surrendered neither.

In 1944, after the tide of the war had changed, some governments of neutral countries – including Switzerland, Sweden, Spain, Portugal, and

[97] Sarfatti 2006, p. 203; Zuccotti 1996, pp. 145–6; Caracciolo 1995, p. 40. Of the approximately 6,500–7,000 foreign Jews in Italy by September 1943, 3,000 had been liberated by the Allies in southern Italy and 1,000 had fled to Switzerland by January 1944. At least 1,915 of the remainder were deported (65–80%, as opposed to about 15% of the Italian Jews). This calculation is based on figures given in Voigt 1987, esp. pp. 46–8. See also Toscano 1995, p. xli.

[98] Michaelis 1978, pp. 233–4, 255–6; indictment of April 23, 1971, StA Kammergericht Berlin 1 Js 1/65, pp. 256, 371.

[99] Steur 1997, p. 113; for the context see Knox 2007, pp. 56–69; for their status see the recollections of Gabi Deleon and Lea Sorger in *We Survived*, vol 3, pp. 215, 270.

[100] Fischer 1999, pp. 87, 238; Kotani 1995, pp. 43–56; Schlemmer and Woller 2005, p. 185. For internment experiences see the recollections of Rukula Bencion and Mila Karaoglanović in *We Survived*, vol. 3, pp. 429, 445.

[101] Pearson 2005, pp. 250, 258, 325.

[102] Miller 1975, p. 100. This might also explain why the Bulgarian representative, Belev, at first agreed to have 20,000 Jews deported – even though there were only close to 12,000 in the annexed territories.

Turkey – turned to issuing protective passports to Jews who did not possess their citizenship. This also often served to save them from deportation.[103] The practice reached its peak in Budapest where several tens of thousands of Jews survived with the help of primarily Swiss and Swedish papers.[104]

But even regimes with viciously anti-Jewish policies exempted certain groups of domestic Jews from persecution and mass murder. In Croatia, those protected included up to 4,000 former Jews who had converted to Christianity, more than 1,000 Jews married to Christians, a "few thousand" people and their immediate families whose expertise as business managers, engineers and physicians was of value, and some one hundred "honorary Aryans." (Altogether 5,000 Jews received protection from the Yugoslav partisans.) Official exemption policies were influenced particularly by the Catholic Church, but also business owners and administrators.[105] While under German occupation, the Hungarian government protected from deportation, with some variation, certain groups of Jewish forced laborers, people with foreign protective passes, some 'honorary Magyars,' and, after 1944, Christian converts.[106]

Some regimes even exempted Jewish specialists and industrialists from internment and deportation. The latter were either left in possession of their businesses or, more frequently, made to serve as managers of their factories after having been dispossessed of them. Such policies were pursued in Slovakia, Croatia and parts of Romania. The justification was usually to prevent or limit damage to the wartime national economy.[107] Here and there, Jewish doctors and pharmacists were spared from deportation and murder for the common good, but in Greater Hungary doctors suffered a higher death rate than others.[108]

Would the mass murder of Jews have been committed without German pressure and organization? Scholarship cannot provide a definitive answer to such counterfactual questions. There are a number of countries in which it probably would not have taken place. In other states, however, it not only would have taken place, it *did* take place – in the summer of 1941 Jews were being killed en masse, independently, in Romania, and, to a lesser degree, in Croatia, at a time when German forces were only just beginning their massacres of the Jewish population in the Soviet

[103] For Turkey see Shaw 1993, pp. 60–250; for Turkish passive help with the flight of Jews from the Greek Aegean see ibid., pp. 250–4; Guttstadt 2008, pp. 253–4.
[104] Braham 1994, pp. 1222–39.
[105] Gitman 2011, esp. pp. xvi, xxiv, xxvii, 14, 48, 54, 61, 67–9, 80–5, 112, 160–8.
[106] See Gerlach and Aly 2002.
[107] Mann 2005, p. 294; Deletant 2006, pp. 157, 162; Gitman 2011, pp. 68–9.
[108] Opfer 2005, p. 279, and the recollections of Rasela Noah-Konfino in *We Survived*, vol. 2, p. 434–5 (Macedonia); Gitman 2011, pp. 80–5; Kovács 1994, pp. xx–xxi.

Union. In several countries, including Hungary and Poland, government policy or important political players sought to resettle their nation's Jews abroad. However, international conditions did not easily allow for their removal. It was imperialist Germany that created such conditions, albeit in a particularly murderous way that was not necessarily supported by every Jew-hater in these other countries. After 1945 the great powers facilitated the creation of another, quite different, outlet, by supporting the foundation of the state of Israel.

Exploitation, displacement, dispossession

As resources became more scarce during the long war, intra-societal struggles ensued in which the Jews were among the most disadvantaged. One way in which governments tried to take advantage of subjugated Jewish minorities was forced labor. But it was usually not the first measure taken; it may be remembered that forced labor was also not a major aspect of the persecution in Germany until 1938 (see Chapter 8). In other countries, too, coerced labor was, in economic terms, a response to the end of mass unemployment and increasing labor shortages brought about by the economic growth that usually came a little later than it did in Germany, often in the early stages of the war. (Therefore, for example, Vichy France and then Free France also intensified forced labor for colonial subjects in northern Africa.[109]) Accordingly, forced Jewish labor was introduced, for instance, in Hungary in 1939, and in 1941, at the latest, in Bulgaria – although these programs were expanded in 1942 and 1943, respectively. Labor camps for foreign emigres (both Jews and non-Jews) were also expanded in democratic Switzerland toward the end of the war, although under quite different conditions. But guards gave camps a punitive character in which hunger and resentment prevailed and some physical abuse took place.[110] In other countries, a large number of Jews who had been forced out of their professions remained unemployed and lived off their possessions, which gave propagandists the opportunity to play on the theme of the idle and parasitic Jew who did not join in the national war effort.

[109] Thomas 1998, pp. 228, 231–2. All colonial powers in Africa expanded forced labor schemes during World War II.

[110] Cornelius 2011, pp. 170, 214. For the Bulgarian labor market see Opfer 2005, pp. 219, 227, for Jews, see pp. 276, 280; for the Hungarian economy and labor markets see Cornelius 2011, pp. 152, 155, 158–60; Gerlach and Aly 2002, p. 161; for Hungary and Romania see Rothschild 1974, pp. 189, 320. For Switzerland see Unabhängige Expertenkommission Schweiz 1999, pp. 161–6, 172–4, 297, 307; Picard 1997, p. 338. Circumstances in Finland were similar from 1942 (Rautkallio 1987, pp. 113–19).

The forced labor of Jews was organized in special military labor units in a number of countries like Hungary, Romania and Turkey (where the units were dissolved in 1942).[111] In other states such as Croatia, Slovakia, Vichy France, Italy and, to a small degree, Turkey, Jews were interned in camps and then assigned compulsory work. In Bulgaria the Ministry of Interior took over work units formerly organized by the military in 1941.[112] As organization by the military already suggests, it was men, for the most part, who became subject to (or were considered able to perform) forced labor. Many Jews served alongside other interned or independently mobilized minorities such as Serbs and Romanians in Hungary; Christian minorities in Turkey; Roma, Turks, Pomaks, Greeks and Serbs in Bulgaria (44,000 of them by November 1942); and refugees of other backgrounds in Switzerland and France.[113] However, for Jews (unlike other groups) internment for labor service could result in deportation to German extermination camps, as was the case for foreign Jews interned in France in the summer of 1942.[114]

As already indicated, the forced labor of Jews had aspects other than economic ones. Labor was designed to be a measure of discrimination, debasement and punishment and to give non-Jews the satisfaction of knowing that they were not the only ones who had to obey orders, and sweat and suffer for the war effort. Accordingly it was often manual, unqualified, heavy, dirty and dangerous work that Jews were forced to do. Although all forced labor was degrading, differences in treatment were immense. While up to 44,000 Jews in the labor service of the Hungarian army died from overwork, want, abuse, from being made to perform dangerous tasks like clearing minefields, or in Soviet captivity,[115] there are no comparable reports about the Romanian or Turkish military labor services. Coerced labor in Bulgarian, Swiss or French camps was generally not lethal; whereas it led to the deaths of many Romanian Jews in Transnistria, and the forced labor of Jews in Croatian camps resembled that in German concentration camps after 1941 with mass killings of the unfit and few survivors.[116]

[111] Braham 1977a; Guttstadt 2008, pp. 199–201; Ancel 2007, pp. 119–20, 147–8, 332–45.

[112] For Bulgaria see Chary 1972, p. 50; see also Collotti 2006, pp. 113–17. For the limited implementation of forced labor for Jews in Italy see Zuccotti 1996, p. 64.

[113] Cornelius 2011, p. 170; Opfer 2005, p. 282.

[114] Shaw 1993, p. 58.

[115] See Braham 1977a, esp. pp. 36–9. There is a debate about the number of Hungarian Jews who died as POWs in Soviet captivity.

[116] Ancel 2011, pp. 395–416; for Croatia see the contributions in *Jasenovac Memorial Site*. But in Turkey there were at least twenty-one deaths among the more than 2,000 able-bodied male internees who had failed to pay a wealth tax that applied only to non-Muslims, including Jews (Shaw 1993, pp. 39–41).

Several governments allied with Germany, such as Bulgaria, refused to have their Jews deported to German camps because they needed their labor for their own war efforts.[117] The same applied to Hungary, where the forced labor service was expanded from about 14,000 people in 1941 to 106,000 in 1943, and even more Jews (but also non-Jews) were conscripted in the spring of 1944.[118] Even the Hungarian fascist Arrow Cross Party argued that all Hungarian Jews should remain in the country as forced laborers and opposed the deportations of hundreds of thousands (to Auschwitz) in May and June 1944.[119] The party based its argument on official German statements expressing their wish that foreign Jews be used for labor in Germany.

However, there was another twist to this sort of thinking that historians have not yet systematically analyzed. In several cases, governments agreed to the deportation of Jews from their country to German-controlled areas at crucial moments when they wished to avoid, or limit, the sending of non-Jewish nationals to Germany for labor. Either this, or they demanded the return of non-Jews in exchange. The reason for such bargaining was that forced labor in Germany was increasingly regarded with hostility because of the poor or insufficient food, the excessive strenuousness of the work, the restrictions imposed on laborers' movement and activities, and the racist attitudes displayed by the Germans. The desire to repatriate non-Jewish citizens in exchange for Jews is one of the reasons for the deportations of Jews from Slovakia after February 1942; and from Hungary, under the Sztójay government, in May 1944, and then under Szálasi in November 1944.[120] When the Germans demanded from the French authorities in Tunisia 8,000 workers for the construction of fortifications in January 1943, French officials made a disproportionate demand for 3,000 men from the Jewish community.[121] For France, Croatia and Greece, there are at least some indications of this connection. The mass deportations of Jews from France commenced in June 1942 – at the same time that Germany was demanding many more laborers than it had before, and at the same time the French government

[117] For Bulgaria see Steur 1997, pp. 96, 102, 108, 211, 214–16; for Slovakia see Hradská 1996, pp. 84–7.

[118] Cornelius 2011, p. 109; Gerlach and Aly 2002, pp. 162, 310–12.

[119] Szöllösi-Janze 1989, p. 426 and "Lagebericht aus Ödenburg und Umgebung" (copy) with cover letter of July 31, 1944, PA AA R100408; this was also the Arrow Cross Party's position when it took power in October 1944 (Nagy-Talavera 2001, p. 326).

[120] For Slovakia see Lipscher 1979, pp. 100, 109; Bauer 1993, pp. 65–6; for Hungary under Sztójay see Gerlach and Aly 2002, pp. 171–2; for Hungary under Szálasi see Cornelius 2011, p. 337.

[121] Abitbol 1983, p. 146. The German Security Police demanded that all Jewish men aged between seventeen and fifty be included, but the real number never exceeded 4,500–5,000 (Sabille 1954, pp. 69, 82–3; Abitbol 1983, pp. 137, 141).

announced the *relève* (according to which the Germans freed French POWs in exchange for French civilian workers being sent to Germany). In fact, from June to mid-August France supplied only 40,000 workers for the *relève* compared to about 18,000 Jews.[122] An Italian general commented that Vichy France preferred sending Jews for forced labor to surrendering French non-Jews.[123] It is also worth noting that the first deportation transports from France to arrive at Auschwitz contained largely able-bodied men. In 1942, Germany demanded more laborers from Croatia, but Zagreb wanted to send primarily Serbs, especially from areas where partisans were operating, and in August 1942 they also shipped close to 5,000 Jews to Germany. Nonetheless, most of the laborers provided were ethnic Croats.[124] During the deportation of Jews from Salonica in the spring of 1943, there were official, and violent popular protests against (non-Jewish) Greek laborers being sent to Germany, and in the summer of 1942 several thousand Jewish men were sent for forced labor after the Greek Inspector General for Macedonia complained that ethnic Greeks were being used for hard labor.[125]

Government paternalism for ethnically favored groups thus played into their selective hierarchy of who should be sacrificed first, as well as their readiness to have Jews deported. A similar effect is visible for other groups. In June 1942, shortly before Croatia agreed to have Jews deported to Germany in July, Operation Viking started. This involved the Croats deporting approximately 10,000 prisoners, mostly Serbs (but no Jews), from their concentration camp at Jasenovac to Germany in order to replenish the German labor force. (In addition the Croats murdered all of the Roma workers in Jasenovac in July and largely replaced them with new Serbian prisoners, mostly civilians, interned during a large German-Croat anti-partisan operation at Kozara.)[126] The French authorities selected political refugees, especially Spaniards, Italian and Polish emigres and north Africans, for work in Germany and German fortification and road building in France. The Germans seem to have adapted their deportation policies to French preferences in this regard.[127]

[122] Mariot and Zalc 2010, pp. 150, 160–1, 183; Griffioen and Zeller 2011, p. 890; Zielinski 1995b, p. 33; Zielinski 1995a, pp. 86–9, 95, 126.

[123] Steinberg 1992, p. 153.

[124] See Schölzel 2013, pp. 44–5, 51–6, 82. For the following, see Safrian 1997, p. 229.

[125] Gerlach 2010, pp. 242–3; Safrian 1997, p. 229; Loulos 1999, p. 149.

[126] Goldstein 2006, p. 128; Lengel-Krizman 2006, p. 166.

[127] Ory 1976, p. 44; Kletzin 1996, S. 201; Zielinski 1995a, p. 127; see notes about a meeting between Hitler and Himmler, December 10, 1942, and comments in Witte *et al.* 1999 pp. 636–7; telegram from Himmler to Hitler through Bormann, December 18, 1942, BA NS 19/1929, pp. 61–3.

Such mechanisms, similar to some German policies (see Chapter 10), can also be observed in the housing sector. Apartments in urban areas became scarce as cities grew during the war-related economic boom (the war effort allowed for little in the way of construction of housing, and aerial bombardments – especially late in the war – destroyed many buildings). Some of the population resided in buildings that were more precarious than those of their middle-class Jewish compatriots. In Osijek, Croatia, Jews were evicted from their apartments in the city center to the suburbs due to "the housing crisis."[128] The same happened to thousands of Jews in Bratislava (Slovakia), Vichy France, Romania and Lithuania.[129] In part, governments merely legalized squatters' unauthorized seizures of apartments as, for example, in Hungary and the Romanian-occupied Soviet city of Odessa, where ethnic Germans seized housing. French fascists in Tunisia were a little more circumspect and requested the German-Italian occupiers hand them the houses of Jews.[130]

The logic of the forced movements of Jews was a product of conflicting interests pertaining to housing, exposure to bombing, internment for forced labor or the security threats Jews allegedly posed, and concentration prior to deportation – as the twists in Bulgaria and Hungary illustrate. In Bulgaria, as an alternative to deportation to Germany, Jews (who constituted 10% of the capital's population) were evicted from Sofia to internment camps in the countryside for labor and for so-called security purposes; this occurred in mid 1943 at a time when further armament efforts increased the demand for labor. From the end of 1943, many Jews were admitted back to Sofia after the Allied air raids had begun and after much of the population had left the capital.[131] In Hungary, the swift concentration of Jews in the provinces in 1944 mostly served the impending deportations, and in each region it was organized shortly before the trains left. However, for a long time there was no concentration of Jews in Budapest since the deportations had been stopped before they affected the metropolis. Competing ghettoization plans from the

[128] Recollections of Mirko Najman in *We Survived* 2006, p. 240; see also Braham 1992 (p. 133) for Croatia.

[129] Hilberg 1992a, pp. 91–2; for a case from Užtiltę, Lithuania, in August 1941, see Levinson 2006, p. 173.

[130] Gerlach and Aly 2002, pp. 201–3; "Vereinbarung über die Stellung der deutschen Volksgruppe," signed by Alexianu and Hoffmeyer, August 14/30, 1942, in Völkl 1996, pp. 117–18; Sebag 1991, p. 245.

[131] Chary 1972, p. 29; Opfer 2005, pp. 227, 280; Steur 1997, pp. 104, 110–11; Hilberg 1992a, p. 91. Larger bombardments started in the fall of 1943 and by April 1944 three-quarters of the inhabitants of Sofia had left the capital (Opfer 2005, p. 197–8). Schmider 2002 (pp. 360–1) and Müller 2007 (p. 80) time the bulk of the non-Jewish exodus as January 1944. The press also argued in 1942 that Jews should be removed from Sofia to free up housing: Hilberg 1994a, pp. 802–3.

summer of 1944 had different objectives: some were aimed at freeing up apartment space, especially higher quality lodgings; some were aimed at concentrating Jews in order to isolate them; yet others were aimed at dispersing them in an effort to deter Allied air raids. Some wanted Jews placed close to factories (the Allies were supposed to spare Jews from attack), while others wanted them kept away from factories since Jews were also suspected of signaling to Allied planes. Under the Arrow Cross, two ghettos were finally established for isolating Jews and stripping them of attractive apartments.[132] Similarly, but unsuccessfully, the fascist Françistes movement in France demanded the ghettoization of Jews, and that several Polish or Romanian Jewish immigrants be killed for each victim of Allied aerial attacks.[133] The Romanian government considered deporting almost all of the Jews from southern Transylvania in order to improve the housing situation for Romanian refugees from northern Transylvania. However, little seems to have been done to help the former Romanian refugees in Bukovina.[134] But the Romanian deportation of tens of thousands of Jews – who were consequently murdered – from Odessa, in the winter of 1941–42, has been linked to easing the housing situation.[135] As in the case of labor policies, governments tried to mitigate the burden that the war placed upon the housing sector, substituting policies against Jews for social policy, and satisfying some of the popular envy directed against Jews. These feelings among the population, and their impact on government policies, are better documented in the field of housing than in the field of labor.

In the course of dispossessing Jews, governments intended to channel all of the confiscated property through official means and control the redistribution of seized assets (for Germany, see Chapter 10). For example, authorities organized the confiscation of foreign currency – which would be exchanged at artificially low rates by official changing stations.[136] However, it was often hard to tell whether the proceeds of gendarmerie and police confiscations of Jewish property went into official or private hands –as was the case in Southern Bukovina, Romania. One of the major points of criticism of Romanian behavior – by Romanians and foreigners – was that the confiscations amounted to anarchic pillage; civil servants had little success in bringing this under control or in trying to ensure that seized property went to the state. Some prefects who were supposed to guarantee the state's interests misappropriated Jewish

[132] The best study on this is Cole 2003.
[133] Cohen 1992, pp. 111–12.
[134] Benyamin 2001, p. 148; Deletant 2006, p. 165.
[135] Angrick 2003, p. 284.
[136] For the Romanian case see Ioanid 2001, pp. 74, 89.

property for themselves.[137] One aspect of the corrupt character of expropriation in Romania was that it was carried out unevenly in different regions of the country.[138] In Bulgarian-annexed Thrace and Macedonia, the national bank held confiscated valuables and the proceeds of the immediate liquidation of Jewish property; even household goods were sold off to citizens. In Greece, too, the national bank, the Bank of Greece, held the assets of deported Jews in accordance with German plans.[139] In Lithuania, the Citizens' Committee of Vilnius resolved at the end of July 1941 to distribute Jewish property to public institutions at a time when locals still claimed national sovereignty. In some other places, local authorities simply handed Jewish property over to ethnic Lithuanians.[140]

As I have already shown with regard to legislation, anti-Jewish economic policies, when stripped of their benevolent rhetoric, showed little regard for the lower class. Few benefited from the legislation, but those that did benefited greatly. Romanian state-controlled welfare organizations founded in October 1940 were supposed to distribute Jewish property to the needy, but there is little evidence for resources actually reaching poor non-Jews. The Protective Council for Social Works had to compete for resources with the military, the National Center for Romanization and the Central Office for Jewish Affairs.[141] The larger schemes for socializing Jewish property, which were often adopted in response to dissatisfaction with lopsided redistribution processes, came too late (mid 1944) to be effective in Hungary.[142] The earlier expropriation of Jewish-owned land for agriculture and forestry had, at best, benefited a limited number of rural dwellers. It had served, rather, to deflect interest from the lack of far-reaching land reform.[143]

One challenge to wartime social policy was inflation. To use the example of Slovakia – which had entered the war against the Soviet Union in June 1941 – the war turned out to be unexpectedly expensive. But a special tax on Jews covered five-sixths of the costs incurred. This helped combat inflation,[144] a scourge that menaced the urban lower class in particular. But the effect was only temporary. In Slovakia, public dissatisfaction with the 'Aryanization' policy grew. In a broader sense,

137 Ioanid 2001, pp. 83, 92–3 (for the gendarmes); Deletant 2006, pp. 146, 162, 165, 179–80.
138 Benyamin 1997, pp. 6–7; Iancu 1997, p. 259.
139 Plaut 1996, p. 57; Molho 2002, p. 217 (notes of March 7 and 10, 1943).
140 Brandišauskas 2003, p. 57–9.
141 Hausleitner 2004, esp. pp. 38–42, 44.
142 Kádár and Vági 2005, pp. 58, 70.
143 For Poland (1936) see Melzer 1997, p. 131; for Hungary see Gerlach and Aly 2002, pp. 61–73.
144 Aly 2006a, pp. 226–7.

restricting the economic activities of Jews, placing various burdens on them, and stripping them of their property, were, to a degree, symbolic practices that substituted for a lack of social policy.

Jewish victims among others

As it was with German policies, Jewish citizens (and foreigners) were not the only people persecuted by non-German governments and societies. Aside from the above-mentioned mass expulsions by Bulgaria, Croatia and Hungary, Bosnian Serbs and Kosovo Albanians, Italian, Hungarian, Bulgarian and Croatian troops, in particular, each killed tens of thousands of partisans, suspected partisans and leftists.[145] A look at these other persecutions is telling in that it reveals some connections and overlapping motives, as well as some differences, in comparison with anti-Jewish policies, and it also shows that in many countries Jews were the most fiercely persecuted group while in others they weren't.

Like Jews in 1941, Sinti and Roma (so-called 'gypsies') became targets of cross-national persecution a year later. No attention has been paid to this because research has so far concentrated on the German persecution, and little has been done in terms of international comparison. The Roma in Croatia, though subject to the mid 1941 race laws, were targeted for arrest only in May 1942, and most had been killed by October. While interventions by Islamic clergy saved a sizable number of Muslims among them, 25,000–27,000 of a total of between 28,000 and 30,000 (at least three-quarters) were stabbed, beaten or starved to death in local death camps. Their death rate was at least as high as that of the Croatian Jews. And as with Jews, close to 50% of the dead were female, and 94% of those who perished were killed in camps.[146] Due to their wandering, criminal records, unemployment and lifestyle, roughly 41,000 of the approximately 250,000 Roma in Romania were registered as dangerous or undesirable by May 1942. Some 11,141 nomads were deported to Transnistria between June and August 1942, as were 13,176 sedentary Roma from September to October 14; the deportation was stopped simultaneously with that of the Jews. Between 50% and 75% of those deported (i.e., 12,000–18,000 people, or 5–7% of all of the

[145] For mass killings of Soviet civilians during anti-partisan warfare by the French Infantry Regiment 638, see Müller 2007, pp. 120–9; for Slovak troops see Gerlach 1999, pp. 886–7.

[146] Biondich 2002, pp. 34–42; Fings *et al.* 1992, pp. 22–6; 97% of all Roma and 75–80% of all Jews in the Croatian state died, according to Trifković 2008, p. 63. According to Biondich 2005 (p. 72 note 4) the percentage of Roma killed was between 53% and 96%. The last sentence is based on partial data in Cvetković 2008, pp. 364–5.

country's Roma) perished in Transnistria, mainly from hunger and diseases.[147] In Slovakia, only those among the approximately 100,000 Roma who led migrant lives, or had no job, were subject to persecution in 1940. Many were impoverished because their traditionally Jewish employers or business partners had been deported, and this fueled the popular notion that Roma were 'useless' and lazy. Following a decree in 1941, village communities handed Roma over to the authorities; from the summer of 1942 to 1943 they also chased them away. During the suppression of the 1944 national uprising, German forces killed many for their alleged aid to the insurgents.[148] In Bulgarian-annexed Macedonia, Roma were forced to convert to Christianity from January 1942, subjected to forced labor from May 1942, and from August 1942 their freedom of movement was curtailed because of the alleged danger they posed by spreading epidemics.[149] In the Czech lands and in Hungary, Sinti and Roma fell victim to violence in other time periods.[150]

Roma held different positions in society than Jews did, but some of the same factors made them targets of violence: including ethnic homogenization, impoverishment, an alleged role in spreading epidemics, alleged laziness, alleged unreliability and imagined security risks. Remarkably, the wave of persecutions in Croatia, Romania, Slovakia and Bulgaria in 1942 took place before the Germans began systematically deporting Sinti and Roma to Auschwitz in early 1943 – although it was after 1941 when German soldiers and police started to shoot Roma in the occupied Soviet territories and in Serbia, and began to starve or gas 5,000 Austrian 'gypsies' in the Wartheland.[151]

Behind the Eastern Front, the Hungarian army supplied many of the occupation forces in the areas under German administration in northern Ukraine and southwestern Russia.[152] Hungarian troops were also important in parts of the Balkans. The Hungarian military's operations against resistance were connected in different theaters to massacres of local non-Jews – and also Jews – who were collectively suspected of supporting insurgency. Hungarian troops battling an insurgency triggered by Hungarian annexation and the deportation of at least 30,000 Serbs in the summer of 1941 conducted a raid in Novisad in late January 1942, arrested locals according to lists prepared earlier, and shot them

[147] Achim 2001, pp. 101–11; Achim 2004, pp. 169–79.
[148] Hübschmanová 1999, pp. 156–8; for the uprising see also Zimmermann 1996, pp. 290, 383.
[149] Opfer 2005, p. 282.
[150] Nečas 1999, pp. 169–71; Karsai 2005, pp. 105, 114; Gerlach and Aly 2002, pp. 429–30.
[151] For the German part see Zimmermann 1996, pp. 225–7, 248–76.
[152] Müller 2007, p. 48.

in remote places along a river bank. Of the more than 3,300 victims, 810 were Jews – about 20% of the Jewish population of the affected towns, as compared to the 2.7% of local Slavs who were among the executed.[153] Hungarian troops, who killed at least 18,000 locals (most of whom were non-Jews) in northern Ukraine from late 1941 to the summer of 1942 – massacring more than even many German units did – were not untainted by racism, although they did not do so as a result Nazi indoctrination. Thus, it is not surprising that Jews – including, for example, ninety people in the Korinkivka district in December 1941 – were among their victims. In the area of Vinnitsa, Hungarian troops participated in half a dozen 'actions' in which 2,000 Jews were shot.[154] While the number of killings committed by Hungarian soldiers on Soviet territory receded after mid 1942, in 1944 the Hungarian military murdered Romanians in the temporarily conquered areas of southern Transylvania; they also massacred 120 Jews in Sărmaş, most of whom were beaten or stabbed to death.[155]

The presumption that Jews supported resisters and guerrillas was in connection with fierce anti-communist policies. For instance, many Jews apprehended in Croatia and Hungarian-annexed Voivodina in 1941 were, according to their surviving relatives, active leftists or involved in resistance activities. Hundreds of (Serb and Croat) communists were killed in the summer of 1941.[156] The connection was not always strong. The Danish government, for example – one in which social democrats played a leading role – did not persecute Jewish nationals, but it did turn on the communists (who had condemned the regime's cooperation with the German occupiers), joined the Anti-Comintern Pact in 1941, and outlawed the Communist Party in August 1941. Of the 250 Communists interned, 150 were deported together with some Danish Jews in October 1943.[157] Danish authorities surrendered some Jewish refugees to German authorities between 1940 and 1943.[158] A regiment in the Waffen-SS made up largely of Danes, the recruitment for which the Danish government lent some support, burned down villages and shot civilians

153 Wuescht 1975, pp. 18–21, 38; Braham 1994, pp. 214–22.

154 Anderson 1999, esp. p. 353; similarly Ungváry 2005b (esp. pp. 99–101), who finds, however, that the Hungarian commanders were not racists.

155 Nagy-Talavera 2001, p. 308.

156 Pavlowitch 2008, p. 26; arrests are frequently mentioned in *We survived*, vol. 2; see also the recollections of Edo Neufeld, vol. 3, p. 169. In Yugoslavia, the Communist Party had been outlawed since 1921 but had continued to act through some legal organizations (Pavlowitch 2008, p. 6).

157 Law of August 22, 1941, in Lemkin 1944, pp. 381–3; Kirchhoff 1994, p. 108; Schulze 2007, pp. 59–60.

158 Yahil 1983, pp. 197–8.

during anti-guerrilla operations carried out under German command in the Soviet Union in 1943.[159] Simultaneously with the Danish move, German and French authorities outlawed the French Communist Party in the occupied as well as the unoccupied zone in 1941. In November and December 1941 alone, French police arrested close to 13,000 communists.[160] Italy banished 15,000 anti-fascists and kept 150,000 under surveillance.[161] The Romanian government persecuted Jews in Bukovina and Bessarabia for their alleged support of the Soviets and shot tens of thousands of Jews and non-Jews after mines planted by the Soviets in Odessa exploded in October 1941. The fact that there was no systematic arrest of communists in Transnistria – who were supposed to check in with the police weekly – and that some communists were employed in the civil service (despite an official ban) points to some moderation of Romania's violent anti-communism after 1941. The total number of communist sympathizers arrested in Romania between 1940 and 1944 was about 2,000.[162] Numbers of communists killed by non-German governments are hard to come by, but in many countries they ran into the thousands.

As the previous examples have indicated, the connection between the violence against leftists and insurgents, on the one hand, and that against Jews, on the other hand, was not always close. The Bulgarian army and police fiercely suppressed resistance in occupied Yugoslav Macedonia, Serbia and Greek Macedonia and Thrace, killing several tens of thousands of people and expelling or putting to flight 300,000 Greeks and Serbs.[163] Yet these operations hardly affected Jews in 1941–42, and when the Jews from Macedonia and Thrace were deported in March 1943, it was seemingly not rationalized in terms of their supposed help for partisans. Some propaganda in Finland linked Jews and Bolshevism, and, historically, Finnish Jews came largely from Russia – but two hard fought wars against the Soviet Union in 1939–40 and 1941–44 did not lead to legal discrimination or persecution of local Jews or deportation to German-controlled areas. By contrast, more than 18,000 of 64,000 Soviet POWs (28%) perished in Finnish captivity; some were shot by Finnish troops. Between a quarter and a half of the Slav population in reconquered Karelia, the whole of which would be expelled, were interned

[159] Müller 2007, pp. 145–7.

[160] German Military Commander in France, Ic, Supplements to political situation reports, October 30 and December 25, 1941, and public announcement by German Military Commander, August 14, 1941, in Delacor 2000a, pp. 150, 174, 216.

[161] Longhi 2010, p. 66 note 6.

[162] Dallin 1998, pp. 179–80; for the total number see Deletant 2006, p. 72.

[163] Miller 1975, pp. 127–8; Mitrovski *et al.* 1971, esp. pp. 122–3, 132–6, 156 (11,170 people were killed by Bulgarians in Serbia alone).

in Finnish camps from 1941 to 1944 – as many as 24,000 at one time, and at least 4,000 perished. (Soviet sources put the number of deaths at 12,000; following the Finnish civil war of 1918 leftists suffered from similarly brutal internment.) In the early 1940s there were plans to settle eastern Karelia by "a racially pure stock of people organically part of Finland." Additionally, about 2,900 politically suspicious Soviet POWs and immigrants – including at least sixty-six Jews among the POWs and eight Jewish refugees from central Europe – were handed over to the German Security Police (who probably killed most of them).[164] Military officers, right-wing parties and supporters of the Agrarian Party – as well as the right wing of the socialists – dreamed of a Greater Finland that included the Kola peninsula.[165] In Turkey there was low-level persecution of Jews and Christian middlemen minorities (especially Greeks), and ethnic homogenization policies forced most of the approximately 5,000 Jews from Thrace to flee to other parts of the country in 1934. But by far the bloodiest violence targeted Kurds during the Dersim uprising of 1937–38, when Turkish troops massacred about 30,000 people.[166]

Unlike Hungary, Italian empire-building did not lead to lethal persecution of Jews. In the French colony of Tunisia, the Italian Foreign Ministry even prevented Vichy government measures from applying to Jews with Italian citizenship, for Jews comprised a large part of the Italian presence (and Italy, committed to expanding her influence in Tunisia, wanted to protect her economic interests).[167] While fascist Italy, which persecuted Jews, nevertheless protected them from German deportation until 1943, Italian troops killed thousands of civilians in operations against guerrilla resistance in Yugoslavia, Greece and the Soviet Union. They razed many villages, shot all of the male inhabitants and interned entire populations in some areas. The Italian military took the same brutal measures as German units, although they shot fewer hostages.[168] In the Dalmatian camp of Rab alone, 30,000 people were interned – including close to 3,000 Jews – and every tenth inmate died of deprivation, with Slovenes faring much worse than Jews. As many as 7,000 Slovenes may have died of the 400,000 who may have passed through Italian

164 "POW Camps 1939–1944," available at: http://geocities.com/finnmilpge/fmp_pow_camps.html?200919 (accessed May 19, 2009); Laine 1994, pp. 319–33; Laine 2002, esp. pp. 139–48 (quote from p. 139); Silvennoinen 2008, esp. pp. 157–8, 219–20; Rautkallio 1987; Förster 2005, p. 96. There was also a eugenic program in Finland (Hösch 2001, p. 252).

165 Aspelmeier 1967, p. 104.

166 McDowall 2004, pp. 207–9.

167 See note by Italian Foreign Ministry, department IV, May 30, 1942, in Carpi 1999, p. 79; memo from the Italian embassy in Berlin, September 2, 1942, in Sabille 1954, pp. 187–8; Abitbol 1983, p. 128.

168 Pavlowitch 2008, pp. 140–5; Burgwyn 2005, pp. 93, 104, 111, 137–8, 154, 288, 292, 301; for the Soviet territories see Schlemmer 2005, p. 37.

internment camps.[169] At the front, Italian troops repeatedly shot captured Soviet soldiers.[170] Racism was not alien to Italy or Italian fascism; it played a major role in the murders that Italians committed during colonial conquest and rule. In Libya and Ethiopia, massacres of the local population and operations (including chemical warfare) to crush resistance led to tens of thousands of deaths – including those of at least 1,423 Christian priests in Ethiopia in 1937. Between 350,000 and 760,000 Ethiopians died from war and occupation. In the Cyrenaica region alone, a minimum of 40,000 people, or a quarter of the population, perished in Italian internment camps from hunger and mistreatment between 1930 and 1933 – long before the so-called racist turn in Italian fascism.[171] Such mass internment was later applied again, in Dalmatia and in 1938 after the conquest of Abyssinia, at a time when the greatest reach of Italian colonialism corresponded to a new ideological quality and when racist laws of a quasi-apartheid character were extended to cover not only Africans but also Jews.[172]

Non-German governments (primarily Romania, Croatia and Hungary) were responsible for the deaths of at least 300,000 Jews, and 50,000 died in pogroms in the summer of 1941. The number of non-Jews killed under these non-German regimes[173] was even higher. The Croatian and Italian governments were responsible for killings in six-digit figures; the policies of Hungarian, Romanian, Bulgarian, Turkish and Finnish authorities killed tens of thousands of non-Jews. In several countries, like Romania and Hungary, Jews were the group with the largest number of unnatural deaths for non-combatants both in relative terms as well as in absolute numbers. However, in some states, other groups suffered a higher mortality than did Jews. For example, it was more dangerous to be a Soviet POW in Finland, or a Slav in Karelia, than to be a Jew. A similar point can be made about Italy with reference to Libya. In the Independent State of Croatia the percentage of Roma who were murdered seems to have been equal to or higher than for Jews, and many more Serbs (more than 300,000) were killed than either Jews or Roma, although Serbs had a relatively higher chance of survival.[174] Many Jews, Serbs, Roma and Croat opponents were interned together in camps like the Jasenovac

169 Ahonen *et al.* 2008, p. 47; Gitman 2011, p. 143; Steinberg 1992, pp. 174–6; Pavlowitch 2008, p. 141.

170 Schlemmer 2005, pp. 44–6.

171 Collotti 2006, pp. 22–39; Del Boca 2004, esp. pp. 194–7; Mattioli 2004, pp. 218–19; Di Sante 2008; Schlemmer and Woller 2005, p. 199; Mann 2005, pp. 308–9. The thesis of racism having been alien to Italians, or even insignificant, can be found in de Felice 1995, p. xv; Ahonen *et al.* 2008, p. 45.

172 Del Boca 1995, esp. p. 339; Raspin 1986, p. 79.

173 I leave out Allied states from these considerations.

174 For Roma see Chapter 14, note 146 above.

complex.[175] Authorities and citizens of Romania and Croatia, the countries with the most murderous anti-Jewish programs (after Germany), also killed the most Roma. As with Croatia, Bulgarians killed more Greeks and Yugoslavs than Jews, even if one assigns to them responsibility for the deaths of the Jews deported from Thrace and Macedonia to Bulgaria. If one takes all of the victim groups into account, any ideas about the moral immunity of societies such as those in Finland, Bulgaria, Italy, Denmark and Turkey to racism, or to generating violence, have to be abandoned.

What is even more important is that there were many connections between the persecution of Jews and non-Jews, although this nexus differed from country to country. These links mainly involved the following elements: an attempted consolidation of the nation state or empire building, racism, ethnic homogenization, xenophobia, economic protectionism, the efforts of a commercial middle class and intelligentsia to rise socially, and combating armed resistance and anti-leftist polices. Such attitudes and interests also contributed to the fact that some of these governments agreed to hand part of their Jewish population over to the Germans. And despite all the differences, the policies of non-German regimes were in many ways similar to German ones.

[175] Cvetković 2008, p. 367.

15 In the labyrinths of persecution: Survival attempts

This chapter focuses on Jewish action and the possibilities of Jewish survival, but also the lack thereof. Concentrating on survival, as such, is unrepresentative because most Jews did not survive. Close to 6 million were murdered; about 1.3 million Jews once living under German rule – or in countries allied with Germany – lived to see the end of the war in 1945 (see Chapter 5). Also, the experiences of the survivors are not always representative of all the persecuted. For instance, living in a camp – so prominent in survivors' accounts and the imagination of today's public – was far from a universal Jewish experience (unlike other victim groups, like Soviet POWs and Polish and Soviet forced laborers). A majority of Jews were in camps, but I estimate that 2.5 million never so much as spent a single night in a camp.[1] This number includes those Jews, predominantly in the occupied Soviet territories, who Germans and their helpers massacred close to their towns; and those who were deported to extermination camps and murdered within hours of their arrival. Life in confinement of other kinds (in ghettos, Jewish neighborhoods, or 'Jew houses') was more typical. But as this chapter also deals with many failed attempts to survive, and the reasons for these failures, it does account for Jewish responses in general to German and Axis persecution, which has been covered before.

The perspective of this chapter is narrow in that it does not offer a full account of Jewish life and emotions during the persecution. Like most other parts of this book, it analyzes actions, as a principle, and tries to explain their background, also in terms of ideas and emotions. But, like elsewhere, I do not elaborate much on thoughts, attitudes and emotions that did not lead to action. I think that a total history of that side of life, in all its aspects, remains to be written (as it does for perpetrators too). In particular, we have not fully understood the everyday lives of the persecuted in which, it seems to me, not everything was related to

[1] Even most Jewish *survivors* from France, Germany and Romania were never camp inmates.

being persecuted. This would have to have been so. Psychologically, their everyday lives can be understood in terms of an instinctive distancing of themselves from the dangers they faced. As Gustawa Jarecka wrote in the Warsaw ghetto, "Already then [April 18, 1942] we marveled about the defiant continuation of the everyday. The everyday was like the water, on which no trace remains. After each new loss, after each new blow it closed with frightening indifference."[2]

There was no purely individualistic survival. Survival required social interaction, just as persecution did, and it could not happen without relations with non-Jews. This was even the case, or especially so, for sizable Jewish rescue organizations.[3] In this sense, Jews strove for social integration with non-Jews. But they ran into difficulties beyond the official German policies aimed at isolating them. Their efforts began with little things. When German Jews were deported from the Rhineland to Riga, they repeatedly tried to make contact with others during stops at railway stations in order to obtain water and arrange for letters to be sent.[4] Having non-Jewish friends could enable one to go into hiding.[5] A Lithuanian newspaper complained in mid 1943 that non-Jewish Lithuanians still supplied their Jewish acquaintances with food and that farmers still traded with them.[6] For the early post-war analyst Samuel Gringauz, the elites in Polish ghettos were what he called "contact people," i.e., those in business relationships with Germans, employees of the Germans, or their proteges in the German-controlled Jewish self-administrations.[7] Survival, even in the short term – which included having sufficient food provisions, rescue from arrest, and a secure hiding place – could also depend on good relations within the Jewish community.[8]

The methods that Jews employed in trying to survive were based on their attempts to understand the logics of persecution and respond to them.[9] The most successful strategies, relatively speaking, were, first, reliance on the open or tacit protection of non-German governments and their citizens; second, legal and illegal cross-border emigration; third,

[2] Gustawa Jarecka, "The last stage of resettlement is death" (*c.* second half of 1942) in Sakowska 1993, p. 232.

[3] For France see Cohen 1994, esp. p. 16.

[4] Report by Police Captain Salitter, December 26, 1941, in Hilberg 1981, p. 132.

[5] See the account by Barbara Gorá in Śliwowska 1999, pp. 71–2; see the account of Riva Blumbergiene-Cvibakaite in *With a Needle* 2003, p. 43.

[6] Diary of A. Jerushalmi, July 9, 1943, in Grossman and Ehrenburg 1994, pp. 569–70.

[7] Gringauz 1949, p. 13; see Kassow 2010, p. 284.

[8] This is obvious from the fate of the members of the Oyneg Shabat archive in Warsaw; see Kassow 2010, pp. 239–331.

[9] Fein 1979 (pp. 197–325) described Jewish behavior as a rational choice.

going into hiding or living illegally or with guerrilla groups; and, fourth, forced labor in German or other camps.[10]

Since there were different logics of persecution, a definitive and decisive counter strategy was hard to come by. The same person might need more than one strategy to survive. The paths that led to survival were narrow and twisted,[11] and they ended in many different places – one could not always predict which alleyways would lead to safety. But in many places, staying put held little promise. In the Polish cities of Lublin, Białystok and Łódź, only 1.5%, 0.3% and 0.5% of the pre-war Jewish population that had lived in each, respectively, and had remained there for the duration of the war, were liberated by Soviet troops.[12] By far the most successful option for Polish Jews was to emigrate, flee, be evacuated or even be deported to the Soviet Union. The next three most successful options combined (camps on Polish soil, camps in Germany and illegally living among non-Jews) produced fewer survivors. A small number stayed with, or under, the protection of partisans.[13]

The picture was similar in Vilnius and the Lithuanian-Belarusian borderlands, but with telling differences: most survivors escaped to the Soviet side; some outlasted persecution "in the ghetto," the forests or with the partisans; and very few were hidden by non-Jews. People from small towns had a much lower chance of survival in all of these categories, except for life in the forest or with the partisans.[14] In Zagreb, Croatia, the best chance turned out to be in camps, prisons and forced labor institutions; followed by joining the partisans and living clandestinely. Others fled abroad. In Sarajevo, most survivors endured by way of Italian protection or by joining the partisans. The protection of the Croatian state for Jews deemed important to the national economy, or for those in mixed marriages, also resulted in many surviving in Croatia.[15] In Serbia, some managed to hold out with the partisans while others fled (many to Italy) or survived as POWs (in Germany), in hiding, or in mixed marriages.[16] For Jews in Paris, flight to Vichy France and illegal life there, or remaining in the city – illegally or legally (an option available almost exclusively to French citizens) – helped more than half to survive; employment with the officially recognized organization of French Jews, or with the

[10] This is adapted from Hilberg 1992a, pp. 206–7, who did not discuss emigration at this point.
[11] See, for example, Bauer 2013, pp. 193–216.
[12] Dobroszycki 1994, pp. 3–4.
[13] See Dobroszycki 1994, pp. 13, 19, 68, 76–83; Paulsson 2004, p. 393.
[14] Lejzer Ran, "Der gerettete Überrest von Wilna und Umgebung," *Blätter über Wilna*, 1946, German translation in StA Hannover 2 Js 388/65, pp. 1734–41.
[15] Goldstein 2004, p. 58; Gitman 2011, pp. 67–8, for Sarajevo see ibid., p. 61.
[16] See Pavlowitch 2008, p. 70; for the town of Zemun see Fogel 2007, p. 160.

German military, was more risky. Armed struggle in the city also led to death.[17] The fate of Hungarian Jews was no different in that few survived in hiding and a large number lived under the very unreliable protection of national governments; it was atypical because relatively many Jews from Hungary (about 110,000 plus approximately 15,000 hostages) survived as forced laborers under German control.[18]

The widely varying survival rates testify to extremely different conditions. Some 99% of the Jews from Denmark survived; 80% from Italy; 75% from France; 67% from Germany; 67% from Romania (not counting those from Romanian-occupied Ukraine); 66% from Austria; 60% from Belgium; close to half from Norway; 36% from Greater Hungary; 34% from Austria; 25% from the Netherlands; 25% from Croatia, Bosnia, and Herzegovina; 20% from all of Yugoslavia; approximately 15% from Greece; about 20% from Soviet Belarus (but only 3.5% in German-controlled territory); about 10% from western and central Poland (4% in German-controlled territory); 6–7% from Lithuania (4% in German-controlled territory); 5–6% from Volyn (1.5% in German-controlled territory); and about 40% from Soviet Ukraine (hardly more than 5% in German-controlled territory).[19]

Major survival strategies

Geographic mobility was a traditional means of survival for Jews in times of emergency and also a way to seek a better life. According to one source, from 1900 to 1914 alone, 3 million Jews had changed their country of residence. Most had left eastern Europe where poverty and hostility had increased.[20] As described above, emigration numbers from 1933 to 1945 were much lower as a result of, among other reasons, the general tightening of immigration restrictions in the context of growing xenophobia and socioeconomic insecurity after World War I. Jews in particular were targeted by legal and unofficial immigration restrictions. In total, about 300,000 Jews may have survived by migrating to countries that German troops or policies never reached; before 1941, these were mainly Germans

[17] See Adler 1989, pp. 14, 45, 189, 198–9, 201, 217, 219.
[18] See Gerlach and Aly 2002, p. 409.
[19] For Austria see Moser 1966, p. 52, and Friedländer 1998, p. 241; for Hungary see Gerlach and Aly 2002, pp. 50, 409; for Croatia, Bosnia and Herzegovina see Gitman 2011, p. 24; for Greece see Lewkowicz 2006, p. 69, and Plaut 1996, pp. 54, 71, 95; for Belarus see Gerlach 1999, pp. 380–1, 740–5, and Smilovitsky 2003; for Poland see the data compiled in Dobroszycki 1994, esp. pp. 25–6; for Lithuania see Dieckmann 2011, pp. 308–9, 1538, and Levinson 2006, p. 14; for Volyn see Spector 1990a, pp. 53–5, 337, 357–8; for Ukraine see Kruglov 2010, pp. 273, 284.
[20] Report to the Women's Section of DELASEM, October 1941, in Sarfatti 2006, p. 261.

and Austrians (see Chapter 3). This does not include those German Jews who fled to neighboring countries and were later trapped by invading German troops, or those who returned to Nazi Germany after emigration. Some 16,000 of the 53,000 Jews who had left in 1933 later returned, and 6,000 of those Jews who had migrated from Germany to Poland from 1933 to 1938 came back because of the hostile atmosphere in Poland.[21] Overall emigration figures were much lower: 25,000 for Czech Jews from 1939 to 1941, and relatively few Polish, French, and Italian Jews emigrated legally after the beginning of their persecution in 1939, 1940 and 1938, respectively.[22] From 1940 to 1943, about 40,000–60,000 left illegally for Switzerland and Spain, among them many from Italy and France, including foreign Jews residing in these countries. Sweden took in about 6,000 Danish and Norwegian Jews.[23] Many thousand tried to escape from one Axis country to another, where the conditions were supposedly less threatening: for example, from Poland to Hungary in 1939–40; from Slovakia to Hungary in 1941–42; from German- to Romanian-occupied Soviet territory in 1942; and from Hungary to Slovakia or Romania in 1944.[24] Many Jews left small German towns in the 1930s for cities where life was supposedly still bearable.[25]

In addition to the 1.3 million survivors just mentioned, another 1.6–1.7 million Jews narrowly escaped destruction in the Soviet Union in 1941, and some more in 1942, by being evacuated or fleeing on their own as German troops approached (see also Chapter 4). This was close to 40% of the Jewish population in the affected areas; the percentage was lower in the west and higher in the east.[26] To illustrate the impact, Germans and Romanians murdered 1.6 million of Ukraine's Jews; a million survived, 90% of them by fleeing to the east.[27] Jews were overrepresented among the 10–15 million Soviet evacuees and refugees because many of them resided in cities (and, so, were close to railway stations),

21 Marrus 1985, p. 135.

22 For the Czech Jews see Kárný 1982, p. 174; for Poland see Gutman 1982, p. 18. For the emigration of 90,000 Polish Jews to Palestine in 1930–39 see Mendelsohn 1983, p. 79.

23 For Spain see Rother 2001, pp. 130–2, who revised other estimates downward (ibid., pp. 5–7); for Switzerland see Unabhängige Expertenkommission 1999, pp. 24–5; for Norway see Abrahamsen 1991, pp. 2, 16.

24 For flight from and to Hungary see Gerlach and Aly 2002, pp. 31, 306–7; for escape to areas under Romanian occupation see Grossman and Ehrenburg 1994 (for example, pp. 83–5), and Zabarko 2005, pp. 33–4.

25 See Wildt 2007, for example, pp. 285–90.

26 See Arad 2009 (pp. 72–87) for 1941; for Belarus see Gerlach 1999, pp. 378–81. German troops caught up with some of those evacuated in 1941, but there were new evacuees in 1942. Thus, the 1941 figures may give an accurate overall picture of how many survived this way.

27 Kruglov 2010, p. 273.

often belonged to groups, such as civil servants and factory workers that were given priority in the evacuation, and more Jews may have made an effort to be evacuated than non-Jews. Only occasionally did saving Jews from future persecution play a role in the considerations of Soviet authorities. More than half of all those surviving Jews living in areas that came at some point under German or Axis control were evacuated Soviet Jews. Their evacuation belonged to the Jewish social tradition of flight and emigration from threat. Many Jews had already fled or been evacuated from the same areas when German and Austrian troops approached in 1914–16 during World War I[28] (although others stayed behind in 1941 because German troops had, in their experience, behaved decently during World War I).

In the end, emigration and flight were the most successful survival strategies. But pursuing them depended on realizing that the situation was grave enough to risk the loss of homeland, wealth and social networks. Emigration was not possible for, or practiced by, everybody; the old, the poor and women were disproportionately left behind, and Jews from other countries had less time and fewer opportunities than those from Greater Germany. Large families were also disadvantaged and disproportionately often arrested.[29] Among Soviet Jews, those from the recently annexed western borderlands and from remote places had little chance. To flee abroad implied seeking protection from foreign governments, but this was not always successful, especially if these belonged to the Axis.

Non-German governments, where they were still in place, did offer some protection to their Jewish nationals. The Bulgarian and Romanian regimes rejected deportation of their Jewish citizens from their mainlands. This was also true for some years of the Italian and Hungarian governments. The French government, administration and police increasingly obstructed the arrest and transportation of Jewish co-nationals (see Chapter 5). Slovak, Croatian, Italian and Hungarian leaders insisted (even after deportations had started) on exempting certain categories of Jews from the worst of the persecution. These often included Christian converts, those in mixed marriages, intellectuals and business elites.[30] As outlined above, these policies were often backed or demanded by various elites, although many members of these same elites had not objected in principle to discrimination against Jews (see Chapters 13 and 14).

28 See Prusin 2010, pp. 55–8.

29 This is suggested by a study on Lens in northern France: Mariot and Zalc 2010, pp. 97, 127.

30 For exemptions in Italy see Michaelis 1978, pp. 255–6, and Longhi 2010, pp. 32, 84; for Croatia see Gitman 2011, pp. 56, 67–8; for Romania see Ancel 1984, p. 407.

Maintaining close contacts with national elites was useful for mobilizing support. For example, 27% of adult Jewish Italians were members of the Fascist Party before 1938, and more than 43% were married to non-Jews. Jews had served as important and respected government ministers after emancipation.[31] In Romania, Wilhelm Filderman, leader of the Jewish community, issued hundreds of petitions, and several members of the ruling non-Jewish circles sought to maintain friendly relations with Jews in 1942.[32] Such governmental-cum-social protection enabled 50,000–60,000 Jews in German-occupied France, 30,000 of them in Paris, to live in legally declared residences until 1944; only about 3,000 Jews were arrested in that city between January and July of that year.[33] Negotiations and petitions with the regime were less successful inside Germany, but they did take place in the 1930s and led to regulations like the Haavara agreement that enabled many to emigrate.[34] Even in 1942, when extermination was under way, German and French Jews contested their 'racial' assessments in court. This strategy was not always without success, leading bureaucrats to consider prohibiting such challenges.[35] Accordingly, the Zionist Rescue Committee in Budapest claimed to have worked out a plan of action shortly after the German occupation of Hungary in which three out of the six recommended survival strategies required elite contacts: negotiations with German officials and Hungarian "forces," and appeals to non-Axis governments and the International Committee of the Red Cross.[36]

Such protection was less reliable for Jews who did not hold the citizenship of their country of residence. Part of the reason was their lesser social integration. For example, French Jews and Jewish immigrants to France did not live in the same neighborhoods, often spoke different languages, had different social statuses, held different sorts of jobs, and joined different organizations.[37] From 1933 to 1936, before becoming the target of persecution themselves, some functionaries of French Jewish organizations made xenophobic remarks about Jewish immigrants and advocated the repatriation of German Jews.[38] One concern among French Jews was

[31] Longhi 2010, pp. 32, 36 note 35; Zuccotti 1996, pp. 15–18.

[32] Ancel 2011, p. 169; Ancel 1984, p. 388.

[33] Zuccotti 1993, pp. 161, 199; Adler 1989, p. 219; for France see Poznanski 1997, p. 554.

[34] See Friedländer 1998, pp. 60–5; Barkai 1988, pp. 47–8, 75–8.

[35] See undated memo (after August 17, 1942), BA 15.09, Nr. 20, pp. 12–22, and Military Commander in France, Abt. Wi I to Commissariat General for Jewish Questions, October 2, 1942, BA 15.09, Nr. 2, p. 36.

[36] Quoted in Gerlach and Aly 2002, pp. 299–300. The other strategies mentioned were the preparation of hideouts and false identity papers, flight to Romania and Tito's partisans, and unspecified "active and passive resistance" of Hungarian Jews.

[37] Dreyfus 1981, p. 244.

[38] Caron 1999, pp. 94–116; Marrus and Paxton 1981, p. 189.

that Jewish immigration would give rise to anti-Jewish attitudes in general. Later, the General Association of Israelites in France made helping French Jews a priority and supported Jewish immigrants only when pressed.[39] In Germany, many Jewish intellectuals were prejudiced against Jewish immigrants from eastern Europe, and before the Nazi era some advocated sending them back eastward.[40] Tensions between immigrant and non-immigrant Jews also existed in other countries.[41] What was true within Jewish populations was even more the case outside them.

The consequences for immigrants were striking, at least in western Europe. In France, the death rate among Jews in general was 24%; among those with French citizenship it was 12.6%; among alien Jews it was 41%. But the 12.6% figure includes 8,000 naturalized Jews and another 8,000 born in France to foreign Jews. If one counts these two groups as alien, then more than half of the Jews of recent foreign origin died, but less than one-tenth of autochthonous French Jews did.[42] In other words, less than 10% of the Jews from France who perished were not of direct foreign extraction. The fact that the Germans murdered a higher percentage of the Jews from Belgium than of those from France also correlates with the higher proportion of foreign Jews residing in Belgium (90%) than in France (50%).[43] In Italy, foreign Jews ran double the risk of being killed compared to Jewish Italian nationals.[44] But the high mortality rate among Dutch Jews, 85% of whom originated from the Netherlands, does not follow the same pattern.[45]

Another traditional protective strategy that enabled a smaller number of Jews to survive was conversion to Christianity: this saved tens of thousands of lives.[46] One reason the number wasn't larger was the Nazi racist concept itself –according to which descent, not religion, mattered, which rendered a change of religion irrelevant. However, this was not the case in many countries allied with Germany where converted Jews

[39] Adler 1989, p. 110.
[40] See Aschheim 1982, pp. 33–4, 85; for romantization as a countertrend see ibid., pp. 185–214.
[41] Picard 1997, p. 283.
[42] The calculation is based on figures in Zuccotti 1993, pp. 3, 207, 237; see also Meyer 2000, p. 34.
[43] Blom 1989, p. 286.
[44] See Sarfatti 2006, p. 203 and Chapter 14 of this book. Once deported, however, foreign Jews had a higher survival rate (22% versus 8%; Toscano 1995, p. xli), probably as a result of their language abilities, adaptability and age.
[45] Maxwell 1998, p. 3.
[46] For Italy in 1938–39 see Longhi 2010, p. 58 note 138, and Michaelis 1978, p. 258; for Austria in 1938 see SD situation report for 1938, MadR, vol. 1, p. 67; for Hungary see Gerlach and Aly 2002, p. 313, and Braham 1994, pp. 496, 895–900; for Slovakia see Hradská 1996, p. 83.

had legal protection, and, at times, German authorities respected these laws because of overriding foreign policy interests. Another equally grave reason for the small number of conversions was the clergy's disinclination to baptize Jews. To some degree, the Croatian Catholic Church has been cited as an exception.[47] In the German-occupied Soviet territories, where converting Jews required a great deal of courage, a few priests tried to help as many Jews as they could by, among other things, providing them with baptismal certificates.[48] The scarcity of Christian charity was one way in which the social environment of Jews obstructed pathways of survival.

Making Jews indispensable to German authorities, as forced laborers, was not a traditional method of survival. This was the controversial basic strategy of many Jewish councils like those in Łódź, Vilnius and Białystok.[49] It sometimes meant abandoning children and the elderly and sick. The strategy saved only a few people, and for a number of interrelated reasons. Most Jews were employed as unskilled laborers, if at all, and, thus, were replaceable. Moreover, the SS took over control of most Jewish forced laborers and held them in grossly undersupplied camps (where conditions were much worse than in ghettos and where they endured the most violent treatment). As a result, only a few of those selected for work stayed alive (see Chapter 9). Forced labor saved a sizable group only among the Hungarian Jews because they were in German hands for a relatively short time.[50]

Forced labor organized by other Axis countries also saved relatively few. Jewish workers either suffered conditions similar to those in SS camps – and often died, as in Croatia and Romanian-occupied Transnistria – or they eventually fell into German hands, as in France, Slovakia and Hungary; or there were few Jewish forced laborers in the first place, as in Italy. Many Jews in hiding also needed to find work for sustenance. In southern France they found employment as teachers, traveling salesmen, office staff and salespersons; young boys and girls in occupied Poland found work as farmhands, mainly tending cattle. This difference highlights how much more desperate the situation of Jews was in Poland than in France.[51]

47 Gitman 2011, pp. 109–12.
48 Grossman and Ehrenburg 1994, p. 63 (Berdichev, Ukraine) and 777 (Lithuania).
49 Trunk 1972, pp. 400–13; for East Upper Silesia see Steinbacher 2000, pp. 296–7; for France see Adler 1989, pp. 44, 198–9.
50 See Gerlach and Aly 2002, pp. 375–414.
51 For France see Poznanski 1997, pp. 159–65, and Kaspi 1997, pp. 166–72; for Poland see various survivors' accounts in Śliwowska 1999, pp. 4, 76, 84–6.

Tremendous difficulties in living in hiding

The question why Jews did not simply run away is often posed. But life in hiding was very difficult.[52] One reason is that Jews who lived clandestinely, even though many were able to find non-Jewish helpers, were frequently denounced by other non-Jews, especially in eastern Europe. One child survivor said that he was reported several times.[53] Jews were revealed in their hiding places, but also in villages, the forest, on city streets and in church by strangers, as well as acquaintances.[54] In Lvov there was an extensive spy network for such purposes, whereas, purportedly, there was not in other Ukrainian cities like Kharkov and Kiev.[55] The dedication of denouncers, and insecurity for Jews, could reach as far as that of the neighbor who reported Doba Belozovskaya's children to the German authorities during the Germans' preparations for the retreat from Kiev in the fall of 1943. The children were never seen again.[56] Not everyone denounced Jews. Still, the story of several farmers warning Jewish refugees in Ladyzhin, Vinnitsa *oblast*, Ukraine, of an approaching killing squad, only for the group to be denounced by an elderly man from the same village, is not uncharacteristic.[57] On the basis of a small sample, Gunnar Paulsson concluded that Jews in Warsaw ran a higher risk of being betrayed or murdered than of being discovered by German or Polish officials.[58] Reporting by private individuals and local party officials, rather than through raids or discovery by the Gestapo, led to about 20–40% of police cases against Jews in Germany.[59] Denunciations of Jews were also very frequent in France and Hungary (see Chapter 13).

In Poland, some non-Jews not only reported escaped Jews, they also murdered them. Maria Kopel from Krasnobrody recalled that her father was killed by villagers who also let her five-year-old brother freeze to death, tried to drown her sister, and handed another brother over to the

[52] A good description can be found in Młynarczyk 2007, pp. 293–322.
[53] See the account of Roman Lewin in Śliwowska 1999, pp. 193–9.
[54] See the accounts of Leszek Leon Allerhand in Śliwowska 1999, pp. 157–8; Leon Czerwonka in Hochberg-Mariańska and Grüss 1996, p. 197; Vladimiras Kobrinas in *With a Needle* 2003, p. 187.
[55] R. Fraerman's report on Lvov can be found in Grossman and Ehrenburg 1994, pp. 184–7.
[56] See Doba Belozovskaya's account in Zabarko 2005, p. 18. For a similar story from Vienna see Königseder 1996, p. 207.
[57] See the account of Regina Leshchinskaya (Sudobitskaya) in Zabarko 2005, p. 161.
[58] Paulsson 2002, p. 213.
[59] Johnson and Reuband 2005, pp. 301, 405 note 15.

Germans.[60] One man who temporarily survived after escaping from a deportation train on November 8, 1942, while it was on its way from Łukow to the Treblinka extermination camp, reported that non-Jewish Polish farmers attacked the more than 250 fugitives, robbed them, beat them – some to death – and denounced the remainder to the German railroad police who shot all of the escapees they could find.[61]

However, Jews in hiding were not only in danger of outright denunciation; often they were just threatened. They were also endangered by gossip and rumor that could be just as deadly as denunciation (see Chapter 13). This becomes especially clear in a collection of reminiscences of Polish-Jewish child survivors who were interviewed in 1945.[62] These children seem to have been aware of nuances that don't appear in later accounts and the memories of adults. In both small towns and large cities, non-Jews living near Jewish hiding places simply talked too much about where Jews were secretly residing, or they made derogatory remarks.[63] Frequently, and in public, boys loudly called people – minors and adults – Jews.[64] Others – many of them women – threatened to report Jews (sometimes also robbing or blackmailing them)[65] or tried to force neighbors or acquaintances to stop helping Jews.[66] In survivors' accounts, this growing insecurity through rumor, suspicion and open threat is expressed in phrases like "there the ground was crumbling under their feet," or, "when things started to heat up again, we moved."[67] Such practices offset the positive survival effect of the numerous people with good intentions who helped those in hiding. According to one estimate, 160,000 non-Jewish Poles, about half of them in Warsaw, were hiding Jews at different times.[68]

[60] See the account in Hochberg-Mariańska and Grüss 1996, p. 121; see also the survivor account of Herman Amsterdam, ibid., p. 149. Cases from Lithuania are given in the account of Valentina Filipova in *With a Needle* 2003 (pp. 26–7), and one from Ukraine is given by Dovidas Sasoveris, ibid., p. 317.

[61] See Kassow 2010, pp. 433–4.

[62] Hochberg-Mariańska and Grüss 1996.

[63] The accounts of Zygmunt Weinreb and Helena Arbeiter can be found in Hochberg-Mariańska and Grüss 1996, pp. 114, 162; Irina Felgina's account (on eastern Belarus) can be found in *With a Needle* 2003, p. 81–2.

[64] The account of Helena Arbeiter can be found in Hochberg-Mariańska and Grüss 1996, pp. 163–4.

[65] Threats forced Sabina Wylot (Warsaw) to seek a new host on five occasions, see Śliwowska 1999, pp. 144–7. See also the accounts of Szlama Kutnowski, Halina Schütz and Franciszka Guter in Hochberg-Mariańska and Grüss 1996, pp. 78, 99, 167–8.

[66] See the account of Emanuel Elbinger (Nowe Brzesko) in Śliwowska 1999, p. 33; for an account from Belarus see Grossman and Ehrenburg 1994, p. 751.

[67] The account of Pola Elbinger (Nowe Brzesko) can be found in Śliwowska 1999, p. 41 (first quote), and that of Jerzy Alexandrowicz can be found in Hochberg-Mariańska and Grüss 1996, p. 183 (second quote); for another example see the account of Szlama Kutnowski (Warsaw) in ibid., p. 79.

[68] Paulsson 2002, pp. 129–31.

If their secrecy was jeopardized, most Jews felt compelled to move on. Some were chased away.[69] Few reacted like Wilhelm Zienowicz's mother – who insisted on keeping to her story that she was not a Jewess, despite her neighbors shouting at her that she was putting them all at risk.[70] The fact that many Jews reported that they often changed hosts reflects the persistent fear of denunciation and gossip.[71] In the Netherlands, each of the 250 children hidden by a rescue organization needed, on average, five hosts; survivors from Warsaw reported about seven hideouts on average. Individuals required up to thirty-seven hiding places.[72] All of this underlines the fact that seemingly banal practices of social exclusion became a lethal threat for Jews facing German persecution. Habitual hostility toward Jews and reckless thoughtlessness (as displayed by the children whose shouted insults and attacks often appear in survivors' memoirs) could prove deadly in this new context.

Even those survivors who were determined and resourceful enough to make it through, remembered how the hostile environment they had experienced seemed to have left them no way out. Sjoma Spungin from Daugavpils, Lithuania, a thirteen-year-old boy, recalled shortly after the war the situation in May 1942: "We could flee nowhere, our town is small, you cannot hide. And we did not know where there were partisans."[73] Others reinforced this impression. A Jew from Winnitsa, Ukraine, was told by a sympathetic communist political commissar, who had already saved him several times, that the Germans wanted to kill all of the Jews except for a few specialists: "There is nowhere to hide."[74] "The Germans, not without reason, relied on the fact that even upon escape, refugees would have nowhere to go."[75] In the Lithuanian town of Lazdijai, the local police chief told Jewish residents in late October 1941: "Running away is not logical. In every place the German enters,

[69] The accounts of Leon Majblum and Josek Mansdorf can be found in Hochberg-Mariańska and Grüss 1996, pp. 91–2, 107–10.

[70] Zienowicz's account can be found in Śliwowska 1999, p. 312; examples to the contrary are found in the accounts of Dawid Wulf and Jozef Reich in Hochberg-Mariańska and Grüss 1996, pp. 175, 185–7.

[71] See the accounts of Krystyna Budnicka and Jadwiga Fiszbain-Tokarz in Śliwowska 1999, pp. 20, 45–7; those of Tamara Cygler and Fryda Einsiedler are found in Hochberg-Mariańska and Grüss 1996, pp. 87–90, 159–60; various survivors' accounts can be found in *With a Needle* 2003, pp. 111–12, 178–9, 187–9, 199; the account of B.J. Tartakovskaia (Dnjepropetrovsk) is found in Grossman and Ehrenburg 1994, pp. 123–4.

[72] Van Thijn 2001, p. 270; for Warsaw see Paulsson 2004, p. 396. On the Netherlands see Moore 1997, p. 155; Houwink ten Cate 1999, p. 128; Mason 1984, p. 331; on Germany see Benz 1988b, p. 666.

[73] See Spungin's account in Grossman and Ehrenburg 1994, p. 737.

[74] Quoted in Weiner 2001, p. 283.

[75] Smilovitsky 1997 (p. 307) on Belarus.

the Jew is stricken from the list of the living. There is no place where you can hide [...]."[76]

Some of the most harrowing indications of this hopelessness are the many accounts according to which Jews, especially in the German-occupied Soviet territories, escaped from a ghetto or camp but found no better place to flee to than another ghetto or camp.[77] The German entrepreneur Walter Többens, who employed many Jewish textile workers, announced, with some pride, that wealthy Jews in hiding asked him to send them to the Trawniki camp because "they couldn't bear it" among Polish non-Jews.[78] Jews who had fled from the ghetto in Jozefow, Poland, found so little help outside that they fled to a German-controlled labor camp for Jews; inmates reported of these refugees that "in their eyes, we were free and they were captives."[79] In a similar manner, 18,000 Jews in the district of Radom escaped from imminent deportation to their deaths in late 1942, but almost all of them turned themselves in when the German authorities opened new camps and promised to legalize their existence. Most were murdered between January and April 1943.[80] Others even turned themselves in to the Germans or to their local helpers. After having fled just before a mass deportation from Nowe Brzesko near Kraków, "for several days, Jews wandered through the neighboring fields. No one wanted to feed or shelter them. They reported themselves to the police or were captured."[81] Two days after the final massacre in Shamovo near Smolensk on February 2, 1942, four elderly Jews unable to find help went to the local police station and one of them, whose name was Schmuilo, told the officers, "You can bump us off." (A Polish observer from the Zamosc area called this in November 1942 a "common occurrence.") After two massacres that claimed 8,000 Jewish lives in Chmelnik, Ukraine, in January 1942, some Jewish refugees without shelter wandered through the fields until they froze to death.[82]

It is not by accident that these examples are from Poland and the Soviet Union, where German oppression was fierce and denunciations were frequent. In the rural region of Volyn, western Ukraine – which was also

[76] Quoted in Levinson 2006, p. 103.

[77] See Smilowitsky 1997, p. 307 and Gerlach 1999, p. 745 on Belarus; Levin 1985, pp. 114, 131, 180–6, 243–5 on Lithuania; letter by Mikhail Indikt (Dnjepropetrovsk), July 31, 1944, in Grossman and Ehrenburg 1994, p. 113; Bender 2009, p. 90 (Chmielnik, Poland).

[78] Többens's public appeal, March 20, 1943, is quoted in Gutman 1982, pp. 334–5.

[79] Quoted in Silberklang 2004, pp. 163–4.

[80] See Młynarczyk 2007, p. 302, and Seidel 2009, pp. 338, 343.

[81] The account of Emmanual Elbinger can be found in Śliwowska 1999, p. 31.

[82] Report by A.I. Bekker can be found in Grossman and Ehrenburg 1994, p. 81; for Shamovo see pp. 403–4 of the same volume. For Zamosc see Klukowski 1993, p. 226 (diary, November 20, 1942).

torn by civil war –possibly only 9% of those who escaped from the ghettos survived (see Chapter 11).[83] In such areas, only a fraction of those who fled survived or reached the partisans.[84] The hostile attitude of many non-Jews also made underground life for Jews very difficult in Hungary in 1944.[85] The difference between these countries and Yugoslavia is striking. Yugoslavian survivors rarely mentioned denunciations or fleeing from ghetto to ghetto. Instead, raids and roadblocks, followed by attacks by Cetniks, appear in accounts from former Yugoslavia as the main dangers for Jews living illegally.[86] Denunciations seem to have been less frequent there despite the fact that sheltering Jews was punishable by death, at least in German-occupied Serbia.[87] The consequences of denunciation were also apparently less devastating in Italy and France. These comparisons show that the near-impossibility of survival in hiding in the occupied Soviet territories wasn't universal or inevitable; but it also applied to Belarus, so that relations between Jews and non-Jews in that country were not as amicable as many authors, including this one, have portrayed them.[88]

Rumors and denunciations claimed the lives of hundreds of thousands of Jews hidden across Europe. But the impact of them went further. Because of the hostile environment, many Jews didn't even attempt to flee. A Polish social-democratic underground newspaper reported in mid-August 1942 – during the worst wave of deportations from Warsaw to Treblinka – on the widespread resignation among inmates of the Warsaw ghetto and their feeling of being abandoned, caused by the enmity prevailing among Poles outside the ghetto walls.[89] When it became known among the Jews in the Polish town of Wierzbnik in late October 1942 that the ghetto would be liquidated, only a few adults tried to hide and just a few children were put into the care of non-Jews.[90] In western Poland, still fewer Jews tried to live clandestinely than in the central and eastern parts of the country.[91]

83 Spector 1990a, pp. 357–8. But Pohl 2010 (p. 72 note 196) finds Spector's figure of initial refugees exaggerated.

84 For example, see Eckman and Lazar 1977, pp. 85, 90, 136; Ainsztein 1993, pp. 80–8.

85 See Gerlach and Aly 2002, pp. 307–9.

86 This observation is based on the hundred or so accounts in *We Survived*, vols 2 and 3. There are exceptions: see Mirko Najman's account on Osijek in vol. 2, p. 244. This is not to say that there were no raids in Poland; for the German hunts for Jews in Warsaw during the large deportations see the account of Miezzysław Eichel in Hochberg-Mariańska and Grüss 1996, p. 6.

87 German commander in Serbia, order, December 22, 1941, in Lemkin 1944, p. 601.

88 For Belarus see Gerlach 1999, pp. 745–7; similarly Bauer 2013, pp. 220, 226, 228.

89 Friedrich 2006, pp. 244–5.

90 Browning 2010, pp. 76, 79–80, 83–4. For a similar case from Medynia Głogowska see the account of Jozef Leichter in Hochberg-Mariańska and Grüss 1996, pp. 68–9.

91 Krakowski 2007, p. 186. But conditions could make clandestine survival almost impossible, even in countries where compatriots helped many escape abroad. About forty Jews

Based on the observation that the higher the number of Jews who were able to go into hiding, the higher the survival rates were, I assume that decisions not to flee had a significant effect upon the death toll. The large differences among survival rates for Jews in the Netherlands (25%), Belgium (60%), and France (75%) correspond with the differences in the percentages of Jews who went into hiding: 50–56% in France, 36–40% in Belgium, and only 13–20% in the Netherlands.[92] In other words, the fact that so many Dutch Jews didn't even try to escape, a fact due in part to a lack of opportunities (especially before May 1943[93]), explains to a large extent why there were proportionally so many more deaths in the Netherlands than in the two neighboring countries. For example, one study found that approximately the same percentage of Warsaw Jews who went into hiding survived as Dutch Jews in the same situation (taking the different durations of clandestinity into account).[94] According to estimates, 28,000 Jews from Warsaw and more than 100,000 Jews in central Poland went into hiding (5–6% of both populations).[95] Not only were denunciations less common in France and Italy (during the time of German extermination, which started in 1942) but more than half of the Jewish population in France and Italy survived clandestinely, compared to 1–3% in the Polish and Soviet areas. So it is clear that the behavior of non-state agents had a tremendous impact upon Jewish survival chances. Thus, it is crucial for historians to pay attention not only to the activities of German persecutors and foreign governments, but also to the social environment.

Raul Hilberg has argued that major European cities had a saturation level above which it was hard to rescue Jews: the number of surviving Jews was often around 1% but, more generally, between 0% and 3% of the urban population.[96] The point raised by Hilberg's findings is that when Jews formed a large part of the population, as in Poland, Lithuania and Belarus, only a smaller percentage could hide. Hilberg did not make an argument about living clandestinely in cities, he considered all sorts of survival techniques, but, despite all of the opportunities that a city's anonymity offered, it seems that the countryside was a more promising place to hide. In Italy, many Jews (who were mostly urbanites) survived by living illegally

managed to survive inside Norway, and fewer than a hundred inside Denmark (Moore 2010, pp. 81, 96).

92 Data are taken from Griffioen and Zeller 2011, pp. 518, 543, 572, 901 (according to these authors, flights abroad explain little of the differences in survival rates); see also Maxwell 1998, p. 4.

93 See also Griffioen and Zeller 2011, pp. 1008–9; Moore 2010, pp. 234–40.

94 Paulsson 1998, pp. 27–9; Paulsson 2004, p. 383.

95 Paulsson 2004, p. 383; Krakowski 2007, p. 186.

96 Hilberg 1995, pp. 46–8. Budapest would be a counter-example with about 5%.

in the countryside. Only a third of the Jews of Rome hid in the city, and, at best, a third of the Jews of Paris survived in hiding But a larger percentage of both populations stayed alive by going underground outside the city.[97] While this was the trend in some occupied countries (where German police forces were concentrated in cities and towns but had relatively little control in the countryside), the trend was reversed in the German Reich. In Berlin, an estimated 5,000 Jews (8%) went into hiding and 1,500 survived; in Vienna, only about 450 Jews survived underground, but this accounted for three-quarters of all clandestine survivors in Austria; and, in the Old Reich, only 5,000–10,000 Jews outside Berlin even attempted to hide.[98]

The social climate – the readiness of people to hide Jews and not to betray them – was also important because aid organizations could rescue only a minority of those in hiding, let alone of all the Jews. The others in need of help had to find supportive people on their own. For example, there were about 17,000 Jews living illegally in Warsaw in early 1944 of which half received organized help.[99] The percentage was probably lower in the Polish countryside. The capacity of rescue organizations in France was also limited.[100] Scholars have explained the disastrous deportation figures for the Netherlands by a lack of hiding places and the fact that a large clandestine infrastructure emerged only in the spring of 1943.[101] The relatively high survival rate in Belgium has been attributed to strong, early-emerging aid networks.[102] But data on rescuers in Belgium suggest that half of them were not part of any organization.[103] Similarly, according to one estimate, the majority of Jews in Italy survived without help from any organization.[104] Where organized networks did play a large role was in aiding Jews to escape across western European borders (for example those leaving France, Norway and Denmark).[105] The impact of

[97] De Felice 1995, p. xx (a higher estimate for Rome is suggested by Longhi 2010, p. 129 note 65); see also Michaelis 1978, p. 388 for Italy. For about 30,000–35,000 survivors in Paris see Adler 1989, pp. 45, 219; for a refutation of the claim that people in the French countryside were especially hostile toward Jews, see Fogg 2009, pp. 182–3. In the Netherlands, survival rates for Jews from the countryside surpassed those of city dwellers. See Flim 2001, p. 291.

[98] For Berlin see Kosmala 2004, pp. 138–9; for Vienna see Moser 1997; see Benz 1988b, p. 660.

[99] Paulsson 1998, p. 27.

[100] Cohen 1994, pp. 15–21, 24; Eggers 2002, p. 473.

[101] Moore 2010, pp. 234–40.

[102] Zeller and Griffioen 1996, p. 52, and 1997, pp. 32, 34–5, 46; Moore 2010, pp. 218–19.

[103] Paldiel 1998, pp. 310, 314, 317; in contrast see Moore 2010, pp. 176, 178, 187.

[104] Zuccotti 1996, pp. 210–14, 276.

[105] While Moore 2010 shows so much, his claim (p. 7) that most rescuers of Jews in western Europe in general were integrated into organized networks is not supported quantitatively (see also Moore 2004, pp. 389–90). I follow Zuccotti 1993 (pp. 237, 245), who thinks that most Jews hiding in France did so with no, or little, organized help.

organized help in Hungary, outside Budapest, in 1944, was small, while the protection of foreign diplomats allowed many tens of thousands of Jews in the capital to survive legally. In Belarus the communist underground and partisans were only able to help a very limited number of Jews to live in hiding or cross the frontline eastward.[106]

Individual preconditions for survival

Survival was very much about money. Many scholars have described the importance of social hierarchies among Jews: "Social gaps within ghetto society were characteristic of all ghettos."[107] In the Warsaw ghetto, tens of thousands starved to death while businesspeople, smugglers, and, allegedly, functionaries could afford luxuries. This inequality was severely criticized at the time and subsequently.[108] There seems to have been 10,000–30,000 wealthy people, 200,000–250,000 who got by, while 150,000–250,000 were rapidly starving. Until mid 1942, hunger in the ghetto resulted not only from the inhabitants' inability to bring food in but also from many people's inability to buy it.[109] Most of those who starved to death had either already been destitute before the war or had come to the ghetto as refugees or by forced resettlement.[110] Such people were also among those whom the Jewish council at Łódź selected first for the German-imposed deportations to the death camp at Chełmno – labeling them "undesirable elements" and "representatives of the underworld, the scum of society."[111] In Warsaw, destitution was accelerated for thousands of the primarily poor male resettlers whom the Jewish council sent to fill German forced labor assignments and who returned physically and mentally broken.[112] Yehuda Bauer argues that most Jewish survivors from small towns in eastern Poland were from solidly middle-class families because one needed money and relations with non-Jews to save oneself.[113]

The wealth or poverty of Jewish refugees in southern France also had an influence on their survival chances. While many of the poor got caught

[106] See Gerlach 1999, pp. 743–7; Tec 1996; for Hungary see a collection of 800 survivors' accounts at the Lavon Institute archive, Tel Aviv, VII 123/1–5.
[107] Ofer 2009, p. 39.
[108] The account of Wiktoria Śliwowska can be found in Śliwowska 1999, p. 137; see Kassow 2010, pp. 203, 239–331, 382; Gutman 1982, p. 69.
[109] Gutman 1982, pp. 72, 76–7; Kassow 2010, p. 436.
[110] Hilberg 1992a, pp. 188–9; Engelking and Leociak 2009, pp. 314–15.
[111] Quoted in Krakowski 2007, pp. 52, 57.
[112] Gutman 1982, p. 24.
[113] Bauer 2013, p. 36. Middle-class survivors may have also tended more than others to write down or otherwise deposit their memories.

up in French internment camps early on, those who had money and connections could try to survive in hiding.[114] It required money to pay hosts, pay for supplies, travel, and for forged papers and to satisfy blackmailers.[115] This also meant that theft – from the petty larceny of non-Jewish, Polish boys, to professional blackmail and robberies – seriously undermined the chances of survival for Jews in hiding.[116] Money or valuables (gained by embezzlement) were needed to survive as one of the few prisoners in Treblinka, as well as to have a chance to flee from there. Refugees with money abandoned those without, though not always.[117] It may be that the greater wealth, on average, of Jews in western Europe contributed to their higher survival rates.[118]

Observers of the evolution of language in the Łódź ghetto noted the creation of neologisms related to new social hierarchies, e.g., words denoting the relation between the ghetto administration and the rest of the population, between Polish Jews and those deported to the city from other countries, and the existence of certain emaciated people.[119] In many ghettos, Jewish council members and their employees were among those topping the social hierarchy.[120] For example, employees of the Jewish council were assigned the largest food rations – and received the largest actual amounts – in the Warsaw ghetto. Raul Hilberg cites the case of a member of the Jewish council and a Jewish auxiliary policeman accusing each other of unfairly trying to survive thanks to their privileges.[121] Many Jewish policemen in the Warsaw ghetto came from the upper middle class or the intelligentsia.[122] Members of the Police and the Jewish administration improved their (inadequate) salaries through various forms of corruption, as observers bitterly noted.[123] According to one recollection, inmates of Treblinka believed that those with good connections to the

[114] Paxton 2001, p. 182.

[115] See Adler 1989, pp. 43, 48; Paulsson 1998, p. 25.

[116] Examples can be found in the accounts of Miezysław Eichel, Jozef Leichter and Szlama Kutnowski in Hochberg-Mariańska and Grüss 1996, pp. 5, 68, 78; for blackmailers see Paulsson 2002, pp. 148–52.

[117] Sereny 1980, pp. 214, 271–2; see Willenberg 2009, pp. 29, 77, 80–4, 89; for a counter-example from the Chełmno extermination camp see Kassow 2010, p. 465. Jews also looted the property of those murdered at Auschwitz. See Friedler *et al.* 2002, pp. 96, 170, 178.

[118] But Poznanski 1997 (p. 70) points to estimates according to which half of the Jews in France were already without means of subsistence in the fall of 1941.

[119] Löw 2012, pp. 58–67.

[120] Gringauz 1949, p. 13; Hájková 2013, pp. 64, 67, 163.

[121] Hilberg 1992a, pp. 181, 188; Engelking and Leociak 2009, p. 407. For the food supply in Łódź see Alberti 2006, p. 188 note 159.

[122] Gutman 1982, p. 86; Engelking and Leociak 2009, p. 192. For similar observations about janitors see Corni 2002, p. 175.

[123] Kassow 2010, pp. 178–9, 207–8, 360; Engelking and Leociak 2009, p. 198.

Jewish councils, and the wealthy, managed to stay in the ghettos the longest, while all others were deported to their deaths.[124] Jews in France seem to have had a similar expectation. Thus, they entered a "race for protection" by working with the Union Générale des Israélites de France.[125] In the ghettos, the administrations grew because of the many tasks at hand, but also out of self-interest.[126]

All of this differentiation and lack of solidarity had nothing specifically Jewish about it – it could be expected from any social group under extreme distress. Social stratification was pronounced. Class mattered, especially then.[127] But the Nazis portrayed what happened in the Warsaw ghetto (under the German stranglehold) as typical Jewish profiteering, recklessness, dirtiness and moral corruption.[128] In the post-war famine of 1945–47, many non-Jewish Germans displayed similar behavior. During Nazi rule, the waning solidarity among the persecuted reached its peak in the concentration camps of the SS. There, too, most Jews and non-Jews showed the same lack of consideration for their fellow humans.[129] Different Jewish groups, often defined along national lines, also pitted themselves against one another more as the conditions became worse. This prompted one Birkenau survivor, Lello Perugia, to conclude that "this famous ethnic group [the Jews], as some want to call us, doesn't exist."[130] François Wetterwald, a former prisoner in Mauthausen, labeled the groups that he saw emerging as the "powerful," the "capitalists," the "poor," the "oppressed," the "weak," the "clever," the "proud" and the "disinterested." "The solidarity among peoples, [...] between humans from the same country, of the same religion, the same race – one does not believe in it any more if one has been in a concentration camp."[131] Although Jews faced special risks, their survival strategies in these camps resembled those of others: save your energy; avoid German overseers; avoid hard and dangerous work; procure additional food; and hide weakness, disease, and injury. The struggle of all against all led to new relationships of limited trust among a few – the so-called

[124] Willenberg 2009, pp. 126–7.
[125] Adler 1989, p. 44.
[126] Corni 2002, p. 74.
[127] See Corni 2002, pp. 169–94; Hájková 2013, pp. 2, 93–152. By contrast see Gutman 1982, p. 108.
[128] See, for example, the German-produced images in the British documentary film *Warsaw Ghetto* directed by Alexander Bernfes in 1965.
[129] For example, see the memories of Ivona Frajd in *We Survived*, vol. 2, p. 219.
[130] Quoted in Caracciolo 1995, p. 108; see Willenberg 2009 (p. 118) for incessant conflicts among Jewish inmates of Treblinka; see Barkai 1989 for Jews deported from Greater Germany to ghettos in eastern Europe.
[131] Quoted in Freund 1998, p. 874.

substitute families – which provided their members some physical and mental support.[132]

Characteristics other than money were also important for survival. Usually mentioned are non-Jewish looks, good relations with non-Jews and unaccented command of the majority language.[133] Survival as a prisoner in Auschwitz depended on age, duration of internment, physical constitution, profession, class, work assignment and adaptability.[134] For boys and men in hiding, being circumcised meant additional risk. Some survivors later stated that a conscious decision to try to survive, summed up in the formula "rescue was a state of mind," was necessary.[135] "Awareness of danger" was another important attitude.[136] Many demonstrated their irrepressible will to live by their refusal to give up after failed attempts to rescue themselves, before they finally managed to escape from a camp or flee to a foreign country.[137] As a ten-year-old Jewish Lithuanian boy, Edmundas Ruvinas Zeligmanas barely survived at least three mass executions in 1941. The fate of Mikhail Weinschelboim of Berdichev, Ukraine, was similar.[138] In addition to luck, this required extraordinary mental resilience, as did getting through several 'selections.'

Many eastern European Jews spoke Yiddish, or, in the Balkans, Ladino (so-called 'Jew-Spanish') and lacked command of the national language or spoke it with an accent.[139] However, this wasn't true of most Jews from Trianon-Hungary, the Czech lands and Wallachia.[140] Among a section of the Polish Jews, knowledge of Polish had improved in the inter-war period, especially in Warsaw.[141] Those who did not speak the local language properly could not blend in and were easily detected. Thus, Ladino-speaking Jews from Salonica and other places in northern

132 For the Hungarian Jews see Gerlach and Aly 2002, pp. 397–9.
133 See Gutman 1982, p. 285; Paulsson 2004, p. 387; Willenberg 2009, p. 83; Sereny 1980, pp. 273–5; for Italy see Zuccotti 1996, pp. 205, 227.
134 Pawełczyńska 2001, pp. 126–7 note 12.
135 Gitman 2011, p. 52.
136 The account of Jaša Almuli can be found in *We Survived*, vol. 2, p. 405.
137 For flight attempts see the accounts of Pavle Minh and Vilma Jovanović in *We Survived*, vol. 3, pp. 290, 349; another example can be found in Silberklang 2004, pp. 160.
138 See Zeigmana's account in *With a Needle* 2003, p. 367; Weinschelboim's account can be found in Zabarko 2005, pp. 46–50.
139 Concerning Yiddish, see Rothschild 1974 (pp. 35, 89–90) for Poland, Slovakia and Carpatho-Ruthenia; see Deletant 2006 (p. 103) for Bessarabia; see Smilovitsky 2003 (pp. 117–18) for Belarus, including the East; see Mendelsohn 1983 (p. 246) for Latvia. Concerning Ladino see Rothschild 1974 (p. 328), and Troebst 1995 (p. 111) for Bulgaria; see Fleischer 2001 (p. 219) and Plaut 1996 (pp. 24–5) for northern Greece; see Freidenreich 1979 (pp. 7, 17, 53, 57, 215–21) for Yugoslavia (especially Bosnia and Serbia).
140 Rothschild 1974, pp. 192–3; Mendelsohn 1983, pp. 6–7, 87–9.
141 Mendelsohn 1983, pp. 31, 67; Paulsson 2002, p. 30; Kassow 2010, pp. 154, 189.

Greece, for example, hardly tried to escape – in contrast to the Greek speakers from Athens and the south. In the north, virtually all were deported; in the south, only a minority were.[142] Likewise, foreign Jews in France could be recognized by their accents.[143] Speaking a minority language also meant that broader social contacts in everyday life were less frequent.[144] Seine Lupšiciene-Novozeldskyte taught children in the Kaunas ghetto Lithuanian so that the underground movement could more easily place them with Lithuanian families.[145] Of course, it was not language alone that mattered. Many Jews in Bulgaria and in northern Greece spoke Ladino, but only a few of the latter escaped while the former (if they did not reside in the Bulgarian-annexed Greek territories) survived under the protection of Bulgarian elites. Among other reasons, Jews from mainland Bulgaria were mostly lower middle class, and, so, provoked relatively little envy.[146] Bessarabian Jews spoke better Russian than those from Bukovina, but the latter knew more Romanian; when the Romanian authorities deported both groups to Transnistria (western Ukraine), the latter group enjoyed a much higher survival rate than the former because the deportations from Bukovina did not impoverish people as much as those from Bessarabia.[147]

Another prerequisite was knowledge. Two ahistorical, popular misconceptions are that Jews should have known about their imminent destruction in 1938 – or even as early as 1933 – and that Hitler had laid out his intention to exterminate the Jews in his book *Mein Kampf*. In reality, German politicians' violent intentions emerged through a long process that began with plans to expose Jews to a slow decimation process between 1939 and 1941, and later included the plan to exterminate them all between 1941 and 1942. The partially decentralized structure of this process did not help either. In early 1942, Abba Kovner – one of the first and most fervent harbingers of imminent total destruction – was unclear as to why the Germans killed great numbers of Jews in Vilnius but not in nearby Białystok.[148] Knowledge of German intentions, among both Jews and non-Jews, evolved accordingly, and, though it usually followed close behind Nazi decision-making, not everyone was equally informed or even wanted to believe the information that was available to them. In 1944 many Jews deported from Hungary still did not know what took

142 Fleischer 2001, pp. 219–20; Mazower 2004, p. 442.
143 Kaspi 1997, p. 94.
144 See Bowman 2006 (p. 42) on Greece.
145 See her account in *With a Needle* 2003, p. 225.
146 See Brustein and King 2004a, p. 695.
147 See Ofer 1996.
148 Kassow 2010, p. 459.

place at Auschwitz-Birkenau when they arrived there.[149] Dutch underground newspapers had reported since July 1942 that deportation to the East meant death (one even mentioned gas),[150] but it was only in the spring of 1943 that many Jews went underground. There were similar tendencies toward disbelief in France.[151]

Knowledge was distributed very unevenly. An Auschwitz survivor, Ernst Levin, remembered that a Jewish friend deported to Treblinka had managed to send him a letter in Breslau warning him that "here is a camp where humans are treated chemically"; while in 1944 the German manager of an infamous I.G. Farben factory located 12 km from Auschwitz-Birkenau, and who complained to Levin about the smell and was informed that it came from the crematoria, asked, puzzled, "What are they burning?"[152]

Only the great raid on Jews in Paris in July 1942 convinced many foreign Jews (but fewer Jewish French citizens) to leave Paris.[153] Jews from Alsace had a higher survival rate than those in the rest of France, and this has been attributed to the fact that they were exposed to non-lethal German persecution earlier, and, so, had fewer illusions.[154] It took large deportations to prompt many Jews to go into hiding after September 1942 in Warsaw, in late 1942 in the district of Lublin, and in 1942–43 in Berlin and Vienna.[155] Others stayed put, even though they knew what to expect, like, for example, the many Jews in Warsaw who, although ignorant at first, had learned about Treblinka by mid-August 1942. A German military officer observed, "Jewry is informed about its destiny. The dictum of a member of the Jewish council in Lemberg [Lvov] is characteristic: 'All of us carry our death certificate in our pocket – only the date of dying is not yet filled in.'"[156] A survey from the area of Lens, in northern France, suggests that most Jews had already left in 1940, beginning with

149 See Gerlach and Aly 2002, pp. 285–9; the account of Suzana Cenić can be found in *We Survived*, vol. 2, p. 150; for German Jews see the various post-war accounts in Johnson and Reuband 2005; Dörner 2007, pp. 563, 576–7.

150 Hershkovitz 2001, pp. 311, 316–17.

151 Adler 1989, p. 47.

152 The account of Ernst Levin can be found in Johnson and Reuband 2005, p. 81.

153 Adler 1989, p. 43.

154 Dreyfus 2010, p. 380.

155 Paulsson 2002, p. 57; for Lublin see district governor Zörner in General Governors log, December 7, 1942, in Präg and Jacobmeyer 1975, p. 583; for Berlin see Kosmala 2004, p. 140; for Vienna see Moser 1997.

156 *Oberfeldkommandantur* 365, Ia, report of October 17, 1942, BA-MA RH 53-23/39, p. 76. The same source had reported on April 18, 1942, only a month after the beginning of the deportations to the Bełżec extermination camp, "probably the news has gotten around among the Jews that those evacuated never reach the settlement area that they are told about." BA-MA RH 53-23/36, p. 125. See also Klukowski 1993, pp. 189, 191 (March 26 and April 8, 1942). For Warsaw see Gutman 1982, pp. 214, 223.

working-age men. The area's Polish immigrants tended to leave earlier, French citizens and homeowners typically waited until 1942, and people with large families were the most hesitant.[157]

Many did not believe the horrible news. As late as 1944, Jews from Greater Hungary still disregarded BBC reports as well as warnings from escapees about mass gassings at Auschwitz. In Kolozsvár (Cluj), Jews committed one such escapee to a psychiatric ward.[158] In the summer of 1942, Jews in Tłuste, eastern Galicia, refused to believe that all of the Jews in Horodenka, only 35 km away, had been murdered.[159] Returning home having just survived a mass shooting by playing dead in a mass grave in Ponary, near Vilnius, in July 1941, Motl Gdud, although wounded, could not even convince his own father of what had happened.[160] In September 1943, Jewish community leaders in Copenhagen also at first refused to believe warnings of imminent mass arrests and deportation before they finally gave in and organized a successful rescue operation.[161] In neighboring Norway, some of the Jews who were arrested, deported and murdered in the fall of 1942 had fled to neutral Sweden in 1940 but had returned to German-occupied Norway believing promises that nothing would happen to them.[162] But in 1940 there were actually no plans for the murder of Norwegian Jews. Saul Friedländer describes the state of mind of Jews still alive at the end of 1942 as follows: the "overwhelming majority remained torn between temporary realization, perplexity, desperation and recurring new hope."[163] All of these cases illustrate how the uneven evolution and spread of knowledge, as well as protective mental mechanisms, led to poor decision-making.

Loosening cohesion among Jews

There were often great political, economic, religious, linguistic and cultural differences within a country's Jewish populations, especially in eastern Europe – so much so that they could often hardly be called 'communities.'[164] These divisions prevented stronger political action, and thus rendered Jews vulnerable to social pressure.[165] Continuing

[157] Mariot and Zalc 2010, pp. 65–6, 75–6, 79, 85–6.
[158] Gerlach and Aly 2002, pp. 56–7, 304–5; the account of Ivona Frajd can be found in *We Survived*, vol. 2, p. 219.
[159] See the account of Mendel Rosenkranz in Hochberg-Mariańska and Grüss 1996, p. 35.
[160] See Grossman and Ehrenburg 1994, pp. 467–8.
[161] Petrow 1974, pp. 205–7.
[162] Abrahamsen 1991, p. 109.
[163] Friedländer 2006, p. 466.
[164] There is abundant evidence in Mendelsohn 1983; Braham 1994, pp. 77–96; Freidenreich 1979.
[165] For example see Gutman 1982, pp. xviii, 227.

during the Nazi onslaught, inner political conflicts among Jews either hindered coordinated action or prevented much effective action being taken at all.[166] The German-imposed Jewish councils included members of pre-war elites and different political factions.[167]

Persecution and deprivation even undermined social relations within Jewish families. In many cases, the sense of family was very strong, and, in some scholars' opinion, family life intensified in ghettos.[168] But, in the end, it was usually not possible for families to remain together. They had to split up or were separated by force, and, for many, this was the most traumatic experience.[169] In other cases, families did not flee in order to remain together.[170] There were heart-rending scenes of husbands and wives and mothers and children being separated upon their arrival at an extermination camp.[171] In Staraia Uritsa, Ukraine, a hail of blows by German and Ukrainian SS and police did not prevent, as intended, Jews from bidding farewell to relatives and friends before being shot.[172] In a typical account, Jakovas Gauchmanas of Vilnius described his deep concern when it became clear that his family had to separate, and also the great efforts spent in relocating each other.[173] Many survivors' memories devote much space to the search for relatives after the war.

Some family members had lower chances of survival than others. For example, in most Jewish families in Yugoslavia, only one or two members survived out of an average family size in 1938 of 4.11 members.[174] Tragically, loosening cohesion within families is indirectly reflected by the unequal chances of survival that can be inferred from the different death rates for men and women. In the large ghetto of Łódź, women (who are physiologically less vulnerable to famine) succumbed 20% less often than men until the end of 1942, whereas 62% of those sent to the Chełmno annihilation camp in 1942 were women. The tendency that women had a

[166] This can even be seen in studies that place much emphasis on resistance and armed struggle, such as Gutman 1982; see ibid. (pp. 119–44) for the different political organizations in the Warsaw ghetto and pp. 149–54 for a list of periodicals issued in the ghetto originating from more than a dozen separate political groups.

[167] Weiss 1977, pp. 358–65; Trunk 1972, pp. 15–16, 30.

[168] Gringauz 1949, p. 7.

[169] See the account of Krysztyna Budnicka, who had to leave her parents hidden in a sewer, where they perished, in Śliwowska 1999, p. 19; Gerlach and Aly 2002, pp. 288–9; Bauer 2013, pp. 279–80.

[170] For Salonica see Mazower 2004, pp. 437, 442; for Hungary see Gerlach and Aly 2002, p. 308.

[171] See the account of Marek Sznajderman in Śliwowska 1999, p. 243.

[172] Excerpt from the interrogation of Schutzpolizei Captain Salog, May 25, 1944, in Grossman and Ehrenburg 1994, p. 999.

[173] See *With a Needle* 2003, pp. 97–8.

[174] Gordijew 1999, p. 79; similarly in Salonica, Greece: "Census of Jewish population of Salonika in July 1946" in Matarasso 2002 [1948], p. 174.

higher risk than men of being deported to the gas chambers but a lower risk of starving to death was similar in the Warsaw ghetto. For Łódź, the explanation that the Jewish council slated more women for deportation because they were more often unemployed, and therefore in receipt of welfare, is questionable in light of the fact that more men starved to death.[175] In the end, slightly more female than male inmates of the Łódź ghetto survived, a pattern that was not repeated in the rest of Poland. Among Jews from Łódź, more females than males survived in camps and in hiding, but fewer women than men survived as deportees or refugees in the Soviet Union and in armed formations.[176] In Greece, the differences were more pronounced; for every female Jewish survivor in Salonica there were two men.[177] Probably more men than women joined the Greek partisans. Among the Jewish survivors in camps for displaced persons on German soil after 1945, an estimated 40% were women.[178] A slight majority of Hungarian Jewish survivors in the Reich were men, but this was more than offset by the number of females liberated in Budapest.[179] From France and Italy, slightly more Jewish men were deported to Germany than women.[180]

At 0.5%, the chances of survival for Polish-Jewish children living under German rule were still much lower than those for adults. Of course, this was due to the fact that the German authorities mercilessly murdered Jewish children on account of them being unproductive. Most of those who survived were hidden by non-Jews.[181] In the Łódź ghetto, the effort to save children from death by starvation collapsed in the summer of 1941, while at the same time the numbers in Warsaw increased – although they remained on a lower level.[182] Hardly any Jewish children from the ghetto in Vilnius or the surrounding towns saw the end of the war.[183] For Greek Jewish boys and girls, too, it was virtually impossible to survive outside Athens. In Greece (although probably not only there), people over the age of sixty-five had even an smaller survival chance.[184]

175 Hilberg 1992a, pp. 147–8; for Łódź see Unger 1998, pp. 125–6; for employment see ibid., pp. 128, 130.

176 Dobroszycki 1994, pp. 12–14, 85.

177 "Census of Jewish population of Salonika in July 1946" in Matarasso 2002 [1948], p. 174.

178 Bock 2005, p. 10.

179 Gerlach and Aly 2002, pp. 410–11.

180 Hilberg 1992a, p. 320.

181 Dobroszycki 1994, pp. 14–15; Tec 2011, pp. xxv-xxvi.

182 Report by Jewish scientists from late 1941 in Berenstein 1961, p. 140; for Warsaw Oneg Shabat report, "The hell of Polish Jews under the Hitler occupation," June 1942, see Sakowska 1993, p. 210.

183 Report by Basya Finkelstein in Grossman and Ehrenburg 1994, pp. 485–93; Ran (as Chapter 15, note 14).

184 Plaut 1996, pp. 95–6; "Census of Jewish population of Salonika in July 1946" in Matarasso 2002 [1948], p. 174.

The picture was the same for the elderly in the Warsaw ghetto because of famine and, then, gassings. Virtually nobody survived.[185] Practices in the ghetto-camp Theresienstadt clearly disadvantaged elderly people – with the result that more than 90% of the 33,000 victims who died in that place were over the age of sixty.[186] Some 619 Jews survived in hiding in Austria – but only four of them were over the age of seventy.[187] It is a bitter fact that many Jews, and some non-Jews, at least tried to save children but often failed to take care of the aged.[188] As the case of Split, Croatia, shows, their disadvantage started with small steps. When the Croatian authorities registered Jews, it was primarily old people, women with small children, and the helpless who reported – which exposed these groups to further persecution.[189] In Belgium, too, children were disproportionally caught and murdered (more than 70% compared to 40% of all Jews); in France, as elsewhere, however, people often sent their children into hiding first. Possibly as a result of this 86% of Jewish children in France survived (compared to 75% of the adults).[190] There were other groups whose children German forces killed in large numbers: Sinti and Roma, the disabled, those living in areas of anti-partisan warfare, forced laborers and victims of organized starvation (see also Chapters 8, 9 and 11).[191] In some of these cases, more children were killed proportionately than their percentage of the population.

The efforts of Jewish administrations and private social welfare organizations to run soup kitchens, health services and cultural and religious activities more widely[192] were intended to counter this gross inequality and callousness.[193] But these efforts, as heroic and honorable as they were, were on too small a scale in many places to overcome the overwhelming want, poverty and social differences among those Jewish communities and ghettos that were being starved by the German authorities.[194] As with the lack of solidarity under conditions of extreme persecution and shortage, community efforts for mutual aid, education and cultural and

[185] See population figures for July and late November 1942 in Gutman 1982, pp. 270–1; on the misery of children, see also Kassow 2010, pp. 302–3, 407–20.

[186] Hájková 2013, pp. 117–18, 153–4, 298.

[187] Königseder 1996, p. 207. See also Houwink ten Cate 1999, pp. 103–4.

[188] Already in 1930s Germany it had become difficult to meet the increasing demand for homes for the elderly poor: Barkai 1988, pp. 107, 110.

[189] See the account of Silvana Mladinov in *We Survived*, vol. 2, p. 32.

[190] See Maxwell 1998, p. 3, and Fogg 2009, p. 154; see also Poznanski 1997, pp. 472–84.

[191] Pohl 2003, p. 154.

[192] See Kassow 2010, pp. 407–20; Engelking and Leociak 2009, pp. 317–29.

[193] For criticism of this in the Warsaw ghetto see Kassow 2010, pp. 389, 401, 537.

[194] For Warsaw see Kassow 2010, pp. 205, 409–11; Gutman 1982, pp. 40–5, 102–6; for examples from western Ukraine/eastern Poland see Bauer 2013, pp. 27–9, 151–2.

religious life were not specifically Jewish responses.[195] In the Jewish case, these endeavors bought time, but, in the end, saved few lives.

Survival strategies of other persecuted groups

Those under German persecution in World War II found themselves in a labyrinth. There were many blind turns, and many did not find a way out. One could say that for each victim group a different labyrinth existed. But there were intersections between them, as well as parallels.

Between non-Jews and Jews in the concentration camps there were no major differences in coping strategies. The conditions in other types of camps (like the camps for Soviet POWs in late 1941) were at least as bad and the survival strategies, again, were similar. For Soviet POWs there was one way out that Jews did not have, namely, joining auxiliary or even armed service units of the German army or SS. However, in addition to the moral repugnance of doing so, it was highly likely that this would lead to prosecution or repression if the Soviets won the war. Rejecting this option, Soviet POWs and foreign forced laborers on German soil were trapped with virtually no chance to return home during the war, and nowhere to hide for longer time periods.

Others groups went into hiding. When the area of Rome was liberated in early June 1944, up to 10,000 Jews came out of hiding as well as an estimated 400,000 deserters, draft dodgers, forced labor evaders, anti-fascists and escaped POWs.[196] Hundreds of thousands of young French, Dutch and Soviet citizens had lived illegally since 1943 in order to avoid being deported to work in Germany. Some had joined the underground resistance (see Chapters 8 and 11). In eastern Europe, the relatives of those who joined the underground faced German repression in the form of arrest, confiscation of their property and the destruction of their family homes. The Germans threatened with the death penalty all Soviet citizens who sheltered Jews, Soviet military officers or communists.[197]

The persecution which some faced was more localized than it was for Jews. Villagers menaced by German anti-partisan operations in certain areas could theoretically flee if they evaded those German forces that wanted to either kill or deport them for forced labor. However, many of those who slipped through the German lines, or were expelled or

[195] An opposite assessment can be found in Bauer 2013, p. 300. However, similar behavior can also be found in other historic cases of persecution and confinement – like, for example, among North American natives on nineteenth-century reservations.

[196] Longhi 2010, p. 129 note 65.

[197] See the account of Leonid Grips in Zabarko 2005, p. 60.

resettled by the Germans, faced misery and starvation. This made many hesitant to flee. Non-Jews in western Poland who wanted to avoid being resettled eastward spent nights outside their houses with their cattle.[198] In the long run, few of them succeeded. Some groups, like the mentally disabled, had even fewer options for self-protection than did Jews. They could only hope for relatives to petition on their behalf, which did improve their survival chances.[199]

The persecutions of Jews and other groups were in many ways interconnected. This is clear from survivors' accounts. The existence of other sorts of violence gave Jews the opportunity to fake their victimhood, thereby enabling them to gain the support of local authorities, or at least some form of legitimacy. Some pretended to have been bombed out.[200] Others posed as Serbian refugees expelled from Bosnia or Kosovo, or orphaned in the nationalist uprising in Warsaw.[201] Such stories could be convincing because air raids and expulsions caused the sort of mass evacuations and chaos that resulted in many people losing their personal documents.

But these were not always just stories. Jews were sometimes threatened by the same violence as non-Jews. Leszek Leon Allerhand and his mother fled from the Lvov ghetto and found shelter posing as non-Jewish Polish refugees from Ukrainian violence in Volyn. But they had to leave when their refuge became too uncertain after their hosts took in a family of *real* non-Jewish refugees from Volyn. Things went the other way around for Karol Galiński, who came from a village near Lvov. First, he survived an attack by Ukrainian nationalists on a 'Polish' village in which a dozen farmers were killed; then, he pretended to be a Polish orphan among the many Polish rural refugees in Lvov.[202] In Soviet POW camps, Jews shared the grim fate of the other inmates. If they found partisans whom they could join, they were then targeted by German or Axis anti-guerrilla warfare; this could even happen if they lived in areas that were reputedly 'partisan-infested.'[203] After the nationalist uprising of 1944 in Warsaw,

[198] Rutherford 2007, p. 160.

[199] Aly 2013, pp. 39–41, 282.

[200] See the accounts of Mila Karaoglanović (Belgrade/Leskovac and Albania) in *We Survived*, vol. III, pp. 442, 446; of Henoch Lisak (Warsaw) in Śliwowska 1999, p. 101; and van Thijn 2001, p. 271 (Rotterdam). See also Longhi 2010 (p. 93) on Italy. For a woman who was sheltered in Germany as an allegedly bombed-out Polish forced laborer, see Frank 2003, p. 240.

[201] See the account of Juliana Ćirić (Belgrade/Niš) in *We Survived*, vol. 2, p. 390; of Rahela Levi in *We Survived*, vol. III, p. 394; of Lazarz Krakowski in Hochberg-Mariańska and Grüss 1996, p. 126.

[202] Accounts in Śliwowska 1999, pp. 157, 162, 173–4.

[203] Vera Robiček became an Italian hostage held in case of partisan attacks in Albania in 1943. See her account in *We Survived*, vol. 3, p. 262. For the former case, see, for

German forces deported hidden Jews along with all the other citizens, resettled many in the countryside, and brought some to Germany as forced laborers.[204] According to one estimate, 5,000 of the 17,000 Jews hiding in Warsaw died as a result of the insurgency.[205] Periodic round-ups endangered the lives of the inhabitants of Warsaw and Athens, and also the lives of Jews in hiding. When German SS and police, sweeping through the port city of Marseille in January 1943 on the hunt for resisters and criminals, checked the papers of 40,000 locals, most of the 1,600 persons they deported were Jewish refugees.[206] In Italy, Jews were in danger of being caught in manhunts for partisans and deserters.[207] Jews, like others, came under threat when the German military destroyed all usable buildings as it retreated on the Eastern Front.[208] They survived German and Allied air raids and fled elsewhere when their homes were destroyed.[209] Many, especially those in Poland and the Soviet Union, were conscripted as supposedly non-Jewish forced laborers and sent to Germany. Some Jews actively sought out such recruitment, while others were deported against their will.[210]

These examples show, once again, that Jews were not the only people in Europe threatened during World War II. Other persecutions created limited spaces for survival, but also additional risks. If numbers alone tell us that in most places Jews had lower chances of survival than members of most other groups, survival stories bring this fact sharply into focus. For many Soviet and Polish civilians, forced labor in Germany was one of the worst options, whereas some Jews regarded it as a means to save their own lives. Jews disguised themselves as Polish or Soviet forced laborers, but almost never the other way around. Generally speaking, Jews more often than non-Jews joined the partisans (which they did especially in

example, the accounts of Franciszka Guter in Hochberg-Mariańska and Grüss 1996, pp. 169–70, and of Regina Loss-Fisior in Śliwowska 1999, p. 203.

204 Various child survivors' accounts can be found in Śliwowska 1999, pp. 15, 97–8, 109–10, 125, 139, 146–7, 286; see also Schoenfeld 1985, pp. 314–15.

205 Paulsson 1998, p. 28.

206 For Warsaw see the account of Joanna Kaltman in Śliwowska 1999, p. 80; for Athens see Mazower 2001, pp. 344–51; for Marseille see Mazower 2008, p. 440.

207 Longhi 2010, p. 93.

208 See the account of Marian Bobrzyk in Śliwowska 1999, p. 260.

209 See the accounts of Suzana Cenić (Auschwitz, 1944) and Jaša Almuli (Belgrade, 1941) in *We Survived*, vol. 2, pp. 153, 410–16; of Rahela Levi (Belgrade, 1941) in *We Survived*, vol. 3, p. 394.

210 See the accounts of Krystyna Budnicka, Krystyna Chudy and Eugenia Magdziarz in Śliwowska 1999, pp. 20–1, 25–8, 106–7; of Szlama Kutnowski in Hochberg-Mariańska and Grüss 1996, p. 81; of Valentina Filipova (Vitebsk), Viktoras Chramkovas (Brjansk), Fruma Kucinskiene-Vitkinaite (Starodub), Ada Omeljančiuk-Koslovskaja Rozenblat (Minsk) and Feige Spanje-Rozenbergaite (Lithuania) in *With a Needle* 2003, pp. 26, 66, 201, 250, 341.

the Soviet Union, Yugoslavia and Greece) in order to survive. And the strategy often worked. Even in areas characterized by a widespread hostility to Jews, once they made contact with leftist partisans their survival rates were comparatively high.[211] However, the same was not true for isolated armed uprisings organized by Jewish organizations. As a rule, these sporadic and small-scale incidents – such as in the ghetto uprisings of 1943 in Warsaw and Białystok, and as displayed in numerous attempts to break out of small Soviet ghettos – were desperate last-minute attempts at armed resistance and demonstrations of pride. There were few survivors and minimal German losses were inflicted.[212] Other threats, such as aerial bombardment, or forced expulsions along ethno-religious lines, were not a matter of choice. And the German military treated Soviet POWs so badly, especially in 1941, that I know of no single case of a Jew fleeing to a Soviet POW camp.

Another connection between multiple persecutions was that there were fewer opportunities for Jews to hide in countries where the non-Jewish population also suffered from extreme violence. This explains in part the low survival rates for Jews hidden in Poland and the Soviet Union. The punishment in these countries for hiding Jews was much harsher than in central Europe, and often it meant the death penalty (see Chapter 13.) In eastern Europe – and especially the German-occupied Soviet territories – forged identity papers held a greater importance than in other parts of occupied Europe, judging from the prominence given to them in survivors' accounts. Jewish survival was also affected by the mandatory registration of all occupants of every house.[213] Accordingly, some Jewish survivors reported that they left their hosts so as not to endanger them. As Maria Sokol of Kharkov recalled of her quandary, "It is agonizing if one does not know where [to go]. Who would take me in? Who needed me? And [what about] the identity card?"[214] More often than not, Jews were turned away; but there were occasions when Jews were turned

211 For Lithuanian Jews see Dieckmann 2011, p. 1458 (survival rate of 84%); for Yugoslavia see Dulić 2005, p. 359 (75%) and Gordijew 1999, p. 93 (medical personnel with Tito's partisans, 83%); see also Tomasevich 2001, pp. 605–6; Gitman 2011, pp. 167–8; for Slovakia see Rothkirchen 1998, p. 61.

212 See Ainsztein 1993; for Warsaw see also Gutman 1982; for Paris see Adler 1989, pp. 189, 201, 217.

213 See the accounts from Lithuania of Riva Blumbergiene-Cvibakaite and Sulamita Lev in *With a Needle* 2003, pp. 43, 209; various accounts from Ukraine can be found in in Grossman and Ehrenburg 1994, pp. 107, 121–2, 441, 772–4, and in Zabarko 2005, pp. 223–4, 349; the account of Joanna Kaltman can be found in Śliwowska 1999, p. 79. Again, forged papers often required money; for Warsaw see Paulsson 1998, p. 25.

214 See the account in Grossman and Ehrenburg 1994, p. 105–6; see also the accounts of Regina Rück in Hochberg-Mariańska and Grüss 1996, p. 84, and of Ruvim Schtein in Zabarko 2005, p. 349.

away by people who, with tears in their eyes, explained that they simply couldn't take the risk of harboring them.[215]

Conclusion

As with persecution, Jews' chances and strategies for survival depended on many factors. Among these were German anti-Jewish policies, but also the degree of pre-war integration into society, the intensity of hostile feelings against Jews, whether a national government still existed, and, if it did, its policy toward Jews, Jewish population density, individuals' understanding of the dangers, the amount of violence that German forces in an area inflicted on non-Jews, the depth of social crises among non-Jews, and the extent of violence among them. One's geographic location mattered, too; Jews residing outside their home country or in territories annexed or occupied by an Axis power were especially vulnerable when coming under German rule. The social exclusion of Jews was a policy objective of the German and other Axis authorities, but exclusion was also a result of social practices and therefore dependent on the autonomous actions of groups and individuals. In different ways, Jews strove for social integration in response to the persecution, but integrating oneself is difficult where social cohesion is loosened and ethical values are no longer respected. To flee from areas under Nazi control and to rely on the protection of one's national government were, in the end, the most successful survival strategies.

[215] See the accounts of Emanuel Elbinger in Śliwowska 1999, p. 40; of Jozef Leichter in Hochberg-Mariańska and Grüss 1996, pp. 69–70; of Ranana Malchanova-Kleinstein in *With a Needle* 2003, pp. 236, 238; of Rahela Levi in *We Survived*, vol. 3, p. 394; of Eva Gladkaya (Khamara) in Zabarko 2005, p. 55; Krasnoperko 1991, p. 18.

16 Conclusion: Group destruction in extremely violent societies

This book puts the murder of European Jews in much broader contexts than is usual. It describes Germans' mindsets and interests that influenced the destruction. It considers episodes of mass violence against non-Jewish groups and relates and compares them to the fate of Jews. And it takes the policies of non-German states and the behavior of other societies into account. The book's point of departure is that we should analyze modern mass violence as a multi-causal, participatory process that victimizes multiple groups. This approach is meant to uncover dynamics that are not visible when one examines the fate of one persecuted group alone, or when one only examines the history of the state and of political ideas.

As a result, this study emphasizes, more than others, the impact of popular racism (rather than scientific notions of race), nationalism and economic interests on the persecution of Jews and other groups, particularly interests in gains for the non-Jewish bourgeoisie and the educated middle class. My findings suggest that in many regards the background to persecution by Nazi Germany and other countries did not differ as much as is often portrayed. In each country (other than Germany), individual, group and what were perceived as national interests mattered more than Germany's. These national interests did not go uncontested and were sometimes the subject of public debate, as was the violence. Among Germans, these interests were much less contested since there was less social conflict within Germany than there was elsewhere. Facing persecution from forces beyond merely the state, Jews' survival strategies were adapted to deal with the situation of being under threat also from large parts of the population.

Logics of persecution: Economy, ideology and multi-causality

The persecution of European Jews was unusual in many ways; for example, it was a transnational and international action. Yet, like other political processes, it is explainable, since it was structured by a variety of actors with identifiable attitudes and interests. The latter were more changeable than the former, although interests too could have a long-term character and impact. Explanations of the extermination of European Jews will probably always remain controversial. This book has offered elements of an explanation by exploring different logics of the persecution of Jews: racist thought, imperialistic chauvinism, counter-insurgency strategies, various economic-material factors and foreign policy goals. Although I have discussed these threads one by one, they were in reality interwoven.

This book does not claim that economic issues were more important than ideological ones.[1] Such a suggestion would make no sense. If I have discussed pragmatic contributions to persecution more extensively than anti-Jewish attitudes, it is because so much of the literature on the destruction of the Jews either dismisses them out of hand or finds them to be of only secondary importance.[2] Both views are untenable.

Discussions about which factor had priority are unproductive because ideological, material and political considerations were inextricably linked. Most Jews were starved under Nazi rule – both as supposed inferiors, undeserving of more food, and in conditions of real shortage. Most Jewish survivors were exploited as unpaid workers, usually under miserable conditions – often including beatings and humiliation – and their labor was designed as punishment. Among the prejudices against Jews, those of the unfair merchant and exploiter (and, thus, of the unproductive) had been some of the most influential for centuries. Contemporary racist theory would have required establishing whether a person or 'clan' was Jewish through complex examinations, but that would have been too expensive and there were too few 'experts.' There was no ideological sphere called 'anti-Semitism' that was detached from the material world and politics.

Although many stereotypes of Jews were based on perceptions of economic and social status, these were unjust, as all collective ascriptions are. Many Jews worked in trade, but many (or more) did not. Naturally, the same was true of doctors, lawyers and journalists. In eastern Europe many Jews were poor. During World War II, Jewish communities were assaulted as a middlemen minority, although far from all Jews were middlemen; many were, among other things, craftsmen, workers, clerks, housewives and children. Prejudiced observers, however, may have seen in each of these categories a potential for Jews to rise to an elite status

[1] Geiss 1988 (p. 11) implied such a hierarchy for racism in general.
[2] One example is Goldhagen 1997, pp. 158, 160.

since they also believed that Jews had certain inherent qualities. This may partially explain the widespread hostility that Jews faced, in several countries, when they returned after the end of the war (see Chapter 13). German chauvinists and imperialists wanted to take the places of Jewish elites not only at home but also abroad. Many Germans thought, like Hitler, that Jews controlled the Soviet Union and that Germans should replace them. Germans also wanted to supersede Jews as the economic elite in Poland. However, this policy was less pronounced in the many countries where the German authorities agreed to cede the property of Jews to the states in which they resided (see Chapter 10). But many Germans thought that their country's rightful role was that of a hegemonic power for such states, and with their support, the German regime imposed tributes on most that exceeded the total of Jewish property.[3]

The persecution of Jews under the Nazis' rule from 1933 to the summer of 1939 consisted of economic discrimination, social segregation and violent humiliation with the overall goal of driving Jews first out of Germany and then out of its annexed territories (Austria and the Czech lands). These practices incorporated ideas for anti-Jewish measures by the Nazis and by other racists of previous decades (see Chapter 2). Other European countries also adopted such practices, to varying degrees (see Chapter 12). In the fall of 1939, German SS, police, militias and military units killed approximately 7,000 Jews in western Poland. But open mass killings then subsided until June 1941 and the persecution took other forms – particularly ghettoization and deprivation of basic necessities, which claimed many thousands of Jewish lives. Forced emigration continued, despite various schemes to resettle the Jews in a single territory. However, the persecution of other groups was more intense in some ways, and more lethal. Before September 1939 it was first of all political leftists, and later social deviants, who filled the concentration camps, and hundreds of thousands of non-Jews were sterilized. Beginning in September 1939, the largest groups targeted for direct murder were disabled people and the Polish leadership. Such violence continued when, after June 1941, the murder of Jews started with a new intensity (and evolved through several stages) in the Soviet Union. Mass murder in Serbia and deportations of Jews from central to eastern Europe began in October of that year. By January 1942, 900,000 Jews, mostly Soviets, had been killed, while 2 million Soviet POWs had been starved or frozen to death or shot. In the third quarter of 1942, after the SS's plan for total extermination had been put together in the first half of the year and then rapidly implemented, Jews became the largest victim group of German

[3] For the latter point see Aly 2006a.

policies, especially in Poland. Beginning in the fall of 1942, the plan to murder all of the European Jews ran into difficulties, these being primarily the result of the growing hesitancy of various actors in countries allied with Germany. Such passive resistance could be overcome more easily in some cases than it could in others, requiring German persecutors to make decisions about which Jewish groups could be targeted – and in which areas – without prompting too much political upheaval.

Historians have paid much attention to this German decision-making process, and to changes in anti-Jewish policies. Following decades of research it has become clear that there was no Nazi master plan from the beginning and that decision-making was a complex and drawn out process involving many actors at many levels. Thus, historians have emphasized elements of discontinuity. However, it has been difficult to explain the twists and turns in the German persecution of Jews, and others, in terms of ideological factors since racism, prejudices and anti-communism were elements of continuity. What changed more quickly than attitudes, though, were constellations of material, social and political interests.[4] This is why the analysis of such constellations has become important for the debate on anti-Jewish policies. Both interests and attitudes were necessary conditions, without which the mass extermination of Jews, and the mass violence against others, would not have materialized to the extent that they did.

But these interests also contradicted each other. The demand for labor militated against killing Jewish adults (especially after the summer of 1942 when other labor pools dried up), and war-related transportation bottlenecks could be eased by canceling large deportations by train. On the other hand, from the point of view of many Germans, food consumed by Jews could be saved by murdering them (a consideration that was influential in 1941–42, but much less so in 1943–44), which would also free up apartment space, make possible the settlement or resettlement of people, and allow the property of Jews to be used to finance the war effort and combat inflation. In foreign policy, the prevailing view among German players was sometimes that deportations would spur a country's war effort (like Hungary in 1944) and sometimes the contrary (like Denmark in 1942–43).

Germany's capacity for war has been called the "ultimate raison d'être of Nazism," which makes sense given the importance that Hitler assigned to continuous struggle and war. Nazis and a number of other groups saw

[4] The twists in German policies against Jews before early 1942 cannot be explained as mere tactics in implementing a preconceived master plan for total annihilation that persecutors just waited for the right moment to carry into effect (see Chapters 3 and 4).

Jews collectively as among Germany's internal or external enemies in its international conflicts, which made it possible to view the persecution of Jews as part of the war effort, and, therefore, as functional.[5] Again, this was an inaccurate interpretation, for although it was true that hardly any Jews supported the Nazis, or the German occupation of their country, few acted against either. However, the traditional preconception of Jews as traitors or revolutionaries turned into a strong drive for mass murder only after Germany attacked the Soviet Union and (leftist-led) insurgencies started to spread through German-occupied areas in mid 1941. The German military, SS and police needed some time to understand that Jews played no major role among the guerrillas they faced, and this made them adopt new strategies of collective violence against the resistance. Yet the perception that Jews supported uprisings was still influential enough in 1943 to convince German occupation authorities of the need to kill them. It has to be added that perceptions of a Jewish menace reached far beyond armed resistance. Germans at war felt that their country was also threatened by defeatism, propaganda, rumors, jokes, inflation, the black market and so on, all of which were linked to Jews. An interpretation that boils the ideas of a Jewish threat down to political resistance is not in accord with the complex and flexible character of anti-Jewish sentiments.

This was a calamitous effect of the link between material-political interests and negative attitudes toward Jews (and other groups). The perception that certain pressing practical problems could not be solved in other ways made violence against Jews (and others) acceptable – or even desirable – to health and housing officials, food supply functionaries, tax collectors, those occupation administrators who wanted to slightly improve the lot of the general population, occupation troops concerned with counterinsurgency, and diplomats. Different concerns appealed to different groups. This broadened the support base and even increased the pressure for mass murder.

Still, in the German sphere of influence – and even in areas under German occupation – German persecutors did not go "to the ends of the earth to track down each and every living Jew with no regard for the practical consequences."[6] Killing Jews did not have priority over everything else. This is shown by the many postponed deportations and the slow progress deportation trains made, once they were under way, because they had to give way to other, more important, traffic (see Chapter 10). More influential than such organizational factors were the positions of foreign governments. German politicians pursuing the goal

[5] Bloxham 2009, p. 187; for Hitler see Jäckel 1997 [1969], pp. 90–6.

[6] I agree to this statement by Bloxham with reference to the German sphere of influence: see Bloxham 2009, p. 187.

of murdering the Jews did implicate other regimes as accomplices, but not at all costs. Often they did not enforce local support for arrests and deportations because of their interest in foreign cooperation in general. Consequently, the influence of foreign administrations was considerable. The fact that there was, on the whole, so much non-German support for arrests, deportations and murder was the result of national and local political interests and attitudes. These, more than non-Germans' fear of or love for Germans, rendered the German program so disastrously successful.

More than one extremely violent society

German imperialism and policies against Jews do not fully explain the fate of this group. As with every imperialistic nation, Germany's power was not unlimited. It lacked the manpower needed to rule directly all of the areas it conquered, and, so, to appropriate the occupied countries in their totality. Germans needed the cooperation of other governments, administrations and populations. Therefore, other states' policies toward Jews, and the actions of their citizens, were important. This study concludes that anti-Jewish policies and policies of violence against others were more widespread and sweeping than one would have assumed. Many non-German governments, many of which were dictatorial, pursued anti-Jewish policies of their own, often combined with mass violence against other groups. In the 1930s, almost every European country – including many liberal democracies – had anti-Jewish regulations, and at the very least restrictions on Jewish immigration (see Chapter 12.) The number of Jews whose deaths were caused by representatives of countries other than Germany was relatively limited, although not negligible: at least 300,000 (5%) of the total. Romanian forces destroyed about 250,000 Romanian, Moldovan and Ukrainian Jews. In both Croatia and Hungary, officials and government party organizations killed tens of thousands. Up to 50,000 Soviet Jews were killed in popular pogroms from Latvia to the Black Sea – with Romanian and German support – in the summer of 1941 (see Chapters 13 and 14.) The number of Jews shot in 1941 by squads of Soviets under German command is not clear. In particular, the contribution of non-German guards under German command (who were mostly Soviet citizens) in the extermination camps (where Germans were often a minority of the staff)– is not known. This indicates that the activities of Germans and other nationals tended to fuse. But this was no cooperation among equals. While some of the non-Germans in extermination centers may have supported or profited from the former's murderous task, they had usually entered German service in order to themselves escape death in the Soviet POW camps from which they were recruited.

In any case, the actions of non-German states and societies did not only have a direct impact on the killing of Jews. More importantly, they also decisively influenced the chances of escape. On one level, the degree of cooperation of government bureaucracies and police or gendarmerie forces in the arrest, internment and deportation of Jews was a determining factor in how quickly German extermination campaigns succeeded. This was especially true in Slovakia in 1942 and Hungary in 1944. When such cooperation was not forthcoming, the German SS, police and military either had to carry out arduous raids and searches on their own – which slowed down the pace of destruction and allowed more Jews to flee (as happened in Italy) – or German agents were discouraged from pursuing deportation and killing (as in France).

On another level, the social environment created by the behavior of non-Jewish citizens concerning the persecution of Jews had a major influence on the decisions of national governments, police forces and civil servants (making them more hesitant in France, Romania and Bulgaria to support violence), on the chances of Jews being able to survive illegally, and, crucially, on how many Jews tried to hide in the first place (see Chapters 13 and 15.) The experiences of Jews in hiding differed widely not only among individuals, of course, but also from country to country. The stories of Polish, Soviet and Hungarian Jewish survivors reveal enormous insecurity, caused primarily by rumor and denunciation – which is quite in contrast to accounts from Yugoslavia, Italy and France. German threats to kill or severely punish those who assisted Jews, and the general oppression of locals, played no small role in this difference. But although German rule was harsh in Poland and in the occupied Soviet territories, conditions were similar in parts of Yugoslavia, while they were less so in the Netherlands and relatively mild in Hungary (see Chapters 13 and 15). Whereas the percentage of Jewish survivors hiding in large cities does not seem to have differed much internationally, it apparently varied widely in small towns and villages. Raul Hilberg presumed that urban areas had a saturation point for Jews in hiding.[7] Perhaps the same was true in general, because in countries where Jews formed a large part of the population – Poland, Ukraine, Belarus, Lithuania, Latvia, Hungary and Romania – the percentages of Jews who perished were also high. Yet a low percentage of Jews among a population was no guarantee of low death rates – as the Dutch, Slovakian, Czech, Yugoslavian, Greek and Norwegian cases show.

[7] See Hilberg 1995.

As in Germany, other governments' anti-Jewish policies were driven by a variety of partially contradictory interests, as well as deep-seated attitudes. Such anti-Jewish attitudes played into all of this but are hard to measure. According to some questionable assessments, Jews were hated more in Romania than they were in Serbia, Greece, and, one might add, Belarus[8] – but the death rates did not reflect this. Three-quarters of the Dutch Jews perished, compared to a quarter of French Jews; scholars usually do not explain this difference in terms of any greater popularity of anti-Jewish attitudes in the Netherlands. Popular or elite hostility against Jews does not account for all such developments, and especially not the many turns in anti-Jewish policies in countries like Romania and Hungary.

Non-German governments also inflicted mass violence against groups other than Jews, often more than one (see Chapter 14). Bulgarian and Hungarian troops shot tens of thousands each during anti-guerrilla warfare and the combating of resistance; Slovakian troops killed thousands; and Italian forces killed more than 100,000 if one includes the suppression of colonial insurgencies. The Croatian Ustasha regime expelled or murdered hundreds of thousands of Serbs. Romanian, Croatian, and, possibly, Hungarian authorities caused the deaths of thousands of Roma. The Finnish army let 18,000 Soviet POWs die and interned tens of thousands of Slavic civilians. Italy also practiced large-scale internment, especially in Slovenia and Libya. Several countries conducted mass expulsions and other forms of violence, especially in annexed areas.[9] Jews were not always the largest victim group (as in Croatia), not always the worst treated (as in the Italian internment camps in Yugoslavia), and, judging from mortality rates (for example, in Italian Libya and Finland), not always the worst affected in relative terms. More importantly, overarching constellations of violence often affected Jews and non-Jews alike. This was the case in the context of expansion, the attempted incorporation of territories and the foundation of new states (like Slovakia and Croatia) where new elites were favored at the expense of existing ones. In annexed territories settlement needed to be financed, and this was achieved in part by appropriating the property of Jews. During the violent suppression of resistance in these territories, and others, Jews – together with leftists and opposing nationalists – were the targets of reprisals and preemptive violence; Jewish men in particular were collectively suspected of leftist leanings and political unreliability. These constellations often hit Jews especially hard. Consequently they suffered from having to live in a

[8] Déak 2010, p. 225; see also Wannsee Conference 2009, pp. 18–19.
[9] See Gerlach 2012.

climate of insecurity, surveillance and suspicion. Roma, too, were victims of racist persecution – but this was driven by negative perceptions that were quite different from those against Jews, and, dissimilar to the case of the Jews, the persecuted were mostly the very poor and marginalized. In general, all of these persecutions were also fueled by popular racism on the basis of characteristics allegedly inherent to collectives with common ancestry.

Again, these were not just matters of government policies. The widespread partisan wars had a tendency toward civil war, and outright civil war emerged in Yugoslavia, Greece and western Ukraine; while low-intensity conflicts drawn along ethno-religious and class lines simmered in Lithuania and western Belarus. In some cases (like Yugoslavia and Greece), civil conflict created possibilities for Jews to find protection; but elsewhere the survival rates for Jews were lower inside regions of civil war than they were outside them because Jews became engulfed by the conflict. In western Ukraine they were hunted down along with Poles. In a broader sense wars have been described as times of social revolution and transformation.[10] The developments in many countries during World War II undermined solidarity and humanistic values. Rapid geographic and social mobility, impoverishment and the need of many, alongside the increased wealth and social rise of others, led to conflicts.[11] By the end of 1941 the atomization, jealousy, selfishness and suspicion in French society had grown to such an extent that the Chief of State, Pétain, spoke out against the rampant denunciations in his New Year's Eve address of 1942.[12] In German-occupied Poland, human relations became ever more monetized and corrupt, destroying social life and "desocializing Poles," as Jan Gross argued.[13] Overly optimistically in my view, Gross has described the emergence of a so-called underground society in which new organizations promoted new patterns of behavior and a politicization with a tendency toward democracy.[14] Others, however, have described Poland under German rule as increasingly conflict-ridden, even employing the term "civil war."[15] In any case, even if the formation of new groups was as influential as Gross argued, there were many rival

[10] Gross 2006, p. 3.

[11] For the amazing scope of forced migration of different groups in the district of Lublin – where Bełżec and Sobibór were located – see Poprzeczny 2004, p. 236.

[12] Fogg 2009, pp. 31–2.

[13] Gross 1979, pp. 115 (quote), 160, 171–7, 184. For intensified collective stereotypes in cases of sudden social mobility in general, see Bettelheim and Janowitz 1964 [1950], p. 165 (writing on anti-Jewish prejudice); Schumann 2001, p. 18.

[14] Gross 1979, pp. 199–291, esp. 225–6, 291. Accordingly, I would question Gross's conclusion about a "destratification" through general impoverishment (ibid., pp. 171–7).

[15] Pramowska 2010.

groups, and Jews had difficulties joining them, which could result in their death. For example, in the anti-German nationalistic uprising of Warsaw in 1944, some Polish parties refused to cooperate with, and even fought against, each other, and occasionally killed 'outsiders' like communists, Ukrainians and Jews.[16] Many people lost their homes during World War II, and the places to which they fled sometimes also became unstable – as, for example, Montenegro, whose population rose by 60% as a result of an influx of refugees.[17] Jews came under assault in societies where crisis eroded ethical values.

However, this does not mean that there were no niches in the private sphere for many non-Jews to withdraw into. On the contrary, the attempt to retreat into family life and keep away from risks of violence seems to be one characteristic behavior during times of upheaval. Increased numbers of marriages and births are often interpreted as signs of confidence about the future. It is, therefore, not surprising that there was a record number of weddings among non-Jews in Vienna in 1938 during the anti-Jewish hostility after the annexation to Germany.[18] The rebounding of the birth rate in France and Belgium after 1943, under German occupation, to above French pre-war levels, may be more surprising; as is the increasing birth rate in the Netherlands until 1942.[19] Among Polish non-Jews the birth rate dropped, especially in cities; the decline was much smaller in rural areas and in the German-annexed west of the country.[20] There were other signs of optimism – until 1943, the Paris stock exchange experienced one of its most pronounced bull markets.[21]

Connections between abrupt change and mass violence against Jews and others also extended to acute political crises. The deportations of Jews from Bulgaria and northern Greece in the spring of 1943 coincided with internal political upheavals during which moderate politicians were weakened and absorbed with other issues. (In Bulgaria, there was a state of emergency; Greece was in the midst of a change of government.)[22] Developments in Denmark in the fall of 1943 were similar (although most Jews managed to escape with the help of civil society; see Chapters 11 and 13), whereas in Hungary an internal struggle for power contributed to the stopping of deportations of Jews in early July

[16] See the experiences of Willenberg 2009, pp. 187, 192–201.
[17] Pavlowitch 2008, p. 104.
[18] Botz 1975, p. 26.
[19] Sauvy 1978, p. 194; Alary *et al.* 2006, pp. 569–70; for Belgium see Brandt *et al.* 1953, p. 473; for the Netherlands see Hart 1993, p. 28.
[20] Madajczyk 1988, pp. 254–7.
[21] Sanders 2001, p. 23.
[22] For Bulgaria see Opfer 2005, p. 196; for Greece see Nessou 2009, p. 75.

1944.[23] It must be left to future research to describe in details these links between political upheaval and the fate of Jews.

Participatory violence

These conclusions make it evident that the measures of non-German states and the violence against Jews in their societies were of a participatory character. German persecutors needed the support of national elites to carry their anti-Jewish policies into effect, especially the organization of deportations. Often they enjoyed this support, but it was frequently not unequivocal. Societies in crisis were divided in many respects, including their behavior toward Jews. In Romania, Slovakia, France and Bulgaria, those elite factions who preferred not to surrender more Jews – at least not those with national citizenship or from the mainland of the country – held sway in the second half of the war. In Hungary too we observe a zig-zag course in anti-Jewish policies in 1944, but with a very different, murderous outcome (see Chapters 5 and 14).[24] Large parts of the middle classes in all of these countries had advocated anti-Jewish laws in order to damage Jewish competitors – as did Christian churches for religious and political reasons (see Chapters 12 and 13) – but this did not often lead them to support extermination.

But was this not different in Nazi Germany? It is true that German civilians killed fewer Jews in pogroms than other nationals such as Romanians, Ukrainians and Lithuanians did. Altogether, not more than 1% of the Jewish victims of World War II perished in pogroms. In addition, local ethnically German militias in western Poland and in Transnistria killed more than 30,000 Jews under the supervision of the SS and police. German non-state agents made other, indirect, contributions to violence – including the popular prejudices that were important for Nazi racist thinking and practice, and the genealogical research of private associations and churches (see Chapter 7).

However, my conclusions about the participatory character of German violence against Jews and other groups are mainly derived from the structures of policy- and decision-making in life-and-death matters. German persecutors could make their individual contributions to the persecution *through*, rather than needing to bypass, either the state apparatus or Nazi Party organizations. This was so because individuals enjoyed relative autonomy of action, especially in the German-occupied and German-annexed territories, despite the fact that Germany was a

[23] For Hungary see Gerlach and Aly 2002, pp. 339–43.
[24] See Gerlach 2005a.

dictatorship (see Chapter 6). Executive authority was comparatively unhindered by the courts, the press, political opposition and public auditors. (The same was true in other Axis countries.) In this context, the leadership politically enabled even low-level civil servants, military authorities, and SS and police officers (though less so for those in the ranks of military and paramilitary units). In pursuing what they perceived as the best for the German cause, German functionaries in a variety of institutions turned against Jews out of different political motives that connected with images of the "inferior" or "dangerous" Jew. In urging mass murder, these functionaries did not act against the will of the government, except in cases of local conflict over whether Jewish workers should be temporarily allowed to live. In contrast, the guards and camp commandants who let large numbers of Soviet POWs die in the winter of 1941–42, and those who treated eastern European forced laborers so badly in 1942–43 that they were rendered unproductive, came into conflict with the intentions of the regime, although they were not usually punished.

In 1935 and 1938 the Nazi regime had curbed popular, low-level violence against Jews. It did so in part because attacks on Jews and their property drew much criticism by citizens (see Chapter 3). By contrast, popular responses were quite different beginning in 1941, although anti-Jewish violence had intensified greatly. Why did so few oppose mass extermination? It is true that the authorities did not announce the destruction publicly, and that most people within Germany heard only rumors, snippets of information or the claims broadcast on enemy radio stations. In the occupied countries, however – where most of the mass murder took place – the widespread, active support and almost total lack of opposition is remarkable. Fully explaining this remains a task for future research. This book offers only a partial, tentative and general explanation: namely, that German functionaries and soldiers in occupied countries (much more so than non-Germans) tended not to oppose the murder of Jews – or violence against other groups – because it made sense to them in the context of the war, which many regarded as a bitter, deadly struggle of the German nation. The mass violence during the course of anti-guerrilla warfare in the occupied countries appeared similarly justified to almost every German in those countries (veterans defend it to this day), but there, at least, the methods and target groups were sometimes matters of debate.

Another important societal input to mass violence against Jews and others was popular racism. My findings sketch an unusual picture not only of Nazi (and German) practice but also of Nazi theory (see Chapter 7). Even Nazi leaders disagreed on the details of their racist thinking. None of them had a coherent racist doctrine, and the persecution of Jews and others that they organized did not, by and large, apply the contemporary theory of (pseudo-) scientific racism. According to the then prevailing theories, Jews were not a race. In order for race to have guided decisions about violence, racial examinations of individuals or clans would have been necessary. But few groups – like ethnic Germans from eastern Europe, and Roma and Sinti in the Reich – were examined at a level approaching anything like blanket coverage. Rather, Jews were persecuted on the basis of records of their ancestors' religion or their registered ethnicity (as mentioned in Soviet identity papers), and Germans were even less formal in pursuing violence against Soviet POWs, foreign forced laborers and those repressed in the context of anti-guerrilla warfare. Such practices guided violence on the basis of material and political objectives and stereotypes about collectives, which, although more or less traditional, did include biological notions. These borrowings from popular notions of race were expressions of an uninhibited nationalism that manifested itself as xenophobia or imperialism.

Where the attempt to assess anti-Jewish attitudes outside Germany was made, a high level of resentment did not necessarily correlate with hostile behavior. Despite the strong prejudices of rural populations, for example, many Jews found refuge with French and Italian farmers and survived.[25] But, on the other hand, it was not only extremists who contributed to mass murder, as has been shown for many German military and Order Police officers (see Chapter 6). Also, regimes that were not fascist in a narrow sense – Romania and Hungary (before October 1944) – were among those foreign governments who were most murderous or most cooperative with the Germans in their anti-Jewish policies.

Conditions and strategies of survival

At the beginning of the persecution most Jews lived in cities and towns. Urban areas were under particular stress during World War II. In the cities, political oppression was at its fiercest and German authorities and police were at their closest. There was a German gendarmerie post even in many of the small towns in occupied countries. Restrictions on movement in urban areas were more rigid and raids more frequent than in the countryside. In urban areas in occupied Europe, the threat of forced labor conscription was at its most intense, and hunger was worse than in the countryside. In larger towns and cities the danger of aerial bombardment was at its greatest, and the lack of housing and the danger of infectious diseases was at its most severe. These adverse political and socioeconomic

[25] For a Vichy French opinion survey of early 1943 see Adler 1993, pp. 184–7.

conditions in the urban context were in contrast – from the perspective of persecuted people – to advantages like less rigid social control and greater job opportunities.

Many Jews belonged to the middle class (the Jewish leadership certainly did), and middle-class strategies were the most successful ways for Jews to survive. One of these was emigration or long-distance flight. This strategy saved many hundreds of thousands of German, Austrian, Czech, and, later, Soviet Jews; the latter fled eastward in 1941, thereby evading the approaching German troops. By contrast, poor or dependent groups – such as working-class resisters (outside the USSR) and the mentally disabled – could hardly adopt such a strategy. Several hundred thousand Jews – in countries outside Germany with their own governments – survived the war through appeals to national regimes and elites for protection. This protection also extended almost automatically to many POWs. This path was not open to Soviet and Polish Jews, or to the non-Jewish citizens of these countries, forced laborers and Soviet POWs. Both emigration/flight and appeal for protection were traditional responses of Jews to persecution.

Other less common survival strategies were often less successful. Many Jewish councils – counting on German labor needs during the war – tried to present Jews as irreplaceable by virtue of their skilled or unskilled manual labor. This saved no more than about 300,000 Jewish lives, since most Jews lived in areas with – as perceived by German authorities – an oversupply of labor until the summer of 1942 (the time of the worst mass murders); and there was relatively little demand for industrial workers in Poland and the occupied Soviet territories, where most Jews lived. In 1943 the SS took control of the remaining Jewish workers and worksites in most areas, among other reasons to reduce their numbers. Many Jews had little experience as manual workers, and many were used as unskilled forced labor, and, thus, easily replaced. Going underground and living in hiding under false identities saved many thousands in cities from Warsaw to Amsterdam, and even Berlin, but few Jews could hide in the rural areas of many countries, especially Poland, the occupied Soviet territories and Hungary – unlike in Italy and France.

Jews sometimes managed to disguise themselves as different sorts of victims, like those whose homes had been bombed out, refugees of ethnic cleansing, civilian forced laborers or people deported after the Warsaw uprising in 1944. Yet solidarity among victim groups was not guaranteed.[26] The most striking example was in concentration camps, where life epitomized the social disintegration that elsewhere, too, led to competition among groups in distress. In the Netherlands, Jews competed for hiding

[26] For Yugoslavia in general see Pavlowitch 2008, p. ix.

places with non-Jews evading forced labor whom most hosts preferred to shelter.[27] Everyday material concerns often contributed to indifference toward Jews and other victims of persecution in the general population – as, for example, in rural France. Indifference wasn't always the case though; local non-Jewish shop owners and farmers, for example, took an interest in Jewish children in children's homes when they were reliable customers. But beyond material concerns, human bonds were formed between non-Jews and Jews which helped many of the latter to survive.[28] This was apparently less frequent in countries like Poland, but not unheard of. Friendly or neighborly relations between people classified as Jews, and other Europeans, have generally not been in the center of scholarship in recent decades. This may have contributed to fact that understanding the emergence and endurance of such ties during World War II requires more in-depth research.

This is also true for understanding the dissolution of social bonds and their being replaced by hostility. About 80% of the Jews who came under German or Axis control died – they were the group with the highest death rate in Europe. (By way of comparison, slightly more than 50% of Soviet POWs in German hands died.) Among the reasons for this high mortality, and for their persecution on such an international scale, was certainly that resentment against Jews was a very important part of Nazi ideology – and the Nazis were, of course, powerful. However, the active participation by German non-Nazis, and by a variety of non-German states and individuals, also contributed to making the labyrinth of persecution inescapable for many Jews. Jews became the target of collective prejudices that were mobilized in a certain constellation, and at a time when many interests converged against a group that was exposed in a way that few others were; a group whose members held many comfortable or elite positions but little, and decreasing, political power. Jews caused envy, aggression – or at least indifference – among many of those who aimed at social ascent, and also among many who had to endure the misery of wartime crisis. All of this coincided with a general loosening of social solidarity. In this context, the group one was affiliated with became ever more important. This is what made it so difficult for Jews to reintegrate themselves into their own society, or indeed into the ones in which they sought refuge. Social exclusion intensified. Persecution would not have been so sweeping or so traumatic without its participatory character, which reached far beyond the actions of states.

27 Moore 2001, pp. 282–5; see also Moore 2010, p. 231.
28 Fogg 2009, pp. 14, 145–7.

Bibliography

PRIMARY SOURCES

Akten zur deutschen auswärtigen Politik 1918–1945, Serie D, vol. V. 1953 (Baden-Baden: Imprimairie Nationale).

Akten zur deutschen auswärtigen Politik 1918–1945, Serie D, vol. XIII (Part 2). 1970. (Göttingen: Vandenhoeck & Ruprecht).

Arad, Yitzhak, Yisrael Gutman and Abraham Margaliot, eds, 1999. *Documents on the Holocaust* (Lincoln: University of Nebraska Press and Yad Vashem).

Bähr, Hans Walter, ed., 1961. *Die Stimme des Menschen: Briefe und Aufzeichnungen aus der ganzen Welt 1939–1945* (Zurich: Exlibris).

Banse, Ewald, 1939. *Das musst Du von Russland wissen!* (Leipzig: Lindner).

Bauche, Ulrich, Heinz Brüdigam and Ludwig Eiber, eds, 1991. *Arbeit und Vernichtung: Das Konzentrationslager Neuengamme 1938–1945* (Hamburg: VSA).

Berenstein, Tatiana, Artur Eisenbach and Adam Rutkowski, eds, 1957. *Eksterminacja Zydów na Ziemiach Polskich wokresie okupacji hitlerowskiej* (Warsaw: Zydowski Institut Historyczny).

Berenstein, Tatiana, Artur Eisenbach and Bernard Mark, eds, 1961. *Faschismus – Getto – Massenmord* (Berlin: Rütten & Loening).

Blachetta, Walther, 1939. *Das wahre Gesicht Polens* (Berlin: Die Wehrmacht).

Boberach, Heinz, ed., 1984. *Meldungen aus dem Reich: Die geheimen Lageberichte des Sicherheitsdienstes der SS 1938–1945* (Herrsching: Pawlak) (cited in footnotes as: MadR).

Böll, Heinrich, 2001. *Briefe aus dem Krieg 1939–1945*, ed. Jochen Schubert (Cologne: Kipenheuer & Witsch).

Carpi, Daniel, ed., 1999. *Italian Diplomatic Documents on the History of the Holocaust in Greece (1941–1943)* (Jerusalem: Graphit Press).

Centre de documentation juive contemporaine (CDJC), 1982. *Les juifs sous l'occupation: Recueil des textes officiels français et allemands 1940/1944* (Paris: FFDJF).

Ciano, Galeazzo, 1946. *Tagebücher 1939–1943* (Bern: Scherz).

Clogg, Richard, ed., 2002a. *Greece 1940–1949: Occupation, Resistance, Civil War* (Basingstoke and New York: Palgrave).

Clogg, Richard, ed., 2002b. *The Holocaust in Salonika: Eyewitness Accounts* (n.p.: Block).

Delacor, Regina, ed., 2000a. *Attentate und Repressionen: Ausgewählte Dokumente zur zyklischen Eskalation des NS-Terrors im besetzten Frankreich 1941/42* (Stuttgart: Jan Thorbecke).

Der Prozess gegen die Hauptkriegsverbrecher vor dem Internationalen Militärgerichtshof, 1947–49. vols 1–42 (Nuremberg: Internationaler Militärgerichtshof).
Domarus, Max, 1962–1963. *Hitlers Reden und Proklamationen, vol. 1: Triumph (1932–1938)* (1962); and *vol. 2: Untergang (1939–1945)* (1963) (Neustadt a.d. Aisch: Schmidt).
"Es gibt keinen jüdischen Wohnbezirk in Warschau mehr": Stroop-Bericht (Darmstadt: Luchterhand, 1976).
Genoud, François, n.d., ed., "Hitlers Politisches Testament: 'Äusserungen des Führers' im Führerhauptquartier von 4. bis 26. Februar und am 2. April 1945." Available at: http://www.nsjap.com/de/online-buecher/hpt_d.html (accessed September 2, 2013).
Die Tagebücher von Joseph Goebbels: Teil I: Aufzeichnungen 1924–1941, vol. 4 (Munich *et al.*: Saur, 1987); *Teil II: Diktate 1941–1945*, ed. Elke Fröhlich, vols 1 and 2 (Munich: Saur, 1996) (2: 1996b); vol. 4 (Munich: Saur, 1995); vol. 5 (Munich: Saur, 1995) (1995b); vol. 10 (Munich: Saur, 1994).
Goebbels, Joseph, 1941. "Die Juden sind schuld!" *Das Reich* 46, November 16, pp. 1–2.
Gründer, Horst, ed., 1999. *"...da und dort ein neues Deutschland gründen": Rassismus, Kolonien und kolonialer Gedanke vom 16. bis zum 20.* Jahrhundert (Munich: dtv).
Günther, Hans, 1930. *Rassenkunde des jüdischen Volkes* (Munich: J.F. Lehmanns).
Günther, Hans, 1937 [1922]. *Rassenkunde des deutschen Volkes*, revised edition (Munich: J.F. Lehmanns).
Heiber, Helmut, ed., 1958. "Der Generalplan Ost," *VfZ* 6, pp. 281–325.
Heim, Susanne and Götz Aly, eds, 1991. *Bevölkerungsstruktur und Massenmord, BNGS*, vol. 9 (Berlin: Rotbuch).
Hermle, Siegfried and Jörg Thierfelder, eds, 2008. *Herausgefordert: Dokumente zur Geschichte der Evangelischen Kirche in der Zeit des Nationalsozialismus* (Stuttgart: Calwer).
Himmler, Heinrich, 1974. *Geheimreden 1933 bis 1945 und andere Ansprachen*, eds Bradley Smith and Agnes Peterson (Frankfurt a.M.: Propyläen).
Hitler, Adolf, 1961 [1928]. *Hitlers Zweites Buch*, ed. Gerhard Weinberg (Stuttgart: Deutsche Verlags-Anstalt).
Hitler, Adolf, 1982. *Monologe im Führerhauptquartier*, ed. Werner Jochmann (Munich: Heyne).
Hitler, Adolf, 1999 [1925–27]. *Mein Kampf* (Boston and New York: Mariner).
Klarsfeld, Serge, ed., 1977. *Die Endlösung der Judenfrage in Frankreich* (Paris: Beate und Serge Klarsfeld).
Klarsfeld, Serge, ed., 1989. *Vichy – Auschwitz: Die Zusammenarbeit der deutschen und französischen Behörden bei der 'Endlösung der Judenfrage' in Frankreich* (Nördlingen: Greno).
Klee, Ernst, Willi Dressen and Volker Riess, eds, 1988. *"Schöne Zeiten": Judenmord aus der Sicht der Täter und Gaffer*, second edition, Frankfurt a.M.: Fischer).
Klein, Peter, ed., 1997. *Die Einsatzgruppen in der besetzten Sowjetunion 1941/42: Die Tätigkeits- und Lageberichte des Chefs der Sicherheitspolizei und des SD* (Berlin: Edition Hentrich).
Klukowski, Zygmunt, 1993. *Diary from the Years of Occupation 1939–1944* (Urbana and Chicago: University of Illinois Press).

Kulka, Otto Dov and Eberhard Jäckel, eds, 2004. *Die Juden in den geheimen NS-Stimmungsberichten 1933–1945* (Düsseldorf: Droste).

Larsen, Stein Ugelvik, Beatrice Sandberg and Volker Dahm, eds, 2008. *Meldungen aus Norwegen 1940–1945: Die geheimen Lageberichte des Befehlshabers der Sicherheitspolizei und des SD in Norwegen*, vol. II (Münich: Oldenbourg).

Longerich, Peter, ed., 1989. *Die Ermordung der europäischen Juden* (Munich and Zurich: Piper).

Madajczyk, Czesław, ed., 1962. "Generalplan Ost," *Polish Western Affairs* 3 (2), pp. 391–442.

Mallmann, Klaus-Michael, Volker Riess und Wolfram Pyta, eds, 2003. *Deutscher Osten 1939–1945: Der Weltanschauungskrieg in Photos und Texten* (Darmstadt: Wissenschaftliche Buchgesellschaft).

Mendelsohn, John, ed., 1993. *The Holocaust: Selected Documents*, vol. 22 (New York and London: Garland).

Müller, Norbert, ed., 1982. *Deutsche Besatzungspolitik in der UdSSR*, second edition (Cologne: Pahl-Rugenstein).

Obenaus, Herbert and Sybille Obenaus, eds, 1985. *"Schreiben wie es wirklich war...": Die Aufzeichnungen Karl Dürkefäldens aus der Zeit des Nationalsozialismus* (Hannover: Landeszentrale für politische Bildung, 1985).

Overmans, Rüdiger, Andreas Hilger and Pavel Polian, eds, 2012. *Rotarmisten in deutscher Hand* (Paderborn: Schöningh).

Pätzold, Kurt, ed., 1984. *Verfolgung, Vertreibung, Vernichtung* (Frankfurt a.M.: Röderberg).

Pätzold, Kurt and Erika Schwarz, eds, 1992. *Tagesordnung: Judenmord: Die Wannsee-Konferenz am 20. Januar 1942* (Berlin: Metropol).

Picker, Henry, 1977. *Hitlers Tischgespräche im Führerhauptquartier*, revised edition (Stuttgart: Seewald).

Präg, Werner and Wolfgang Jacobmeyer, eds, 1975. *Das Diensttagebuch des deutschen Generalgouverneurs in Polen 1939–1945* (Stuttgart: Deutsche Verlags-Anstalt).

Reese, Willy Peter, 2003. *Mir selber seltsam fremd: Die Unmenschlichkeit des Krieges: Russland 1941–1944*, ed. Stefan Schmitz (n.p.: Claassen).

Röhr, Werner, ed., 1989. *Die faschistische Okkupationspolitik in Polen (1939–1945)* (Cologne: Pahl-Rugenstein).

Rosenberg, Alfred, 1939 [1930]. *Der Mythus des 20. Jahrhunderts* (Munich: Hoheneichen).

Rössler, Mechtild and Sabine Schleiermacher, eds, 1993. *Der "Generalplan Ost": Hauptlinien der nationalsozialistischen Planungs- und Vernichtungspolitik* (Berlin: Akademie).

Roth, Karl Heinz, 1997. "'Generalplan Ost' und der Mord an den Juden: Der 'Fernplan der Umsiedlung in den Ostprovinzen' aus dem Reichssicherheitshauptamt vom November 1939," *1999* 12 (2), pp. 50–70.

Sakowska, Ruth, 1993. *Die zweite Etappe ist der Tod: NS-Ausrottungspolitik gegen die polnischen Juden, gesehen mit den Augen ihrer Opfer* (Berlin: Edition Hentrich).

Schlemmer, Thomas, ed., 2005. *Die Italiener an der Ostfront 1942/43: Dokumente zu Mussolinis Krieg gegen die Sowjetunion* (Munich: Oldenbourg).

Seckendorf, Martin, ed., 1992. *Die Okkupationspolitik des deutschen Faschismus in Jugoslawien, Griechenland, Albanien, Italien und Ungarn (1941–1945)* (Berlin and Heidelberg: Hüthig).

Seraphim, Peter Heinz, 1938. *Das Judentum im osteuropäischen Raum* (Essen: Essener Verlagsanstalt).

Simonow, Konstantin, 1979. *Kriegstagebücher*, vol. 1 (Berlin [East]: Volk und Welt).

Smith, Bradley and Agnes Peterson, eds, 1974. *Heinrich Himmler: Geheimreden 1933 bis 1945* (Frankfurt a.M.: Propyläen).

Spiegelbild einer Verschwörung: Die Kaltenbrunner-Berichte an Bormann und Hitler über das Attentat vom 20. Juli 1944 (Stuttgart: Seewald, 1961).

Stein, Harry, ed., 1992. *Juden in Buchenwald 1937–1942* (Weimar: Gedenkstätte Buchenwald).

Tilitzki, Christian, ed., 1991. *Alltag in Ostpreussen 1940–45: Die geheimen Lageberichte der Königsberger Justiz* (Leer: Rautenberg).

Verbrechen der Wehrmacht, 2002. Edited by Hamburger Institut für Sozialforschung, second revised edition (Hamburg: Hamburger Edition).

Verhandlungen des Reichstags: 4. Wahlperiode 1939, vol. 460: Stenographische Berichte 1939–1942 (Bad Feilnbach: Schmidt Periodicals, 1986).

Vernichtungskrieg: Verbrechen der Wehrmacht 1941–1944, ed., Hamburger Institut für Sozialforschung (Hamburg: Hamburger Edition, 1996).

von Hassell, Ulrich, 1946. *Vom andern Deutschland: Aus den nachgelassenen Tagebüchern 1938–1944* (Zurich and Freiburg: Atlantis).

Witte, Peter, Michael Wildt, Martina Voigt, Dieter Pohl, Peter Klein, Christian Gerlach, Christoph Dieckmann and Andrej Angrick, eds, 1999. *Der Dienstkalender Heinrich Himmlers 1941/42* (Hamburg: Christians).

Yacoel, Yomtov, "In the anteroom of hell: Memoir" in Clogg 2002b, pp. 25–121.

SECONDARY SOURCES (INCLUDING AUTOBIOGRAPHICAL MATERIAL)

Abel, Theodore, 1966 [1938]. *The Nazi Movement* (New York: Atherton).

Abitbol, Michel, 1983. *Les juifs d'Afrique du Nord sous Vichy* (Paris: G.-P. Maisonneuve & Larose).

Abke, Stephanie, 2003. *Sichtbare Zeichen unsichtbarer Kräfte: Denunziationen und Denziationsverhalten 1933–1949* (Tübingen: edition diskord).

Abrahamsen, Samuel, 1991. *Norway's Response to the Holocaust* (New York: Holocaust Library).

Achim, Viorel, 2001. "Die Deportation der Roma nach Transnistrien" in Hausleitner *et al.*, eds, pp. 101–11.

Achim, Viorel, 2004. *The Roma in Romanian History* (Budapest and New York: Central European History Press).

Ackermann, Josef, 1970. *Heinrich Himmler als Ideologe* (Göttingen: Musterschmidt).

Adam, Uwe, 1972. *Judenpolitik im Dritten Reich* (Düsseldorf: Droste).

Adam, Uwe, 1976. "An overall plan for anti-Jewish legislation in the Third Reich?" *YVS* 11, pp. 33–55.

Adler, H.G., 1974. *Der verwaltete Mensch: Studien zur Deportation der Juden aus Deutschland* (Tübingen: Mohr).

Adler, Jacques, 1989. *The Jews of Paris and the Final Solution* (Oxford and New York: Oxford University Press).

Adler, Jacques, 1993. "The changing attitudes of the 'Bystanders' toward the Jews in France, 1940–1943" in John Milfull, ed., *Why Germany? National Socialist*

Anti-Semitism and the European Context (Providence and Oxford: Berg), pp. 171–91.

Adler-Rudel, S., 1968. "The Evian conference on the refugee question," *LBIY* 13, pp. 235–71.

Ahonen, Pertti, Gustavo Corni, Jerzy Kochanowski, Rainer Schulze, Tamás Stark and Barbara Stelzl-Marx, 2008. *People on the Move: Population Movements in Europe in the Second World War and Its Aftermath* (Oxford and New York: Berg).

Ainsztein, Reuben, 1993. *Jüdischer Widerstand im deutschbesetzten Osteuropa während des Zweiten Weltkrieges* (Oldenburg: Bibliotheks- und Informationssystem der Universität Oldenburg).

Alary, Eric, Gilles Gauvin and Bénédicte Vergez-Chaignon, 2006. *Les Français au quotidien 1939–1949* (Paris: Perrin).

Alberti, Michael, 2006. *Die Verfolgung und Vernichtung der Juden im Reichsgau Wartheland 1939–1945* (Wiesbaden: Harrassowitz).

Allen, Michael, 2002. *The Business of Genocide* (Chapel Hill and London: University of North Carolina Press).

Almog, Shmuel, 1990. *Nationalism and Antisemitism in Modern Europe 1815–1945* (Oxford: Pergamon Press).

Altermatt, Urs, 1998. "Das Koordinatensystem des katholischen Antisemitismus in der Schweiz 1918–1945" in Mattioli, ed., (1998a), pp. 465–500.

Aly, Götz, 1987. "Medizin gegen Unbrauchbare" in Götz Aly, Angelika Ebbinghaus, Matthias Hamann, Friedemann Pfäfflin and Gerd Preissler, *Aussonderung und Tod: Die klinische Hinrichtung der Unbrauchbaren*" (*BNGS* 1) (Berlin: Rotbuch), pp. 9–74.

Aly, Götz, 1993. "Erwiderung auf Dan Diner," *VfZ* 41, pp. 621–35.

Aly, Götz, 1999. *Final Solution: Nazi Population Policy and the Murder of European Jews* (London: Arnold).

Aly, Götz, 2005. *Hitlers Volksstaat: Raub, Rassenkrieg und nationaler Sozialismus* (Frankfurt a.M.: Fischer).

Aly, Götz, 2006a. *Hitler's Beneficiaries: Plunder, Racial War, and the Nazi Welfare State* (New York: Metropolitan Books).

Aly, Götz, ed., 2006b. *Volkes Stimme: Skepsis und Führervertrauen im Nationalsozialismus* (Frankfurt a.M.: Fischer).

Aly, Götz, 2011. *Warum die Deutschen? Warum die Juden? Gleichheit, Neid und Rassenhass 1800–1933* (Frankfurt a.M.: Fischer).

Aly, Götz, 2013. *Die Belasteten: "Euthanasie" 1939–1945: Eine Gesellschaftsgeschichte* (Frankfurt a.M.: Fischer).

Aly, Götz, Susanne Heim, Miroslav Kárný, Petra Kirchberger and Alfred Konieczny, 1987. *Sozialpolitik und Judenvernichtung: Gibt es eine Ökonomie der Endlösung?* (*BNGS* 5) (Berlin: Rotbuch).

Aly, Götz and Susanne Heim, 1991. *Vordenker der Vernichtung: Auschwitz und die Pläne für eine neue europäische Ordnung* (Hamburg: Hofmann und Campe).

Ancel, Jean, 1984. "Plans for the deportation of the Rumanian Jews and their discontinuation in light of documentary evidence," *YVS* 16, pp. 381–420.

Ancel, Jean, 1988. "The Romanian way of solving the 'Jewish problem' in Bessarabia and Bukovina, June–July 1941," *YVS* 19, pp. 187–232.

Ancel, Jean, 1992. "The impact of the course of the war on Romanian Jewish policies" in Cohen *et al.*, eds, pp. 177–210.

Ancel, Jean, 1997. "The Romanian campaign of mass murder in Transnistria, 1941–1942" in Braham, ed., pp. 87–133.

Ancel, Jean, 2007. *The Economic Destruction of Romanian Jewry* (Jerusalem: Yad Vashem).

Ancel, Jean, 2011. *The History of the Holocaust in Romania* (Lincoln and Jerusalem: University of Nebraska Press and Yad Vashem).

Anderson, Benedict, 1991. *Imagined Communities: Reflections on the Origin and Spread of Nationalism*, revised edition (London and New York: Verso).

Anderson, Truman, 1995. "Die 62. Infanterie-Division: Repressalien im Heeresgebiet Süd" in Heer and Naumann, eds, pp. 297–323.

Anderson, Truman, 1999. "A Hungarian *Vernichtungskrieg*? Hungarian troops and the Soviet partisan war in Ukraine, 1942," *MGM* 58, pp. 345–66.

Anderson, Truman, 2000. "Germans, Ukrainians and Jews: Ethnic politics in Heeresgebiet Süd, June–December 1941," *War in History* 7 (3), pp. 325–51.

Angrick, Andrej, 2003. *Besatzungspolitik und Massenmord: Die Einsatzgruppe D in der südlichen Sowjetunion 1941–1943* (Hamburg: Hamburger Edition).

Angrick, Andrej, 2005. "Das Beispiel Charkow: Massenmord unter deutscher Besatzung" in Hartmann *et al.*, eds, pp. 117–24.

Angrick, Andrej and Peter Klein, 2006. *Die "Endlösung" in Riga* (Darmstadt: Wissenschaftliche Buchgesellschaft).

Angrick, Andrej, 2013. "Die inszenierte Selbstermächtigung? Motive und Strategie Heydrich's für die Wannsee-Konferenz" in Kampe and Klein, eds, pp. 241–58.

Antonijević, Nenad, 2008. "Holocaust in the area of Kosovo and Methhija during World War II and its context" in *Israeli-Serbian Academic Exchange in Holocaust Research*, pp. 409–15.

Arad, Yitzhak, 1987. *Belzec, Sobibor, Treblinka: The Operation Reinhard Death Camps* (Bloomington and Indianapolis: Indiana University Press).

Arad, Yitzhak, 2009. *The Holocaust in the Soviet Union* (Lincoln and Jerusalem: University of Nebraska Press and Yad Vashem).

Arendt, Hannah, 1986 [1955]. *Elemente und Ursprünge totalitärer Herrschaft* (Munich and Zurich: Piper).

Arlettaz, Silvia and Gérald Arlettaz, 1998. "Die schweizerische Ausländergesetzgebung und die politischen Parteien 1917–1931" in Mattioli, ed., (1998a), pp. 327–56.

Arnaud, Patrice and Michel Fabréguet, 2000. "Les prisonniers de guerre, les travailleurs civils et les concentrationnaires Français entre répression et travail forcé (Novembre 1942-automne 1944)" in Martens and Vaïsse, eds, pp. 419–35.

Aschheim, Steven, 1982. *Brothers and Strangers: The East European Jews in German and German Jewish Consciousness, 1800–1923* (Madison and London: University of Wisconsin Press).

Aspelmeier, Dieter, 1967. *Deutschland und Finnland während der beiden Weltkriege* (Hamburg-Volksdorff: Christoph von der Ropp).

Attali, Jacques, 2010. *The Economic history of the Jewish people* (Portland: ESKA).

Ayaß, Wolfgang, "'Ein Gebot der nationalen Arbeitsdisziplin': Die Aktion 'Arbeitsscheu Reich' 1938" in Wolfgang Ayaß, Reimar Gilsenbach, Ursula Körber, Klaus Scherer, Patrick Wagner and Mathias Winter, eds, *Feinderklärung und Prävention* (*BNGS* 6) (Berlin: Rotbuch), pp. 43–74.

Bailer-Galanda, Brigitte, 2002. "Die Opfer des Nationalsozialismus und die sogenannte Wiedergutmachung" in Tálos *et al.*, eds, pp. 884–901.

Bajohr, Frank, 1995. "Gauleiter in Hamburg: Zur Person und Tätigkeit Karl Kaufmanns," *VfZ* 43, pp. 267–95.

Bajohr, Frank, 1998. *"Arisierung" im Hamburg* (Hamburg: Christians).

Bajohr, Frank, 2001. *Parvenüs und Profiteure: Korruption in der NS-Zeit* (Frankfurt a.M.: Fischer).

Bajohr, Frank, 2003. *"Unser Hotel ist judenfrei": Bäder-Antisemitismus im 19. und 20. Jahrhundert* (Frabkfurt a.M.: Fischer).

Bajohr, Frank and Dieter Pohl, 2006. *Der Holocaust als offenes Geheimnis: Die Deutschen, die NS-Führung und die Alliierten* (Munich: Beck).

Bajohr, Frank and Michael Wildt, eds, 2009. *Volksgemeinschaft: Neue Forschungen zur Gesellschaft des Nationalsozialismus* (Frankfurt a.M.: Fischer).

Balcar, Jaromir and Jaroslav Kučera, 2010. "Von der Fremdbesatzung zur kommunistischen Diktatur: Die personellen Umbrüche in der tschechoslowakischen Wirtschaft nach dem Zweiten Weltkrieg," *JfW* 51 (2), pp. 71–94.

Banken, Ralf, 2009. *Edelmetallmangel und Grossraubwirtschaft: Die Entwicklung des deutschen Edelmetallsektors im "Dritten Reich" 1933–1945* (Berlin: Akademie).

Bankier, David, 1996. *The Germans and the Final Solution: Public Opinion Under Nazism* (Oxford and Cambridge: Blackwell).

Bankier, David, 2011. *Expulsion and Extermination: Holocaust Testimonials from Provincial Lithuania* (Jerusalem: Yad Vashem).

Barkai, Avraham, 1988. *Vom Boykott zur "Entjudung"* (Frankfurt a.M.: Fischer).

Barkai, Avraham, 1989. "German-speaking Jews in eastern European ghettos," *LBIY* 34, pp. 247–66.

Barkai, Avraham, 1991. "German entrepreneurs and Jewish policy in the Third Reich," *YVS* 21, pp. 125–53.

Barkai, Avraham, 1997. "Bevölkerungsrückgang und wirtschaftliche Stagnation" in Avraham Barkai, Paul Mendes-Flohr and Steven Lowenstein, *Deutsch-jüdische Geschichte in der Neuzeit*, vol. IV (Munich: C.H. Beck), pp. 37–49.

Baten, Jörg and Andrea Wagner, 2003. "Mangelernährung, Krankheit und Sterblichkeit im NS-Wirtschaftsaufschwung (1933–1937)," *JfW* 42 (1), pp. 99–123.

Battenberg, Friedrich, 1990. *Das europäische Zeitalter der Juden, vol. II: Von 1650 bis 1945* (Darmstadt: Wissenschaftliche Buchgesellschaft).

Bauer, Yehuda, 1993. *Jews for Sale? Nazi-Jewish Negotiations, 1933–1945* (New Haven and London: Yale University Press).

Bauer, Yehuda, 2001. *Die dunkle Seite der Geschichte: Die Shoah in historischer Sicht, Interpretationen und Re-Interpretationen* (Frankfurt a.M.: Jüdischer Verlag im Suhrkamp Verlag).

Bauer, Yehuda, 2013. *Der Tod des Schtetls* (Frankfurt a.M.: Jüdischer Verlag).

Baum, Herwig, 2011. *Varianten des Terrors: Ein Vergleich zwischen der deutschen und rumänischen Besatzungsverwaltung in der Sowjetunion 1941–1944* (Berlin: Metropol).

Bayraktor, Hatice, 2006. "The anti-Jewish pogrom in Eastern Thrace in 1934: New evidence of the responsibility of the Turkish government," *Patterns of Prejudice* 40 (2), pp. 95–112.

Becker, Felicitas and Jigal Beez, eds, 2007. *Der Maji-Maji-Krieg in Deutsch-Ostafrika 1905–1907* (Berlin: Chr. Links).

Becker, Franz, ed., 2004. *Rassenmischehen – Mischlinge – Rassenmischung: Zur Politik der Rasse im deutschen Kolonialreich* (Stuttgart: Franz Steiner).

Beevor, Antony, 2007. *Ein Schriftsteller im Krieg: Wassili Grossman und die Rote Armee 1941–1945* (n.p.: Bertelsmann).

Bender, Sara, 2009. "Die Juden von Chmielnik unter deutscher Besatzung (1939–1943)" in Dieckmann and Quinkert, eds, pp. 74–96.

Benyamin, Lya, 1997. "Anti-Semitism as reflected in the records of the Council of Ministers, 1940–1944" in Braham, ed., pp. 1–18.

Benjamin, Lya, 2001. "Die 'Judenfrage' in Rumänien im Spiegel des Bukarester Tageblatts" in Hausleitner *et al.*, eds, pp. 139–52.

Benz, Wolfgang, ed., 1988a. *Die Juden in Deutschland 1933–1945* (Munich: Beck).

Benz, Wolfgang, 1988b. "Überleben im Untergrund 1943–1945" in Benz 1988a, pp. 660–700.

Benz, Wolfgang, ed., 1991. *Dimension des Völkermords: Die Zahl der jüdischen Opfer des Nationalsozialismus* (Munich: Oldenbourg, 1991).

Benz, Wolfgang, 1994. "Der Rückfall in die Barbarei: Bericht über den Pogrom" in Pehle, ed., pp. 13–51.

Benz, Wolfgang and Juliane Wetzel, eds, 1996. *Solidarität und Hilfe für Juden während der NS-Zeit: Regionalstudien II* (Berlin: Metropol).

Bergen, Doris, 2003. *War and Genocide: A Concise History of the Holocaust* (Lanham: Rowman and Littlefield).

Berger, Sara, 2013. *Experten der Vernichtung: Das T4-Reinhardt-Netzwerk in den Lagern Belzec, Sobibor und Treblinka* (Hamburg: Hamburger Edition).

Berkhoff, Karel, 2004. *Harvest of Despair: Life and Death in Ukraine Under Nazi Rule* (Cambridge and London: Belknap).

Berliner Geschichtswerkstatt, eds, 2000. *Zwangsarbeit in Berlin 1940–1945: Erinnerungsberichte aus Polen, der Ukraine und Weissrussland* (Erfurt: Sutton).

Bernardini, Gene, 1989. "The origins and development of racial anti-Semitism in fascist Italy" in Marrus, ed., pp. 217–39.

Bettelheim, Bruno and Morris Janowitz, 1964 [1950]. *Social Change and Prejudice* (New York and London: Free Press and Collier Macmillan).

Bićanić, Rudolf, 1944. "The effects of war on rural Yugoslavia," *Geographical Journal* 103 (1/2), pp. 30–45.

Billig, Joseph, 1955. *Le Commissariat Général aux Questions Juives (1941–1944)*, vol. 1 (Paris: Éditions du Centre).

Biondich, Mark, 2002. "Persecution of Roma-Sinti in Croatia, 1941–1945" in *Roma and Sinti: Understudied Victims of Nazism. Symposion Proceedings* (Washington: United States Holocaust Memorial Museum), pp. 33–47.

Biondich, Mark, 2005. "Religion and nation in wartime Croatia: Reflections on the Ustaša policy of forced religious conversions, 1941–1942," *Slavonic and East European Review* 83 (1), pp. 71–116.

Birnbaum, Pierre, 1992. *Anti-Semitism in France: A Political History from Léon Blum to the Present* (Oxford and Cambridge: Blackwell).

Bischof, Günter and Rüdiger Overmans, eds, 1999. *Kriegsgefangenschaft im Zweiten Weltkrieg* (Ternitz-Pottschach: Gerhard Höller).

Bischof, Günter, Stefan Karner and Barbara Stelzl-Marx, eds, 2005. *Kriegsgefangene des Zweiten Weltkrieges: Gefangennahme – Lagerleben – Rückkehr* (Munich and Vienna: Oldenbourg).

Bitterberg, Christoph, 1995. *Der Bielefelder Prozess als Quelle für die deutsche Judenpolitik im Distrikt Bialystok* (unpublished MA thesis, Hamburg).

Black, Peter, 2004. "Die Trawniki-Männer und die 'Aktion Reinhardt'" in Musial, ed., pp. 309–52.

Blättler, Franz, n.d. [1945]. *Warschau 1942: Tatsachenbericht eines Motorfahrers der zweiten schweizerischen Ärztemission 1942 in Polen* (Zurich: Micha).

Blatman, Daniel, 2011. *The Death Marches: The Final Phase of the Nazi Genocide* (Cambridge and London: Belknap).

Blom, J.C.H., 1989. "The persecution of Jews in the Netherlands in a comparative international perspective" in Jozeph Michman, ed., *Dutch Jewish History* (Jerusalem: Hebrew University), pp. 273–89.

Blood, Philip, 2006. *Hitler's Bandit Hunters: The SS and the Nazi Occupation of Europe* (Washington: Potomac).

Bloxham, Donald, 2001. "A survey of Jewish slave labour in the Nazi system," *Journal of Holocaust Education* 10 (3), pp. 25–59.

Bloxham, Donald, 2009. *The Final Solution: A Genocide* (Oxford: Oxford University Press).

Bock, Gisela, 1986. *Zwangssterilisation im Nationalsozialismus* (Opladen: Westdeutscher Verlag).

Bock, Gisela, 2005. "Einleitung" in Gisela Bock, ed., *Genozid und Geschlecht: Jüdische Frauen im nationalsozialistischen Lagersystem* (Frankfurt a.M. and New York: Campus), pp. 7–21.

Böhler, Jochen, 2006. *Auftakt zum Vernichtungskrieg: Die Wehrmacht in Polen 1939* (Frankfurt a.M.: Fischer).

Boll, Bernd and Hans Safrian, 2000. "On the way to Stalingrad: The 6th Army in 1941–42" in Heer and Naumann, eds, pp. 237–71.

Bonwetsch, Bernd, 1985. "Sowjetische Partisanen 1941–1944: Legende und Wirklichkeit des 'allgemeinen Volkskrieges'" in Gerhard Schulz, ed., *Partisanen und Volkskrieg: Zur Revolutionierung des Krieges im 20. Jahrhundert* (Göttingen: Vandenhoeck & Ruprecht), pp. 92–124.

Borejsza, Jerzy, 1989. "Racisme et antislavisme chez Hitler" in François Bedarida, ed., *La politique nazie d'extermination* (Paris: Albin Michel), pp. 57–74.

Borgsen, Werner and Klaus Volland, 1991. *Stalag XB Sandbostel* (Bremen: Edition Temmen).

Borodziej, Włodzimierz, 1999. *Terror und Politik: Die deutsche Polizei und die polnische Widerstandsbewegung im Generalgouvernement 1939 bis 1944* (Mainz: Philipp von Zabern).

Botz, Gerhard, 1975. *Wohnungspolitik und Judendeportation in Wien 1938 bis 1945: Zur Funktion des Antisemitismus als Ersatz nationalsozialistischer Sozialpolitik* (Vienna and Salzburg: Geyer-Edition).

Botz, Gerhard, 1976. *Gewalt in der Politik: Attentate, Zusammenstösse, Putschversuche, Unruhen in Österreich 1918 bis 1934* (Munich: Wilhelm Fink).

Botz, Gerhard, 1986–87."Stufen der Ausgliederung der Juden aus der Gesellschaft: Die österreichischen Juden vom 'Anschluss' bis zum 'Holocaust'," *Zeitgeschichte* 14 (9–10), pp. 359–78.

Bowman, Steven, ed., 2002. *The Holocaust in Salonika: Eyewitness Accounts* (n.p.: Bloch).

Bowman, Steven, 2006. *Jewish Resistance in Wartime Greece* (London and Portland: Valentine Mitchell).

Brachfeld, Sylvain, 2005. "La collaboration de la police anversoise aux arrestations des Juifs de la ville en 1942, sous l'occupation allemande de la Belgique," *Bulletin Trimestrielle de la Fondation Auschwitz* 89, pp. 41–58.

Braham, Randolph, 1973. "The Kamenets Podolsk and Delvidek massacres: Prelude to the Holocaust in Hungary," *YVS* 9, pp. 133–56.

Braham, Randolph, 1977a. *The Hungarian Labor Service System* (New York: East European Quarterly).

Braham, Randolph, 1977b. "The treatment of Hungarian Jews in German-occupied Europe," *YVS* 12, pp. 125–46.

Braham, Randolph, 1983. *Genocide and Retribution: The Holocaust in Hungarian-Ruled Northern Transylvania* (Boston: Kluwer Nijhoff).

Braham, Randolph, 1992. "The influence of the war on the Jewish policies of the German satellite states" in Cohen *et al.*, eds, pp. 125–43.

Braham, Randolph, 1994. *The Politics of Genocide: The Holocaust in Hungary*, revised and enlarged edition (New York: Columbia University Press).

Braham, Randolph, ed., 1997. *The Destruction of Romanian and Ukrainian Jews during the Antonescu Era* (New York: Columbia University Press).

Brakel, Alexander, 2009. *Unter Rotem Stern und Hakenkreuz: Baranowicze 1939–1944* (Paderborn: Schöningh).

Brandes, Detlef, 2006. "Politische 'Kollaboration' im Protektorat Böhmen und Mähren" in Tauber, ed., pp. 453–62.

Brandhuber, Jerzy, 1961. "Die sowjetischen Kriegsgefangenen im Konzentrationslager Auschwitz," *Hefte von Auschwitz* 4, pp. 5–46.

Brandišauskas, Valentinas, 2003. "Neue Dokumente aus der Zeit der Provisorischen Regierung Litauens" in Vincas Bartusevičius, ed., *Holocaust in Litauen* (Cologne: Böhlau), pp. 55–62.

Brandon, Ray and Wendy Lower, eds, 2010. *The Shoah in Ukraine* (Bloomington and Indianapolis: Indiana University Press).

Brandt, Karl, Otto Schiller and Franz Ahlgrimm, 1953. *Management of Agriculture and Food in the German-Occupied and Other Areas of Fortress Europe* (Stanford: Stanford University Press).

Brasz, Chaya and Yosef Kaplan, eds, 2001. *Dutch Jews as Perceived by Themselves and Others* (Leiden: Brill).

Bräutigam, Helmut, 1996. *Fremdarbeiter in Brandenburg in der NS-Zeit* (Brandenburg: RAA).

Bräutigam, Helmut, 2003. "Zwangsarbeit in Berlin 1938–1945" in Helmut Bräutigam, Doris Fürstenberg and Bernt Roder, eds, *Zwangsarbeit in Berlin 1938–1945* (Berlin: Metropol), pp. 17–61.

Brayard, Florent, 2004. *La "solution finale de la question juive"* (Paris: Fayard).

Brechtken, Magnus, 1997. *Madagaskar für die Juden: Antisemitische Idee und Politische Praxis 1885–1945* (Munich: Oldenbourg).

Brechtken, Magnus, 2000. "Französische Kolonien, deutsche Judenpolitik und Umsiedlungsfrage" in Martens and Vaisse, eds, pp. 481–94.

Breitenfellner, Kirstin, 1998. "Der 'jüdische Fuss' und die 'jüdische Nase': Physiognomik, Medizingeschichte und Antisemitismus im 19. und 20. Jahrhundert" in Kirstin Breitenfellner and Charlotte Kolm-Levy, eds, *Wie ein Muster entsteht: Zur Konstruktion des anderen in Rassismus und Antisemitismus* (Bodenheim: Philo), pp. 103–20.

Breitman, Richard, 1992. *The Architect of Genocide: Himmler and the Final Solution* (London: Grafton).

Broszat, Martin, 1965. *Nationalsozialistische Polenpolitik 1939–1945* (Frankfurt a.M.: Fischer).

Broszat, Martin, 1977. "Hitler und die Genesis der 'Endlösung': Aus Anlass der Thesen von David Irving," *VfZ* 25, pp. 739–75.

Browning, Christopher, 1978. *The Final Solution and the German Foreign Office* (New York and London: Holmes and Meier).

Browning, Christopher, 1985. *Fateful Months* (New York and London: Holmes and Meier).

Browning, Christopher, 1986. "Nazi ghettoization policy in Poland," *CEH* 19 (4), pp. 343–68.

Browning, Christopher, 1992. *The Path to Genocide* (Cambridge: Cambridge University Press).

Browning, Christopher, 1993. *Ordinary Men: Reserve Police Battalion 101 and the Final Solution in Poland* (New York: HarperPerennial).

Browning, Christopher, 1998a. *Der Weg zur "Endlösung": Entscheidungen und Täter* (Bonn: Dietz).

Browning, Christopher, 1998b. "Die Debatte über die Täter des Holocaust" in Ulrich Herbert, ed., *Nationalsozialistische Vernichtungspolitik 1939–1945* (Frankfurt a.M.: Fischer), pp. 148–69.

Browning, Christopher, 2000. *Nazi Policy, Jewish Workers, German Killers* (Cambridge: Cambridge University Press).

Browning, Christopher, 2010. *Remembering Survival: Inside a German Slave-Labor Camp* (New York and London: W.W. Norton).

Browning, Christopher with Jürgen Matthäus, 2003. *Die Entfesselung der "Endlösung": Nationalsozialistische Judenpolitik 1939–1942* (Munich: Propyläen).

Brulligny, Arnaud, 2007. "Les Français arrètés au sein de Reich et internés en camps de concentration," *Bulletin Trimestrielle de la Fondation Auschwitz* 94, pp. 9–39.

Brustein, William and Ryan King, 2004a. "Anti-Semitism in Europe before the Holocaust," *International Political Science Review* 25 (1), pp. 35–53.

Brustein, William and Ryan King, 2004b. "Anti-Semitism as a response to perceived Jewish Power: The cases of Bulgaria and Romania before the Holocaust," *Social Forces* 83 (2), pp. 691–708.

Buchholz, Marlies, n.d., "'... und hat unendlich viel Arbeit verursacht': Hannovers Stadtverwaltung und die 'Judenhäuser'," in *Rassismus in Deutschland*, pp. 61–72.

Budrass, Lutz, 2004. "'Arbeitskräfte können aus der reichlich vorhandenen jüdischen Bevölkerung gewonnen werden': Das Heinkel-Werk in Budzyn 1942–1944," *JfW* 45 (1), pp. 41–64.

Buggeln, Marc, 2012. *Das System der KZ-Aussenlager* (Bonn: Friedrich-Ebert-Stiftung).

Burgwyn, H. James, 2005. *Empire on the Adriatic: Mussolini's Conquest of Yugoslavia 1941–1943* (New York: Enigma).

Burleigh, Michael, 1988. *Germany Turns Eastwards: A Study of Ostforschung in the Third Reich* (Cambridge: Cambridge University Press).

Burleigh, Michael and Wolfgang Wippermann, 1991. *The Racial State: Germany, 1933–1945* (Cambridge: Cambridge University Press).

Cahnman, Werner, 1979. "Die Juden in München 1918–1943," *Zeitschrift für bayerische Landesgeschichte* 42, pp. 403–61.

Camera dei deputati, 1989. *La legislazione antiebraica in Italia e in Europa* (Rome: Camera dei deputati).

Camphausen, Gabriele, 1990. *Die wissenschaftliche historische Russlandforschung im Dritten Reich 1933–1945* (Frankfurt a.M: Peter Lang).

Capelli, Anna and Renata Broggini, eds, 2001. *Antisemitismo in Europa negli anni trenta: Legislazioni a confronto* (Milan: FrancoAngeli Storia).

Caracciolo, Nicola, 1995 [1986]. *Uncertain Refuge: Italy and the Jews During the Holocaust* (Urbana and Chicago: University of Illinois Press).

Caron, Vicky, 1999. *Uneasy Asylum: France and the Jewish Refugee Crisis, 1933–1942* (Stanford: Stanford University Press).

Case, Holly, 2006. "The Holocaust and the Transylvanian question in the twentieth century" in Randolph Braham and Brewster Chamberlain, eds, *The Holocaust in Hungary: Sixty Years Later* (New York and Boulder: Columbia University Press), pp. 17–40.

Cecil, Robert, 1972. *The Myth of the Master Race: Alfred Rosenberg and Nazi Ideology* (London: Batsford).

Cépède, Michel, 1961. *Agriculture et alimentation en France durant la IIe guerre mondiale* (Paris: M.-Th. Génin).

Cervi, Alcide, 1956. *Meine sieben Söhne* (Berlin [East]: Dietz).

Césaire, Aimé, 1972. *Discouse on Colonialism* (New York and London: Monthly Review Press).

Cesarani, David, 2007. *Becoming Eichmann: Rethinking the Life, Times and Trial of a "Desk Murderer"* (Cambridge: Da Capo).

Chary, Frederick, 1972. *The Bulgarian Jews and the Final Solution, 1940–1944* (Pittsburgh: University of Pittsburgh Press).

Chiari, Bernhard, 1998. *Alltag hinter der Front: Besatzung, Kollaboration und Widerstand in Weissrussland 1941–1944* (Düsseldorf: Droste).

Chodakiewicz, Marek Jan, 2004. *Between Nazis and Soviets: Occupation Politics in Poland, 1939–1947* (Lanham: Lexington Books).

Cholawski, Shalom, 1982. *Soldiers from the Ghetto* (San Diego: A.S. Barnes and Tantivy Press).

Claussen, Detlev, 1994. *Grenzen der Aufkläörung: Die gesellschaftliche Genese des modernen Antisemitismus* (Frankfurt a.M.: Fischer).

Cohen, Asher, 1987. "Pétain, Horthy, Antonescu and the Jews, 1942–44: Toward a comparative view," *YVS* 18, pp. 163–98.

Cohen, Asher, 1988. "La politique antijuive en Europe (Allemagne exclue) de 1938 à 1941," *Guerres mondiales et conflits contemporaines* 38 (150), pp. 45–59.

Cohen, Asher, 1992. "A history of failures: The fascists in German client and occupied countries" in Cohen *et al.*, eds, pp. 87–123.

Cohen, Asher, 1993. *Persécutions et sauvetages: Juifs et Français sous l'occupation et sous Vichy* (Paris: Éditions du Cerf).

Cohen, Asher, 1994. "Rescuing Jews: Jews and Christians in Vichy France," *British Journal of Holocaust Education* 3 (1), pp. 4–31.

Cohen, Asher, Yehoyakim Cochavi and Yoav Gelber, eds, 1992. *The Shoah and the War* (New York: Peter Lang).

Cole, Tim, 1999. "Constructing the 'Jew', writing the Holocaust: Hungary 1920–1945," *Patterns of Prejudice* 33 (3), pp. 19–27.

Cole, Tim, 2003. *Holocaust City: The Making of a Jewish Ghetto* (London and New York: Routledge).

Collingham, Lizzie, 2011. *The Taste of War: World War II and the Battle for Food* (London: Allan Lane).

Collotti, Enzo, 2006. *Il fascismo e gli ebrei: Le leggi razziali in Italia* (Rome: Editori Laterza).

Conference Report of the International Scientific Conference: The Holocaust Phenomenon, 1999. (Prague: n.p.).

Connelly, John, 1999. "Nazis and Slavs: From racial theory to racial practice," *CEH* 32 (1), pp. 1–33.

Conte, Édouard and Cornelia Essner, 1995. *La quête de la race: Une anthropologie du Nazisme* (Paris: Hachette).

Conway, Martin, 1997. *Catholic Politics in Europe 1918–1948* (London and New York: Routledge).

Conze, Eckart, Norbert Frei, Peter Hayes and Moshe Zimmermann, 2010. *Das Amt und die Vergangenheit: Deutsche Diplomaten im Dritten Reich und in der Bundesrepublik*, second edition (Munich: Blessing).

Cornelius, Deborah, 2011. *Hungary in World War II* (New York: Fordham University Press).

Corni, Gustavo, 2002. *Hitler's Ghettos* (London: Arnold).

Corni, Gustavo and Horst Gies, 1997. *Brot – Butter – Kanonen: Die Ernährungswirtschaft in Deutschland unter der Diktatur Hitlers* (Berlin: Akademie).

Croes, Marnix, 2011. "Researching the survival and rescue of Jews in the Nazi-occupied Europe: A plea for the use of quantitative methods" in Jacques Semelin, Claire Andrieu and Sarah Gensburger, eds, *Resisting Genocide* (New York: Columbia University Press), pp. 65–81.

Crowe, David and John Kolsti, eds, 1991. *The Gypsies of Eastern Europe* (Armonk and London: M.E. Sharpe).

Cüppers, Martin, 2005. *Wegbereiter der Shoah: Die Waffen-SS, der Kommandostab Reichsführer-SS und die Judenvernichtung 1939–1945* (Darmstadt: Wissenschaftliche Buchgesellschaft).

Curilla, Wolfgang, 2006. *Die deutsche Ordnungspolizei und der Holocaust im Baltikum und Weissrussland 1941–1944* (Paderborn: Schöningh).

Cvetković, Dragan, 2008. "Holocaust in Yugoslavia: An attempt at quantification," in *Israeli–Serbian Academic Exchange* 2008, pp. 357–69.

Czech, Danuta, 1989. *Kalendarium der Ereignisse im Konzentrationslager Auschwitz-Birkenau 1939–1945* (Reinbek: Rowohlt).

Dahlmann, Dittmar and Gerhard Hirschfeld, eds, 1999. *Lager, Zwangsarbeit, Deportation und Vertreibung: Dimensionen der Massenverbrechen in der Sowjetunion und in Deutschland 1933 bis 1945* (Essen: Klartext).

Dallin, Alexander, 1998 [1957]. *Odessa, 1941–1944* (Iaşi: Center for Romanian Studies).
Dams, Carsten and Michael Stolle, 2008. *Die Gestapo* (Munich: C.H. Beck).
Datner, Szymon, 1964. *Crimes against POWs: Responsibility of the Wehrmacht* (Warsaw: Zachodnia Agencja Prasowa).
Dawidowicz, Lucy, 1987 [1975]. *The War against the Jews 1933–45* (New York: Penguin, 1987).
Dawletschin, Tamurbek, 2005. *Von Kasan nach Bergen-Belsen* (Göttingen: Vandenhoeck & Ruprecht).
De Felice, Renzo, 1985. *Jews in an Arab Land: Libya, 1835–1970* (Austin: University of Texas Press).
De Felice, Renzo, 1995. "Foreword" in Caracciolo, ed., pp. xv–xxiii.
Déak, István, 2010. "Antisemitism in eastern Europe (excluding Russia and the Soviet empire) since 1848" in Lindemann and Levy, eds, pp. 223–36.
Dean, Martin, 2000. *Collaboration in the Holocaust: Crimes of the Local Police in Belorussia and Ukraine, 1941–1944* (New York: St. Martin's).
Del Boca, Angelo, 1995. "Le leggi razziali nell' imperio di Mussolini" in Del Boca, ed., *Il regime fascista* (Rome and Bari: Editori Laterza), pp. 329–51.
Del Boca, Angelo, 2004. "Faschismus und Kolonialismus: der Mythos von den 'anständigen Italienern'," *Fritz-Bauer-Institut Jahrbuch*, pp. 193–202.
Delacor, Arne, 1994. "Die Lohnpolitik Vichys 1940–1944," *1999* 9 (4), pp. 13–33.
Delacor, Regina, 2000b. "Ausländische Juden – Opfer 'nationaler Prophylaxe'? Zur Verstrickung des *État Français* in die 'Endlösung der Judenfrage' 1942–1944" in Martens and Vaïsse, eds, pp. 495–513.
Deletant, Dennis, 2006. *Hitler's Forgotten Ally: Ion Antonescu and His Regime, Romania 1940–1944* (Basingstoke and New York: Palgrave Macmillan).
Deletant, Dennis, 2010. "Transnistria and the Romanian solution to the 'Jewish problem'" in Brandon and Lower, eds, pp. 156–89.
Demps, Laurenz, 1986. *Zwangsarbeiterlager in Berlin* (Berlin [East]: Kulturbund).
Di Sante, Costantino, 2008. "La 'pacification' Italienne de la Cyrenaïque (1929–1933)," *RHS* 189, pp. 465–96.
Dieckmann, Christoph, 2000 "The war and the killing of the Lithuanian Jews" in Ulrich Herbert, ed., *National Socialist Extermination Policies* (New York and Oxford: Berghahn), pp. 240–75.
Dieckmann, Christoph, 2005. "The murder of Soviet prisoners of war in Lithuania" in Christoph Dieckmann, Vytautas Toliekis and Rimantas Zizas, *Murders of Prisoners of War and of the Civilian Population in Lithuania 1941–1944* (Vilnius: Margi Rastai), pp. 221–59.
Dieckmann, Christoph, 2011. *Deutsche Besatzungspolitik in Litauen 1941–1944* (Göttingen: Wallstein).
Dieckmann, Christoph and Babette Quinkert, eds, 2009. *Im Ghetto 1939–1945* (*BGN* 25) (Göttingen: Wallstein).
Dieckmann, Christoph, Babette Quinkert and Tatjana Tönsmeyer, eds, 2005. *Kooperation und Verbrechen: Formen der "Kollaboration" im östlichen Europa 1939–1945* (*BGN* 19) (Göttingen: Wallstein).
Dietrich, Otto, 1955. *12 Jahre mit Hitler* (Munich: Isar).
Diewald-Kenkmann, Gisela, 1995. *Politische Denunziation im NS-Regime oder Die kleine Macht der "Volksgenossen"* (Bonn: Dietz).

Dmitrów, Edmund, Pawel Machcewicz and Tomasz Szarota, 2004. *Der Beginn der Vernichtung: Der Mord an den Juden in Jedwabne und Umgebung im Sommer 1941* (Osnabrück: Fibre).

Dörner, Bernward, 1998. *"Heimtücke": Das Gesetz als Waffe: Kontrolle, Abschreckung und Verfolgung in Deutschland 1933–1945* (Paderborn: Schöningh).

Dörner, Bernward, 2007. *Die Deutschen und der Holocaust* (Berlin: Propyläen).

Dobroszycki, Lucjan, 1994. *Survivors of the Holocaust in Poland: A Portrait Based on Jewish Community Records* (Armonk and London: M.E. Sharpe).

Dobroszycki, Lucjan and Jeffrey Gurock, eds, 1993. *The Holocaust in the Soviet Union* (Armonk and London: M.E. Sharpe).

Dollmann, Lydia and Susanne Eckelmann, 2000. "Polnische Erinnerungsberichte" in Berliner Geschichtswerkstatt, eds, pp. 17–20.

Don, Yehuda, 1997. "Economic implications of the anti Jewish legislation in Hungary" in David Cesarani, ed., *Genocide and Rescue: The Holocaust in Hungary 1944* (Oxford and New York: Berg), pp. 47–76.

Dower, John, 1986. *War Without Mercy: Race and Power in the Pacific War* (New York: Pantheon).

Drechsler, Horst, 1984. *Aufstände in Südwestafrika* (Berlin [East]: Dietz).

Dreyfus, François Georges, 1981. "Antisemitismus in der Dritten Französischen Republik" in Martin and Schulin, eds, pp. 231–48.

Dreyfus, Jean-Marc, 2007. "La rivalité france-allemande et l' 'aryanisation'," *RHS* 186, pp. 273–90.

Dreyfus, Jean-Marc, 2010. "Elsass-Lothringen" in Wolf Gruner and Jörg Osterloh, eds, *Das "Grossdeutsche Reich" und die Juden: Nationalsozialistische Verfolgung in den "angegliederte" Gebieten* (Frankfurt a.M. and New York: Campus), pp. 363–82.

Drieschner, Axel and Barbara Schulz, eds, 2006. *Stalag IIIB Fürstenwalde (Oder): Kriegsgefangene im Osten Brandenburgs 1939–1945* (Berlin: Metropol).

Droulia, Loukia and Hagen Fleischer, eds, 1999. *Von Lidice nach Kalavryta: Widerstand und Besatzungsterror* (Berlin: Metropol).

Dulić, Tomislav, 2005. *Utopias of Nation: Local Mass Killing in Bosnia and Herzegovina, 1941-42* (Uppsala: Uppsala University).

Durand, Yves, 1999. "Das Schicksal der französischen Kriegsgefangenen in deutschem Gewahrsam" in Bischof and Overmans, eds, pp. 71–8.

Eckman, Lester and Chaim Lazar, 1977. *The Jewish Resistance: The History of the Jewish Partisans in Lithuania and White Russia During the Nazi Occupation 1940–1945* (New York: Shengold).

Eggers, Christian, 2002. *Unerwünschte Ausländer: Juden aus Deutschland und Mitteleuropa in französischen Internierungslagern 1940–1942* (Berlin: Metropol).

Ehrenreich, Eric, 2007. *The Nazi Ancestral Proof* (Bloomington and Indianapolis: University of Indiana Press).

Eichholtz, Dietrich, 1985. *Geschichte der deutschen Kriegswirtschaft, vol II: 1941–1943* (Berlin: Akademie).

Eichholtz, Dietrich, 2001. "Probleme und Praxis der Zwangsarbeit in der deutschen Kriegswirtschaft" in Meyer and Neitmann, eds, pp. 3–21.

Eikel, Markus, 2005. "'Weil die Menschen fehlen': Die deutschen Zwangsarbeitsrekrutierungen und -deportationen in den besetzten Gebieten der Ukraine 1941–1944," *ZfG* 53 (5), pp. 405–33.

Elkins, Catherine, 2005. *Imperial Reckoning: The Untold Story of Britain's Gulag in Kenya* (New York: Henry Holt).

Elsner, Lothar and Joachim Lehmann, 1988. *Ausländische Arbeiter unter dem deutschen Imperialismus 1900 bis 1985* (Berlin [East]: Dietz).

Engelking, Barbara, 2012. "Murdering and denouncing Poles in the Polish countryside, 1942–1945" in Gross, ed., pp. 55–82.

Engelking, Barbara and Jacek Leociak, 2009. *The Warsaw Ghetto: A Guide to the Perished City* (New Haven and London: Yale University Press).

Epstein, Catherine, 2010. *Model Nazi: Arthur Greiser and the Occupation ofWestern Poland* (Oxford: Oxford University Press).

Erin, M.E., 2004. "Russische Historiker über das Schicksal sowjetischer Kriegsgefangener im nationalsozialistischen Deutschland" in V. Selemenev, Ju. Zverev, K.D. Müller and A. Haritonov, eds, *Sowjetische und deutsche Kriegsgefangene in den Jahren des Zweiten Weltkrieges* (Dresden and Minsk), pp. 20–65.

Essner, Cornelia, 1995. "Die Alchimie des Rassenbegriffs und die 'Nürnberger Gesetze'," *JASF* 4, pp. 201–23.

Essner, Cornelia, 2002. *Die "Nürnberger Gesetze" oder Die Verwaltung des Rassenwahns 1933–1945* (Paderborn: Schöningh).

Etherington, Norman, 1984. *Theories of Imperialism* (London: Croom Helm and Barnes & Noble).

Evans, Richard, 2010. "Who remembers the Poles?" *London Review of Books* 32 (21), 4 November, pp. 21–2.

Fabréguet, Michel, 1998. "Entwicklung und Veränderung der Funktionen des Konzentrationslagers Mauthausen" in Herbert *et al.*, eds, pp. 193–214.

Farmer, Kenneth, David Crowe and Richard Blanke, 1985. "National minorities in Poland, 1919–1980" in Horak *et al.*, eds, pp. 35–107.

Fatran, Gila, 2001. "La legislazione antiebraica della Slovacchia di Tiso" in Capelli and Broggini, eds, pp. 70–95.

Fatran, Gila, 2005. "The Jews in the days of the Slovakian national revolt," *Yalkut Moreshet* 3, pp. 42–54.

Faulstich, Heinz, 1998. *Hungersterben in der Psychiatrie 1914–1949* (Freiburg: Lambertus).

Fein, Helen, 1979. *Accounting for Genocide: National Responses and Jewish Victimization during the Holocaust* (New York and London: Free Press and Collier Macmillan).

Felder, Björn, 2009. *Lettland im Zweiten Weltkrieg* (Paderborn: Schöningh).

Ferenc, Tone, 1991. "'Absiedler': Slowenen zwischen 'Eindeutschung' und Ausländereinsatz" in Herbert, ed., pp. 200–9.

Filipkowski, Piotr, 2005. "Polnische Häftlinge im KZ Mauthausen: Versuch einer Typisierung," *BIOS* 18 (1), pp. 128–37.

Fings, Karola, 2006. "Eine 'Wannsee-Konferenz' über die Vernichtung der Zigeuner? Neue Forschungsergebnisse zum 15. Januar 1943 und dem 'Auschwitz-Erlass'," *JASF*, pp. 303–33.

Fings, Karola, Cordula Lissner and Frank Sparing, n.d. [1992]. "*... einziges Land, in dem Judenfrage und Zigeunerfrage gelöst": Die Verfolgung der Roma im faschistisch besetzten Jugoslawien 1941–1945* 15 (Cologne: Rom e.V.).

Fischer, Bernd, 1999. *Albania at War, 1939–1945* (West Lafayette: Purdue University Press).

Fischer, Rolf, 1988. *Entwicklungsstufen des Antisemitismus in Ungarn 1867–1939* (Munich: Oldenbourg).

Fleischer, Hagen, 1986. *Im Kreuzschatten der Mächte: Griechenland 1941–1944* (Frankfurt a.M.: Peter Lang).

Fleischer, Hagen, 1999. "Deutsche 'Ordnung' in Griechenland" in Droulia and Fleischer, eds, pp. 151–224.

Fleischer, Hagen, 2001. "Griechenland: Das bestrittene Phänomen" in Graml, ed., pp. 207–26.

Flim, Bert, 2001. "Opportunities for Dutch Jews to hide from the Nazis" in Brasz and Kaplan, eds, pp. 289–305.

Fogel, Danilo, 2007. *The Jewish Community in Zemun* (Zemun: Jewish Community).

Fogg, Shannon, 2009. *The Politics of Everyday Life in Vichy France* (Cambridge: Cambridge University Press).

Förster, Jürgen, 2005. "Hitlers Verbündete gegen die Sowjetunion und der Judenmord 1941" in Hartmann *et al.*, eds, pp. 91–7.

Frank, Daniel, 2003. "The German 'righteous among the nations': A historical appraisal," *LBIY* 48, pp. 223–47.

Freidenreich, Harriet Pass, 1979. *The Jews of Yugoslavia* (Philadelphia: The Jewish Publication Society of America).

Freund, Florian, 1998. "Häftlingskategorien und Sterblichkeit in einem Aussenlager des KZ Mauthausen" in Herbert *et al.*, eds, pp. 874–86.

Freund, Florian, 2000. "Zwangsarbeit in Österreich 1939–1945" in Rolf Steininger, ed., *Vergessene Opfer des Nationalsozialismus* (Innsbruck: Studien-Verlag, pp. 99–134.

Freund, Florian and Hans Safrian, 2002. "Die Verfolgung der österreichischen Juden 1938–1945" in Tálos *et al.*, eds, pp. 767–94.

Freund, Florian, Bertrand Perz and Karl Stuhlpfarrer, 1993. "Der Bau des Vernichtungslagers Auschwitz-Birkenau: Die Aktenmappe der Zentralbauleitung Auschwitz 'Vorlage: Kriegsgefangenenlager Auschwitz (Durchführung der Sonderbehandlung)' im Militärhistorischen Archiv Prag," *Zeitgeschichte* 20, pp. 187–214.

Friedländer, Saul, 1998. *Nazi Germany and the Jews, Vol. I: The Years of Persecution, 1933–1939* (New York: Harper Perennial).

Friedländer, Saul, 2006. *Die Jahre der Vernichtung: Das Dritte Reich und die Juden, Zweiter Band 1939–1945* (Munich: Beck).

Friedlander, Henry, 1995. *The Origins of Nazi Genocide: From Euthanasia to the Final Solution* (Chapel Hill and London: University of North Carolina Press).

Friedler, Eric, Barbara Siebert and Andreas Kilian, 2002. *Zeugen aus der Todeszone: Das jüdische Sonderkommando in Auschwitz* (Lüneburg: zu Klampen).

Friedrich, Klaus-Peter, 2003. "Zusammenarbeit und Mittäterschaft in Polen 1939–1950" in Dieckmann *et al.*, eds, pp. 113–50.

Friedrich, Klaus-Peter, 2006. "Polen und seine Feinde (sowie deren Kollaborateure): Vorwürfe wegen 'polnischer Kollaboration' und 'jüdischer Kollaboration' in der polnischen Presse (1942–1944/45)" in Tauber, ed., pp. 206–49.

Frykman, Elin, 2000. "The cutting edge: A sterilization campaign in Sweden" in James Kaye and Bo Stråth, eds, *Enlightenment and Genocide* (Brussels: P.I.E. and Peter Lang), pp. 213–42.

Fuchslocher, Kolja, 1998. "'Ich habe Berlin in Schutt und Asche fallen sehn': Der Alltag der Fremd- und Zwangsarbeiter im Luftkrieg" in Scholze-Irrlitz and Noack, eds, pp. 89–102.

Führer, Karl-Christian, 1992. "Mit Juden unter einem Dach? Zur Vorgeschichte des nationalsozialistischen Gesetzes über die Mietverhältnisse mit Juden," *1999*, 7 (1), pp. 51–61.

Führer, Karl-Christian, 1995. *Mieter, Hausbesitzer, Staat und Wohnungsmarkt: Wohnungsmangel und Wohnungswirtschaft in Deutschland 1914–1960* (Stuttgart: Franz Steiner).

Fuhrer, Armin and Heinz Schön, 2010. *Erich Koch: Hitlers brauner Zar* (Munich: Olzog).

Furber, David, 2004. "Near as far in the colonies: The Nazi occupation of Poland," *International History Review* 26 (3), pp. 541–79.

Furber, David and Wendy Lower, 2008. "Colonialism and genocide in Nazi-occupied Poland and Ukraine" in Dirk Moses, ed., *Empire – Colony – Genocide: Conquest, Occupation and Subaltern Resistance in World History* (New York and Oxford: Berghahn), pp. 372–400.

Gailus, Manfred, 2008. *Kirchliche Amtshilfe: Die Kirchen und die Judenverfolgung im "Dritten Reich"* (Göttingen: Vandenhoeck & Ruprecht).

Gailus, Manfred and Armin Nolzen, 2011. *Zerstrittene "Volksgemeinschaft": Glaube, Konfession und Religion im Nationalsozialismus* (Göttingen: Vandenhoeck & Ruprecht).

Ganzenmüller, Jörg, 2005. *Das belagerte Leningrad 1941–1944* (Paderborn: Schöningh).

Garstecki, Martin, 1998. "Polnische Zwangsarbeiter im Spiegel historischer Dokumente: Die Reglementierung des Alltagslebens durch Behörden und Polizei in Brandenburg" in Scholze-Irrlitz and Noack, eds, pp. 73–88.

Gebel, Ralf, 2000. *"Heim ins Reich!": Konrad Henlein und der Reichsgau Sudetenland (1938–1945)* (Munich: Oldenbourg).

Gedye, G., 1942. *Fallen Bastions: The Central European Tragedy* (London: Victor Gollancz).

Geiss, Immanuel, 1988. *Geschichte des Rassismus* (Frankfurt a.M.: Suhrkamp).

Geissbühler, Simon, 2013. *Blutiger Juli: Rumäniens Vernichtungskrieg und der vergessene Massenmord an den Juden 1941* (Paderborn: Schöningh,).

Gellately, Robert, 2002. *Hingeschaut und weggesehen: Hitler und sein Volk* (Stuttgart and Munich: dva).

Genschel, Helmut, 1966. *Die Verdrängung der Juden aus der Wirtschaft des Dritten Reiches* (Göttingen *et al.*: Musterschmidt).

Gentile, Carlo, 2001. "'Politische Soldaten': Die 16. SS-Panzer-Grenadier-Division 'Reichsführer-SS' in Italien 1944," *Quellen und Forschungen aus italienischen Archiven und Bibliotheken* 81, pp. 529–61.

Gerlach, Christian, 1995. "Die deutsche Agrarreform und die Bevölkerungspolitik in den besetzten sowjetischen Gebieten" in Christoph Dieckmann, Christian Gerlach, Joachim Drews, Thomas Bohn and Michael Esch, eds, *Besatzung und Bündnis: Deutsche Herrschaftsstrategien in Ost- und Südosteuropa* (*BNGS* vol. 12) (Berlin and Göttingen: Schwarze Risse and Rote Strasse), pp. 9–60.

Gerlach, Christian, 1997. "Die Einsatzgruppe B" in Klein, ed., pp. 52–70.

Gerlach, Christian, 1998a. *Krieg, Ernährung, Völkermord: Forschungen zur deutschen Vernichtungspolitik im Zweiten Weltkrieg* (Hamburg: Hamburger Edition).

Gerlach, Christian, 1998b. "The Wannsee conference, the fate of German Jews, and Hitler's decision in principle to exterminate all European Jews," *JMH* 70 (4), pp. 759–812.

Gerlach, Christian, 1999. *Kalkulierte Morde: Die deutsche Wirtschafts- und Vernichtungspolitik in Weissrussland 1941 bis 1944* (Hamburg: Hamburger Edition).

Gerlach, Christian, 2000. "Men of 20 July and the war in the Soviet Union" in Heer and Naumann, eds, pp. 127–45.

Gerlach, Christian, 2005a. "A magyarországi zsidóság deportálásának döntéshozatali mechanizmusa" in Judit Molnár, ed., *A holokauszt Magyarországon európai perspektívában* (Budapest: Balassi Kiadó), pp. 469–78.

Gerlach, Christian, 2005b. "Die Verantwortung der Wehrmachtführung: Vergleichende Betrachtungen am Beispiel der sowjetischen Kriegsgefangenen" in Hartmann *et al.*, eds, pp. 40–9.

Gerlach, Christian, 2010. *Extremely Violent Societies: Mass Violence in the Twentieth Century World* (Cambridge: Cambridge University Press).

Gerlach, Christian, 2012. "Annexations in Europe and the persecution of Jews, 1939–1944," *CEH* 39, pp. 137–56.

Gerlach, Christian and Götz Aly, 2002. *Das letzte Kapitel: Realpolitik, Ideologie und der Mord an den ungarischen Juden 1944/1945* (Stuttgart and Munich: dva).

Gerlach, Christian and Nicolas Werth, 2009. "State violence – violent societies" in Michael Geyer and Sheila Fitzpatrick, eds, *Beyond Totalitarianism: Stalinism and Nazism Compared* (Cambridge: Cambridge University Press), pp. 133–79.

Gerwarth, Robert, 2008. "The central European counter-revolution: Paramilitary violence in Germany, Austria and Hungary after the Great War," *Past and Present* 200, pp. 175–209.

Gerwarth, Robert, 2011, *Reinhard Heydrich* (Munich: Siedler).

Giltner, Patrick, 2010. "Beyond the racial state: Rethinking Nazi Germany," *Bulletin of the German Historical Institute in Washington* 46, pp. 163–70.

Gitman, Esther, 2011. *When Courage Prevailed: The Rescue and Survival in the Independent State of Croatia 1941-1945* (St Paul: Paragon House).

Giusti, Maria Teresa, 2003. *I prigionieri italiani in Russia* (Bologna: il Mulino).

Glass, Heidrun, 2001. "Die Rezeption des Holocaust in Rumänien (1944–1947)" in Hausleitner *et al.*, eds, pp. 153–65.

Glees, Anthony, 1995. "The 1944 plotters and the war of genocide," *Holocaust Education* 4 (1), pp. 51–73.

Goffman, Erving, 1961. *Asylums: Essay on the Social Situation of Mental Patients and Other Inmates* (Garden City: Doubleday).

Golczewski, Frank, 1996. "Die Revision eines Klischees: Die Rettung von verfolgten Juden im Zweiten Weltkrieg durch Ukrainer" in Benz and Wetzel, eds, pp. 9–82.

Goldhagen, Daniel, 1997. *Hitler's Willing Executioners: Ordinary Germans and the Holocaust* (New York: Vintage).

Goldstein, Ivo, 2004. "Restoring Jewish life in communist Yugoslavia, 1945–1947," *East European Jewish Affairs* 34 (1), pp. 58–71.

Goldstein, Ivo, 2006. "Jews in the Jasenovac camp" in *Jasenovac Memorial Site*, pp. 108–38.

Gordijew, Paul Benjamin, 1999. *Voices of Yugoslav Jewry* (Albany: SUNY Press).

Gottwaldt, Alfred and Diana Schulle, 2005. *Die "Judendeportationen" aus dem Deutschen Reich 1941–1945* (Wiesbaden: Marix).

Grabher, Michael, 2006. *Irmfried Eberl*, second revised edition (Frankfurt a.M.: Peter Lang).

Grabitz, Helge and Wolfgang Scheffler, 1993. *Letzte Spuren: Ghetto Warschau, SS-Arbeitslager Trawniki, Aktion Erntefest*, second revised edition (Berlin: Hentrich).

Grabowski, Hans-Ludwig, 2008. *Das Geld des Terrors: Geld und Geldersatz in deutschen Konzentrationslagern und Gettos 1933 bis 1945* (Regenstauf: Battenberg).

Graml, Hermann, 1988. *Reichskristallnacht: Antisemitismus und Judenverfolgung im Dritten Reich* (Munich: dtv).

Graml, Hermann, ed., 2001. *Vorurteil und Rassenhass. Antisemitismus in den faschistischen Bewegungen Europas* (Berlin: Metropol).

Griffioen, Pim and Ron Zeller, 2011. *Jodenverfolging in Nederland, Frankrijk en België 1940–1945: Overeenkomsten, verschillen, oorzaken* (Amsterdam: Boom).

Gringauz, Samuel, 1949. "The ghetto as an experiment of Jewish social organization," *JSS* 11 (1), pp. 3–20.

Gross, Jan, 1979. *Polish Society Under German Occupation: The Generalgouvernement, 1939–1944* (Princeton: Princeton University Press).

Gross, Jan, 1988. *Und wehe, du hoffst...: Die Sowjetisierung Ostpolens nach dem Hitler-Stalin-Pakt 1939–1941* (Freiburg: Herder).

Gross, Jan, 2001. *Neighbors: The Destruction of the Jewish Community in Jedwabne, Poland* (Princeton and Oxford: Princeton University Press).

Gross, Jan, 2006. *Fear* (Princeton: Princeton University Press).

Gross, Jan, 2012a. *Golden Harvest* (Oxford: Oxford University Press).

Gross, Jan, ed., 2012b. *The Holocaust in Occupied Poland* (Frankfurt a.M.: Peter Lang).

Grosse, Pascal, 2000. *Kolonialismus, Eugenik und bürgerliche Gesellschaft in Deutschland 1850–1918* (Frankfurt a.M.: Campus).

Grossman, Wassili and Ilja Ehrenburg, 1994. *Das Schwarzbuch: Der Genozid an den sowjetischen Juden* (Reinbek: Rowohlt).

Grüttner, Michael, 2001. "Faschismus, Franquismus und Antisemitismus in Spanien" in Graml, ed., 2001, pp. 95–118.

Gruner, Wolf, 1997. *Der Geschlossene Arbeitseinsatz deutscher Juden: Zur Zwangsarbeit als Element der Verfolgung* (Berlin: Metropol).

Gruner, Wolf, 2000a. "Die Grundstücke der 'Reichsfeinde': Zur Arisierung von Immobilien durch Städte und Gemeinden 1938–1945" in Irmtrud Wojak and Peter Hayes, eds, *"Arisierung" im Nationalsozialismus* (Frankfurt a.M. and New York: Campus), pp. 123–56.

Gruner, Wolf, 2000b. "Die Judenverfolgung und die Kommunen: Zur wechselseitigen Dynamisierung von zentraler und lokaler Politik 1933–1941," *VfZ* 48 (1), pp. 75–126.

Gruner, Wolf, 2001. "Der Zwangsarbeitseinsatz von Juden in der Region Berlin/Brandenburg 1938/39–1943" in Meyer and Neitmann, eds, pp. 47–68.

Gruner, Wolf, 2004. "Von der Kollektivausweisung zur Deportation der Juden aus Deutschland" in Kundrus and Meyer, eds, pp. 21–62.

Gruner, Wolf, 2005. "Das Protektorat Böhmen und Mähren und die antijüdische Politik 1939–1941: Lokale Initiativen, regionale Massnahmen, zentrale Entscheidungen im Grossdeutschen Reich," *TSD*, pp. 27–62.

Gruner, Wolf, 2010. "Protektorat Böhmen und Mähren" in Gruner and Osterloh, eds, pp. 139–73.

Gruner, Wolf and Jörg Osterloh, eds, 2010. *Das Grossdeutsche Reich und die Juden: Nationalsozialistische Verfolgung in den angegliederten Gebieten* (Frankfurt a.M.: Campus).

Gryglewski, Marcus, 1996. *Die Gestapoleitstelle Breslau und die Judendeportationen in Schlesien*, unpublished MA thesis, Freie Universität Berlin.

Grynberg, Michał, 1984. *Żydzi w rejencji ciechanowskiej 1939–1942* (Warsaw: Państwowe Wydawnictwo Naukowe).

Guckes, Jochen, 1999. "Le rôle des chemins de fer dans la déportation des juifs de France," *RHS* 165, pp. 29–110.

Gumbrecht, Emil, 1980 [1922]. *Vier Jahre politischer Mord* (Heidelberg: Wunderhorn).

Guth, Stefan, 2009. *Zwischen Konfrontation und Verständigung: Der deutsch-polnische Historikerdialog im 20. Jahrhundert*, PhD thesis, University of Bern.

Gutman, Yisrael, 1982. *The Jews of Warsaw, 1939–1943* (Brighton: Harvester).

Gutman, Yisrael and Michael Berenbaum, eds, 1994. *Anatomy of the Auschwitz Death Camp* (Bloomington and Indianapolis).

Guttstadt, Corry, 2008. *Die Türkei, die Juden und der Holocaust* (Berlin and Hamburg: Assoziation A).

Haas, Gaston, 1994. *"Wenn man gewusst hätte, was sich drüben im Reich abspielte…": 1941–1943 – Was man in der Schweiz von der Judenvernichtung wusste* (Basel and Frankfurt a.M.: Helburg & Lichtenhahn).

Haase, Norbert and Brigitte Oleschinski, eds, 1995. *Torgau – Ein Kriegsende in Europa* (Bremen: Edition Temmen).

Haberer, Eric, 2001. "The German police and genocide in Belorussia, 1941–1944," Part I, *JGR* 3 (1), pp. 13–29; Part II, *JGR* 3 (3), pp. 207–18.

Hadziiossif, Christos, "Griechen in der deutschen Kriegsproduktion" in Herbert, ed., 1991, pp. 210–33.

Hájková, Anna, 2013. *Prisoner Society in the Terezin Ghetto, 1941–1945*, PhD thesis, University of Toronto.

Hałgas, Kazimiersz, 1987. "Die Arbeit im 'Revier' für sowjetische Kriegsgefangene in Auschwitz: Ein Bericht," *Die Auschwitz-Hefte*, 1 (Weinheim and Basel: Beltz), pp. 167–72.

Hammermann, Gabriele, 2002. *Zwangsarbeit für den "Verbündeten": Die Arbeits- und Lebensbedingungen der italienischen Militärinternierten in Deutschland 1943–1945* (Tübingen: Niemeyer).

Hammermann, Gabriele, 2005. "Zur Situation der italienischen Militärinternierten aus sozialhistorischer Perspektive" in Bischof *et al.*, eds, pp. 438–55.

Hansch-Singh, Annegret, 1991. *Rassismus und Fremdarbeiter im Zweiten Weltkrieg*, PhD thesis, Free University of Berlin.

Hart, Nicky, 1993. "Maternal nutrition and infant mortality: A re-examination of the Dutch hunger winter," *Population Studies* 47 (1), pp. 27-46.

Harten, Hans-Christian, Uwe Neirich and Matthias Schwerendt, 2006. *Rassenhygiene als Erziehungsideologie des Dritten Reiches* (Berlin: Akademie).

Hartmann, Christian, 2001. "Massensterben oder Massenvernichtung? Sowjetische Kriegesgefangene im 'Unternehmen Barbarossa'. Aus dem Tagebuch eines Lagerkommandanten," *VfZ* 49, pp. 97–158.

Hartmann, Christian, Johannes Hürter and Ulrike Jureit, eds, 2005. *Verbrechen der Wehrmacht: Bilanz einer Debatte* (Munich: C.H. Beck).

Hartog, L.J., 1997 [1994]. *Der Befehl zum Judenmord* (Bodenheim: Syndikat).

Harvey, Elizabeth, 2003. *Women and the Nazi East: Agents and Witnesses of Germanization* (New Haven and London: Yale University Press).

Hasenclever, Jörn, 2006. "Die Befehlshaber der rückwärtigen Heeresgebiete und der Mord an den sowjetischen Juden" in Timm Richter, ed., *Krieg und Verbrechen* (Munich: Martin Meidenbauer), pp. 207–18.

Hasenclever, Jörn, 2010. *Wehrmacht und Besatzungspolitik in der Sowjetunion: Die Befehlshaber der rückwärtigen Heeresgebiete 1941–1943* (Paderborn: Schöningh).

Hausleitner, Mariana, 2001a. *Die Rumänisierung der Bukowina: Die Durchsetzung des nationalstaatlichen Anspruchs Grossrumäniens 1918–1944* (Munich: Oldenbourg).

Hausleitner, Mariana, 2001b. "Grossverbrechen im rumänischen Transnistrien 1941–1944" in Hausleitner *et al.*, eds, pp. 15–31.

Hausleitner, Mariana, 2003. "Auf dem Weg zur Ethnokratie: Rumänien in den Jahren des Zweiten Weltkrieges" in Dieckmann *et al.*, eds, pp. 78–112.

Hausleitner, Mariana, 2004. "Wohltätigkeit mit geraubtem Eigentum: Maria Antonescu und die Juden in Rumänien," *JASF* 13, pp. 37–50.

Hausleitner, Mariana, Brigitte Mihok and Juliane Wetzel, eds, 2001. *Rumänien und der Holocaust: Zu den Massenverbrechen in Transnistrien 1941–1944* (Berlin: Metropol).

Headland, Ronald, 1992. *Messages of Murder: A Study of the Reports of the Einsatzgruppen of the Security Police and Security Service, 1941–1943* (London and Toronto: Farleigh Dickinson University Press).

Hecht, Cornelia, 2003. *Deutsche Juden und Antisemitismus in der Weimarer Republik* (Bonn: Dietz).

Heer, Hannes, 1995. "Die Logik des Vernichtungskrieges: Wehrmacht und Partisanenkampf" in Heer and Naumann, eds, pp. 104–38.

Heer, Hannes and Klaus Naumann, eds, 1995. *Vernichtungskrieg: Verbrechen der Wehrmacht 1941–1944* (Hamburg: Hamburger Edition).

Heer, Hannes and Klaus Naumann, eds, 2000. *War of Extermination: The German Military in World War II 1941–1944* (New York and London: Berghahn).

Heiden, Detlev, 1995. "Von der Kleinsiedlung zum Behelfsheim: Wohnen zwischen Volksgemeinschaft und Kriegsalltag" in Heiden and Mai, eds, pp. 348–74.

Heiden, Detlev and Gunter Mai, eds, 1995. *Nationalsozialismus in Thüringen* (Weimar: Böhlau).

Heim, Susanne und Götz Aly, 1987. "Die Ökonomie der 'Endlösung'" in Aly *et al.*, eds, pp. 11–90.

Heim, Susanne, 1999. "Vertreibung, Raub und Umverteilung: Die jüdischen Flüchtlinge aus Deutschland und die Vermehrung des 'Volksvermögens'" in Susanne Heim, Insa Meinen, Ahlrich Meyer and Horst Kahrs, eds, *Flüchtlingspolitik und Fluchthilfe* (*BNSP* vol. 15) (Berlin: Schwarze Risse and Rote Strasse), pp. 107–38.

Heinemann, Isabel, 2003. *"Rasse, Siedlung, deutsches Blut": Das Rasse- und Siedlungshauptamt der SS und die rassenpolitische Neuordnung Europas* (Göttingen: Wallstein).

Heinemann, Winfried, "Der militärische Widerstand und der Krieg," *DRZW* 9/1 (Munich: dva), pp. 743–892.

Heinen, Armin, 2001. "Gewalt – Kultur: Rumänien, der Krieg und die Juden (Juni bis Oktober 1941)," in Hausleitner *et al.*, eds, 2001, pp. 33–52.

Herbert, Ulrich, 1985. *Fremdarbeiter: Politik und Praxis des "Ausländer-Einsatzes" in der Kriegswirtschaft des Dritten Reiches* (Bonn: Dietz).

Herbert, Ulrich, 1989. "Arbeiterschaft im 'Dritten Reich': Zwischenbilanz und offene Fragen," *GuG* 15, pp. 320–60.

Herbert, Ulrich, ed., 1991. *Europa und der "Reichseinsatz": Ausländische Zivilarbeiter, Kriegsgefangene und KZ-Häftlinge in Deutschland 1938–1945* (Essen: Klartext).

Herbert, Ulrich, 1991. "Einleitung" in Herbert, ed., pp. 7–25.

Herbert, Ulrich, 1993. "Arbeit und Vernichtung: Ökonomisches Interesse und Primat der 'Weltanschauung' im Nationalsozialismus" in Dan Diner, ed., *Ist der Nationalsozialismus Geschichte?* (Frankfurt a.M.: Fischer), pp. 198–236.

Herbert, Ulrich, 1996. *Best: Biographische Studien über Radikalismus, Weltanschauung und Vernunft, 1903–1989* (Bonn: Dietz).

Herbert, Ulrich, Karin Orth and Christoph Dieckmann, eds, 1998. *Die nationalsozialistischen Konzentrationslager* (Göttingen: Wallstein).

Herczl, Moshe, 1997. *Christianity and the Holocaust of Hungarian Jewry* (New York: New York University Press).

Herf, Jeffrey, 2005. "'Der Krieg und die Juden': Nationalsozialistische Propaganda im Zweiten Weltkrieg," *DRZW*, 9/2 (Munich: dva), pp. 159–202.

Herf, Jeffrey, 2006. *The Jewish Enemy: Nazi Propaganda During World War II and the Holocaust* (Cambridge and London: Belknap).

Hershkovitz, Roni, 2001. "The persecution of the Jews, as reflected in Dutch underground newspapers" in Brasz and Kaplan, eds, 2001, pp. 307–22.

Herzstein, Robert Edwin, 1989. "Anti-Jewish propaganda in the Orel region of Great Russia, 1942–1943: The German army and its Russian collaborators," *SWCA* 6, pp. 33–55.

Hilberg, Raul, 1981. *Sonderzüge nach Auschwitz* (Mainz: Dumjahn).

Hilberg, Raul, 1992a. *Täter, Opfer, Zuschauer. Die Vernichtung der Juden 1933–1945* (Frankfurt a.M.: Fischer).

Hilberg, Raul, 1992b. *Perpetrators, Victims, Bystanders: The Jewish Catastrophe 1933–1945* (New York: HarperPerennial).

Hilberg, Raul (1994a). *Die Vernichtung der europäischen Juden*, revised and enlarged edition (Frankfurt a.M.: Fischer).

Hilberg, Raul (1994b), "Auschwitz and the final solution" in Yisrael Gutman and Michael Berenbaum, eds, *Anatomy of the Auschwitz Death Camp* (Bloomington and Indianapolis: Indiana University Press), pp. 81–92.

Hilberg, Raul, 1995. "The fate of Jews in the cities" in Betty Rogers Rubenstein and Michael Berenbaum, eds, *What Kind of God? Essays in Honor of Richard L. Rubenstein* (Lanham: University Press of America), pp. 41–51.

Hildebrand, Klaus, 1973. *Deutsche Aussenpolitik 1933–1945*, revised edition, (Stuttgart: Kohlhammer).

Hilger, Andreas, 2000. *Deutsche Kriegsgefangene in der Sowjetunion, 1941–1956: Kriegsgefangenenpolitik, Lageralltag und Erinnerung* (Essen: Klartext).

Hill, Alexander, 2005. *The War Behind the Eastern Front: The Soviet Partisan Movement in North-Western Russia 1941–1944* (London and New York: Frank Cass).

Hillgruber, Andreas, 1996. *Der Zweite Weltkrieg, ed. Bernd Martin*, sixth revised and enlarged edition, Stuttgart: Kohlhammer).

Hionidou, Violetta, 2006. *Famine and Death in Occupied Greece, 1941–1944* (Cambridge: Cambridge University Press).

Hirschfeld, Gerhard, 1984. *Fremdherrschaft und Kollaboration: Die Niederlande unter deutscher Besatzung 1940–1945* (Stuttgart: dva).

Hirschfeld, Gerhard, 1991. "Kollaboration in Frankreich – Einführung" in Hirschfeld and Marsh, eds, pp. 7–22.

Hirschfeld, Gerhard and Patrick Marsh, eds, 1991. *Kollaboration in Frankreich* (Frankfurt a.M.: Fischer).

Hochberg-Mariańska, Maria and Noe Grüss, eds, 1996. *The Children Accuse* (London and Portland: Vallentine Mitchell).

Hochschild, Adam, 1998. *King Leopold's Ghost* (Boston: Houghton Mifflin).

Hösch, Edgar, 2001. "Faschismus und Antisemitismus in Finnland" in Graml, ed., pp. 227–52.

Hoffmann, Christhard, 2001. "Die reine Lehre einer politischen Sekte: Antisemitismus in der norwegischen 'Nasjonal Samling'" in Graml, ed., pp. 253–73.

Hoffmann, Jens, 2008. *"Das kann man nicht erzählen": Aktion 1005 – Wie die Nazis die Spuren ihrer Massenmorde in Osteuropa beseitigten* (Hamburg: Konkret).

Hoffmann, Katharina, 2001. *Zwangsarbeit und ihre gesellschaftliche Akzeptanz in Oldenburg 1939–1945* (Oldenburg: Isensee).

Holler, Martin, 2009. *Der nationalsozialistische Völkermord an den Roma in der besetzten Sowjetunion (1941–1944)* (Heidelberg: Dokumentations- und Kulturzentrum Deutscher Sinti und Roma).

Holz, Klaus, 2001. *Nationaler Antisemitismus: Wissenssoziologie einer Weltanschauung* (Hamburg: Hamburger Edition).

Hoppe, Hans-Joachim, 1979. *Bulgarien – Hitlers eigenwilliger Verbündeter* (Stuttgart: dva).

Horak, Stephan, ed., 1985. *Eastern European National Minorities 1919–1980* (Littleton: Librarires Unlimited).

Horne, John and Alan Kramer, 2001. *German Atrocities, 1914* (New Haven: Yale University Press).

Hortzitz, Nicoline, 1988. *"Früh-Antisemitismus" in Deutschland (1789–1871/72): Strukturelle Untersuchungen zu Wortschatz, Text und Argumentation* (Tübingen: Max Niemeyer).

Horváth, Franz, 2008. "Volkstumspolitik, soziale Kompensation und wirtschaftliche Wiedergutmachung: Der Holocaust in Nordsiebenbürgen" in Hürter and Zarusky, eds, pp. 115–50.

Houwink ten Cate, Johannes, 1999. "Mangelnde Solidarität gegenüber Juden in den besetzten niederländischen Gebieten?" in Wolfgang Benz and Juliane Wetzel, eds, *Solidarität und Hilfe für Juden während der NS-Zeit: Regionalstudien 3* (Berlin: Metropol), pp. 87–133.

Hradská, Katarína, 1996. "Vorgeschichte der slowakischen Transporte nach Theresienstadt," *TSD*, pp. 82–97.

Hübschmanová, Milena, 1999. "Roma in the Slovak state in survivor reports" in *Conference Report of the International Scientific Conference*, pp. 156–9.

Hürter, Johannes and Jürgen Zarusky, eds, 2008. *Besatzung, Kollaboration, Holocaust* (Munich: Oldenbourg).

Hull, Isabel, 2005. *Absolute Destruction: Military Culture and the Practices of War in Imperial Germany* (Ithaca and London: Cornell University Press).

Humburg, Martin, 1998. *Das Gesicht des Krieges: Feldpostbriefe von Wehrmachtssoldaten aus der Sowjetunion 1941–1944* (Opladen: Westdeutscher Verlag).

Iancu, Carol, 1997. "The Jews of Romania during the Antonescu regime as reflected in French diplomatic documents" in Braham, ed., pp. 251–67.

"Ich werde es nie vergessen": Briefe sowjetischer Kriegsgefangener 2004–2006, ed. Verein Kontakte e.V. (Berlin: Christoph Links), 2007.

Ingrao, Christian, 2012. *Hitlers Elite: Die Wegbereiter des nationalsozialistischen Massenmords* (Berlin: Propyläen).

Ioanid, Radu, 1997. "The fate of Romanian Jews in Nazi-occupied Europe" in Braham, ed., pp. 217–36.

Ioanid, Radu, 2000. *The Holocaust in Romania* (Chicago: Ivan R. Dee).

Ioanid, Radu, 2001. "The deportation of the Jews to Transnistria" in Hausleitner *et al.*, eds, pp. 69–100.

Israeli–Serbian Academic Exchange in Holocaust Research, 2008 (Belgrade: Museum of Genocide Victims).

Jäckel, Eberhard, 1966. *Frankreich in Hitlers Europa* (Stuttgart: Deutsche Verlags-Anstalt).

Jäckel, Eberhard, 1986. *Hitlers Herrschaft: Vollzug einer Weltanschauung* (Stuttgart: dva).

Jäckel, Eberhard, 1997 [1969]. *Hitler's World View: A Blueprint for Power* (Cambridge and London: Harvard University Press).

Jansen, Christian and Arno Weckbecker, 1992. *Der "Volksdeutsche Selbstschutz" in Polen 1939–1940* (Munich: Oldenbourg).

Jansen, Hans, 1997. *Der Madagaskar-Plan* (Munich: Langen Müller).

Jasch, Hans-Christian, 2012. *Staatssekretär Wilhelm Stuckart und die Judenpolitik* (Munich: Oldenbourg).

Jasenovac Memorial Site, 2006 (Jasenovac: Jasenovac Memorial Site).

Jelinek, Yeshayahu, 1989. "The Holocaust and the internal policies of the Nazi satellites in eastern Europe: A comparative study" in Marrus, ed., pp. 291–6.

Jellonnek, Burkhard, 1990. *Homosexuelle unter dem Hakenkreuz* (Paderborn: Schöningh).

Jersak, Tobias, 1999. "Die Interaktion von Kriegsverlauf und Judenvernichtung: Ein Blick auf Hitlers Strategie im Spätsommer 1941," *Historische Zeitschrift* 268 (2), pp. 311–74.

Jobst, Herbert, 1939. "Lateinamerika – Verlorenes Paradies der Juden" in Könitzer and Trurnit, eds, pp. 207–25.

Jochmann, Werner, 1988a. *Gesellschaftskrise und Judenfeindschaft in Deutschland 1870–1945* (Hamburg: Christians).

Jochmann, Werner, 1988b. "Struktur und Funktion des deutschen Antisemitismus 1878–1914" in Strauss and Kampe, eds, pp. 99–142.

Jockheck, Lars, 2006. *Propaganda im Generalgouvernement: Die NS-Besatzungspresse für Deutsche und Polen 1939–1945* (Osnabrück: Fibre).

Johnson, Eric and Karl-Heinz Reuband, 2005. *What We Knew: Terror, Mass Murder, and Everyday Life in Nazi Germany: An Oral History* (Cambridge MA: Basic Books).

Jonca, Karol, 1996. "Deportations of German Jews from Breslau 1941–1944 as described in eyewitness testimonies," *YVS* 25, pp. 275–316.

Jordan, Rudolf, 1971. *Erlebt und erlitten: Weg eines Gauleiters von München nach Moskau* (Leoni: Druffel).

Kádár, Gábor and Zoltán Vági, 2005. "Theorie und Praxis: Die ökonomische Vernichtung der ungarischen Juden" in Mihok, ed., pp. 89–102.

Kaienburg, Hermann, 1996. "Jüdische Arbeitslager an der Strasse der SS," *1999*, 11 (1), pp. 13–39.

Kalinin, P.S., 1968. *Die Partisanenrepublik* (Berlin [East]: Dietz).

Kallis, Aristotle, 2005. "Race 'value' and the hierarchy of human life: Ideological and structural determinants of National Socialist policy-making," *JGR* 7 (1), pp. 5–29.

Kallis, Aristotle, 2009. *Genocide and Fascism: The Eliminationist Drive in Fascist Europe* (New York and London: Routledge).

Kamenec, Ivan, 2003. "Die Grundzüge des Arisierungsprozesses in der Slovakei," *TSD*, pp. 307–20.

Kamenec, Ivan, 2007 [1991]. *On the Trail of Tragedy: The Holocaust in Slovakia* (Bratislava: H & H).

Kampe, Norbert and Peter Klein, eds, 2013. *Die Wannsee-Konferenz am 20. Januar 1942* (Cologne: Böhlau).

Kaneko, Martin, 2008. *Die Judenpolitik der japanischen Reichsregierung* (Berlin: Metropol).

Karay, Felicja, 2004. "The conflict among German authorities over Jewish slave labor camps in the General Government," *Yalkut Moreshet* 2, pp. 221–45.

Karner, Stefan, 1995. *Im Archipel GUPVI: Kriegsgefangenschaft und Internierung in der Sowjetunion 1941–1956* (Vienna and Munich: Oldenbourg).

Kárný, Miroslav, 1982. "Die 'Judenfrage' in der nazistischen Okkupationspolitik," *Historica* 21, pp. 137–92.

Kárný, Miroslav, 1987. "'Vernichtung durch Arbeit': Sterblichkeit in den NS-Konzentrationslagern" in Aly *et al.*, eds, pp. 133–58.

Kárný, Miroslav, 1994. "Die Rolle der Kollaboration in der deutschen Okkupationspolitik im Protectorat Böhmen und Mähren" in Röhr, pp. 149–63.

Kárný, Miroslav, 1998. "Die Ausschaltung der Juden aus dem öffentlichen Leben des Protektorats und die Geschichte des Ehrenariertums," *TSD*, pp. 7–39.

Karsai, László, 2005. "Zentrale Aspekte des Völkermordes an den ungarischen Roma" in Mihok, ed., pp. 103–14.

Kaspi, André. 1997. *Les juifs pendant l'occupation* (Paris: Éditions du Seuil).

Kassow, Samuel, 2010. *Ringelblums Vermächtnis: Das geheime Archiv des Warschauer Ghettos* (Reinbek: Rowohlt).

Kasten, Bernd, 1993. *"Gute Franzosen": Die französische Polizei und die deutsche Besatzungsmacht im besetzten Frankreich 1940–1944* (Sigmaringen: Jan Thorbecke).

Kasten, Bernd, 2000. "Das Verhältnis zwischen deutscher und französischer Polizei in den Regionen von der Besetzung Südfrankreichs bis zur Invasion" in Martens and Vaïsse, eds, pp. 113–27.

Katz, Jacob, 1980. *From Prejudice to Persecution: Anti-Semitism, 1700–1933* (Cambridge: Harvard University Press).

Katz, Shlomo, 1973. "Public opinion in western Europe and the Evian conference of July 1938," *YVS* 9, pp. 105–32.

Kay, Alex, 2006. *Exploitation, Resettlement, Mass Murder: Political and Economic Planning for German Occupation Policy in the Soviet Union, 1940–1941* (New York and Oxford: Berghahn).

Keller, Rolf, n.d. [1994]. "'Die kamen in Scharen hier an, die Gefangenen': Sowjetische Kriegsgefangene, Wehrmachtsoldaten und deutsche Bevölkerung in Norddeutschland 1941/42" in *Rassismus in Deutschland*, pp. 35–60.

Keller, Rolf, 2011. *Sowjetische Kriegsgefangene im Deutschen Reich 1941/42* (Göttingen: Wallstein).

Kershaw, Ian, 1998. *Hitler: 1889–1936* (Stuttgart: dva).

Kershaw, Ian, 2008. *Hitler, the Germans, and the Final Solution* (New Haven and London: Yale University Press).

Kettenacker, Lothar, 1973. *Nationalsozialistische Volkstumspolitik im Elsass* (Stuttgart: dva).

Kiełboń, Janina, 2004. "Judendeportationen in den Distrikt Lublin" in Musial, ed., pp. 111–40.

Kiernan, V.G., 1995. Imperialism and its Contradictions, ed. Harvey Kaye (New York and London: Routledge).

Kilian, Katrin, 2005. "Kriegsstimmungen: Emotionen einfacher Soldaten in Feldpostbriefen," *DRZW* 9/2, pp. 251–88.

Kingston, Paul, 1991. "Die Ideologen: Vichy-Frankreich 1940–1944" in Hirschfeld and Marsh, eds, pp. 60–86.

Kirchhoff, Hans, 1994. "Die dänische Staatskollaboration" in Röhr, ed., pp. 101–18.

Kistenmacher, Hans, 1959. *Die Auswirkungen der deutschen Besetzung auf die Ernährungswirtschaft Frankreichs während des Zweiten Weltkrieges* (Tübingen: Institut für Besatzungsfragen).

Klarsfeld, Serge, 1982. "Post-face" in *CDJC*, pp. i–ii.

Klarsfeld, Serge, 1992. "The influence of the war on the final solution in France" in Cohen *et al.*, eds, pp. 271–81.

Klausch, Hans-Peter, 1993. *Antifaschisten in SS-Uniform: Schicksal und Widerstand der deutschen politischen KZ-Häftlinge, Zuchthaus- und Wehrmachtgefangenen in der SS-Sonderformation Dirlewanger* (Bremen: Temmen).

Klein, Peter, 2009. *Die "Ghettoverwaltung Litzmannstadt" 1940–1944* (Hamburg: Hamburger Edition).

Kleman, Hein and Sergey Kudryashov, 2012. *Occupied Economies: An Economic History of Nazi-Occupied Europe* (London and New York: Berg).

Kletzin, Birgit, 1996. *Trikolore unterm Hakenkreuz: Deutsch-französische Kollaboration 1940–1944 in den diplomatischen Akten des Dritten Reiches* (Opladen: Leske + Budrich).

Kletzin, Birgit, 2000. *Europa aus Rasse und Raum: Die nationalsozialistische Idee der "neuen Ordnung"* (Münster: LIT).

Klinkhammer, Lutz, 1993. *Zwischen Besatzung Bündnis: Das nationalsozialistische Deutschland und die Republik von Salò 1943–1945* (Tübingen: Max Niemeyer).

Knox, MacGregor, 2007. "Das faschistische Italien und die 'Endlösung' 1942/43," *VfZ* 55, pp. 55–92.

Königseder, Angelika, "Österreich – ein Land der Täter?" in Benz and Wetzel, eds, pp. 173–229.

Königseder, Angelika, 2001. "Faschistische Bewegungen in Österreich vor 1938" in Graml, ed., pp. 75–93.

Könitzer, Willi and Hansgeorg Trurmt, eds, 1939. *Weltentscheidung in der Judenfrage* (Dresden: Zwinger Verlag Rudolf Glöss).

Kochan, Thomas, 1998. "Topographie der möglichen Begegnungen: Zwangsarbeiter und Zwangsarbeiterlager in der Erinnerung der deutschen Anwohner" in Scholze-Irrlitz and Noak, eds, pp. 28–34.

Kohlhaas, Elisabeth, 1995. "Die Mitarbeiter der regionalen Staatspolizeistellen" in Paul and Mallmann, eds, pp. 219–35.

Kokoška, Stanislav, 1997. "Zwei unbekannte Berichte aus dem besetzten Prag über die Lage der jüdischen Bevölkerung im Protektorat," *TSD*, pp. 31–49.

Konieczny, Alfred, 1996. "The transit camp for Breslau Jews at Rieburg in Lower Silesia (1941–1943)," *YVS* 25, pp. 317–42.

Koonz, Claudia, 2006. "Respectable racism – state-sponsored anti-Jewish research 1935–1940," *SDIY* V, pp. 399–423.

Koonz, Claudia, 2007. *The Nazi Conscience* (Cambridge and London: Belknap).

Korb, Alexander, 2013. *Im Schatten des Weltkriegs: Massengewalt der Ustaša gegen Serben, Juden und Roma in Kroatien, 1941–1945* (Hamburg: Hamburger Edition).

Kosmala, Beate, 2001."Gewalt gegen Juden in Nachkriegspolen 1944–1947: Kriegserfahrungen, Bürgerkrieg und antisemitisches Erbe" in Graml, ed., pp. 313–29.

Kosmala, Beate, 2004. "Zwischen Aachen und Wien: Flucht vor der Deportation (1941–1943)" in Kundrus and Meyer, eds, pp. 135–59.

Kosyk, Wolodymyr, 1993. *The Third Reich and Ukraine* (New York: Peter Lang).

Kotani, Apostol, 1995. *Albania and the Jews* (Tirana: Eureka).

Kotzageorgi, Xanthippi and Georgios Kazamias, 1994. "The Bulgarian occupation of the prefecture of Drama (1941–1944) and its consequences on the Greek population," *Balkan Studies* 35 (1), pp. 81–112.

Kotzageorgi, Xanthippi, 1996. "Population changes in eastern Macedonia and in Thrace: The legislative 'initiatives' of the Bulgarian authorities (1941–1944)," *Balkan Studies* 37 (1), pp. 133–64.

Kovács, Mária, 1994. *Liberal Professions and Illiberal Politics: Hungary from the Habsburgs to the Holocaust* (Washington: Oxford University Press).

Krakowski, Shmuel, 1992. "The fate of the Jewish POWs of the Soviet and Polish armies" in Cohen *et al.*, eds, pp. 218–31.

Krakowski, Shmuel, 2007. *Das Todeslager Chełmno/Kulmhof* (Göttingen: Wallstein).

Kramer, Alan, 2010. "Prisoners in the First World War" in Sibylle Scheipers, ed., *Prisoners in War* (Oxford: Oxford University Press), pp. 75–90.

Kranig, Andreas, 1986. "Die NS-Arbeitseinsatzordnung" in Ulrich Herbert and Gerhard Lind, eds, *Arbeitsrecht und Nationalsozialismus* (Bergisch-Gladbach: Gustav-Stresemann-Institut), pp. 23–41.

Krasnoperko, Anna, 1991. *Briefe meiner Erinnerung: Mein Überleben im jüdischen Ghetto von Minsk 1941/42* (Schwerte: Haus Villigst).

Krausnick, Helmut and Hans-Heinrich Wilhelm, 1981. *Die Truppe des Weltanschauungskrieges: Die Einsatzgruppen der Sicherheitspolizei und des SD 1938–1942* (Stuttgart: dva).

Kreuzmüller, Christoph, 2008. "Die Erfassung der Juden im Reichskommissariat der besetzten niederländischen Gebiete" in Hürter and Zarusky, eds, pp. 31–44.

Kroener, Bernhard, 1999. " 'Menschenbewirtschaftung', Bevölkerungsverteilung und personelle Rüstung in der zweiten Kriegshälfte (1942–1944)," *DRZW*, 5/2 (Stuttgart: dva), pp. 777–1001.

Kroll, Frank-Lothar, 1998. *Utopie als Ideologie: Geschichtsdenken und politisches Handeln im Dritten Reich* (Paderborn: Schöningh).

Kruglov, Alexander, 2010. "Jewish losses in Ukraine, 1941–1944" in Brandon and Lower, eds, pp. 272–90.

Kubatzki, Rainer, 2001a. "Topographie und Nutzungsgeschichte der 700 Zwangsarbeiterlager in und um Berlin 1939 bis 1945" in Meyer and Neitmann, eds, pp. 89–109.

Kubatzki, Rainer, 2001b. *Zwangsarbeiter und Kriegsgefangenenlager: Standorte und Topographie in Berlin und im brandenburgischen Umland* (Berlin: Berlin).

Kühl, Stefan, 1994. *The Nazi Connection: Eugenics, American Racism, and German National Socialism* (New York and Oxford: Oxford University Press).

Kühl, Stefan, 2004. "Rassenforschung im Rahmen der internationalen eugenischen Bewegung" in Peter Martin and Christine Alonzo, eds, *Zwischen Charleston and Stechschritt: Schwarze im Nationalsozialismus* (Hamburg and Munich: Dölling and Galitz), pp. 495–507.

Kühne, Thomas, 2006. *Kameradschaft: Die Soldaten des nationalsozialistischen Krieges und das 20. Jahrhundert* (Göttingen: Vandenhoeck & Ruprecht).

Kumanev, Georgy, 1991. "The Nazi genocide of the Jewish population in the occupied territory of the Soviet Union," *Soviet Jewish Affairs* 21 (1), pp. 59–68.

Kundrus, Birthe, 2009. "Regime der Differenz: Volkstumspolitische Inklusionen und Exklusionen im Warthegau und im Generalgouvernement 1939–1944" in Bajohr and Wildt, eds, pp. 105–23.

Kundrus, Birthe and Beate Meyer, eds, 2004. *Die Deportation der Juden aus Deutschland* (*BGN* 20) (Göttingen: Wallstein).

Kunz, Norbert, 2005. *Die Krim unter deutscher Herrschaft 1941–1944: Germanisierungsutopie und Besatzungsrealität* (Darmstadt: Wissenschaftliche Buchgesellschaft).

Kury, Patrick, n.d. [2003]. *Über Fremde reden: Überfremdungsdiskurs und Ausgrenzung in der Schweiz 1900–1945* (Zurich: Chronos).

Kuss, Susanne, 2011. *Deutsches Militär auf kolonialen Kriegsschauplätzen*, second revised edition (Berlin: Ch. Links).

Kvist, Karin, 2000. "A study of antisemitic attitudes within Sweden's wartime Utlänningsbyrån," *Holocaust Education* 9 (2/3), pp. 199–211.

Kwiet, Konrad, 1984. "The ultimate refuge: Suicide in the Jewish community under the Nazis," *LBIY* 29, pp. 135–67.

Kwiet, Konrad, 1991. "Forced labour of German Jews in Nazi Germany," *LBIY* 36, pp. 389–410.

Lafont, Max, 1987. *L'extermination douce: La mort de 40,000 Malades Menteaux dans les Hôpiteaux Psychiatriques en France, sous le régime de Vichy* (Éditions de l'AREFPPI).

Lagrange, Maurice, 1977. "Le rapatriement des réfugiés après l'exode (juillet-septembre 1940)," *Revue de l'histoire de la deuxième guerre mondiale* 27 (107), pp. 39–52.

Lagrou, Pieter, 2002. "La guerre, les mots et le deuil: Bilan chiffré de la Seconde Guerre Mondiale" in Stephane Rouzeau, Annette Becker, Christian Ingrao and Henry Rousso, eds, *La violence de guerre, 1914–1945* (Brussels: Complexe), pp. 313–27.

Laine, Antti, 1994. "Finnland als Okkupationsmacht in Sowjetkarelien und die Kollaboration der Karelier" in Röhr, ed., pp. 319–33.

Laine, Antti, 2002. "Finland and the contribution of Germany to the enemy image in the great patriotic war" in Laine and Mikka Ylikangas, eds, *Rise and Fall of Soviet Karelia* (Helsinki: Kikimora), pp. 133–52.

Lang, Ralf, 1996. *Italienische "Fremdarbeiter" im nationalsozialistischen Deutschland 1937–1945* (Frankfurt a.M.: Peter Lang).

Lange, Karl, 1965. "Der Terminus 'Lebensraum' in Hitlers '*Mein Kampf*'," *VfZ* 13, pp. 426–37.

Lappenküper, Ulrich, 2000. "Der 'Schlächter von Paris': Carl-Albrecht Oberg als Höherer SS- und Polizeiführer in Frankreich 1942–1944" in Martens and Vaïsse, eds, pp. 129–45.

Laqueur, Walter, 1980. *The Terrible Secret* (London: Weidenfeld and Nicholson).

Lasik, Alexander, 1994. "Historical-sociological profile of the Auschwitz SS" in Gutman and Berenbaum, eds, pp. 271–87.

Latzel, Klaus, 1998. *Deutsche Soldaten – nationalsozialistischer Krieg? Kriegserlebnis – Kriegserfahrung 1939–1945* (Paderborn: Schöningh).

Lauerwald, Hannelore, 1996. *In fremdem Land: Kriegsgefangene im Stalag VIIIA Görlitz 1939–1945: Tatsachen, Briefe, Dokumente* (Görlitz: Viadukt).

Lavi (Loewenstein), Th., 1960. "Documents on the struggle of Rumanian Jewry for its rights during the Second World War," *YVS* 4, pp. 261–315.

Lehnstaedt, Stephan, 2007. "'Ostnieten' oder Verwaltungsexperten? Die Auswahl der deutschen Staatsdiener für den Einsatz im Generalgouvernement Polen 1939–1944," *ZfG* 55, pp. 701–21.

Lehnstaedt, Stephan, 2008. "Alltägliche Gewalt: Die deutschen Besatzer in Warschau und die Ermordung der jüdischen Bevölkerung" in Hürter and Zarusky, eds, pp. 81–102.

Lemkin, Raphael, 1944. *Axis Rule in Occupied Europe* (Washington: Carnegie Endowment for International Peace).

Lengel-Krizman, Narcisa, 2006. "Genocide carried out on the Roma – Jasenovac 1942" in *Jasenovac Memorial Site*, pp. 154–70.

Leniger, Markus, 2006. *Nationalsozialistische "Volkstumsarbeit" und Umsiedlungspolitik 1933–1945: Von der Minderheitenbetreuung zur Siedlerauslese* (Berlin: Frank & Timme).

Lenski, Mordechai, 1959. "Problems of disease in the Warsaw ghetto," *YVS* 3, pp. 283–301.

Lerner, Pablo and Alfredo Mordechai Rabello, 2006–07. "The prohibition of ritual slaughtering (kosher shechita and halal) and freedom of religion of minorities," *Journal of Law and Religion* 22 (1), pp. 1–62.

Levin, Dov, 1979. "The fighting leadership of the *Judenräte* in the small communities of Poland" in Yisrael Gutman and Cynthia Haft, eds, *Patterns of Jewish Leadership in Nazi Europe, 1933–1945* (Jerusalem: Yad Vashem), pp. 133–49.

Levin, Dov, 1985. *Fighting Back: Lithuanian Jewry's Armed Resistance to the Nazis 1941–1945* (New York and London: Holmes and Meier).

Levin, Dov, 1992. "Unique characteristics of Soviet Jewish soldiers in the Second World War" in Cohen *et al.*, eds, pp. 233–44.

Levine, Paul, 2000. "Attitudes and administration: Comparing the responses of mid-level bureaucrats to the Holocaust," *Holocaust Education* 9 (2/3), pp. 212–36.

Levinson, Joseph, ed., 2006. *The Shoah (Holocaust) in Lithuania* (Vilnius: Vilna Gaon Jewish State Museum).

Levy, Richard, 2010. "Political antisemitism in Germany and Austria, 1848–1914" in Lindemann and Levy, eds, pp. 121–35.

Lewkowicz, Lea, 2006. *The Jewish Community of Salonika: History, Memory, Identity* (London and Portland: Vallentine Mitchell).

Liberman, Peter, 1996. *Does Conquest Pay? The Exploitation of Occupied Industrial Societies* (Princeton: Princeton University Press).

Libionka, Dariusz, 2004. "Antisemitismus und antijüdische Gewalt im polnischen Nordosten in den 1930er Jahren: Das Verhalten des Klerus in der Diözese Łomża," *JASF* 13, pp. 15–35.

Lieb, Peter, 2007. *Konventioneller Krieg oder NS-Weltanschauungskrieg? Kriegführung und Partisanenbekämpfung in Frankreich 1943/44* (Munich: Oldenbourg).

Liesenberg, Carsten, 1995. "'Wir täuschen uns nicht über die Schwere der Zeit...': Die Verfolgung und Vernichtung der Juden" in Heiden and Mai, eds, pp. 443–62.

Lifton, Robert, 1986. *The Nazi Doctors* (New York: Basic Books).

Lilienthal, Georg, 1992. "Arier oder Jude? Geschichte des erb- und rassekundlichen Abstammungsgutachtens" in Propping and Schott, eds, pp. 66–84.

Lindemann, Albert and Richard Levy, eds, 2010. *Antisemitism* (Oxford: Oxford University Press).

Linkow, G., 1956. *Die unsichtbare Front* (Berlin [East]: Volk und Welt).

Lipscher, Ladislav, 1972. "Die Verwirklichung der antijüdischen Massnahmen in den vom Dritten Reich beeinflussten Staaten" in Karl Bosl, ed., *Das Jahr 1941 in der europäischen Politik* (Munich and Vienna: Oldenbourg), pp. 121–41.

Lipscher, Ladislav, 1979. *Die Juden im Slowakischen Staat 1939–1945* (Munich: Oldenbourg).

Litani, Dora, 1967. "The destruction of the Jews in Odessa in the light of Rumanian documents," *YVS* 6, pp. 135–54.

Lösch, Niels, 1997. *Rasse als Konstrukt: Leben und Werk Eugen Fischers* (Frankfurt a.M.: Peter Lang).

Löw, Andrea, 2012. "Die Erfahrung der radikalen Ungleichheit: Vom sprachlichen Umgang mit dem Gettoleben in Litzmannstadt (Łódź)" in Nicole Kramer and Armin Nolzen, eds, *Ungleichheit im "Dritten Reich"* (*BGN* 28) (Göttingen: Wallstein), pp. 48–68.

Löwe, Heinz-Dietrich, 1981. "Antisemitismus in der ausgehenden Zarenzeit" in Martin and Schulin, eds, pp. 184–208.

Longerich, Peter, 1998a. *Politik der Vernichtung: Eine Gesamtdarstellung der nationalsozialistischen Judenverfolgung* (Munich and Zurich: Piper).

Longerich, Peter, 1998b. *Die Wannsee-Konferenz vom 20. Januar 1942: Planung und Beginn des Genozids an den europäischen Juden* (Berlin: Edition Hentrich).

Longerich, Peter, 2001. *Der ungeschriebene Befehl: Hitler und der Weg zur 'Endlösung'* (Munich and Zurich: Piper).

Longerich, Peter, 2006. *"Davon haben wir nichts gewusst!" Die Deutschen und die Judenverfolgung 1933–1945* (Munich: Siedler).

Longerich, Peter, 2008. *Heinrich Himmler* (Munich: Siedler).

Longerich, Peter, 2010. *Joseph Goebbels* (Munich: Siedler).

Longhi, Silvano, 2010. *Die Juden und der Widerstand gegen den Faschismus in Italien (1943–1945)* (Berlin: LIT).

Lorenz, Einhart, 2007. "Antisemitische Judenbilder und die norwegische Haltung zur Deportation," *JASF* 16, pp. 217–38.

Lotfi, Gabriele, 2000. *KZ der Gestapo: Arbeitserziehungslager im Dritten Reich* (Stuttgart and Munich: dva).

Loulos, Konstantin, 1994. "Politische, wirtschaftliche und soziale Aspekte der Kollaboration in Griechenland 1941–1944" in Röhr, ed., pp. 397–414.

Loulos, Konstantin, 1999. "Vergeltungsmassnahmen der Besatzungsmächte und 'endogene' Repressalien in Griechenland 1941–1944" in Droulia and Fleischer, eds, pp. 137–50.

Lower, Wendy, 2005. *Nazi Empire-Building and the Holocaust in Ukraine* (Chapel Hill: University of North Carolina Press).

Lozowick, Yaakov, 1987. "Rollbahn Mord: The early activities of Einsatzgruppe C," *HGS* 2, pp. 221–41.

Lynch, Edouard, 2012. "Food stocks, the black market, and town and country tensions in France during two world wars and beyond" in Paul Brassley, Yves

Segers and Leen van Molle, eds, *War, Agriculture and Food: Rural Europe from the 1930s to the 1950s* (New York and London: Routledge), pp. 229–44.

Mächler, Stefan, 1998. "Kampf gegen das Chaos – die antisemitische Bevölkerungspolitik der eidgenössischen Fremdenpolizei und Polizeiabteilung 1917–1954" in Mattioli, ed., (1998a), pp. 357–421.

MacKenzie, S.P., 1994. "The treatment of prisoners of war in World War II," *JMH* 66, September, pp. 487–520.

Madajczyk, Czesław, 1988. *Die Okkupationspolitik Nazideutschelands in Polen 1939–1945* (Cologne: Pahl-Rugenstein).

Madajczyk, Czesław, 1994. "Kann man in Polen 1939–1945 von Kollaboration sprechen?" in Röhr, ed., (1994a), pp. 133–48.

Maderegger, Sylvia, 1973. *Die Juden im österreichischen Ständestaat 1934–1938* (Vienna and Salzburg: Geyer-Edition).

Mahler, Raphael, 1944. "Jews in public service and the liberal professions in Poland, 1918–1939," *JSS* VI (4), pp. 291–350.

Maifreda, Germano, 2001. "Aspetti economici della legislazione antiebraica italiana nel quadro delle legislazioni europee" in Capelli and Broggini, eds, pp. 261–88.

Maksudov, Sergej, 1993. "The Jewish population losses of the USSR from the Holocaust" in Dobroszycki and Gurock, eds, pp. 207–13.

Malinowski, Stephan, 2003. *Vom König zum Führer: Sozialer Niedergang und politische Radikalisierung im deutschen Adel zwischen Kaiserreich und NS-Staat*, revised edition (Berlin: Akademie).

Mallmann, Klaus-Michael, 2004. "'...Missgeburten, die nicht auf diese Welt gehören': Die deutsche Ordnungspolizei in Polen 1939–1941" in Mallmann and Musial, eds, pp. 71–89.

Mallmann, Klaus-Michael and Bogdan Musial, eds, 2004. *Genesis des Genozids: Polen 1939–1941* (Darmstadt: Wissenschaftliche Buchgesellschaft).

Mallmann, Klaus-Michael and Martin Cüppers, 2006. *Halbmond und Hakenkreuz: Das Dritte Reich, die Araber und Palästina* (Darmstadt: Wissenschaftliche Buchgesellschaft).

Mallmann, Klaus-Michael, Jochen Böhler and Jürgen Matthäus, 2008. *Einsatzgruppen in Polen* (Darmstadt: Wissenschaftliche Buchgesellschaft).

Mann, Michael, 2005. *The Dark Side of Democracy: Explaining Ethnic Cleansing* (Cambridge: Cambridge University Press).

Manoschek, Walter, 1993. *"Serbien ist judenfrei": Militärische Besatzungspolitik und Judenvernichtung in Serbien 1941/42* (Munich: Oldenbourg).

Marcus, Joseph, 1983. *Social and Political History of the Jews in Poland, 1919–1939* (Berlin: Mouton).

Marguairaz, Michel, 1991. "Deutschland, Vichy und die ökonomische Kollaboration" in Hirschfeld and Marsh, eds, pp. 109–29.

Mariot, Nicolas and Claire Zalc, 2010. *Face à la persecution: 991 Juifs dans la guerre* (Paris: Odile Jacob).

Marrus, Michael, 1985. *The Unwanted: European Refugees in the Twentieth Century* (New York and Oxford: Oxford University Press).

Marrus, Michael, ed., 1989. *The Nazi Holocaust, Vol. 4/1, The Final Solution Outside Germany* (Westport and London: Meckler).

Marrus, Michael and Robert Paxton, 1981. *Vichy France and the Jews* (New York: Basic Books).

Marrus, Michael and Robert Paxton, 1982. "The Nazis and the Jews in occupied western Europe, 1940–1944," *JMH* 54 (4), pp. 687–714.

Martens, Stefan and Maurice Vaïsse, eds, 2000. *Frankreich und Deutschland im Krieg (November 1942-Herbst 1944)* (Bonn: Bouvier).

Martin, Bernd, 1969. *Deutschland und Japan im Zweiten Weltkrieg* (Göttingen: Musterschmidt).

Martin, Bernd and Ernst Schulin, eds, 1981. *Die Juden als Minderheit in der Geschichte* (Munich: dtv).

Martin, Peter, 1999. "'...auf jeden Fall zu erschiessen': Schwarze Kriegsgefangene in den Lagern der Nazis," *Mittelweg 36*, 8 (5), pp. 76–91.

Mason, Henry, 1984. "Testing the human bonds within nations: Jews in the occupied Netherlands," *Political Science Quarterly* 99 (2), pp. 315–43.

Mason, Timothy, 1978. *Sozialpolitik im Dritten Reich: Arbeiterklasse und Volksgemeinschaft*, second edition (Opladen: Westdeutscher Verlag).

Matarasso, Isaac Aaron, 2002. "'...and yet not all of them died...': The destruction of Salonika's Jews during the German occupation" in Bowman, ed., pp. 125–233.

Mataušić, Nataša, 2006. "The Jasenovac concentration camp" in *Jasenovac Memorial Site*, pp. 47–54.

Mathieu, G. Bording, 1981. "The secret anti-Judaism Sondernummer of 21st May 1943," *LBIY* 26, pp. 291–300.

Matkovski, Aleksandar, 1959. "The destruction of Macedonian Jewry in 1943," *YVS* 3, pp. 203–58.

Matthäus, Jürgen, Konrad Kwiet, Jürgen Förster and Richard Breitman, eds, 2003. *Ausbildungsziel Judenmord? "Weltanschauliche Erziehung" von SS, Polizei und Waffen-SS im Rahmen der "Endlösung"* (Frankfurt a.M.: Fischer).

Mattioli, Aram, ed., 1998a. *Antisemitismus in der Schweiz 1848–1960* (Zurich: Orell Füssli).

Mattioli, Aram, 1998b. "Antisemitismus in der Geschichte der modernen Schweiz – Begriffserklärungen und Thesen" in Mattioli, ed., (1998a), pp. 3–22.

Mattioli, Aram, 2004."Die vergessenen Kolonialverbrechen des italienischen Faschismus in Libyen," *Fritz-Bauer-Institut Jahrbuch*, pp. 203–26.

Maurer, Trude, 1994. "Abschiebung und Attentat: Die Ausweisung der polnischen Juden und der Vorwand für die Kristallnacht" in Pehle, ed., pp. 52–73.

Maxwell, Elisabeth, 1998. "The rescue of Jews in France and Belgium during the Holocaust," *Holocaust Education* 7 (1/2), pp. 1–18.

Mazower, Mark, 2000. *Dark Continent: Europe's Twentieth Century* (New York: Vintage).

Mazower, Mark, 2001 [1993]. *Inside Hitler's Greece: The Experience of Occupation, 1941–1944* (New Haven and London: Yale University Press).

Mazower, Mark, 2004. *Salonica: City of Ghosts* (London: HarperCollins).

Mazower, Mark, 2008. *Hitler's Empire* (New York: Penguin).

McDowall, David, 2004. *A Modern History of the Kurds*, third enlarged and revised edition (London and New York: IBTauris).

Mehringer, Hartmut, 1998. *Widerstand und Emigration: Das NS-Regime und seine Gegner*, second edition (Munich: dtv).

Meinen, Insa, 2008. "Die Deportation der Juden aus Belgien und das Devisenschutzkommando" in Hürter and Zarusky, eds, pp. 45–79.

Melichar, Peter, 2005. "Who is a Jew? Antisemitic defining, identifying and counting in pre-1938 Austria," *LBIY* 50, pp. 149–74.

Melson, Robert, 1992. *Revolution and Genocide: On the Origins of the Armenian Genocide and the Holocaust* (Chicago and London: Chicago University Press).

Melzer, Emanuel, 1997. *No Way Out: The Politics of Polish Jewry 1935–1939* (Cincinnati: Hebrew Union College Press).

Mendelsohn, Ezra, 1983. *The Jews of East Central Europe Between the World Wars* (Bloomington: Indiana University Press).

Merridale, Catherine, 2000. *Night of Stone: Death and Memory in Russia* (London: Granta).

Meyer, Ahlrich, 2000. *Die deutsche Besatzung in Frankreich 1940–1944: Widerstandsbekämpfung und Judenverfolgung* (Darmstadt: Wissenschaftliche Buchgesellschaft).

Meyer, Beate, 1999. *"Jüdische Mischlinge": Rassenpolitik und Verfolgungserfahrung 1933–1945* (Hamburg: Döring and Galitz).

Meyer, Hermann Frank, 2008. *Blutiges Edelweiss: Die 1. Gebirgs-Division im Zweiten Weltkrieg* (Berlin: Christoph Links).

Meyer, Winfried and Klaus Neitmann, eds, 2001. *Zwangsarbeit während der NS-Zeit in Berlin und Brandenburg* (Potsdam: Verlag für Berlin-Brandenburg).

Meyer zu Uptrup, Wolfram, 2003. *Kampf gegen die "jüdische Weltverschwörung": Propaganda und Antisemitismus der Nationalsozialisten 1919–1945* (Berlin: Metropol).

Michaelis, Meir, 1978. *Mussolini and the Jews: German-Italian Relations and the Jewish Question in Italy 1922–1945* (Oxford: Oxford University Press).

Michlic, Joanna, 2006. *Poland's Threatening Other: The Image of the Jew from 1880 to the Present* (Lincoln and London: University of Nebraska Press).

Michman, Dan, ed., 1998. *Belgium and the Holocaust* (Jerusalem: Yad Vashem).

Michman, Joseph, 1986. "Planing for the final solution against the background of developments in Holland in 1941," *YVS* 17, pp. 145–80.

Mierzejewski, Alfred, 2001. "A public enterprise in the service of mass murder: The Deutsche Reichsbahn and the Holocaust," *HGS* 15 (1), pp. 33–46.

Mihok, Brigitte, ed., 2005. *Ungarn und der Holocaust* (Berlin: Metropol).

Mihovilović, Dorde and Jelka Smreka, 2006. "About the 'list of individual victims of the Jasenovac concentration camp'" in *Jasenovac Memorial Site*, pp. 218–19.

Miller, Marshall Lee, 1975. *Bulgaria During the Second World War* (Stanford: Stanford University Press).

Milotova, Jaroslava, 1996. "Die Protektoratspresse und die Judenfrage," *TSD*, pp. 153–85.

Milotova, Jaroslava, 2002. "Zur Geschichte der Verordnung Konstantin von Neuraths über das jüdische Vermögen," *TSD*, pp. 75–115.

Milton, Sybil, 1984. "The expulsion of Polish Jews from Germany, October 1938 to July 1939," *LBIY* 29, pp. 169–99.

Mitrovski, Boro, Venceslav Glišic and Tomo Ristovski, 1971. *Das bulgarische Heer in Jugoslawien 1941–1945* (Belgrade: Medjunarodna Politika).

Młynarczyk, Jacek, 2007. *Judenmord in Zentralpolen: Der Distrikt Radom im Generalgouvernement* (Darmstadt: Wissenschaftliche Buchgesellschaft).

Mohrmann, Walter, 1972. *Antisemitismus: Ideologie und Geschichte im Kaiserreich und in der Weimarer Republik* (Berlin: Deutscher Verlag der Wissenschaften).

Molho, Mentes, 2002. "Assets of Jews of Salonika" in Steven Bowman, ed., *The Holocaust in Salonika: Eyewitness Accounts* (n.p.: Bloch), pp. 212–33.

Mommsen, Hans, 1997. "Hitler's Reichstag speech of 30 January 1939," *History and Memory* 9 (1/2), pp. 147–61.

Mommsen, Hans and Dieter Obst, 1988. "Die Reaktion der deutschen Bevölkerung auf die Verfolgung der Juden 1933–1943" in Hans Mommsen and Susanne Willems, eds, *Herrschaftsalltag im Dritten Reich* (Düsseldorf: Schwann), pp. 374–421.

Mommsen, Wolfgang, 1987. *Imperialismustheorien*, third revised edition (Göttingen: Vandenhoeck & Ruprecht).

Moore, Bob, 1997. *Victims and Survivors: The Nazi Persecution of the Jews in the Netherlands 1940–1945* (London: Arnold).

Moore, Bob, 2001. "The Dutch churches, Christians and the rescue of Jews in the Netherlands" in Brasz and Kaplan, eds, pp. 277–88.

Moore, Bob, 2003. "The rescue of Jews from Nazi persecution: A western European perspective," *JGR* 5 (2), pp. 293–308.

Moore, Bob, 2004. "The rescue of Jews in Nazi-Occupied Belgium, France and the Netherlands," *Australian Journal of Politics and History* 50 (3), pp. 385–95.

Moore, Bob, 2010. *Survivors: Jewish Self-Help and Rescue in Nazi-Occupied Western Europe* (Oxford: Oxford University Press).

Morandi, Elia, 2004. *Italiener in Hamburg: Migration, Arbeit und Alltagsleben vom Kaiserreich bis zur Gegenwart* (Frankfurt a.M.: Peter Lang).

Moser, Gwyn, 1997. "Jewish *U-Boote* in Austria, 1938–1945," available at: http://motlc.wiesenthal.com/site/pp.asp?c=gvKVLcMVIuG&b=395003 (accessed January 12, 2014).

Moser, Jonny, 1966. *Die Judenverfolgung in Österreich 1938–1945* (Vienna: Europa).

Mosse, George, 1990 [1978]. *Die Geschichte des Rassismus in Europa* (Frankfurt a.M.: Fischer).

Mühlberger, Detlef, 2003. *The Social Bases of Nazism 1919–1933* (Cambridge: Cambridge University Press).

Müller, Rolf-Dieter, 1991. *Hitlers Ostkrieg und die deutsche Siedlungspolitik* (Frankfurt a.M.: Fischer).

Müller, Rolf-Dieter, 2007. *An der Seite der Wehrmacht: Hitlers ausländische Helfer beim "Kreuzzug gegen den Bolschewismus" 1941–1945* (Berlin: Chr. Links).

Müller, Sven Oliver, 2005. "Nationalismus in der deutschen Kriegsgesellschaft 1939 bis 1945," *DRZW*, 9/2, pp. 9–92.

Musial, Bogdan, 1999. *Deutsche Zivilverwaltung und Judenverfolgung im Generalgouvernement: Eine Fallstudie zum Distrikt Lublin 1939–1944* (Wiesbaden: Harrassowitz).

Musial, Bogdan, ed., 2004. *"Aktion Reinhardt": Der Völkermord an den Juden im Generalgouvernement 1941–1944* (Osnabrück: fibre).

Nagy-Talavera, Nicholas, 2001. *The Green Shirts and the Others: A History of Fascism in Hungary and Romania* (Iaşi: Center for Romanian Studies).

Nečas, Ctibor, 1991. "Preparation and execution of the genocide of Roma from the Czech lands in the years of Nazi occupation" in *Conference Report of the International Scientific Conference*, pp. 169–73.

Nedelsky, Nadya, 2001. "The wartime Slovak state: A case study in the relationship between ethnic nationalism and authoritarian patterns of government," *Nations and Nationalism* 7 (2), pp. 215–34.

Neitzel, Sönke, 2005. *Abgehört: Deutsche Generäle in britischer Kriegsgefangenschaft 1942–1945* (Berlin: Ullstein).

Neliba, Günter, 1992. *Wilhelm Frick: Der Legalist des Unrechtsstaates* (Paderborn: Schöningh).

Nessou, Anestis, 2009. *Griechenland 1941–1944: Deutsche Besatzungspolitik und Verbrechen gegen die Zivilbevölkerung – eine Beurteilung nach dem Völkerrecht* (Osnabrück: Universitätsverlag Osnabrück).

Neugebauer, Wolfgang, 2002. "Der NS-Terrorapparat" in Tálos *et al.*, eds, pp. 721–43.

Neumann, Boaz, 2010. *Die Weltanschauung der Nazis: Raum, Körper, Sprache* (Göttingen: Wallstein).

Niewyk, Donald, 1980. *The Jews in Weimar Germany* (Manchester: Manchester University Press).

Nimmo, William, 1988. *Behind a Curtain of Silence: Japanese in Soviet Custody, 1945–1956* (New York: Greenwood).

Nissen, Mogens, 2006. "Danish food production in the German war economy" in Frank Trentmann and Flemming Just, eds, *Food and Conflict in Europe in the Age of the Two World Wars* (London and New York: Palgrave Macmillan), pp. 172–92.

Niznansky, Eduard, 1998. "Die Deportation der Juden in der Zeit der autonomen Slowakei im November 1938," *JASF* 7, pp. 20–45.

Nordlund, Sven, 2000. " 'The war is over – now you can go home!' Jewish refugees and the Swedish labour market in the shadow of the Holocaust," *Holocaust Education* 9 (2/3), pp. 171–98.

Nova, Fritz, 1986. *Alfred Rosenberg: Nazi Theorist of the Holocaust* (New York: Hippocrene).

Nyssen, Elke, 1979. *Schule im Nationalsozialismus* (Heidelberg: Quelle und Meyer).

Obst, Dieter, 1991. *"Reichskristallnacht": Ursachen und Verlauf des antisemitischen Pogroms vom November 1938* (Frankfurt a.M.: Peter Lang).

Ofer, Dalia, 1996. "Everyday life in the ghettos of Transnistria," *YVS* 25, pp. 175–208.

Ofer, Dalia, 2009. "The ghettos in Transnistria and ghettos under German occupation in eastern Europe" in Dieckmann and Quinkert, eds, pp. 30–53.

Ogorreck, Ralf, 1992. *Die Einsatzgruppen der Sicherheitspolizei und des SD im Rahmen der "Genesis der Endlösung": Ein Beitrag zur Entschlussbildung der "Endlösung der Judenfrage" im Jahre 1941*, PhD thesis, Free University of Berlin.

Oldenburg, Manfred, 2004. *Ideologie und militärisches Kalkül: Die Besatzungspolitik der Wehrmacht in der Sowjetunion 1942* (Cologne: Böhlau).

Oleksy, Krystyna, 1995. "Salman Gradowski – Ein Zeuge aus dem Sonderkommando," *TSD*, pp. 121–35.

Olshausen, Klaus, 1973. *Zwischenspiel auf dem Balkan: Die deutsche Politik gegenüber Jugoslawien und Griechenland von März bis Juli 1941* (Stuttgart: dva).

Opfer, Björn, 2005. *Im Schatten des Krieges: Besatzung oder Anschluss – Befreiung oder Unterdrückung: Eine komparative Untersuchung über die bulgarische Herrschaft in Vardar-Makedonien 1915–1918 und 1941–1944* (Münster: LIT).

Oprach, Marc, 2006. *Nationalsozialistische Judenpolitik im Protektorat Böhmen und Mähren* (Hamburg: Dr Kovač).

Oren, Nissan, 1968. "The Bulgarian exception: A reassessment of the salvation of the Jewish community," *YVS* 7, pp. 83–106.

Orlowski, Hubert, 1996. *"Polnische Wirtschaft": Zum deutschen Polendiskurs der Neuzeit* (Wiesbaden: Harrassowitz).

Orth, Karin, 1997. "Rudolf Höss und die 'Endlösung der Judenfrage'," *WerkstattGeschichte* 6 (18), pp. 45–57.

Orth, Karin, 1999. *Das System der nationalsozialistischen Konzentrationslager* (Hamburg: Hamburger Edition).

Orth, Karin, 2000. *Die Konzentrationslager-SS: Sozialstrukturelle Analysen und biographische Studien* (Göttingen: Wallstein).

Ory, Pascal, 1976. *Les collaborateurs 1940–1945* (Paris: Éditions du Seuil).

Osterloh, Jörg, 1997. *Ein ganz normales Lager: Das Kriegsgefangenen-Mannschaftsstammlager 304 (IVH) Zeithain bei Riesa/Sa. 1941 bis 1945* (Leipzig: Gustav Kiepenheuer).

Otto, Reinhard, 1998. *Wehrmacht, Gestapo und sowjetische Kriegsgefangene im deutschen Reichsgebiet 1941/42* (Munich: Oldenbourg).

Otto, Reinhard, Rolf Keller and Jens Nagel, 2008. "Sowjetische Kriegsgefangene in deutschem Gewahrsam 1941–1945: Zahlen und Dimensionen," *VfZ* 56 (4), pp. 557–602.

Overmans, Rüdiger, 1999. "Die Rheinwiesenlager 1945: 'Ein untergeordneter Eintrag im Leidensbuch der Geschichte?'" in Bischof and Overmans, eds, pp. 233–64.

Overmans, Rüdiger, 2005. "Die Kriegsgefangenenpolitik des Deutschen Reiches 1939 bis 1945," *DRZW*, 9/2 (Munich: dva), pp. 729–875.

Overy, Richard, 1995. *Why the Allies Won* (New York and London: W.W. Norton).

Overy, Richard, Gerhard Otto and Johannes Houwink ten Cate, eds, 1997. *Die "Neuordnung Europas": NS-Wirtschaftspolitik in den besetzten Gebieten* (Berlin: Metropol).

Pätzold, Kurt and Erika Schwarz, 1994. *"Auschwitz war für mich nur ein Bahnhof": Franz Novak, der Transportoffizier Adolf Eichmanns* (Berlin: Metropol).

Pagenstecher, Cord, Bernhard Bremberger and Gisela Wenzel, 2008. *Zwangsarbeit in Berlin: Archivrecherchen, Nachweissuche und Entschädigung* (Berlin: Metropol).

Paldiel, Mordechai, 1998. "The rescue of Jewish children in Belgium during World War II" in Michman, ed., pp. 307–25.

Palty, Sonja, 1995. *Jenseits des Dnjestr: Jüdische Deportationsschicksale aus Bukarest in Transnistrien 1942–1943*, ed. Erhard Roy Wiehn (Constance: Hartung-Gorre).

Paucker, Arnold, 1988. "Die Abwehr des Antisemitismus in den Jahren 1893–1933" in Strauss and Kampe, eds, pp. 143–71.

Paul, Gerhard, 2002. "Von Psychopathen, Technokraten des Terrors und 'ganz gewöhnlichen' Deutschen: Die Täter der Shoah im Spiegel der Forschung" in idem, *Die Täter der Shoah* (Göttingen: Wallstein), pp. 13–90.

Paul, Gerhard and Klaus-Michael Mallmann, eds, 1995. *Die Gestapo – Mythos und Realität* (Darmstadt: Wissenschaftliche Buchgesellschaft).

Paulsson, Gunnar, 1998. "The rescue of Jews by non-Jews in Nazi-occupied Poland," *Holocaust Education* 7 (1/2), pp. 19–44.

Paulsson, Gunnar, 2002. *Secret City: The Hidden Jews ofWarsaw, 1940–1945* (New Haven and London: Yale University Press).

Paulsson, Gunnar, 2004. "Das Verhältnis zwischen Polen und Juden im besetzten Warschau, 1940–1945" in Musial, ed., pp. 383–404.

Pavlowitch, Stevan, 2008. *Hitler's New Disorder: The Second World War in Yugoslavia* (London: Hurst & Co).

Pavone, Claudio, 1992. *Una guerra civile: Saggio storico sulla moralità nella Resistenza* (Torino: Bollati Boringhieri).

Pavunovski, Vladimir, 2001. "La legislazione antisemita in Bulgaria durante la seconda guerra mondiale" in Capelli and Broggini, eds, pp. 96–138.

Pawełczyńska, Anna, 2001. *Werte gegen Gewalt: Betrachtungen einer Soziologin über Auschwitz* (Oświęcim: Staatliches Museum Auschwitz-Birkenau).

Paxton, Robert, 2001 [1992]. *Vichy France: Old Guard and New Order 1940–1944* (New York: Columbia University Press).

Pearson, Owen, 2005. *Albania in Occupation and War: From Fascism to Communism 1940–1945* (London and New York: IB Tauris).

Pehle, Walther, ed., 1994 [1988]. *Der Judenpogrom 1938* (Frankfurt a.M.: Fischer).

Pekesen, Berna, 2012. *Nationalismus, Türkisierung und das Ende der jüdischen Gemeinden in Thrakien 1918–1942* (Munich: Oldenbourg).

Penkower, Monty Noam, 1988. *The Jews Were Expendable* (Detroit: Wayne State University Press).

Penter, Tanja, 2004. "Arbeiten für den Feind in der Heimat – der Arbeitseinsatz in der besetzten Ukraine 1941–1944," *JfW* 45 (1), pp. 65–94.

Perz, Bertrand and Florian Freund, 2004. "Auschwitz neu? Pläne und Massnahmen zur Wiedererrichtung der Krematorien von Auschwitz-Birkenau in der Umgebung des KZ Mauthausen im Februar 1945," *Dachauer Hefte* 20, pp. 58–70.

Perz, Bertrand and Thomas Sandkühler, 1999. "Auschwitz und die 'Aktion Reinhard' 1942–45: Judenmord und Raubpraxis in neuer Sicht," *Zeitgeschichte* 26 (5), pp. 283–316.

Peschanski, Denis, 2002. *La France des camps: L'internement 1938–1946* (Paris: Gallimard).

Peschanski, Denis, 2010 [1994]. *Les Tsiganes en France 1939–1946* (Paris: CNRS Éditions).

Peterson, Christopher, Steven Maier and Martin Seligman, 1993. *Learned Helplessness: A Theory for the Age of Personal Control* (New York and Oxford: Oxford University Press).

Petrick, Fritz, 1994. "Die norwegische Kollaboration 1940–1945" in Röhr, ed. (1994a), pp. 119–30.

Petrick, Fritz, 1995. "Die DAF und die Gewerkschaften in von Deutschland besetzten Ländern," *BBGFW* 4, pp. 1–33.

Petrick, Fritz, 1998. *"Ruhestörung": Studien zur Nordeuropapolitik Nazideutschlands* (Berlin: Edition Organon).

Petrow, Richard, 1974. *The Bitter Years: The Invasion and Occupation of Denmark and Norway, April 1940–May 1945* (New York: William Morrow).

Picard, Jacques, 1997. *Die Schweiz und die Juden 1933–1945* (Zurich: Chronos).

Picciotto Fargion, Liliana, 1989. "The anti-Jewish policy of the Italian social republic (1943–1945)" in Marrus, ed., pp. 255–87.

Pilichowski, Czesław, 1982. "Verbrauch von Nahrungsmitteln durch jüdische Bevölkerung und Häftlinge der Okkupationslager im besetzten Polen," *Studia Historiae Oeconomicae* 17, pp. 205–15.

Pingel, Falk, 1978. *Häftlinge unter SS-Herrschaft* (Hamburg: Hoffmann & Campe).

Piper, Ernst, 2005. *Alfred Rosenberg: Hitlers Chefideologe* (Munich: Blessing).

Plaut, Joshua, 1996. *Greek Jewry in the Twentieth Century, 1913–1983: Patterns of Jewish Survival in the Greek Provinces Before and After the Holocaust* (Madison: Farleigh Dickinson University Press and Associated University Press).

Pohl, Dieter, 1993. *Von der "Judenpolitik" zum Judenmord: Der Distrikt Lublin des Generalgouvernements 1939–1944* (Frankfurt a.M.: Peter Lang).

Pohl, Dieter, 1996. *NS-Judenverfolgung in Ostgalizien 1941–1944* (Munich: Oldenbourg).

Pohl, Dieter, 1998. "Die grossen Zwangsarbeitslager der SS- und Polizeiführer für Juden im Generalgouvernement 1939–1945" in Herbert *et al.*, eds, pp. 415–38.

Pohl, Dieter, 2000. "Schauplatz Ukraine: Der Massenmord an den Juden im Militärverwaltungsgebiet und im Reichskommissariat 1941–1943" in Norbert Frei, Sybille Steinbacher and Bernd Wagner, eds, *Ausbeutung, Vernichtung, Öffentlichkeit: Neue Studien zur nationalsozialistischen Lagerpolitik* (Munich: Saur), pp. 135–73.

Pohl, Dieter, 2003. *Verfolgung und Massenmord in der NS-Zeit 1933–1945* (Darmstadt: Wissenschaftliche Buchgesellschaft).

Pohl, Dieter, 2010. "The murder of Ukraine's Jews under German military administration and in the Reich Commissariat Ukraine" in Brandon and Lower, eds, pp. 23–76.

Pohl, Dieter, 2011. *Die Herrschaft der Wehrmacht: Deutsche Militärbesatzung und einheimische Bevölkerung in der Sowjetunion 1941–1944* (Frankfurt a.M.: Fischer).

Poliakov, Leon, 1953. "An opinion poll on anti-Jewish measures in Vichy France," *JSS* 15 (2), pp. 135–50.

Poliakov, Léon, 1974. *The Aryan Myth: A History of Racist and Nationalist Ideas in Europe* (London: Chatto + Heinemann).

Polian, Pavel, 2005a. "Sowjetische Juden als Kriegsgefangene" in Bischof *et al.*, eds, pp. 487–505.

Polian, Pavel, 2005b."The internment of returning Soviet prisoners of war after 1945" in Bob Moore and Barbara Hately-Brown, eds, *Prisoners of War, Prisoners of Peace* (Oxford and New York: Berg), pp. 123–39.

Polian, Pavel, 2007. "Die Repatriierung der sowjetischen Kriegsgefangenen" in *Ich werde es nie vergessen*, pp. 36–42.

Polian, Pavel, 2008. "Hätte der Holocaust beinahe nicht stattgefunden? Überlegungen zu einem Schriftwechsel im Wert von über zwei Millionen Menschenleben" in Hürter and Zarusky, eds, pp. 1–19.

Poprzeczny, Joseph, 2004. *Odilo Globocnik: Hitler's Man in the East* (Jefferson and London: McFarland).

Poznanski, Renée, 1997. *Les juifs en France pendant la seconde guerre mondiale* (Paris: Hachette).

Pramowska, Anna, 2010. *Civil War in Poland, 1942–1948* (Basingstoke and New York: Palgrave).

Pressac, Jean-Claude, 1989. *Auschwitz: Techniques and Operation of the Gas Chambers* (New York: Beate Klarsfeld Foundation).

Pressac, Jean-Claude, 1995. *Die Krematorien von Auschwitz*, second edition (Munich and Zurich: Piper).

Propping, Peter and Heinz Schott, eds, 1992. *Wissenschaft auf Irrwegen: Biologismus – Rassenhygiene – Eugenik* (Bonn and Berlin: Bouvier).

Prusin, Alexander, 2003. "Revolution and ethnic cleansing in western Ukraine: The OUN-UPA assault against Polish settlements in Volynia and eastern Galicia, 1943–1944" in Steven Béla Várdy and T. Hunt Tooley, eds, *Ethnic Cleansing in Twentieth Century Europe* (New York: Columbia University Press), pp. 517–35.

Prusin, Alexander, 2007. "A community of violence: The Sipo/SD and its role in the Nazi terror system in Generalbezirk Kiev," *HGS* 21 (1), pp. 1–30.

Prusin, Alexander, 2010. *The Lands Between: Conflict in the East European Borderlands, 1870–1992* (Oxford: Oxford University Press).

Pryce-Jones, David, 1991. "Paris unter der deutschen Besatzung" in Hirschfeld and Marsh, eds, pp. 23–42.

Pulzer, Peter, 1966. *Die Entstehung des politischen Antisemitismus in Deutschland und Österreich 1867–1914* (Gütersloh: Sigbert Mohn).

Quadflieg, Peter, 2009. "Luxemburg – Zwangsrekrutiert ins Deutsche Reich: Luxemburgs nationale Identität und ihre Prägung durch den Zweiten Weltkrieg" in von Lingen, pp. 172–88.

Raspin, Angela, 1986. *The Italian War Economy 1940–1943: With Particular Reference to Italian Relations With Germany* (New York and London: Garland).

Rass, Christoph, 2003. *"Menschenmaterial": Deutsche Soldaten an der Ostfront* (Paderborn: Schöningh).

Rass, Christoph, 2005. "Verbrecherische Kriegführung an der Front: Eine Infanteriedivision und ihre Soldaten" in Hartmann *et al.*, eds, pp. 80–96.

Rassismus in Deutschland, n.d. [1994] (*Beiträge zur Geschichte der nationalsozialistischen Verfolgung in Norddeutschland*, no. 1) (Bremen: Edition Temmen).

Rautkallio, Hannu, 1987. *Finland and the Holocaust* (New York: Holocaust Library).

Rechnitz Koffler, Florette and Richard Koffler, 1995. "Introduction" in Caracciolo, pp. xxv-xxxiv.

Reemtsma, Jan Philipp, 2008. *Vertrauen und Gewalt: Versuch über eine besondere Konstellation der Moderne* (Hamburg: Hamburger Edition).

Reichardt, Sven, 2002. *Faschistische Kampfbünde: Gewalt und Gemeinschaft im italienischen Squadrismus und in der deutsche SA* (Köln u.a.: Böhlau).

Reinhardt, Klaus, 1972. *Die Wende vor Moskau: Das Scheitern der Strategie Hitlers im Winter 1941/42* (Stuttgart: dva).

Reitlinger, Gerald, 1961 [revised English edition 1953] *Die Endlösung* (Berlin: Colloquium)

Reitlinger, Gerald, 1963. *Ein Haus auf Sand gebaut: Hitlers Gewaltpolitik in Russland 1941–1944*, second edition (Gütersloh: Bertelsmann).

Reznikova, Irina, 2000. "Repression während der Leningrader Blockade," *1999* 15 (1), pp. 117–41.

Rieger, Berndt, 2007. *Creator of the Nazi Death Camps: The Life of Odilo Globocnik* (London and Portland: Vallentine Mitchell).

Ries, Markus, 1998. "Katholischer Antisemitismus in der Schweiz" in Mattioli, ed., pp. 45–57.

Riess, Volker, 1995. *Die Anfänge der Vernichtung "lebensunwerten Lebens" in den Reichsgauen Danzig-Westpreussen und Wartheland 1939/40* (Frankfurt a.M.: Peter Lang).

Roberts, Sophie, 2006. "Jews, Vichy and the Algiers insurrection of 1942," *Holocaust Education* 12 (3), pp. 63–88.

Robinson, Roland, 1972. "Non-European foundations of European imperialism: Sketch for a theory of collaboration" in Roger Owen and Bob Sutcliffe, eds, *Studies in the Theory of Imperialism* (London: Longman), pp. 117–40.

Röhr, Werner, ed., 1994a. *Okkupation und Kollaboration 1938–1945* (Berlin and Heidelberg: Hüthig).

Röhr, Werner, 1994b. "Gewittersturm über Warschau – Politische Akzenten des Aufstands 1944," *BBGFW* 3, pp. 1–55.

Röhr, Werner, 1997. "System oder organisiertes Chaos? Fragen einer Typologie der deutschen Okkuptionsregimes im Zweiten Weltkrieg" in Robert Bohn, ed., *Die deutsche Herrschaft in den "germanischen" Ländern 1940–1945* (Stuttgart: Franz Steiner), pp. 11–45.

Röhr, Werner, 2002. "'Reichsgau Wartheland' 1939–1945: Vom 'Exerzierplatz des praktischen Nationalsozialismus' zum 'Mustergau'?" *Bulletin für Faschismus- und Weltkriegsforschung* 18, pp. 28-54.

Römer, Felix, 2008. *Der Kommissarbefehl: Wehrmacht und NS-Verbrechen an der Ostfront 1941/42* (Paderborn: Schöningh).

Romano, Jaša and Ladoslav Kadelburg, 1977. "The Third Reich: Initiator, organizer and executor of anti-Jewish measures and genocide in Yugoslavia" in *The Third Reich and Yugoslavia* (Belgrade: Institute for Contemporary History), pp. 670–90.

Romanovski, W., 1984. *Natsistskaya politika genotsida i "vyshtshennoi semli" v Belorussii 1941–1944* (Minsk: Belarus).

Rose, Romani, ed., 2003. *Der nationalsozialistische Völkermord an den Sinti und Roma*, second edition (Heidelberg: Dokumentations- und Kulturzentrum deutscher Sinti und Roma).

Roseman, Mark, 2002. *The Villa, the Lake, the Meeting: Wannsee and the Final Solution* (London: Penguin).

Rosenkötter, Bernhard, 2003. *Treuhandpolitik: Die "Haupttreuhandstelle Ost" und der Raub polnischen Vermögens 1939–1945* (Essen: Klartext).

Rossino, Alexander, 2003. *Hitler Strikes Poland: Blitzkrieg, Ideology and Atrocity* (Lawrence: University of Kansas Press).

Rost, Karl Ludwig, 1992. "Der propagandistische Missbrauch des Begriffes 'Erbkrankheit' im NS-Staat" in Propping and Schott, eds, pp. 44–65.

Roth, Markus, 2009. *Herrenmenschen: Die deutschen Kreishauptleute im besetzten Polen* (Göttingen: Wallstein).

Rother, Bernd, 2001. *Spanien und der Holocaust* (Tübingen: Max Niemeyer).

Rothkirchen, Livia, 1998. "The situation of Jews in Slovakia between 1939 and 1945," *JASF* 7, pp. 46–70.

Rothkirchen, Livia, 2005. *The Jews of Bohemia and Moravia: Facing the Holocaust* (Lincoln and Jerusalem: University of Nebraska Press and Yad Vashem).

Rothschild, Joseph, 1974. *East Central Europe Between the Two World Wars* (Seattle and London: University of Washington Press).

Roumani, Maurice, 2008. *The Jews of Libya: Coexistence, Persecution, Resettlement* (Brighton and Portland: Sussex Academic Press).

Rozen, Minna, 2005. "Jews and Greeks remember their past: The political career of Tsevi Koretz (1933–43)," *JSS* 12 (1), pp. 111–66.

Rozenblum, Thierry, 2003. "Une cité si ardente: L'administration communale de Liège et la persecution des Juifs, 1940–1942," *RHS* 179, Septembre–Decembre, pp. 9–74.

Rückerl, Adalbert, ed., 1977. *NS-Vernichtungslager im Spiegel deutscher Strafprozesse* (Munich: dtv).

Rürup, Reinhard, 1975. *Emanzipation und Antisemitismus* (Göttingen: Vandenhoeck & Ruprecht).

Rürup, Reinhard, 1988. "Emanzipation und Antisemitismus: Historische Verbindungslinien" in Strauss and Kampe, eds, pp. 88–98.

Rupnow, Dirk, 2000. *Täter, Gedächtnis, Opfer: Das "Jüdische Zentralmuseum" in Prag 1942–1945* (Vienna: Picus).

Rupnow, Dirk, 2006. "Antijüdische Wissenschaft im 'Dritten Reich' – Wege, Probleme und Perspektiven der Forschung," *SDIY* V, pp. 539–98.

Rutherford, Phillip, 2007. *Prelude to the Final Solution: The Nazi Program for Deporting Ethnic Poles, 1939–1941* (Lawrence: University Press of Kansas).

Sabatello, Eitan, 1989. "Le conseguenze sociale ed economiche delle persecuzioni sugli ebrei in Italia" in Camera dei deputati, pp. 79–94.

Sabille, Jean, 1954. *Les juifs de Tunisie sous Vichy et l'occupation* (Paris: Éditions du Centre).

Safrian, Hans, 1997. *Eichmann und seine Gehilfen* (Frankfurt: Fischer Taschenbuch).

Saller, Karl, 1961. *Die Rassenlehre des Nationalsozialismus in Wissenschaft und Propaganda* (Darmstadt: Progress).

Sanders, Paul, 2001. *Histoire du marché noir 1940–1946* (n.p. [Paris]: Perrin).

Sanders, Paul, 2005. *The British Channel Islands under German Occupation 1940–1945* (n.p.: Jersey Heritage Trust).

Sarfatti, Michele, 1994. *Mussolini contro gli ebrei: Cronaca dell' elaborazione delle leggi del 1938* (Torino: Silvio Zamorani).

Sarfatti, Michele, 2006. *The Jews in Mussolini's Italy* (Madison: University of Wisconsin Press).

Sarraute, P. and P. Tager, 1982. "Introduction" in CDJC, pp. 1–12.

Sauvy, Alfred, 1978. *La vie économique des Français de 1939 à 1945* (Paris: Flammarion).

Schäfer, Annette, 2000. *Zwangsarbeiter und NS-Rassenpolitik: Russische und polnische Arbeitskräfte in Württemberg 1939–1945* (Stuttgart: Kohlhammer).

Schafft, Gretchen, 2004. *From Racism to Genocide: Anthropology in the Third Reich* (Urbana and Chicago: University of Illinois Press).

Schaller, Helmut, 2002. *Der Nationalsozialismus und die slawische Welt* (Regensburg: Friedrich Pustet).

Schechtman, Joseph, 1946. *European Population Transfers 1939–1945* (New York: Oxford University Press).

Scheck, Raffael, 2008. *Hitler's African Victims: The German Army Massacres of Black French Soldiers in 1940*, second edition. (Cambridge: Cambridge University Press).

Scheffler, Wolfgang, 1985. "The forgotten path to the 'final solution': The liquidation of the ghettos," *SWCA* 2, pp. 31–51.

Scheffler, Wolfgang, 1988. "Wege zur 'Endlösung'" in Strauss and Kampe, eds, pp. 186–214.

Scheffler, Wolfgang, 1997. "Die Einsatzgruppe A" in Klein, ed., pp. 29–51.

Scheffler, Wolfgang and Helge Grabitz, 1993. *Der Ghetto-Aufstand Warschau 1943 aus der Sicht der Täter und Opfer in Aussagen vor deutschen Gerichten* (Munich: Goldmann).

Schelvis, Jules, 1998. *Vernichtungslager Sobibór* (Berlin: Metropol).

Schenk, Dieter, 2000. *Hitlers Mann in Danzig: Albert Forster und die NS-Verbrechen in Danzig-Westpreussen* (Bonn: Dietz).

Schiefelbein, Dieter, n.d. (1993). *Das "Institut zur Erforschung der Judenfrage Frankfurt am Main": Vorgeschichte und Gründung 1935–1939* (Frankfurt a.M.: Stadt Frankfurt a.M.).

Schildt, Axel, 1998. "Wohnungspolitik" in Hans Günther Hockerts, ed., *Drei Wege zur Sozialstaatlichkeit: NS-Diktatur, Bundesrepublik und DDR im Vergleich* (Munich: Oldenbourg), pp. 151–89.

Schlarp, Karl-Heinz, 1986. *Wirtschaft und Besatzung in Serbien 1941–1944* (Stuttgart: Franz Steiner).

Schlemmer, Thomas and Hans Woller, 2005. "Der italienische Faschismus und die Juden 1922 bis 1945," *VfZ* 53 (2), pp. 165–201.

Schleunes, Karl, 1992. "1939: The making of war and the final solution" in Cohen *et al.*, eds, pp. 25–34.

Schmider, Klaus, 2002. *Partisanenkrieg in Jugoslawien 1941–1944* (Hamburg: E.S. Mittler & Sohn).

Schmuhl, Hans-Walter, 2005. *Grenzüberschreitungen: Das Kaiser-Wilhelm-Institut für Anthropologie, menschliche Erblehre und Eugenik 1927–1945* (Göttingen: Wallstein).

Schneider, Hubert, 2010. *Die "Entjudung" des Wohnraums – "Judenhäuser" in Bochum* (Münster: LIT).

Schölzel, Christian, 2013. "Zwangsarbeit und der 'Unabhängige Staat Kroatien'" in Sanela Hodzic and Christian Schölzel, eds, *Zwangsarbeit und der "Unabhängige Staat Kroatien" 1941–1945* (Berlin: LIT), pp. 3–127.

Schoenfeld, Joachim, 1985. *Holocaust Memoirs: Jews in the Lwów Ghetto, the Janowski Concentration Camp, and as Deportees in Siberia* (Hoboken: KTAV).

Scholze-Irrlitz, Leonore and Karoline Noack, eds, 1998. *Arbeit für den Feind: Zwangsarbeiter-Alltag in Berlin und Brandenburg (1939–1945)* (Berlin and Brandenburg: be.bra).

Schreiber, Beate, 2007. "'Arisierung' in Berlin 1933–1945: Eine Einführung" in Christof Biggeleben, Beate Schreiber and Kilian Steiner, eds, *"Arisierung" in Berlin* (Berlin: Metropol), pp. 13–53.

Schreiber, Gerhard, 1996. *Deutsche Kriegsverbrechen in Italien* (Munich: Beck).

Schröder, Hans-Joachim, 1992. *Die gestohlenen Jahre: Erzählgeschichten und Geschichtserzählung – Interview: Der Zweite Weltkrieg aus der Sicht ehemaliger Mannschaftssoldaten* (Tübingen: Max Niemeyer).

Schulle, Diana, 2001. *Das Reichssippenamt* (Berlin: Logos).

Schulte, Jan Erik, 2001. *Zwangsarbeit und Vernichtung: Das Wirtschaftsimperium der SS* (Paderborn: Schöningh).

Schulte, Theo, 2000. "Korück 582" in Heer and Naumann, eds, pp. 314–28.

Schulz, Kristina, 2012, *Die Schweiz und die literarischen Flüchtlinge 1933–1945* (Berlin: Akademie).

Schulze, Birgit, 2007. "Das Schicksal dänischer Deportierter in nationalsozialistischen Konzentrationslagern," *Dachauer Hefte* 23, pp. 57–72.

Schumann, Dirk, 2001. *Politische Gewalt in der Weimarer Republik 1918–1933* (Essen: Klartext).

Schwarze, Gisela, ed., 2005. *Die Sprache der Opfer: Briefzeugnisse aus Russland und der Ukraine als Quelle der Geschichtsschreibung* (Essen: Klartext).

Sebag, Paul, 1991. *Histoire des Juifs de Tunisie* (Paris: L'Harmattan).

Seckendorf, Martin, 2001. "Deutsche Baltikumkonzeptionen 1941–1944 im Spiegel von Dokumenten der zivilen Okkupationsverwaltung: Eine Dokumentation," *1999*, 16 (1), pp. 140–72.

Seeger, Andreas, 1996. *"Gestapo-Müller": die Karriere eines Schreibtischtäters* (Berlin: Metropol).

Segbers, Klaus, 1987. *Die Sowjetunion im Zweiten Weltkrieg* (Munich: Oldenbourg).

Seidel, Robert, 2006. *Deutsche Besatzungspolitik in Polen: Der Distrikt Radom 1939–1945* (Paderborn: Schöningh).

Seidler, Horst and Andreas Rett, 1982. *Das Reichssippenamt entscheidet: Rassenbiologie im Nationalsozialismus* (Vienna and Munich: Jugend und Volk).

Sereny, Gitta, 1980. *Am Abgrund* (Frankfurt a.M.: Ullstein).

Shapiro, Paul, 1997. "The Jews of Chişinău (Kishinev): Romanian reoccupation, ghettoization, deportation" in Braham, ed., pp. 135–93.

Shaw, Stanford, 1993. *Turkey and the Holocaust* (New York: New York University Press).

Shelach, Menachem, 1992. "The murder of Jews in Serbia and the Serbian uprising in July 1941" in Cohen *et al.*, eds, pp. 161–75.

Shepherd, Ben, 2004. *War in the Wild East: The German Army and Soviet Partisans* (Cambridge and London: Harvard University Press).

Sigg, Marco, 2011. *"Der Unterführer als Moltke im Taschenformat": Auftragstaktik im deutschen Heer 1935–1945*, PhD dissertation, University of Bern.

Silberklang, David, 2004. "Die Juden und die ersten Deportationen aus dem Distrikt Lublin" in Musial, ed., pp. 141–64.

Silvennoinen, Oula, 2008. *Geheime Waffenbrüderschaft: Die sicherheitspolizeiliche Zusammenarbeit zwischen Finnland und Deutschland 1933–1944* (Darmstadt: Wissenschaftliche Buchgesellschaft).

Sinnreich, Helene, 2004. *The Supply and Distribution of Food in the Łódź Ghetto: A Case Study in Nazi Jewish Policy, 1939–1945*, PhD thesis, Brandeis University.

Şiperco, Andrei, 1997. *Crucea Roşie Internaţională şi România în perioada celui de-al doilea război mondial (1 septembrie 1939 – 23 august 1944)* (Bucarest: Editura Enciclopedică).

Śliwowska, Wiktoria, ed., 1999. *The Last Eyewitnesses: Children of the Holocaust Speak* (Evanston: Northwestern University Press).

Smilovitsky, Leonid, 1997. "Righteous Gentiles, the partisans and Jewish survival in Belorussia, 1941–1944," *HGS* 11 (3), pp. 301–29.

Smilovitsky, Leonid, 2003. "A demographic profile of the Jews in Belorussia from the pre-war to the post-war time," *JGR* 5 (1), pp. 117–29.

Smith, Woodruff, 1986. *The Ideological Origins of Nazi Imperialism* (New York and Oxford: Oxford University Press).

Snyder, Timothy, 1999. "'To resolve the Ukrainian problem once and for all': The ethnic cleansing of Ukrainians and Poles, 1943–1947," *Journal of Cold War Studies* 1 (2), pp. 86–120.

Snyder, Timothy, 2010a. *Bloodlands: Europe Between Hitler and Stalin* (New York: Basic Books).

Snyder, Timothy, 2010b. "The life and death of the western Volhynian Jewry, 1931–1945" in Brandon and Lower, eds, pp. 77–113.

Solonari, Vladimir, 2007a. "An important new document on the Romanian policy of ethnic cleansing during World War II," *HGS* 21 (2), pp. 268–97.

Solonari, Vladimir, 2007b. "Patterns of violence: The local population and the mass murder of Jews in Bessarabia and northern Bukovina, July–August 1941," *Kritika* 8 (4), pp. 749–87.

Solonari, Vladimir, 2010. *Purifying the Nation: Population Exchange and Ethnic Cleansing in Nazi-Allied Romania* (Washington and Baltimore: Woodrow Wilson Centre Press and Johns Hopkins University Press).

Speckner, Hubert, 2003. *In der Gewalt des Feindes: Kriegsgefangenenlager in der "Ostmark" 1939 bis 1945* (Munich: Oldenbourg).

Speckner, Hubert, 2005. "Kriegsgefangenenlager in der 'Ostmark'" in Bischoff *et al.*, eds, pp. 329–51.

Spector, Shmuel, 1990a. *The Holocaust of Volhynian Jews 1941–1944* (Jerusalem: Yad Vashem).

Spector, Shmuel, 1990b. "Aktion 1005 – effacing the murder of millions," *HGS* 5, pp. 157–73.

Spector, Shmuel, 1993. "Jews in the resistance and partisan movements in the Soviet Ukraine," *YVS* 28, pp. 127–43.

Spengler-Axiopoulos, Barbara, 2011. "Griechen ohne Heimat: Am Ende stand die Entwurzelung – das wenig bekannte Schicksal der 'Bürgerkriegskinder'," *Neue Zürcher Zeitung*, 5, May, p. 49.

Spoerer, Mark, 2001. *Zwangsarbeit unter dem Hakenkreuz* (Stuttgart and Munich: dva).

Spoerer, Mark and Jochen Fleischhacker, 2002. "Forced laborers in Nazi Germany: Categories, numbers, and survivors," *Journal of Interdisciplinary History* 33 (2), pp. 169–204.

Stark, Tamás, 1999. "Ungarische Gefangene in der Sowjetunion" in Bischof and Overmans, eds, pp. 407–16.

Stark, Tamás, 2001. "Population movements in Hungary during the war years," in *Jahrbuch des Italienisch-deutschen Historischen Instituts in Trient* 27, pp. 619–32.

Stark, Tamás, 2005. "Ungarische Zivilisten in sowjetischer Kriegsgefangenschaft" in Bischoff *et al.*, eds, pp. 109–22.

Stein, George, 1978. *Geschichte der Waffen-SS* (Königstein: Athenäum).

Stein, Harry, 1998. "Funktionswandel des Konzentrationslagers Buchenwald im Spiegel der Lagerstatistiken" in Herbert *et al.*, eds, pp. 167–92.

Steinbacher, Sybille, 2000. *"Musterstadt" Auschwitz: Germanisierungspolitik und Judenmord in Ostoberschlesien* (Münich: K.G. Saur).

Steinberg, Jonathan, 1992. *Deutsche, Italiener und Juden* (Göttingen: Steidl).

Steinberg, Maxime, "The Jews in the years 1940–1944: Three strategies for coping with a tragedy" in Michman, ed., pp. 347–72.

Steiner, John and Jobst von Cornberg, 1998. "Willkür in der Willkür: Befreiung von den antisemitischen Gesetzen," *VfZ* 46, pp. 143–87.

Steinert, Marlis, 1970. *Hitlers Krieg und die Deutschen* (Düsseldorf and Vienna: Econ).

Steinweis, Alan, 2006. *Studying the Jew. Scholarly Antisemitism in Nazi Germany* (Cambridge and London: Harvard University Press).

Stern, Fritz, 1965. *The Politics of Cultural Despair: A Study in the Rise of Germanic Ideology* (Garden City: Doubleday).

Steur, Claudia, 1997. *Theodor Dannecker: Ein Funktionär der "Endlösung"* (Essen: Klartext).

Stiller, Alexa, 2009. "Grenzen des 'Deutschen': Nationalsozialistische Volkstumspolitik in Polen, Frankreich und Slowenien während des Zweiten Weltkriegs" in Mathias Beer, Dietrich Beyrau and Cornelia Rauh, eds, *Deutschsein als Grenzerfahrung* (Essen: Klartext), pp. 61–84.

Stoltzfus, Nathan, 1996. *Resistance of the Heart: Intermarriage and the Rosenstrasse Protest in Nazi Germany* (New York and London: W.W. Norton).

Strauss, Herbert, 1980. "Jewish emigration from Germany: Nazi policies and Jewish responses (I)," *LBIY* 25, pp. 313–61.

Strauss, Herbert, 1987. *Essays on the History, Persecution and Emigration of the German Jews* (New York: Saur).

Strauss, Herbert and Norbert Kampe, eds, 1988. *Antisemitismus: Von der Judenfeindschaft zum Holocaust* (Bonn: Bundeszentrale für politische Bildung).

Streit, Christian, 1991 [1978]. *Keine Kameraden: Die Wehrmacht und die sowjetischen Kriegsgefangenen 1941–1945* (Bonn: Dietz).

Strugar, Vlado, n.d [1969]. *Der jugoslawische Volksbefreiungskrieg 1941 bis 1945* (Berlin [East]: Deutscher Militärverlag).

Strzelecki, Andrzej, 1994. "The plunder of victims and their corpses" in Gutman and Berenbaum, eds, pp. 246–66.

Sulik, Alfred, 1991. "Volkstumspolitik und Arbeitseinsatz: Zwangsarbeiter in der Grossindustrie Oberschlesiens" in Herbert, ed., pp. 106–26.

Szita, Szabolcs, 1999. *Verschleppt, verhungert, vernichtet: Die Deportation von Juden auf das Gebiet des annektierten Österreich 1944–1945* (Vienna: Eichbauer).

Szöllösi-Janze, Margit, 1989. *Die Pfeilkreuzlerbewegung in Ungarn* (Munich: Oldenbourg).

Tálos, Emmerich, Ernst Hanisch, Wolfgang Neugebauer and Reinhard Sieder, 2002. *NS-Herrschaft in Österreich* (Vienna: öbv & hpt).

Tauber, Joachim, ed., 2006. *"Kollaboration" in Nordeuropa: Erscheinungsformen und Deutungen im 20. Jahrhundert* (Wiesbaden: Harrassowitz).

Tauber, Joachim, 2008. "Die litauische Verwaltung und die Juden in Vilnius 1941–1943" in Hürter and Zarusky, eds, pp. 103–14.

Tec, Nechama, 1996. *Bewaffneter Widerstand: Jüdische Partisanen im Zweiten Weltkrieg* (Gerlingen: Bleicher).

Tec, Nechama, 2011. "Introduction" in Patricia Heberer, ed., *Children During the Holocaust* (Lanham: AltoMira), pp. xxi–xli.

Teichova, Alice, 1997. "Instruments of economic control and exploitation: The German occupation of Bohemia and Moravia" in Overy *et al.*, eds, pp. 83–108.

Terry, Nicholas, 2005. *The German Army Group Center and the Soviet Civilian Population 1942–1944: Forced Labour, Hunger and Population Displacement on the Eastern Front*, PhD dissertation, University of London.

Thalmann, Rita, 1999. *Gleichschaltung in Frankreich 1940–1944* (Hamburg: Europäische Verlagsanstalt).

The Power of Civil Society in a Time of Genocide: Proceedings of the Holy Synod of the Bulgarian Orthodox Church on the Rescue of Jews in Bulgaria 1940–1944, 2005 (Sofia: Sofia University Press St. Kliment Ohridski).

Ther, Philipp, 2011. *Die dunkle Seite der Nationalstaaten: "Ethnische Säuberungen" im modernen Europa* (Göttingen: Vandenhoeck & Ruprecht).

Thomas, Martin, 1998. *The French Empire at War 1940–45* (Manchester and New York: Manchester University Press).

Thum, Gregor, 2006. "Mystische Landschaften: Das Bild vom 'deutschen Osten' und die Zäsuren des 20. Jahrhunderts" in Gregor Thum., ed., *Traumland Osten: Deutsche Bilder vom östlichen Europa im 20. Jahrhundert* (Göttingen: Vandenhoeck & Ruprecht), pp. 181–213.

Thum, Gregor, 2013. "Megalomania and angst: The nineteenth-century mythization of Germany's eastern borderlands" in Omer Bartov and Eric Weitz, eds, *Shatterzones of Empires* (Bloomington and Indianapolis: Indiana University Press), pp. 42–60.

Tönsmeyer, Tatjana, 2003. *Das Dritte Reich und die Slowakei: Politischer Alltag zwischen Kooperation und Eigensinn* (Paderborn: Schöningh).

Tokarska-Bakir, Joanna, 2012. "Cries of the mob in the pogroms in Rzeszów (June 1945), Cracow (August 1945) and Kielce (July 1946) as a source for the state of the mind of the perpetrators" in Gross, ed. (2012b), pp. 205–29.

Tomasevich, Jozo, 2001. *War and Revolution in Yugoslavia, 1941–1945: Occupation and Collaboration* (Stanford: Stanford University Press).

Tooze, Adam, 2007. *Ökonomie der Zerstörung: Die Geschichte der Wirtschaft im Nationalsozialismus* (Munich: Siedler).

Toscano, Mario, 1995. "The Jews in Italy and anti-Semitic Policy of Fascism" in Caracciolo, ed., pp. xxxv–xli.

Toury, Jacob, 1986. "Die Entstehungsgeschichte des Austreibungsbefehls gegen die Juden der Saarpfalz und Badens (22./23. Oktober 1940 – Camp de Gurs)," *Jahrbuch des Instituts für deutsche Geschichte* 15, pp. 431–64.

Traverso, Enzo, 1999. *Understanding the Nazi Genocide: Marxism After Auschwitz* (London and Sterling: Pluto Press).

Traverso, Enzo, 2003. *Moderne und Gewalt: Eine europäische Genealogie des Nazi-Terrors* (Cologne: ISP).

Trienekens, Gerardus, 1985. *Tussen ons volk en de honger: De voedselvoorziening, 1940–1945* (Utrecht: Stichting Matrijs).

Trifković, Srda, 2008. "Balkan bloodbath before Wannsee: Croatia 1941 revisited" in *Israeli–Serbian Academic Exchange in Holocaust Research*, pp. 47–64.

Troebst, Stefan, 1995. "Antisemitismus im 'Land ohne Antisemitismus': Staat, Titularnation und jüdische Minderheit in Bulgarien 1887–1993" in Mariana Hausleitner and Monika Katz, eds, *Juden und Antisemitismus im östlichen Europa* (Wiesbaden: Harrassowitz), pp. 109–25.

Trolle, Jörgen, 1994. *Die verschwundene Ordnungsmacht: Gestapo-Terror gegen die dänische Polizei vom 19.9.1944 bis Mai 1945* (Frankfurt a.M.: Haag + Herchen).

Trubeta, Sevasti, 2003. "'Gypsiness', racial discourse and persecution: Balkan Roma during the Second World War," *Nationalities Papers* 31 (4), pp. 495–514.

Trunk, Isaiah, 1972. *Judenrat: The Jewish Councils in Eastern Europe Under German Occupation* (New York and London: Macmillan).

Tuchel, Johannes, 1992. *Am Grossen Wannsee 56–58: Von der Villa Minoux zum Haus der Wannsee-Konferenz* (Berlin: Edition Hentrich).

Tumarkin, Nina, 1994. *The Living and the Dead: The Rise and Fall of the Cult of World War II in Russia* (New York: Basic Books).

Turan, Serbulent and Donald Dutton, 2010. "Psychic freezing to lethal malevolent authority," *Journal of Aggression, Conflict and Peace Research* 2 (3), pp. 4–15.

Tyaglyy, Mikhail, 2004. "The role of antisemitic doctrine in German propaganda in the Crimea, 1941–1944," *HGS* 18 (3), pp. 421–59.

Ueberschär, Gerd and Wolfram Wette, eds, 1991. *Der deutsche Überfall auf die Sowjetunion* (Frankfurt a.M.: Fischer).

Ultee, Wout, Frank van Tubergen and Ruud Luijkx, 2001. "The unwholesome theme of suicide: Forgotten statistics of attempted suicide in Amsterdam and Jewish suicides in the Netherlands for 1936–1943" in Brasz and Kaplan, eds, pp. 325–53.

Unabhängige Expertenkommission Schweiz – Zweiter Weltkrieg, 1999. *Die Schweiz und die Flüchtlinge zur Zeit des Nationalsozialismus* (Bern: UEK).

Unger, Michal, 1998. "The status and plight of women in the Lodz ghetto"in Dalia Ofer and Leonore Weitzman, eds, *Women in the Holocaust* (New Haven and London: Yale University Press), pp. 123–42.

Ungváry, Krisztián, 2005a. "Der Getriebene und der Treiber: Das Verhältnis zwischen ungarischer Politik und deutschen Deportationsplänen" in Mihok, ed., pp. 41–54.

Ungváry, Krisztián, 2005b. "Das Beispiel der ungarischen Armee: Ideologischer Vernichtungskrieg oder militärisches Kalkül?" in Hartmann *et al.*, eds, pp. 98–106.

Urban, Rudolf, 1939. "Das Ende einer 'Oase': Die Judenfrage in Sudentengau und im Reichsprotektorat Böhmen und Mähren" in Könitzer and Trurnit, eds, pp. 70–6.

van Laak, Dirk, 2003. "Die Mitwirkenden bei der 'Arisierung': Dargestellt am Beispiel der rheinisch-westfälischen Industrieregion 1933–1940" in Ursula Büttner, ed., *Die Deutschen und die Judenverfolgung im Dritten Reich* (Frankfurt a.M.: Fischer), pp. 273–304.

van Laak, Dirk, 2005. *Über alles in der Welt: Deutscher Imperialismus im 19. und 20. Jahrhundert* (Munich: Beck).

van Thijn, Ed, 2001. "Memories of a hidden child: A personal reflection" in Brasz and Kaplan, eds, pp. 265–76.

Vegesack, Siegfried, 1965. *Als Dolmetscher im Osten* (Hannover: Hirschheydt).

Völkl, Ekkehard, 1996. *Transnistrien und Odessa (1941–1944)* (Regensburg: Lassleben).

Voigt, Klaus, 1987. "Refuge and persecution in Italy, 1933–1945," *SWCA* 4, pp. 3–64.

Volkmann, Hans-Erich, 1984. "Landwirtschaft und Ernährung in Hitlers Europa 1939–1945," *MGM* 35, pp. 9–74.

Volkov, Shulamit, 1990. *Jüdisches Leben und Antisemitismus im 19. und 20.Jahrhundert* (Munich: Beck).

Volovici, Leon, 1997. "The victim as eyewitness: Jewish intellectual diaries during the Antonescu period" in Braham, ed., pp. 195–213.

von Herwarth, Hans, 1982. *Zwischen Hitler und Stalin: Erlebte Zeitgeschichte 1931 bis 1945* (Frankfurt a.M. *et al.*: Propyläen).

von Lingen, Kerstin, 2009. *Kriegserfahrung und nationale Identität in Europa nach 1945* (Paderborn u.a.: Schöningh).

von Trotha, Trutz, 1997. "Zur Soziologie der Gewalt" in Trutz von Trotha, ed., *Soziologie der Gewalt* (Opladen: Westdeutscher Verlag), pp. 9–56.

von Xylander, Marlen, 1989. *Die deutsche Besatzungsherrschaft auf Kreta 1941–1945* (Freiburg: Rombach).

von Zitzewitz, Hasso, 1992. *Das deutsche Polenbild in der Geschichte* (Cologne: Böhlau).

Vulesica, Marija, 2008. "Antisemitismus im ersten Jugoslawien," *JASF* 17, pp. 131–52.

Vynokurova, Faina, 2010. "The fate of Bukovinian Jews in the ghettos and camps of Transnistria, 1941–1944: A review of the sources at the Vinnytsa Oblast state archive," *Holocaust and Modernity* 2 (8), pp. 18–26.

Wachsmann, Nikolaus, 2004. *Hitler's Prisons: Legal Terror in Nazi Germany* (New Haven and London: Yale University Press).

Wagner, Patrick, 1996. *Volksgemeinschaft ohne Verbrecher: Konzeption und Praxis der Kriminalpolizei in der Zeit der Weimarer Republik und des Nationalsozailismus* (Hamburg: Christians).

Wagner, Thorsten, 2001. "Ein vergebliches Unterfangen? Der Antisemitismus und das Scheitern des dänischen Nationalsozialismus" in Graml, ed., pp. 275–96.

Walk, Joseph, ed., 1981. *Das Sonderrecht für Juden im NS-Staat* (Heidelberg and Karlsruhe: Müller).

Walter, Dirk, 1999. *Antisemitische Kriminalität und Gewalt: Judenfeindschaft in der Weimarer Republik* (Bonn: Dietz).

Wannsee Conference and the Genocide of European Jews, 2009. House of the Wannsee Conference Memorial and Educational Site, ed. (Berlin).

Wardzyńska, Maria, 1993. *Sytuacja ludności polskiej w Generalnym Komisariacie Litwy, czerwiec 1941–lipiec 1944* (Warsaw: Główna Komisja Badania Zbrodni).

We survived ... Yugoslav Jews on the Holocaust, 2006 (vol. 2) and 2009 (vol. 3) (Belgrade: Jewish Museum).

Weber, Peter, 2004. "Eyewitness testimonies as source of a historical analysis of the deportations to Transnistria, 1941–1943," *Balkan Studies* 45, pp. 28–43.

Wechsler, Harold, 1984. "The rationale for restriction: Ethnicity and college admission in America, 1910–1980," *American Quarterly* 36 (5), pp. 643–87.

Weikart, Richard, 2004. *From Darwin to Hitler: Evolutionary Ethics, Eugenics, and Racism in Nazi Germany* (Palgrave Macmillan: New York and Basingstoke).

Weikart, Richard, 2009. *Hitler's Ethic: The Nazi Pursuit of Evolutionary Progress* (New York: Palgrave Macmillan).

Weindling, Paul, 1989. *Health, Race and German Politics Between National Unification and Nazism, 1870–1945* (New York: Cambridge University Press).

Weindling, Paul, 2000. *Epidemics and Genocide in Eastern Europe 1890–1945* (Oxford: Oxford University Press).

Weiner, Amir, 2001. *Making Sense of War: The Second World War and the Fate of the Bolshevik Revolution* (Princeton and Oxford: Princeton University Press).

Weinert, Rainer, 1993. *"Die Sauberkeit der Verwaltung im Kriege": Der Rechnungshof des Deutschen Reiches 1938–1946* (Opladen: Westdeutscher Verlag).

Weingarten, Ralph, 1981. *Die Hilfeleistung der westlichen Welt bei der Endlösung der deutschen Judenfrage: Das "Intergovernmental Committee on Political Refugees" (IGC) 1938–1939* (Bern: Peter Lang).

Weiss, Aharon, 1977. "Jewish leadership in occupied Poland – postures and attitudes," *YVS* 12, pp. 335–65.

Welzer, Harald, with collaboration of Michaela Christ, 2005. *Täter: Wie aus ganz normalen Menschen Massenmörder werden* (Frankfurt a.M.: Fischer).

Wenzel, Mario, 2007. "Ausbeutung und Vernichtung: Zwangsarbeitslager für Juden im Distrikt Krakau 1942–1944," *Dachauer Hefte* 23, pp. 189–207.

Westermann, Edward, 2005. *Hitler's Police Battalions: Enforcing Racial War in the East* (Lawrence: University of Kansas Press).

Wetzel, Juliane, 1988. "Auswanderung aus Deutschland" in Benz, ed. (1988a), pp. 412–98.

Wielenga, Friso, 2009. "Die 'Guten' und die 'Bösen': Niederländische Erinnerungskultur und nationale Identität nach 1945" in von Lingen, pp. 246–64.

Wiesinger, Barbara, 2008. *Partisaninnen: Widerstand in Jugoslawien (1941–1945)* (Vienna: Böhlau).

Wildt, Michael, 1995. *Die Judenpolitik des SD 1935 bis 1938* (Munich: Oldenbourg).

Wildt, Michael, 2003. *Generation des Unbedingten: Das Führungskorps des Reichssicherheitshauptamtes* (Hamburg: Hamburger Edition).

Wildt, Michael, 2007. *Volksgemeinschaft als Selbstermächtigung: Gewalt gegen Juden in der deutschen Provinz 1919 bis 1939* (Hamburg: Hamburger Edition).

Willems, Susanne, 2000. *Der entsiedelte Jude: Albert Speers Wohnungsmarktpolitik für den Berliner Hauptstadtbau* (Berlin: Edition Hentrich).

Willenberg, Samuel, 2009. *Treblinka: Lager, Revolte, Flucht, Warschauer Aufstand* (Hamburg and Münster: Unrast).

Williams, Maurice, 2005. *Gau, Volk und Reich: Friedrich Rainer und der österreichische Nationalsozialismus* (Klagenfurt: Geschichtsverein Kärnten).

Winkler, Heinrich August, 1981. "Die deutsche Gesellschaft der Weimarer Republik und der Antisemitismus" in Martin and Schulin, eds, pp. 271–89.

Wistrich, Robert, 1991. *Antisemitism* (London: Thames Methuen).

With a Needle in the Heart: Memoirs of Former Prisoners of Ghettos and Concentration Camps, 2003 (Vilnius: Garnelis).

Witt, Sabine, 2012. *Apostel der Reinheit: Die kulturelle Praxis nationalsozialistischer Intellektueller in der Slowakei, 1918 bis 1945*, PhD thesis, University of Bern.

Witte, Peter, 1995. "Zwei Entscheidungen in der 'Endlösung der Judenfrage': Deportationen nach Łódź und Vernichtung in Chelmno," *TSD*, pp. 38–68.

Witte, Peter and Stephen Tyas, 2001. "A new document on the deportation and murder of Jews during 'Einsatz Reinhardt' 1942," *HGS* 15 (3), pp. 468–86.

Wnuk, Rafal, n.d., "Recent Polish historiography on Polish–Ukrainian relations during World War II and its aftermath," available at: http://ece.columbia.edu/files/ece/images/wnuk-1.pdf (accessed January 22, 2013).

Wuescht, Johann, 1969. *Jugoslawien und das Dritte Reich* (Stuttgart: Seewald).

Wuescht, Johann, 1975. *Die mayarische Okkupation der Batschka 1941–1944* (Kehl: Selbstverlag).

Yahil, Leni, 1983 [1969]. *The Rescue of Danish Jewry* (Philadelphia: Jewish Publication Society of America).

Zabarko, Boris, ed., 2005. *Holocaust in the Ukraine* (London and Portland: Vallentine Mitchell).

Zabarko, Boris, 2014. "Die letzte Generation der Überlebenden und das Gedenken an den Holocaust in der Ukraine" in Babette Quinkert and Jörg Morré, eds, *Deutsche Besatzung in der Sowjetunion 1941–1944: Vernichtungskrieg, Reaktionen, Erinnerung* (Paderborn: Schöningh), pp. 383–99.

Zagovec, Rafael, 2005. "Gespräche mit der 'Volksgemeinschaft': Die deutsche Kriegsgesellschaft im Spiegel westalliierter Frontverhöre," *DRZW* 9/2, pp. 289–381.

Zariz, Ruth, 1987. "Officially approved emigration from Germany after 1941: A case study," *YVS* 18, pp. 275–91.

Zarusky, Jürgen, 2007. "Die 'Russen' im KZ Dachau: Bürger der Sowjetunion als Opfer des NS-Regimes," *Dachauer Hefte* 23, pp. 105–39.

Zbikowski, Andrzej, 1993. "Local anti-Jewish pogroms in the occupied territories of eastern Poland, June–July 1941" in Dobroszycki and Gurock, eds, pp. 173–9.

Zeidler, Manfred and Ute Schmidt, eds, 1999. *Gefangene in deutschem und sowjetischem Gewahrsam 1941–1956* (Dresden: Hannah-Arendt-Institut für Totalitarismusforschung).

Zeller, Ron and Pim Griffioen, 1996 and 1997. "Judenverfolgung in den Niederlanden und in Belgien während des Zweiten Weltkriegs: Eine vergleichende Analyse," Part I in *1999*, 10 (3), 1996, pp. 30–54; Part II in *1999*, 11 (1), 1997, pp. 29–48.

Zellhuber, Andreas, 2006. *"Unsere Verwaltung treibt einer Katastrophe zu…": Das Reichsministerium für die besetzten Ostgebiete und die deutsche Besatzungsherrschaft in der Sowjetunion 1941–1945* (München: Ernst Vogel).

Zielinski, Bernd, 1995a. *Staatskollaboration: Vichy und der Arbeitskräfteeinsatz im Dritten Reich* (Münster: Westfälisches Dampfboot).

Zielinski, Bernd, 1995b. "Arbeitslosenpolitik in Frankreich unter deutscher Besatzung (1940–42)," *1999* 10 (3), pp. 15–34.

Ziemann, Benjamin, 2003. "Germany after the First World War – a violent society? Results and implications of recent research on Weimar Germany," *Journal of Modern European History* 1 (1), pp. 80–95.

Zimmerer, Jürgen, 2001. *Deutsche Herrschaft über Afrikaner: Staatlicher Machtanspruch und Wirklichkeit im kolonialen Namibia* (Hamburg: LIT).

Zimmerer, Jürgen, 2005. "The birth of the Ostland out of the spirit of colonialism: A postcolonial perspective on the Nazi policy of confinement and extermination," *Patterns of Prejudice* 39 (2), pp. 197–219.

Zimmermann, Michael, 1995. "Die Gestapo und die regionale Organisation der Judendeportationen" in Paul and Mallmann, eds, pp. 357–72.

Zimmermann, Michael, 1996. *Rassenutopie und Genozid: Die nationalsozialistische 'Lösung der Zigeunerfrage'* (Hamburg: Christians).

Zizas, Rimantas, 2005. "Persecution of non-Jewish citizens of Lithuania, murder of civilian population" in Dieckmann *et al.*, eds, pp. 289–383.

Zmarzlik, Hans-Günter, 1981. "Antisemitismus im Kaiserreich 1871–1918" in Martin and Schulin, eds, pp. 249–70.

Zürcher, Regula, 2004. *"Wir machten die schwarze Arbeit des Holocaust": Das Personal der Massenvernichtungsanlagen von Auschwitz* (Nordhausen: Traugott Bautz).

Zuccotti, Susan, 1993. *The Holocaust, the French and the Jews* (New York: Basic Books).

Zuccotti, Susan, 1996 [1987]. *The Italians and the Holocaust* (Lincoln: University of Nebraska Press).

Zwergbaum, Aaron, 1960. "Exile in Mauritius," *YVS* 4, pp. 191–257.

Index

For EU product safety concerns, contact us at Calle de José Abascal, 56–1°,
28003 Madrid, Spain or eugpsr@cambridge.org.

www.ingramcontent.com/pod-product-compliance
Ingram Content Group UK Ltd.
Pitfield, Milton Keynes, MK11 3LW, UK
UKHW020345140625
459647UK00019B/2316

* 9 7 8 0 5 2 1 7 0 6 8 9 6 *